安藤忠雄の建築　0

Tadao

TADAO ANDO 0 Process and Idea

First published in Japan on March 31, 2010

TOTO Publishing (TOTO LTD.)
TOTO Nogizaka Bldg., 2F,
1-24-3 Minami-Aoyama, Minato-ku,
Tokyo 107-0062, Japan
[Sales]Telephone: +81-3-3402-7138 Facsimile: +81-3-3402-7187
[Editorial]Telephone: +81-3-3497-1010
URL: http://www.toto.co.jp/bookshop/

Author: Tadao Ando
Publisher: Nobuyuki Endo
Book Designer: Tetsuya Ohta
Printing Director : Noboru Takayanagi
Printer: Tokyo Inshokan Printing Co., LTD.

Printed in Japan
ISBN978-4-88706-309-9

Ando 0

Process and Idea

Tadao Ando 0 Process and Idea

Contents
目次

Legend ／凡例
1. Location 所在地
2. Design period 設計期間
3. Construction period 施工期間

1990s

2000s

TADAO ANDO

Process and Idea

Tadao Ando

There are times when I am attracted to something though I do not understand the reason for the attraction.

My visit to the monastery of La Tourette by Le Corbusier on my first trip to the West in 1965 was just such a time.

Rough concrete rose from a slope. The courtyard was a strange landscape of cones and cylinders. Inside the building was revealed a visionary, geometrical world bathed in light and colors. Individual scenes were exciting and moving, but I was unable to come to any conclusion of my own as to what the building as a whole was saying. I visited the space repeatedly over several days but finally left La Tourette without finding an answer.

It was later, when I discovered in a biography of Corbusier a record of a conversation with Father Couturier, that I was able to arrive at an answer of my own. To the friar who played the role of patron in his two religious projects—La Tourette and Ronchamp—Corbusier spoke passionately about the Monastery of Ema near Florence which he had visited in youth.

A memory of the simple, untarnished dwellings of monks situated quietly in the pastoral landscape of Tuscany had in the course of decades matured in the mind of the great architect and flowered in the guise of that strange space of worship. Corbusier's architecture, overflowing with vitality, had its origin, not in a theory of form, but in memory that had been thoroughly assimilated and transmuted into flesh and blood.

Since starting my architectural practice in the 1970s, I have always wanted to take on new challenges and to create things that went beyond what I had already done. My goal has always been a building that could only have been created in a certain place at a certain time.

However, if I look back to see how each project was conceived—the process by which the design was arrived at—it seems to me I too began, not with a blank slate, but with memory transmuted into flesh and blood.

When I was commissioned to design an apartment building in Kobe and visited the site in the foothills of the Rokko Mountains, I was strongly attracted to, not the level land that had already been prepared, but the steep slope behind it. I no doubt felt that way because there were subconscious memories in my mind of beautiful communities I had experienced in the past such as villages on the islands of Santorini and dwellings carved into rock in Cappadocia.

When the image of a black, castle-like silhouette came into my head as I was developing a concept for the theater called Kara-za, leading me to design a movable theater in that image using scaffolding pipes that could be leased anywhere, it was probably because Kara Juro's shocking crimson tent which I had experienced in real time in my twenties had made such a deep impression on me.

The past influences the present, and the present helps create the future—I believe the world of architectural imagination exists in such a continuous flow of time.

Of course architecture cannot be created out of image alone. First, keeping in mind the conditions of the program, I read the site. I get a sense of scale and register what the natural conditions are; then to give shape to vague images I make sketches, models and hard-line drawings. Through repeated studies, I clarify the intention of the architectural space that is to come into being.

When the organizational schema becomes evident, I then begin to grapple with technology and laws and regulations.

In Rokko Housing, after I had conceived the idea of adapting a cubical frame to the topography, a process of giving physical expression to that idea followed. That was the most creative and intense period in the project.

First, a soil survey of the site and the surrounding area was carried out. Analyzing a steep, 60-degree slope is extremely complex and would have been nearly impossible with a conventional method of calculation. However, the problem was solved through the introduction of a computer, the use of which was still relatively rare in the late 1970s.

Then there were laws and regulations. On a site in an area designated a category 1 exclusively residential district, building regulations limited the height to ten meters and the building coverage to 40 percent. The idea of covering the entire slope with a building was not likely to be approved if the application were made in the usual way. However, those limits would not present a problem if the method used to establish the ground level, the criterion for calculating building height and building coverage, could be interpreted more broadly in keeping with the special condition of the site. Confident that the building I was trying to create would not damage the environment, I used this strategy in negotiating with the concerned authorities. It took approximately three years to reach a conclusion.

A lengthy design period can only be economically disadvantageous for a small office. However, despite the difficulty, as we advance toward the realization of the imagined landscape, solving each problem in this way, the initial idea is made more perfect and our love for the building becomes more profound.

It is precisely this process through which an idea passes, this process of turmoil, that is architecture.

Since the mid-1990s, the full-fledged introduction of the computer has accelerated everything, and today the sense of craftsmanship that existed in the past is no longer to be found on most building sites. I am well aware that discussing an unsophisticated, analog process is itself anachronistic in this day and age.

However, though the means by which buildings are made may have become digitalized, human beings are the ones who conceive, and ultimately make and use, buildings. If buildings are to be created for those imperfect beings full of contradictions, then ideas born of flesh and blood, ideas that are at times violent and tenacious, at other times so subtle and sympathetic as to seem irrational, are surely also necessary.

No matter how perfect the world inside a computer monitor is, no matter how precise and beautiful those drawings are, they cannot communicate the nature of an idea as well as a sketch drawn in earnest by a human being nor are they as trustworthy as drawings made with true feeling by hand.

Efforts to use advances in information technology to improve productivity and to develop new architectural forms are all well and good, but we must not become addicted to their convenience and forget this important truth about architecture, that they originate in the ideas of human beings, in ideas born of flesh and blood.

The Japanese architectural world, which has been the center of my practice, is entering a period of unprecedented change. Environmental problems and imbalances in the international economic and political structure now suddenly evident in the twenty-first century are the price we are paying for having continued to build relentlessly under capitalism in the twentieth century. Amid our present global recession, doubts are being raised about not only the pernicious practice of scrap-and-build but even the reason for being of the building industry itself.

The foundation of Japan's building industry today was indeed laid in the postwar period of growth, when the devastated country was in need of reconstruction. No matter how social circumstances may change in the future, a contraction of the industry in both scale and form seems inevitable.

Many of those who nevertheless want to continue to create architecture may end up going overseas in pursuit of work. Those concerned find it impossible to tell what the future will bring.

However, architecture continues to be an integral part of culture, which is the driving force of human history. It is precisely because these are difficult times, that we, the creators of things, ought to take pride in our profession. We ought to believe in the dream of creation. The dream that human beings have always cherished since ancient times is worthy of belief even in an age full of anxiety.

We must give full play to our imagination and give shape to as-yet unseen visions. I ardently pray that human beings will still feel the joy and anguish of the process by which architecture is conceived a hundred years in the future.

発想の過程

安藤忠雄

わからないけれども惹かれるということがある。

1965年の初めての渡欧の際、ル・コルビュジエのラ・トゥーレット修道院を訪れたときがまさにそうだった。

斜面に屹立する荒々しい表情のコンクリート。角錐や円筒で構成される不思議な中庭の風景。その内部には、光と色彩が降り注ぐ幻想的な幾何学の世界が広がっている——個々のシーンは刺激的で心を動かされたのだが、全体としてそれが何を語るものなのか、自分なりの結論が出せない。数日間通ってその空間で過ごしたが、結局答えは見つからないまま、ラ・トゥーレットを去った。

私なりに答えが出せたのは、後に、コルビュジエの伝記の中で、クチュリエ神父との対話の記録を見つけたときだ。ラ・トゥーレットとロンシャン、ふたつの宗教施設で、パトロン的役割を果たしてくれたこの神父に対し、コルビュジエは若い頃に訪れたフィレンツェのエマの修道院のことを熱心に語っていた。

トスカーナ地方の牧歌的な風景の中にひっそりと佇む、素朴で清廉な修道士達の住まい——その記憶が数十年かけて偉大な建築家の中で熟成され、開花した結果が、あの不思議な祈りの空間だった。単なる造形理論ではない、肉体化された記憶こそが、コルビュジエの生命力あふれる建築の原点だった。

1970年代から建築活動をスタートして以来、いつも新しいことに挑戦したい、次は今の仕事を超えるものをつくりたいと考えてきた。その場所でそのときにしかできない建築を目指して奔ってきた。

だがそうしてつくってきたひとつひとつの仕事をいかに発想したか、その過程を振り返れば、始まりは決してゼロからというのでなく、やはり自身の肉体化された記憶が原点だったように思う。

例えば神戸の六甲で集合住宅の依頼を受け、山裾の敷地を訪れた時、用意されていた平坦な土地ではない、背後の急斜面に強いインスピレーションを感じたのは、やはりサントリーニ島の集落やカッパドキアの洞窟住居といった過去に体験した美しい集落の記憶が無意識下にあったからだろう。

唐十郎の芝居小屋を構想していたとき、真っ黒な鳥城のようなシルエットが自然と頭に浮かび、それをリース可能な仮設用の単管パイプを使って、移動式劇場としてつくろうと考えたのは、20代にリアルタイムで体験した唐十郎の紅テント、あの衝撃的な印象が心に深く刻まれていたからだろう。

過去が現在に影響を与え、未来が創られていく――そんな連続する時間の流れの中に、建築のイマジネーションの世界もまた、あるのだと私は思う。

無論、イメージだけでは建築はつくれない。まずはプログラム等の条件を頭におきながら敷地を読む。スケール感覚を掴み、自然の条件を感じ取り――その茫漠としたイメージをかたちにするために、スケッチを描き、模型をつくり、ハードラインで図面を描いていく。そうしてスタディを重ねながら、つくるべき建築空間の意図を明らかにしていく。

構成の図式が見えてきたら、次は技術と法規との格闘だ。

六甲の集合住宅では、立方体フレームで地形をなぞるというアイディアを見つけた後の、この具現化のプロセスが最も創造的で、濃密な時間だった。

まずは周辺を含めた敷地の地質調査。60度の急勾配の解析は極めて複雑なもので、従来の手計算では不可能と実現性が危ぶまれたが、この問題は70年代末当時にはまだ珍しかったコンピュータを導入することで解決を見た。

そして法規である。第一種住居専用地域の敷地には、最高10mの高さ制限があり、また建物を建てられる範囲、建ぺい率は40％以内に、との建築規制があった。普通に申請したのでは、斜面全体を建築で覆うアイディアは通らない。だが、高さと建ぺい率を算出する基準となる地盤面の設定方法を、特殊な敷地状況に応じて拡大解釈して考えることが出来れば、規定値をクリアできる。つくろうとしている建築が周辺環境を損なうようなものではないと確信はしていたから、この戦略をもって、行政との交渉に臨んだ。それが決着するのに約3年間かかった。

小さな事務所の経済を考えれば、設計期間が長期におよぶことは不利益でしかない。だが、そうしてひとつひとつ問題を解決しながら、思い描いた風景の実現に向って進んでいく苦しい時間の中で、アイディアはより研ぎ澄まされ、私たち自身の建築への愛情が深まっていく。

この発想の過程、葛藤の過程こそが建築だ。

90年代半以来のコンピュータの本格的な導入ですべてがスピード化し、建築の現場もかつてのモノづくりの感覚から乖離する一方の現代にあって、泥臭い、アナログ的なプロセスを語ること自体が時代錯誤であることは充分理解している。

しかし、つくる手段がデジタルであれ、建築をつくろうと思うのは人間であり、それをつくるのも、また使うのも人間である。矛盾に満ちた、不完全な存在の人間のための建築をつくるならば、ときに暴力的で執念深く、ときに非合理的なほどに繊細で温かな、人間の生身の思考、身体による発想も必要だろう。

どれだけコンピュータのモニタの中の世界が完璧で、どれだけその図面が精緻で美しい仕上がりであっても、人間が本気で描いたスケッチほどには内容が伝わらないし、思いを込めた手描きの図面ほどに確かなものではないのだ。

ITの進歩を生産性の向上、新たな建築のかたちの開発につなげる努力もいいが、その便利さに溺れて、人間の思い、身体による発想という、重要な建築の本質を忘れてはならない。

今、私が活動の拠点としてきた日本の建築界は、かつてない大きな転機を迎えつつある。資本主義の下にひたすら“つくり続けた”20世紀を経て、そのツケが環境問題や世界構造のアンバランスというかたちで一挙に表れることとなった21世紀——とりわけ、2010年現在の世界的な経済不況の中で、スクラップアンドビルドの悪慣習とともに、建築業の社会的存在理由そのものに疑念がもたれはじめているのだ。

確かに、現在の日本の建築産業の基盤は、荒廃した国を立て直すべく戦後社会の成長期につくられたものである。今後社会情勢がどのように変化していくのであれ、その規模と形態が収縮の方向に進んでいくのはやむを得ないことだろう。

それでも建築をつくり続けようとする人間は、その多くが仕事を求めて日本国外に出て行くことになるかもしれない。関係者にとっては本当に、まったく先が見えない状態だ。

だが、建築が人間の歴史を担う文化の一部であることは変らない事実である。今のこの困難なときだからこそ、誰よりもつくり手である私たち自身が、自らの職業に＜誇り＞をもちたい。つくることの＜夢＞を信じたい。古代から延々と紡がれてきたその＜夢＞は、不安ばかりの今の時代にあってなお、信じる価値のある＜夢＞だ。

想像力を無限に膨らませ、まだ見ぬ心の風景をかたちにしていく——この建築を発想する過程の喜びと苦しみが、100年先の未来にも続いていくことを、今は切に願うばかりである。

DETAIL
TADAO ANDO

1970s

Row House in Sumiyoshi
Tezukayama House
Tezukayama Tower Plaza
Fuku House
Wall House
STEP
Glass Block House
Rokko Housing I
Rokko Housing II
Rokko Housing III 0
Matsutani House
Koshino House

Row House in Sumiyoshi
住吉の長屋

1. Osaka, Osaka, Japan 大阪府大阪市
2. 1975.1-1975.8
3. 1975.10-1976.2

This is a small house with a floor area of about 20 *tsubo* ($66m^2$), built a few years after I established my office. Taking the theme of how to realize a living space as a microcosm within a tiny building on a cramped site, I proposed a composition in which the existing row house is replaced by a two-level concrete box, and this box is then divided in three with the center as an open void.

事務所を開設して数年目につくった20坪ほどの小住宅である。狭小な敷地に建つ極小の建築の内に、いかにしてミクロコスモスとしての住空間を実現するかを主題とし、既存長屋を2層分のコンクリートの箱に置き換え、その箱を3分割した中央をヴォイドとする構成を提案した。

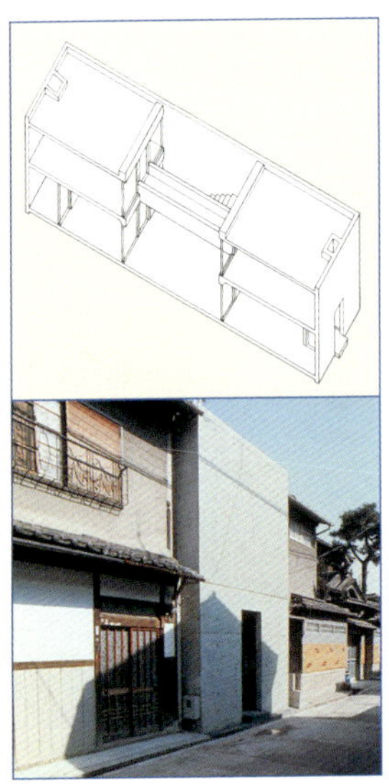

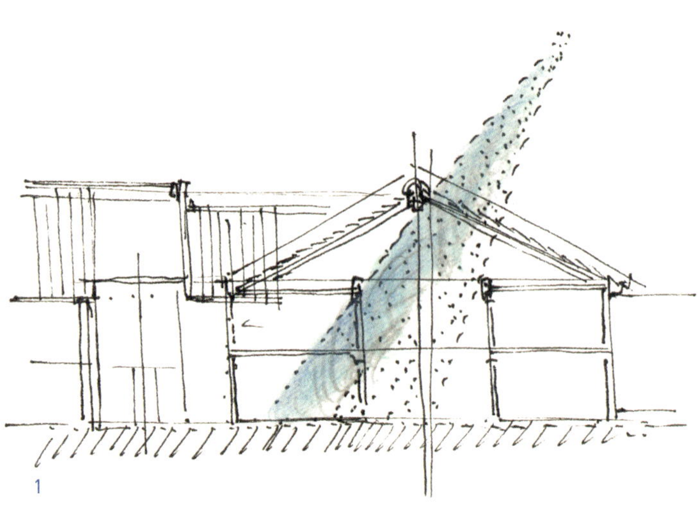

1

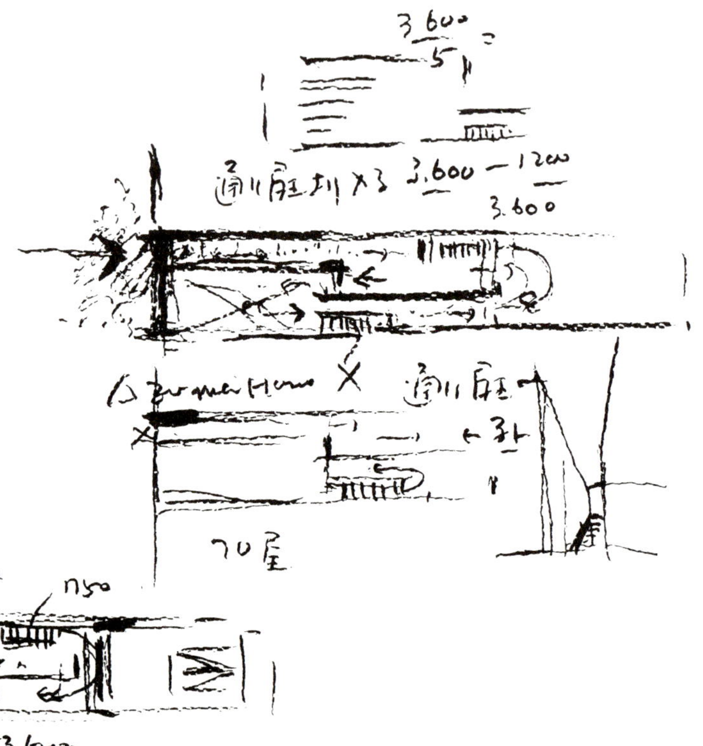

2

1 Sketch superimposing the elevation and section. Conceptual sketch of a residence in which the nucleus is an inner courtyard that pulls "nature" into the living areas.
2 Reinvigorating the row house format, characteristic of this area, as contemporary architecture. Exploratory sketches of the plans.
3 Image sketch of the exterior. A concrete box embedded in the clusters of low wooden houses of downtown Osaka.
4 Image sketch of the composition. Showing the wind paths in plan and section.

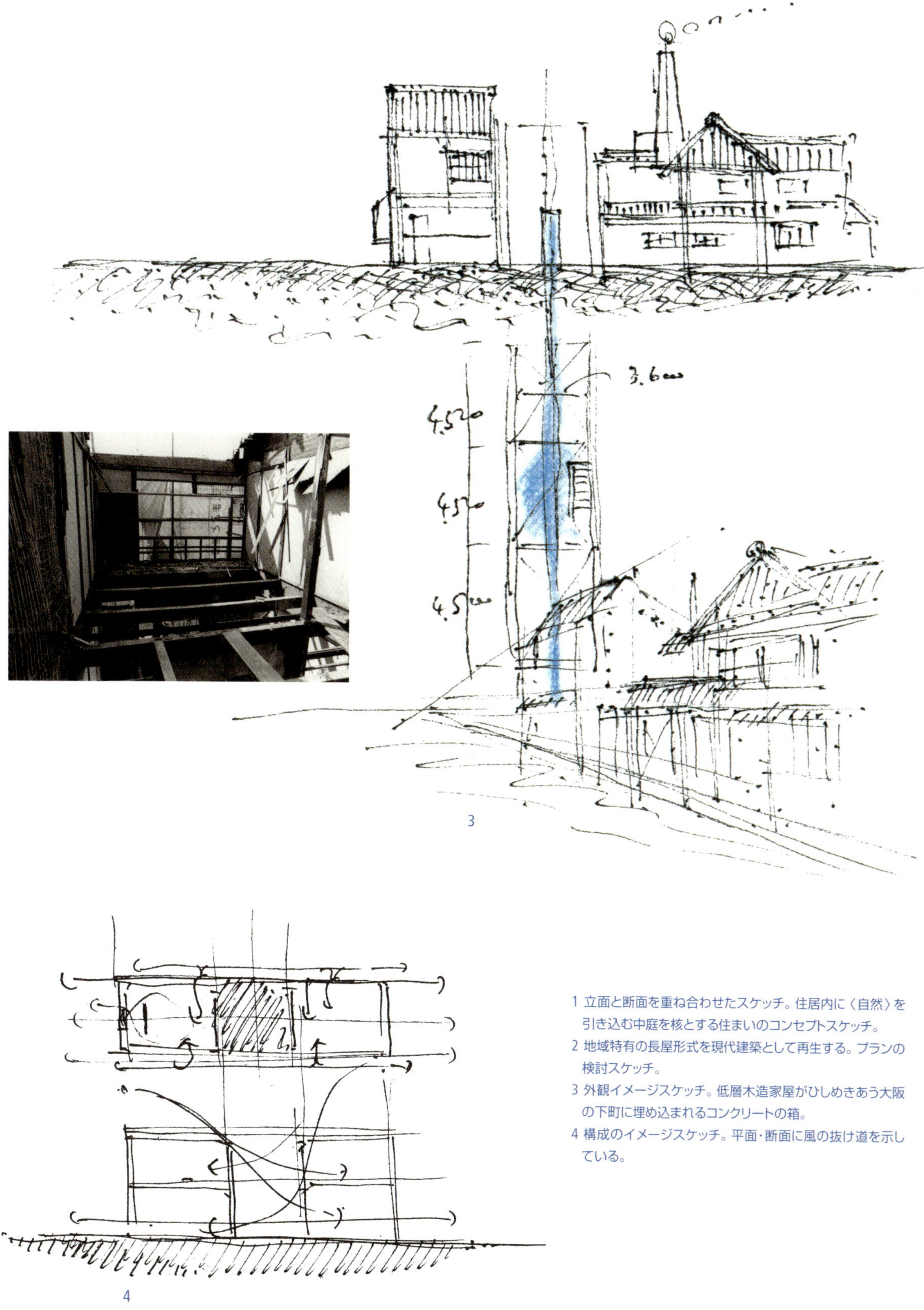

3

4

1 立面と断面を重ね合わせたスケッチ。住居内に〈自然〉を引き込む中庭を核とする住まいのコンセプトスケッチ。
2 地域特有の長屋形式を現代建築として再生する。プランの検討スケッチ。
3 外観イメージスケッチ。低層木造家屋がひしめきあう大阪の下町に埋め込まれるコンクリートの箱。
4 構成のイメージスケッチ。平面・断面に風の抜け道を示している。

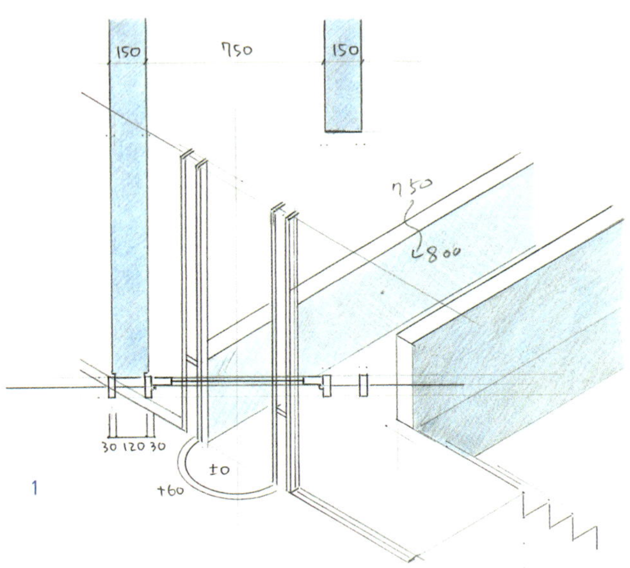

1

The multiple, complex spatial experiences developed within the simple composition, the vigor of nature abstracted as light and wind drawn within the expression of closed concrete walls. The image that was to become the starting point for my subsequent architecture emerged in the process of constructing this small urban house.

単純な構成とその内に展開する複雑多様な空間体験、コンクリート壁の閉ざされた表情とその内に息づく光、風による抽象化された自然の生命力。その後の私の建築の原点となるイメージが、この小さな都市住宅建設のプロセスの中で生まれた。

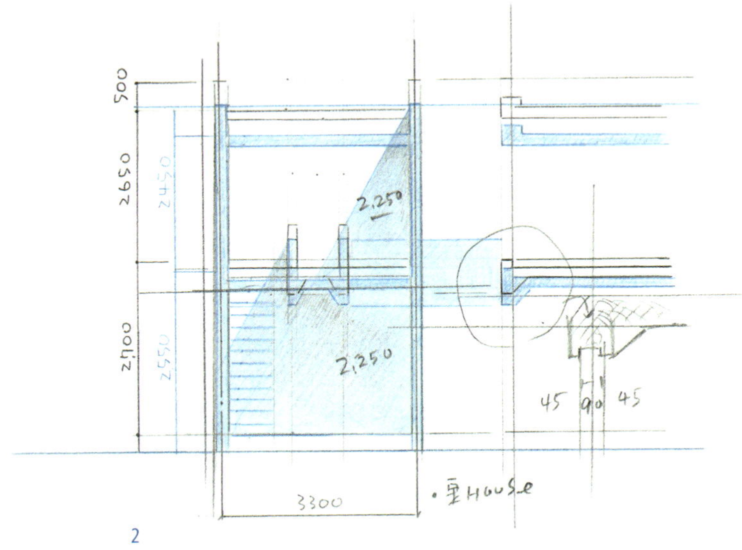

2

1, 2 Exploratory sketch of the details. With tolerance limits that do not allow even a single millimeter to be wasted, studies to hone the details were made right up until the building was completed.
3 Detailed cross section.

1, 2 ディテールの検討スケッチ。1mm の無駄も許されない極限の寸法条件ゆえに、ディテールを研ぎ澄ますスタディは建物が完成するギリギリまで続けられた。
3 断面詳細図。

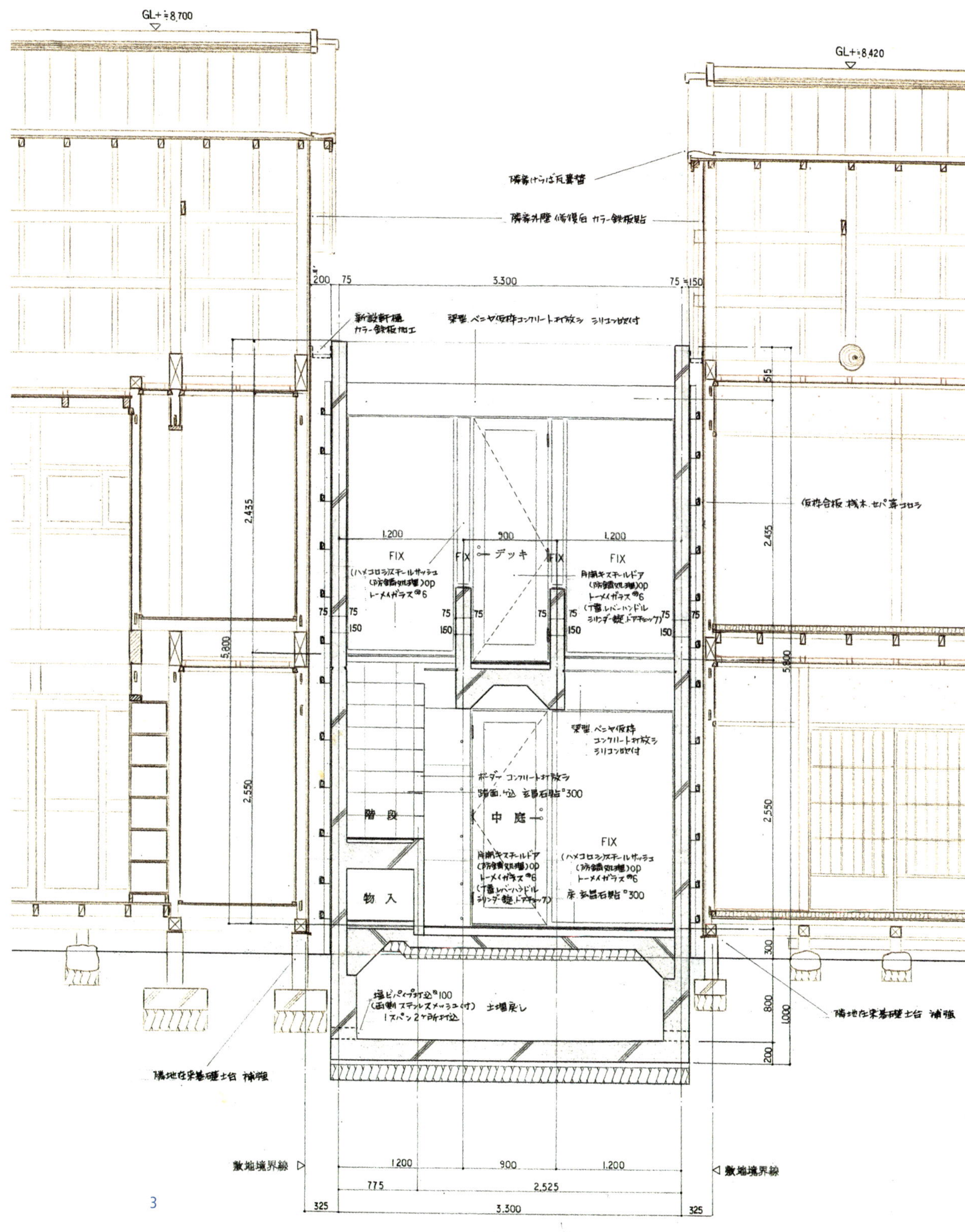

3

Tezukayama House
帝塚山の家

1. Osaka, Osaka, Japan　大阪府大阪市
2. 1976.3-1977.3
3. 1977.4-1977.9

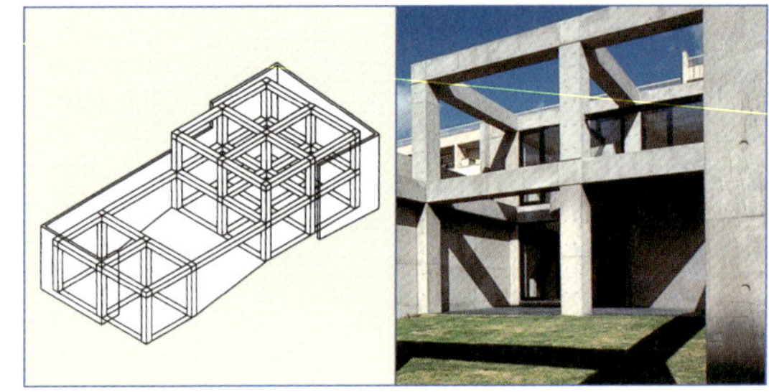

This is a house built in the Abeno district of downtown Osaka. In tiny urban houses such as the Row House in Sumiyoshi, the theme is the creation of a microcosm surrounded and enclosed by walls on all sides of a narrow site, but on the generous site for the Tezukayama House, a frame has been introduced in as a main element in addition to the walls, a compositional experiment in which a three-dimensional lattice and independent walls are superimposed. This is a work that made me reconsider the perennial architectural questions of columns and walls.

大阪の下町、阿倍野区につくった住宅。「住吉の長屋」などの極小都市住宅では狭い敷地いっぱいに壁をまわし、囲われた小宇宙をつくり出すことをテーマとしたが、敷地に余裕のある「帝塚山の家」では、壁に加えてもうひとつ、主たる要素としてフレームを取り入れ、立体格子と自立壁が重なり合う構成を試みた。柱と壁という建築の普遍的な問題を改めて考えさせられた仕事となった。

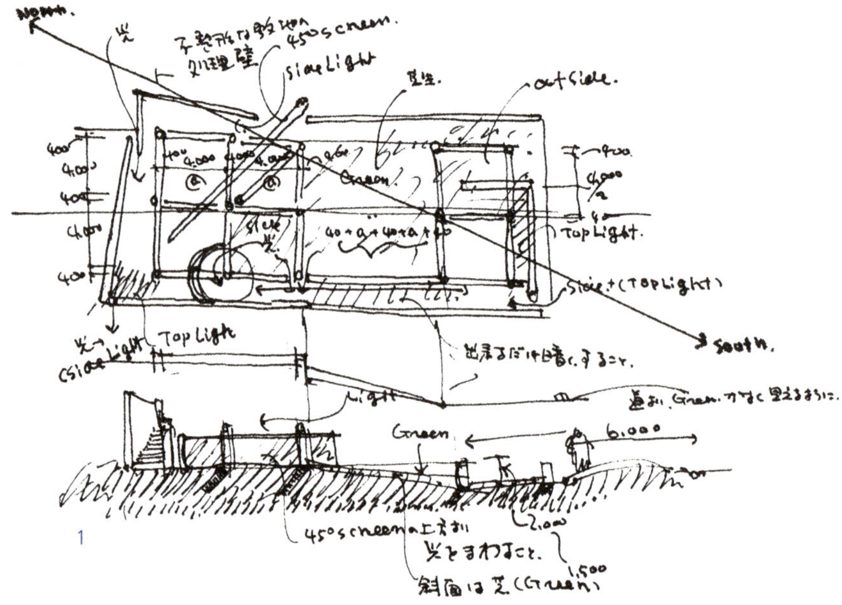

1

1, 2 Concept sketches summarizing the compositional idea. Irregularly shaped walls intrude into a three-dimensional lattice. The slippages arising there produce a varied spatial sequence.
3 Detailed plan drawing.
4 From above: second floor plan, first floor plan, cross section.

1, 2 構成のアイディアが凝縮されたコンセプトスケッチ。立体格子の中に不整形の壁が干渉する。そこに生じるズレが多様な空間のシークエンスを生み出す。
3 平面詳細図。
4 上から2階平面図、1階平面図、断面図。

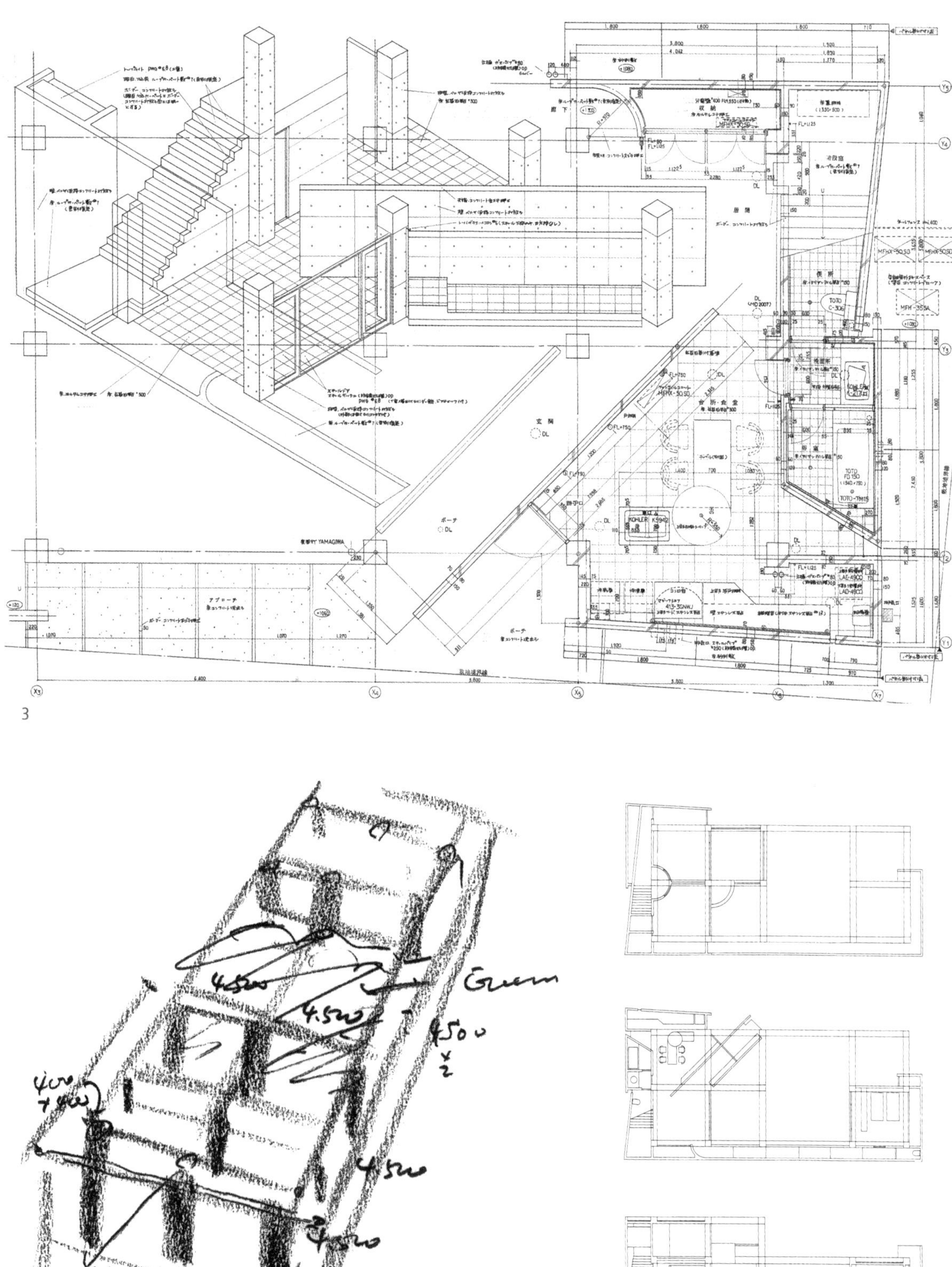

3

2

4

Tezukayama Tower Plaza
帝塚山タワープラザ

1. Osaka, Osaka, Japan 大阪府大阪市
2. 1975.2-1976.1
3. 1976.2-1976.9

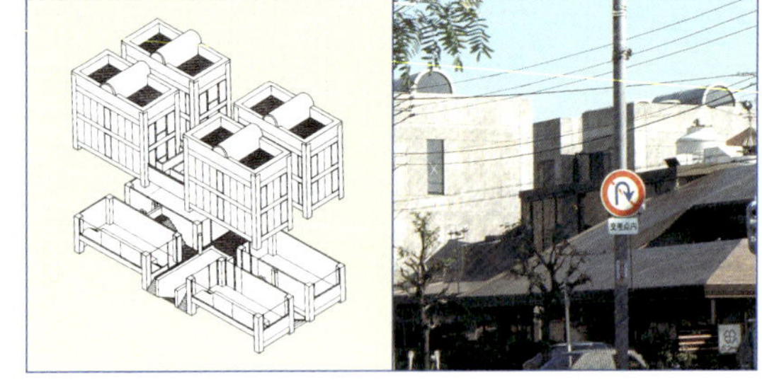

A small-scale mixed residential and commercial facility built in Osaka's Sumiyoshi district. Four towers, each with one basement floor and three floors above ground, are arrayed at intervals. The lower parts are commercial, the second and third floors are maisonette residences, and decks connect the second-floor levels. This composition emerged from the idea of pulling the street into the building.

大阪住吉区につくった小規模な商住の複合施設。地下1階、地上3階のタワーを4本、間隔をおいて並べ、下層部を商業に、2、3階をメゾネットの住居として、2階レベルをデッキで結ぶ。建物の中に街路を引き込むという発想から生まれた構成である。

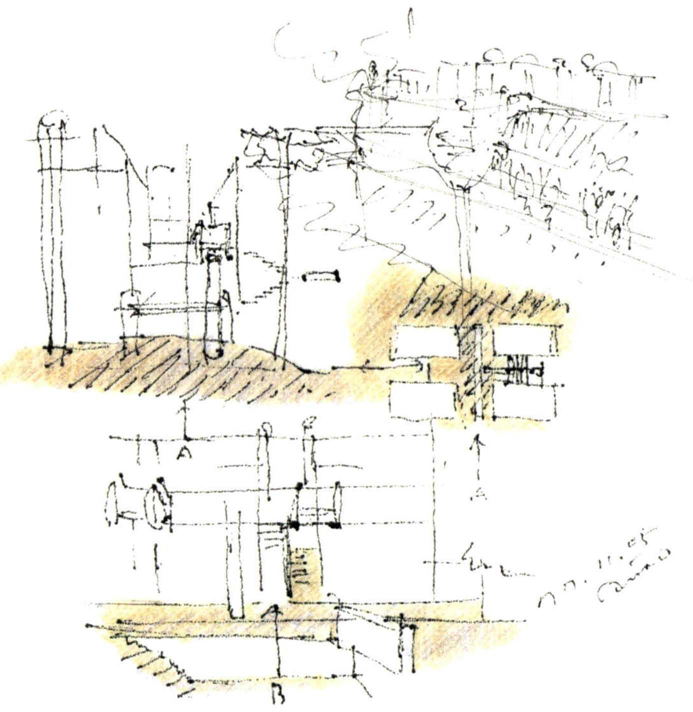

Fuku House
福邸

1. Wakayama, Wakayama, Japan　和歌山県和歌山市
2. 1978.10-1979.4
3. 1979.8-1980.6

Built at the end of the 1970s, this is a comparatively large-scale private residence in Wakayama Prefecture. A plan using a three-dimensional lattice and brightly lit spaces with glass block walls—by superimposing ideas that I had earlier tried in tiny houses, I conceived living spaces appropriate to this scale.

70年代の終わりに和歌山につくった比較的大規模の個人住宅。立体格子によるプランニング、ガラスブロックの壁による光の空間——といったそれまで小規模の住宅で試みてきたアイディアを重ね合わせ、スケールにふさわしい抑揚のある住空間をつくろうと考えた。

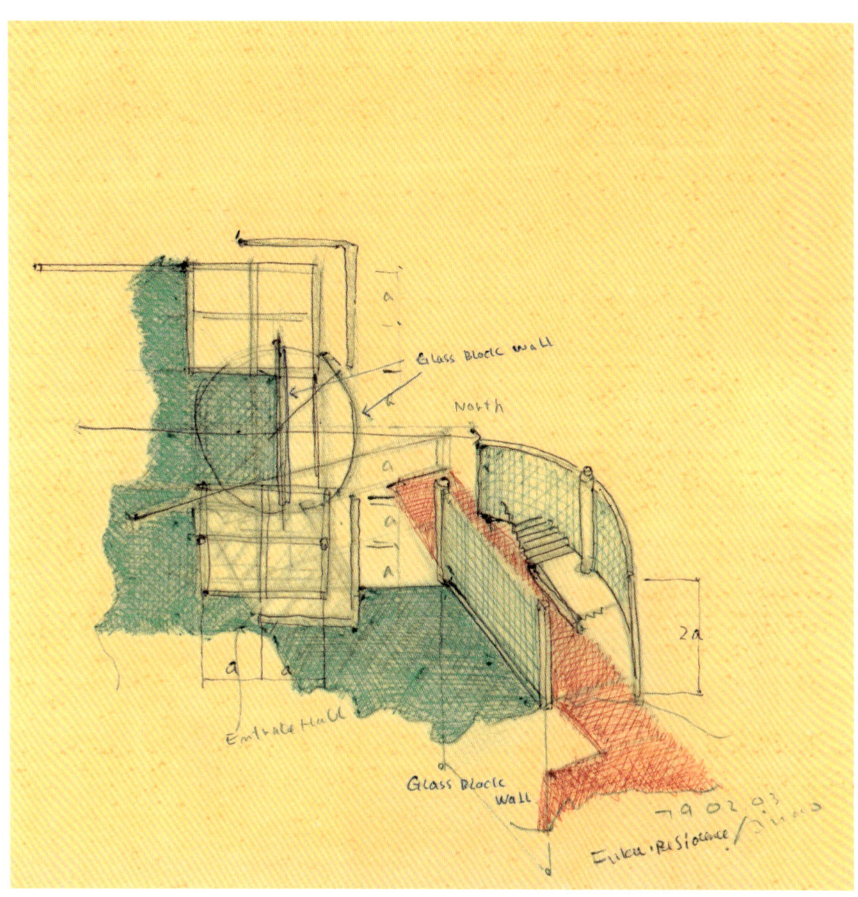

Image sketches of the spatial composition. Two blocks of a three-dimensional frame are placed in axial symmetry. To the south is a courtyard garden enclosed by walls, to the north are the hall and staircase, connected by two glass block walls.

空間構成図式のイメージスケッチ。軸対称に置かれた2棟の立体フレーム。南側は壁で囲われた中庭とし、北側は2枚のガラスブロック壁によってホールと階段室をつないでいる。

Wall House
領壁の家

1. Ashiya, Hyogo, Japan　兵庫県芦屋市
2. 1976.6-1977.2
3. 1977.2-1977.7

In the 1970s, around the time I began my architectural activities, I conceived a housing model using the theme of a "Twin Wall" as if dwelling inside one thick wall. Though differing in shape from the Row House in Sumiyoshi, this house also uses that idea.

1970年代、建築活動をスタートした頃、「ツインウォール」と題して厚い1枚の壁の中に住み込むような住居モデルを考えた。そのアイディアを、住吉の長屋とまた違うかたちで試みたのが、この住宅である。

1 Exploratory sketches of the composition. Architecture with a linear form embedded in a sloping site covered with foliage. Living spaces created by a three-dimensional lattice of posts and beams are interposed between two freestanding walls, with a cylinder as the roof. The architectural expression suggests that a concept has been directly converted into a shape.
2 From above: first floor plan, second floor plan, cross section.
3 Detailed elevation drawing.

1 構成の検討スケッチ。木々の生い茂る傾斜地に埋め込まれたリニアなフォルムの建築。柱・梁の立体格子による住空間を2枚の自立した壁が挟み込み、屋根にはシリンダーが載る。概念がそのままかたちとなって現れたような建築の表現。
2 上から1階平面図、2階平面図、断面図。
3 立面詳細図。

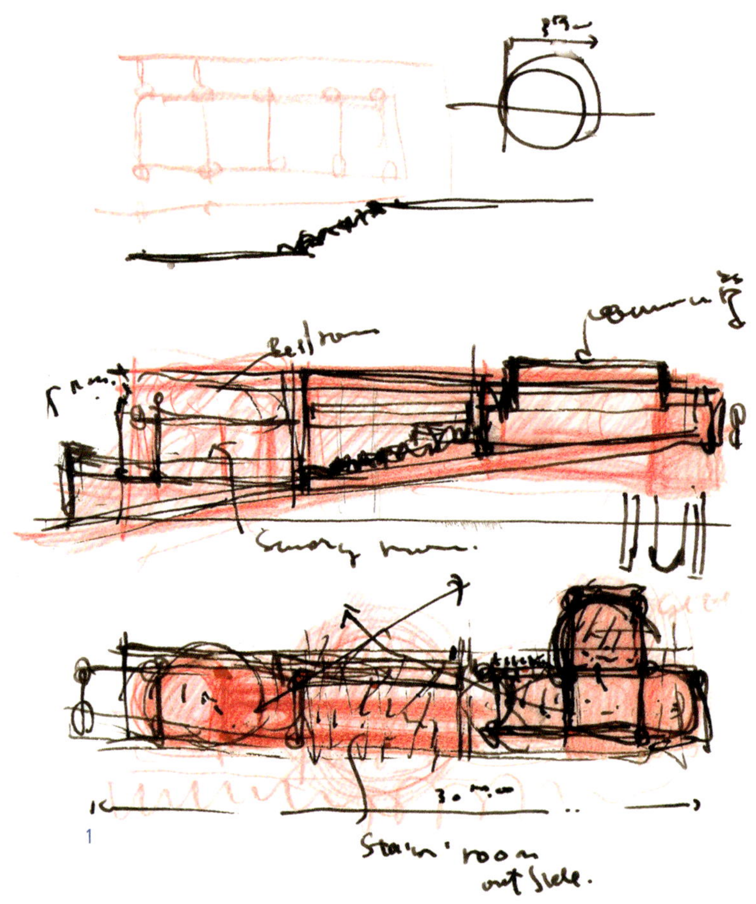

1

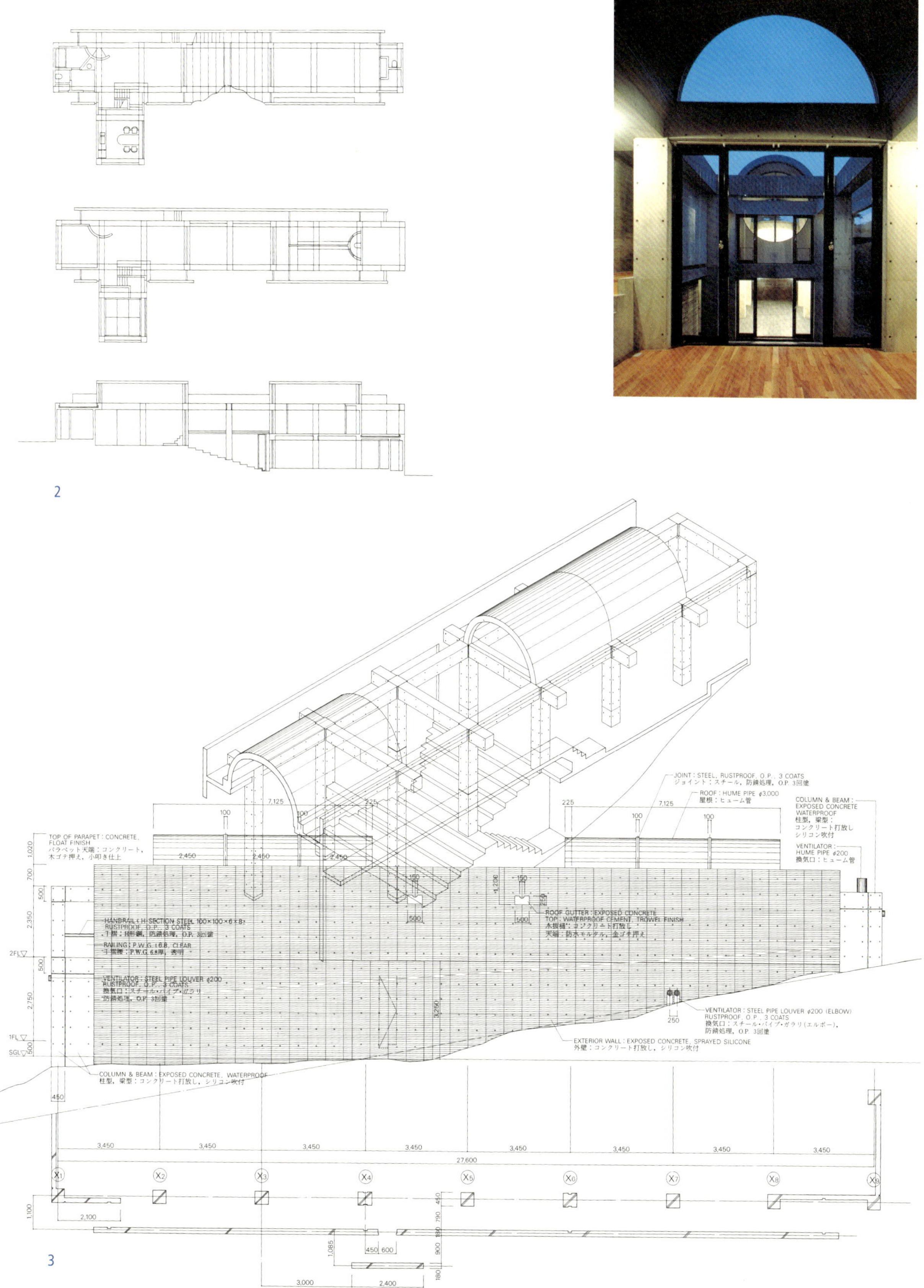

TOP OF PARAPET : CONCRETE, FLOAT FINISH
パラペット天端：コンクリート，木ゴテ押え，小叩き仕上
HANDRAIL : H-SECTION STEEL 100×100×6×8, RUSTPROOF, O.P., 3 COATS
RAILING : P.W.G. 6.8, CLEAR
手摺腰：P.W.G. 6.8厚，透明
VENTILATOR : STEEL PIPE LOUVER ¢200 RUSTPROOF, O.P., 3 COATS
COLUMN & BEAM : EXPOSED CONCRETE, WATERPROOF
柱型，梁型：コンクリート打放し，シリコン吹付
JOINT : STEEL, RUSTPROOF, O.P., 3 COATS
ジョイント：スチール，防錆処理，O.P. 3回塗
ROOF : HUME PIPE ¢3,000
屋根：ヒューム管
COLUMN & BEAM : EXPOSED CONCRETE WATERPROOF
柱型，梁型：コンクリート打放し シリコン吹付
VENTILATOR : HUME PIPE ¢200
換気口：ヒューム管
ROOF GUTTER : EXPOSED CONCRETE
TOP : WATERPROOF CEMENT, TROWEL FINISH
VENTILATOR : STEEL PIPE LOUVER ¢200 (ELBOW)
RUSTPROOF, O.P., 3 COATS
換気口：スチール・パイプ・ガラリ(エルボー)，
防錆処理，O.P. 3回塗
EXTERIOR WALL : EXPOSED CONCRETE, SPRAYED SILICONE
外壁：コンクリート打放し，シリコン吹付
2FL
1FL
SGL
27,600

2

3

STEP
STEP

1. Takamatsu, Kagawa, Japan　香川県高松市
2. 1977.4-1978.10
3. 1979.2-1980.3

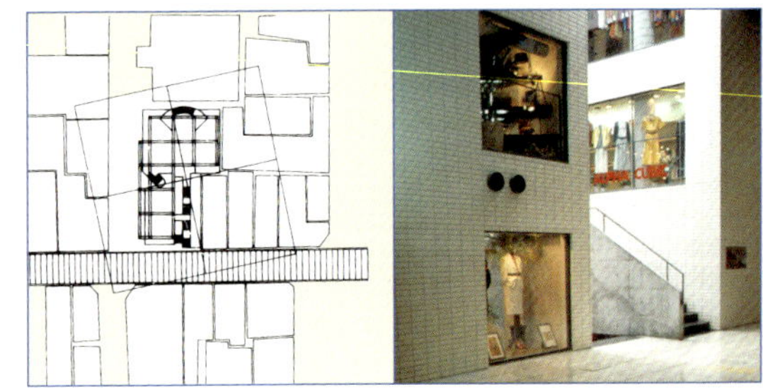

This is a commercial facility built within a shopping arcade in Takamatsu City. Here, against the background of typical shopping streets in a Japanese provincial city, I thought of making an intense space piercing this monotony. This is the 4m-wide three-dimensional alley space created in the middle of the four-story building. Because there is no roof over it, wind and rain enter directly. Centered around a staircase that ascends as one goes deeper, exterior space is drawn into the building interior and another city is created —this is related to my later commercial building projects such as FESTIVAL and GALLERIA [akka].

高松市のアーケードの中につくった商業施設である。ここでは日本の地方都市に典型的な書き割り的な商店街の風景の中にあって、その単調さを突き破るような激しい空間をつくりたいと考えた。それが4階建ての建物中央に設けた、幅4mほどの立体路地の空間である。屋根を架けていないため、風雨はそのまま入り込んでくる。奥に進むにつれて上昇するこの階段を中心として、建物内に外部空間を引き込み、もうひとつの都市をつくり出す——この仕事が後の「フェスティバル」や「GALLERIA [akka]」といった私の商業建築へとつながっていった。

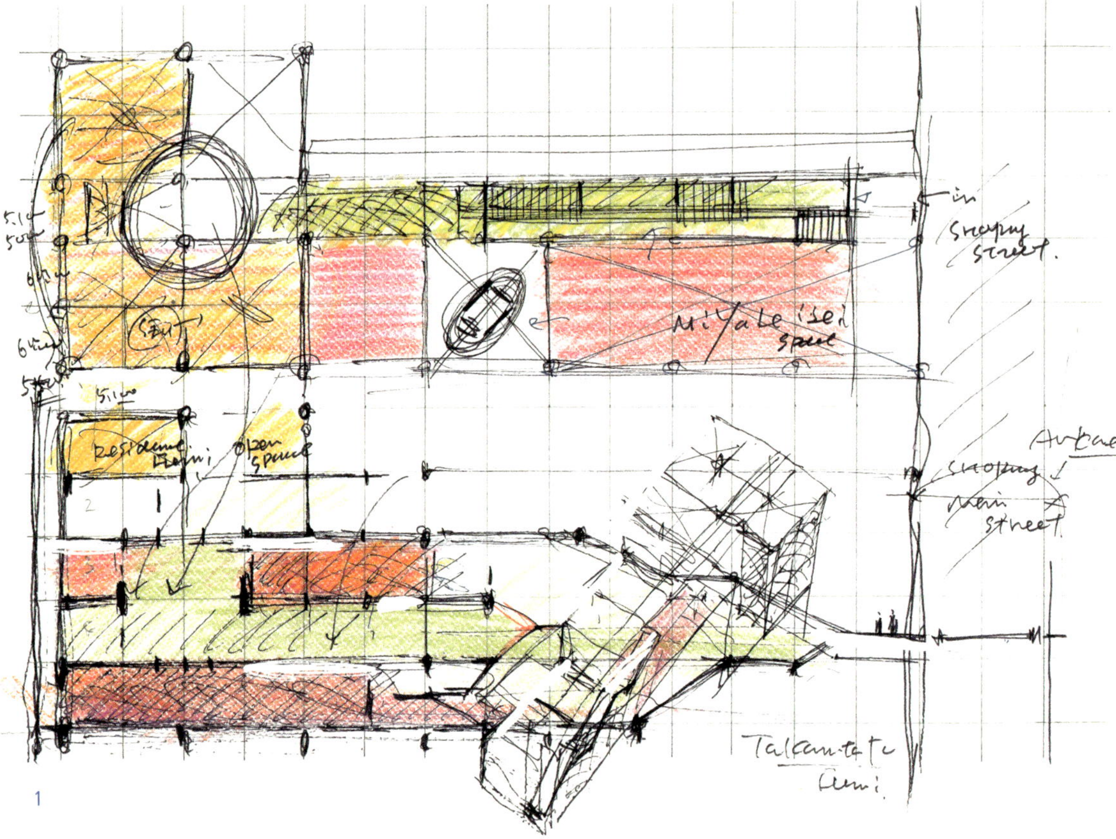

1

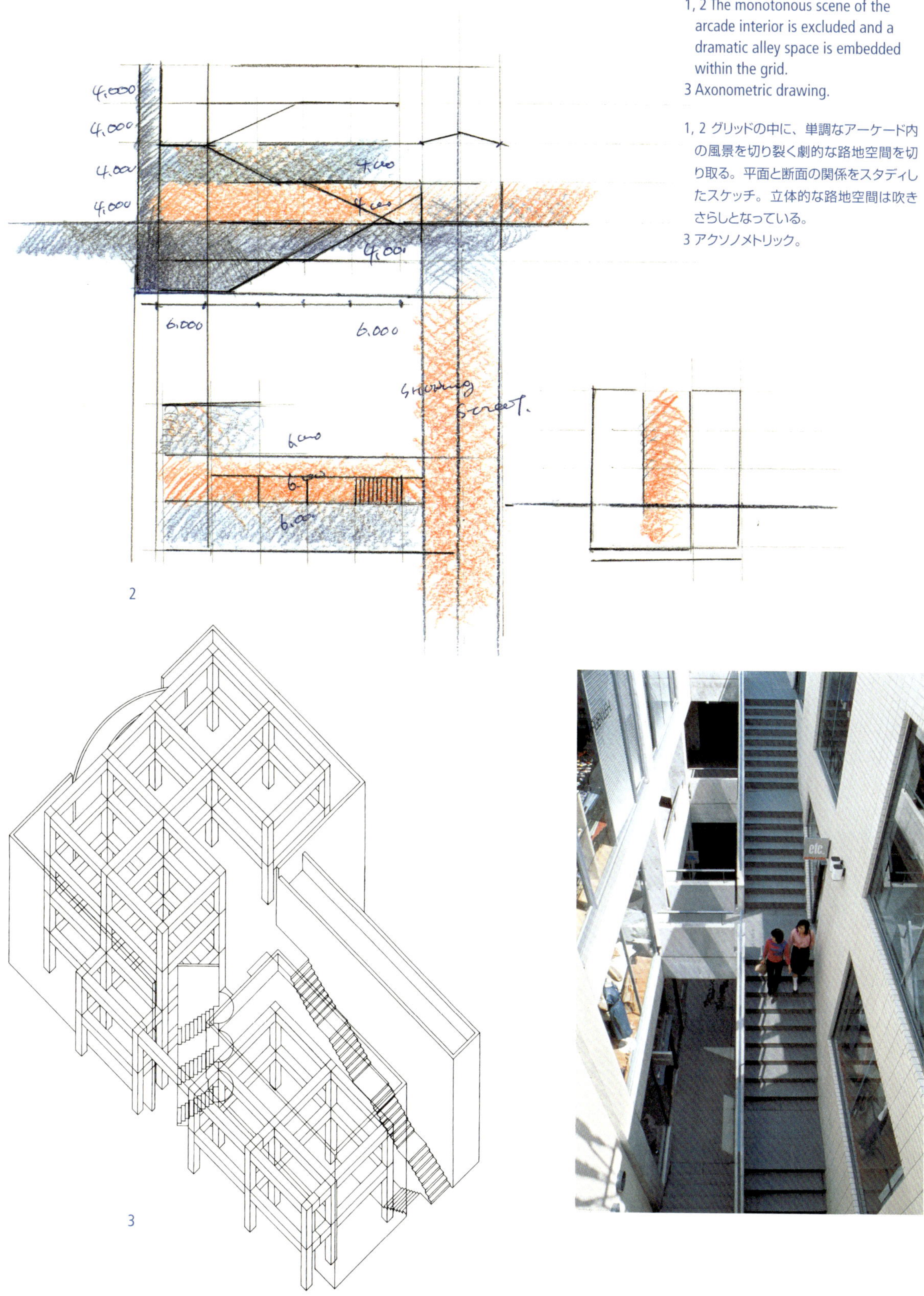

2

3

1, 2 The monotonous scene of the arcade interior is excluded and a dramatic alley space is embedded within the grid.
3 Axonometric drawing.

1, 2 グリッドの中に、単調なアーケード内の風景を切り裂く劇的な路地空間を切り取る。平面と断面の関係をスタディしたスケッチ。立体的な路地空間は吹きさらしとなっている。
3 アクソノメトリック。

Glass Block House
ガラスブロックの家

1. Osaka, Osaka, Japan　大阪府大阪市
2. 1977.7-1978.4
3. 1978.6-1978.12

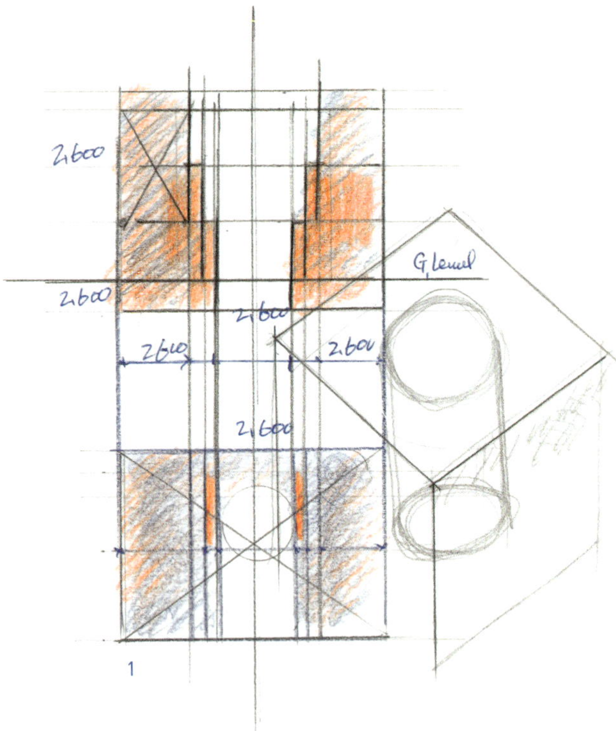

1

This is a two-generation residence built on a rectangular site in a disorderly townscape crowded with small- to medium-size factories and shops. Attempting to make the house an independent microcosm, I began with the composition of a volume filling the entire site containing a courtyard in the middle, but it is difficult to bring daylight to the lower parts of a three-story building. Accordingly, I adopted a cross-sectional composition in which rooms facing the courtyard on the higher floors are progressively set back. Glass blocks are used for the funnel-shaped light garden thus achieved, as well as for the partitions inside the house. I imagined a space as if light had been given a shape.

中小の町工場、商店が建て込む雑然とした街中の矩形の敷地につくった2世帯住宅である。自立した小宇宙としての住まいをつくろうと、敷地いっぱいにヴォリュームを立ち上げ、その中央を中庭とする構成で考え始めたが、3層では下まで光が届きにくい。そこで中庭に面する室が上階にいくにつれてセットバックする断面構成をとった。そうしてできる漏斗型の光庭の空間と住宅内部を区切る材料にはガラスブロックを用いた。光をかたちにしたような空間をイメージしていた。

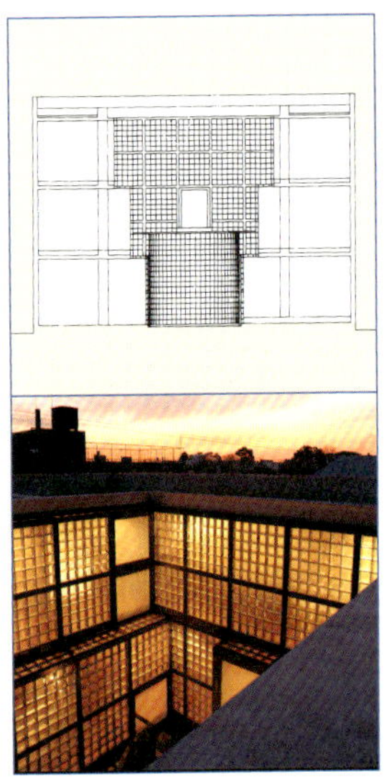

2

1, 2 Study sketches of the spatial composition diagram with a void at the center. Delineating the essence of the architectural intentions.

3 The architecture is regulated by the standardized 200mm-square module of glass blocks. A cross-sectional detail overlaid on an axonometric in order to accurately grasp detail problems that are difficult to draw in plan and cross section.

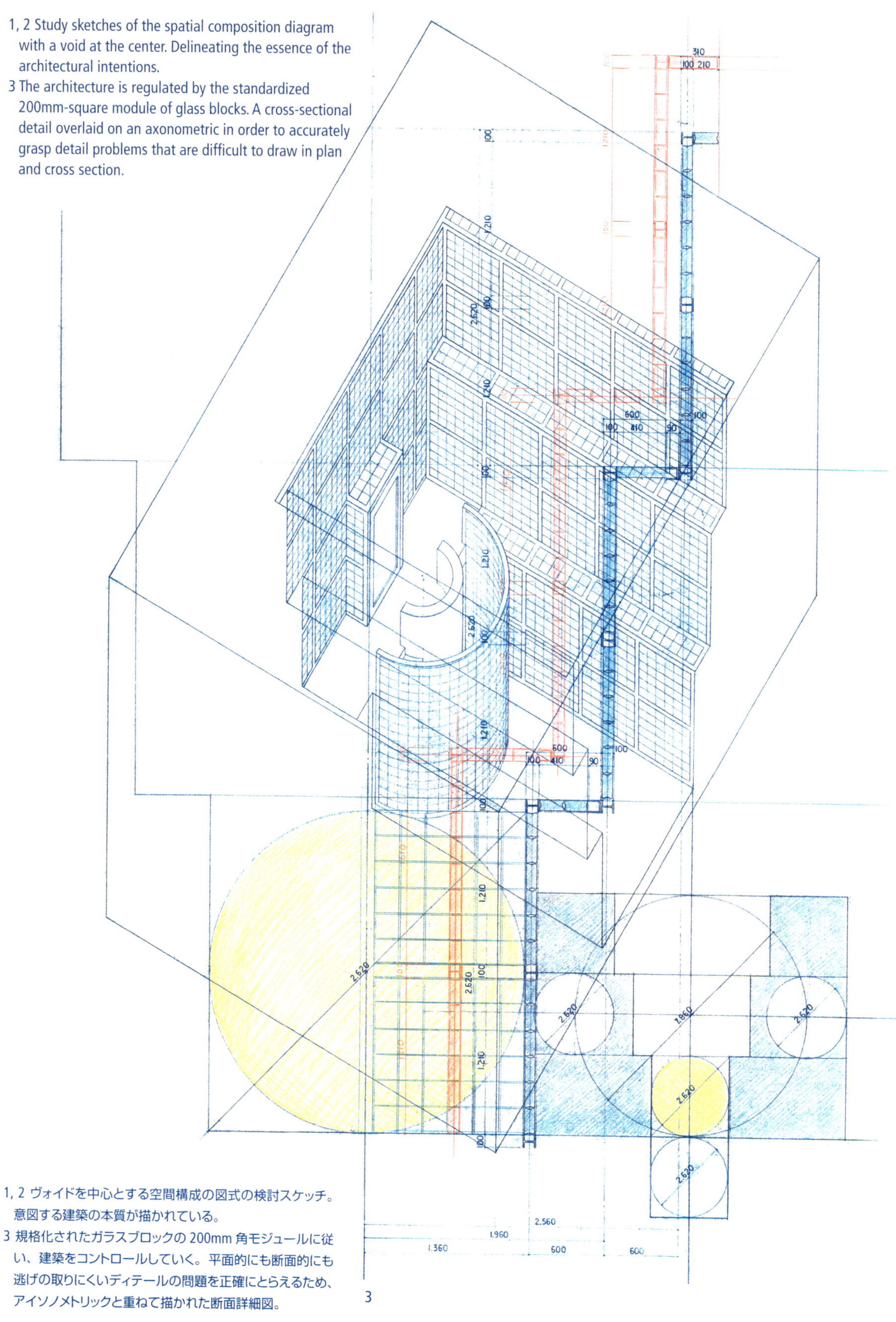

3

1, 2 ヴォイドを中心とする空間構成の図式の検討スケッチ。意図する建築の本質が描かれている。

3 規格化されたガラスブロックの 200mm 角モジュールに従い、建築をコントロールしていく。平面的にも断面的にも逃げの取りにくいディテールの問題を正確にとらえるため、アイソノメトリックと重ねて描かれた断面詳細図。

Rokko Housing I
六甲の集合住宅 I

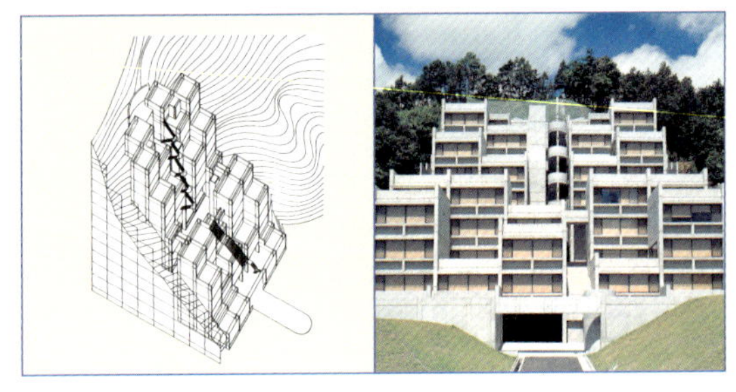

1. Kobe, Hyogo, Japan　兵庫県神戸市
2. 1978.10-1981.10
3. 1981.10-1983.5

The site is a slope with a 60-degree incline located at the foot of Mt. Rokko in Kobe. This is mass housing project based on a total of eighteen maisonettes. A building on a flat site at the foot of the slope was initially requested, but I felt that the slope at the rear of the site had a larger potential. Having convinced the client, the project began. A composition that traces a slope with geometric shapes, using concrete post-and-beam units as the basic module, was an idea I had been thinking about since the Okamoto Housing of the mid-1970s.

敷地は、神戸六甲山の麓、60度の勾配をもった急斜面に位置する。全18戸のメゾネットを基本とした集合住宅である。当初は斜面下の平坦地に建築を依頼されたが、現地で背後の斜面の方に大きな可能性を感じ、クライアントを説き伏せてこのプロジェクトをスタートした。コンクリート・ラーメンのユニットを基本単位とする幾何学形態で斜面をなぞる構成は、70年代半ばの岡本ハウジングから考えていたアイディアだった。

Initial image sketches. The shape of the slope is converted into geometric forms. Architecture with an appearance similar to that of an Italian hilltop town. The slippages in plan and section, generated as a result of adjusting the simple geometric units to the slope, give hints for the composition.

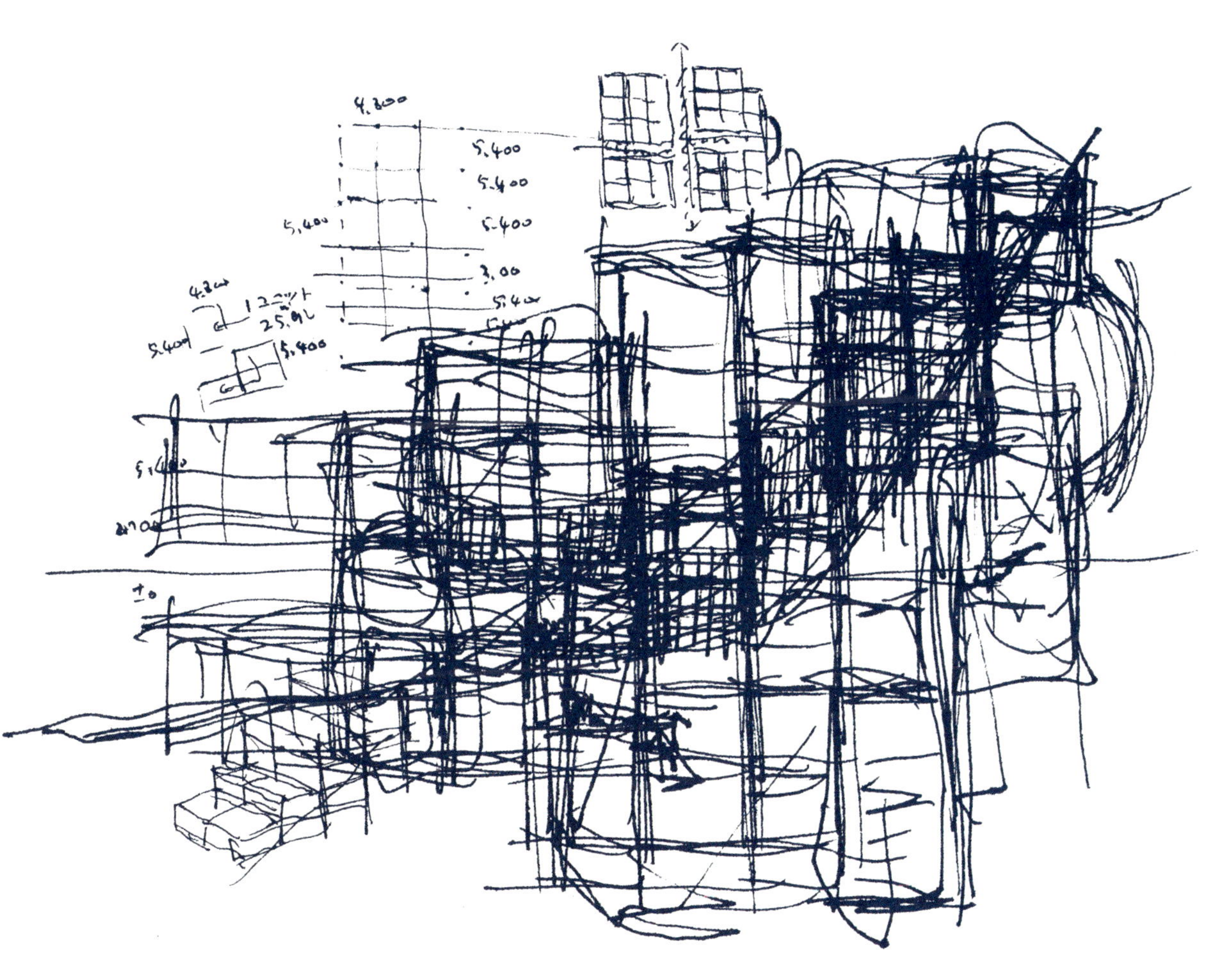

初期のイメージスケッチ。斜面形状を幾何学形態に変転する。イタリア山岳地帯の集落のような建築の佇まい。単純なユニットの幾何学を斜面になじませる結果生じる平断面のズレを、構成の手がかりとしていく。

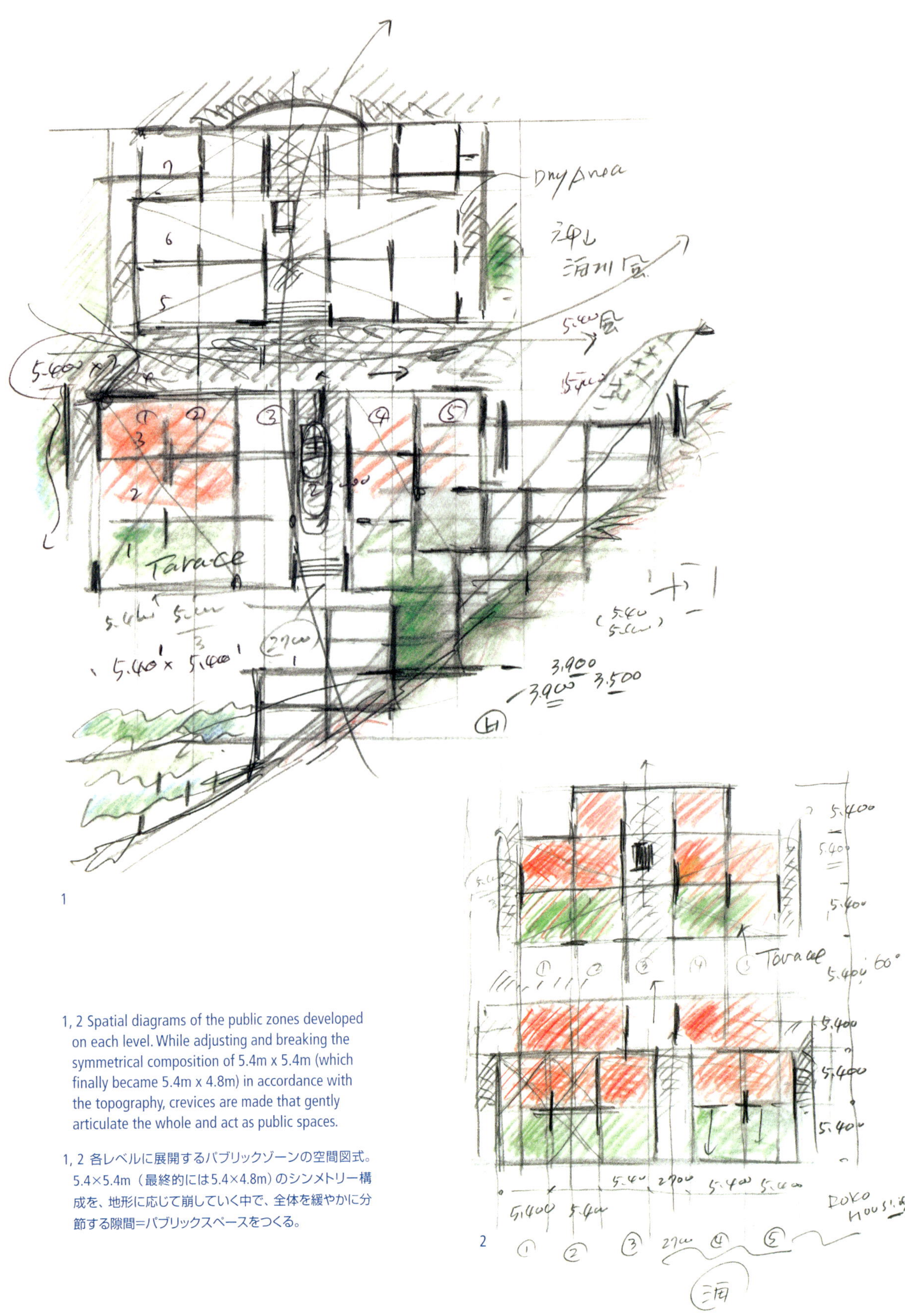

1

2

1, 2 Spatial diagrams of the public zones developed on each level. While adjusting and breaking the symmetrical composition of 5.4m x 5.4m (which finally became 5.4m x 4.8m) in accordance with the topography, crevices are made that gently articulate the whole and act as public spaces.

1, 2 各レベルに展開するパブリックゾーンの空間図式。5.4×5.4m（最終的には5.4×4.8m）のシンメトリー構成を、地形に応じて崩していく中で、全体を緩やかに分節する隙間＝パブリックスペースをつくる。

3 Cross section. Based on maisonettes that make full use of the slope, the dwellings have many variations created by inserting roof terraces into the plans. The fissure-like spaces that run between the housing units are buffer zones that delineate a subtle gradation between public and private, and also function as devices that draw nature into the building.
4 Plans of each floor.

3 断面図。住戸は斜面を活かしたメゾネットを基本とし、ルーフテラスをプランに組み込むことで、多様なヴァリエーションをつくる。亀裂のように走る住棟間のスペースは、公私の間に微妙なグラデーションを描く緩衝領域であるのと同時に、建物内に自然を引き込む装置として機能する。
4 各階平面図。

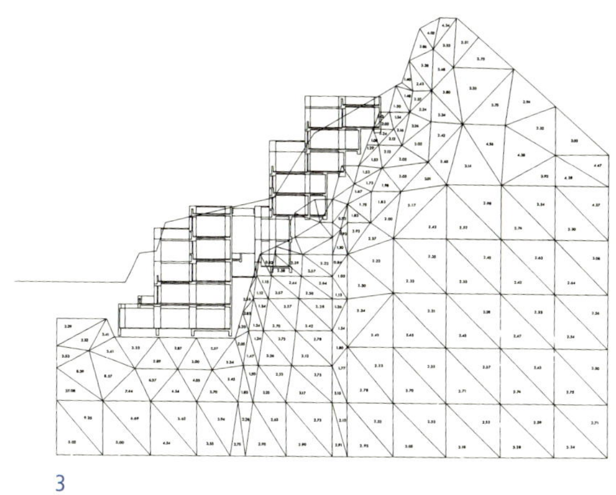

3

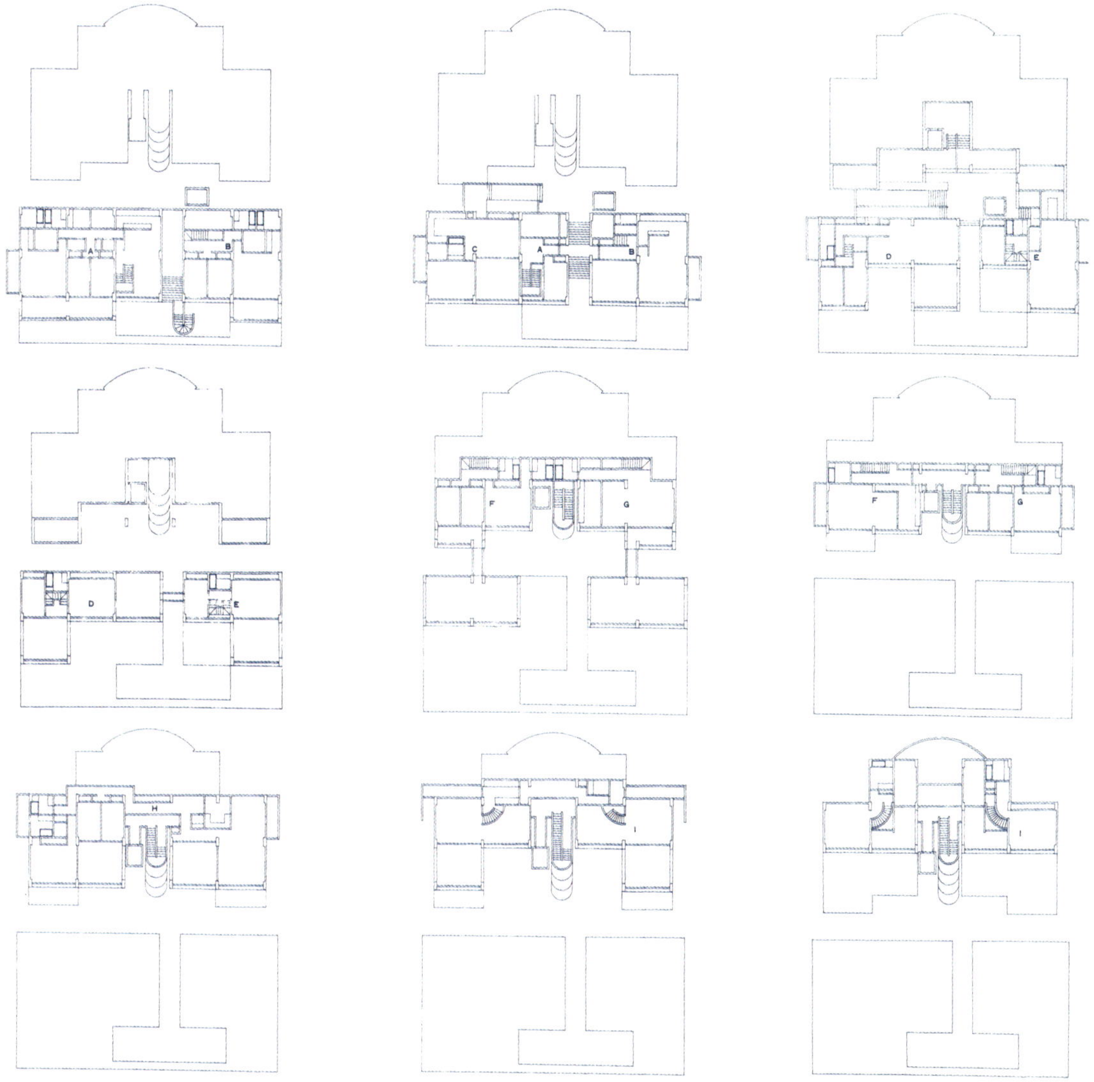

4

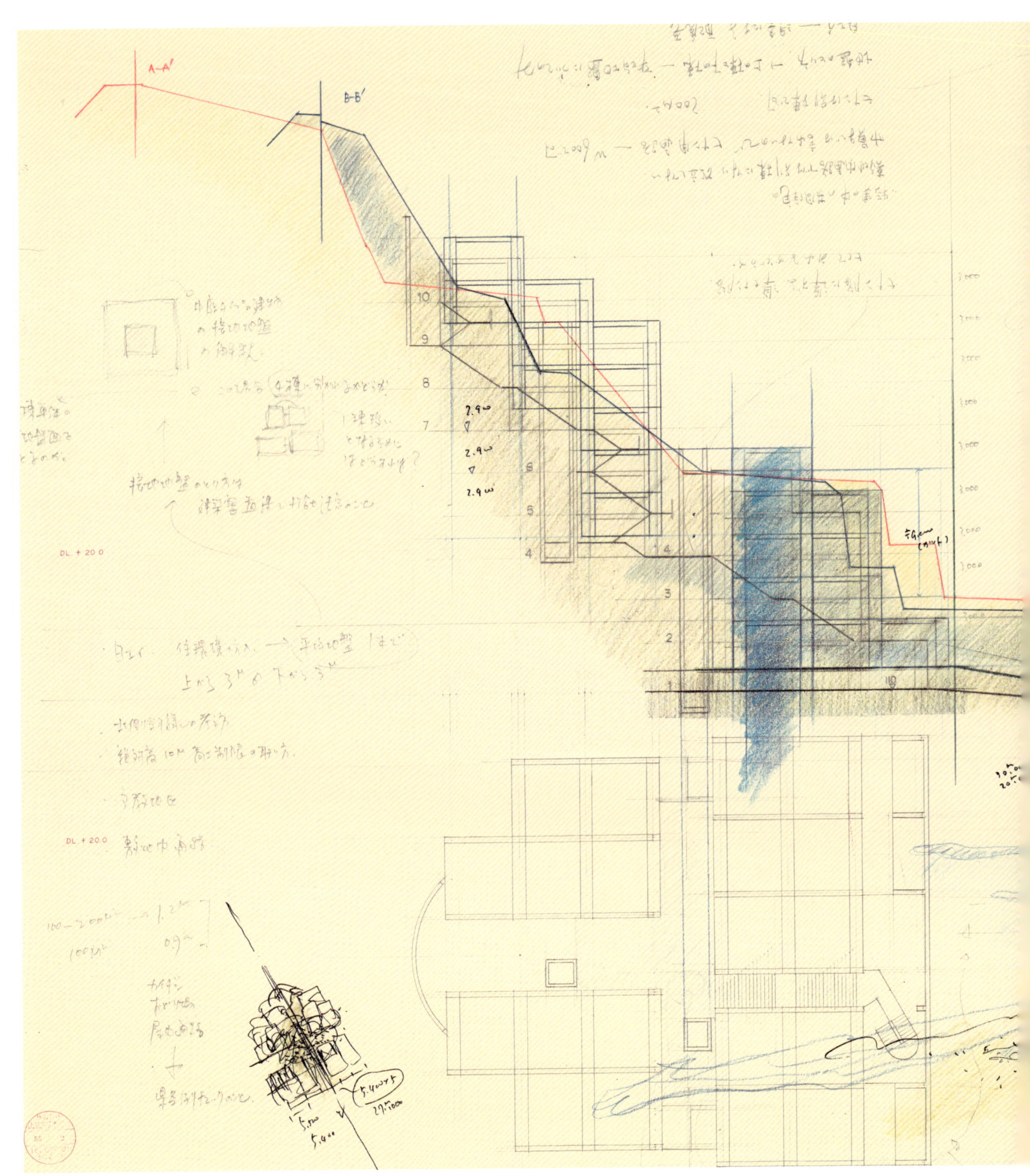

Draft of the cross-sectional layout, drawn for a meeting with the contractor prior to the start of construction. By overlaying the necessary information, it becomes a single sheet that plainly expresses the main points of the architecture.

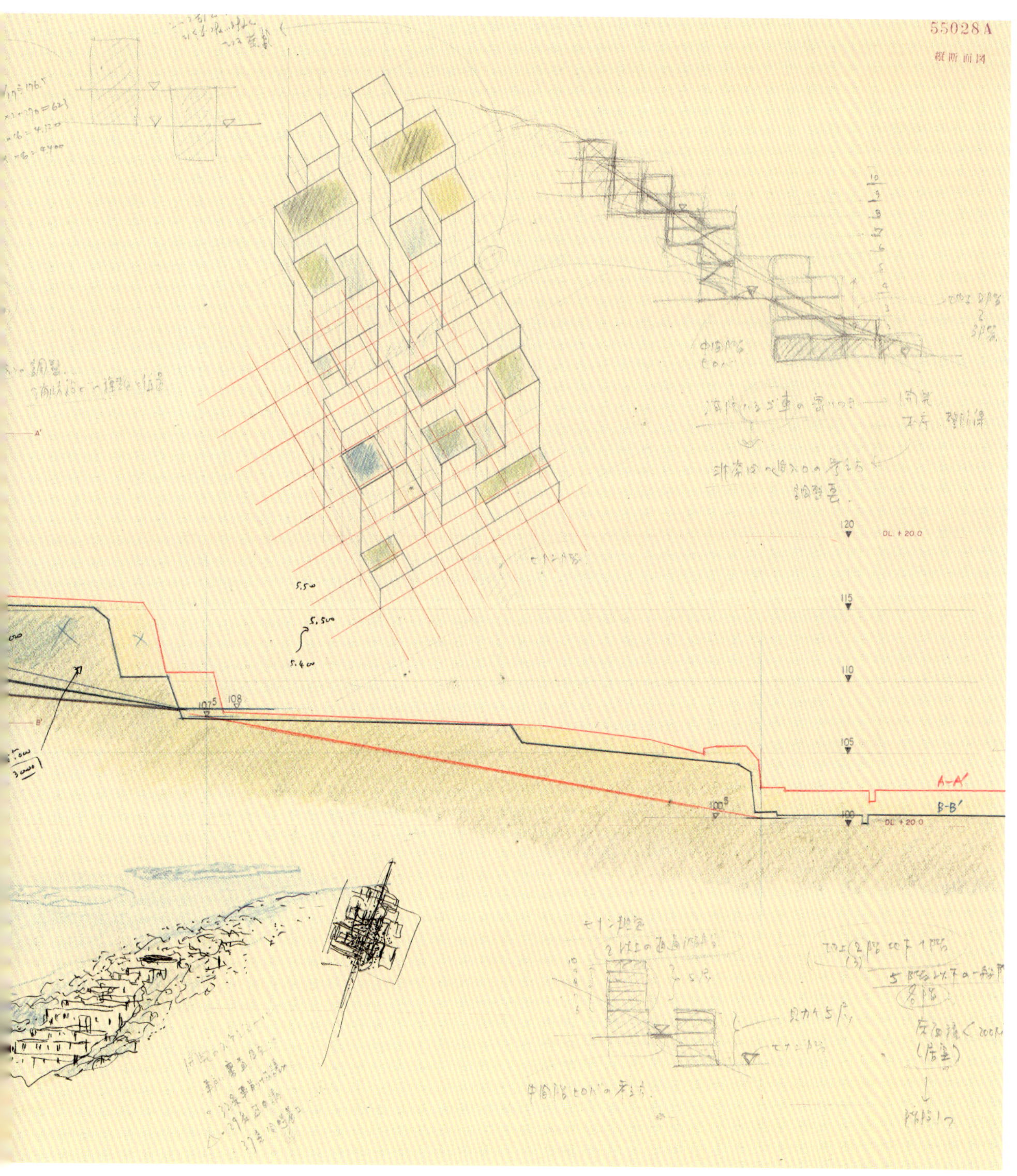

工事着手時、施工会社との打ち合わせのために描かれた断面配置検討図。必要な情報が書き重ねられていく中で、建築の要点が端的に表現された1枚となった。

1 Axonometric cross section.
2 Exploratory sketch of the central staircase. Made while considering issues such as the effects of natural light in each place and views of the scenery from the stair landings, which give a sense of pleasure to climbing by foot.

1 断面アクソノメトリック。
2 中央階段検討スケッチ。足で上ることの楽しさを感じられる階段として踊り場から見る風景、各所の光の効果などを考えてつくられている。

1

2

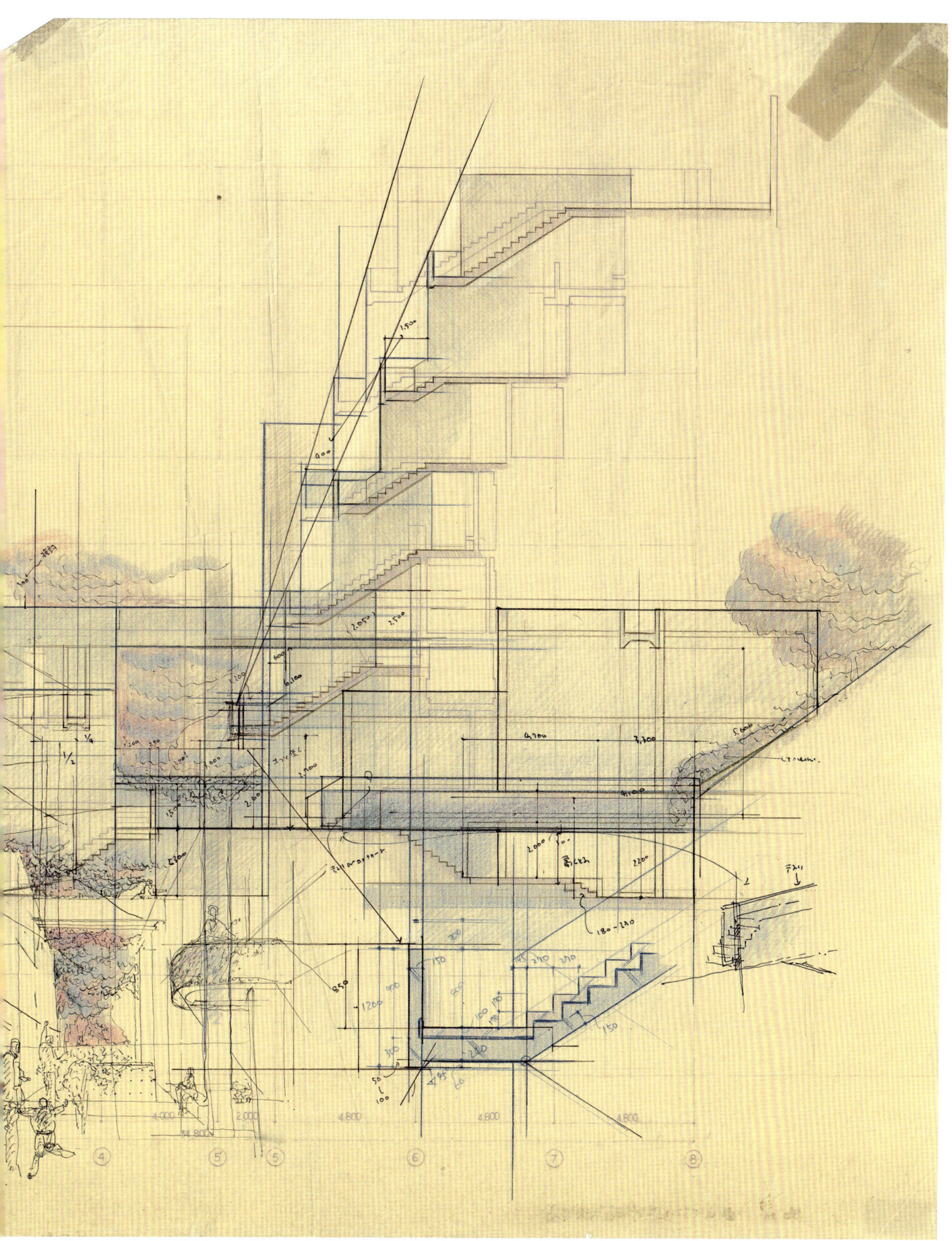

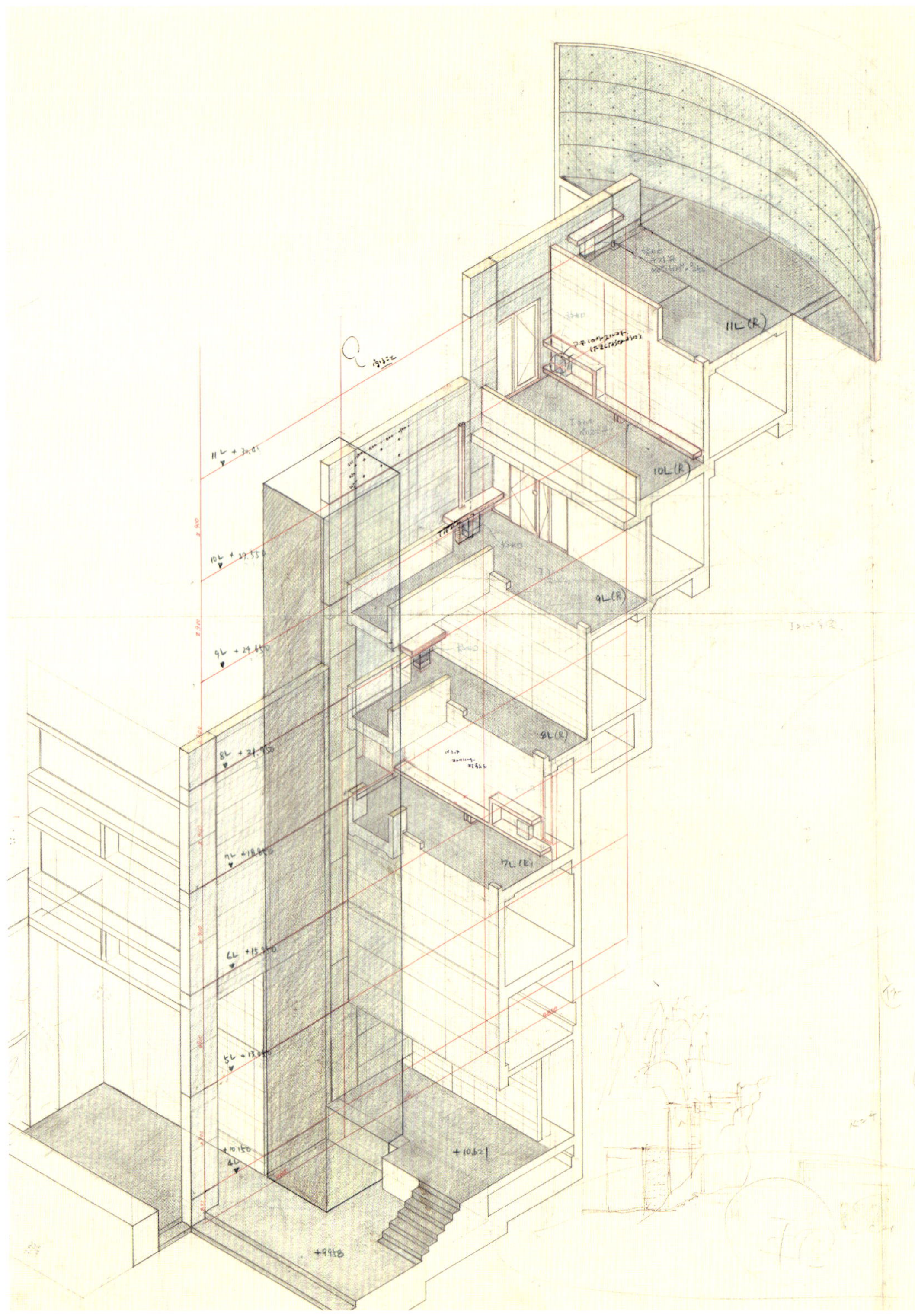

1

1 Exploratory sectional drawing of the setback parts.
2 Exploratory drawing of the elevation. The strict geometry continues all the way to the corners.

2

1 セットバック部分の断面検討図。
2 立面検討図。厳格な幾何学のシステムが隅々まで貫かれている。

Rokko Housing II
六甲の集合住宅 II

1. Kobe, Hyogo, Japan　兵庫県神戸市
2. 1985.8-1987.4
3. 1989.10-1993.5

In 1983, around the time Rokko Housing I was completed, an entirely different entrepreneur offered me a commission that sounded like a joke: "I want to make a similar housing project for the adjacent slope." With a site area about three times larger, a total allowable floor area about four times larger, and fifty units, the conditions provided more flexibility than phase I, in which legal regulations such as the allowable building envelope had been strict. Given this opportunity, rather than simply repeating phase I, all my effort was thrown into trying to make a stronger development of that idea.

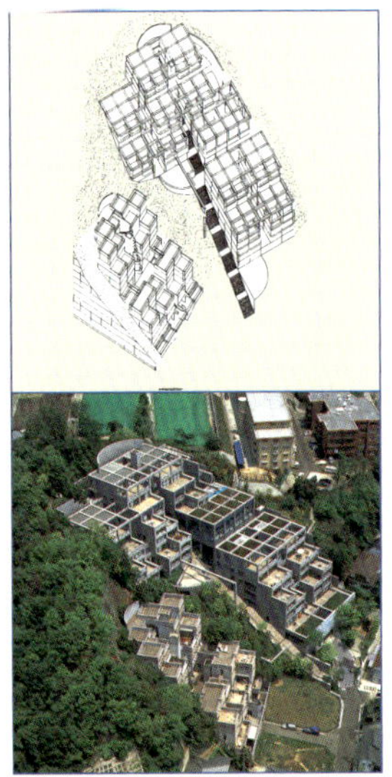

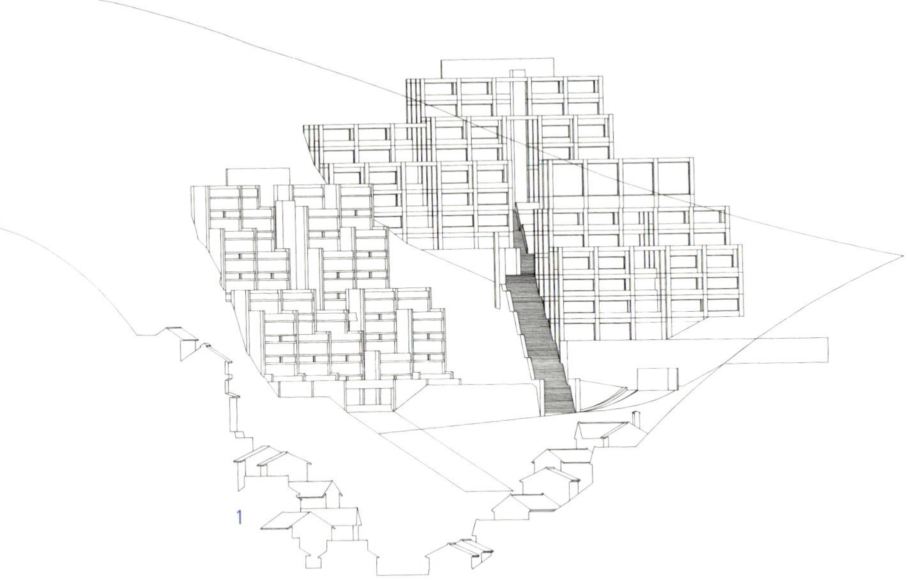

1

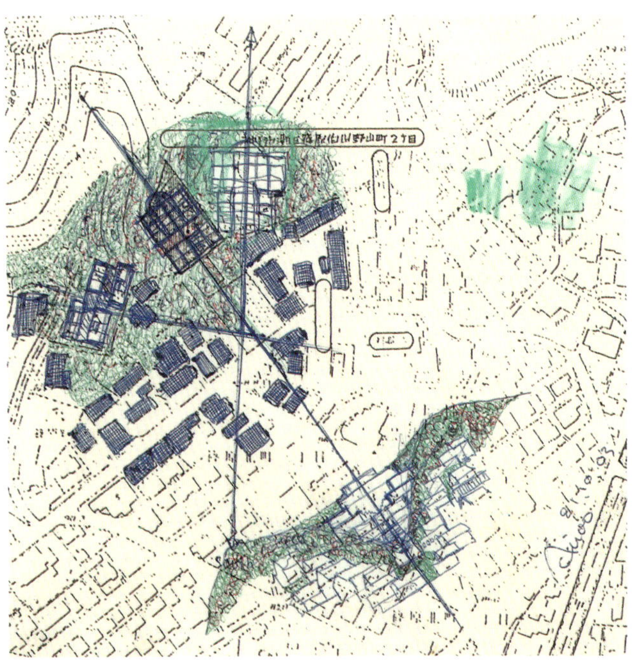

2

1 Elevation. The architecture of phase II was conceived as if producing new scenery by considering the site to include phase I, in an exponential relationship.
2 Study for the layout of phase II, which is guided by the topography along an axis shifted about 30 degrees from phase I. Making an architectural scene that could be called an urban edge, at the foot of the Kobe mountains.
3 Photograph during construction (November 1991).

1 立面図。I 期も含めて敷地とみなし、それぞれが累乗的に関係しあい、新たな風景をつくり出すようなII期の建築を考える。
2 地形から導かれるI 期と約30度角度を振った軸線に沿うII期の配置を検討。神戸の山の手に、都市のエッジともいうべき建築の風景をつくっていく。
3 工事中の写真（91年11月）。

1983年、六甲の集合住宅Ⅰの完成に前後して、まったく別の事業者から「隣接する斜面地に同じく集合住宅をつくりたい」という冗談のような仕事の依頼がきた。敷地面積約3倍、延床面積約4倍の50戸の規模で斜線制限等の法的規制が厳しかったⅠ期よりもかなり余裕のある条件だった。これをチャンスとして「単にⅠ期の反復をするのではなく、そのアイディアをより強く、発展させたものをつくろう」と力いっぱい取り組んだ。

3

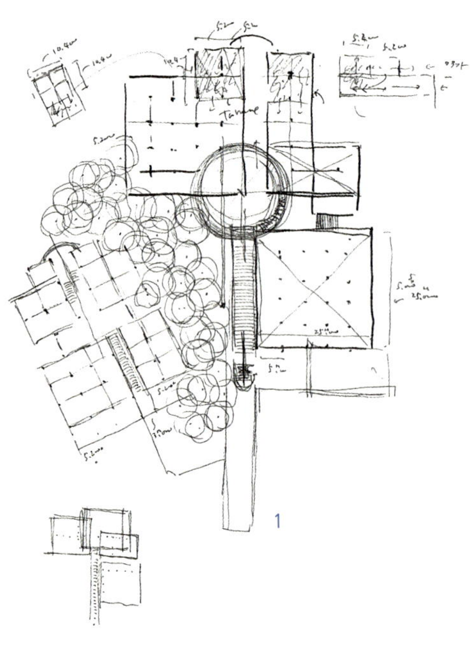

1

2

1 As in phase I, slippage is created by embedding the unit frames in the topography, then taking the intermediate space as an axis in order to produce a richly varied assemblage.

2 Compositional diagrams of the sizes, plans, and varied dwelling units. Beyond the given program, phase II is an attempt to augment the public spaces, such as an indoor public pool from which the sea is visible.

1 Ⅰ期同様、ユニットのフレームを地形に埋め込んでいくことでズレを生じさせ、その余白の空間を軸に、変化に富んだ集合体をつくり出す。

2 大きさ、プランとも多様な住戸のユニットの構成ダイアグラム。海の見える屋内プールなど、Ⅱ期ではプログラムの上でもパブリックスペースのさらなる充実が試みられている。

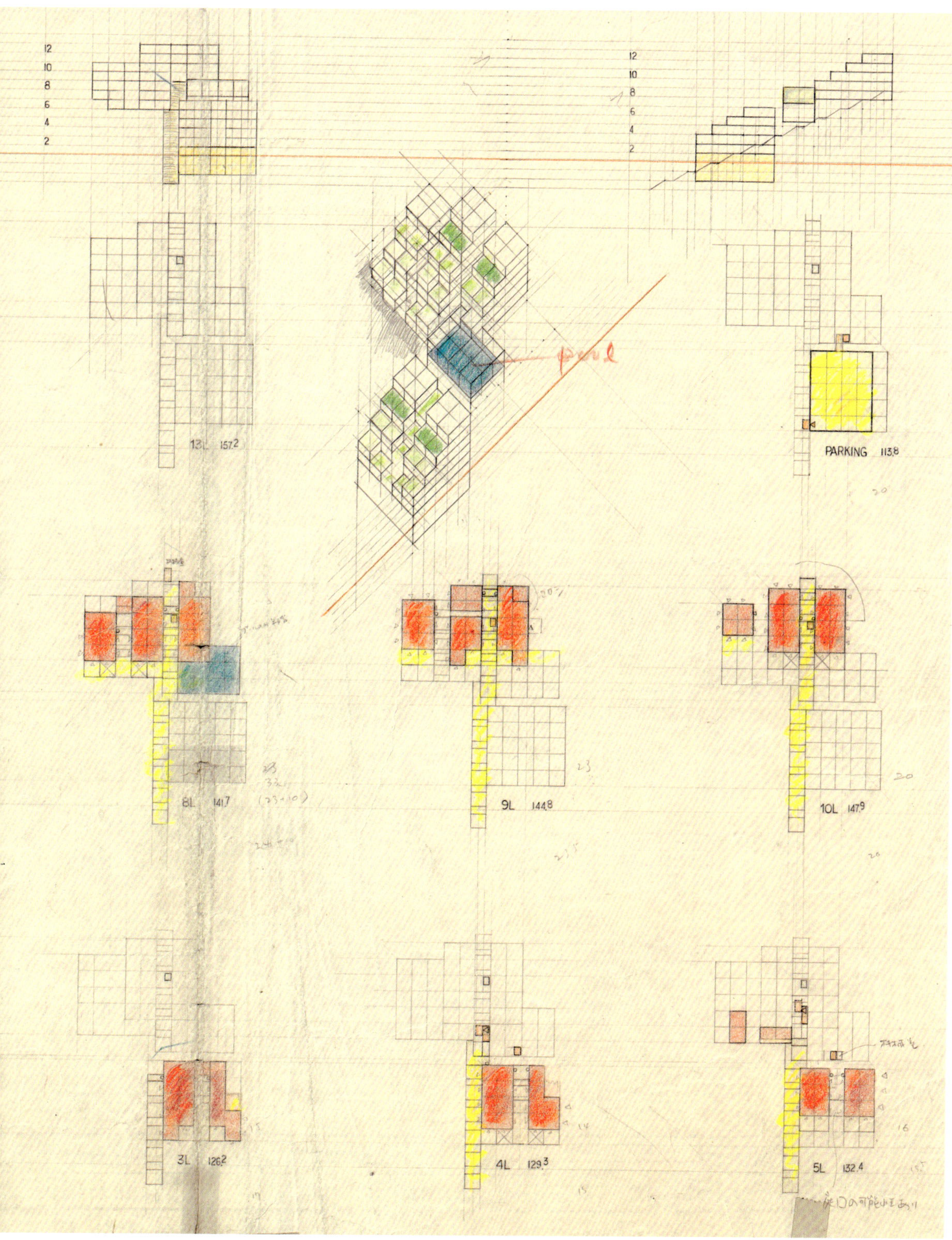

12
10
8
6
4
2
12
10
8
6
4
2
pool
13L 157.2
PARKING 113.8
8L 141.7
9L 144.8
10L 147.9
3L 126.2
4L 129.3
5L 132.4

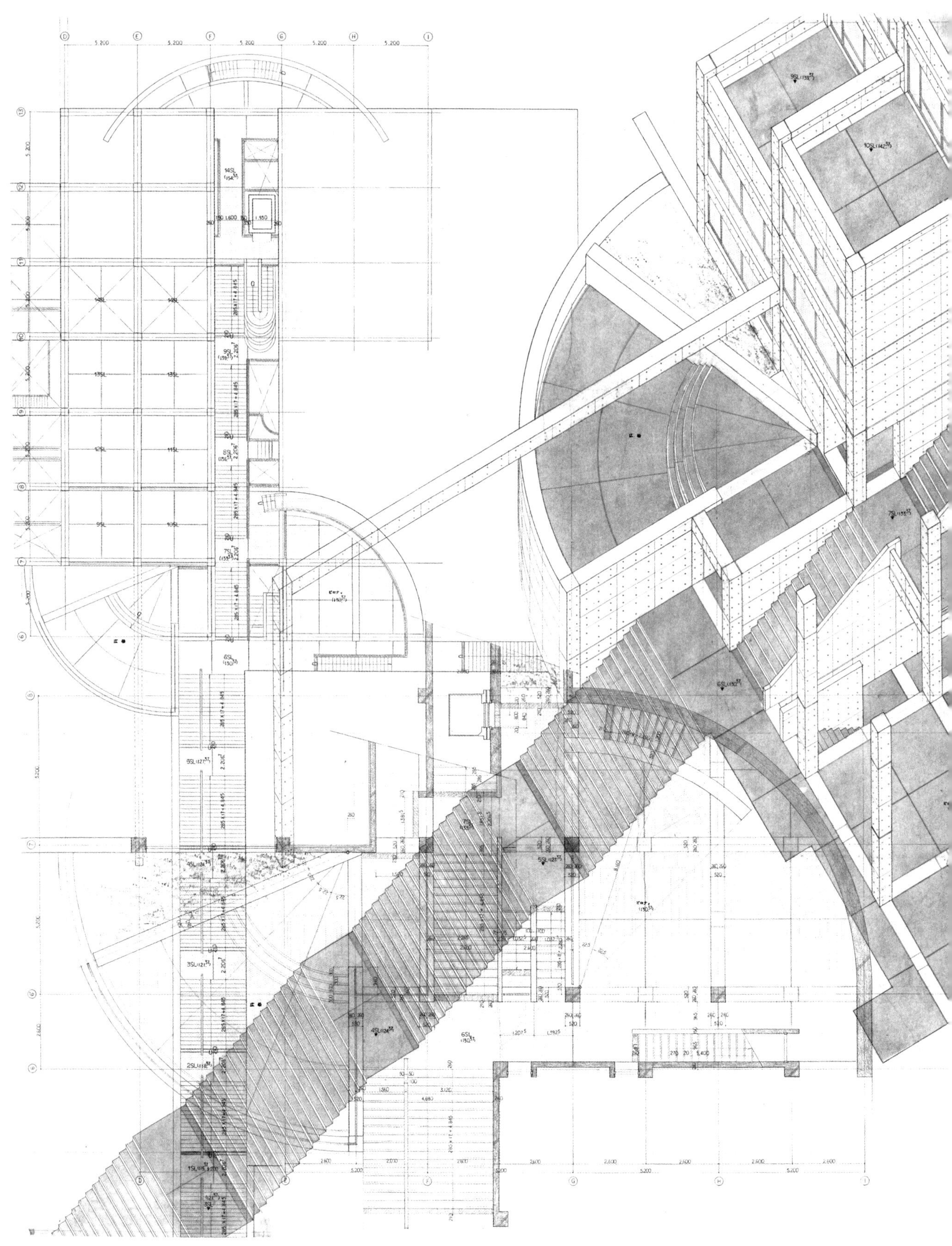

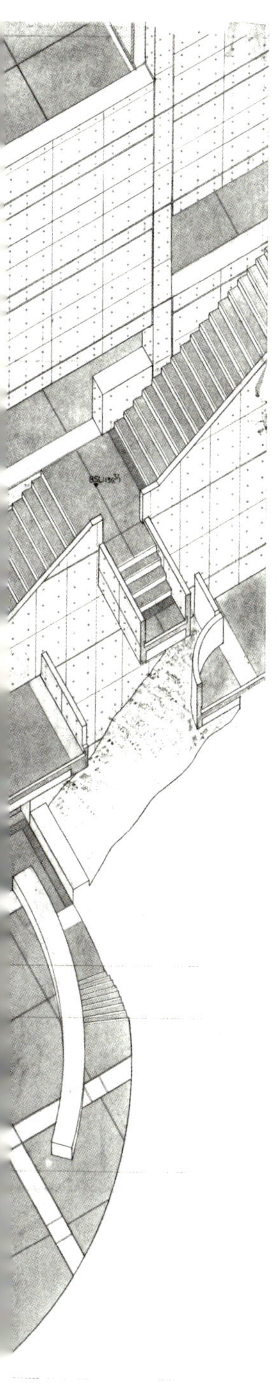

Detailed study of the central plaza that is the nucleus of the public spaces traversing the housing blocks.

住棟間を巡るパブリックスペースのひとつの核となる中央プラザの検討詳細図。

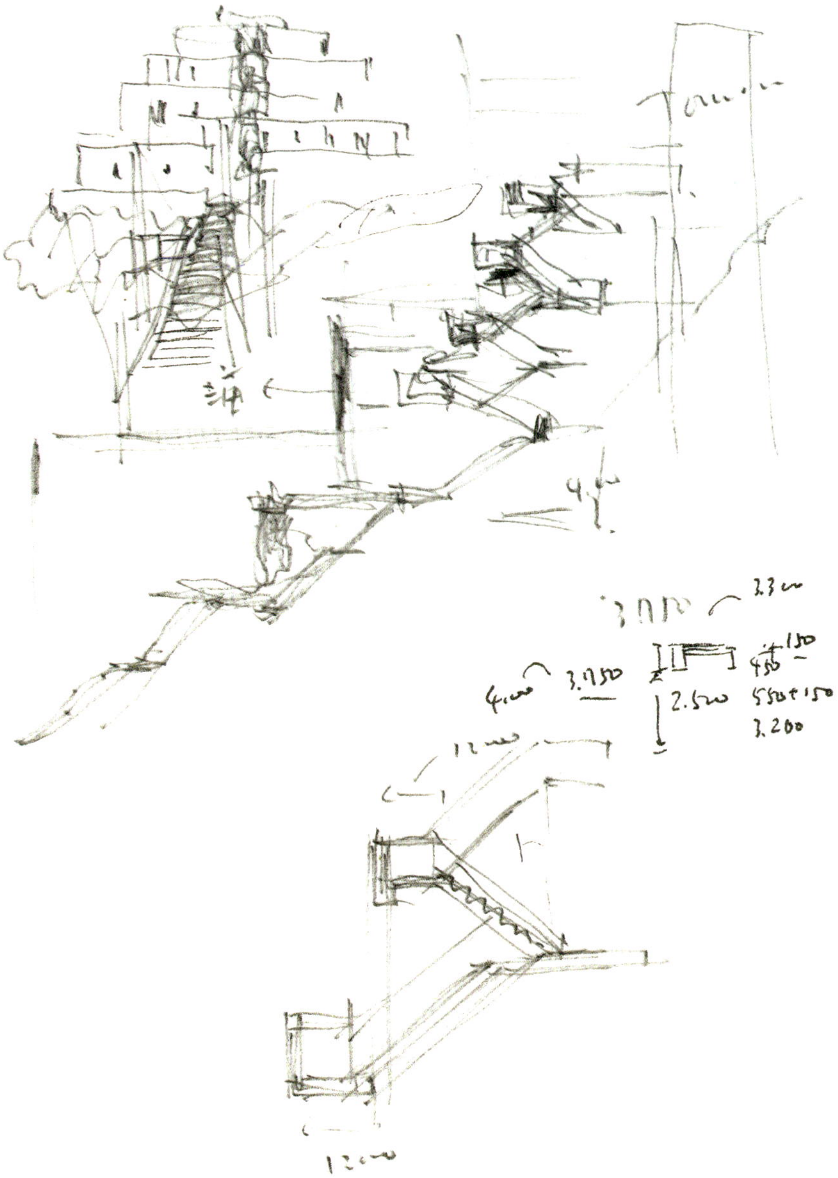

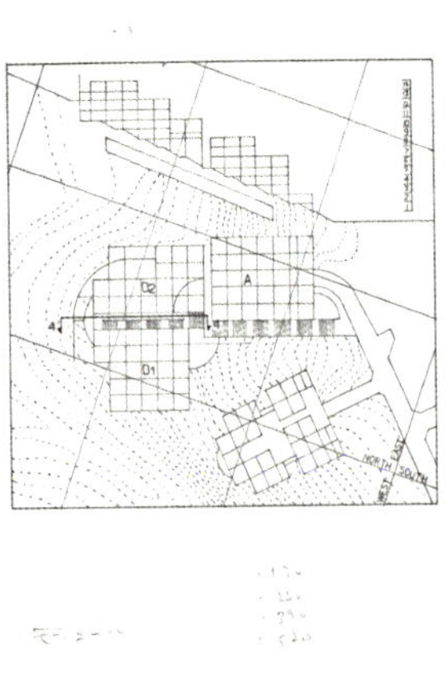

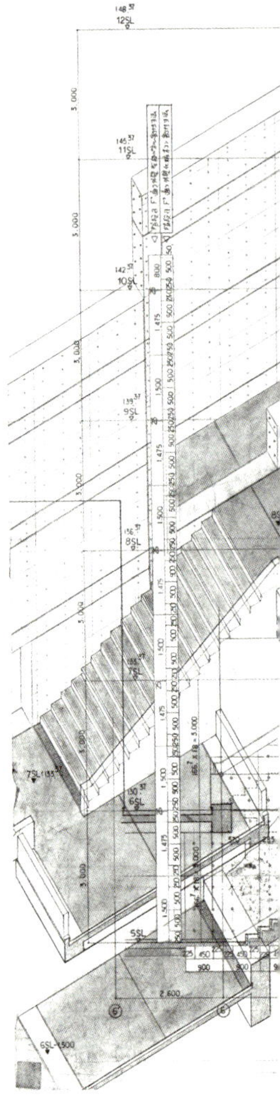

Detailed study drawing of the main external staircase in which diverse spatial sequences are implemented like three-dimensional alleys. The dimensions of the stair treads and risers were carefully determined while giving consideration to comfort when descending.

立体路地のように多様な空間のシークエンスを実現する、メインの屋外階段の詳細検討図。階段の蹴上げ・踏み面寸法は、下りていくときの快適さも考慮して、慎重に決定された。

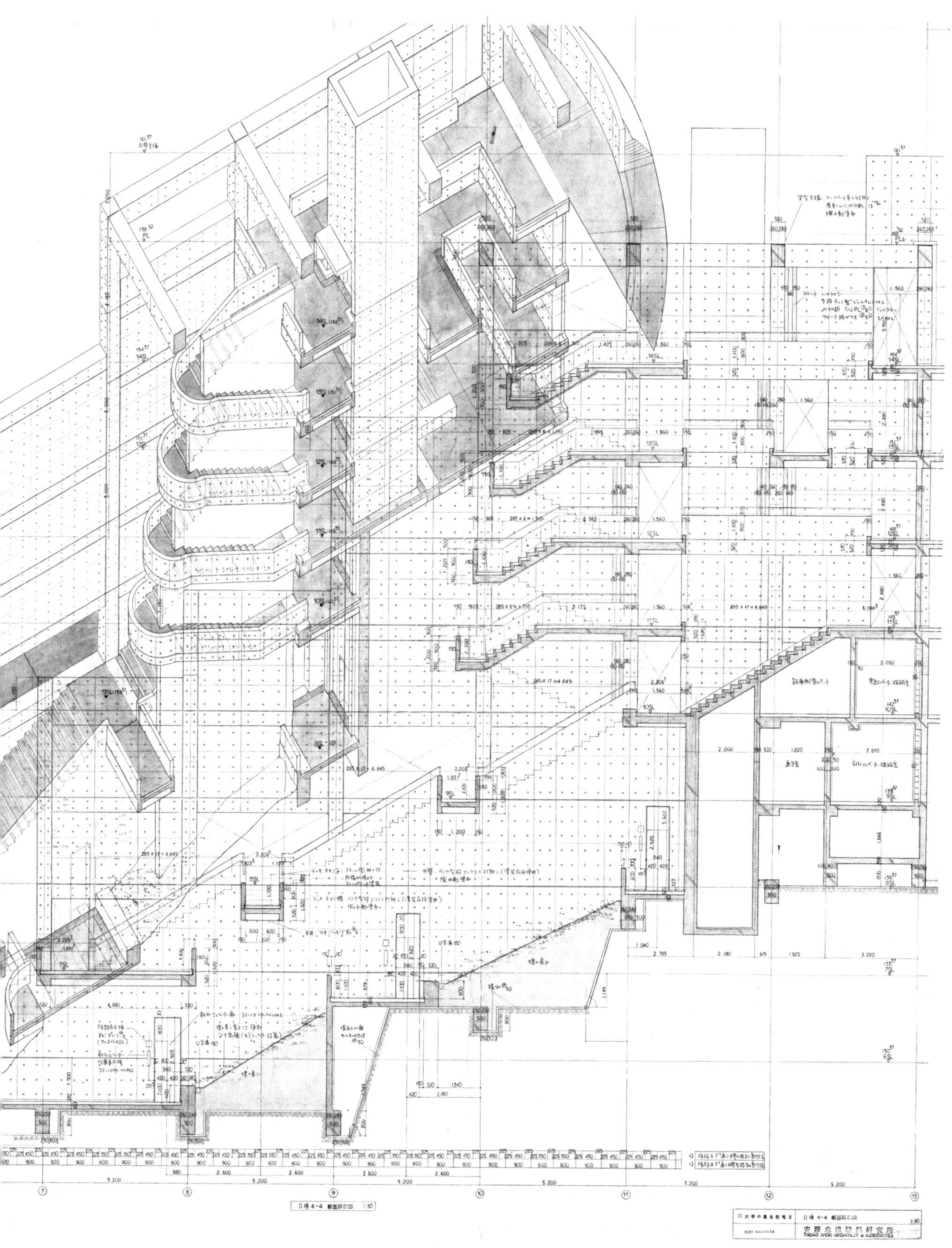

Rokko Housing III 0
六甲の集合住宅 III 0（初期案）

1. Kobe, Hyogo, Japan　兵庫県神戸市
2. 1992.8-1995.1

Following the good fortune of having been able to build phase I and phase II housing projects in the same place, I went on to conceive a plan for phase III on an adjoining site, for which I had not been commissioned. Assuming a site and scale that exceeds that of phase II, I conceived mass housing with an abundance of public facilities and spaces as if becoming a town in itself—this study is connected to the reconstruction projects following the Great Hanshin Awaji Earthquake of 1995, which began in connection with Rokko Housing III.

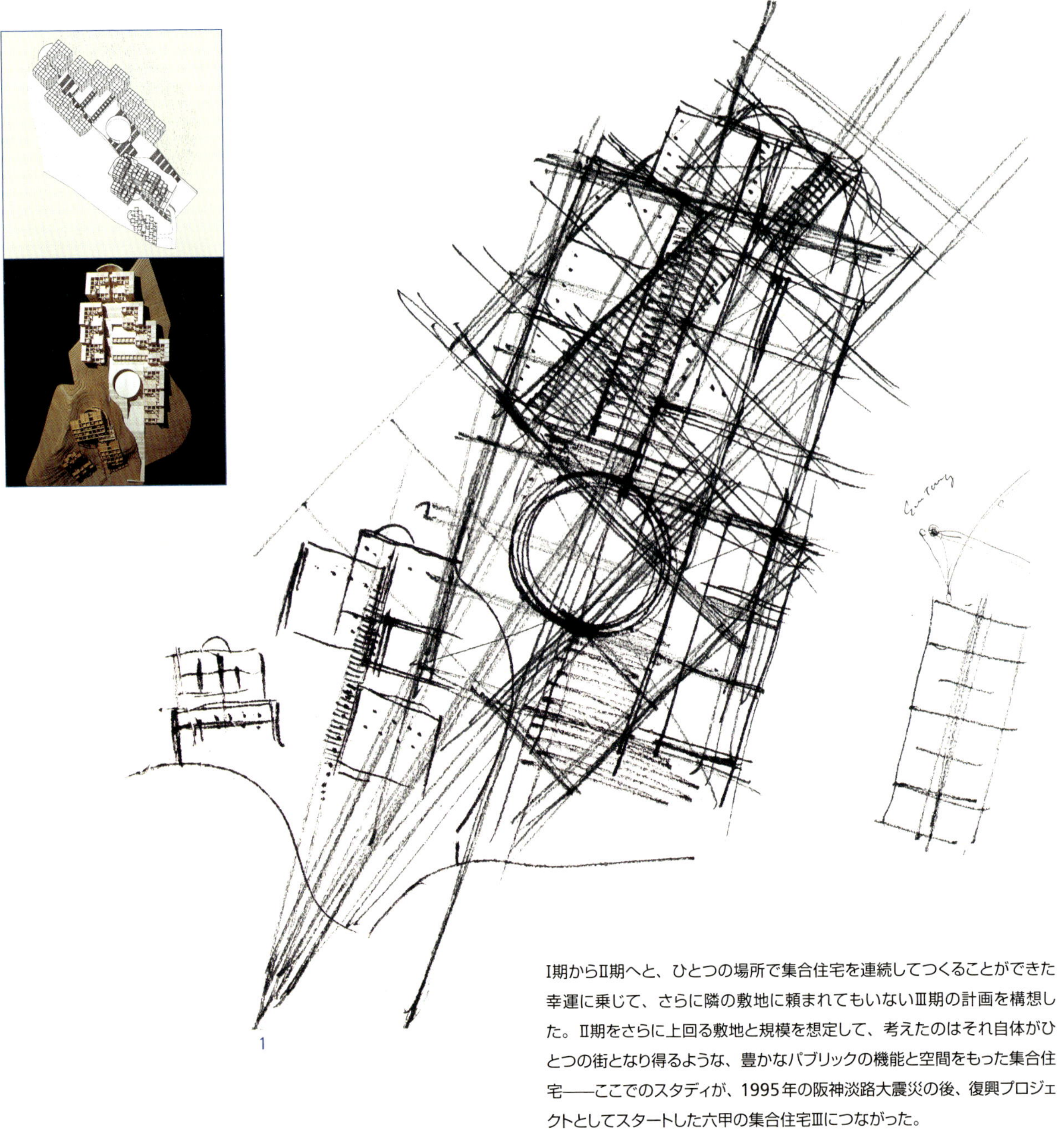

1

I期からII期へと、ひとつの場所で集合住宅を連続してつくることができた幸運に乗じて、さらに隣の敷地に頼まれてもいないIII期の計画を構想した。II期をさらに上回る敷地と規模を想定して、考えたのはそれ自体がひとつの街となり得るような、豊かなパブリックの機能と空間をもった集合住宅——ここでのスタディが、1995年の阪神淡路大震災の後、復興プロジェクトとしてスタートした六甲の集合住宅IIIにつながった。

2

1, 2 Exploratory sketches of the site plan composition. A collection of residences becomes a block, and a collection of blocks is composed into a group, expressing a grouping logic.

1, 2 配置構成の検討スケッチ。住戸の集まりがブロックとなり、そのブロックの集まりがグループを構成して、一定の集合の論理を表現する。

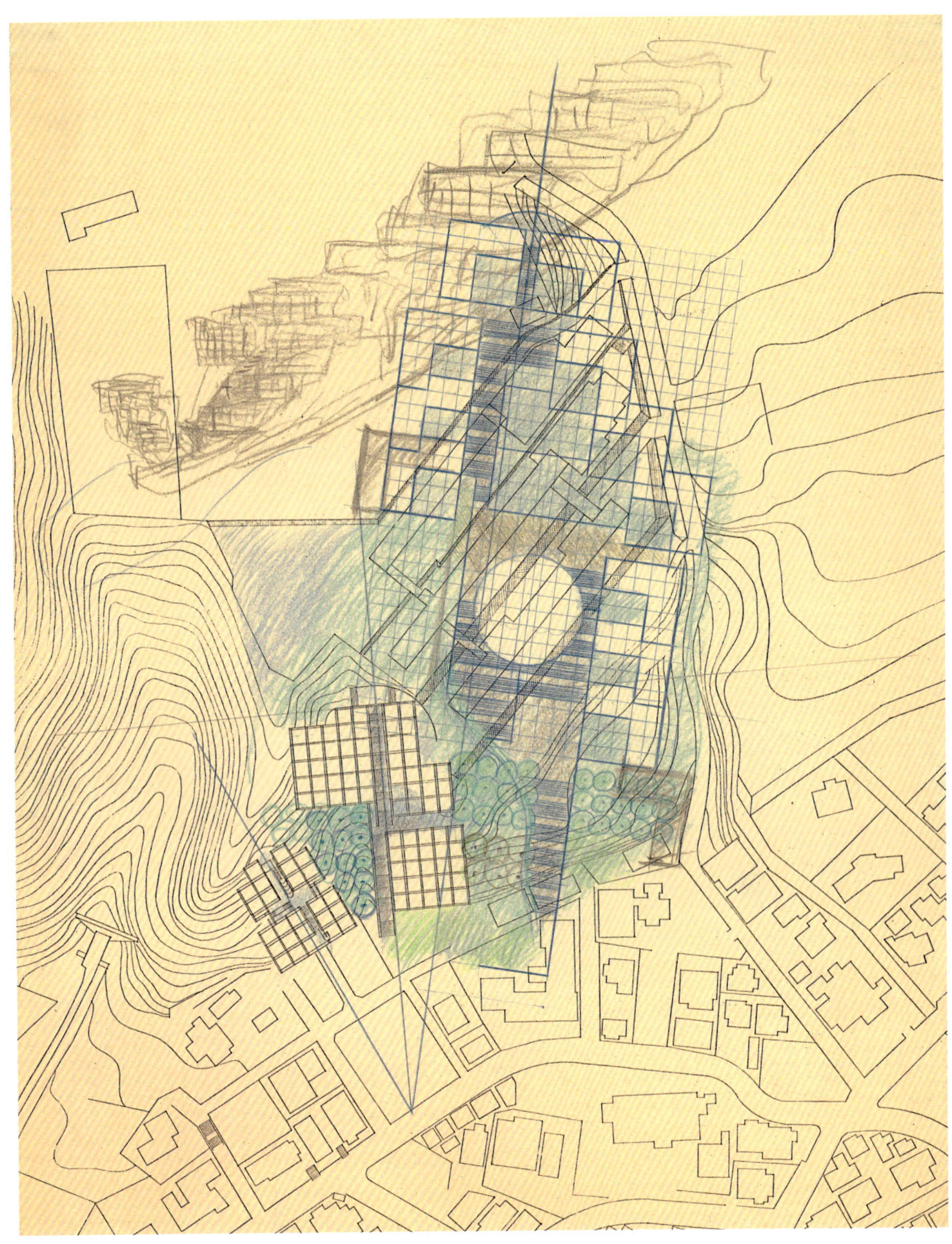

Exploratory sketch of the site plan. The stair plaza is placed on a central axis shifted 13 degrees from the axis of phase II, and L-shaped housing blocks are layered as if surrounding it.

配置検討図。II期の軸線から13度振られた中心軸に沿って、階段広場が配され、それを囲むようにL字型の住戸ブロックが重層する。

Matsutani House
松谷邸

1. Kyoto, Kyoto, Japan　京都府京都市
2. 1978.7-1979.3 (phase Ⅰ) / 1989.7-1990.1 (phase Ⅱ)
3. 1979.8-1979.11 (phase Ⅰ) / 1990.2-1990.5 (phase Ⅱ)

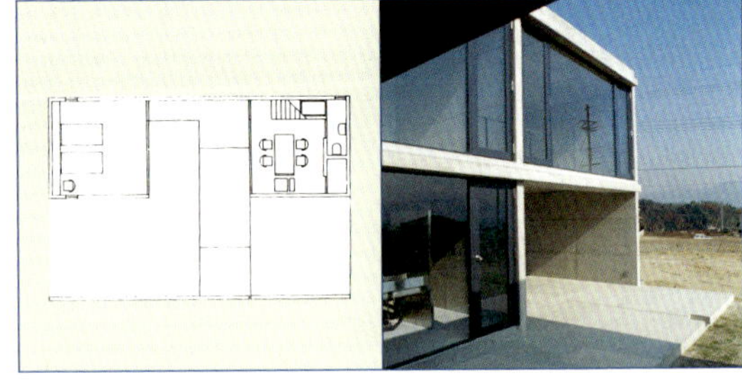

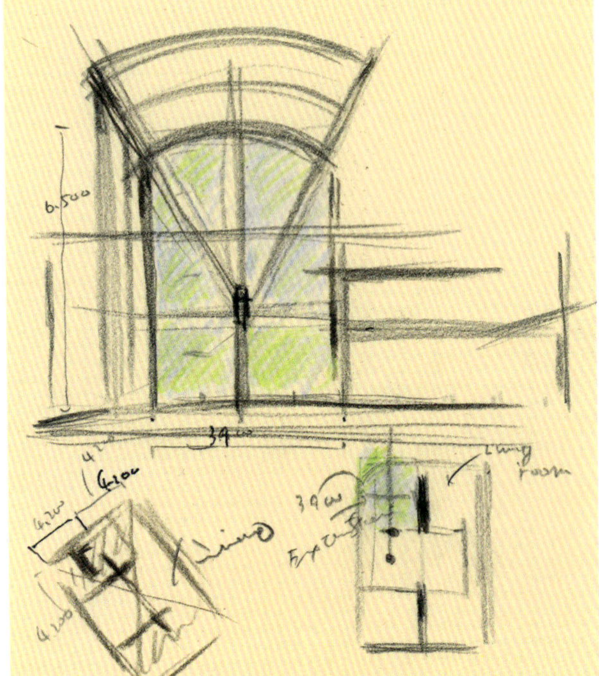

1

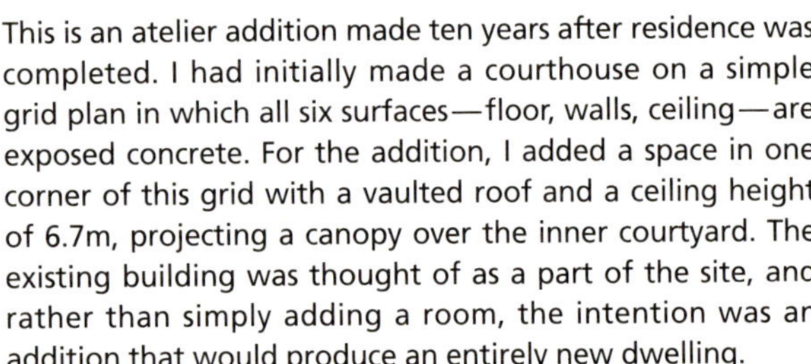

This is an atelier addition made ten years after residence was completed. I had initially made a courthouse on a simple grid plan in which all six surfaces—floor, walls, ceiling—are exposed concrete. For the addition, I added a space in one corner of this grid with a vaulted roof and a ceiling height of 6.7m, projecting a canopy over the inner courtyard. The existing building was thought of as a part of the site, and rather than simply adding a room, the intention was an addition that would produce an entirely new dwelling.

竣工10年後にアトリエを増築した住宅である。最初につくったのは、単純なグリッドプランで床・壁・天井の6面をコンクリート打ち放しとしたコートハウス。増築では、そのグリッドの一角に、中庭に大きく突き出すキャノピーをもった天井高さ6.7mのヴォールト屋根の空間を加えた。既存の建物を敷地の一部と考え、単に部屋をひとつ加えるというのではなく、まったく新しい住まいをつくるつもりで増築した。

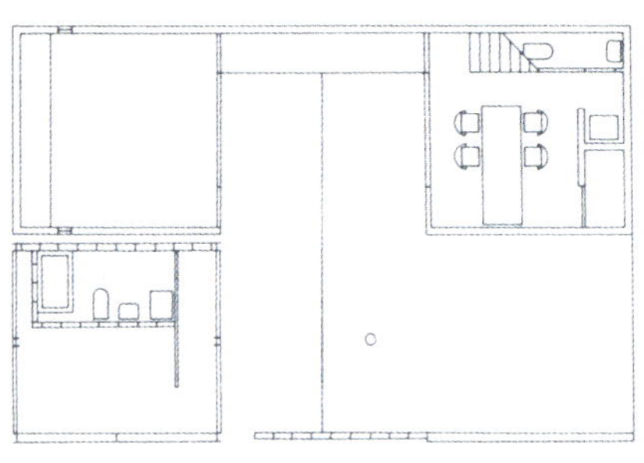

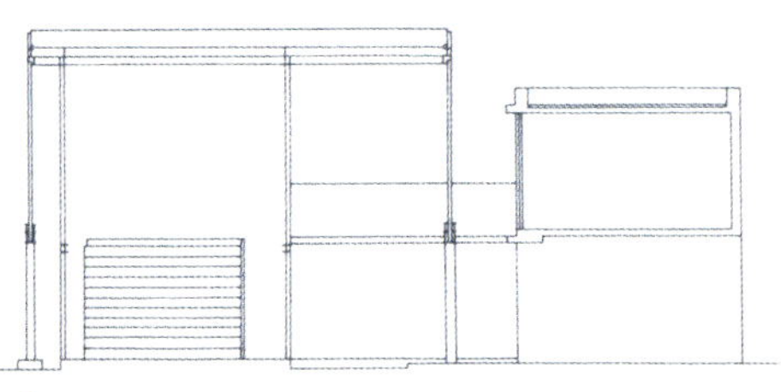

2

1 Image sketch. Symbolic Y-shaped steel columns support the roof.
2 Section and plan after the addition (the upper frame shows the plan prior to the addition).
3 Detailed drawing of the addition. Because the original residence had an extremely simple composition, the addition creates a dramatic spatial transformation.

1 イメージスケッチ。象徴的な鉄骨のY字柱が屋根を支える。
2 増築後平面図と断面図（※上部枠内は増築前平面図）
3 増築部詳細図。もとの住宅がシンプル極まりない構成ゆえ、増築による空間の変化は劇的である。

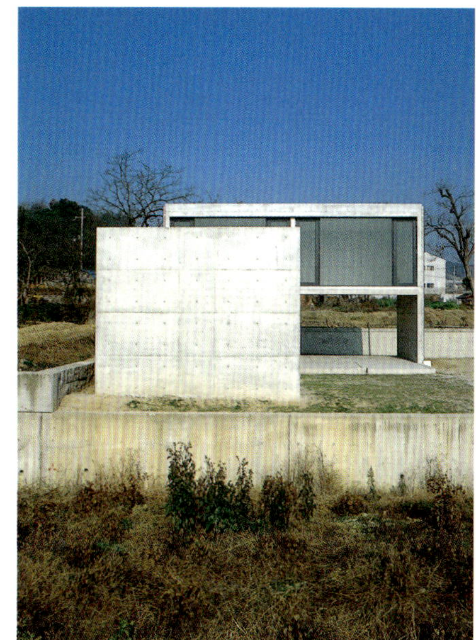

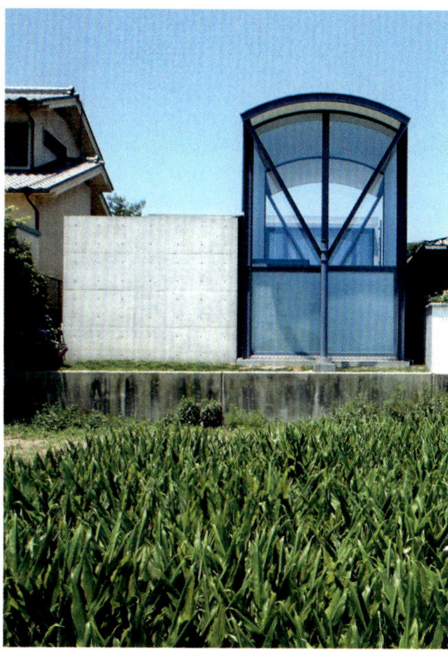

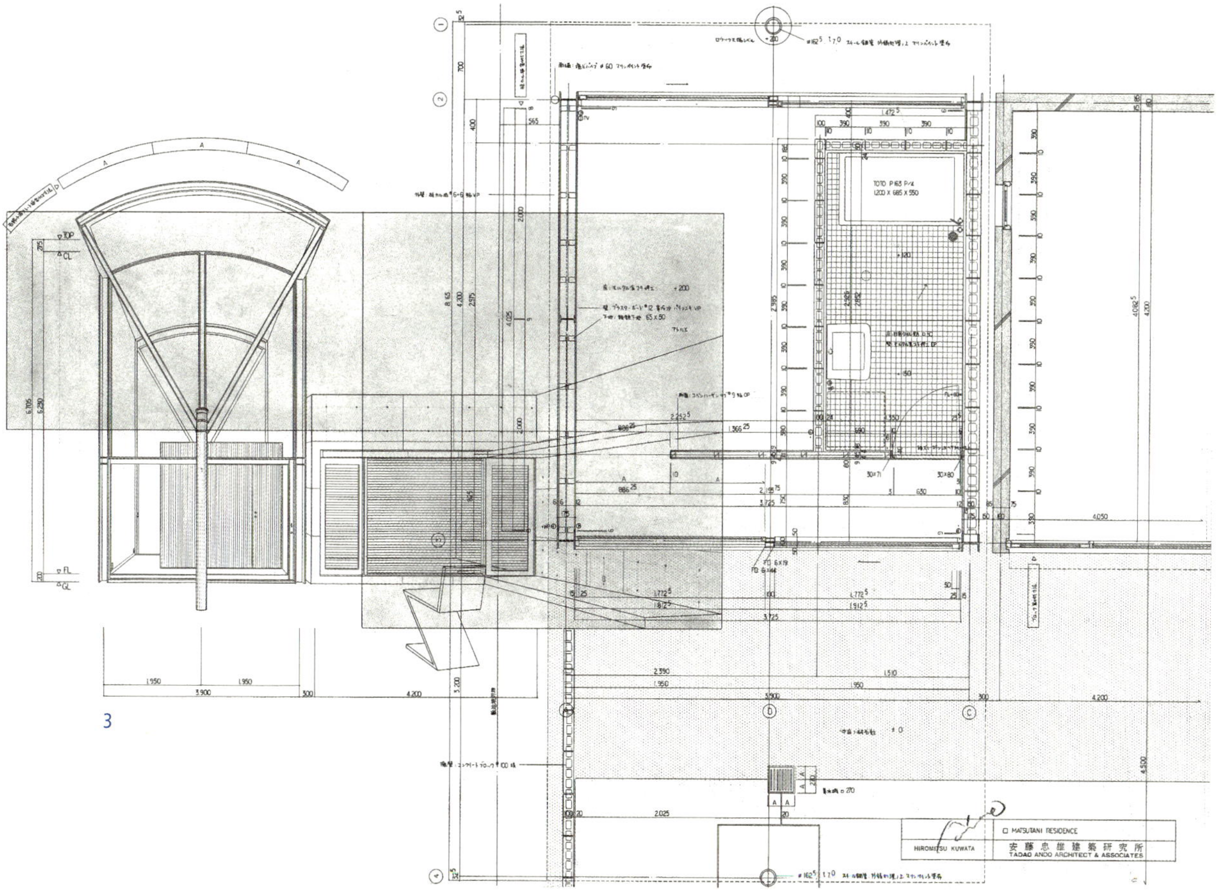

TOTO P163 P/4
1200 X 685 X 550
MATSUTANI RESIDENCE
HIROMITSU KUWATA
安藤忠雄建築研究所
TADAO ANDO ARCHITECT & ASSOCIATES

3

Koshino House
小篠邸

1. Ashiya, Hyogo, Japan　兵庫県芦屋市
2. 1979.9-1980.4 (phase Ⅰ) / 1983.1-1983.6 (phase Ⅱ)
3. 1980.7-1981.3 (phase Ⅰ) / 1983.11-1984.3 (phase Ⅱ)

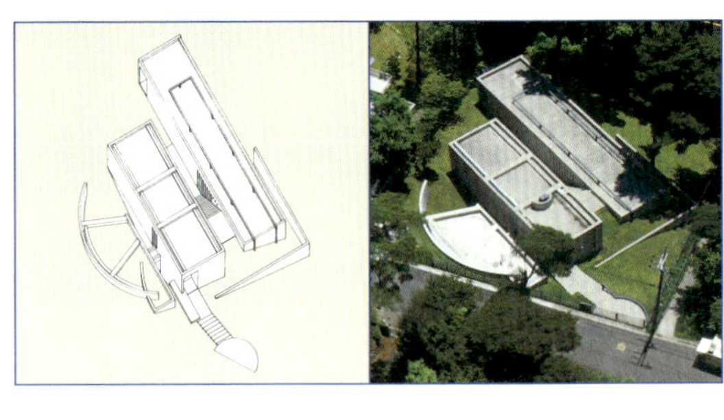

On a site located in the slopes of a verdant mountain in Ashiya, Hyogo Prefecture, this is a residence for fashion designer Hiroko Koshino. Given the rich natural environment of this site and a program with a high degree of freedom, I thought of living spaces characterized by light, and the theme of "place" in contemporary architecture. How much "expression" can be achieved in architecture with a composition of limited materials and elements? This was a task in which I discovered things linked to new developments in my architecture.

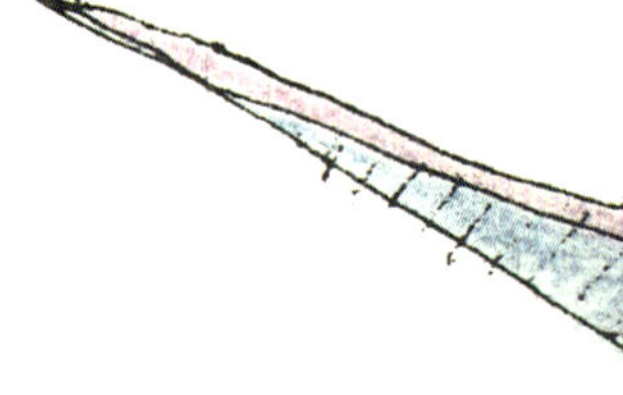

1

1, 2 Two concrete boxes aligned parallel along the slope of the site. Image of architecture embedded in the topography.
3 Iterative studies of sublime spatial drama contained in a regular repetition of primary geometric shapes. Traces of conflicting
ideas between the abstract (= geometry) and the concrete (= life).

敷地は兵庫県芦屋の緑深い山の斜面に位置する。ファッションデザイナーのコシノ・ヒロコのための住宅。自然豊かな立地環境、自由度の高いプログラムの中で考えたのは、光によって特徴付けられる住空間と、現代建築における場所という主題である。素材も要素も限定した構成の中で、建築はどこまで〈表現〉できるのか——自身の建築の新たな展開につながるものを見い出し得た仕事だった。

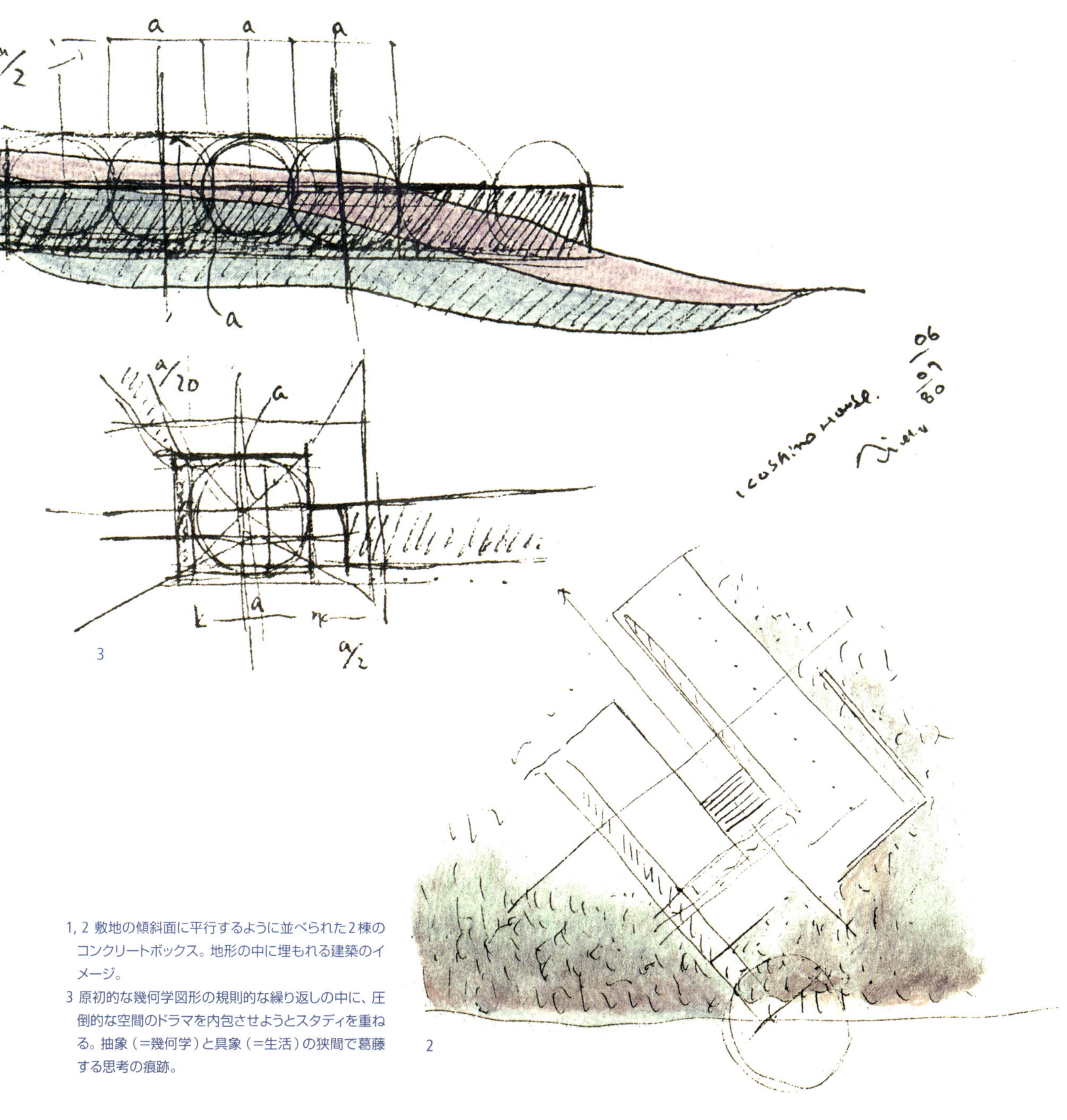

1, 2 敷地の傾斜面に平行するように並べられた2棟のコンクリートボックス。地形の中に埋もれる建築のイメージ。

3 原初的な幾何学図形の規則的な繰り返しの中に、圧倒的な空間のドラマを内包させようとスタディを重ねる。抽象（＝幾何学）と具象（＝生活）の狭間で葛藤する思考の痕跡。

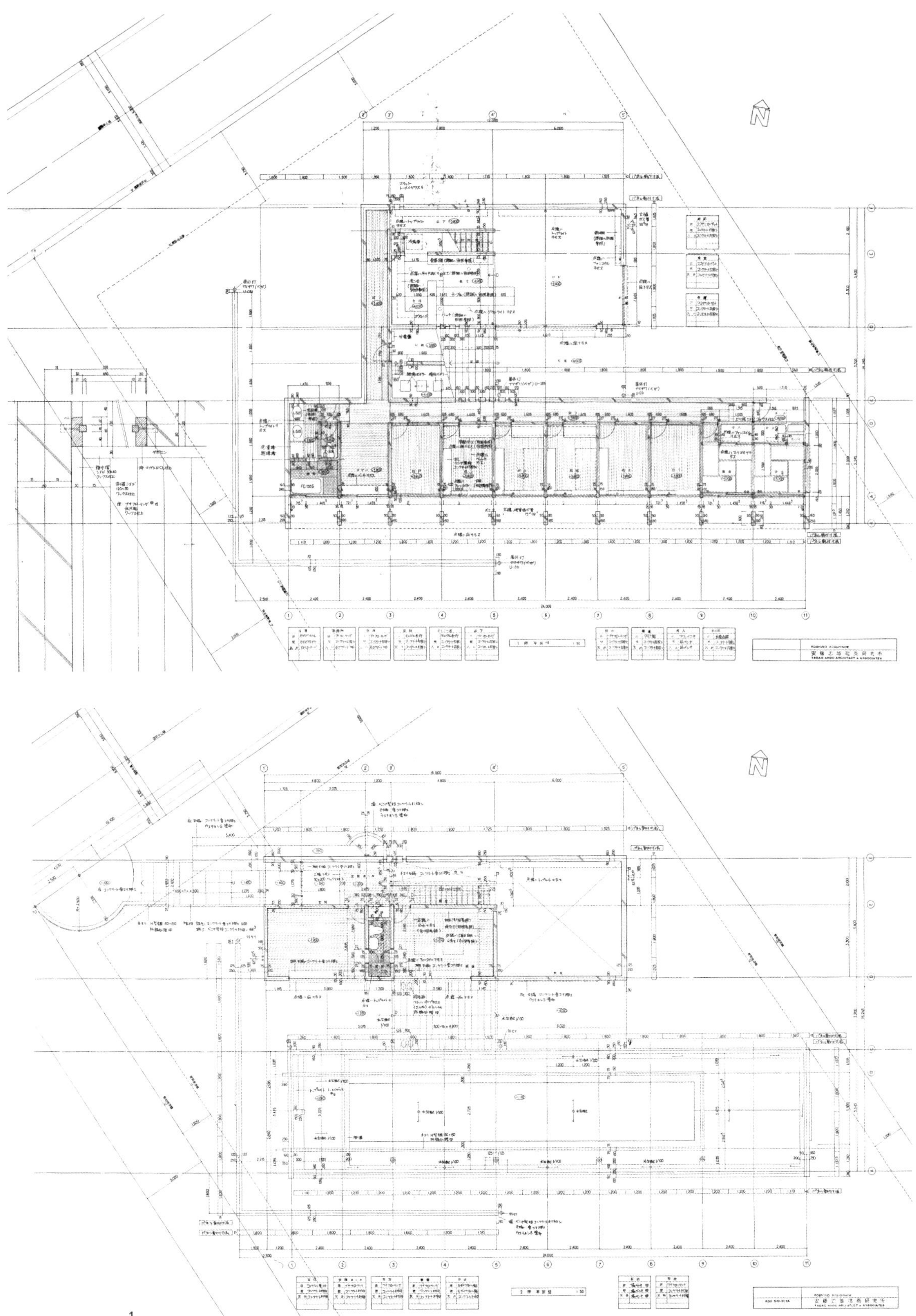

1

1 From above: second floor plan, first floor plan.
2 Exploratory sketch of the composition. The wide exterior staircase, which connects the living room block with the rooftop of the private room block, has an important significance as a form and as the core of the composition connecting building and place.
3 Section.

2

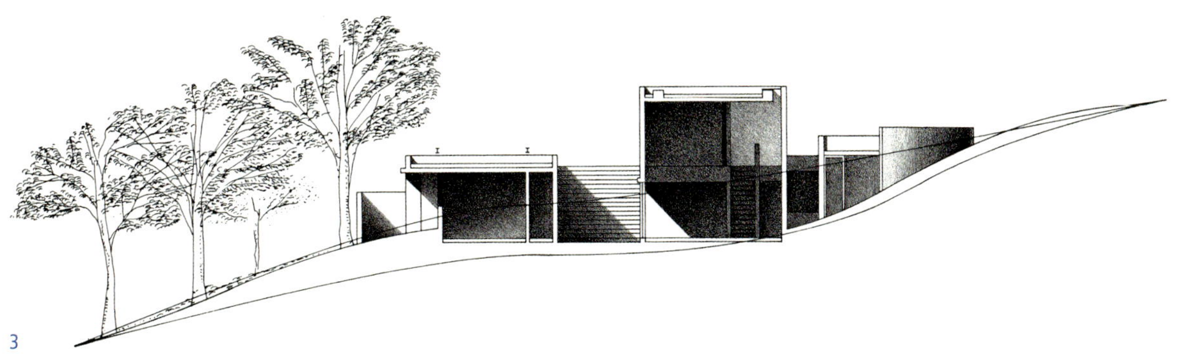

3

1 上から2階平面図、1階平面図。
2 構成の検討スケッチ。リビング棟と個室群棟の屋上をつなぐ幅広の屋外階段が、造形として、また建物と場所を結びつける構成の核として、重要な意味をもつ。
3 断面図。

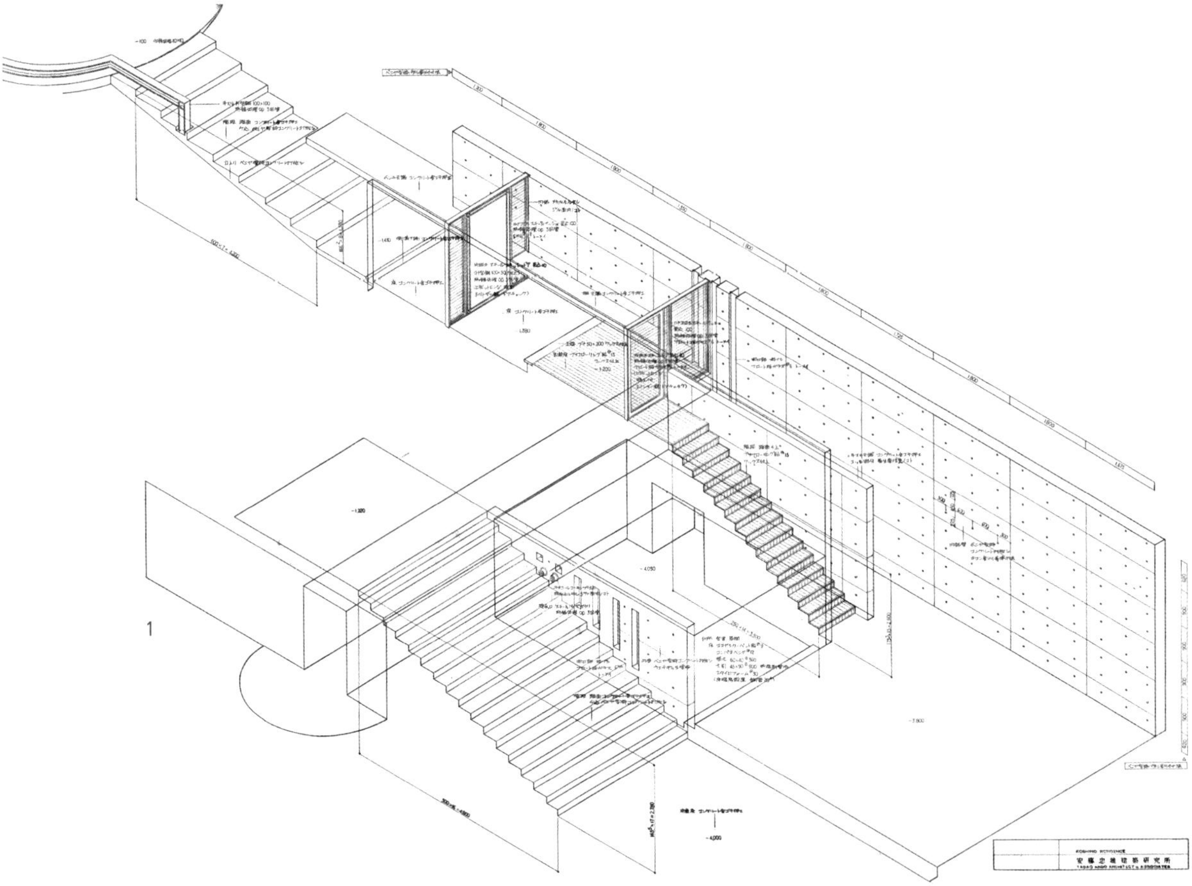

1

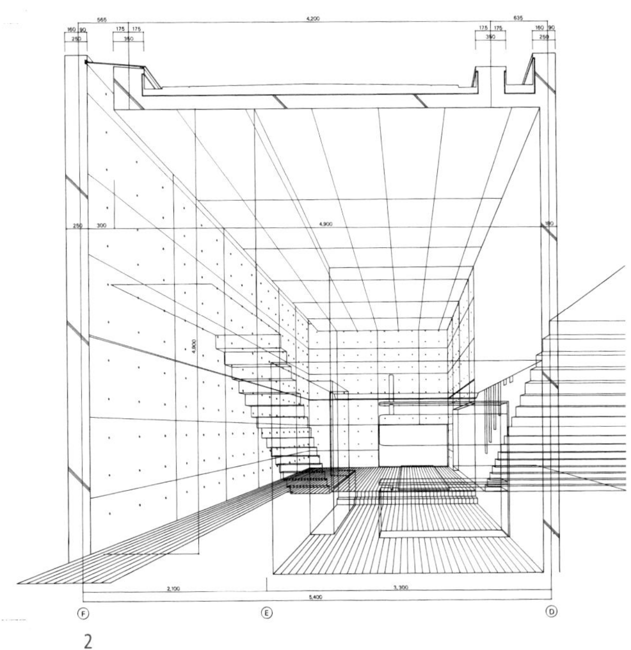

2

Le Corbusier said, "Architecture is the masterly, correct, and magnificent play of masses brought together in light." In the Koshino House, I tried to make a residence through the single-minded pursuit of light alone.

ル・コルビュジエは、「建築とは、光のしたに集められたヴォリュームの、知的で、正確で、壮大な遊びである」と言った。小篠邸では、ただ光を徹底的に追い求めることで、ひとつの住まいをつくろうと考えていた。

1, 2 Drawings of the composition of the living spaces.
3 Image sketches of the variety of light, giving character to each place. By creating natural scenes in which the sources of light and field of vision are purified and abstracted, paradoxically, the rich variations of the four seasons are recreated.

1, 2 リビング空間の構成検討図。
3 各所を特徴づけるさまざまな光のイメージスケッチ。光源と視界を純化し、抽象化された自然の風景をつくり出すことで、逆説的に豊かな四季の変化が映し出される。

3

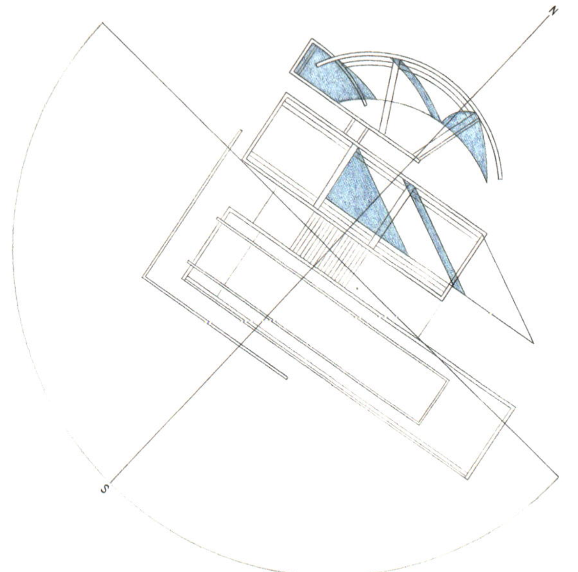

Four years after completion, an atelier was added. This was an unanticipated task, but taking the existing blocks as part of the site, it was engaged as a new building on a new site. I conceived an architecture with an arc motif in order to achieve a complete contrast with the rectilinear composition of the existing part in terms of shape and the quality of light. Making an addition with my own hands to a previously completed work is interesting in ways that differ from building something new.

竣工4年後にアトリエを増築した。予定外の仕事だったが、既存の棟を敷地の一部ととらえ、新しい敷地に新築するつもりで取り組んだ。考えたのは既存部の直線的構成と、かたちの上でも光の質の上でも好対照をなす、円弧をモチーフとした建築。一旦完結した仕事に、自身で手を加える増築の仕事は、新築とはまた違った面白さがあっていい。

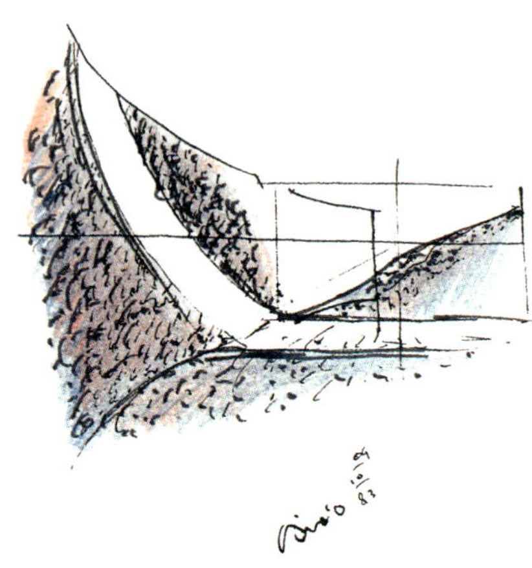

The space is enclosed by a wall that describes a quarter circle on the ground. A skylight slot pierces the ceiling along the arc, and a powerful geometry of light is drawn across the concrete walls. The added space has a character that contrasts with the existing part.

4分の1の円弧を描く壁が地盤を受け止め、空間を囲い取る。円弧に沿って、天井にはスリット状のトップライトが穿たれ、コンクリートの壁に力強い光の幾何学が描かれる。既存部と対比的な性格をもつ増築部分の空間。

1980s

FESTIVAL
Atelier in Oyodo
Atelier in Oyodo II
Tea House for Soseikan
Umemiya House
Town House in Kujo
Kidosaki House
Doll's House
Atelier Yoshie Inaba
Kaneko House
TIME'S I+II
Town House in Saikudani
Chapel on Mt. Rokko
Kara-za
Church on the Water
Theater on the Water
GALLERIA [akka]
COLLEZIONE
Tea House in Oyodo
Church of the Light+Sunday School
Izu Project
Children's Museum, Hyogo
Benesse House / Naoshima
Museum of Literature, Himeji
Suntory Museum+Plaza
Water Temple
Forest of Tombs Museum, Kumamoto

FESTIVAL
フェスティバル

1. Naha, Okinawa, Japan　沖縄県那覇市
2. 1980.1-1983.2
3. 1983.3-1984.9

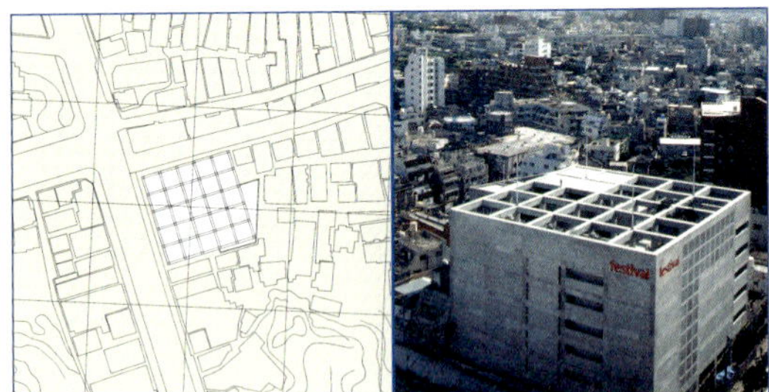

Okinawa has a subtropical climate with an average temperature of about 22°C and a minimum temperature of about 15°C. Before beginning the design, I first went from Osaka to Okinawa by boat in order to personally experience the sense of separation from the mainland. For several days after arriving in Naha, I patiently walked around the city and made sketches of the scenes I witnessed of people leading their lives. An image emerged of the architecture I should make for the strong light, wind, and tree shadows on this southern island.

沖縄は平均気温22℃、最低気温15℃前後の亜熱帯気候風土にある。設計開始当初、まず本土との距離を身体で知るために、大阪から沖縄まで船で行った。那覇に到着した後は数日かけて、ひたすら街の中を歩き、目にする人々の生活の風景をスケッチした。南国ならではの強い光、風、木陰――それらの向こうに、つくるべき建築のイメージが見えてきた。

1

3

1, 2 Image sketch drawn during the first visit to the site in the center of Naha. Delineating the image of a building resembling a plaza where people will gather.
3-6 Sketches of vernacular houses, *shiisa* [lion-shaped roof ornaments found in Okinawa], and people in traditional dress.

4

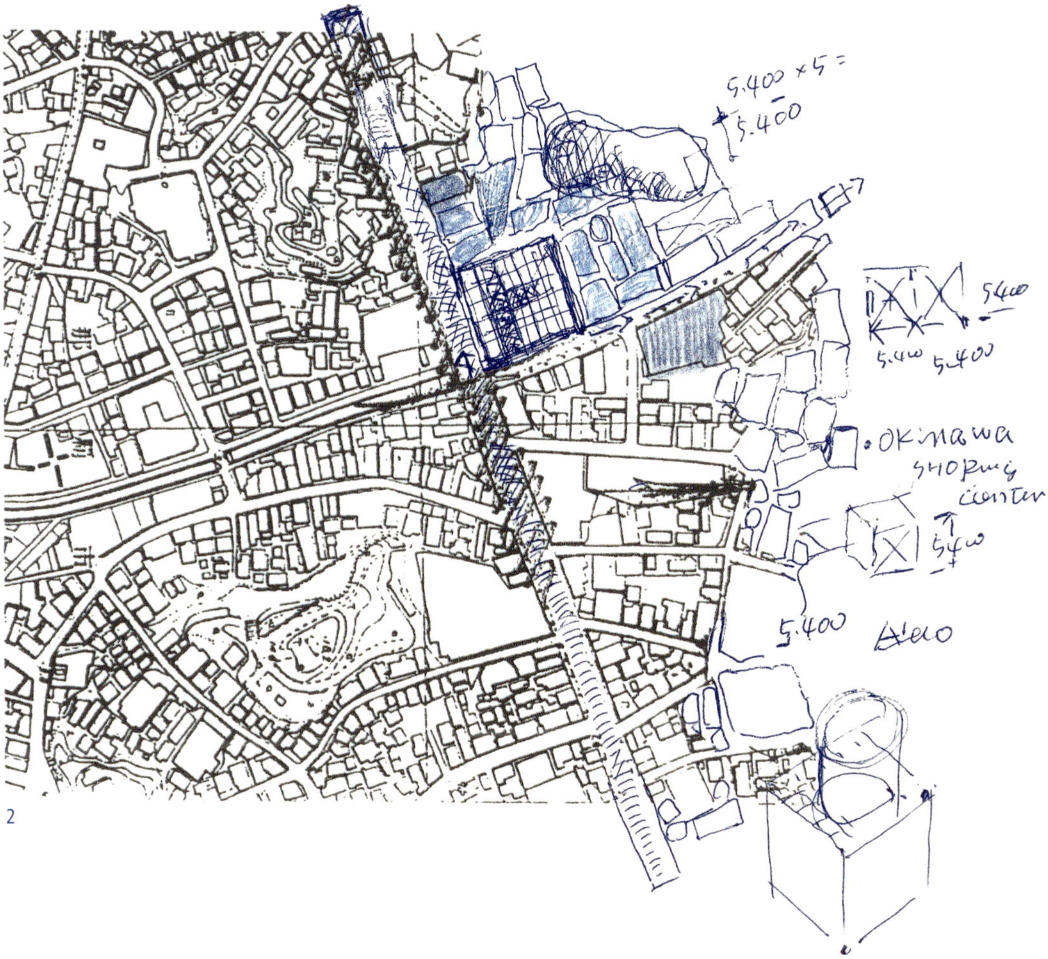

2

5

1, 2 那覇市中心部の敷地を初めて訪れた際に描かれたイメージスケッチ。人々が集まる広場のような建物のイメージが描かれている。

3-6 民家やシーサー、民族衣装を描いたスケッチ。

6

The strongest impression that remained after walking around Naha was the large number of concrete block buildings, and the importance placed on sunshine and good ventilation. I wanted to make architecture like a banyan tree, producing a shaded space with a pleasant feeling where people would gather to relax—from such thoughts emerged the image of a "breathing box" using concrete blocks with holes across every surface, into which wind, light, and shadow naturally enter.

那覇の街を歩いていて、強く印象に残ったのは、コンクリートブロックの建物が多く、日影と風通しのよさが非常に大事にされている点だった。人々が涼を求めて集まってくる、心地よい影の空間をつくり出すガジュマルの木のような建築をつくりたい——そんな思いから生まれたのが、穴あきコンクリートブロックを全面的に使い、風と光、影が自在に入り込む、呼吸する箱のイメージだった。

1

1 The conceptual starting point is a solid volume composed of a homogenous grid frame. Within this geometric operation, how to excise voids containing an abundance of ever-changing deep shadows? Iterative studies exploring the spatial diagram.
2, 3 Image sketch of the "breathing box." An image of excised spaces that allow light to be taken inside the building and wind to pass through.

1 発想の原点は均質なグリッドフレームによる立体。その幾何学的操作の中でどれだけ陰影深い変化に富んだヴォイドを切り取れるか。空間の図式を模索するスタディが繰り返された。
2, 3〈呼吸する箱〉のイメージスケッチ。光が建物内部にまで入り込み、風がすり抜けていく、抜けた空間のイメージ。

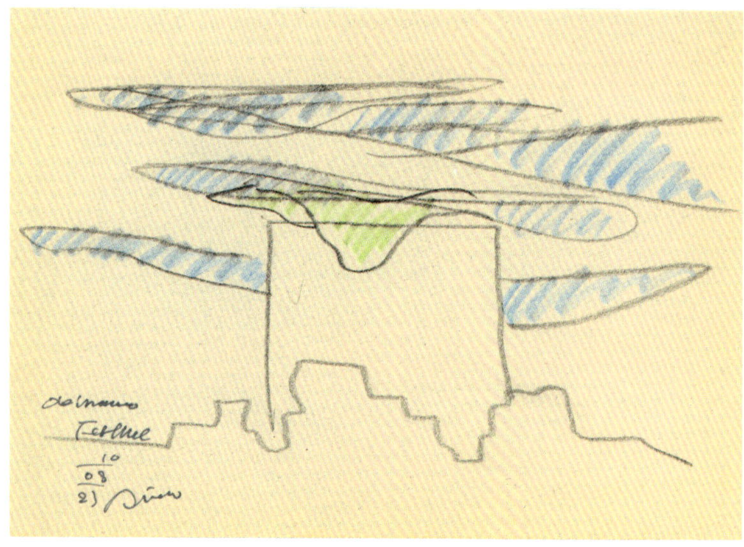

2

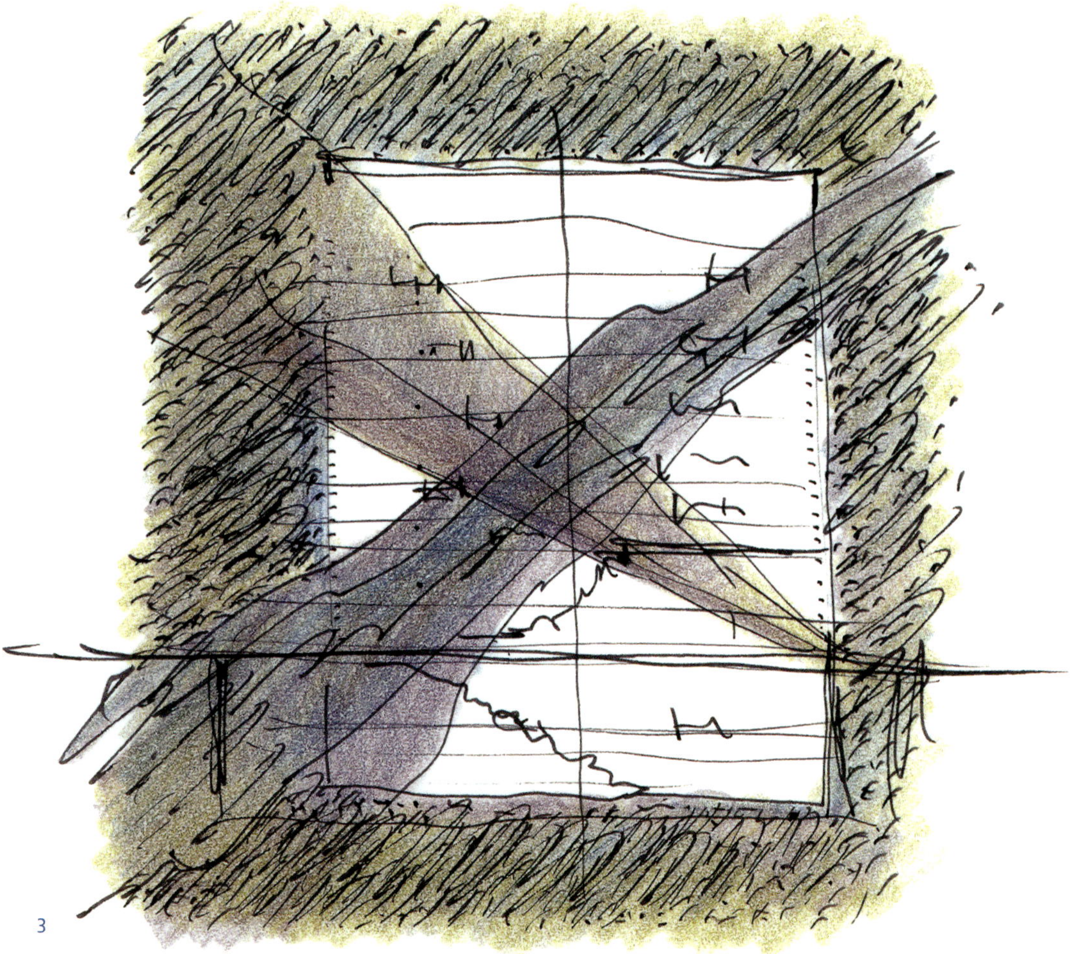

3

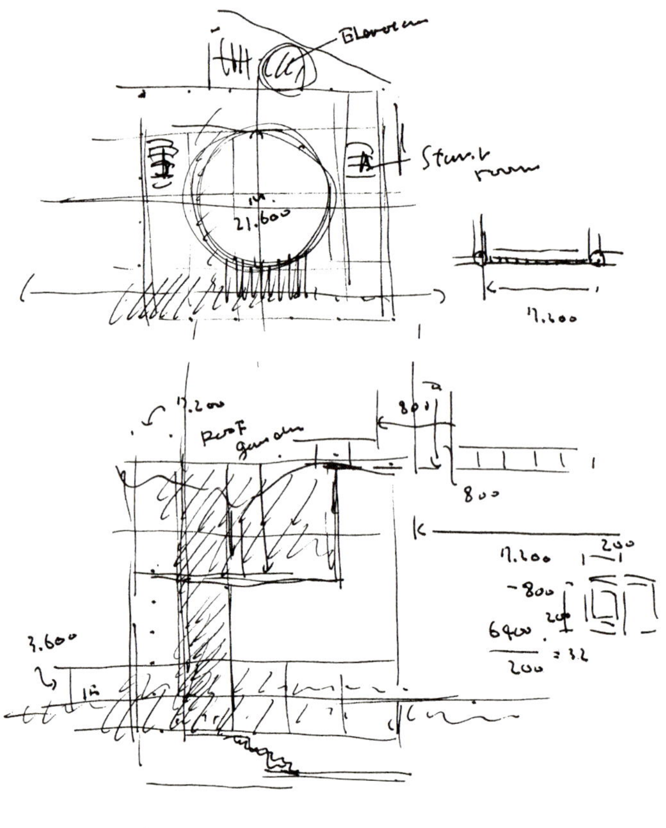

1

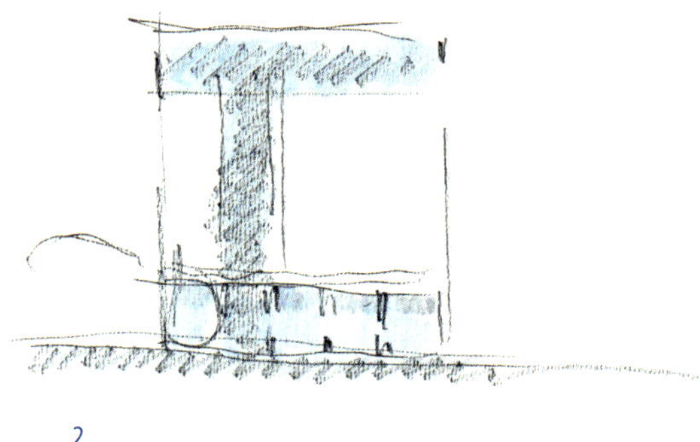

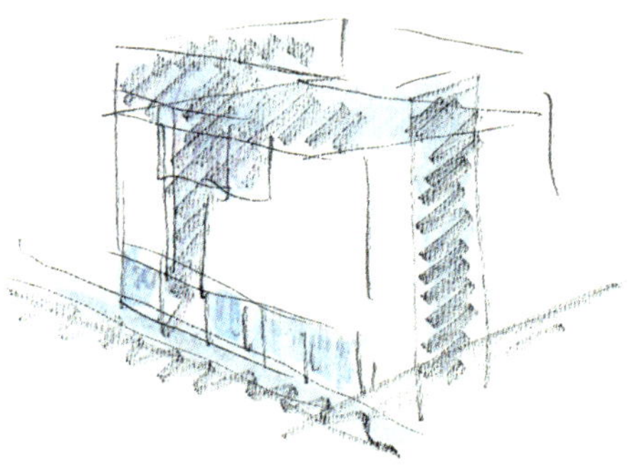

2

1, 2 The public path areas are connected through the voids into three-dimensional streets, producing exterior spaces without air-conditioning equipment. The upper two levels contain an open court in which banyan trees have been planted.
3 Images of the eight-storey-high void containing three-dimensional streets. Through the iteration of a simple geometric operation, a stair-shaped plaza resembling an artificial ravine is made inside the building.
4 The outer layer of the void is a screen of concrete blocks with holes. The purpose of the materials, the purpose of the details —sketches conveying the intentions of the designer.

1, 2 パブリックの通路部分は吹き抜けでつながる立体街路とし、空調設備は設けない屋外空間とする。最上部の2層はオープンコートとして、ガジュマルの木を植える。

3 8層吹き抜けの立体街路のイメージ。単純な幾何学的操作の繰り返しの中で、建物内に人工の渓谷のような段状の広場をつくり出す。

4 ヴォイドの表皮を覆うのが穴あきコンクリートブロックのスクリーン。何のための材料か、何のためのディテールか——設計者の意思を伝えるためのスケッチ。

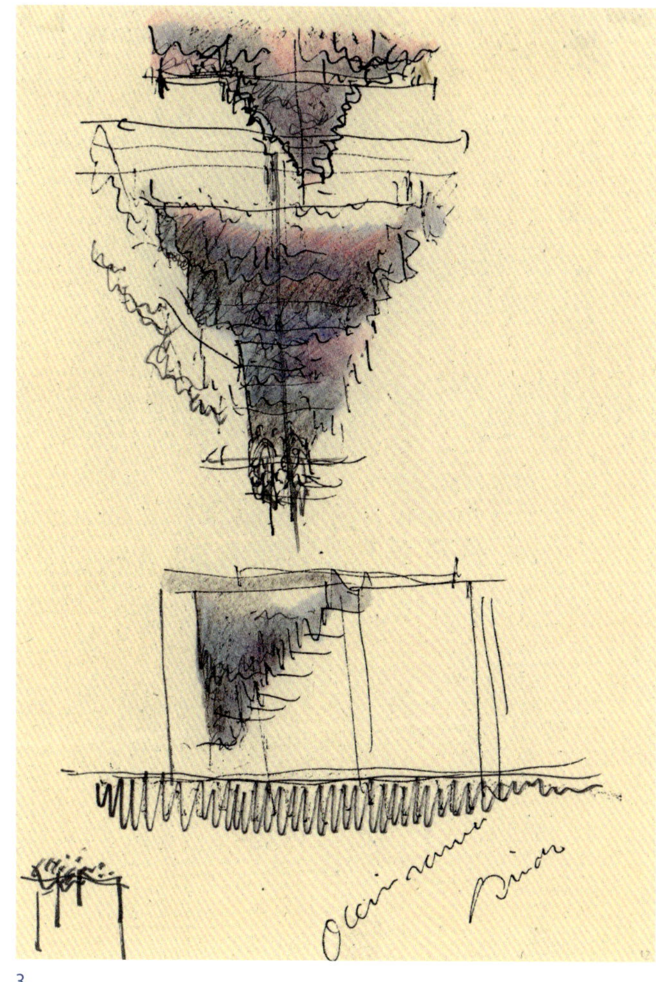

3

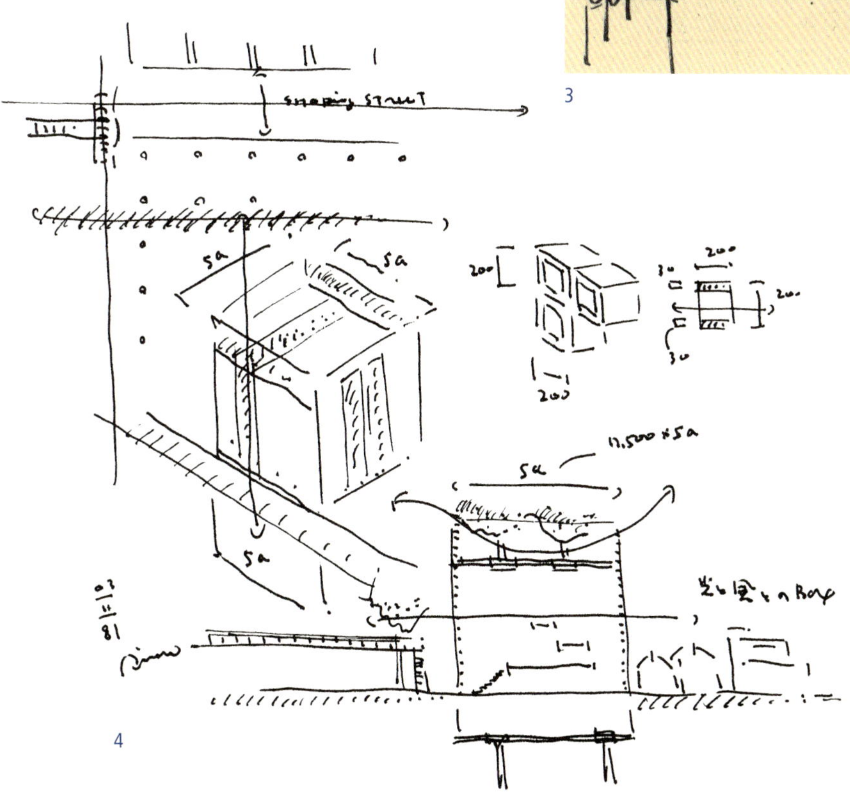

4

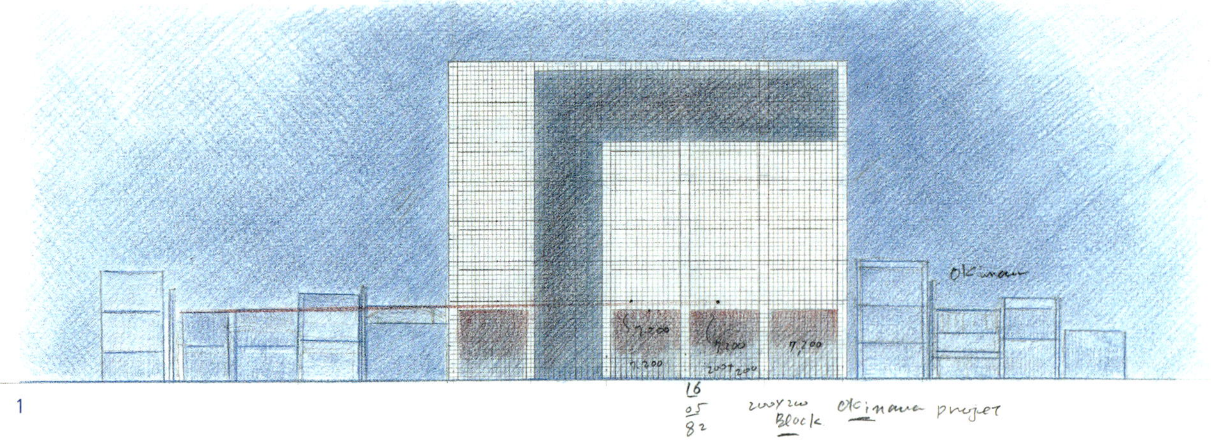

1

1 Image sketch of the exterior. A façade that can bring in exterior space from the surroundings.
2, 5 Axonometric. The whole is an enormous cube measuring 36m per side. This structure is organized by the 200mm-per-side module of the concrete blocks. Taking as one of its themes the details of the integration of the whole and the parts, Festival is architecture that shows Ando's tenacity at its best.
3, 4 Sections.

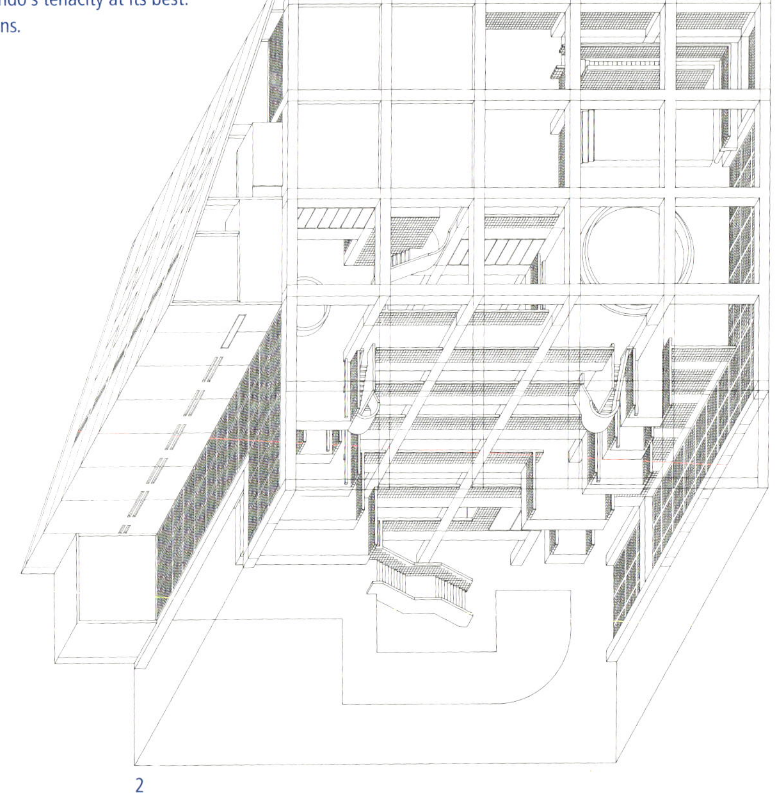

2

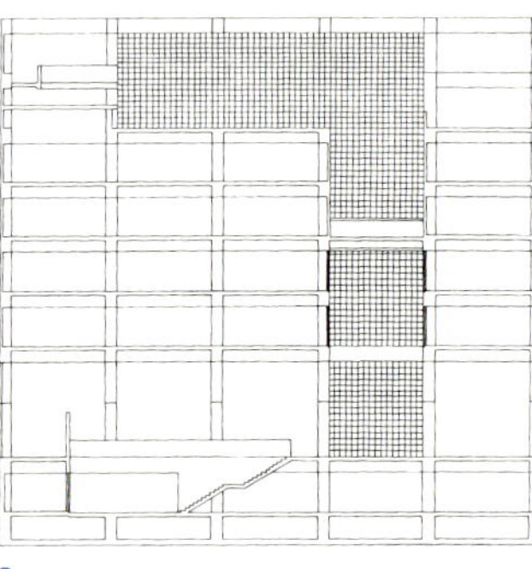

3

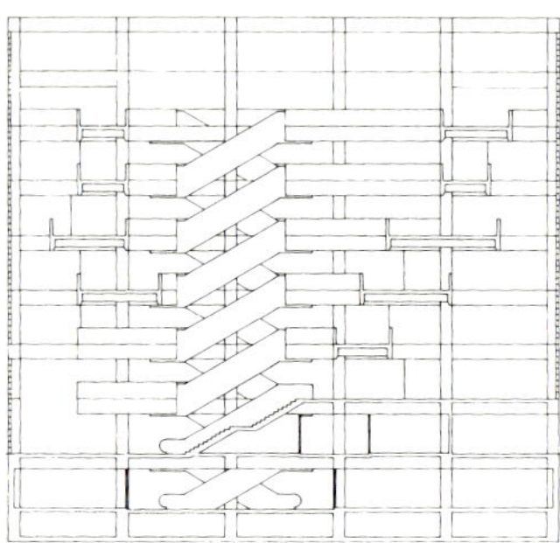

4

1 外観イメージスケッチ。内包する屋外空間が周囲からもうかがえるファサード。
2, 5 アクソノメトリック。全体は1辺36mの巨大な立方体。その構造体を1辺200mmのコンクリートブロックのモジュールに従って再構成していく。「フェスティバル」は全体と部分の統合をディテールのひとつのテーマとする、安藤の執念が最もよく表れた建築である。
3, 4 断面図。

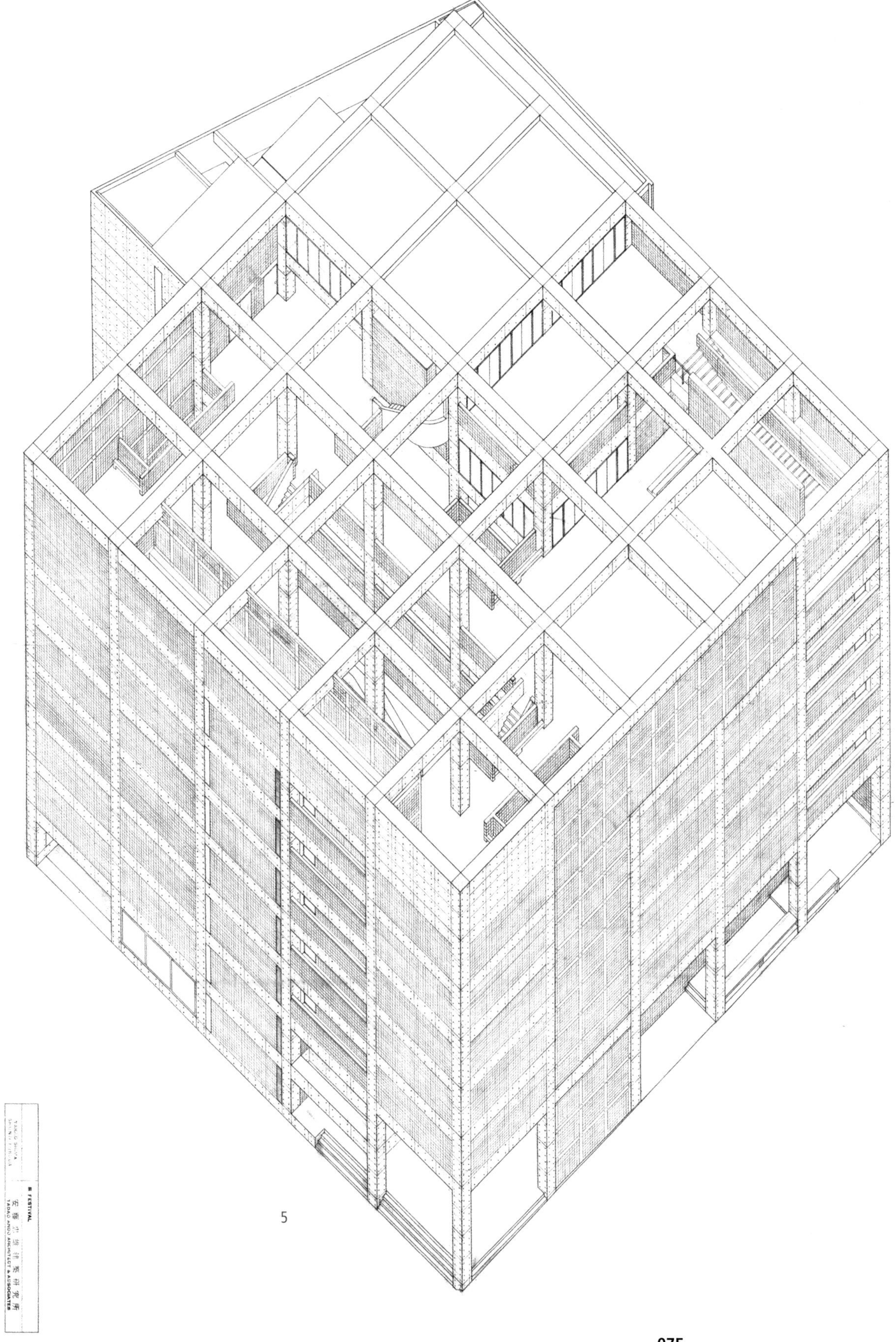

5

Sketches of the movement spaces around the void. Layered spatial images delineating the struggle between the concrete block screens and the columns and beams. A thought process alternating between the whole and the parts is revealed.

吹き抜けまわりの移動空間のスケッチ。空間のイメージに重ねて、コンクリートブロックのスクリーンと、柱梁との取り合いが描かれている。全体と部分を行き来する思考のプロセスがうかがえる。

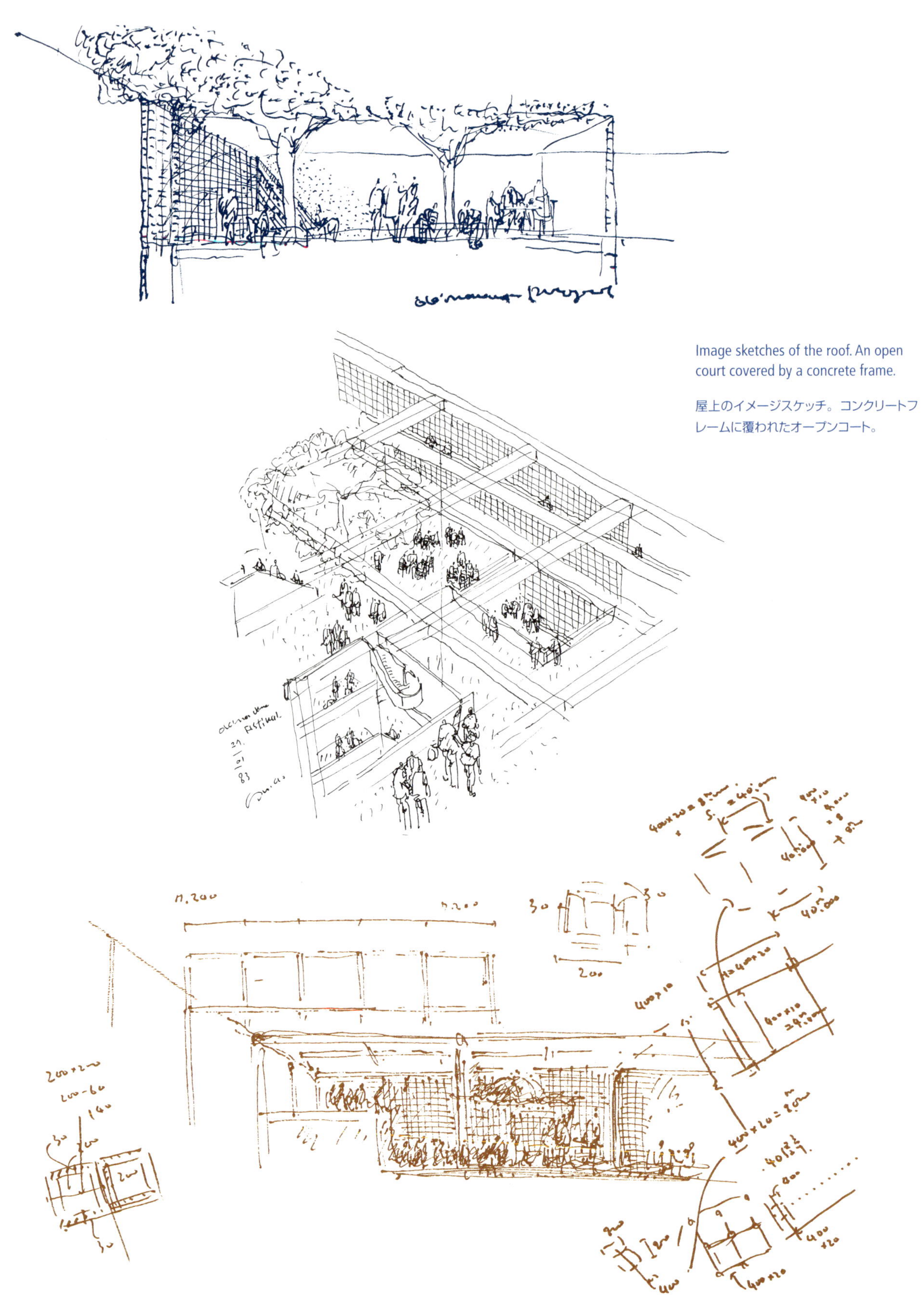

Image sketches of the roof. An open court covered by a concrete frame.

屋上のイメージスケッチ。コンクリートフレームに覆われたオープンコート。

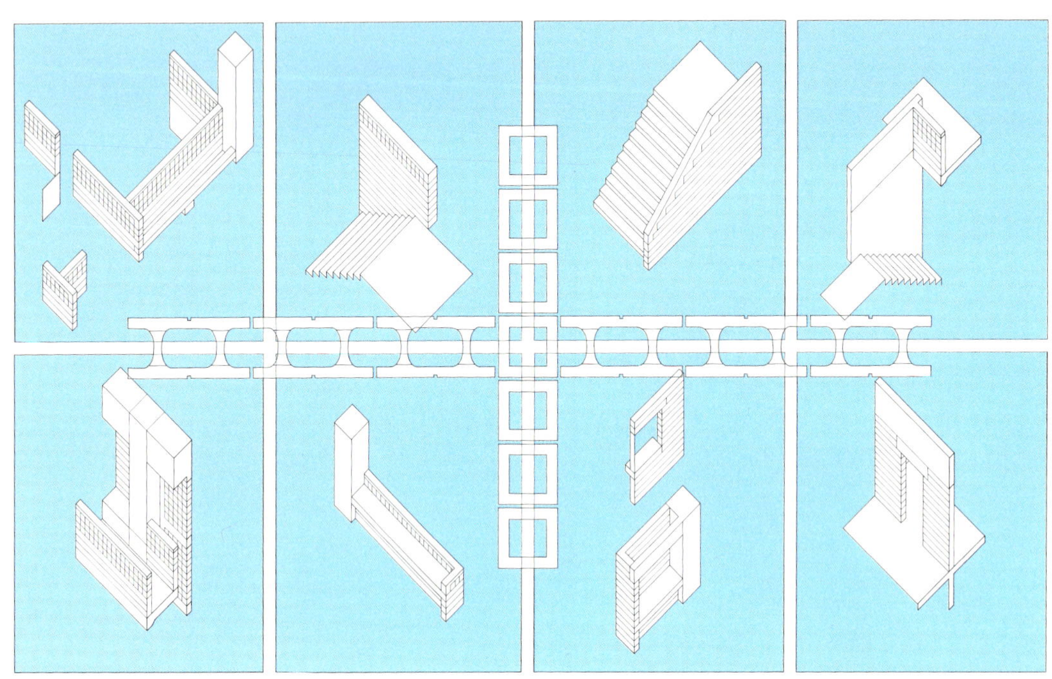

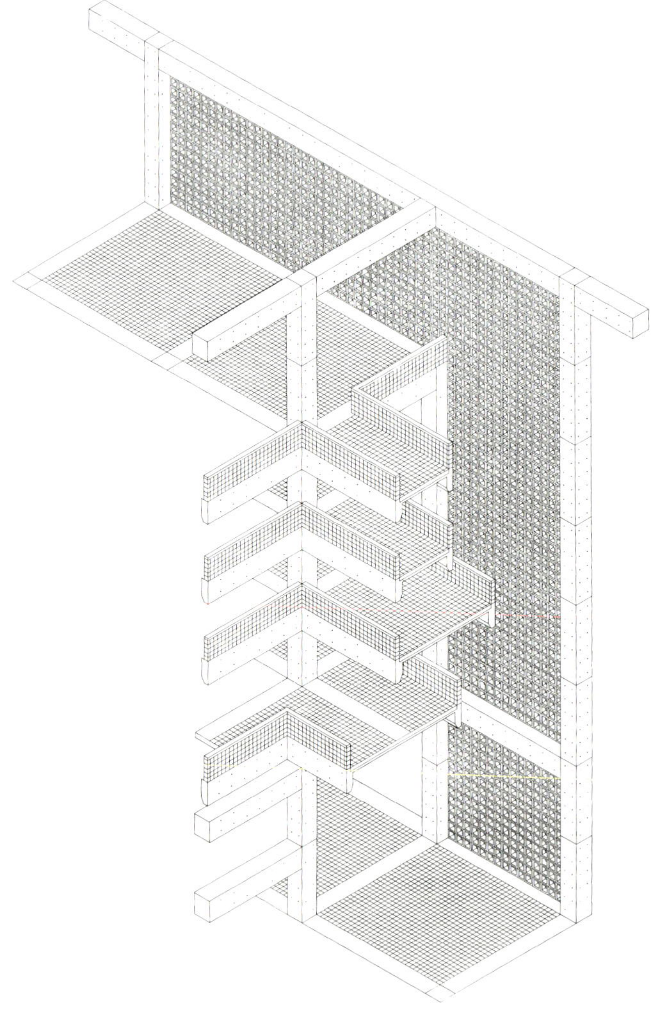

Axonometric delineating architectural elements of concrete blocks. A building of light and wind, integrated under a clear ordering system.

コンクリートブロックによる建築エレメントを描いたアクソノメトリック。明快な秩序の下に統合される、光と風の建築。

Atelier in Oyodo
大淀のアトリエ

1. Osaka, Osaka, Japan　大阪府大阪市
2. 1980.1-1980.8 (phase Ⅰ)/1981.3-1981.9 (phase Ⅱ)/1986.1-1986.5 (phase Ⅲ)
3. 1980.9-1981.3 (phase Ⅰ)/1981.10-1982.2 (phase Ⅱ)/1986.6-1986.9 (phase Ⅲ)

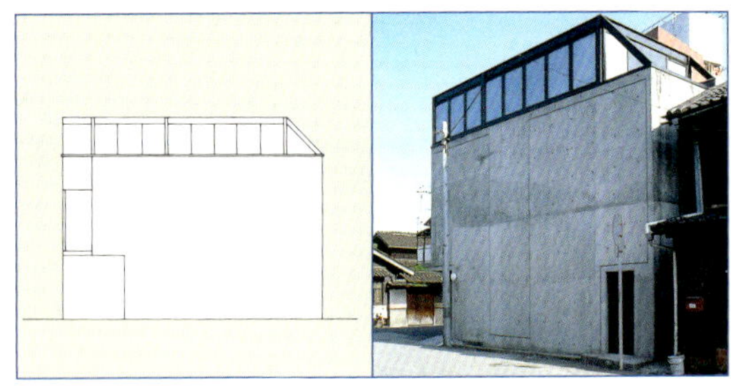

I purchased one of my very early houses (Tomishima House) from the client, and turned into my own atelier. In the process of using it, I made a number of extensions and alterations. In the first stage, a roof was extended over the rooftop deck; in the second stage, a new connecting wing was built on an adjacent site; in the third stage, a penthouse with a vaulted roof was suspended between the two wings. This accumulation of improvised alterations created discontinuous spaces that elicit surprise from visitors.

ごく初期につくった住宅（冨島邸）をクライアントより買い取り、自身のアトリエとしたもの。使いこなしていく過程で、逐次増改築を行い、第Ⅰ期では屋上に屋根を架け、第Ⅱ期では隣接地に新築棟を建てて連結、第Ⅲ期には2棟間にヴォールト屋根のペントハウスを架け渡した。即興的な改造の積み重ねは、来訪者の意表をつく不連続な空間をつくり出した。

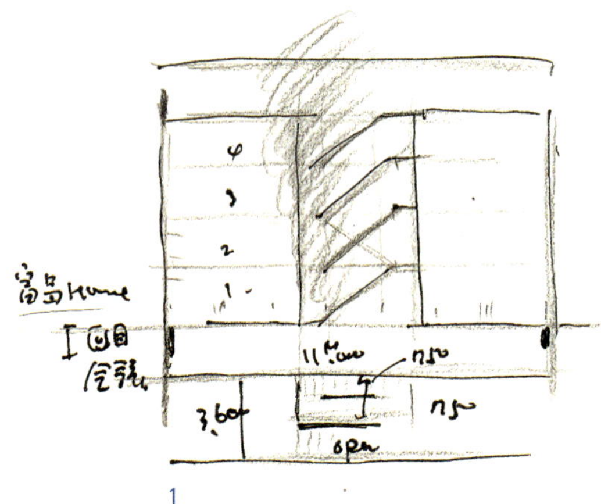

1

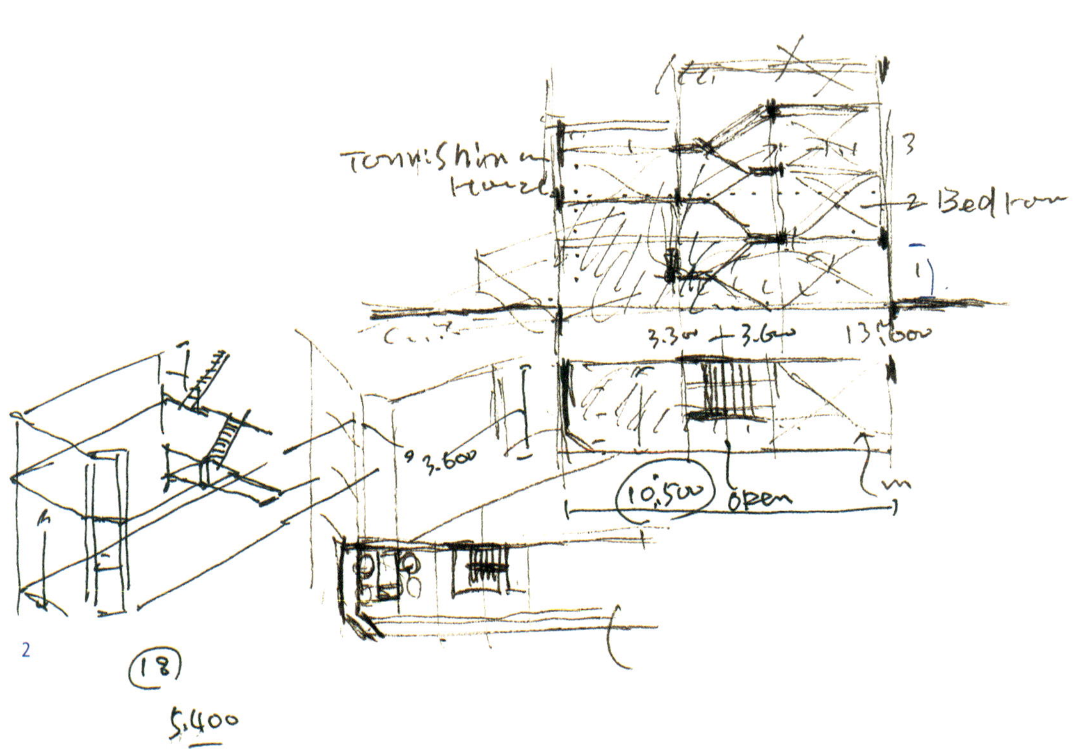

2

1, 2 Sketches made during the studies for the first stage addition. The Tomishima House has a composition in which the block is divided in three equal parts, with a stair well interposed in the center and each room connected by offset floors. First, a steel frame was used to span the rooftop deck, then a rooftop level was created by enclosing it with frosted glass.

3, 4 Sketches made during the studies for the second stage addition. A new wing was built on an adjoining site and connected to the existing wing.

3

1, 2 第Ⅰ期増築を検討中のスケッチ。冨島邸は棟を3等分した真ん中の吹き抜け階段を挟んで各部屋をスキップフロアでつなげる構成。まずはその屋上に鉄骨フレームを掛け渡し、スリガラスで囲われた屋上階を増築。

3, 4 第Ⅱ期増築を検討中のスケッチ。隣接地に新たな棟をつくり既存棟と連続させる。

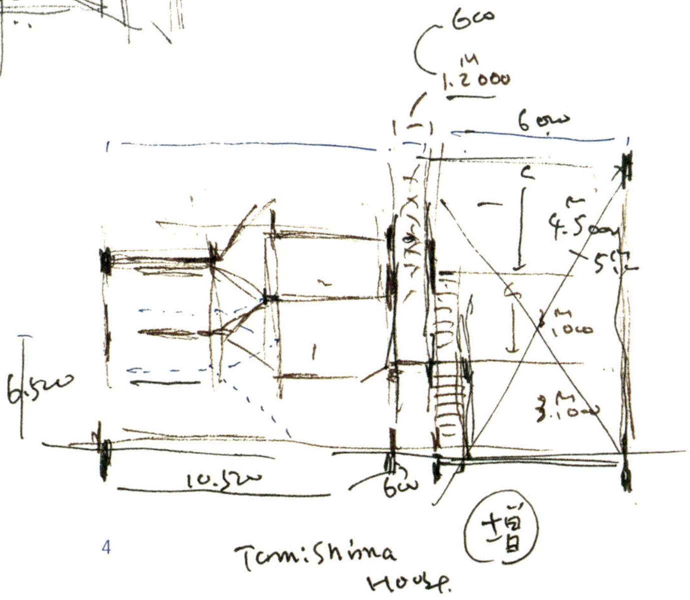

4

1

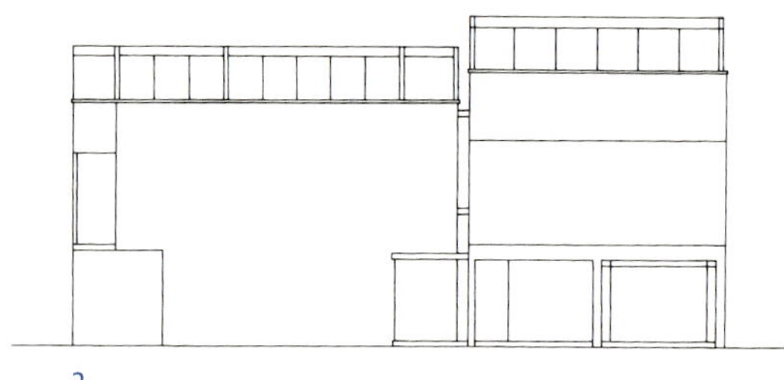

2

The volume of the newly built wing is defined by a wall following the shape of the site and an L-shaped wall connected to the existing wing. The center of the composition is a light garden placed at the rear. By setting walls across the sightlines to the upper part, a rich expression of light changing over time may be felt within.

新築棟のヴォリュームは敷地形状に沿った円弧の壁と、既存棟と接するL字型の壁で決められた。構成の中心は奥に設けた光庭。上部に視線を遮る壁を架け渡すことで、時とともに変化する光の豊かな表情が室内で感じられる。

3

1 Exploratory sketches of the second stage plans.
2 Second stage elevation.
3 Image sketches of the second stage interior. Studying the ways light will enter.
4 Second stage cross section.
5 Exploratory sketch of the entry porch connecting the two wings.

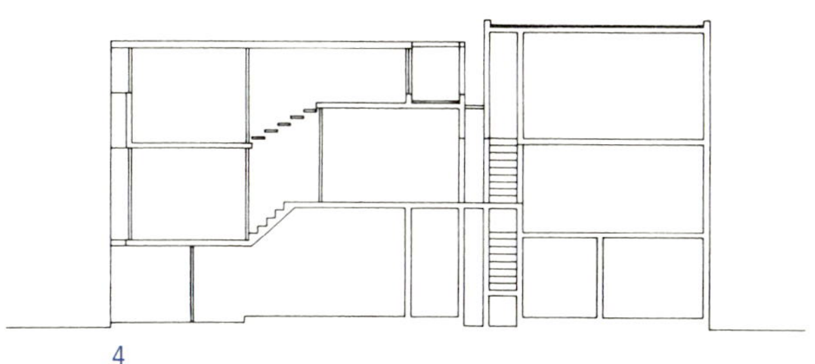

4

1 Ⅱ期のプラン検討スケッチ。
2 Ⅱ期の立面図。
3 Ⅱ期の内部イメージスケッチ。光の入れ方を検討している。
4 Ⅱ期の断面図。
5 2棟を連結する玄関ポーチの検討スケッチ。

5

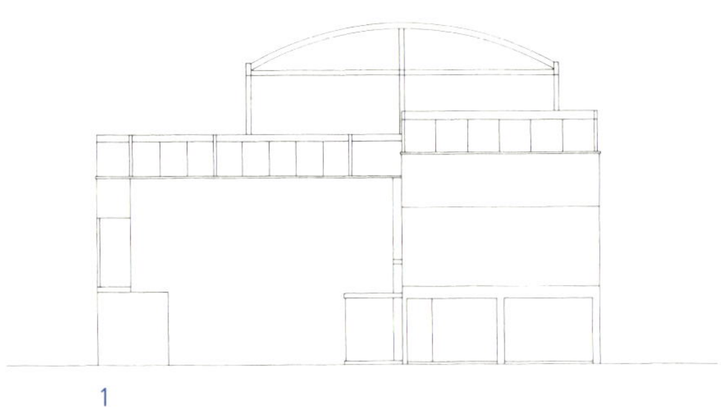

Resolving the slippages between the two wings in plan and in section during the repeated renovations caused unexpected spaces to arise in unforeseen places, such as the ladders up and down the walls, or the toilet located in the connection between the two wings. While being the base for my activities, this is also a place for personal architectural experiments.

2棟の断面的、平面的ズレを納めながら、改造を重ねていくうちに、壁伝いに上り下りするはしごや、2棟の連結部に位置するトイレなど、思いもよらぬ場所に意外な空間が生まれた。この建築は、私にとって活動の拠点であるのと同時に、個人的な建築実験の場であった。

1 Third stage elevation.
2 Third stage plans.

1 Ⅲ期の立面図。
2 Ⅲ期の平面図。

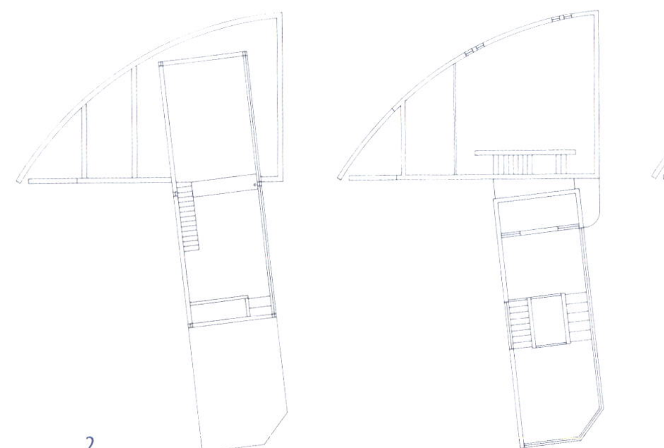

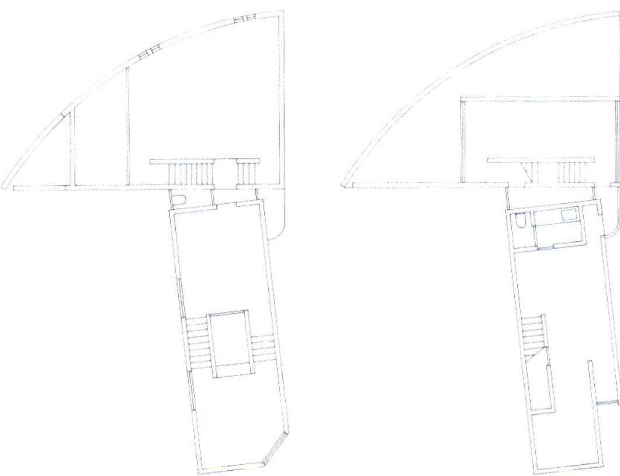

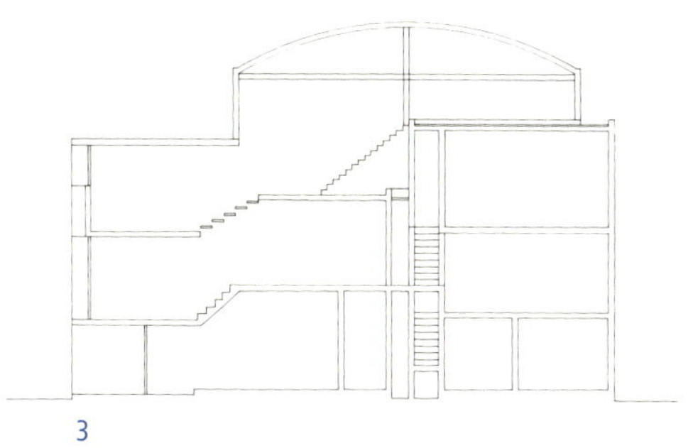

3

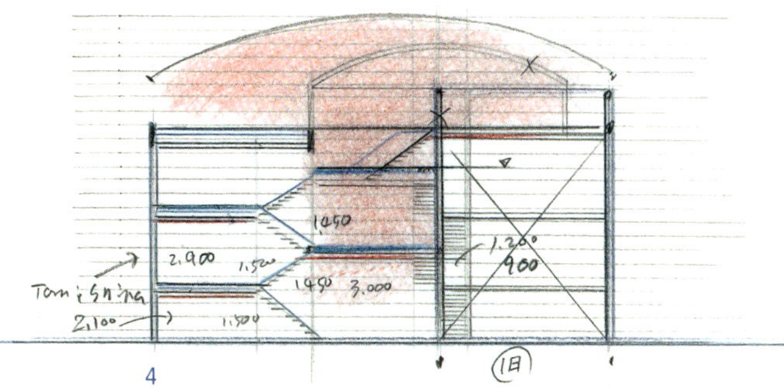

4

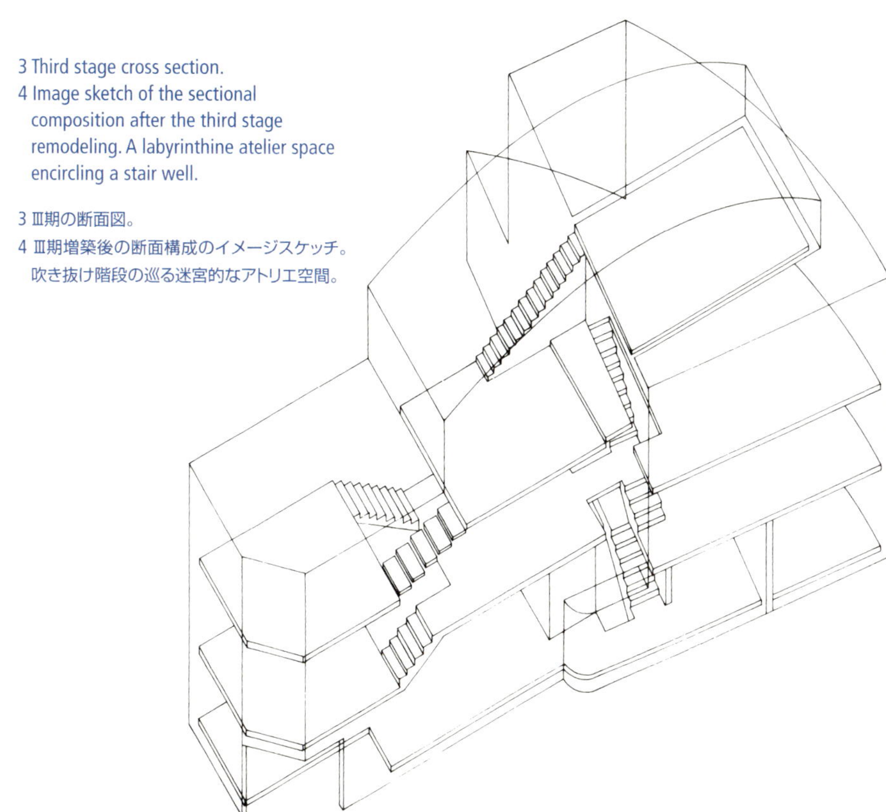

3 Third stage cross section.
4 Image sketch of the sectional composition after the third stage remodeling. A labyrinthine atelier space encircling a stair well.

3 Ⅲ期の断面図。
4 Ⅲ期増築後の断面構成のイメージスケッチ。吹き抜け階段の巡る迷宮的なアトリエ空間。

Atelier in Oyodo II
大淀のアトリエ II

1. Osaka, Osaka, Japan　大阪府大阪市
2. 1989.6-1990.5
3. 1990.6-1991.4

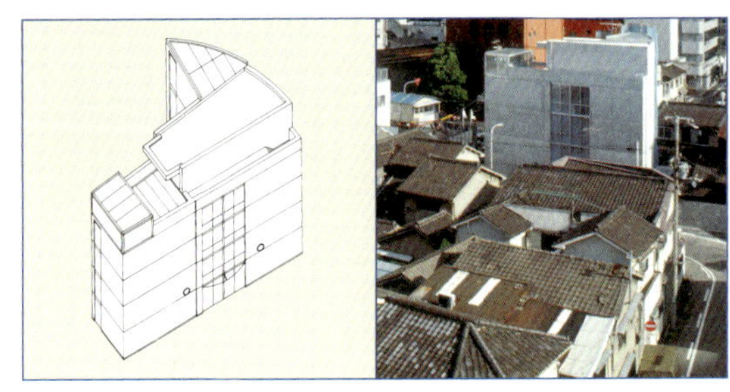

Atelier in Oyodo was demolished in order to build something entirely new. The outline of the plan remains unchanged, and the interior also basically follows the composition of the previous atelier. The stairwell space piercing all floors on the east side of the building is the nucleus. Stacked in a stepping configuration, each floor faces this stairwell and is connected to the stairs by bridges. I wanted to make a single, continuous space that always allowed a sense of unity between the twenty-or-so staff members and myself.

大淀のアトリエを解体し、全面的に新築したものである。建物の平面的な輪郭はそのまま、内部も基本的には前のアトリエの構成を踏襲した。核となるのは、建物東側の全階を貫く吹き抜け階段の空間。各フロアはこの吹き抜けに面して、段状にセットバックしながら重なり、ブリッジを介して階段と結ばれる。20名余りのスタッフと私とが常に一体感を感じられるような、ワンルームの空間をつくりたかった。

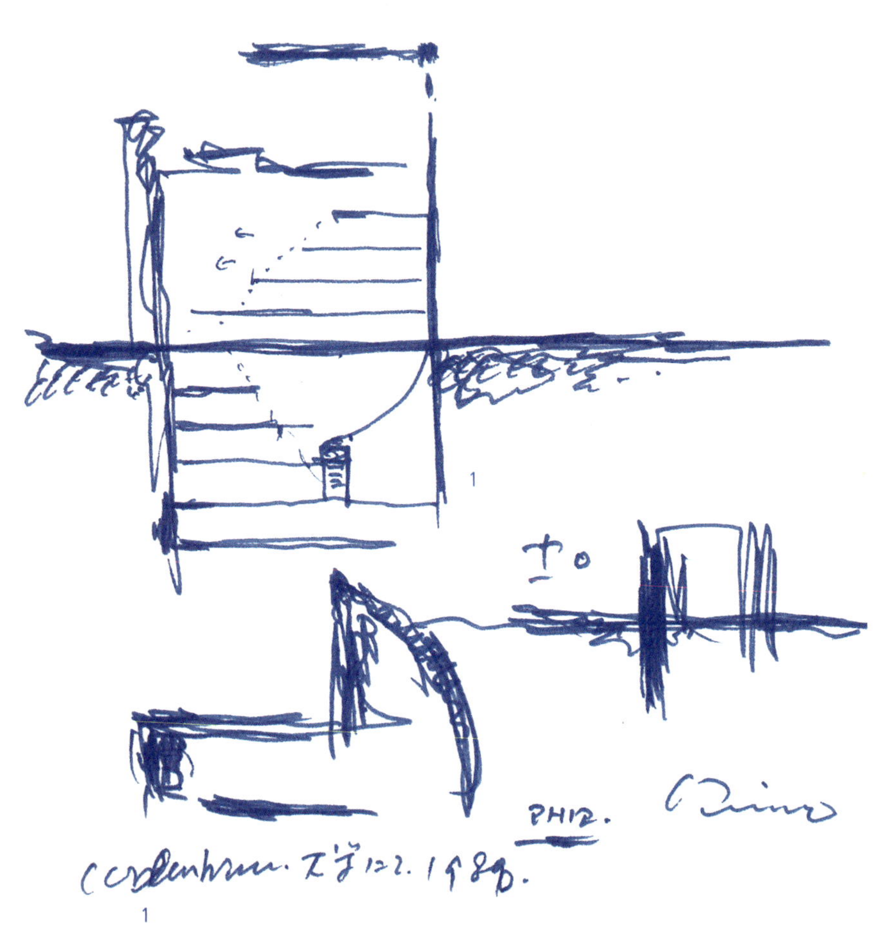

1

1

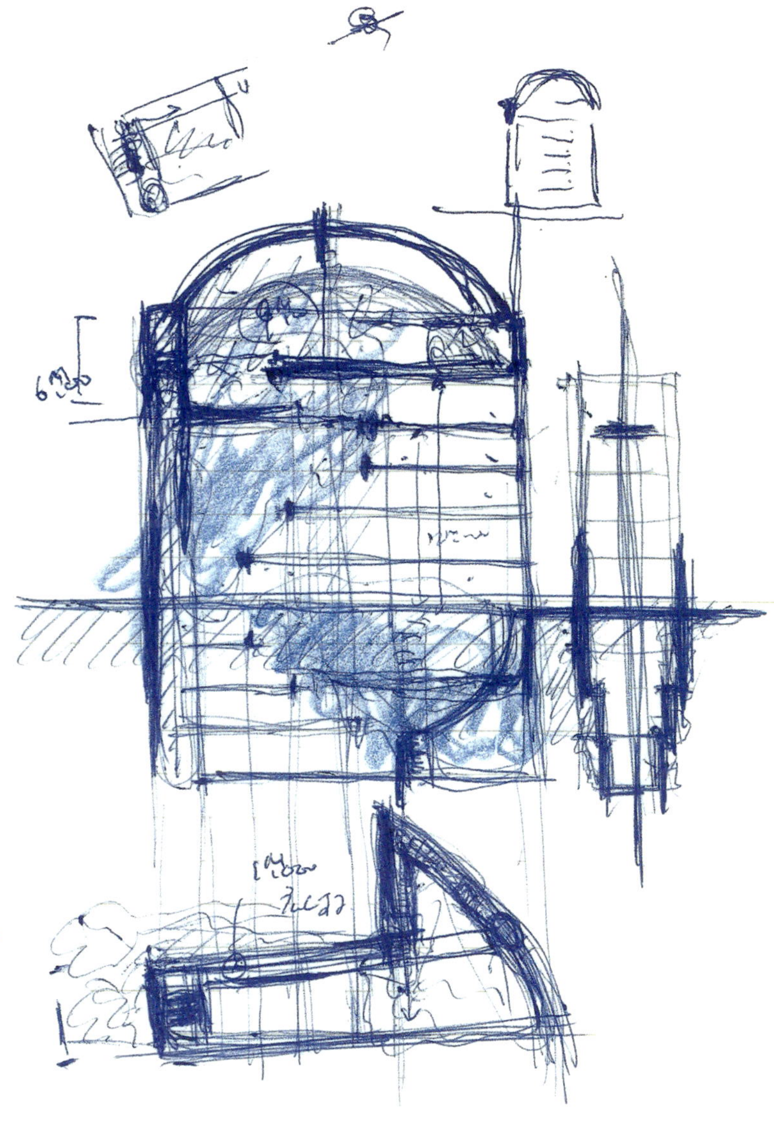

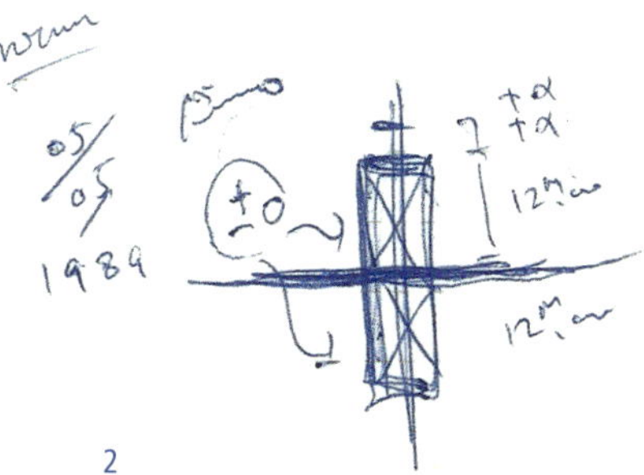

2

1 From the outset, the image was of a bowl-shaped stairwell space contained between walls, and I thought of inverting the shape of this compositional diagram for the underground levels.

2 How to bring light into this stairwell space? Studies of variations for the roof shape on the roof-deck level. Like the previous atelier, a vaulted roof proposal was explored.

1 当初より、壁に挟まれたすり鉢型の吹き抜け空間がイメージとしてあり、その構成図式を反転させたかたちに地下をつくろうと考えていた。

2 吹き抜けの空間に、いかにして光を導くか。最上階の屋根形状のさまざまなヴァリエーションを検討。前のアトリエと同じ、ヴォールト屋根にする案も検討された。

1

1 Sectional drawing done when the design had been mostly decided. In terms of cost and technology, it was difficult to build the underground levels exactly like the image, but without giving up, a proposal for four basement levels was investigated.

2 Section, plans. It finally became a building with five levels above ground and two basement levels. The entire upper part of the stairwell is a skylight, and light entering the apex reaches the deepest parts of the building. Ando's desk sits at the bottom of this well of light.

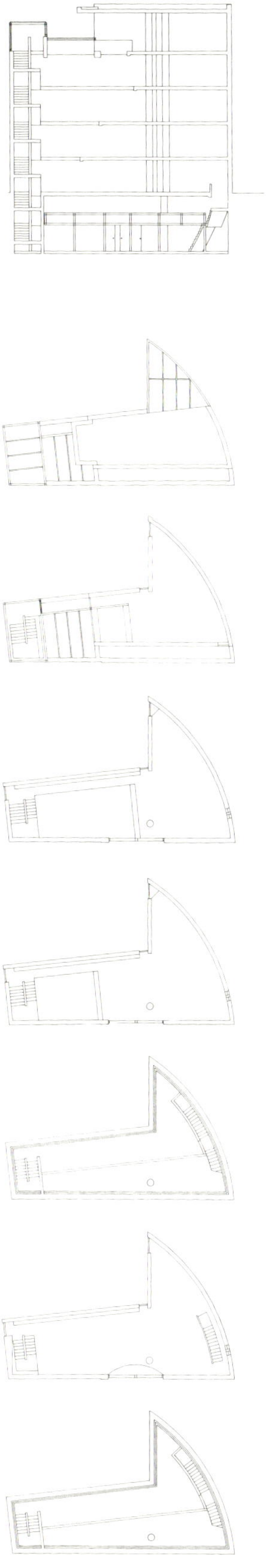

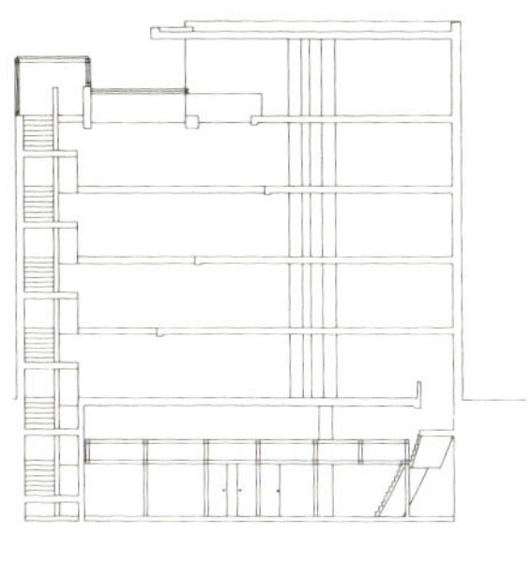

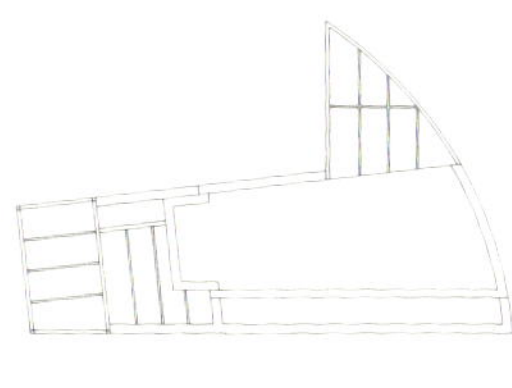

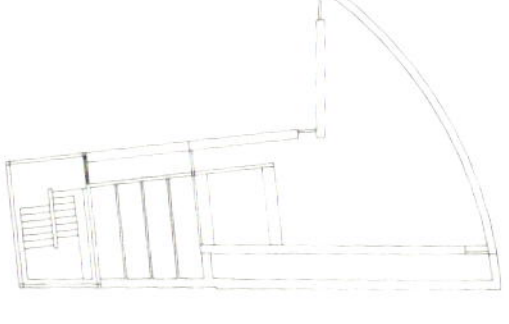

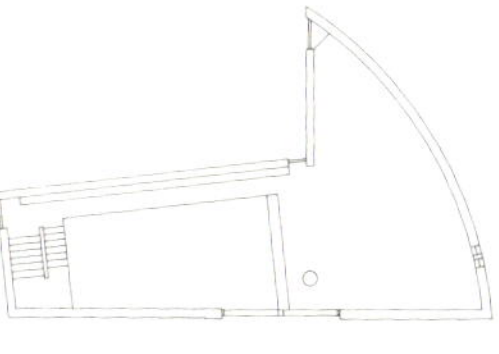

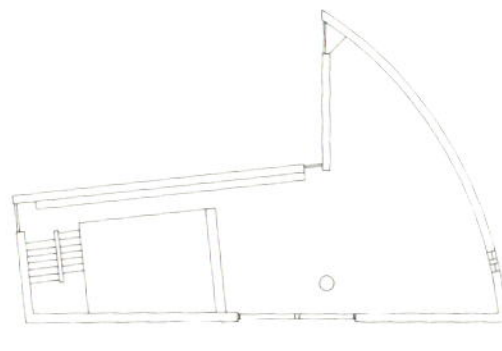

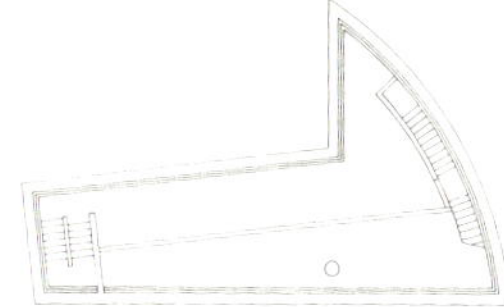

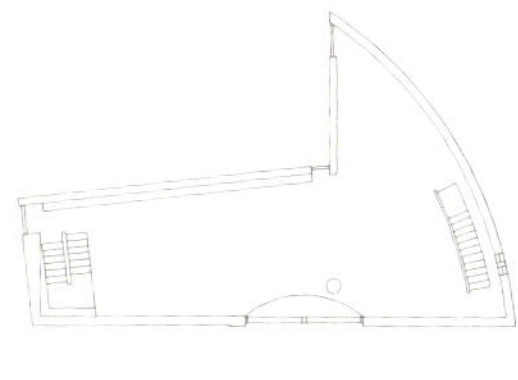

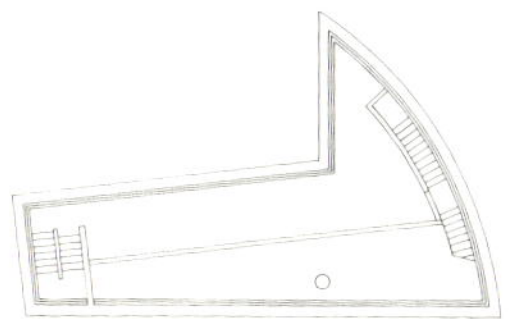

2

1 設計がほぼ固まった時期に描かれた断面ドローイング。コスト的、技術的にイメージ通りの地下をつくるのは難しかったが、あきらめられず、地下4階の案を検討している。

2 断面図、平面図。最終的には地上5階、地下2階の建物となった。吹き抜け階段の上部は全面トップライトとして、頭上からの光が建物内部深くまで入り込む。この光の井戸の底に安藤のデスクがある。

Tea House for Soseikan
双生観の茶室

1. Takarazuka, Hyogo, Japan　兵庫県宝塚市
2. 1981.5-1982.2
3. 1982.3-1982.7

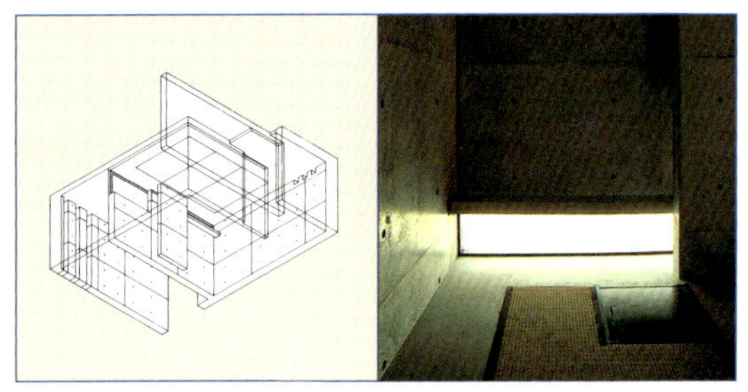

This is a tearoom added to the east wing of Souseikan, one of my early houses. The floor, ceiling, and walls enclosing the three tatami-mat space are all made of exposed concrete. Through this simple composition, I tried to make a microcosm within which one may sense the depths of infinity in a tiny space by means of a refined combination of overlapping walls and apertures.

私の初期の住宅「双生観」の東棟寄りに増築した茶室である。畳3畳の空間を囲う壁、天井、床のすべてをコンクリート打ち放しとしている。単純な構成の中で、壁の重なりと開口部のあり方、その組み合わせを練り上げることで、極小のスペースの中に無限の奥行きを感じさせる小宇宙をつくろうとしていた。

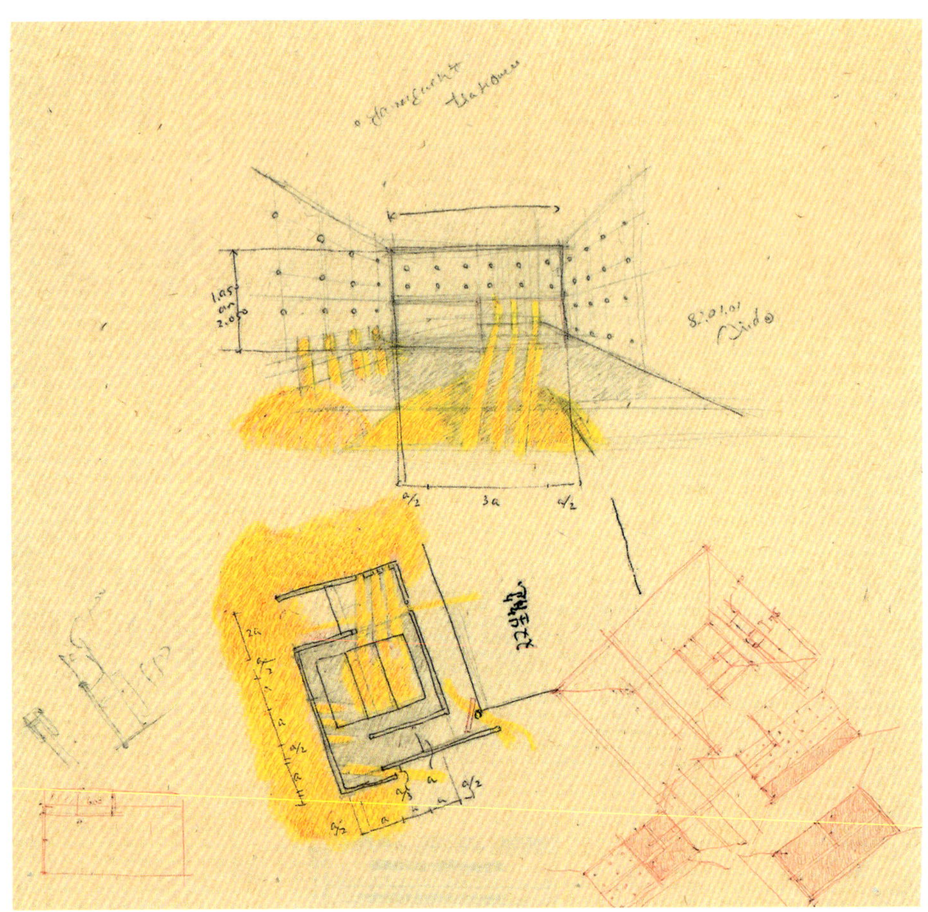

Because it is tiny, a dimensioning system based on the size of a human body was carefully and closely considered.

極小であるがゆえ、人間の身体尺度に則した寸法体系が、慎重かつ厳密に考えられている。

Umemiya House
梅宮邸

1. Kobe, Hyogo, Japan　兵庫県神戸市
2. 1981.6-1982.9
3. 1982.10-1983.3

This is an attempt to compose a house using nothing but the partitioning and combining of squares. Within a simple division of rooms, the idea was to create a deep living space through the way they are each connected, including their relationships with the outside.

正方形の分割、組み合わせのみによる構成を試みた住宅である。単純な部屋割りの中で、それぞれのつながり方、外部との関係に変化をつけ、奥行きのある住空間をつくろうと考えた。

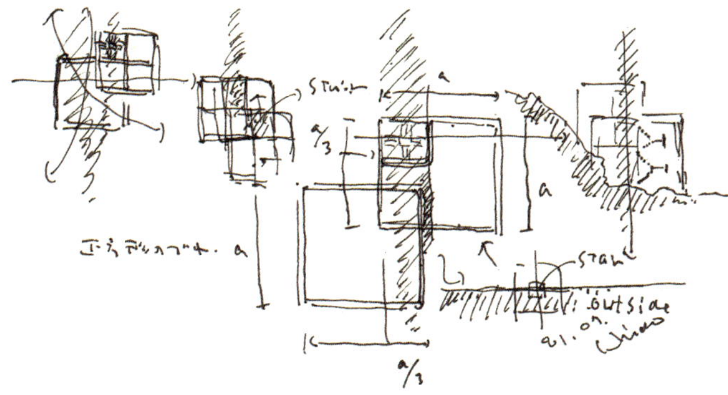

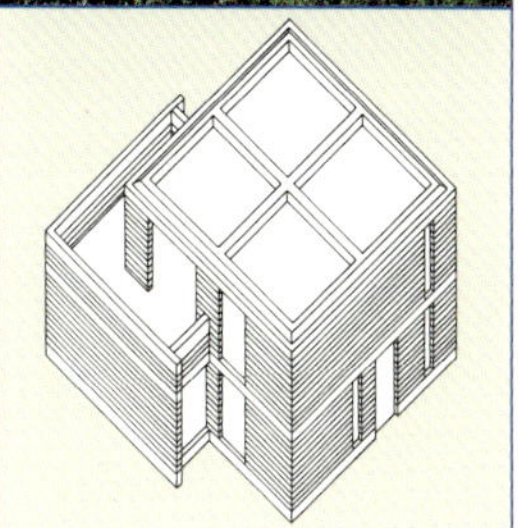

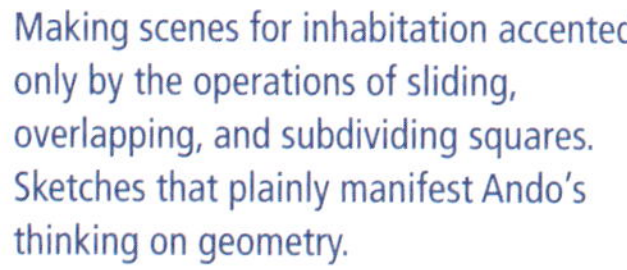

Making scenes for inhabitation accented only by the operations of sliding, overlapping, and subdividing squares. Sketches that plainly manifest Ando's thinking on geometry.

正方形をズラし、重ねて分割する操作のみで抑揚ある住まいのシーンをつくり上げていく。幾何学による安藤の思考が端的に表れたスケッチ。

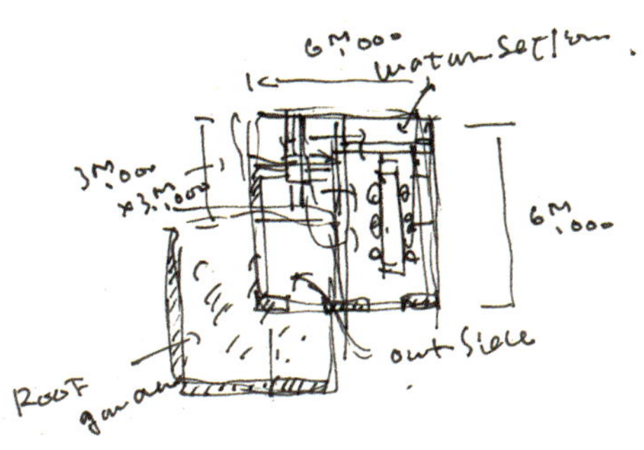

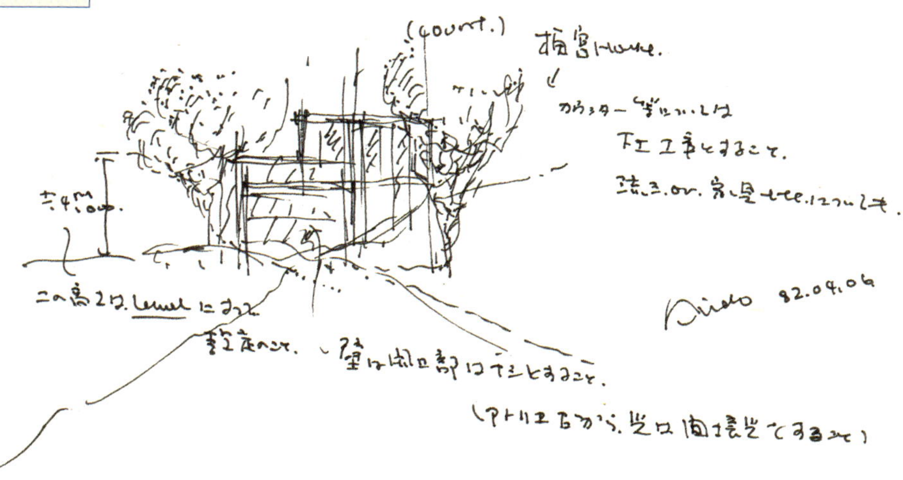

Town House in Kujo
九条の町屋

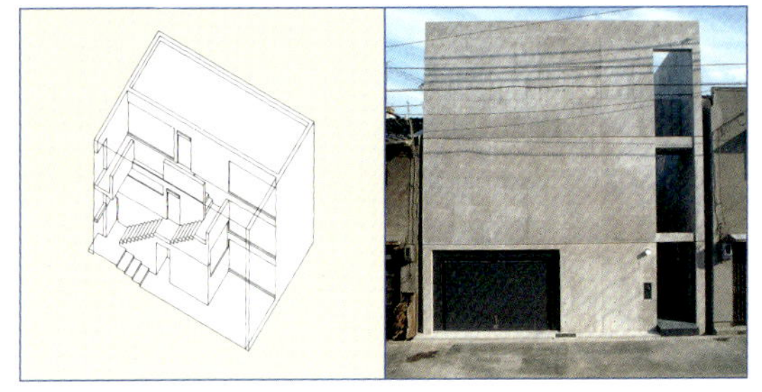

1. Osaka, Osaka, Japan　大阪府大阪市
2. 1981.11-1982.4
3. 1982.5-1982.10

A residence for two households (a couple, and their son and his wife) built in downtown Osaka. Taking half of the volume surrounded by a three-story-high wall as an inner courtyard, I conceived the access to each dwelling as if passing through a "drawn-in road space." The rooms are stacked on three levels, and gently tied by exterior steps traversing the inner courtyard. This is one prototype for the series of *machiya*-type houses that I experimented with following the Row House in Sumiyoshi.

大阪下町につくった2世帯（夫婦とその息子夫婦）のための住宅。3層分の高さの壁で囲ったヴォリュームの2分の1を中庭にあて、各住居へのアクセスを〈引き込まれた街路空間〉を経るように考えた。3層に積み重ねた室は、中庭を巡る外階段によって緩やかに結ばれる。「住吉の長屋」以来試みてきた一連の町屋型住宅の、ひとつのプロトタイプである。

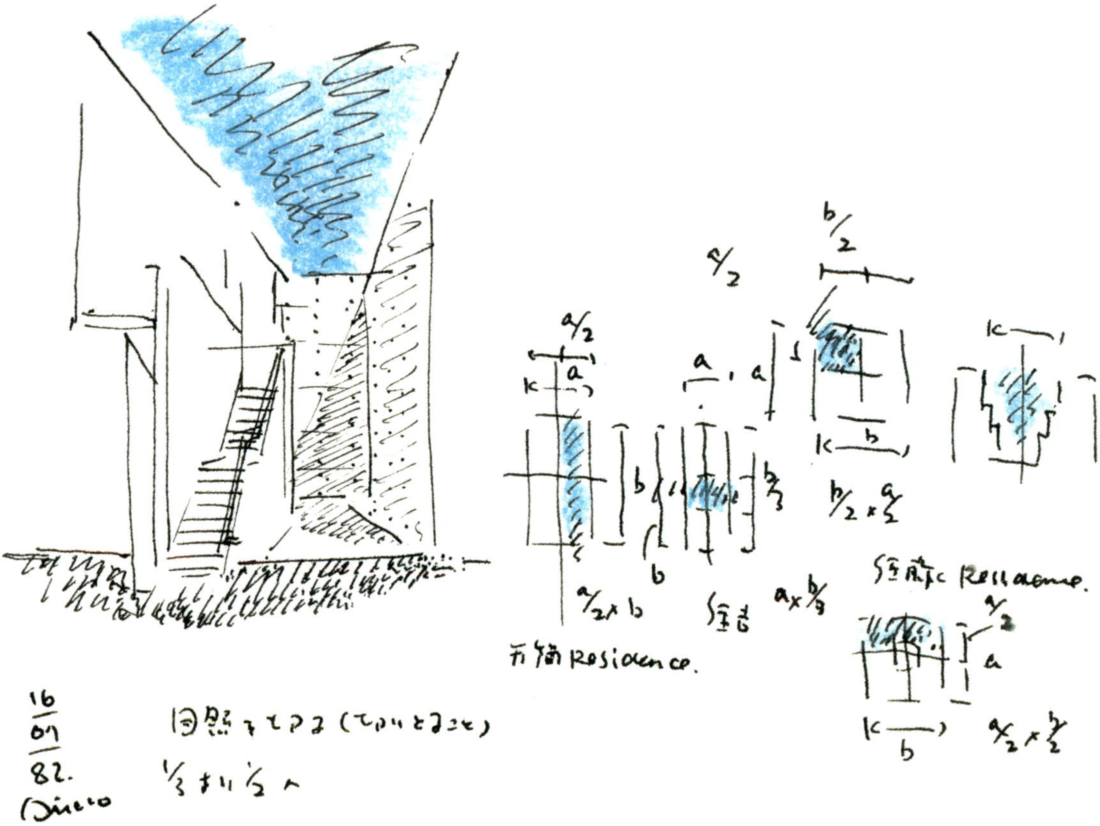

1

1 Study sketches of spatial diagrams based on the ways the void may be introduced.
2 Embedded window frame detail for the only aperture made in the box.
3 Exploratory drawing of the exterior space focused on the inner courtyard.
4 Exploratory drawing of the cross section.
5 Exploratory drawing of the façade and the inner courtyard elevation.
6 Exploratory drawing of the plan.

1 ヴォイドの取り方による空間図式の検討スケッチ。
2 ボックスに穿たれた唯一の開口部にはめ込まれるサッシュのディテール。
3 中庭を中心とした屋外部分の検討図。
4 断面検討図。
5 ファサード、中庭エレベーションの検討図。
6 平面検討図。

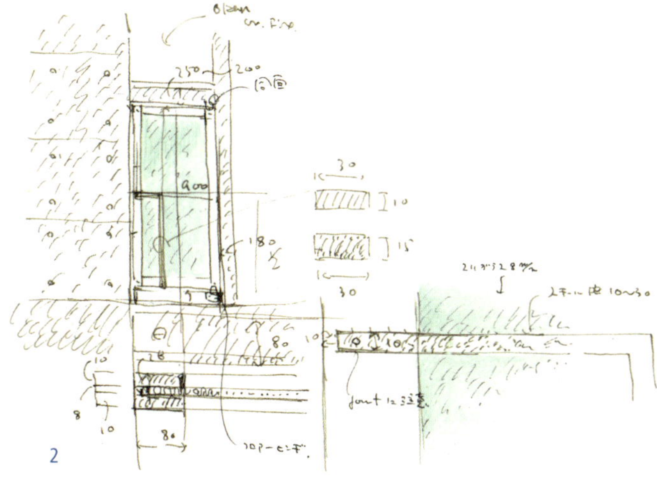

2

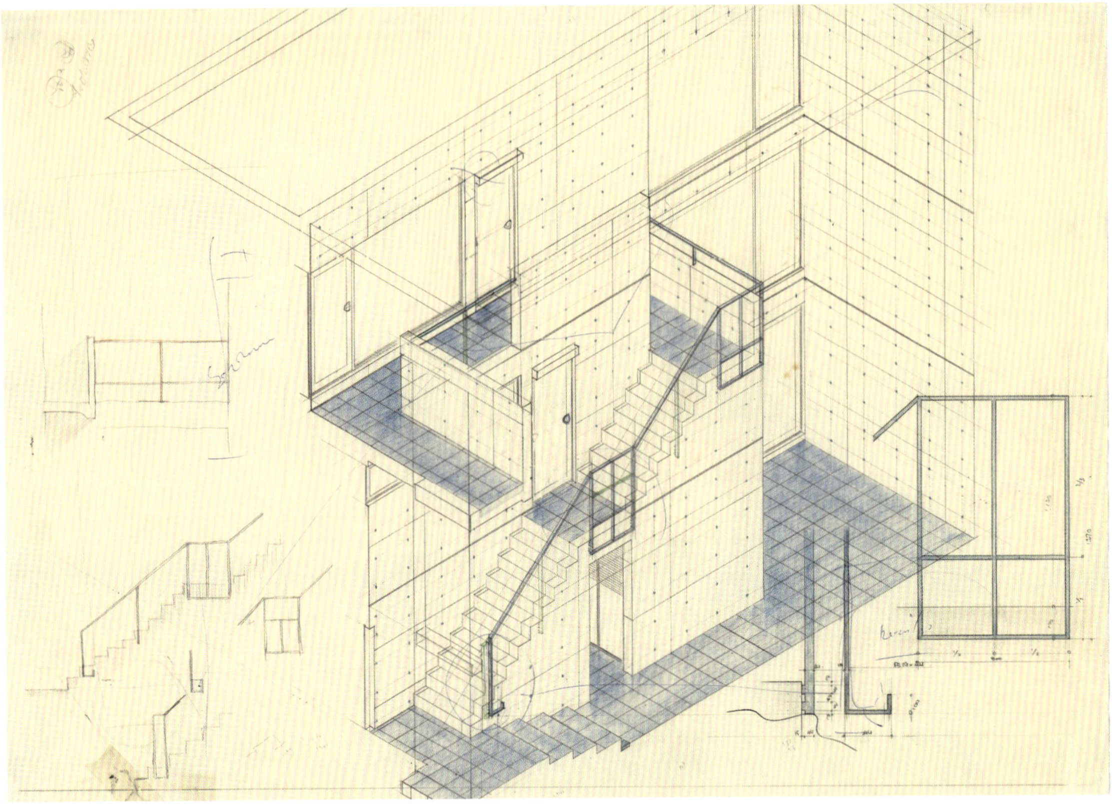

3

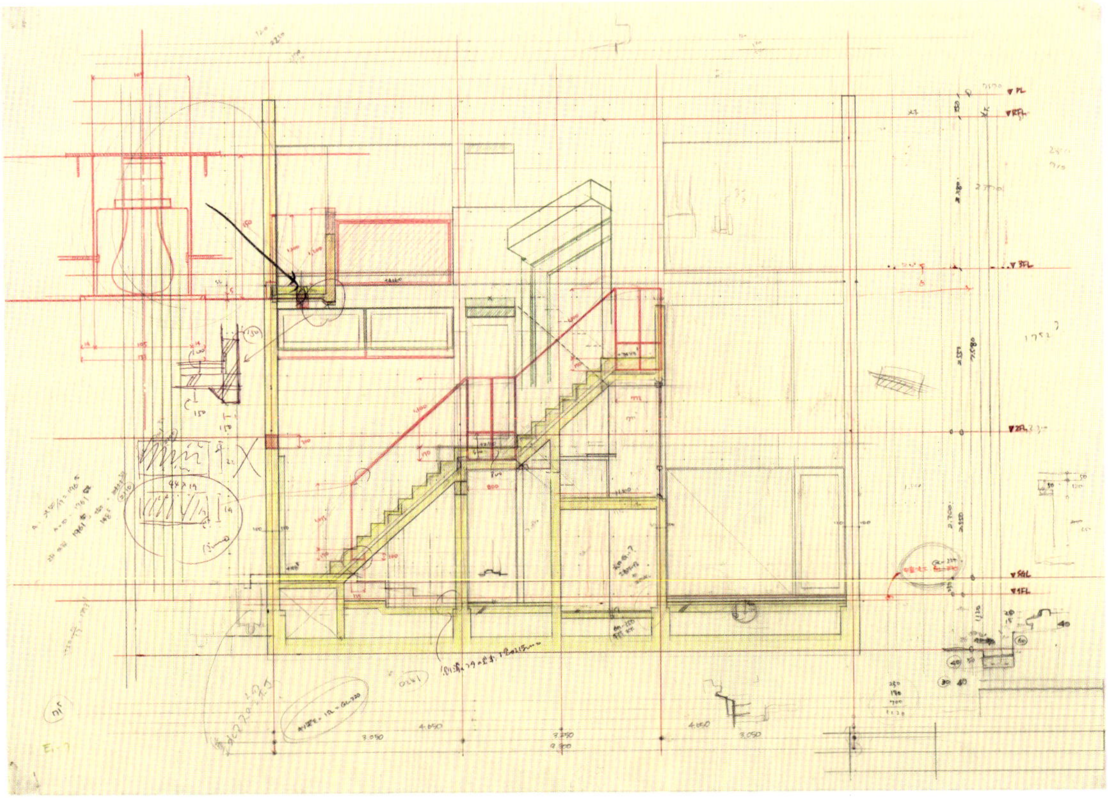

4

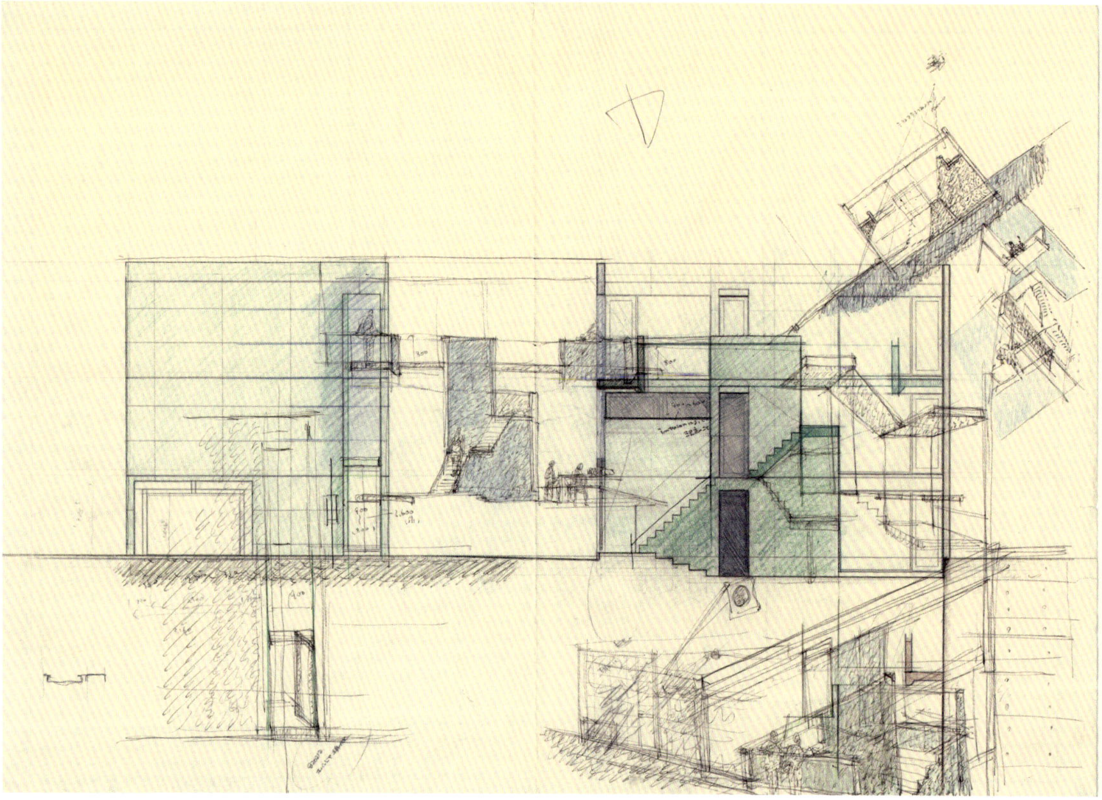

5

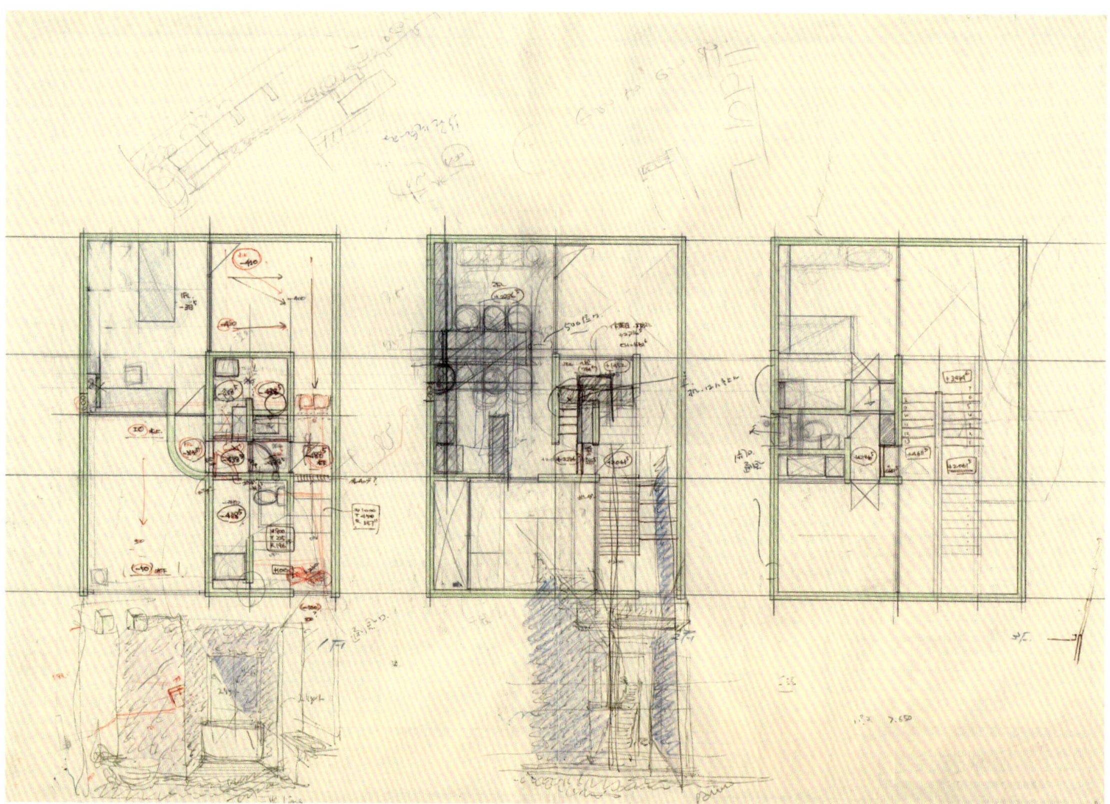

6

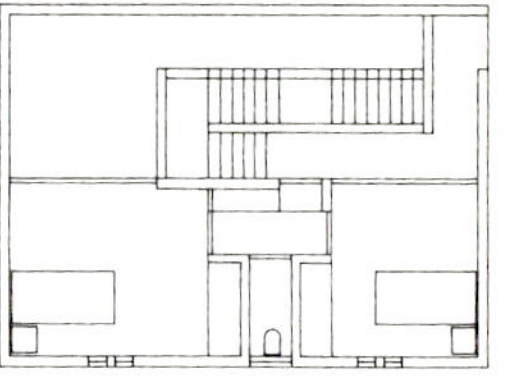

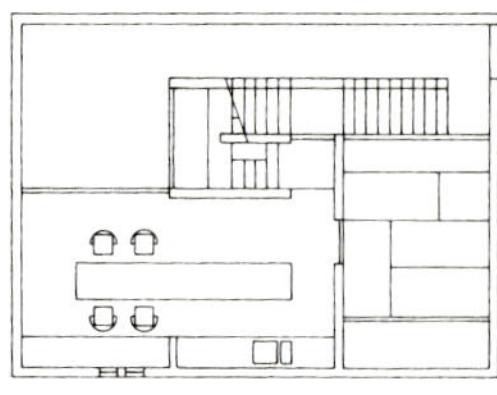

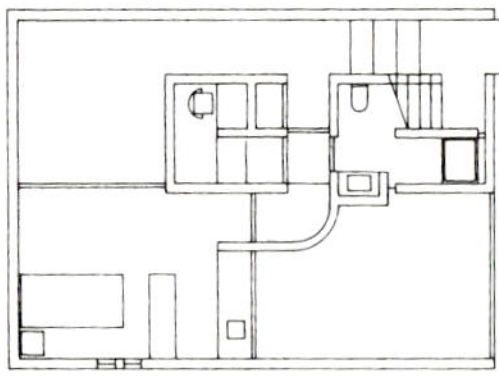

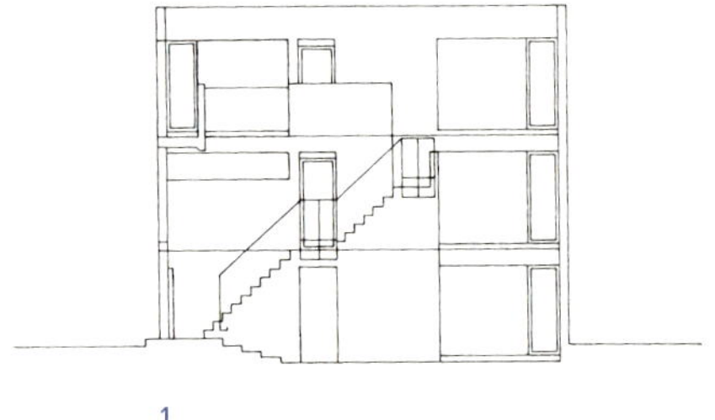

1

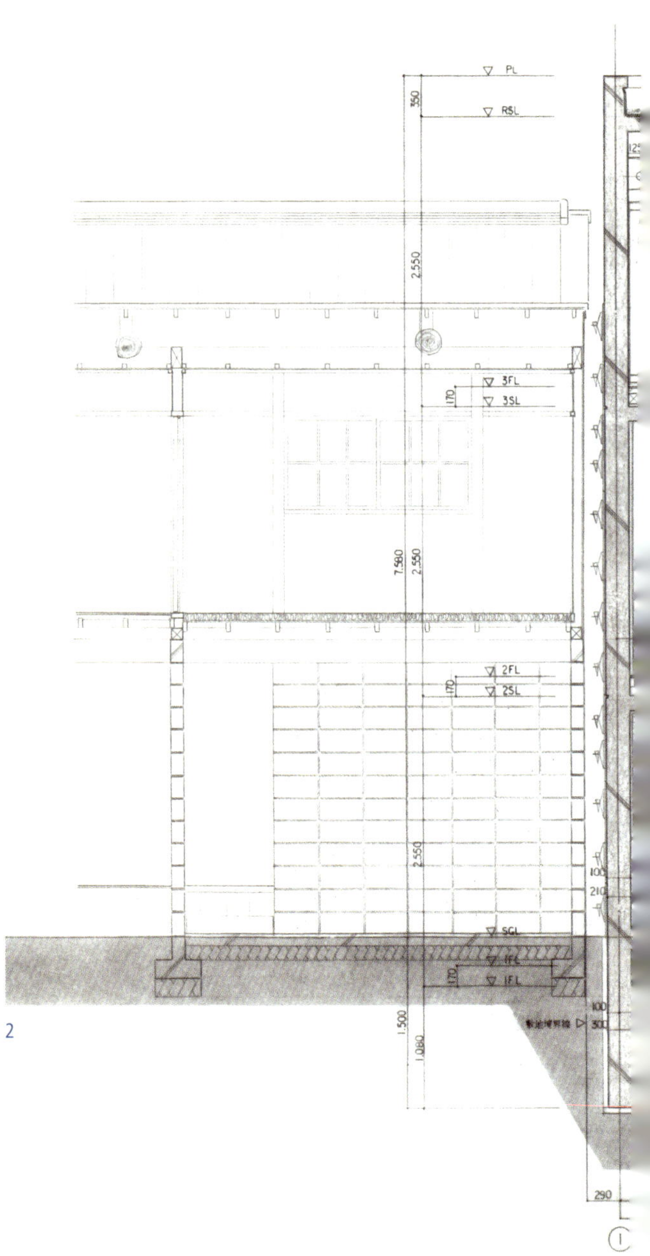

2

1 From below: cross section, first floor plan, second floor plan, third floor plan.
2 Detailed cross section.

1 下から断面図、1階・2階・3階平面図。
2 断面詳細図。

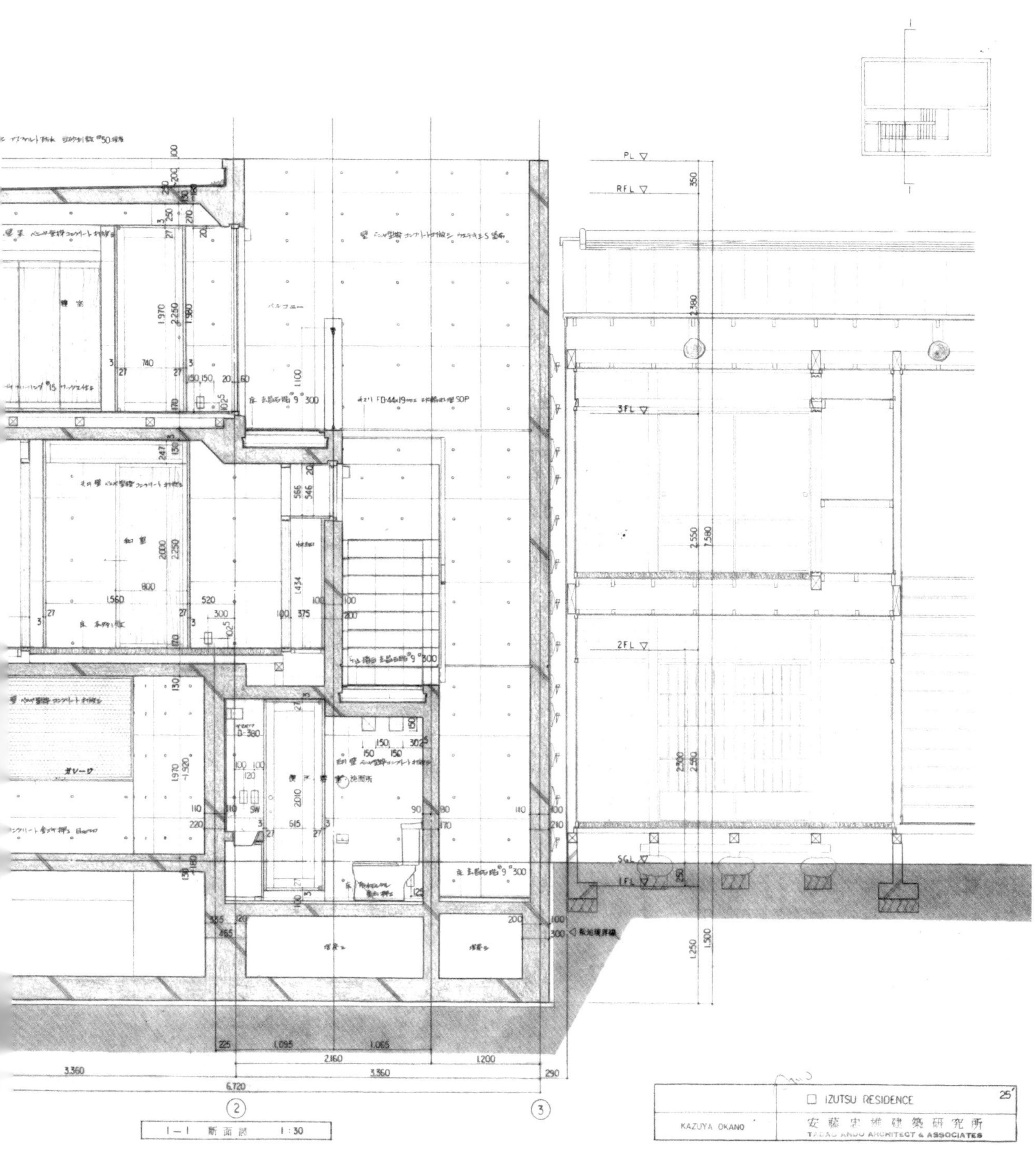
PL
RFL
3FL
2FL
SGL
1FL
IZUTSU RESIDENCE
KAZUYA OKANO
安藤忠雄建築研究所
TADAO ANDO ARCHITECT & ASSOCIATES
1－1 断面図 1:30

Kidosaki House
城戸崎邸

1. Setagaya-ku, Tokyo, Japan　東京都世田谷区
2. 1982.10-1985.10
3. 1985.10-1986.10

The site is located in a quiet residential area in the Setagaya district of Tokyo. This is a house for three households: the client couple and their respective parents. While ensuring privacy and independence for each family, by making abundant void spaces in the interstices I conceived a plan for a single residential complex containing all these lives bound together.

敷地は世田谷区の閑静な住宅地の中に位置する。クライアント夫婦とその両親たち3世帯のための住宅である。それぞれの家族が、プライバシーを確保して独立しながらも、その隙間のヴォイドの空間を豊かにすることで、ひとつに結びあった生活を営めるひとつの共同住宅の計画として考えた。

1

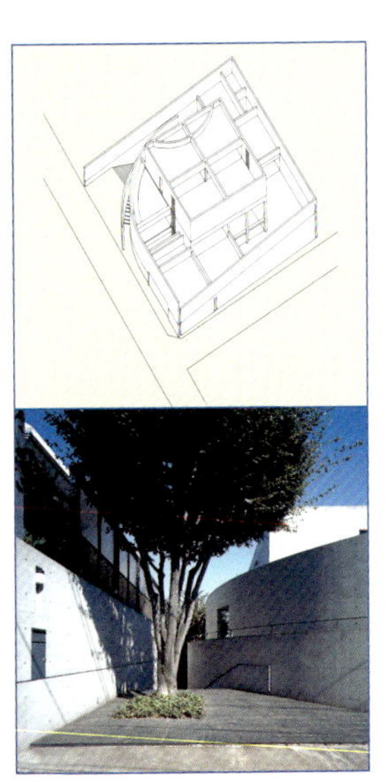

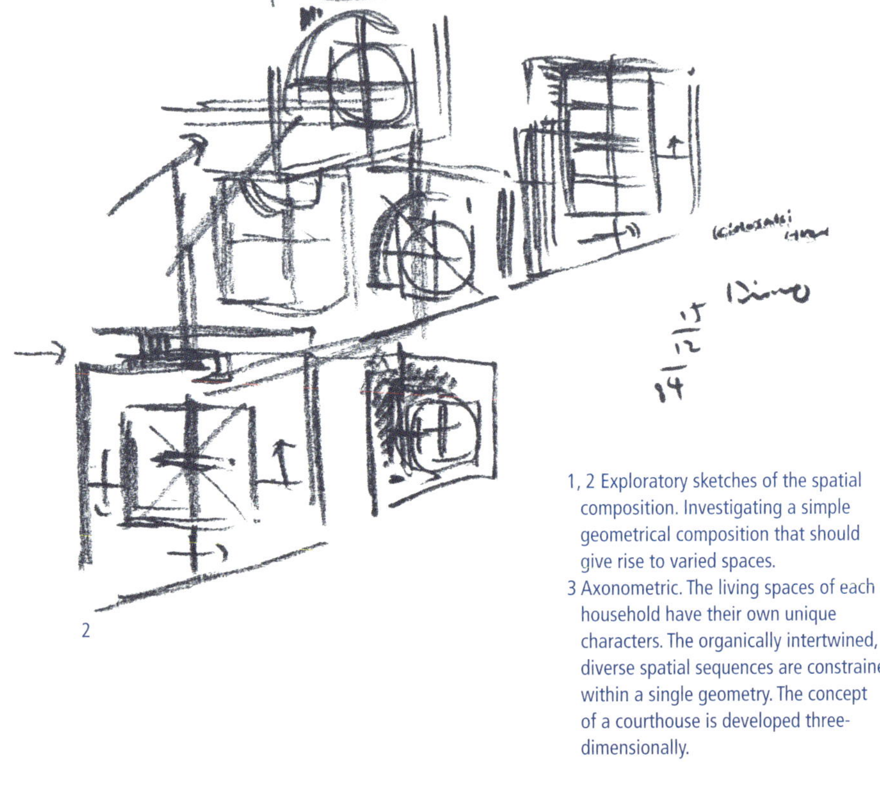

2

1, 2 Exploratory sketches of the spatial composition. Investigating a simple geometrical composition that should give rise to varied spaces.
3 Axonometric. The living spaces of each household have their own unique characters. The organically intertwined, diverse spatial sequences are constrained within a single geometry. The concept of a courthouse is developed three-dimensionally.

1, 2 空間構成の検討スケッチ。複雑な空間を実現すべき、単純な構成の幾何学を模索している。

3 アクソノメトリック。各世帯の生活空間がそれぞれに独自の性格をもって、有機的に絡み合う、多様な空間のシークエンスを、ひとつの幾何学の中に封じ込めていく。3次元に展開するコートハウスのコンセプト。

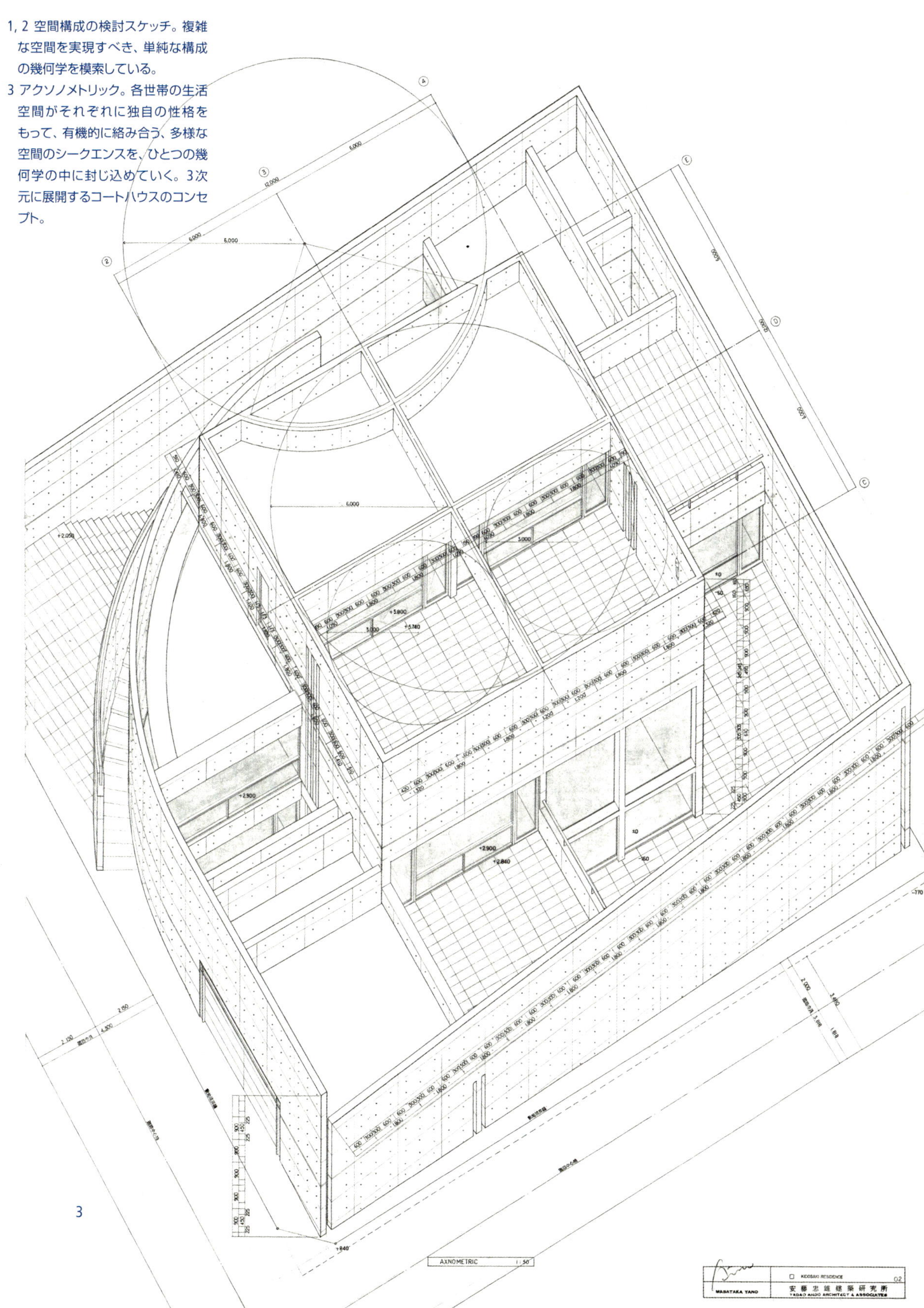

3

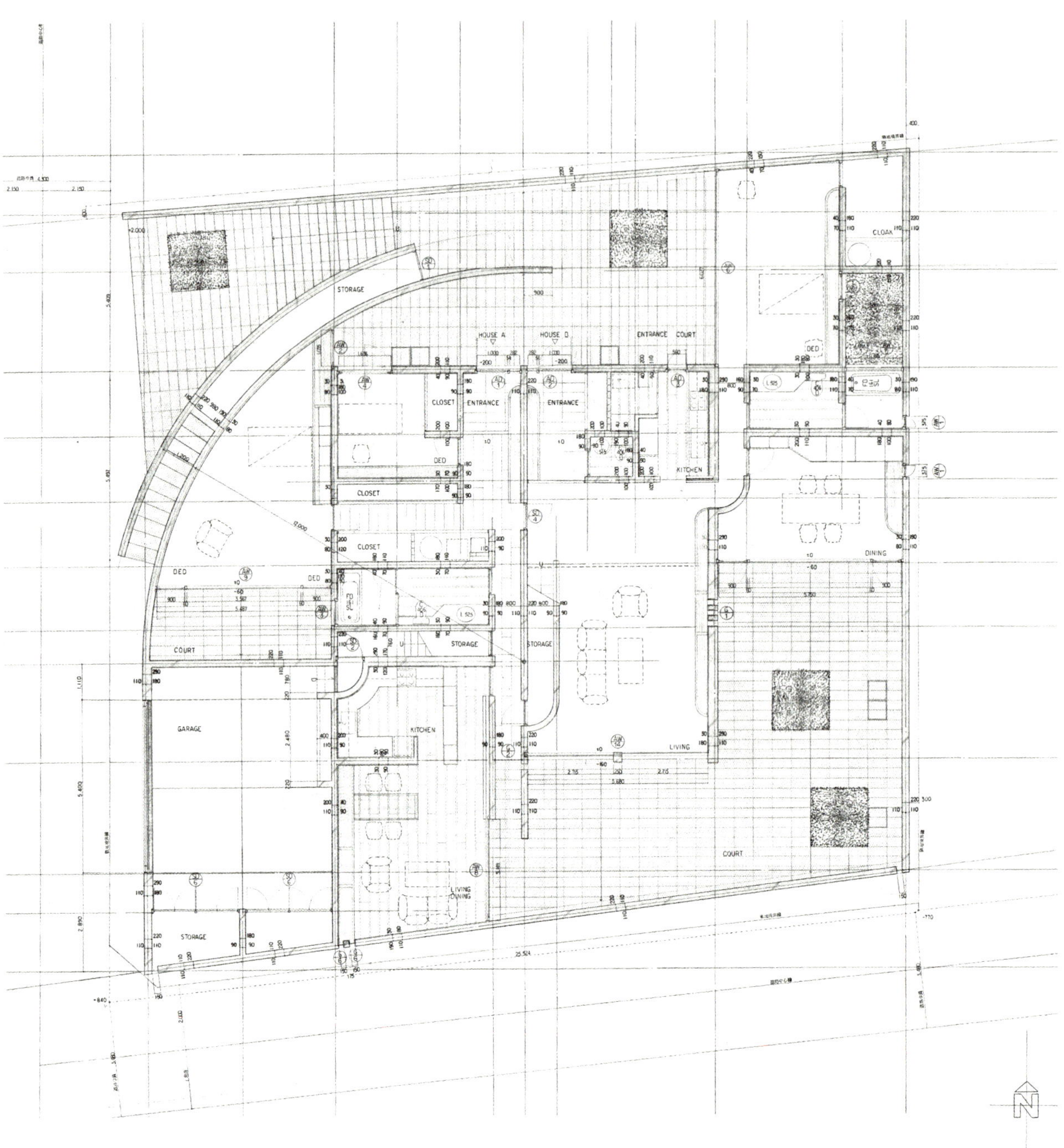

Detailed first floor plan

1階平面詳細図

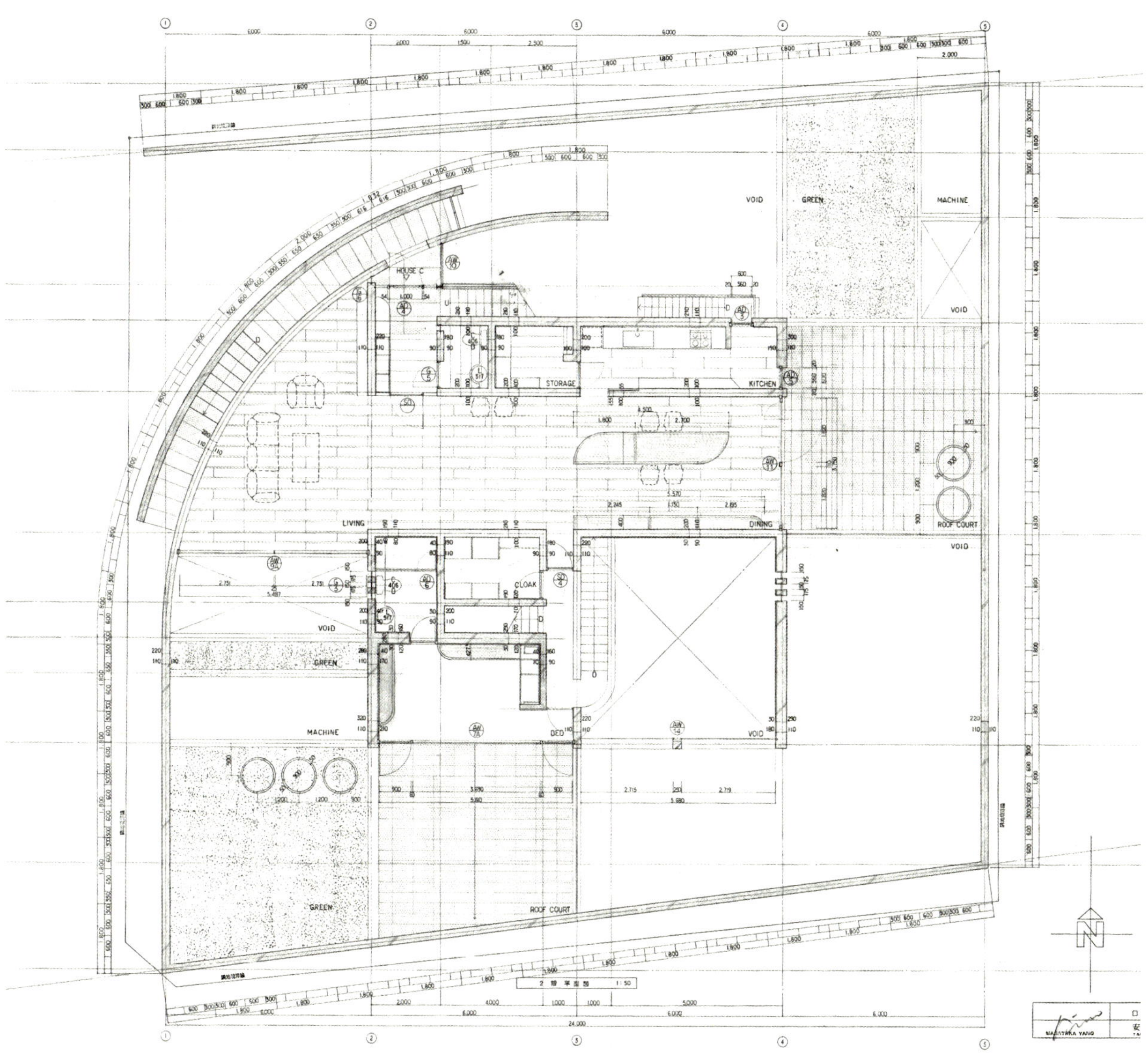

Detailed second floor plan

2階平面詳細図

Doll's House
ドールズハウス

2. 1982

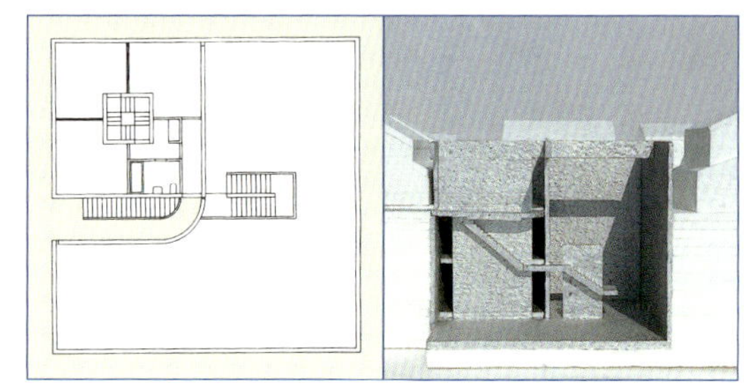

This is a proposal submitted for an ideas competition on the theme of "a house designed for dolls." Reinterpreting the presence of dolls as scale-less humans, I conceived a residential space that may accommodate an occupant as small as a grain of sand or as large as Gulliver.

「人形のための住居計画」というテーマのアイディアコンペに提出した案である。人形という存在をノンスケールの人間として読み替え、居住者が粒のようになってもガリバーのように大きくなっても住宅足り得る空間を考えた。

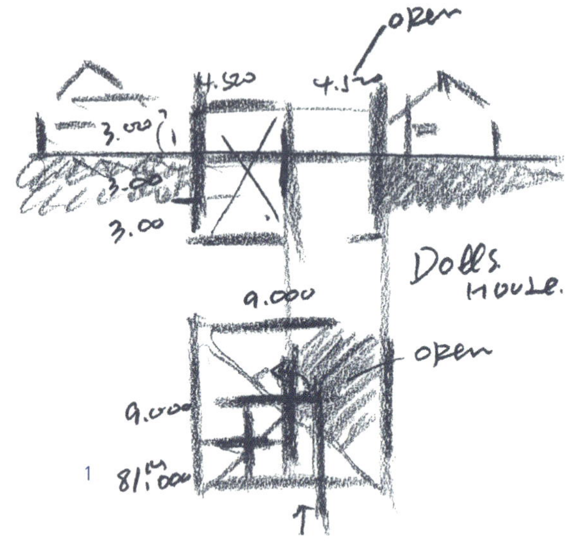

1

1, 2 Image sketches.
3 Axonometric drawing. A house produced by geometrical processes of enlarging and shrinking squares.

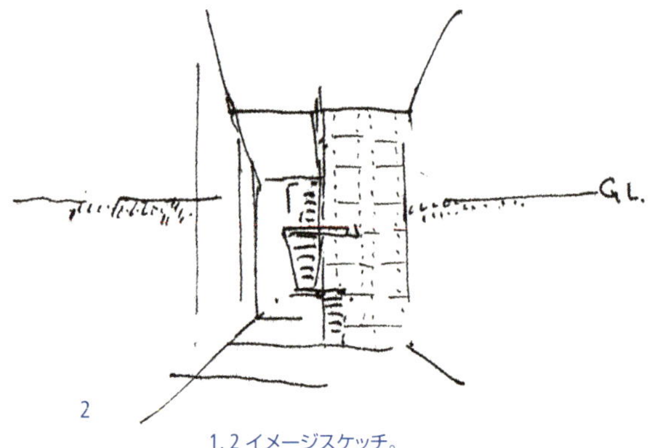

2

1, 2 イメージスケッチ。
3 アクソノメトリックドローイング。正方形が拡大、縮小する幾何学的展開の中に成立する住居。

3

Atelier Yoshie Inaba
アトリエ・ヨシエ・イナバ

1. Shibuya-ku, Tokyo, Japan　東京都渋谷区
2. 1983.5-1984.4
3. 1984.5-1985.4

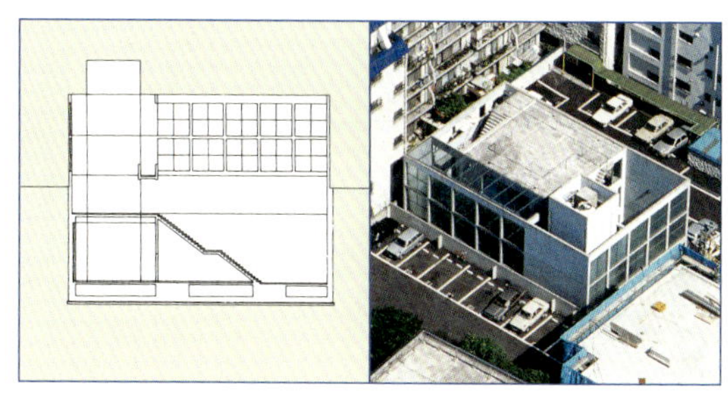

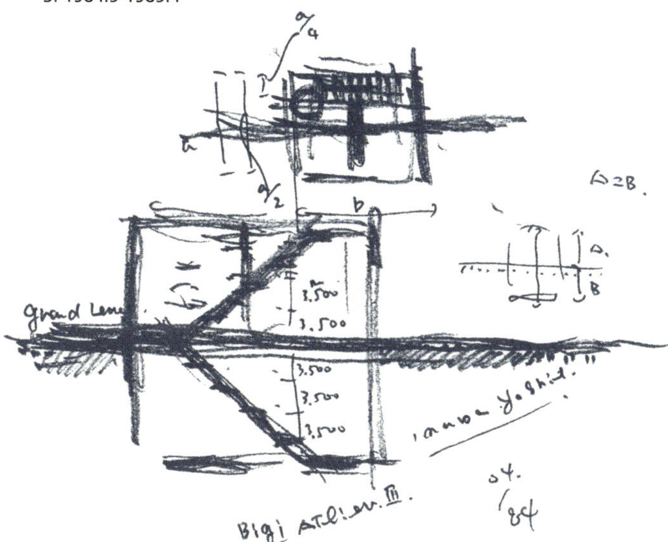

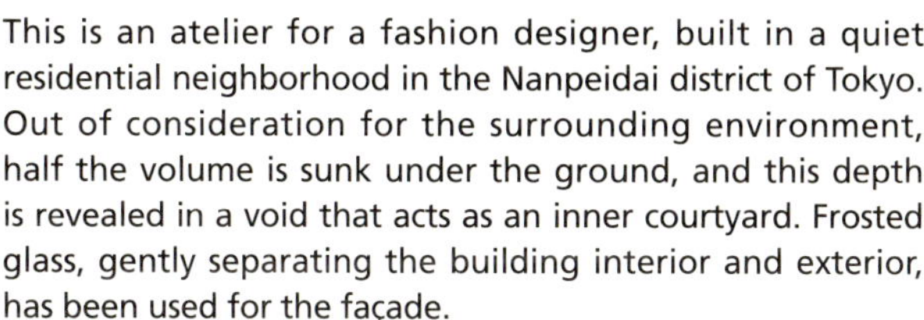

This is an atelier for a fashion designer, built in a quiet residential neighborhood in the Nanpeidai district of Tokyo. Out of consideration for the surrounding environment, half the volume is sunk under the ground, and this depth is revealed in a void that acts as an inner courtyard. Frosted glass, gently separating the building interior and exterior, has been used for the façade.

東京南平台の閑静な住宅地につくったファッションデザイナーのアトリエである。周辺環境への配慮から全体のヴォリュームの半分を地下に沈め、その深さをそのまま表すヴォイドを中庭とした。ファサードには、建物内外を緩やかに隔てるスリガラスのスクリーンを用いた。

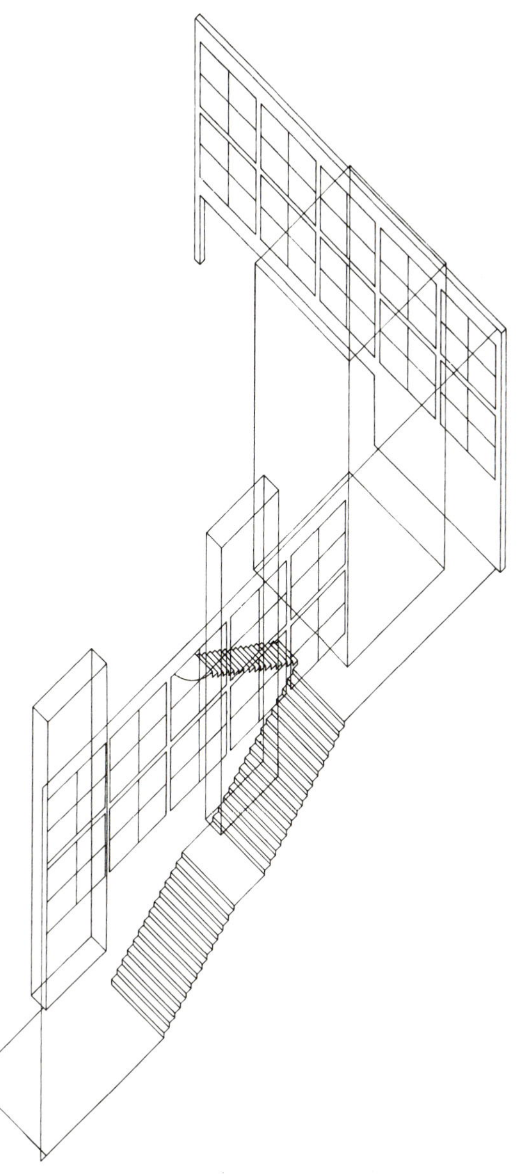

Kaneko House
金子邸

1. Shibuya-ku, Tokyo, Japan　東京都渋谷区
2. 1982.11-1983.4
3. 1983.5-1983.11

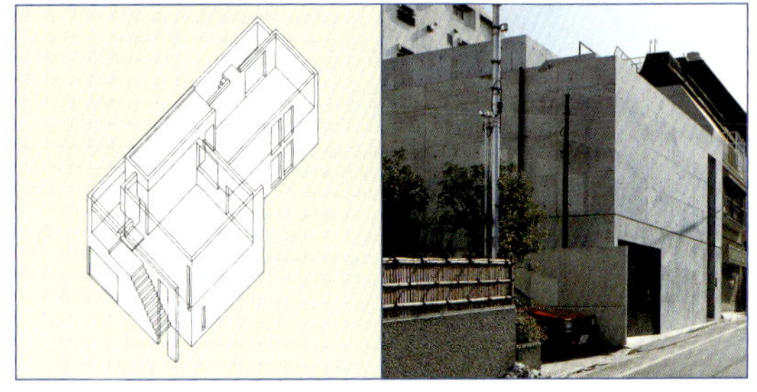

A house built facing a small road in a verdant residential area of Tokyo's Shibuya district. Through subtle differences in floor height and the expression of open and closed walls, I concentrated on the movement spaces connecting the rooms, thinking to make a house with great depth, as if beyond one wall the spaces for daily life extend in a relaxed way from the entrance hall to the living room, dining room, and garden beyond.

緑の多い、渋谷の住宅街の小道に面してつくった住宅。微妙な床の高低差や壁の開閉の表情など、部屋と部屋を結ぶ移動空間のあり方を徹底して煮詰めることで、1枚の壁の向こうに、玄関から居間・食堂、その先の庭へと生活空間がゆったりと広がっていくような、奥行き深い住まいをつくろうと考えた。

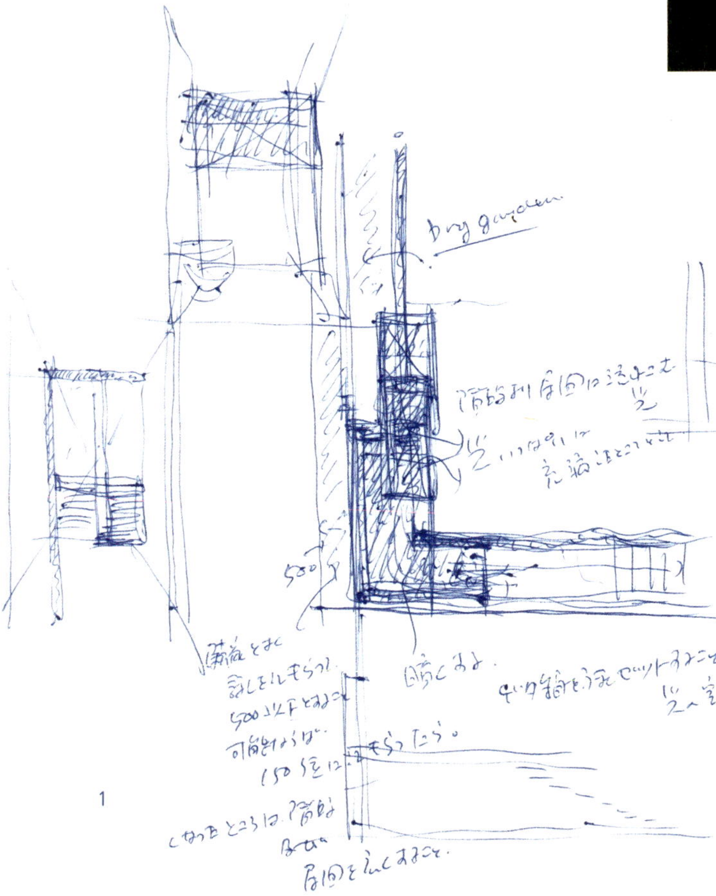

1

1 Compositional sketches. The focus of the study is movement spaces such as stairs and corridors. Each room is three-dimensionally interlocked, and the theme is to create expansive living spaces.

1 構成のスケッチ。スタディの中心は階段、廊下などの移動空間。各室を立体的に組み合わせ、広がりのある住空間をつくり出すことがテーマとされた。

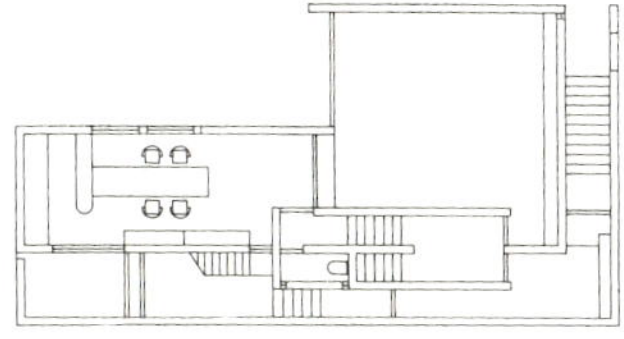

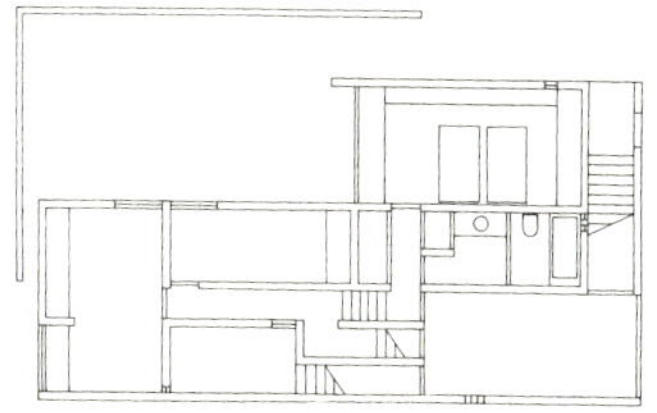

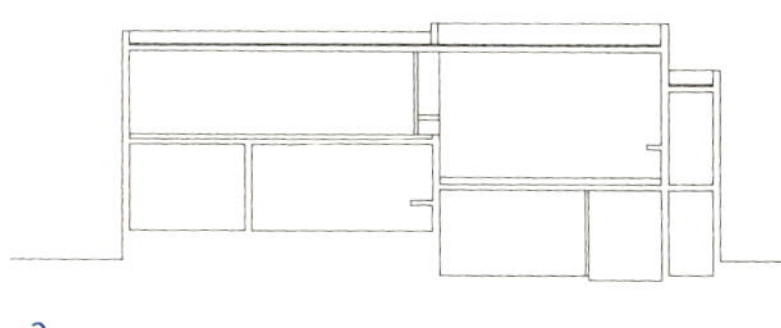

2

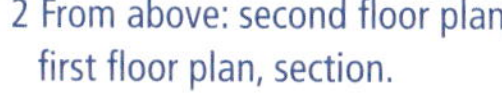

2 From above: second floor plan, first floor plan, section.
3 Spatial perspective from the entrance to the living room and dining room.

2 上から2階平面図、1階平面図、断面図。
3 エントランスから、リビング、ダイニングに至る空間のパースペクティブ。

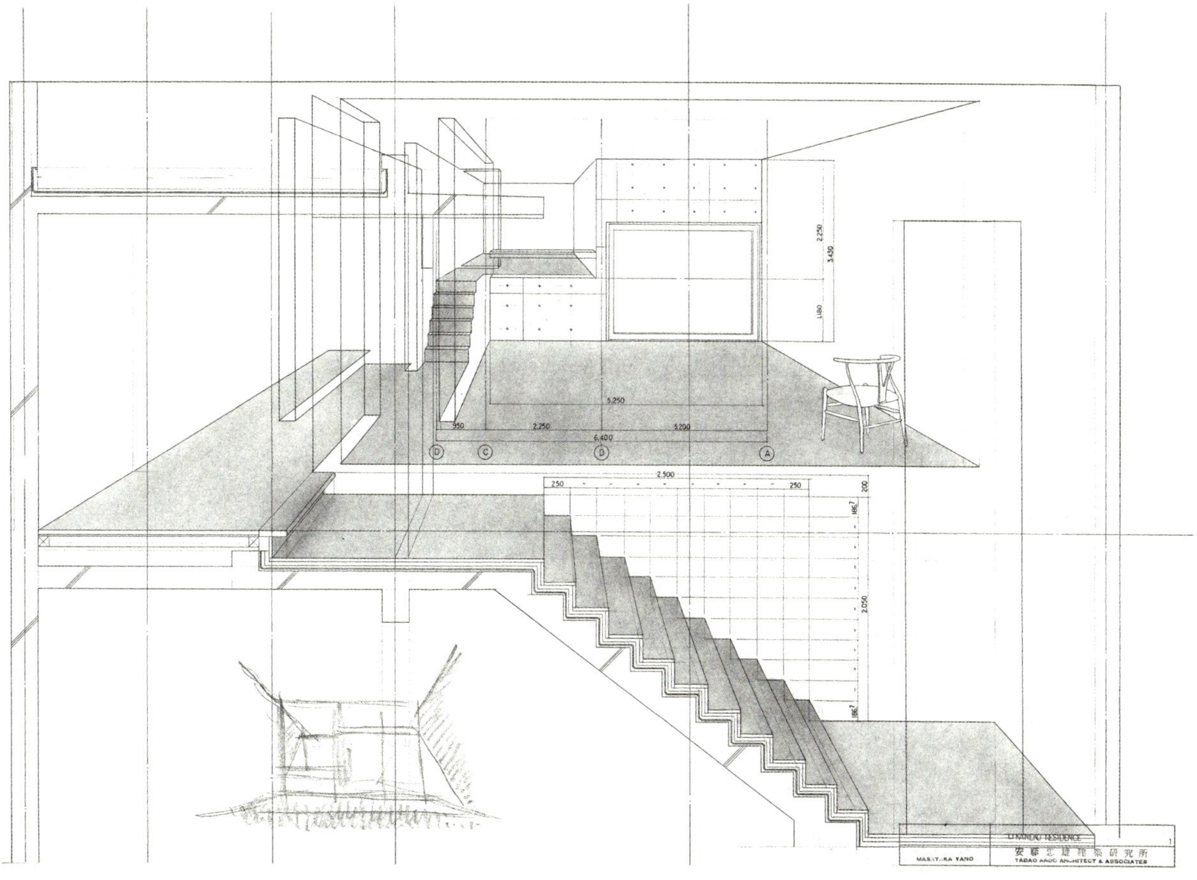

3

TIME'S I+II
TIME'S I+II

1. Kyoto, Kyoto, Japan　京都府京都市
2. 1983.4-1983.10 (phase Ⅰ) / 1984.10-1990.7 (phase Ⅱ)
3. 1983.11-1984.9 (phase Ⅰ) / 1990.8-1991.9 (phase Ⅱ)

The site is located in the center of Kyoto, in the vicinity of the Sanjo Bridge across the Takase River. This is a plan for a commercial facility constructed in two phases. In a district of Kyoto subject to ongoing urbanization, the main theme here was architecture integrated with the river, recapturing for the city this river that had become detached from the citizens' everyday lives.

敷地は京都市中心部、高瀬川に架かる三条小橋のほとりに位置する。Ⅱ期にわたって建設された商業施設の計画である。近代都市化の進む京都の市街地にあって、ここでは人々の日常から遠ざけられていた川を都市に取り戻すこと、川と一体化する建築を主題とした。

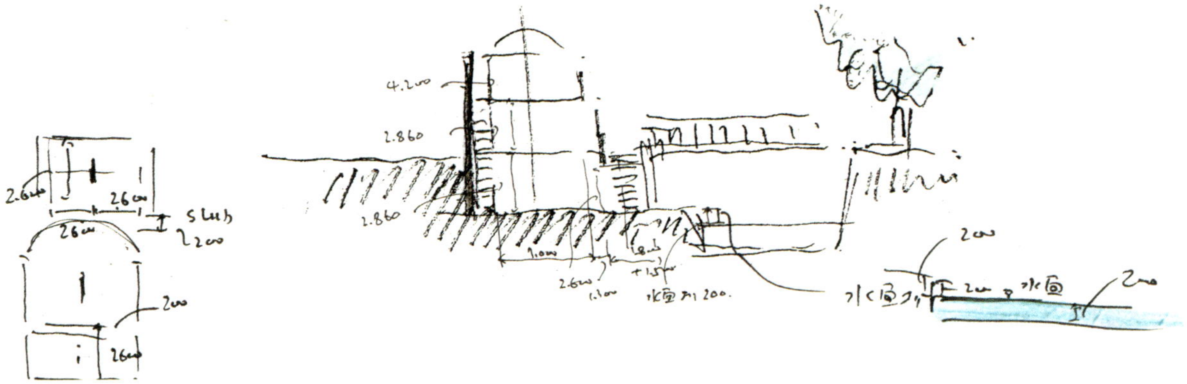

1

1 Sectional study sketches, architectural volumes responding to the sense of scale of the river.
2 Axonometric.
3 From above: third floor plan, second floor plan, first floor plan.

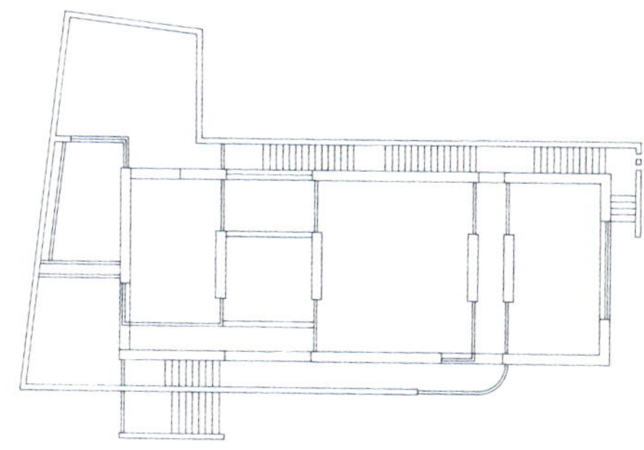

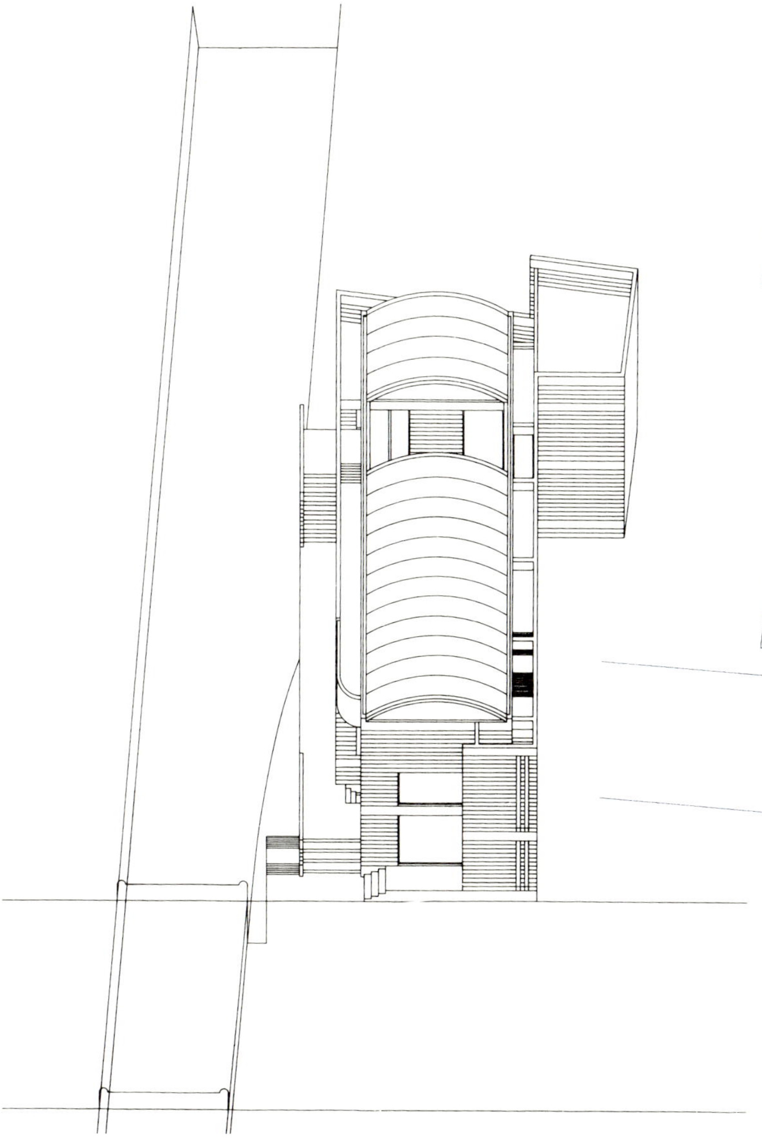

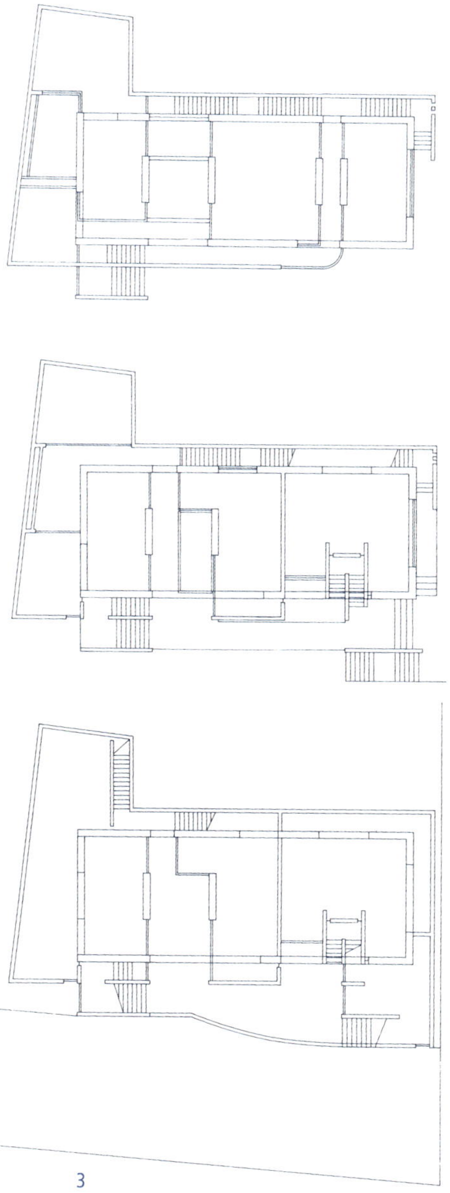

3

2

1 川のスケール感に応える建築ヴォリューム、断面形状の検討スケッチ。
2 アイソノメトリック。
3 上から3階、2階、1階平面図。

An attempt to respond to the sense of scale of the Takase River. The height of the building is constrained by excavating the entire site down to the water level, giving one floor below ground level and two floors above. It is a simple composition centered on a regular volume covered with a vaulted roof, but the "margins" surrounding it are architecturalized as stairs and alleys, and by connecting the shop spaces to the complex intertwining of interior and exterior in the three-dimensional alley spaces, I thought to make a place wherein the river may be encountered from various viewpoints.

1

高瀬川のスケール感に応えるよう。敷地全体を水面レベルまで掘り下げ、建物は地下1階、地上2階の高さに抑えて計画した。ヴォールト屋根を冠した整形のヴォリュームを中心とする単純な構成だが、その周囲を取り巻く〈余白〉を階段や通路として建築化し、店舗間を内外空間の入り組む立体的な路地空間でつないでいくことで、さまざまな視点で〈川〉と出合える場所をつくろうと考えた。

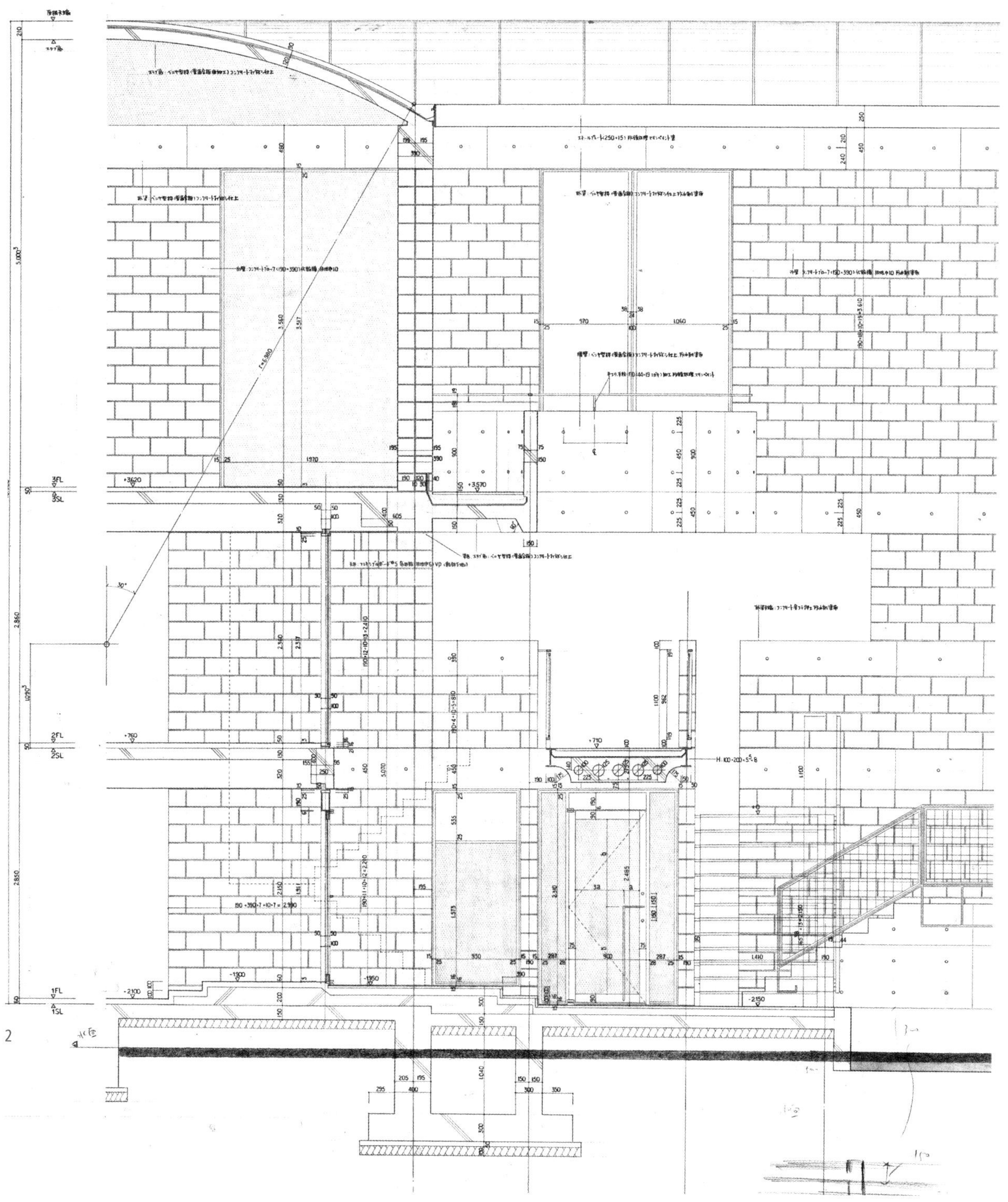

1 Study sketches of the details of the vaulted roof. As human-scale architecture, careful attention has been paid to the sense of scale of the details.
2 Detailed cross section.

1 ヴォールト屋根のディテールの検討スケッチ。ヒューマンスケールの建築ゆえ、細部の寸法感覚に細心の注意が払われる。
2 断面詳細図。

For the expansion plan from phase I to phase II, which took place seven years later, a "thoroughfare" connecting Sanjo Street to Ryoma Street was implemented by means of architecture. Architecturalizing the street context—literally, this is architecture that opens up the city.

I期からII期へ、7年越しに行われた拡張計画の際には、建築を介しての三条通りと竜馬通りを結ぶ〈通り抜け〉が実現した。街の文脈を建築化する——文字通り、都市に開かれた建築である。

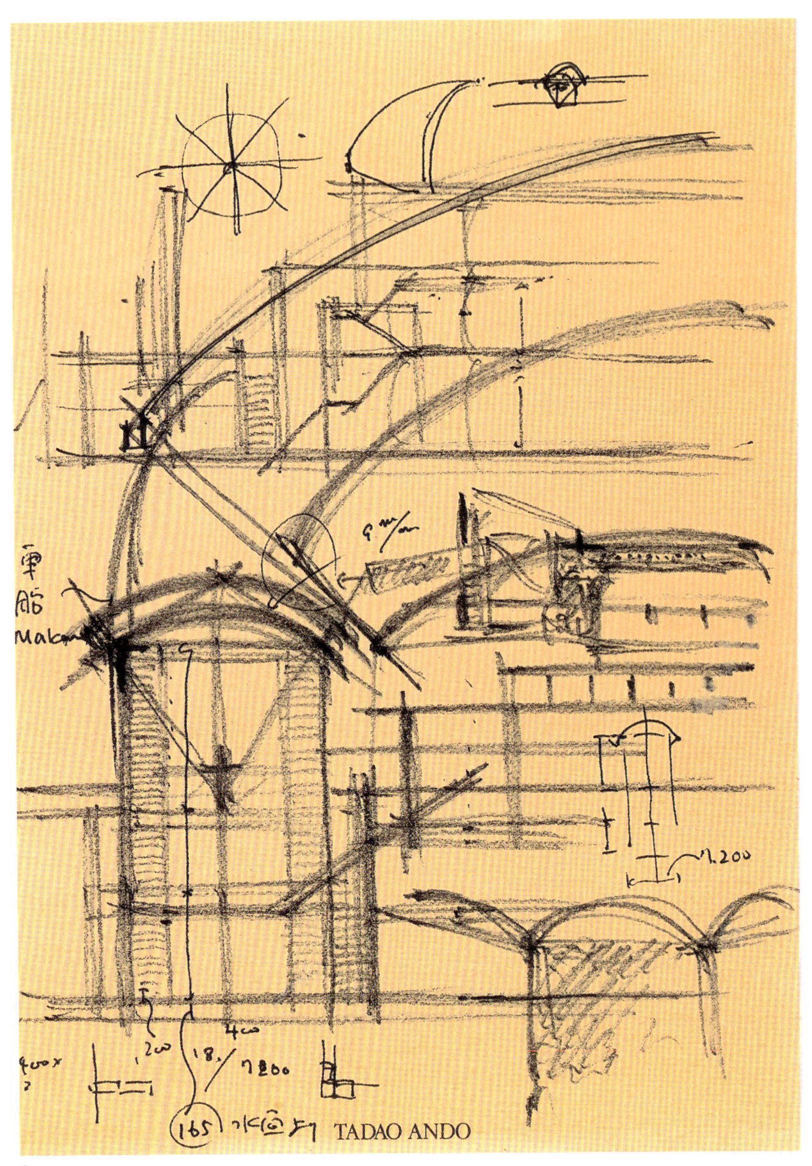

1

1 Exploratory sketches of the roof shape of phase II. The sense of materiality focused on concrete blocks, the curved roof, and so on, all conceived following the vocabulary of phase I.
2 Detailed section.
3 Elevation.

1 II期の屋根形状の検討スケッチ。コンクリートブロックを中心とする素材感、曲面屋根等、すべてI期のヴォキャブラリーを踏襲するよう考えられている。
2 断面詳細図。
3 立面図。

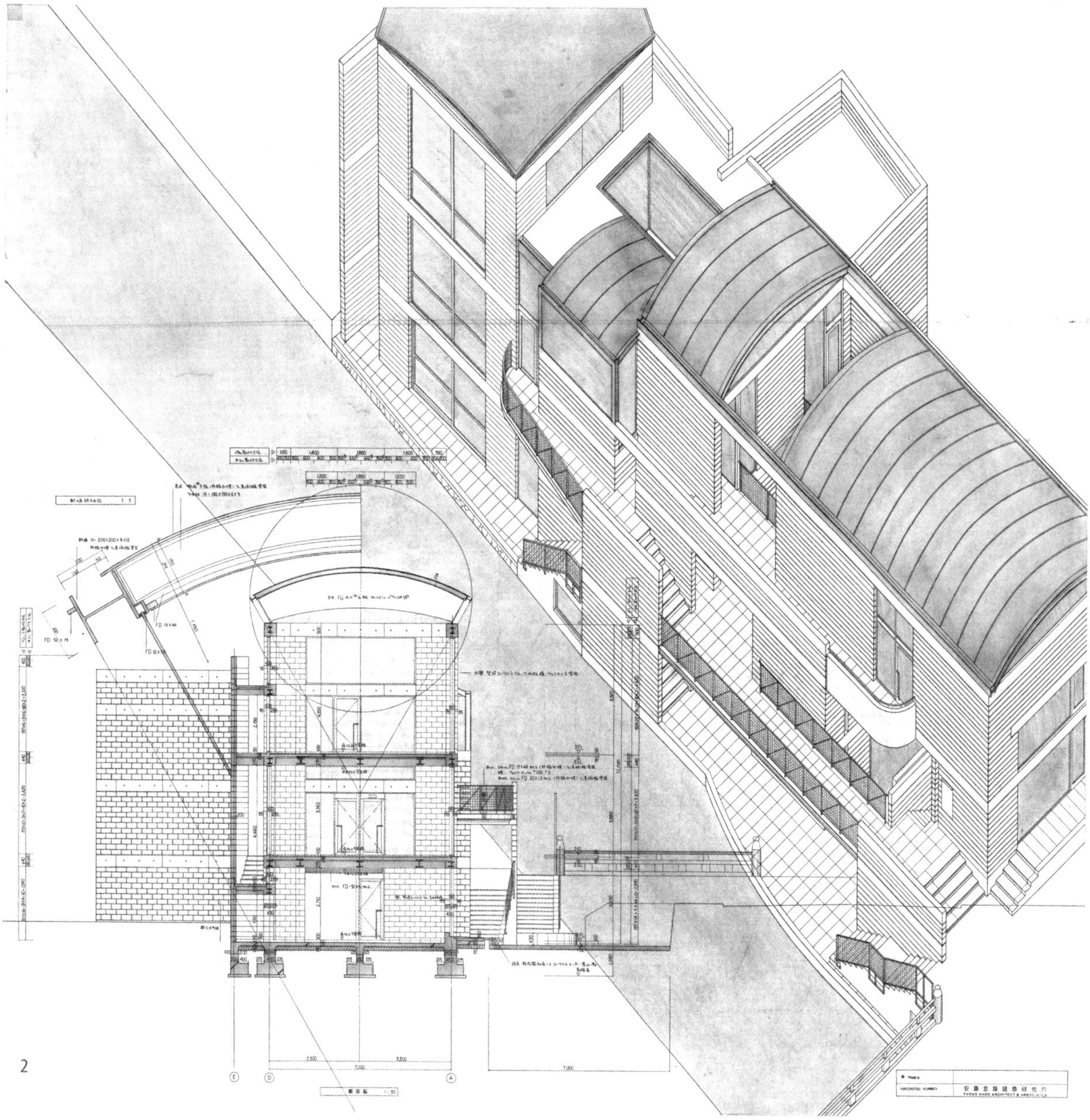

2

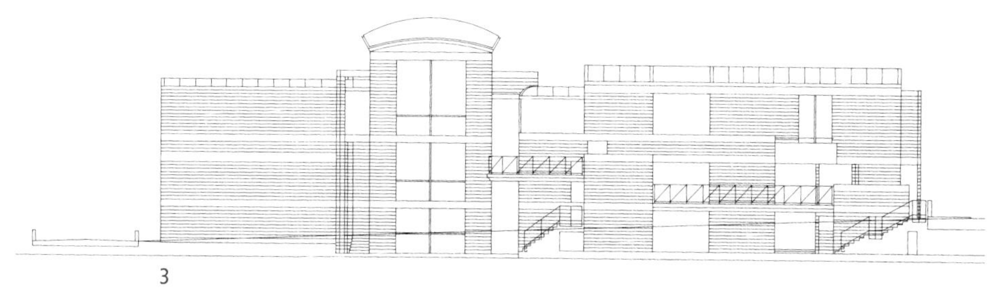

3

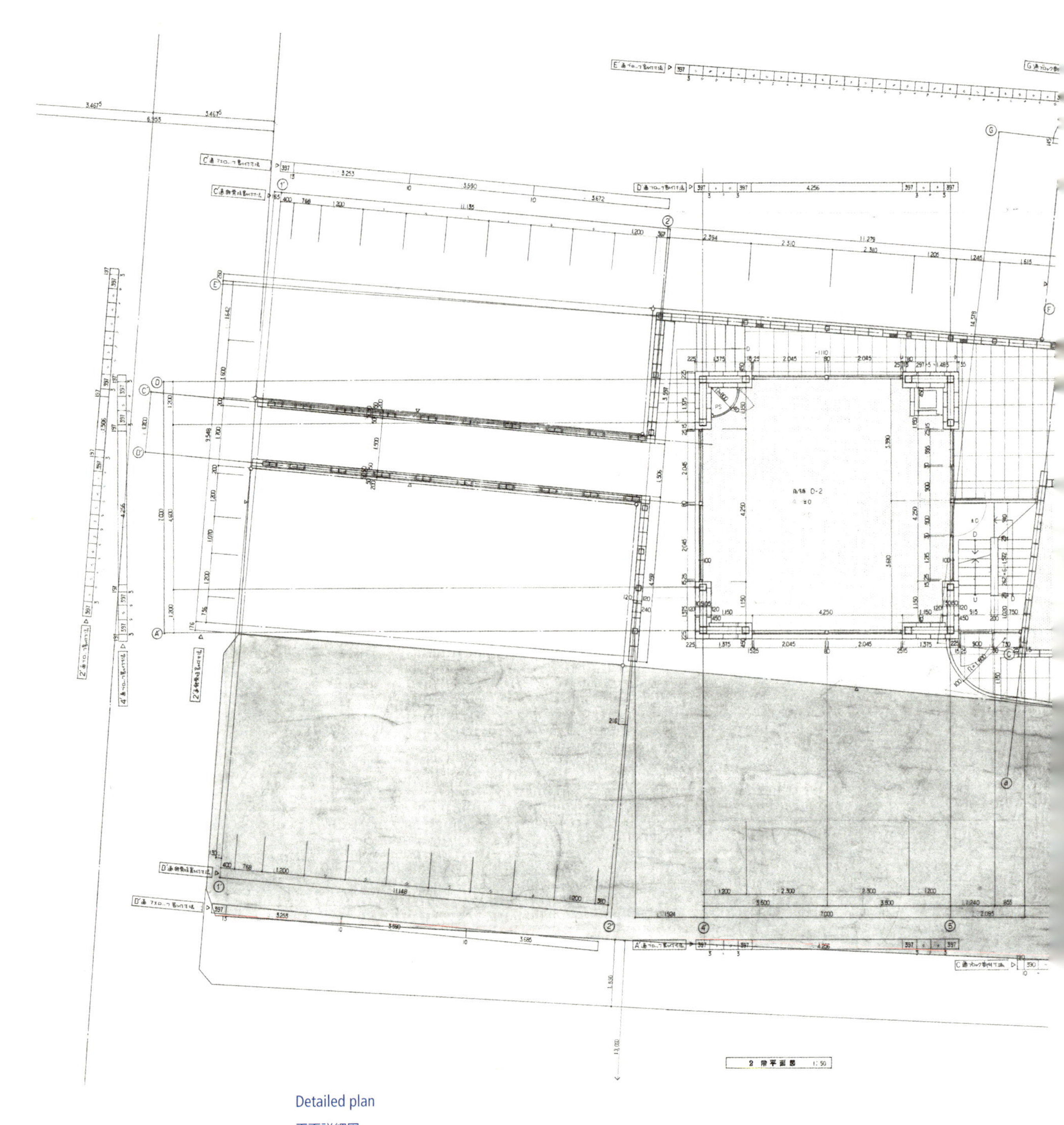

Detailed plan

平面詳細図

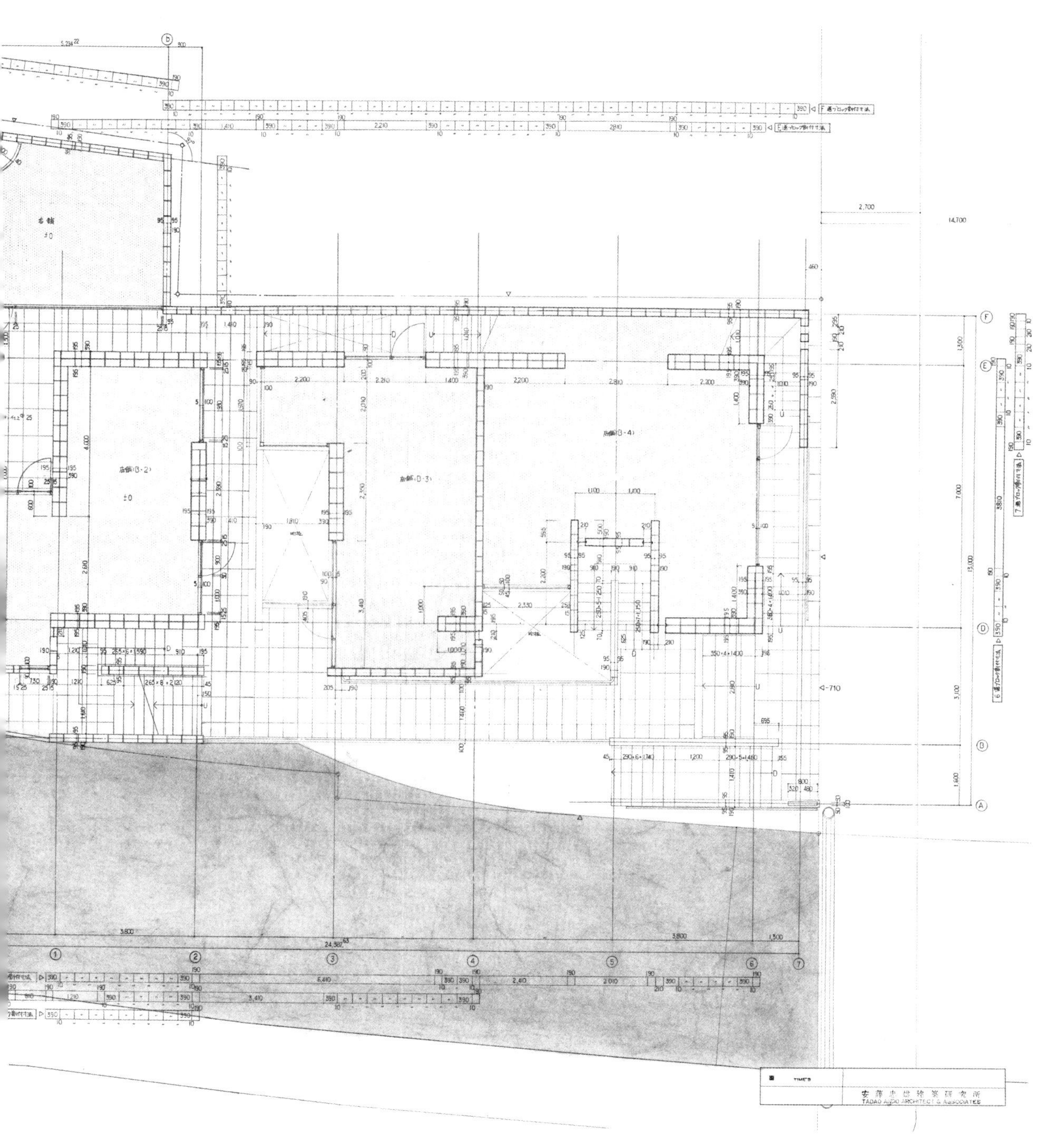
安藤忠雄建築研究所
TADAO ANDO ARCHITECT & ASSOCIATES

Town House in Saikudani
細工谷の家

1. Osaka, Osaka, Japan　大阪府大阪市
2. 1985.5-1985.9
3. 1985.10-1986.5

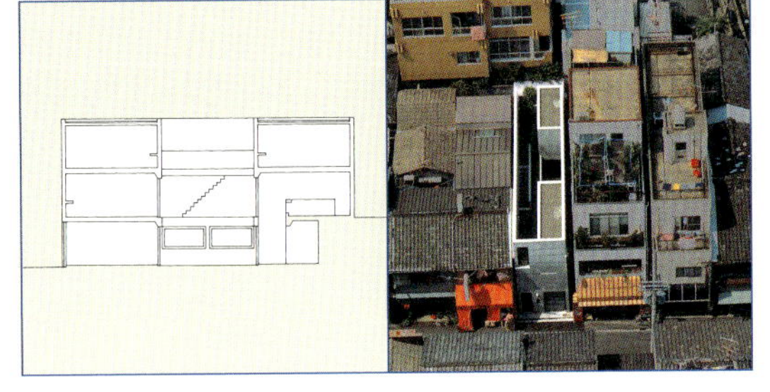

The site is a typical downtown shopping district in Osaka, where a wooden townhouse on one lot was torn down and a 3.5m-wide, 15m-deep, three-storey concrete box inserted. The whole has been divided into three equal parts, and in addition to making the center a void, it has been divided longitudinally in two, with one half as exterior space. I thought of trying to connect each room directly to the outside.

敷地は大阪の典型的な下町商店街、その一画の木造長屋を切り取り、間口3.5m、奥行き15mのコンクリート3階建ての箱を挿入した。全体を3等分して中央をヴォイドとした上で、さらに長手方向も2分して半分を戸外とし、どの部屋も屋外に直に接するよう考えた。

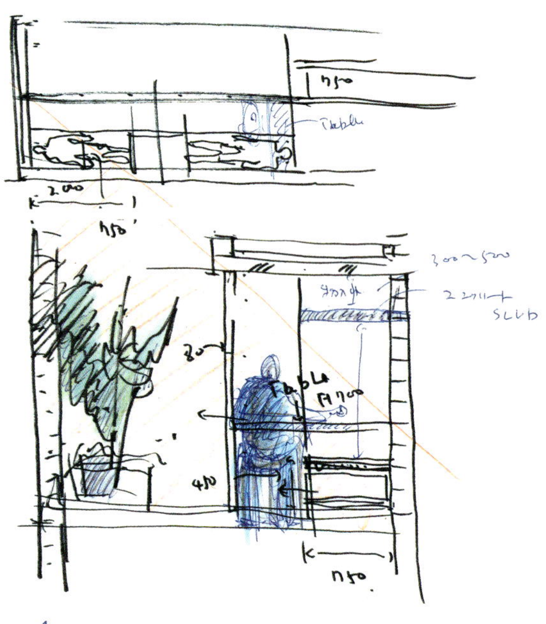

1

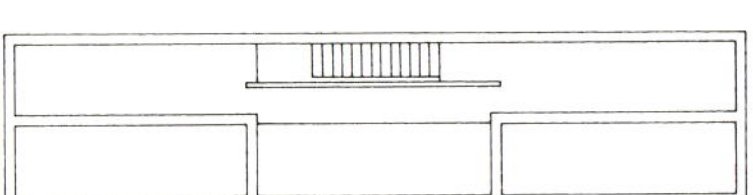

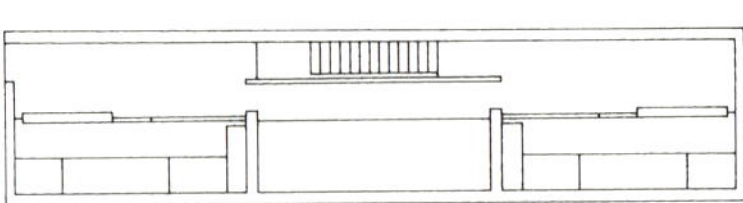

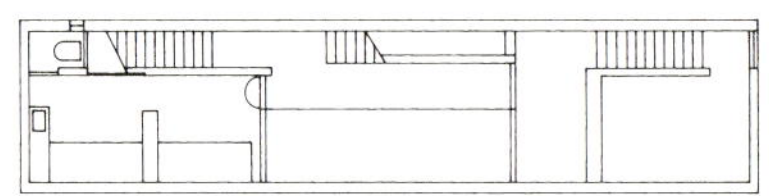

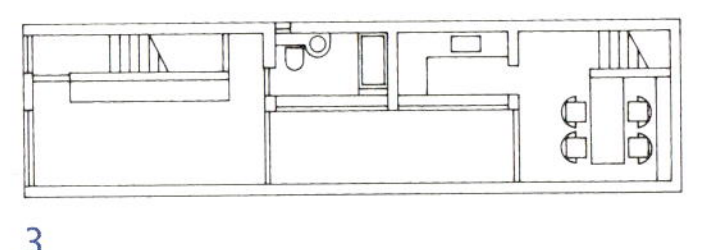

3

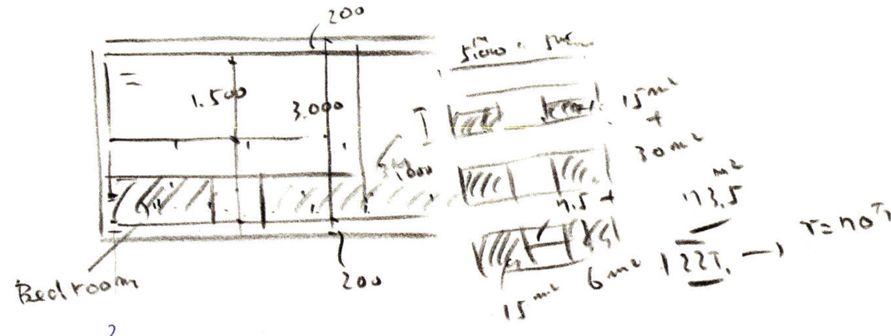

2

1, 2 Study sketches of the plan detail dimensions for the bedroom. On the third floor and the rooftop floor, the full expanse of 15m has been taken as a living space. Because this is the maximum space, iterative studies were made to determine the detailed dimensions, measured in millimeters.
3 From above: roof plan, third floor plan, second floor plan, first floor plan.
4 Perspective of the inner courtyard.

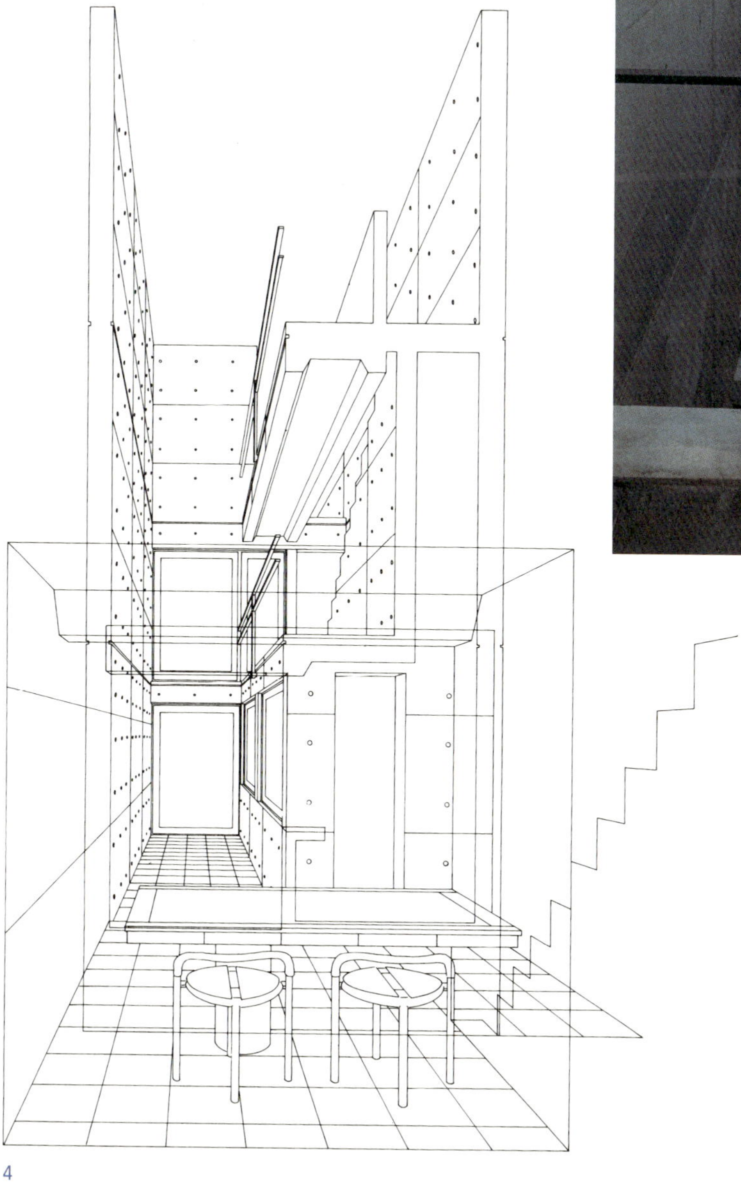

4

1, 2 寝室の平面詳細寸法の検討スケッチ。3階、屋上階では15mの距離がそのまま住空間として取り入れられている。極限のスペースゆえ、細部寸法の決定にはミリ単位で検討が重ねられた。
3 上から屋根伏、3、2、1階平面図。
4 中庭のパースペクティブ。

Chapel on Mt. Rokko
六甲の教会

1. Kobe, Hyogo, Japan　兵庫県神戸市
2. 1985.1-1985.7
3. 1985.8-1986.3

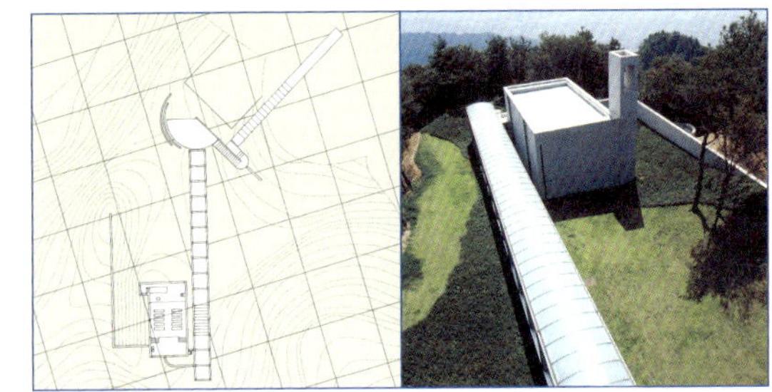

The site is located on a verdant slope in the vicinity of the peak of Mt. Rokko in Kobe. This was my first design for church architecture. Taking the imagery of medieval Romanesque monasteries, by abstracting the essence of those spaces I wanted to make my own "space of prayer" resolved as a composition of simple elements.

敷地は神戸の六甲山の頂き近辺の緑豊かな斜面地に位置する。私が初めて設計した教会建築である。イメージとして中世ロマネスクの修道院を参照しつつ、その空間のエッセンスを抽出し、単純な要素の構成に還元して私なりの〈祈りの空間〉をつくろうと考えた。

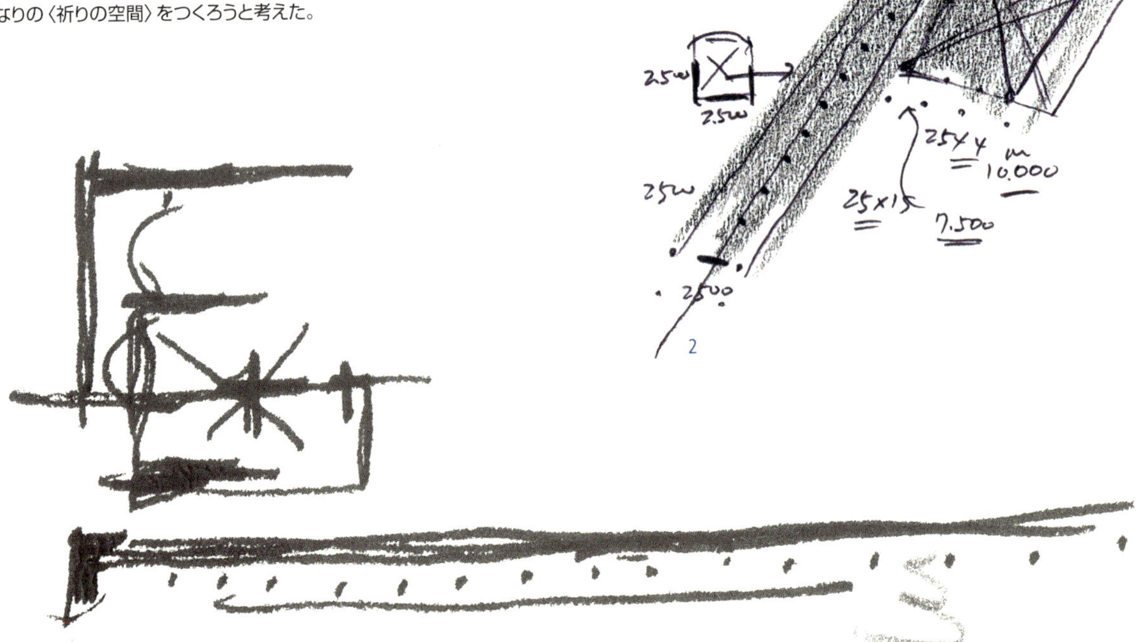

2

1

1 Placing the nave at the periphery of the worship hall is a typical format for church architecture, but here they are separated with a Romanesque cloister format.
2 The volumes of the worship hall, the bell tower, and the extended glass colonnade. Exploration of the balance and proportional relationships of these elements embedded in the slope.
3 Departing the everyday world toward a space of tranquil prayer—a study of this very important approach space. From thinking about how to utilize the lush greenery of the surroundings, a glass colonnade proposal emerged.

1 教会堂建築は、礼拝堂の周囲に身廊をもつのが一般的な形式であるが、ここでは両者を分離、ロマネスクの回廊形式が取られている。
2 礼拝堂のマッスと鐘楼、引き伸ばされたガラスのコロネード。斜面地にはめ込まれる要素のバランス、比例関係の検討。
3 日常の世界を離れ、静謐な祈りの空間へ——最も重要なアプローチ空間のスタディ。周囲の豊かな緑をいかに活かすか、思考する中でガラスのコロネード案が生まれる。

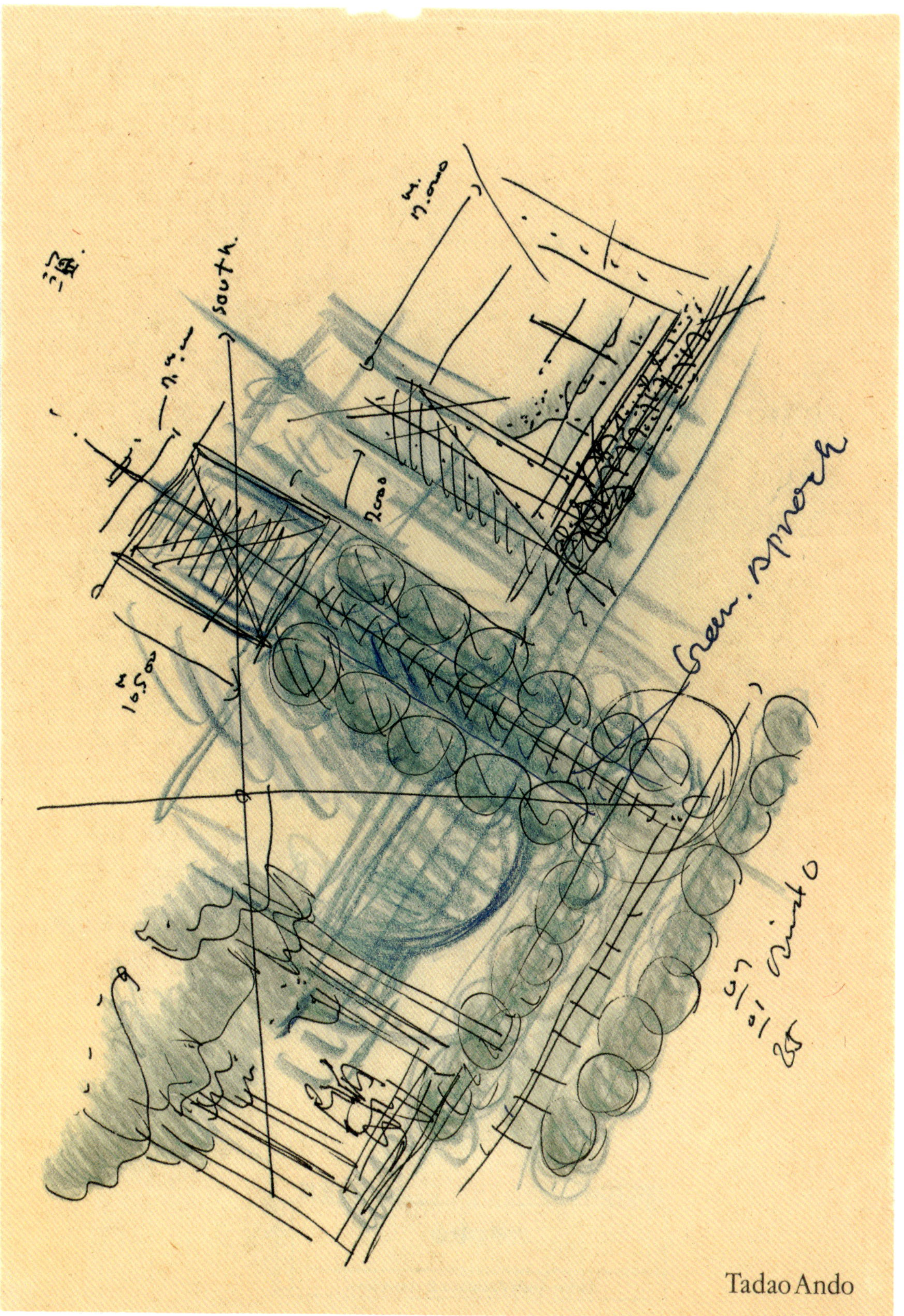

3

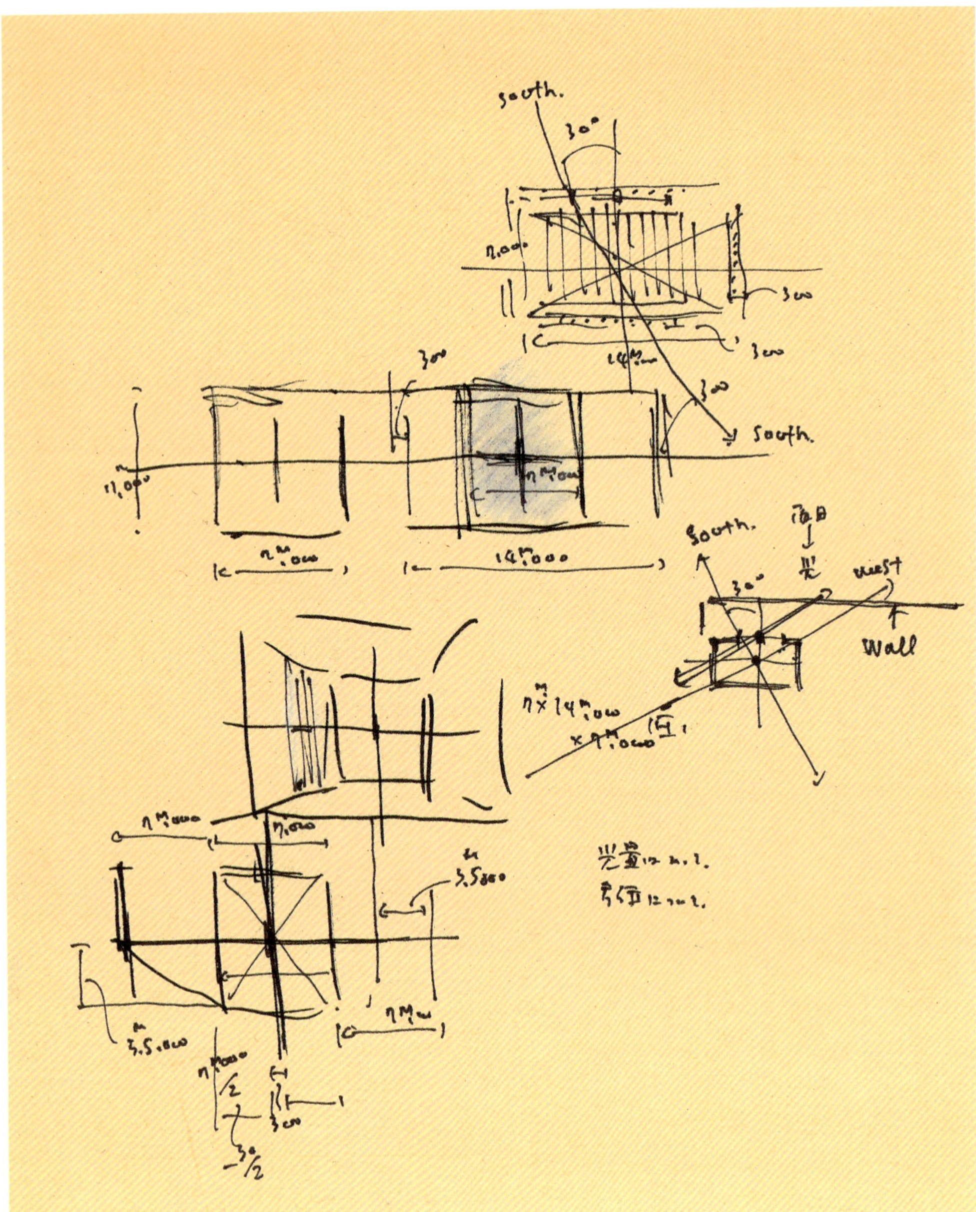

1

1 Exploratory sketch of the proportions of the worship hall. In order to limit the visible elements, awareness is focused on the sense of scale.

2 Vaulted roof colonnade extending toward the worship hall. The walls on either side are made of frosted glass, gently excluding the surrounding nature. The circular terrace is a device to shift the axis of the colonnade with regard to the adjacent hotel.

1 礼拝堂のプロポーションの検討スケッチ。登場する要素は限られているため、その寸法感覚に意識は集中する。

2 礼拝堂へ至るヴォールト屋根のコロネード。両壁面はスリガラスとし、緩やかに周囲の自然と隔てられる。円形をかたどるテラスは、隣接するホテル棟に対し、コロネードの軸をずらすための仕掛け。

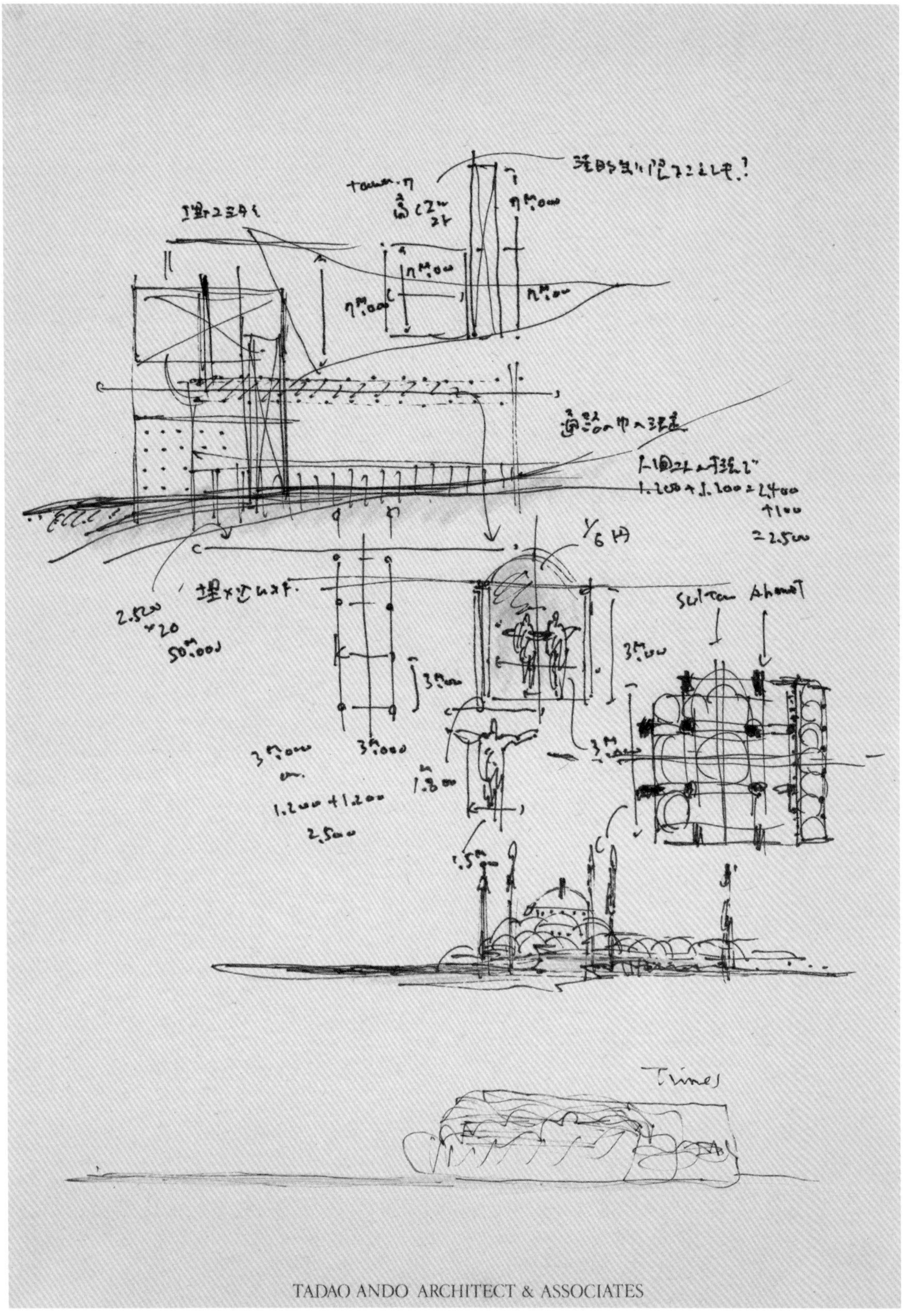

2

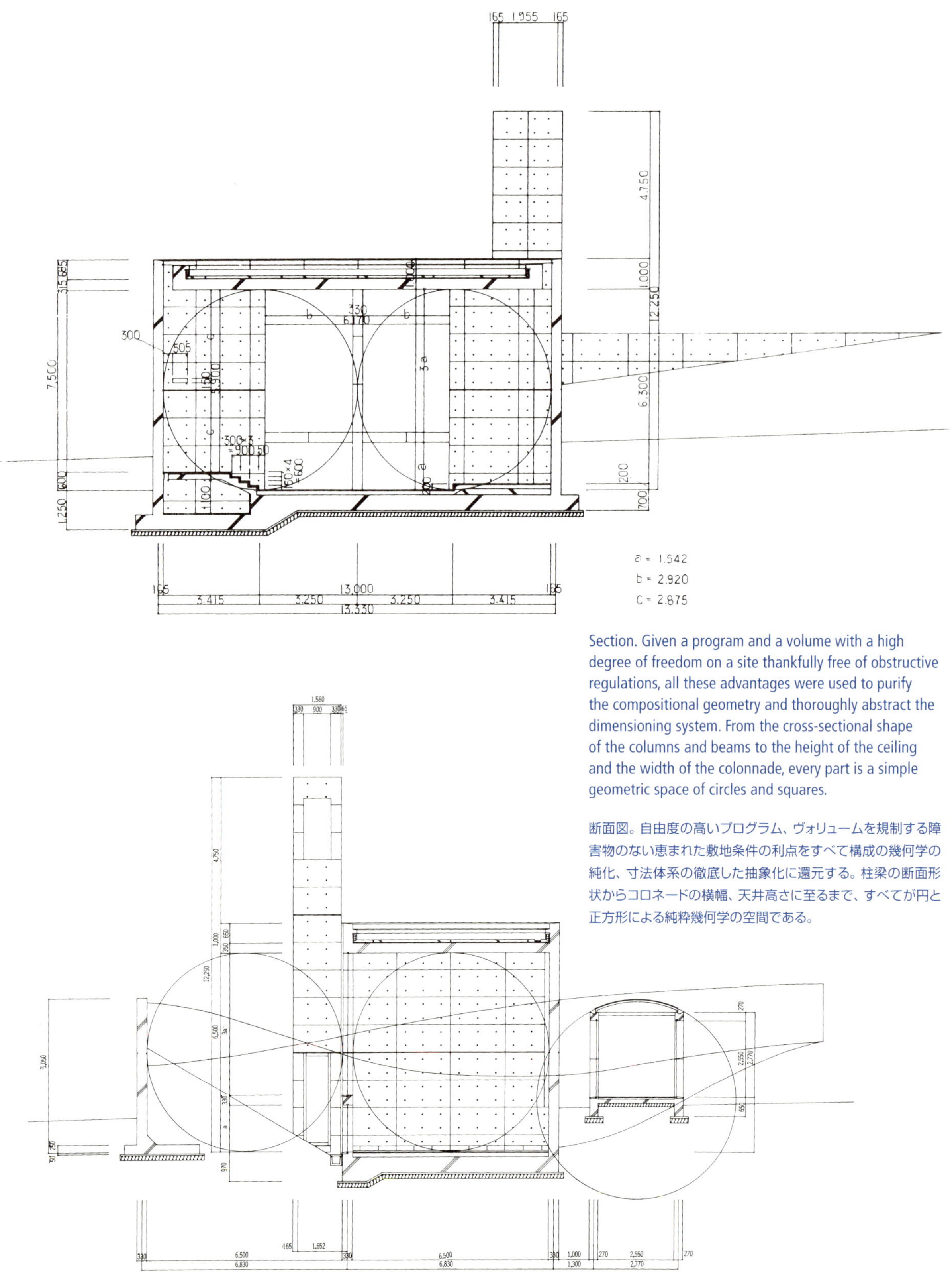

Section. Given a program and a volume with a high degree of freedom on a site thankfully free of obstructive regulations, all these advantages were used to purify the compositional geometry and thoroughly abstract the dimensioning system. From the cross-sectional shape of the columns and beams to the height of the ceiling and the width of the colonnade, every part is a simple geometric space of circles and squares.

断面図。自由度の高いプログラム、ヴォリュームを規制する障害物のない恵まれた敷地条件の利点をすべて構成の幾何学の純化、寸法体系の徹底した抽象化に還元する。柱梁の断面形状からコロネードの横幅、天井高さに至るまで、すべてが円と正方形による純粋幾何学の空間である。

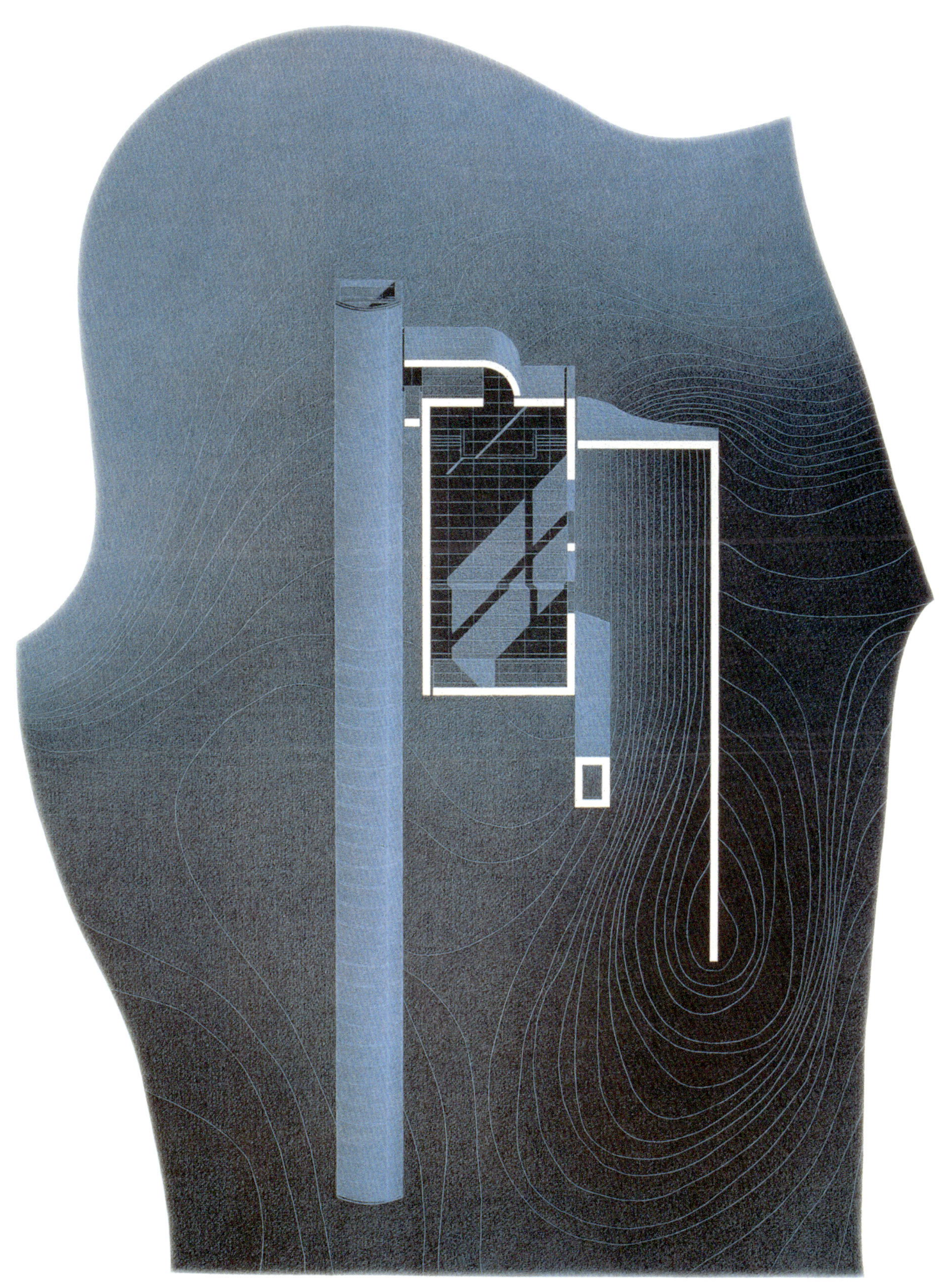

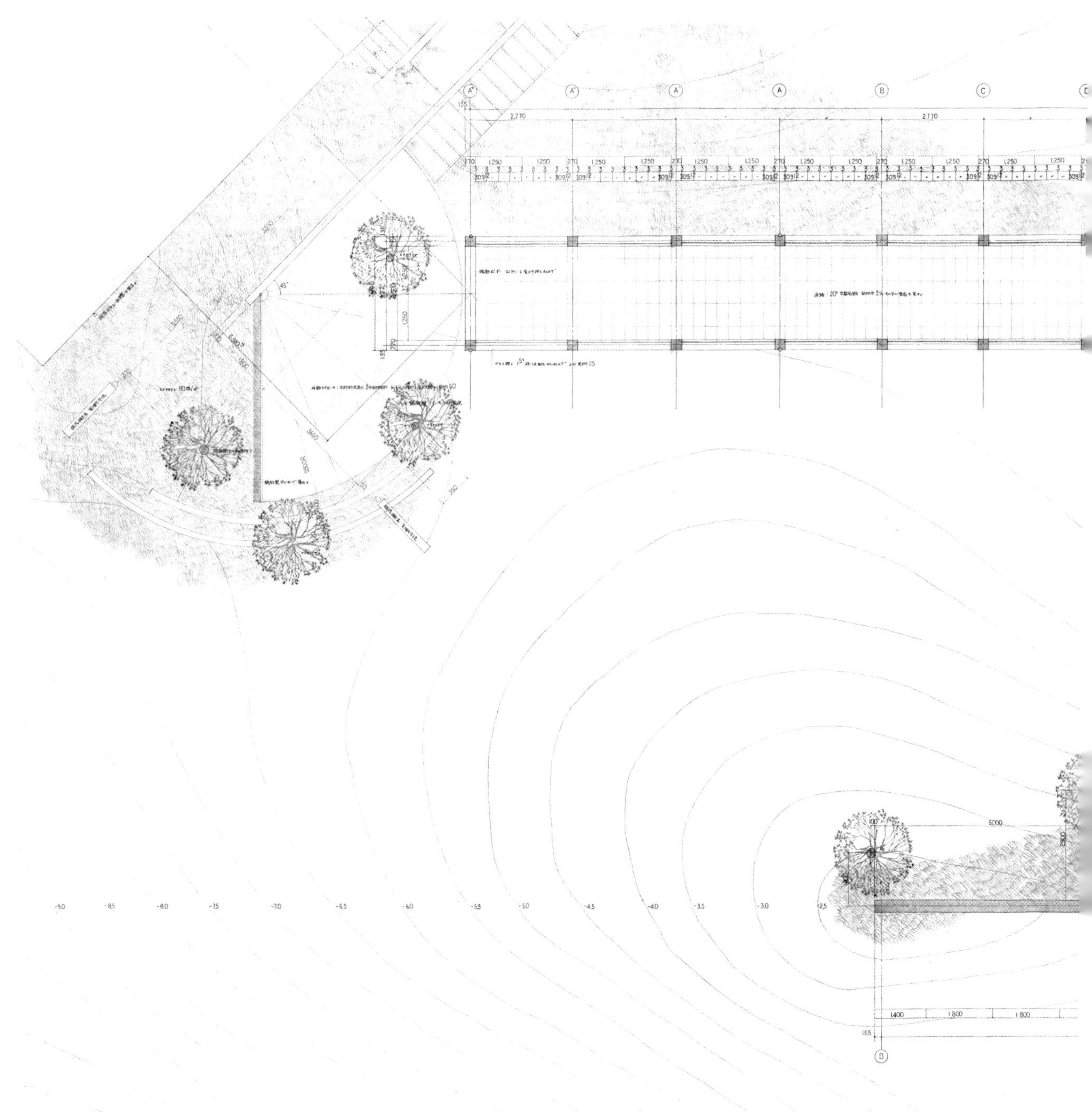

Detailed drawing of the plan

平面詳細図

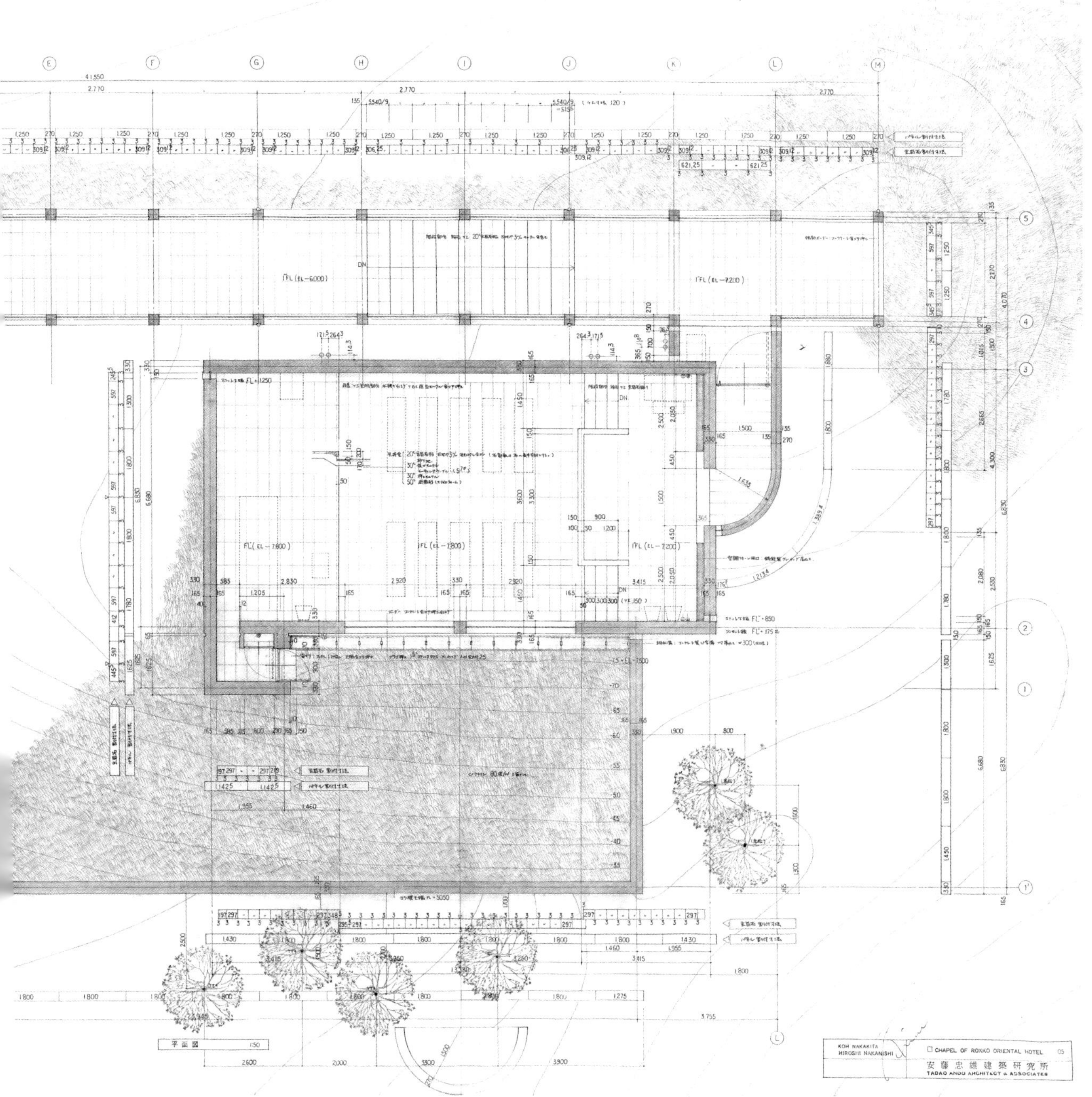
KOH NAKAKITA
HIROSHI NAKANISHI
CHAPEL OF ROKKO ORIENTAL HOTEL 05
安藤忠雄建築研究所
TADAO ANDO ARCHITECT & ASSOCIATES

Kara-za
唐座

1. Sendai, Miyagi, Japan / Taito-ku, Tokyo, Japan
   宮城県仙台市／東京都台東区
2. 1985.7-1987.4
3. 1987.5-1987.06 (Sendai) / 1988.2-1988.3 (Taito-ku)

This is a movable theater for Juro Kara, a figure at the vanguard of underground theater. Since the 1960s, Juro Kara has consistently attempted to secede from traditional artistic concepts through a passionate form of drama that expresses naked, raw humanity. As a place to contain this energy, it was appropriate to create an extraordinary space similar to his "Red Tent" situated playhouse, that is to say, an architecture that is a foreign substance in the city. The planning of Shitamachi Kara-za began in the summer of 1985.

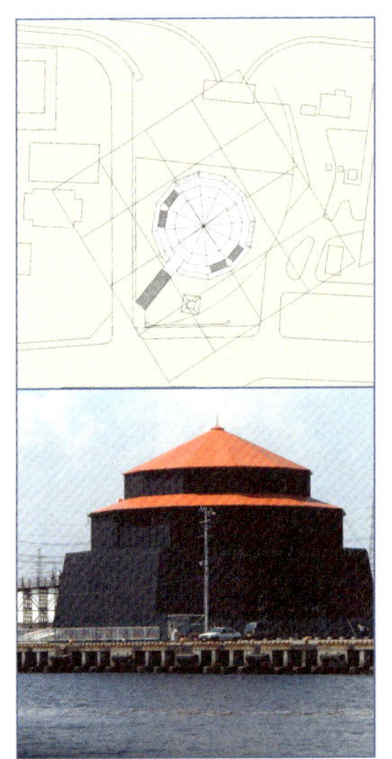

1

1, 4 Initial image sketches. Delineating architecture with an archaic, extraordinary appearance, like a fortress from Japan's Warring States period (1467-1568).
2, 3 Sketches drawn when visiting Egypt and Greece during the design. A prototype of a spatial theater that may become the image of Karaza appears in the superimposition of scenes from foreign countries.

2

アングラ演劇の旗手、唐十郎のための移動式芝居小屋である。60年代以来、唐十郎が一貫して試みてきたのは旧来の芸術観念からの離脱、人間のむき出しの生を表現する情念の舞台だった。そのエネルギーを受け止める場として、ふさわしいのは赤テントの状況劇場のような、非日常の空間、すなわち、都市の異物としてある建築——。1985年夏、下町唐座の計画はスタートした。

3

4

1, 4 初期イメージスケッチ。戦国時代の砦のような非現代的、非日常的な佇まいの建築が描かれている。
2, 3 設計期間中、訪れたエジプトとギリシアで描かれたスケッチ。異国の風景と重ね合わせ、劇場空間の原型となるべき唐座のイメージが登場する。

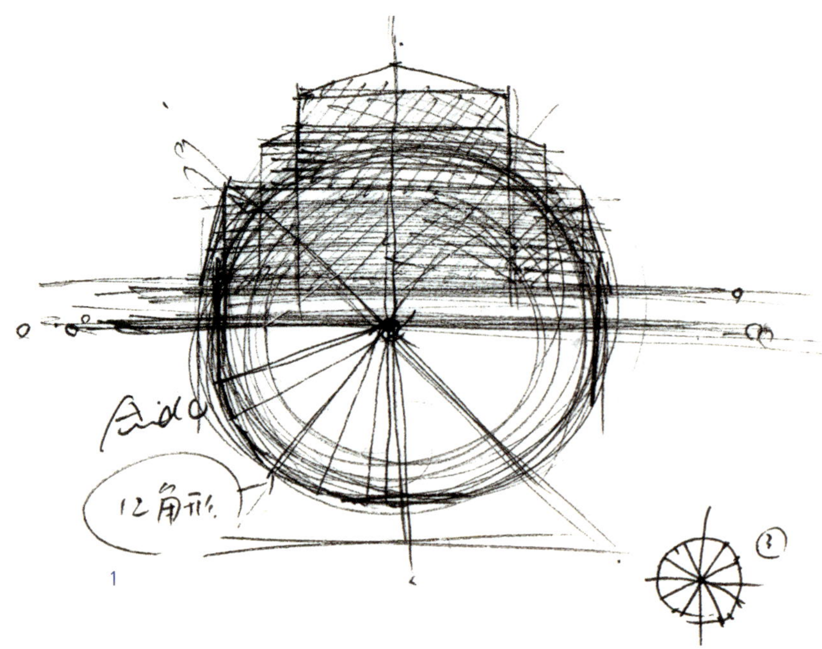

1

1-3 Initial image sketches. A tangible form of architecture that differs from the lineage of Ando previous works. It was initially conceived as a dodecagonal wood structure.

1-3 初期イメージスケッチ。それまでの安藤作品の系譜とは異なる具象的なフォルムの建築。当初は、12角形平面の木造で検討されていた。

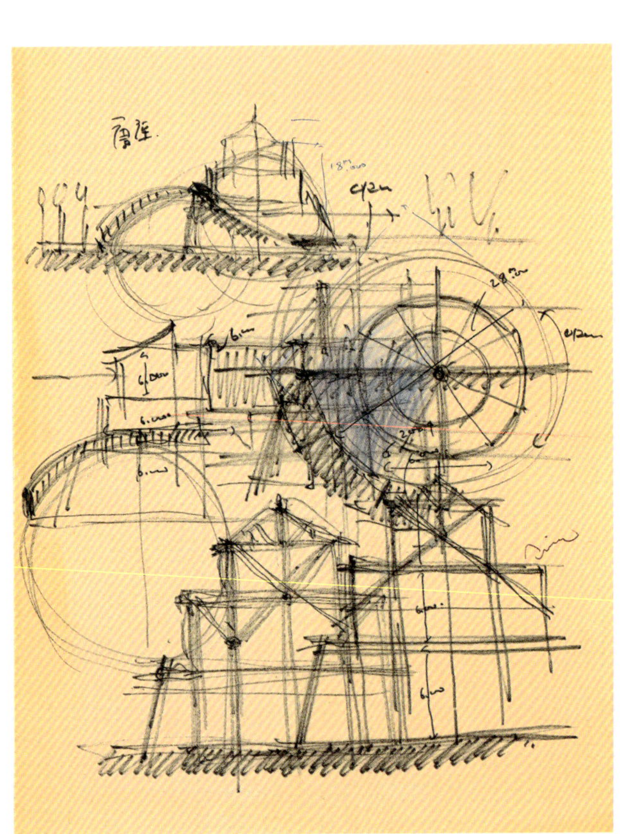

2

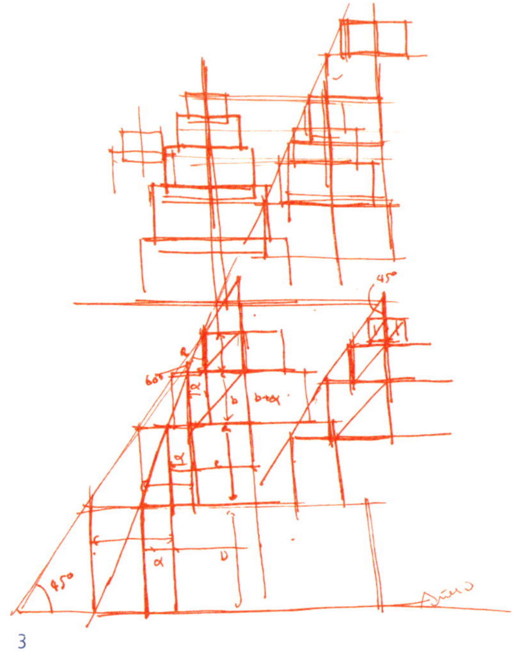

3

4

5

4, 5 A pointed roof placed on a dodecagonal wooden assemblage that is 40m in internal diameter and 23m in height. The approach route is an arched bridge floating in the air. At this point in time, the image of the architecture became fixed, including the materials and the colors.

4, 5 内径40mの12角形平面、高さ23mの木造架構の上にとんがり屋根をかぶせる。アプローチは宙に浮かぶ太鼓橋。色調、素材を含め、この時点でつくるべき建築のイメージは固まっていた。

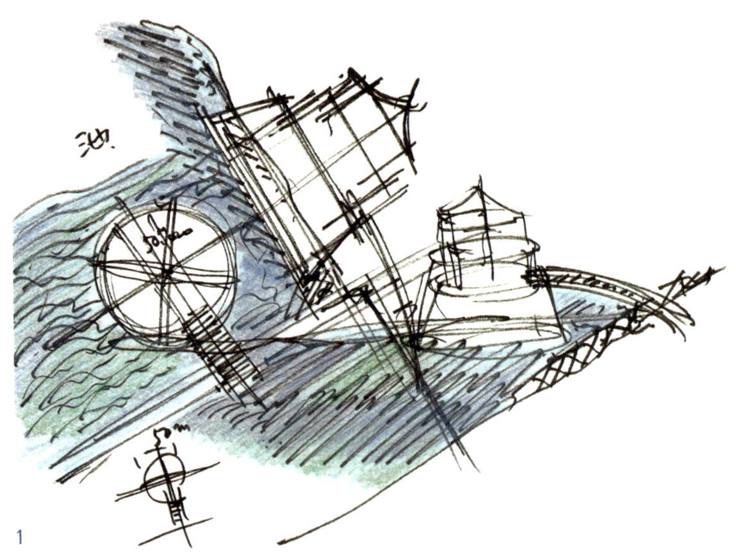

1

Because nothing had been decided except for the site being in Asakusa, I walked around the area looking for the most appropriate place for this theater. Shinobazu Pond, Sumida River, the Asakusa precinct... the project itself was a dreamlike discussion with a slim chance of being realized. Precisely because of this, I wanted to make a design that was as extreme as possible.

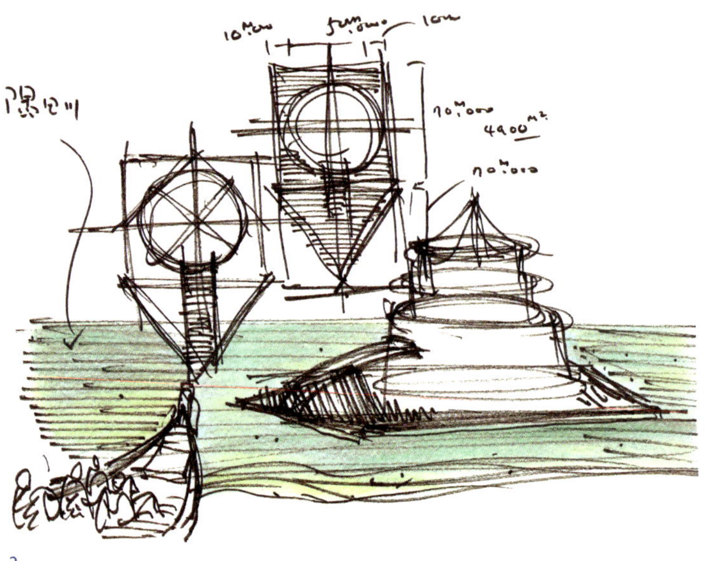

2

敷地は浅草という以外決まっていなかったため、この劇場に最もふさわしい場所をと、地元を歩いて探し回った。不忍池、隅田川、浅草境内……プロジェクト自体が夢のような話で実現の可能性は薄い。だからこそできるだけ途方もないものを設計してやろうと考えていた。

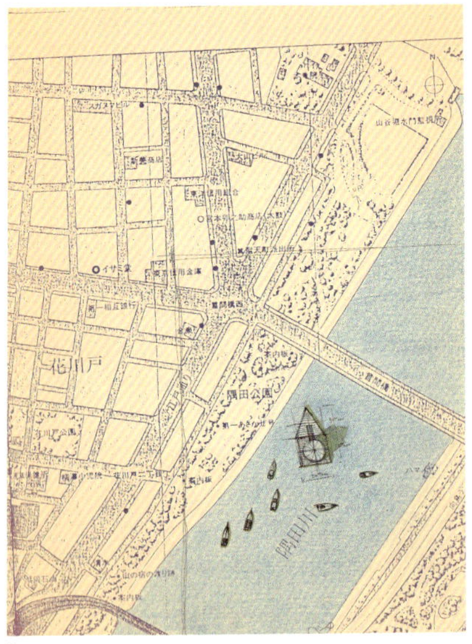

3

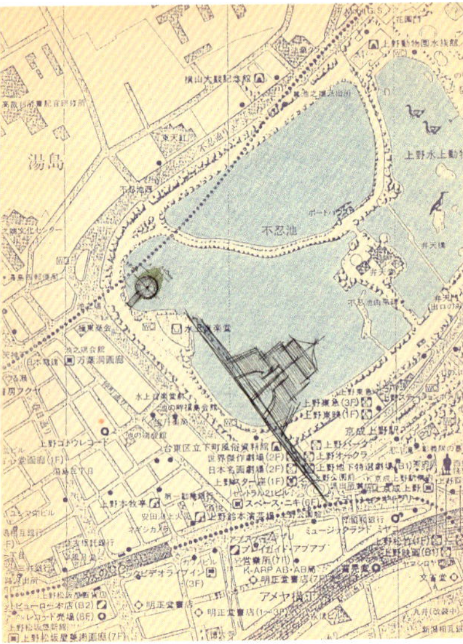

4

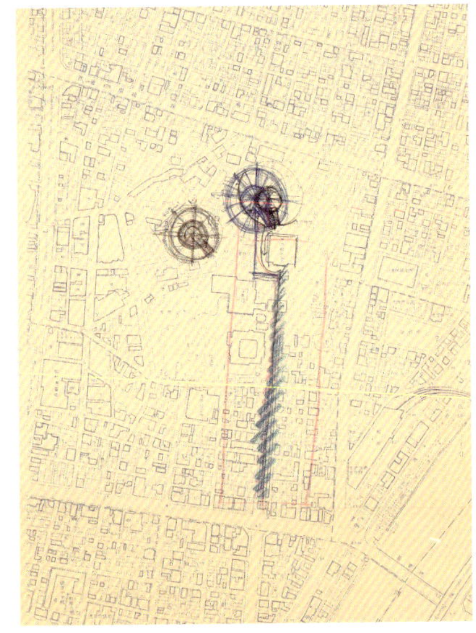

5

In the grounds of Sensou-ji temple, I thought of involving the residents in a downtown renewal plan. On the day of the performance, the streetlights in the area were all turned off. Walking around darkness-shrouded Asakusa looking for candles, I was greeted by the light of burning torches in the grounds, and there the flame of Juro Kara's passion flared —this imagery incessantly expanded, but somehow did not become a real project.

浅草寺の境内では、下町の復興計画として住人にも参加してもらうことを考えた。芝居の上演日は町中の電気をすべて消す。闇に包まれた浅草をロウソクをたよりに歩いていくと、境内の松明の灯りが出迎える、そこに唐十郎の情念の炎が燃え上がる——イメージはいくらでも膨らんだが、なかなか現実の仕事として動かない。

6

1, 3 Kara-za floating on Sumida River.
2, 6 Kara-za built on the grounds of Sensou-ji temple.
4, 5 Kara-za floating in Shinobazu Pond.

1, 3 隅田川のいかだの上の唐座。
2, 6 浅草境内に建つ唐座。
4, 5 不忍池に浮かぶ唐座。

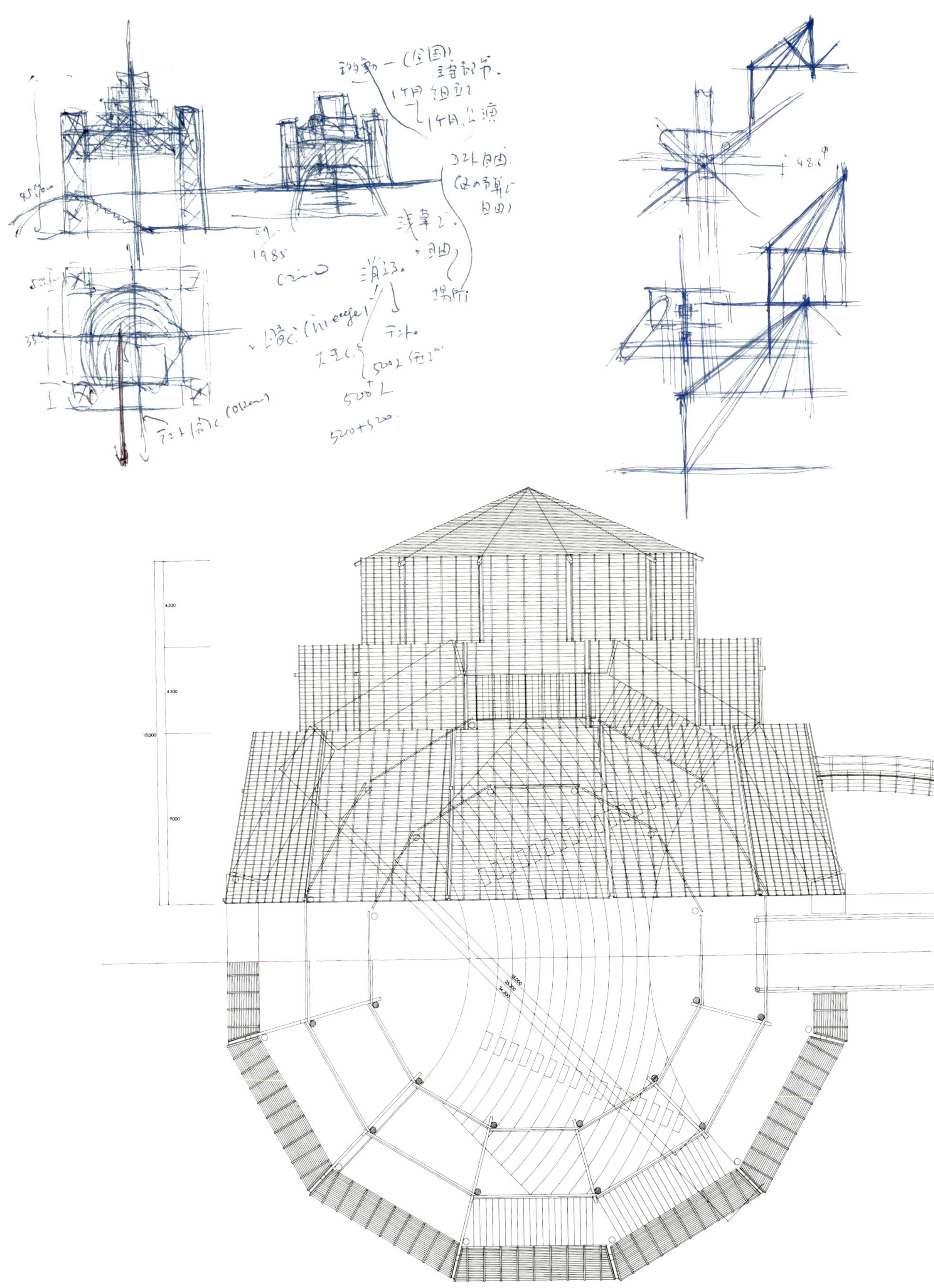

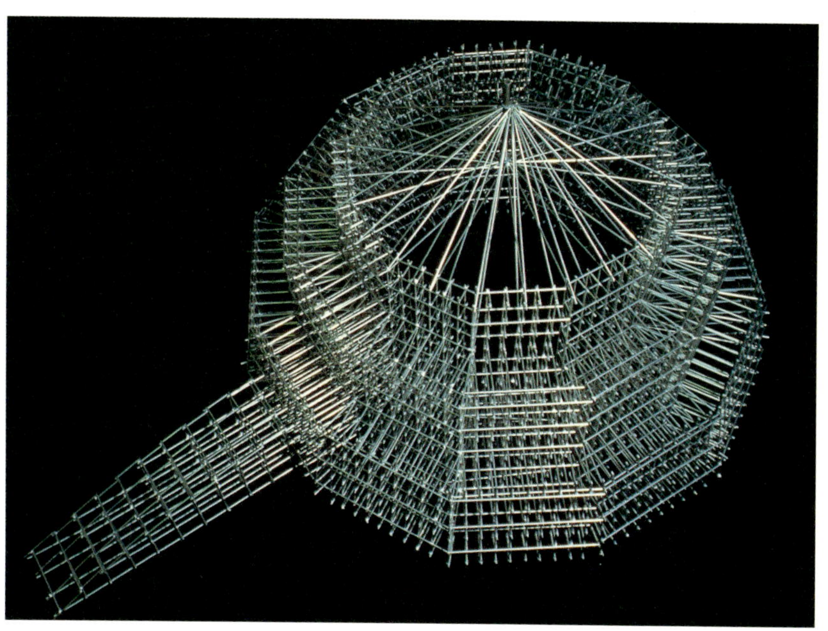

After many changes due to problems with securing land, the project in Asakusa was finally cancelled in the autumn of 1985 due to budgetary problems. Then in the winter of 1986, the Saison Group offered their assistance. The building was first made as a pavilion for that group in a 1987 exhibition in Sendai, then dismantled at the end of the exhibition, brought to Asakusa and reassembled as a theater. At that time, mobility—that is, a structure that could be easily dismantled and constructed—became an important architectural issue. What came to mind was a structure made of the steel pipes used for scaffolding on construction sites.

土地確保の問題で二転三転した挙句、1985年の秋には予算の問題から浅草でのプロジェクトは頓挫した。すると1986年の冬、セゾングループから援助の話がもち上がった。まずは翌1987年の仙台の博覧会の同グループのパビリオンとしてつくり、会期終了後にそれを解体、浅草ににもってきて劇場として再度組み立てるという計画だ。この時点で、移動性、つまり解体、組み立てが容易にできる構造が重要な建築条件となった。そして浮かんだのが、建設現場の足場を組む鉄パイプによる構造である。

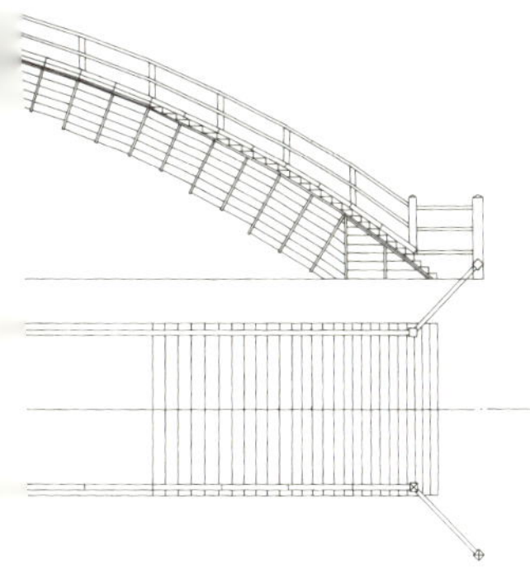

As an assemblage of generic, standardized items such as steel pipes, the construction period will be brief, and by conveying the assembly method alone, it may be reproduced anywhere in the world. In addition to these planning advantages, the sensibility of unrefined industrial materials such as steel pipes is appropriate for the appearance of Shitamachi Kara-za at unexpected places.

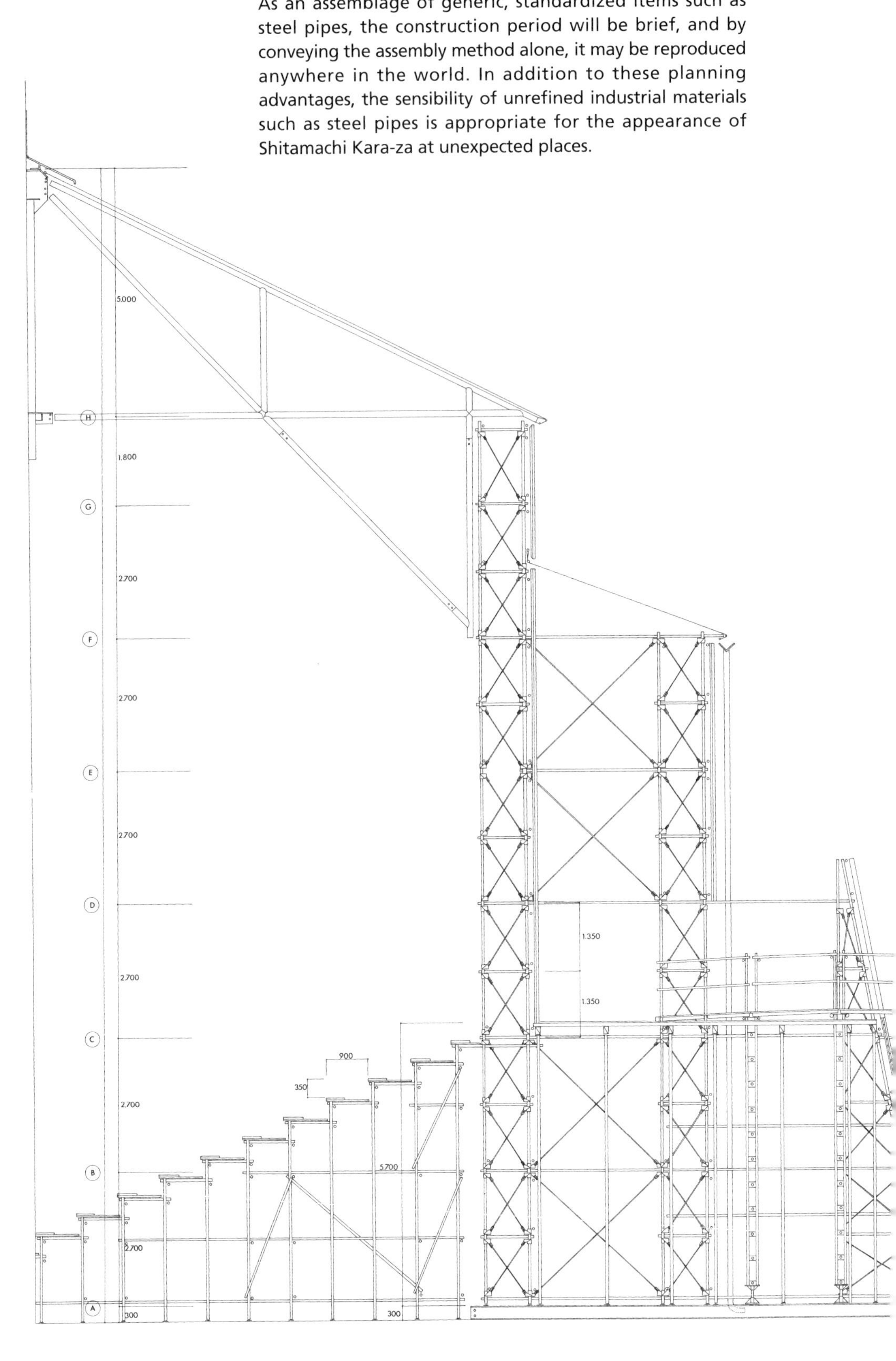

鉄パイプという汎用的な規格品の組み合わせならば工期は短くて済むし、組み立ての方法さえ伝えれば、世界のどこでも再現できる。こうした計画上の利点以上に、鉄パイプという無骨な工業素材の感性が、神出鬼没の下町唐座に似つかわしい。

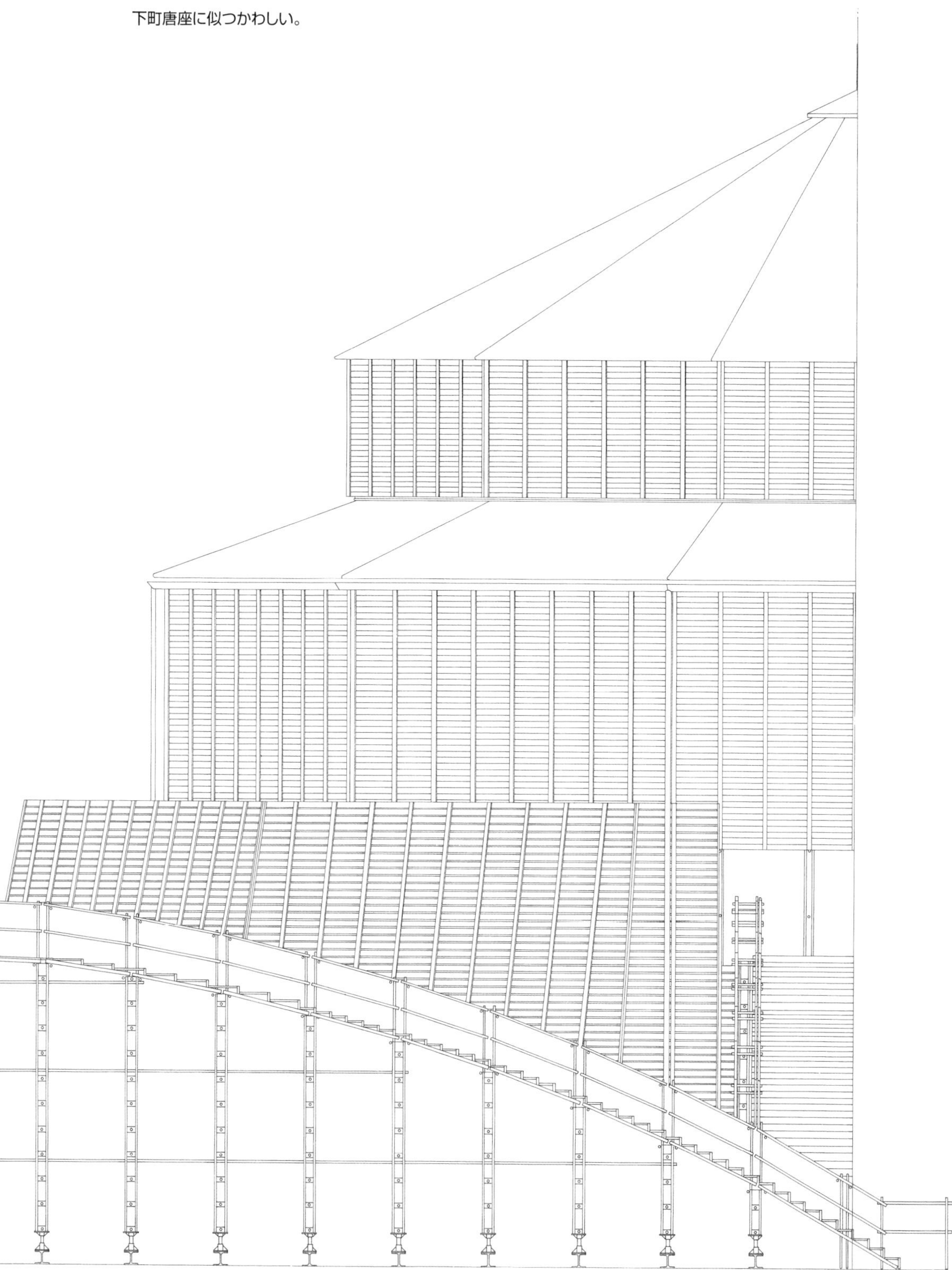

On April 8, 1988, the musical program for opening night was "Jennie." The spirited performance of the troupe, lead by Juro Kara, exploded with enough force to energize the city itself. Yet following this, the movable theater Shitamachi Kara-za was not materialized in any other city. It was a dream-like project that momentarily flared within the "bubble economy."

1988年4月8日、こけら落としの演目は「さすらいのジェニー」。唐十郎率いる一座の気迫の演技は、都市を刺激する十分なエネルギーを爆発させた。だが、移動劇場〈下町唐座〉が、その後どこかの都市に再び現れることはなかった。バブル経済のただ中に一瞬沸き起こった、夢のようなプロジェクトだった。

下町唐座

Church on the Water
水の教会

1. Yufutsu-gun, Hokkaido, Japan　北海道勇払郡
2. 1985.9-1988.4
3. 1988.4-1988.9

The Church on the Water originally began as a fantasy project for the Kobe seaside. At the time, it was an expression of my interest in considering a completely opposite kind of site, for example a church floating on water. The intention was to make a simple study, but the idea inflated as it progressed, and finally I made a large model and presented it in an exhibition. The task of an architect is not only to build the commissions received. Sometimes, an architect must pressure society by saying, "this is the kind of thing I would like to make." Projects may also begin in this way.

1 This is not a real work but a fantasy project, so the geometry of the composition was purified into something bolder and simpler. Within the basic unit of a 5m grid, this is a compact architecture formed from nothing but squares, circles, and L-shaped walls.
2, 3 Image sketches made when the opportunity arose to start the project. At that time, a site where one may look down from Mt. Rokko to the Kobe seashore was chosen, and the idea was for the entire water garden of the worship hall to run down an embankment and connect to the sea.

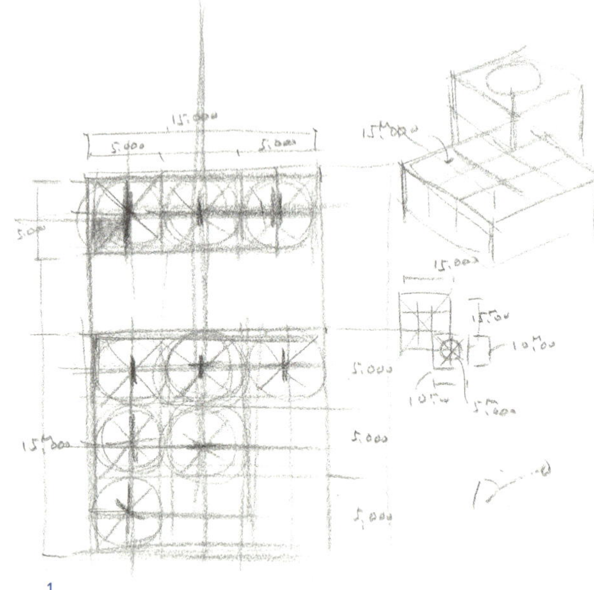

1

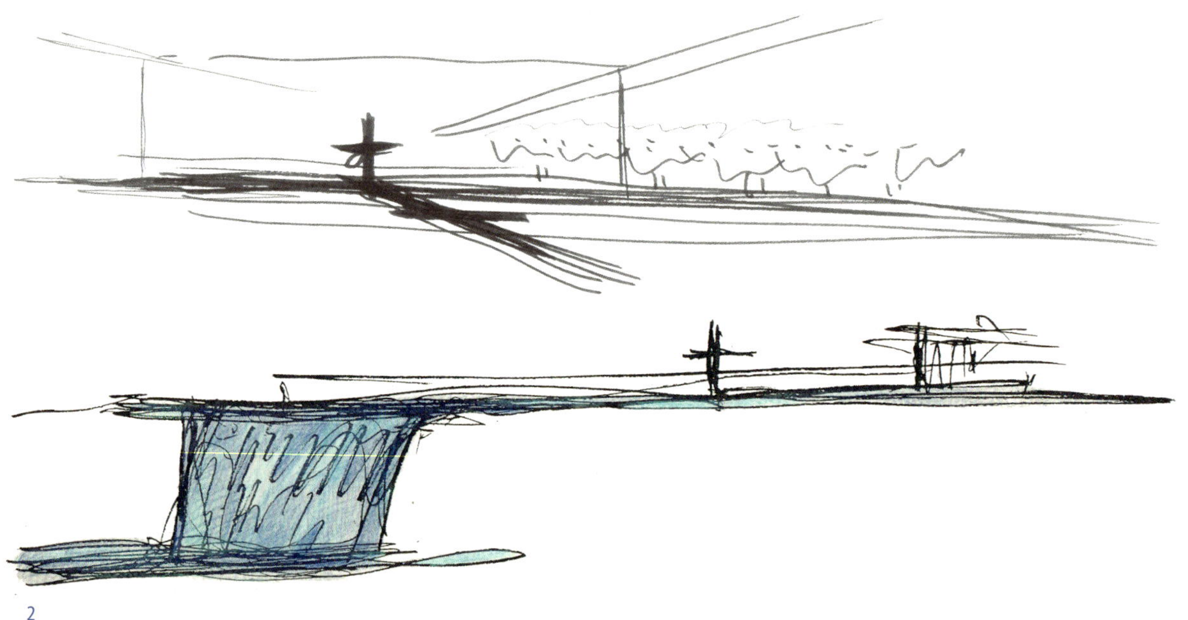

2

「水の教会」は、もとは神戸の海際で架空のプロジェクトとして始めたものだった。そのときはまったく正反対の立地で、例えば水の上に浮かぶ教会を考えるのも面白いだろうという発想だった。簡単なスタディのつもりが、進めるほどにアイディアが膨らんでいき、ついには大きな模型をつくって、展覧会で発表することとなった。依頼を受けてつくるばかりが建築家の仕事ではない。「自分はこんなものをつくりたい」と、ときには建築家の側から社会に働きかけ、そこから始まる仕事があってもいいだろう。

3

1 現実の仕事ではない、架空のプロジェクトであるがゆえ、構成の幾何学はより力強く、単純なものへと純化される。1辺5mのグリッドを基本単位とした中に、正方形と円、L型の壁のみでかたちづくられる、簡潔極まりない建築。

2, 3 プロジェクトを始めるきっかけとなったイメージスケッチ。当初は六甲山から見下ろす神戸の海の突端を敷地として、礼拝堂全面の水庭が護岸を流れ落ち、海へとつながるというアイディアだった。

In spring 1987, when the proposal for the Church on the Water was shown at an exhibition, a developer from Tomamu (Hokkaido), who happened to visit the venue, offered to have it realized on his own property. The site provided by the client was literally in the middle of nature, concealed from its surroundings by lush greenery, and in winter it becomes an unbroken snowscape. There is no sea, but if water could be drawn from a small river in the vicinity, it would be possible to make a scene of a crucifix standing still on a quiet, mirror-like lake surface rather than a crucifix floating on the waves of the sea. Because of the serene environment, no significant adjustments were necessary in the basic composition, scale, and proportions, and the project got underway in a form almost the same as the original image.

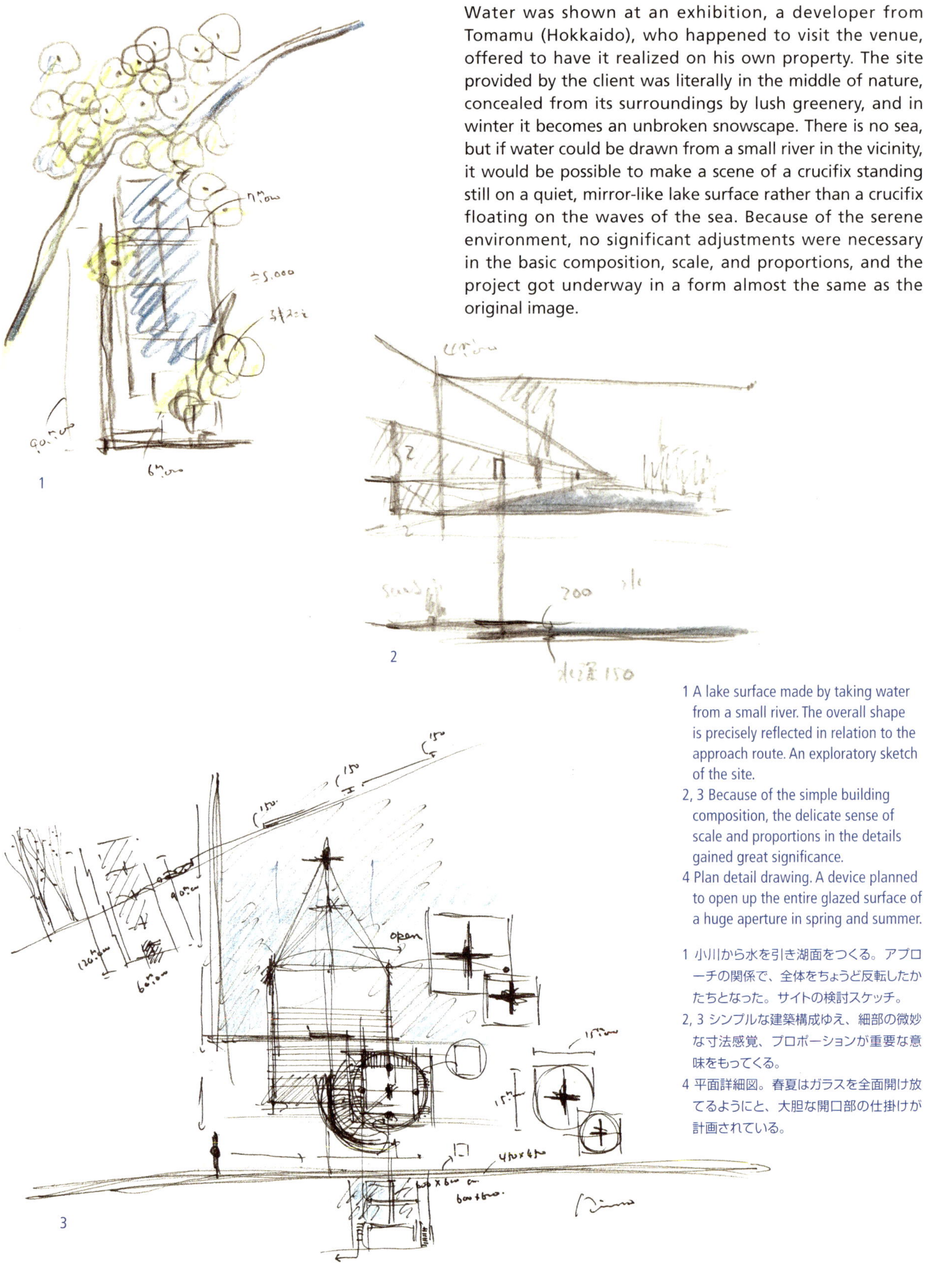

1 A lake surface made by taking water from a small river. The overall shape is precisely reflected in relation to the approach route. An exploratory sketch of the site.

2, 3 Because of the simple building composition, the delicate sense of scale and proportions in the details gained great significance.

4 Plan detail drawing. A device planned to open up the entire glazed surface of a huge aperture in spring and summer.

1 小川から水を引き湖面をつくる。アプローチの関係で、全体をちょうど反転したかたちとなった。サイトの検討スケッチ。

2, 3 シンプルな建築構成ゆえ、細部の微妙な寸法感覚、プロポーションが重要な意味をもってくる。

4 平面詳細図。春夏はガラスを全面開け放てるようにと、大胆な開口部の仕掛けが計画されている。

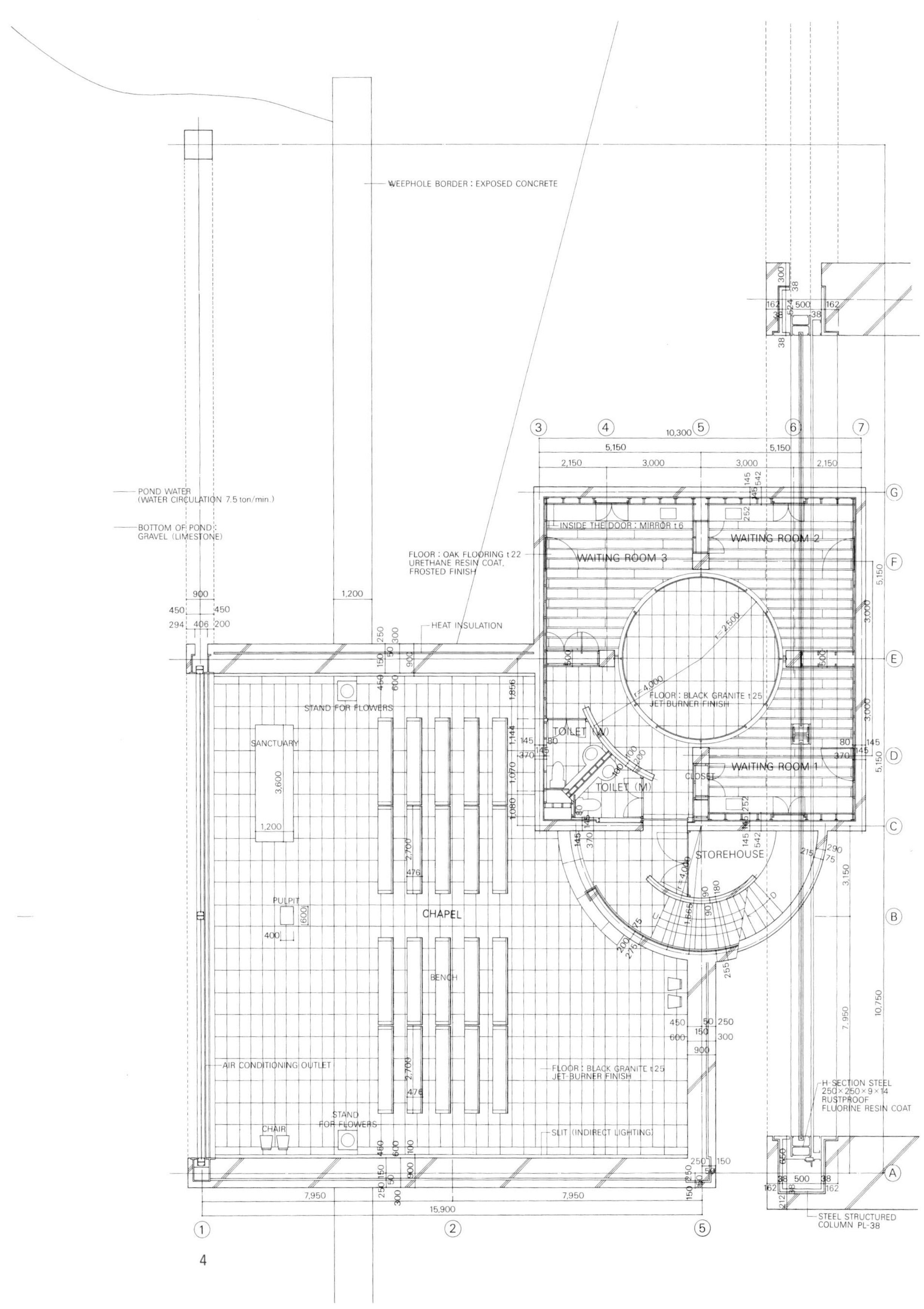
WEEPHOLE BORDER : EXPOSED CONCRETE
POND WATER (WATER CIRCULATION 7.5 ton/min.)
BOTTOM OF POND : GRAVEL (LIMESTONE)
FLOOR : OAK FLOORING t22 URETHANE RESIN COAT, FROSTED FINISH
HEAT INSULATION
INSIDE THE DOOR : MIRROR t6
WAITING ROOM 3
WAITING ROOM 2
WAITING ROOM 1
FLOOR : BLACK GRANITE t25 JET-BURNER FINISH
TOILET (W)
TOILET (M)
CLOSET
STOREHOUSE
STAND FOR FLOWERS
SANCTUARY
PULPIT
CHAPEL
BENCH
AIR CONDITIONING OUTLET
CHAIR
SLIT (INDIRECT LIGHTING)
H-SECTION STEEL 250×250×9×14 RUSTPROOF FLUORINE RESIN COAT
STEEL STRUCTURED COLUMN PL-38

4

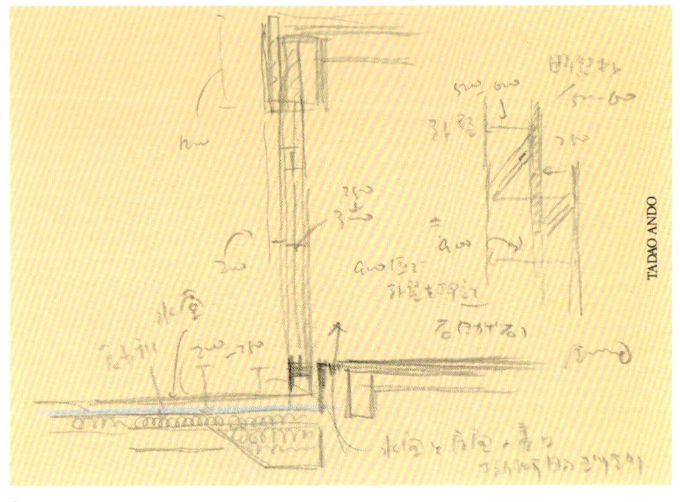

1

1, 2 Exploratory sketch of the front aperture details. For reasons of strength, the large glass is hung from the structure above.
3 Section overlaid with a detail drawing.

1, 2 前面開口部ディテールの検討スケッチ。強度的な理由から、大ガラスを上部より吊る構造となった。
3 ディテールと重ねて描かれた断面詳細図。

1987年の春、「水の教会」の計画案を展覧会で発表したところ、たまたま会場を訪れた北海道トマムの開発者から「ぜひ自分の所で」という申し出があった。クライアントが用意した敷地は、周囲を豊かな緑に覆われ、冬には一面の銀世界となる、文字通りの大自然の只中。海はないが、近くの小川から水を引けば、海の波間に浮かぶ十字架とはまた異なる、鏡面のように静かな湖面に佇む十字架の風景をつくることができる。おおらかな環境ゆえ、基本的な構成、スケール、プロポーションともに大きな調整も必要なく、プロジェクトはほぼ当初のイメージのまま、現実の仕事として動き出した。

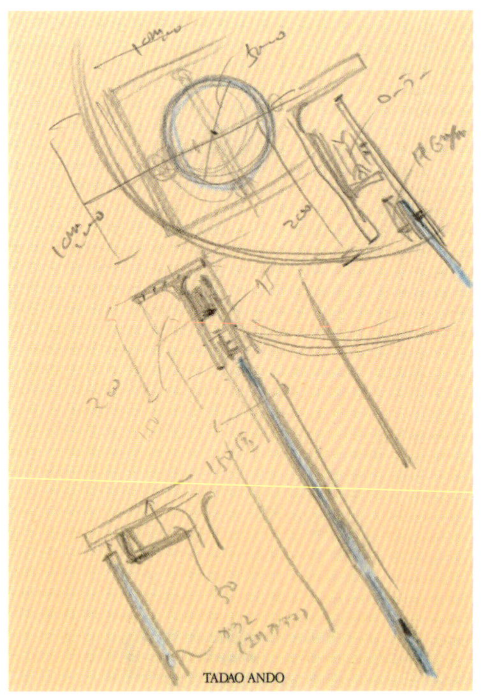

2

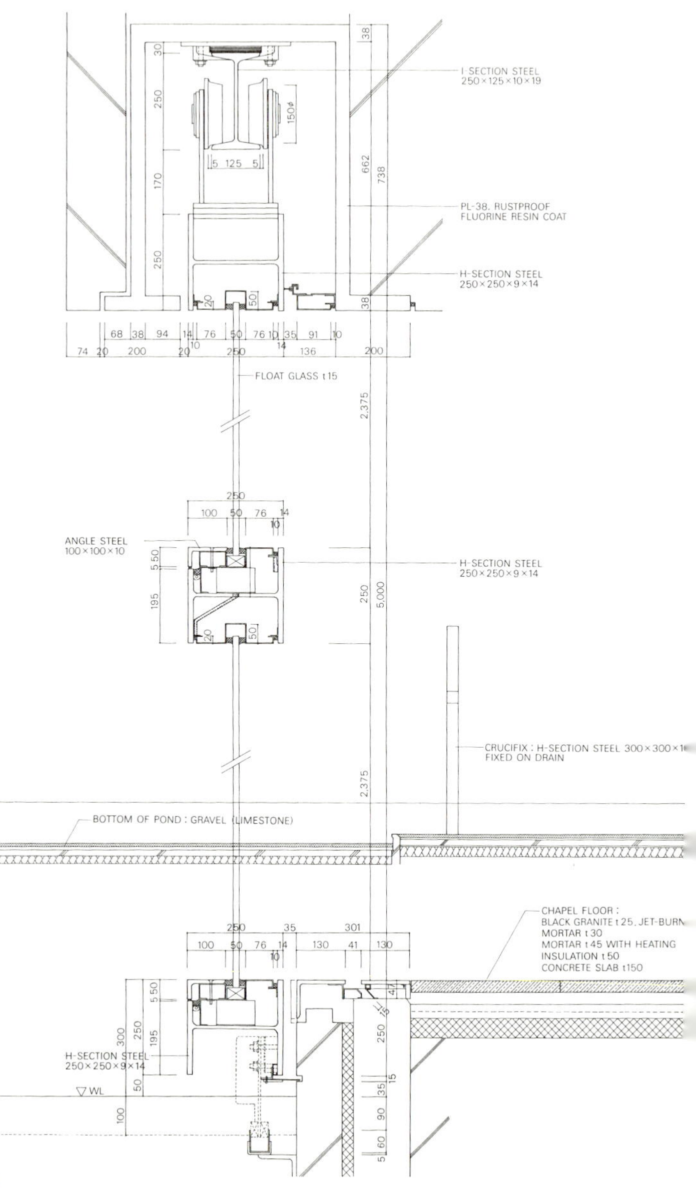

3

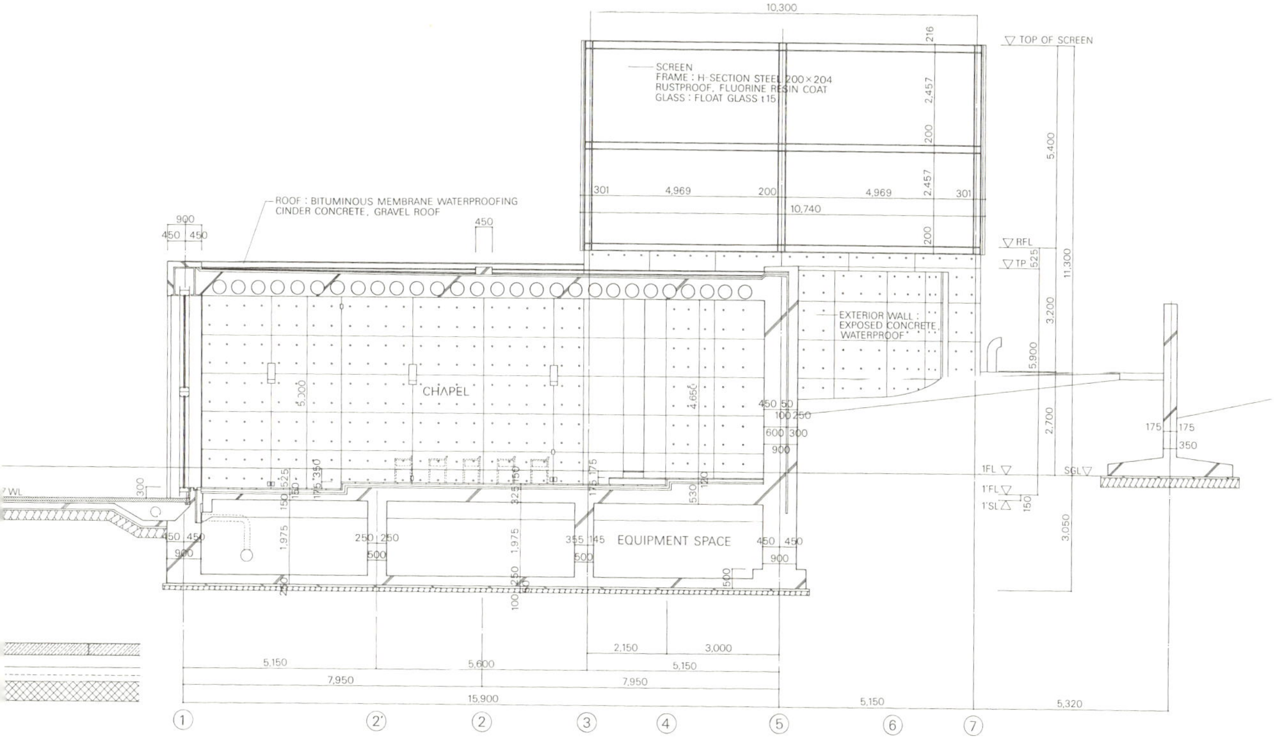

SCREEN
FRAME : H-SECTION STEEL 200×204
RUSTPROOF, FLUORINE RESIN COAT
GLASS : FLOAT GLASS t15

TOP OF SCREEN

ROOF : BITUMINOUS MEMBRANE WATERPROOFING
CINDER CONCRETE, GRAVEL ROOF

EXTERIOR WALL :
EXPOSED CONCRETE
WATERPROOF

CHAPEL

EQUIPMENT SPACE

Theater on the Water
水の劇場

1. Yufutsu-gun, Hokkaido, Japan　北海道勇払郡
2. 1987.08

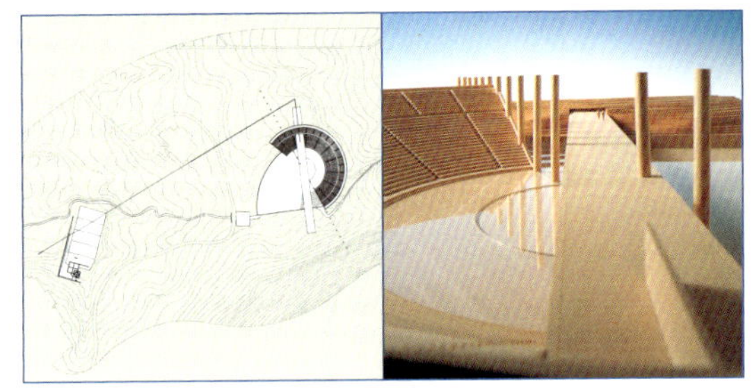

During construction of the Church on the Water, I talked about wanting to build something else based on the same concept, and so the Theater on the Water project began. Making an artificial lake upstream on the river that leads to the Church on the Water, seating to accommodate 6000 people is created as if surrounding this body of water. Against a background of nature, this proposal for a theater on water becomes an outdoor venue in warm seasons and a skating rink in winter. Finally, this plan was not implemented, but ten years later I was able to try and realize the idea of an open-air theater in Awaji Yumebutai.

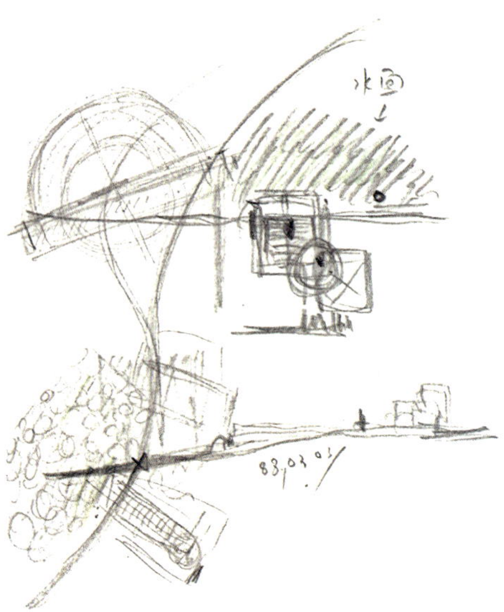

The centripetality of a circular shape and the centrifugality produced by a row of columns. A space with a sense of tension is produced by thoroughly honing this composition comprising a minimum of elements.

円形がもつ求心性と、列柱の醸し出す遠心性。最小限の要素による構成を徹底的に研ぎ澄ますことで、緊張感ある空間をつくり出す。

「水の教会」の建設中、同じコンセプトでもうひとつ何かつくりたいという話になり、この「水の劇場」プロジェクトが始まった。「水の教会」とつながる川の上流に扇形の人工湖をつくり、その水面を囲むように6000人収容の観覧席を設ける。大自然を背景に、暖かい時期は野外劇場、冬はスケートリンクとなる水上の広場の計画だ。結局この計画は実現しなかったが、10年後、「淡路夢舞台」でこの野外劇場のアイディアを実際に試みることとなった。

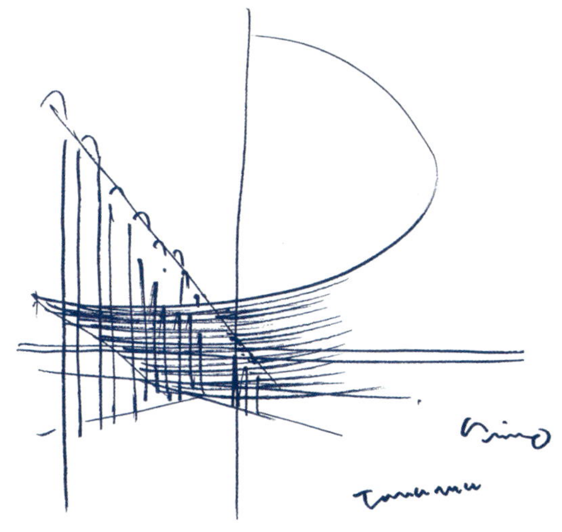

GALLERIA [akka]
GALLERIA [akka]

1. Osaka, Osaka, Japan　大阪府大阪市
2. 1985.10-1987.3
2. 1987.3-1988.4

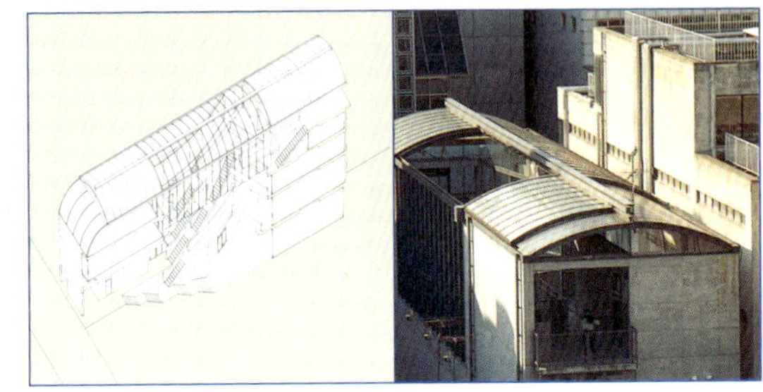

This is a retail complex constructed on a site 8m wide and 40m deep, in Osaka's Minami commercial district. Thinking it would be interesting if this were a humble building that blended into the disorderly streetscape but betrayed expectations by containing an overwhelming labyrinthine space, I proposed architecture with a six-story-high void occupying half the building footprint, which gained the client's approval for implementation.

大阪ミナミの繁華街の、間口8m、奥行き40mの敷地につくった商業施設である。雑然とした街並みの中に溶け込むささやかなビルの中に、予想を裏切る圧倒的な迷宮空間があったら面白いだろうと、全容積の2分の1を占める6層吹き抜けのヴォイドをもつ建築を提案、クライアントの理解を得て実現した。

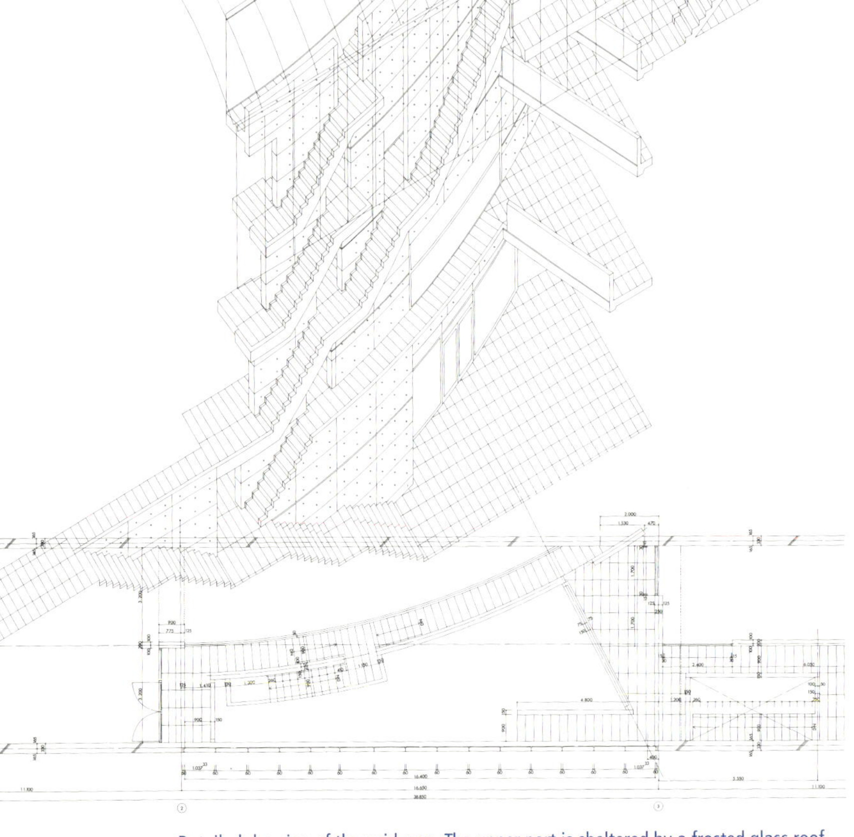

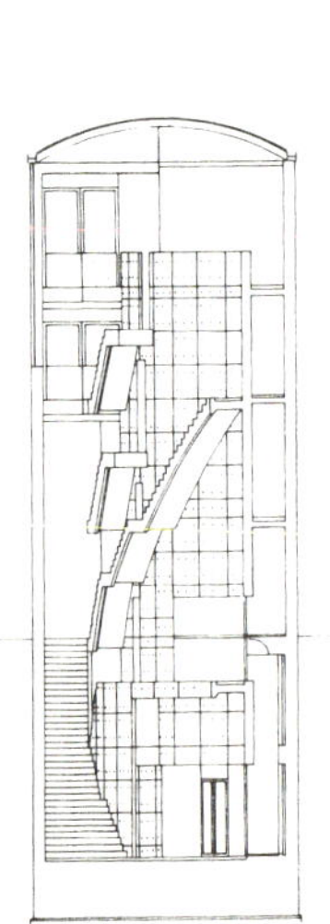

Detailed drawing of the void area. The upper part is sheltered by a frosted glass roof.

吹き抜け部の詳細図。上部にはスリガラスのヴォールト屋根が架かる。

COLLEZIONE
COLLEZIONE

1. Minato-ku, Tokyo, Japan　東京都港区
2. 1986.3-1987.8
3. 1987.9-1989.9

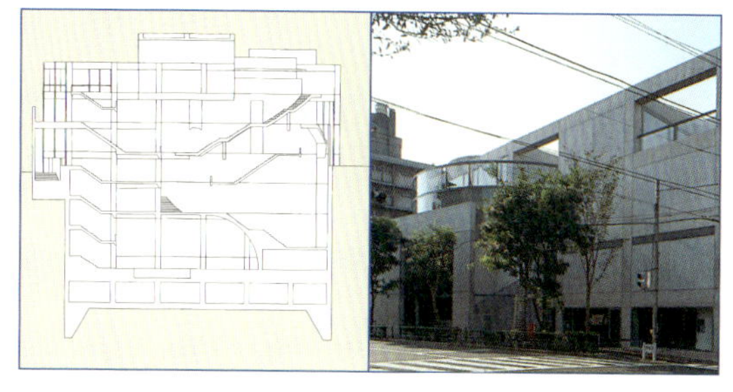

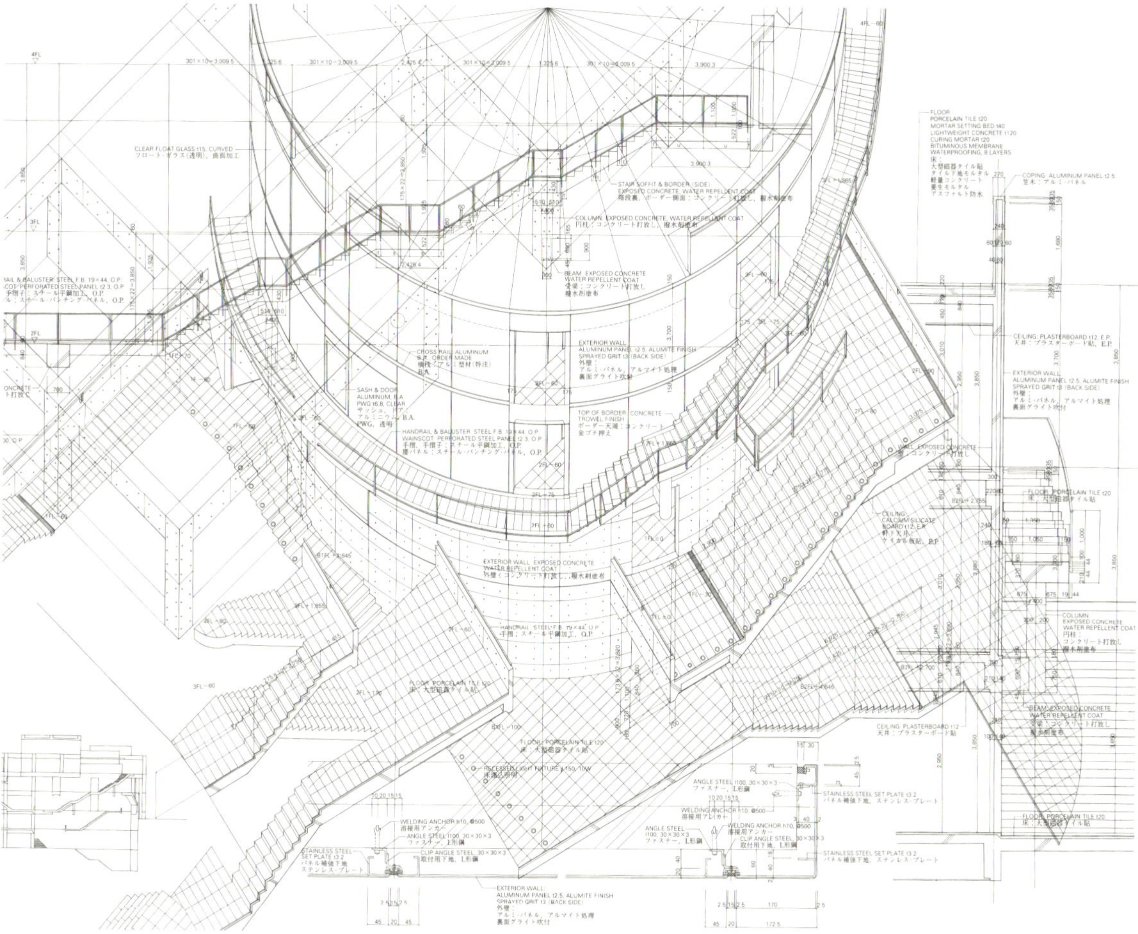

Detailed drawing of the public space.
パブリックスペースの詳細図。

This is a commercial complex built on a main street in the Minami Aoyama district of Tokyo, based on the theme of a spatial composition that expands below ground. The idea of interlocking a rectangular volume and a cylinder, with a three-dimensional public maze traversing the gaps between them, originated in my experiments with the unrealized Art Gallery Complex and Shibuya Project.

東京南青山のメインストリートに建つ地下へと展開する空間構成をテーマとした複合商業施設である。矩形ヴォリュームとシリンダーをかみ合わせ、その隙間にパブリックの立体迷路を巡らせるアイディアは、非実現に終わったアート・ギャラリー・コンプレックスと渋谷プロジェクトの試みに端を発したものだった。

Tea House in Oyodo
大淀の茶室

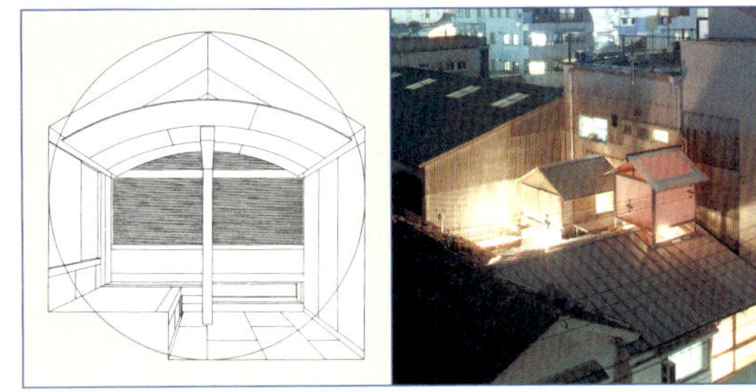

1. Osaka, Osaka, Japan　大阪府大阪市
2. 1985.4-1985.10 (veneer) / 1985.5-1986.10 (block) / 1987.1-1988.4 (tent)
3. 1985.12 (veneer) / 1986.10-1986.11 (block) / 1988.4 (tent)

In the mid-1980s, acting as my own client, I made three *chashitsu* (tea houses) as additions to a row house near my office. The main materials were all everyday things that can be easily obtained: plywood, concrete blocks, and tent fabric. This was temporary architecture very different from the ordinary image of a "tea house" but I wanted to give a personal expression to the spirit of the tea house by making extraordinary places through a pursuit of the ultimate limits of spatiality.

1980年代半ば、自らクライアントとなり、事務所近くの長屋を増築して3軒の〈茶室〉をつくった。主たる素材は、ベニヤ、コンクリートブロック、テントと日常一番手に入りやすいものばかり。一般的な〈茶室〉のイメージとは大きく異なる仮設建築だったが、極限の空間性を追い求めることで非日常の場をつくり出そうという、茶室の精神を自分なりに表現しようと考えつくった。

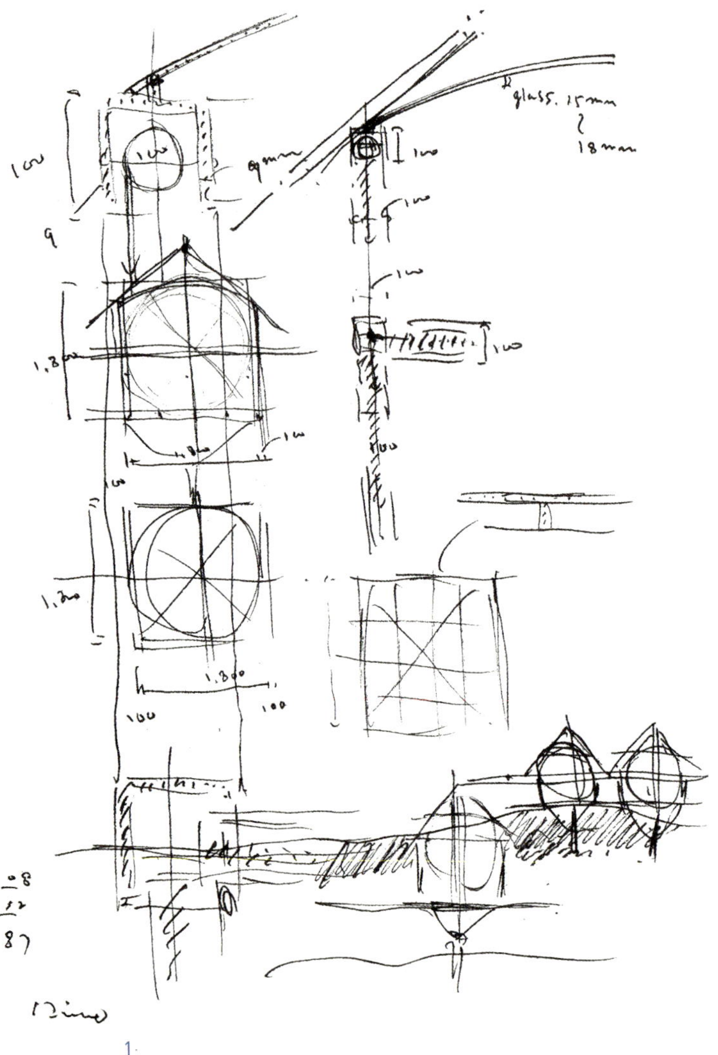

1

1 Exploratory sketches for the tent tea house. An Ando-style tea house made with exceedingly simple modern materials and details.
2 Overall cross section. First, a tea house using linden plywood for all the floors, walls, and ceilings was added to the roof of a wooden row house. Next, a block tea house, enclosed by walls of polished concrete blocks, was made on the first floor of the row house. Following that, a tent tea house was made on the roof as an annex to the plywood tea house.

1 テントの茶室の検討スケッチ。極めて簡素な現代的素材とディテールでつくられた安藤流の茶室。
2 全体断面図。最初に、木造長屋の屋根の上に床・壁・天井すべてシナベニヤの茶室を増築した。次に、長屋の1階に研ぎ出しコンクリートブロックの壁で囲ったブロックの茶室をつくり、その後に再び屋根上に、ベニヤの茶室と隣り合うかたちでテントの茶室がつくられた。

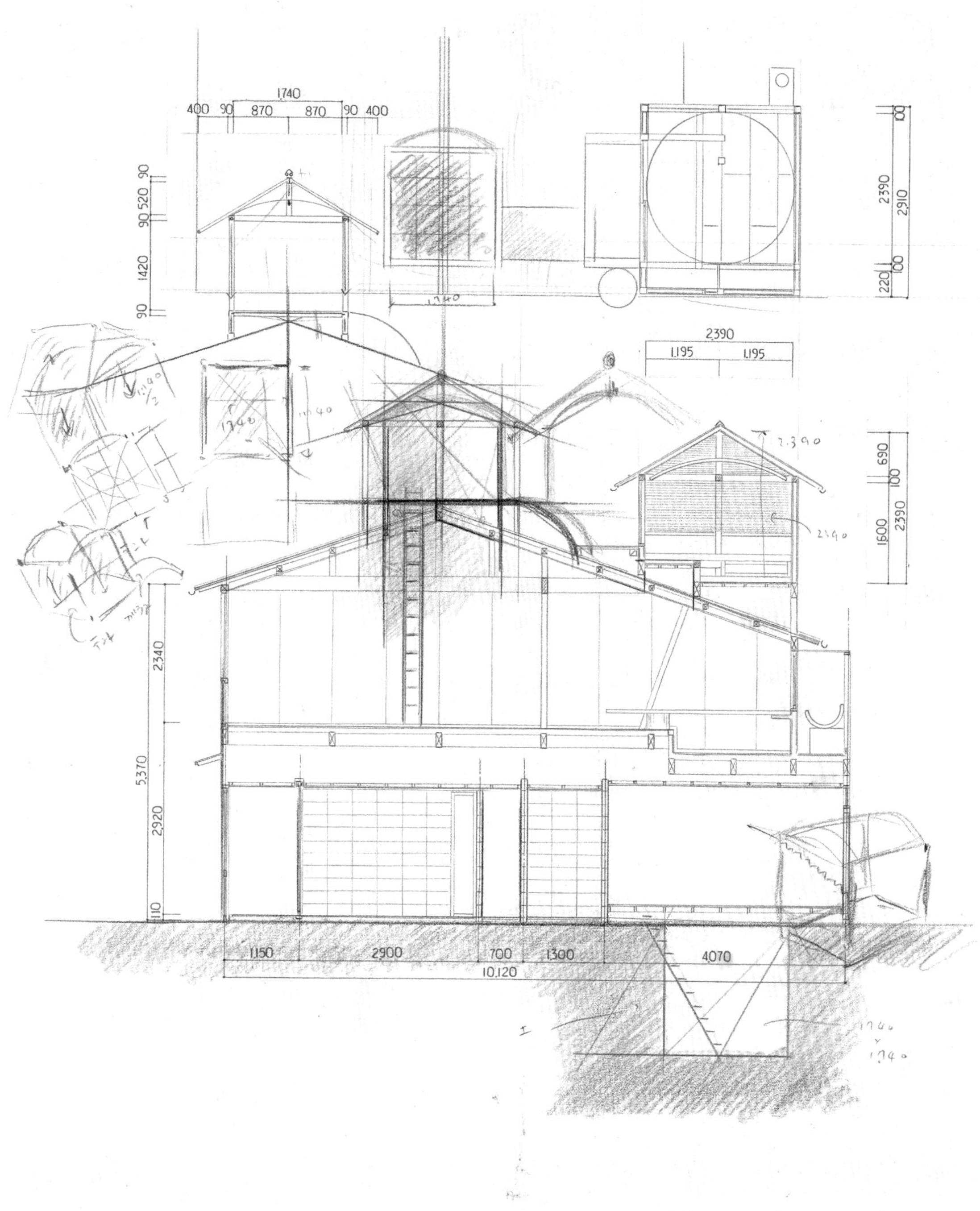

1,740
400 90 870 870 90 400
2390
2910
1,195 1,195
690
1600
2340
5,370
2920
1,150
2900
700
1300
4070
10,120

2

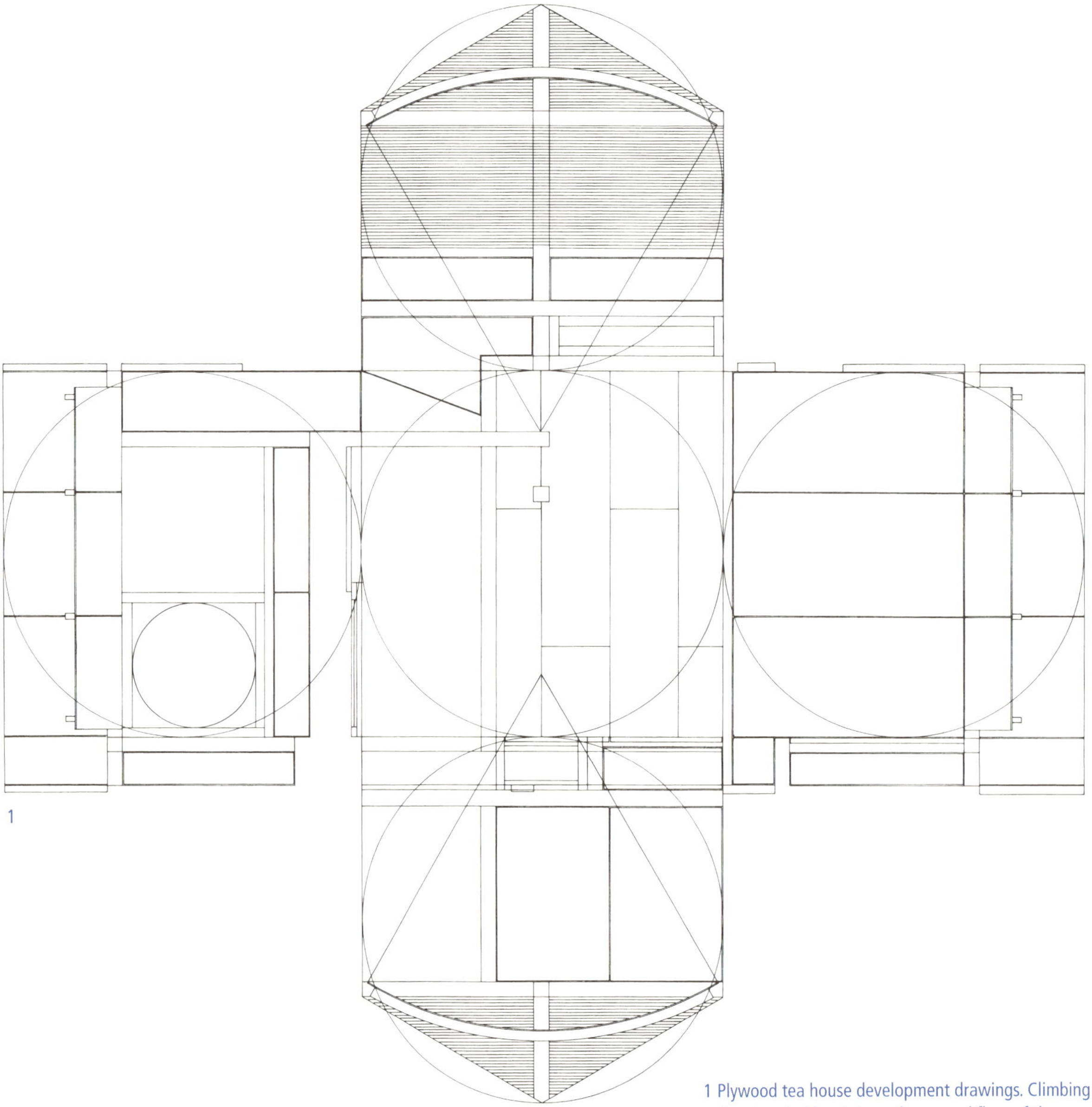

1

1 Plywood tea house development drawings. Climbing the steep ladder-stair on the second floor of the row house, the 1/6th-circle vaulted ceiling floats in the soft light that envelops the six-sided plywood volume. The scale of the plywood teahouse (the size inscribed by a 2390mm-diameter sphere) was determined through a comparative study with Tai-an tea house at Myouki-an Temple [the only extant tea house attributed to famed sixteenth century tea master Sen Rikyu].

2 Axonometric. An arched bridge of strengthened glass is suspended from the window of the plywood tea house, straddling the roof at the other end, and the tent tea house is constructed by affixing a glass ceiling and floor to steel roof trusses.

3 Cross section of the tent tea house. The ceiling height and the internal plan dimensions use the traditional module of 5 *shaku* 8 *sun* [approximately 1545mm]. Isolated from the tumult of downtown Osaka by a gentle filter, this small space provides an extraordinary, mysterious sensation.

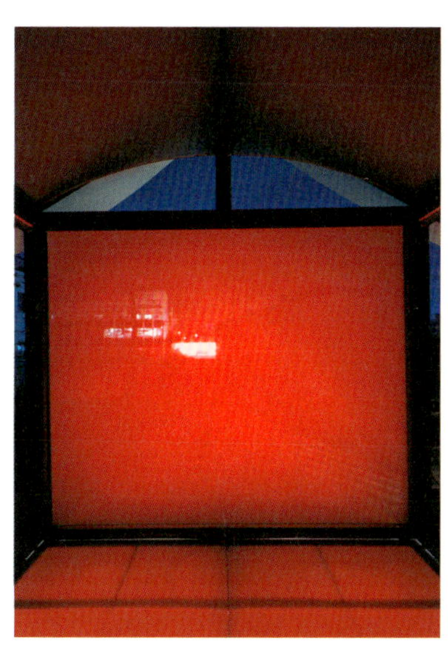

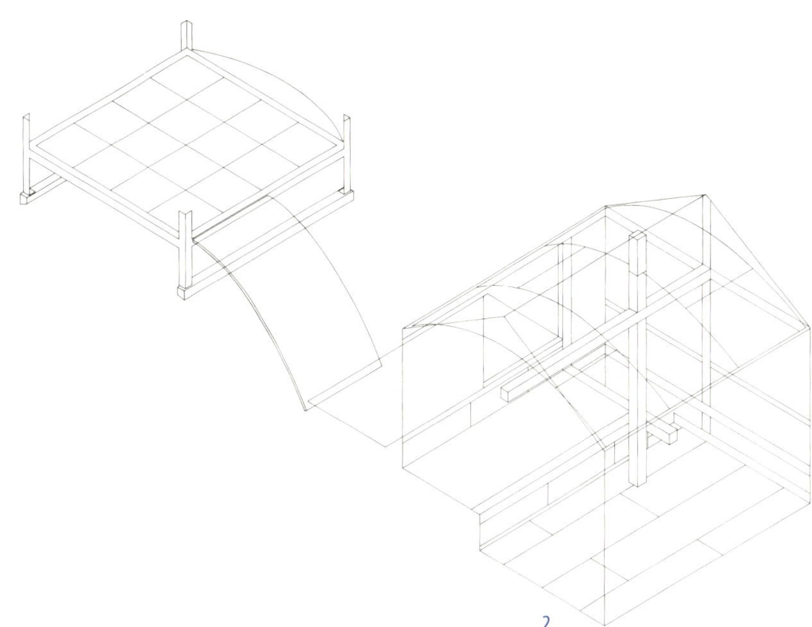

2

1 ベニヤの茶室展開図。長屋2階の急なはしご階段を上ると、ベニヤの6面体が包み込む柔らかな光の間に6分円のヴォールト天井が浮かぶ。ベニヤの茶室のスケール（直径2390mm の球体が内接する大きさ）は、妙喜庵待庵との比較検討により決定された。

2 アクソノメトリック。ベニヤの茶室の窓から強化ガラスの太鼓橋が架かり、その先に屋根の棟にまたがって、鉄骨の小屋組みにガラスの天井と床を組み合わせたテントの茶室がつくられた。

3 テントの茶室断面図。平面の内法寸法と天井高さは伝統的モジュールの5尺8寸。大阪下町の喧騒から柔らかなフィルターで切り取られた小空間が、非日常の不思議な感覚をもたらす。

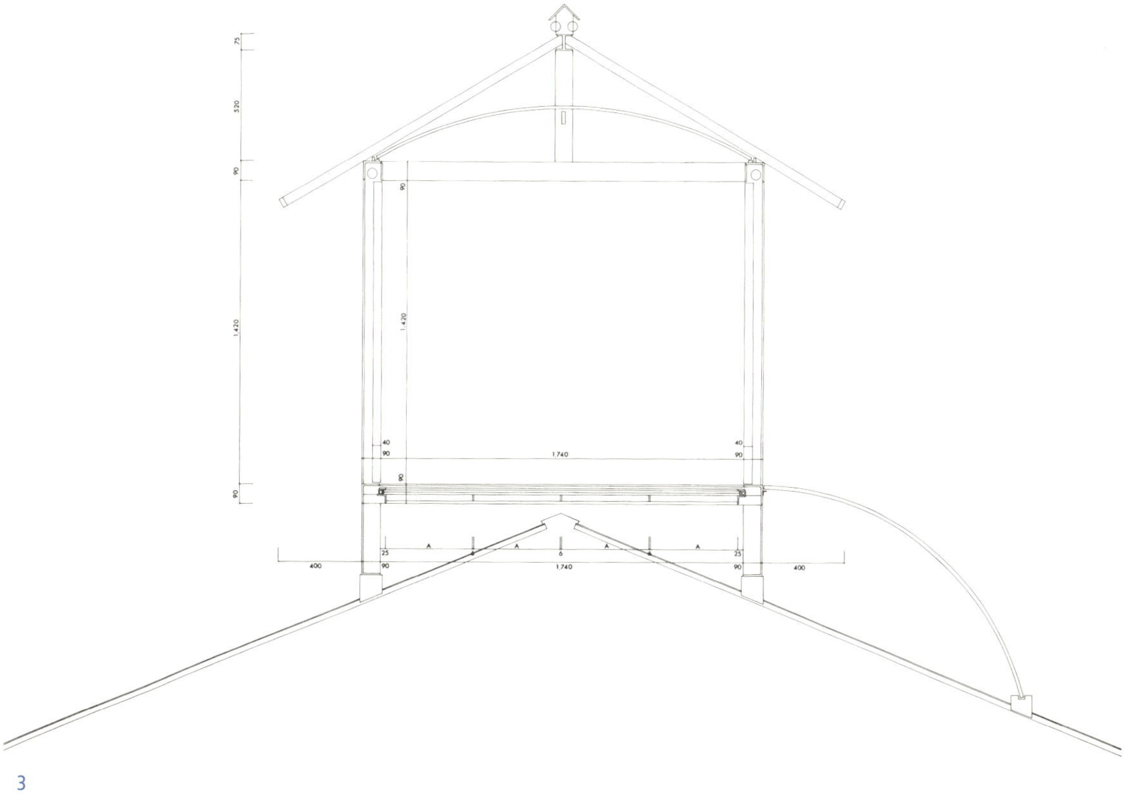

3

Church of the Light + Sunday School
光の教会＋日曜学校

1. Ibaraki, Osaka, Japan　大阪府茨木市
2. 1987.1-1988.5 (phase Ⅰ) / 1997.3-1998.5 (phase Ⅱ)
3. 1988.5-1989.4 (phase Ⅰ) / 1998.5-1999.2 (phase Ⅱ)

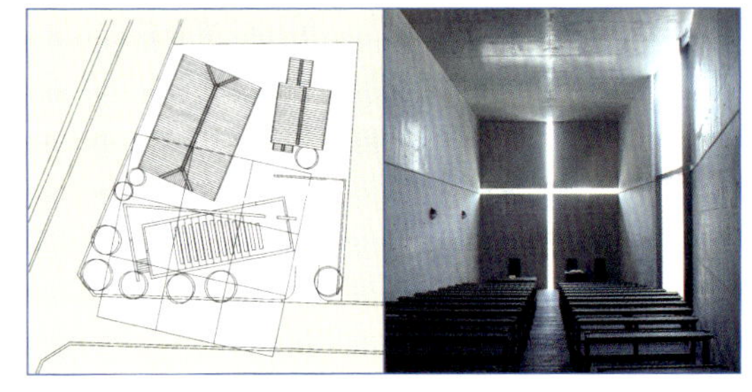

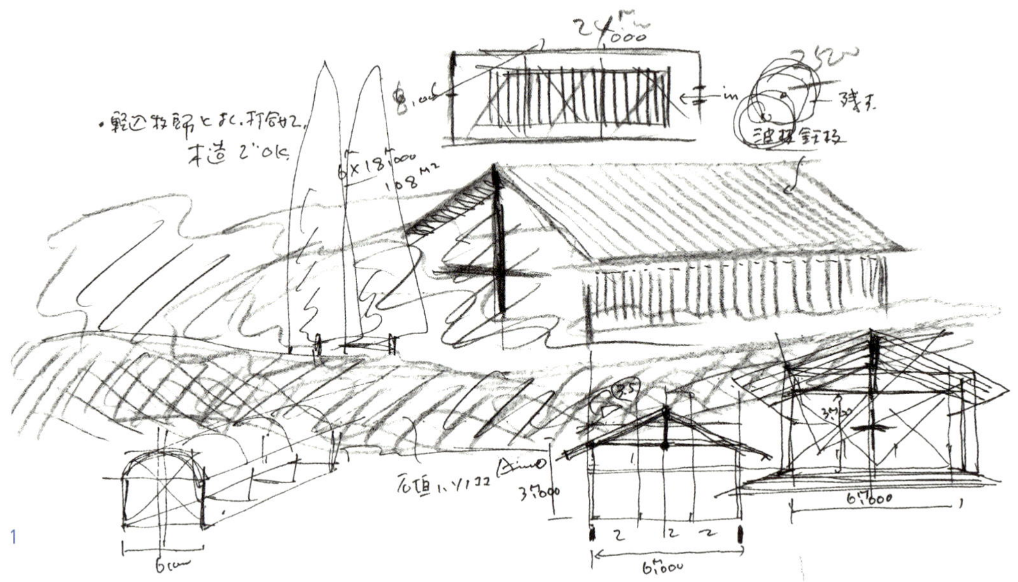

1

2

1 Early image sketches, conceived as a wood structure.
2 Sketches drawn during a visit to the site visit before beginning the design.
3, 4 In terms of budget, it could only be a simple box shape. The question therefore became how to create a sacred space inside that box appropriate as a place where people gather and pray—the architect's dilemmas appeared as multiple, overlapping lines.

1 木造で考えていた初期イメージスケッチ。
2 計画前、敷地を訪れた際に描かれたスケッチ。
3, 4 予算の都合上、単純な箱型とせざるを得ない。ならばその箱の中に、いかにして人々が集い、祈りを捧げる場所にふさわしい神聖な空間を生み出すか——建築家の葛藤が幾重にも重ねられた線となって表れた。

I received this commission in 1987, at exactly the same time that the plan for the Church on the Water got underway. The scale is small, and the local environment is a very ordinary suburban residential area. The budget was truly precarious. Despite the harsh conditions, I was struck by the strong desires of the parishioners hoping for new architecture, and so I undertook the task. Initially I thought of a wood structure, but somehow could not achieve the shape I had in mind. Having become stumped, I decided to build it in concrete. Adjusting to the budget, I reduced the volume and everything else to the bare minimum. This is architecture that challenges the limitations of cost.

1987年、ちょうど「水の教会」の計画が動き始めたと同時期に依頼を受けた。規模は小さく、立地環境もごく普通の郊外住宅地。予算は実に心許ない。厳しい条件であったが、新たな建築を願う信者たちの強い思いに打たれ、仕事を引き受けた。当初は木造で考えていたが、なかなか思うようなかたちに納まらず、迷った末にコンクリートでつくろうと決めた。予算に合わせて容積も何もかも極限まで絞り込む。コストの限界に挑戦する建築だった。

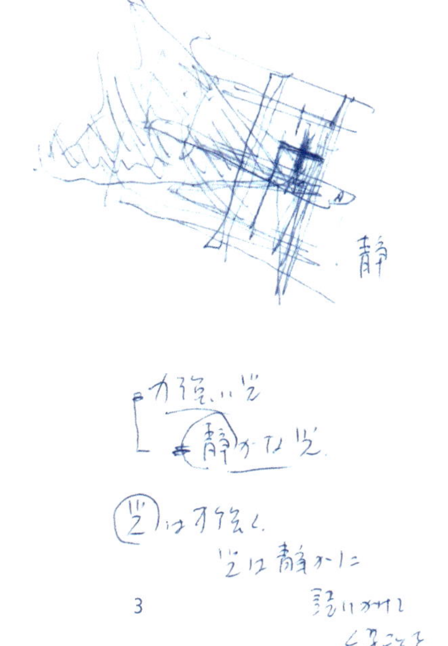

3

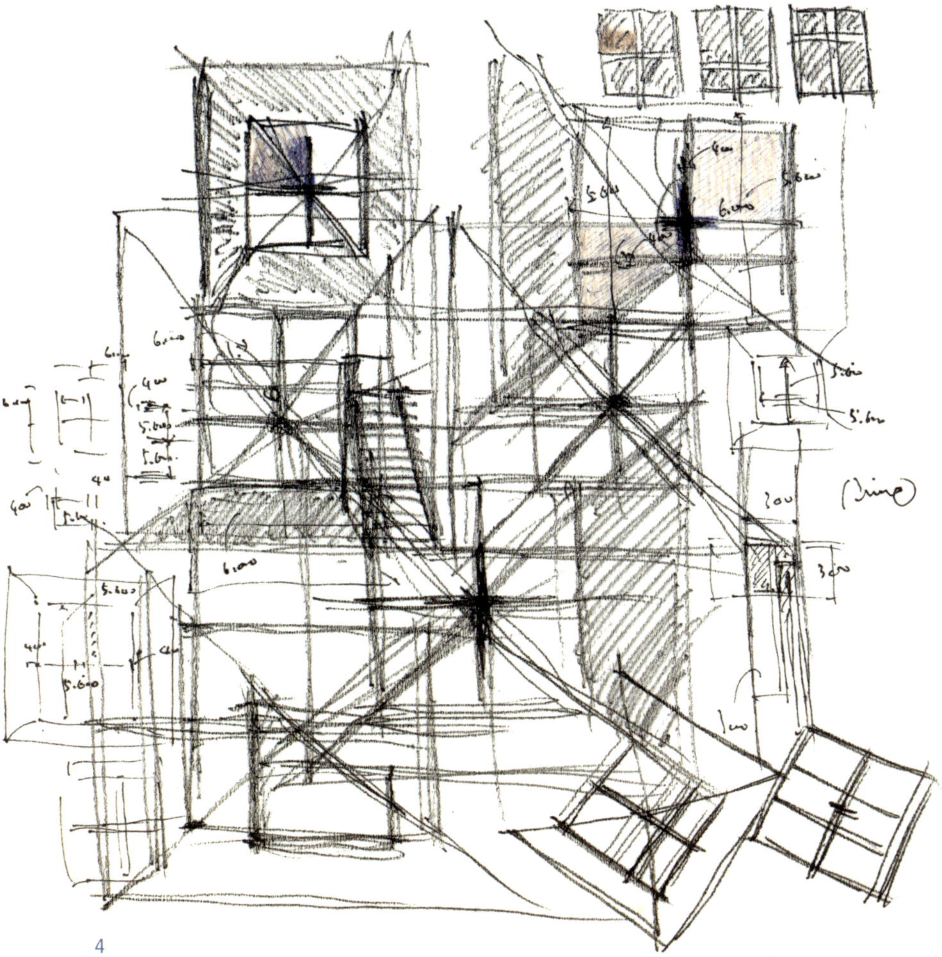

4

For more than a year after receiving the commission, I struggled with a composition in which a concrete wall slices through the box diagonally, articulating the entrance part from the single-space worship hall, within which a stepping floor is excavated.

It is a naked space reduced to the minimum, without any ornamental elements. Only the crucifix-shaped incision piercing the front wall projects the symbol of a church within the gloomy space.

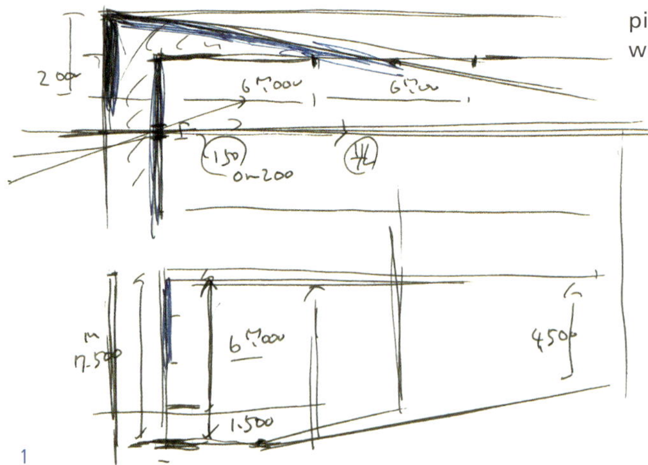

1

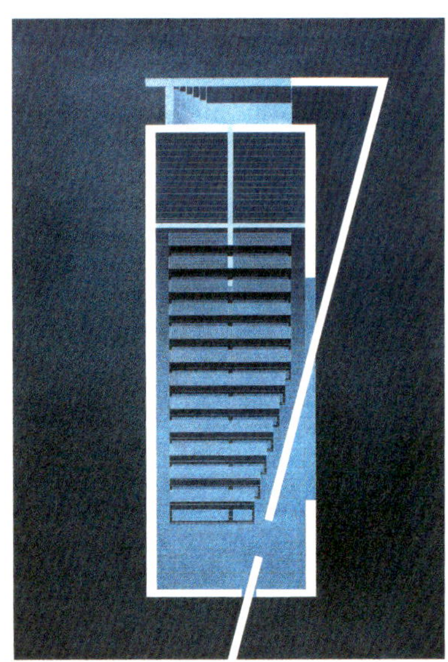

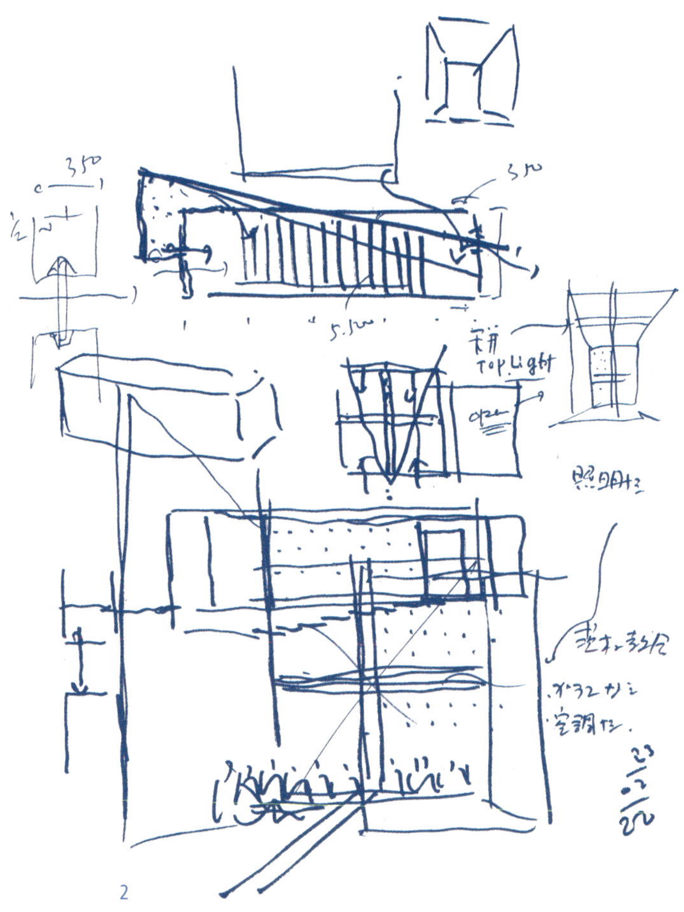

2

1, 2 Sketches drawn with the intention of instructing my staff. The composition became fixed, and entered the stage of studying actual spatial dimensions.

3, 4 Image sketches of a "cross of light" made by slots piercing the concrete.

1, 2 スタッフへの指示の目的で描かれたスケッチ。構成が固まり、具体的な空間寸法の検討段階に入る。

3, 4 コンクリートに穿かれたスリットによる〈光の十字架〉のイメージスケッチ。

依頼を受けてから１年余り後にたどり着いたのが、１枚のコンクリートの壁が箱を斜めに貫き、内部を階段状に床を掘り下げたワンルームの礼拝堂とエントランス部分とに分節する構成。
装飾的な要素が一切ない、極限まで削ぎ落とされた裸形の空間だった。唯一、正面の壁に穿たれた十字の切り込みが薄暗い空間に教会のシンボルを映し出す。

3

4

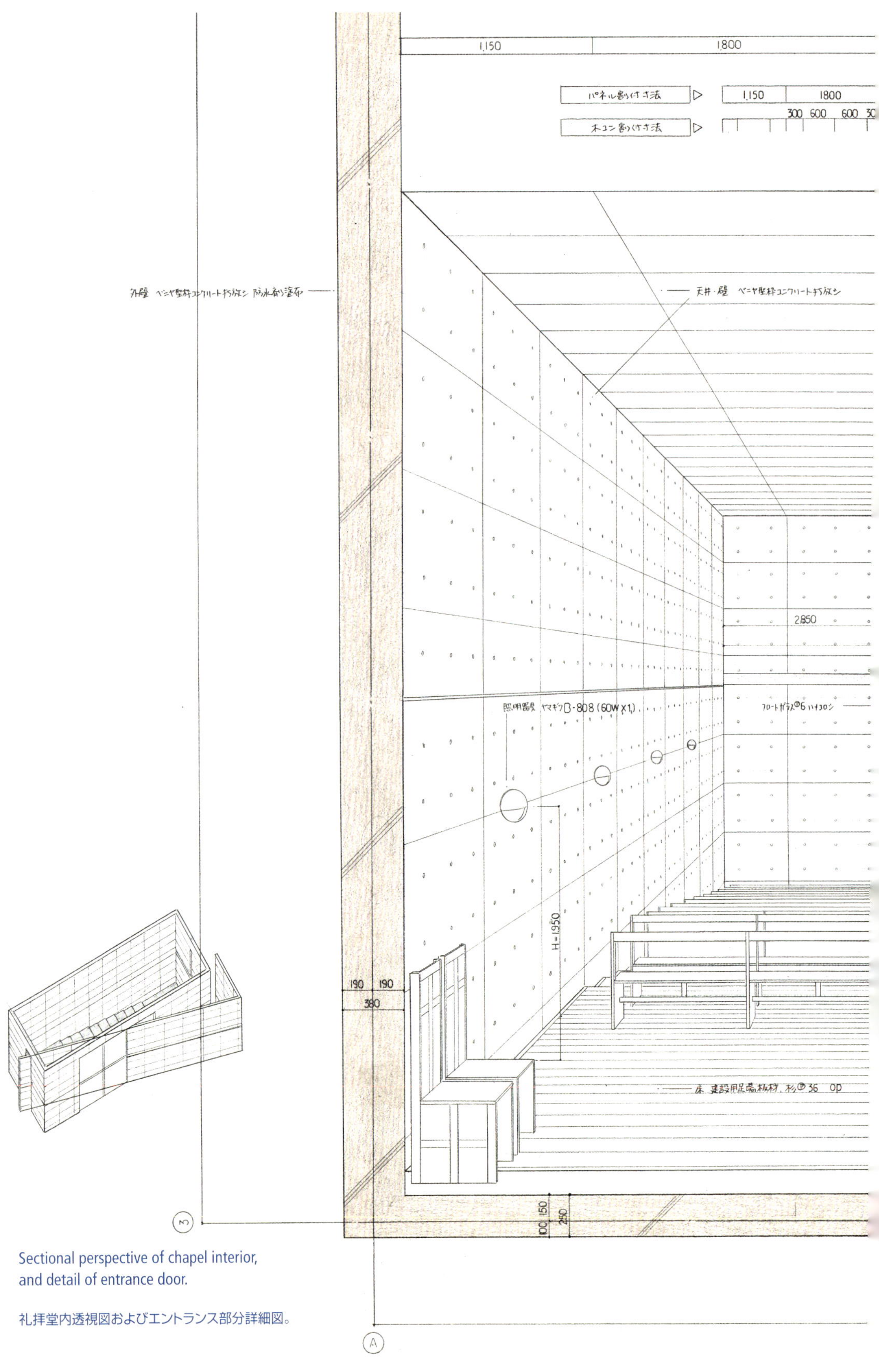

Sectional perspective of chapel interior,
and detail of entrance door.

礼拝堂内透視図およびエントランス部分詳細図。

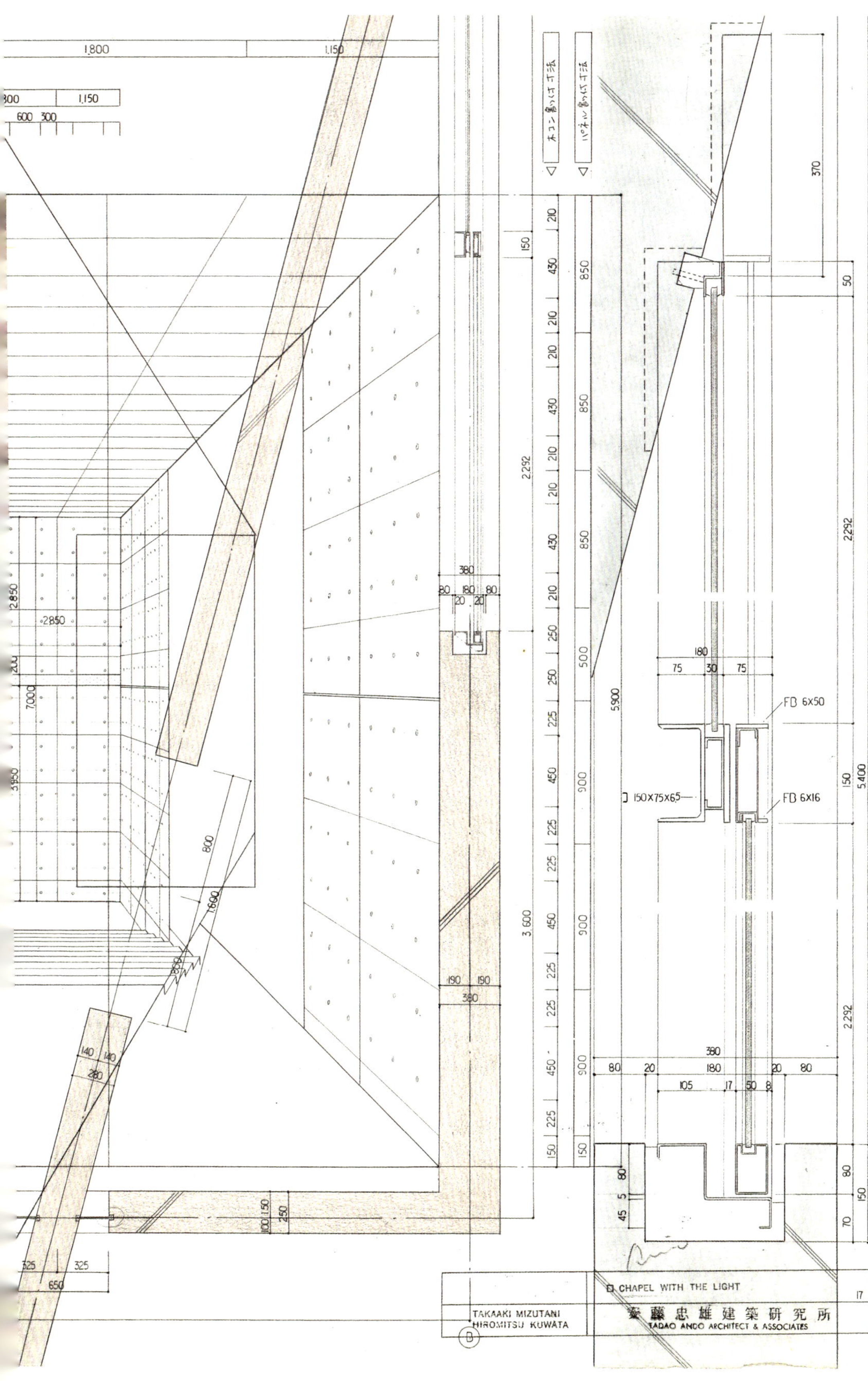

木コン割付け寸法
パネル割付け寸法
FB 6X50
[150X75X6.5
FB 6X16
CHAPEL WITH THE LIGHT
TAKAAKI MIZUTANI
HIROMITSU KUWATA
安藤忠雄建築研究所
TADAO ANDO ARCHITECT & ASSOCIATES

Twelve years after the completion of Church of the Light, it was expanded with a meeting facility attached to the church. Not a merely an addition, I aimed at a building that would contrast with the Church of the Light, giving a tense relationship between the new and old buildings, but with an awareness of a complete "repetition of the worship hall" in their exterior appearance. Conversely, for the interior of the building, I thought of overturning that impression through a space of light. I wanted to make a Sunday School suffused with bright light in emphatic contrast to the symbolic cross of light floating in the gloomy space of the worship hall.

「光の教会」完成から12年後、教会付属の集会施設を増設した。単なる継ぎ足しの増築ではない、緊張感ある新旧建物の関係性、光の教会と対となるような建物を目標とし、外観においては徹底して〈礼拝堂の反復〉を意識した。逆に建物内部においては、あえてその印象を覆すような光の空間を考えた。象徴的な十字の光を浮かび上がらせる礼拝堂の闇の空間とは好対照をなす、明るい光に満ちた「日曜学校」をつくりたかった。

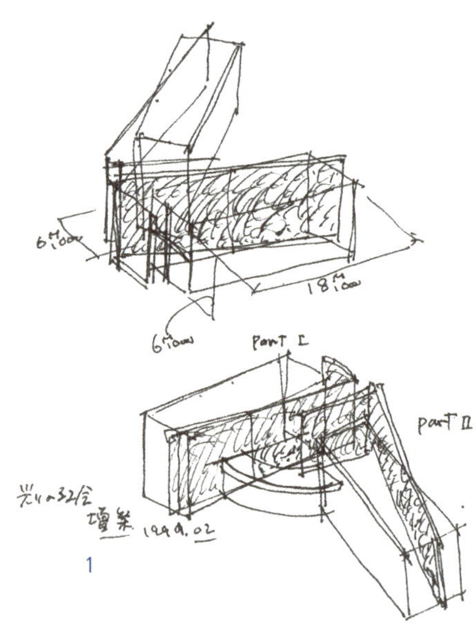

1

1 Study sketches of the relationship between the new and old building volumes. While following the worship hall, the scale and composition create a "new" space.
2 Study sketch of the site layout. A positive meaning is given to the buffer space between the new and the old.
3 Detailed plan.

1 新旧の建物ヴォリュームの関係の検討スケッチ。スケール、構成ともに、礼拝堂を踏襲しつつ、〈新しい〉空間を生み出す。
2 配置検討スケッチ。新旧の間の余白のスペースに積極的な意味を与える。
3 平面詳細図

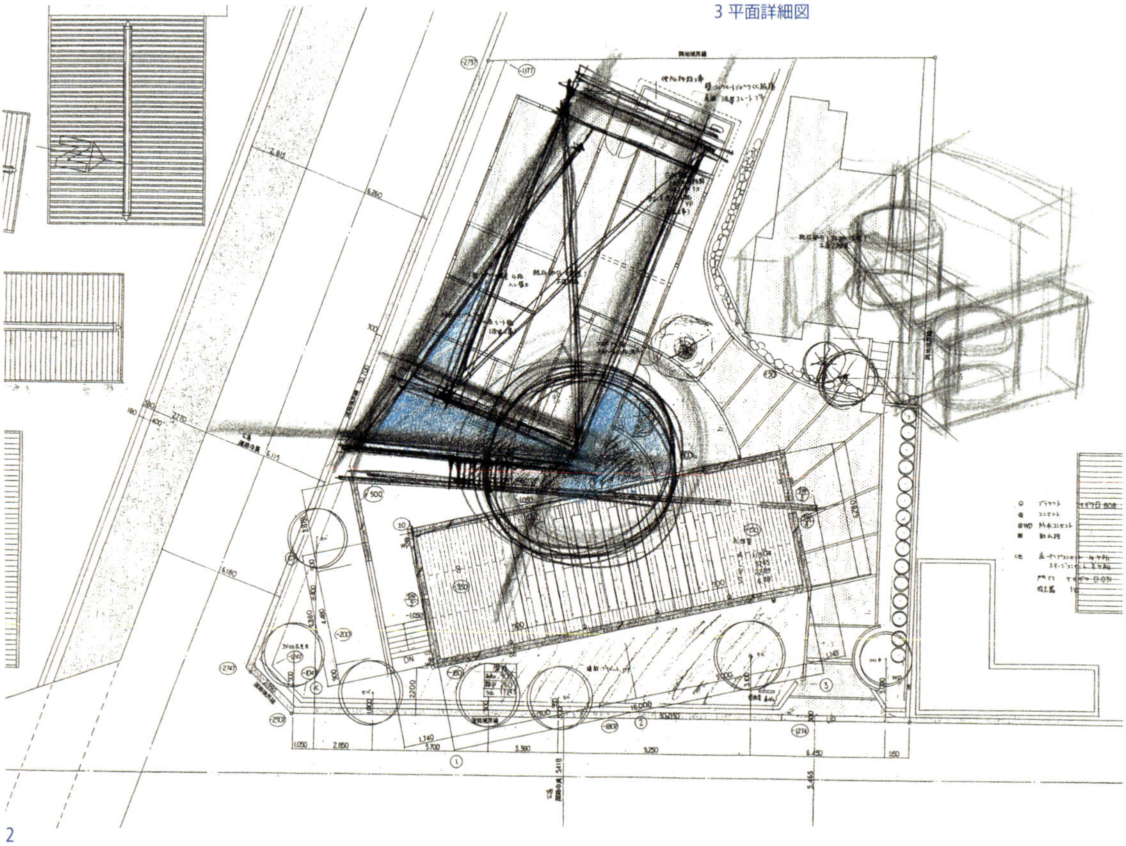

2

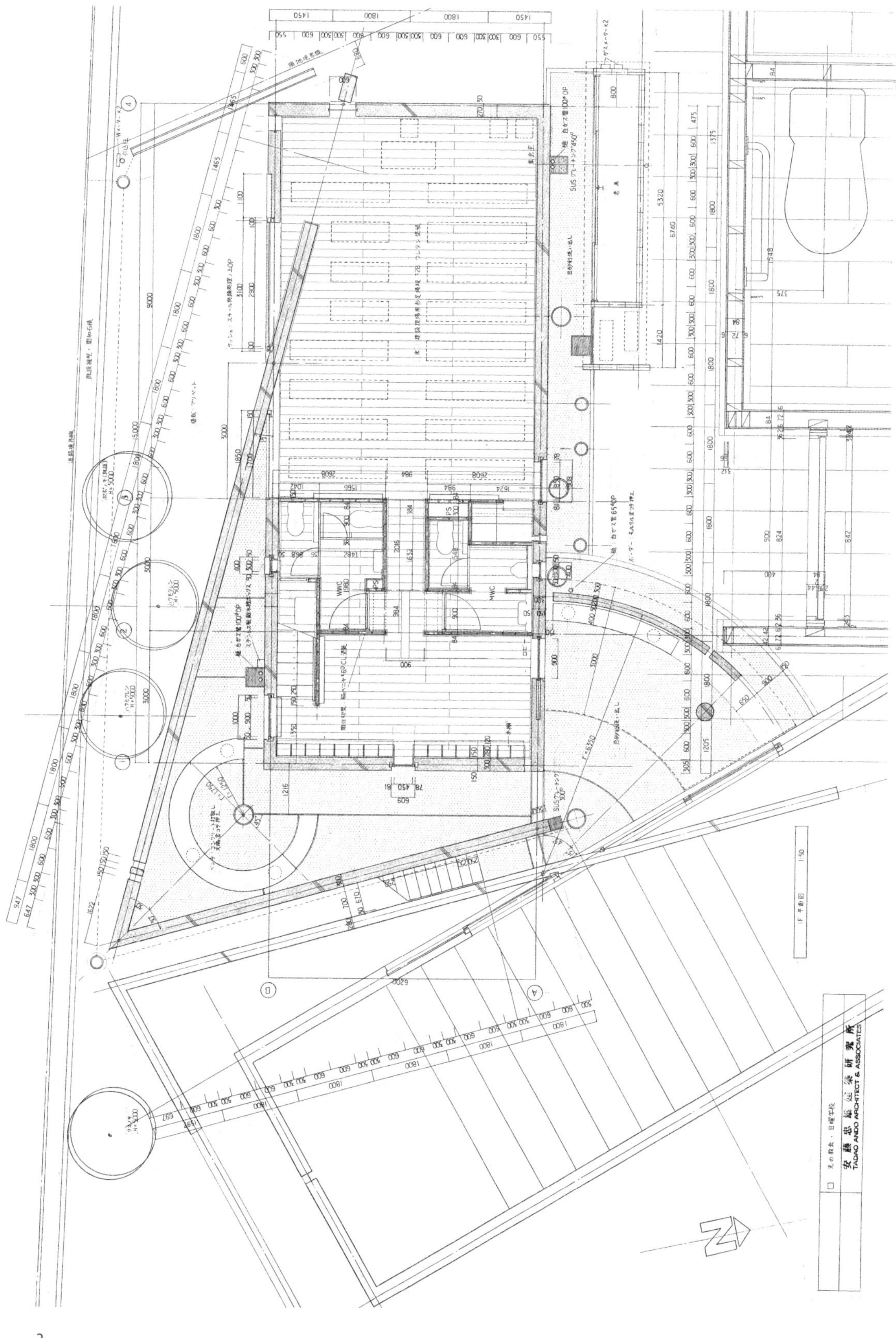

3

Izu Project
伊豆プロジェクト

1. Kamo-gun, Shizuoka, Japan 静岡県賀茂郡
2. 1987.6-1989.12

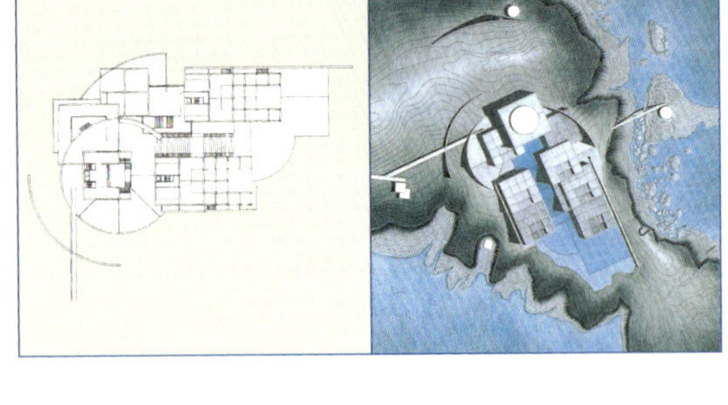

1

This is a hotel design that I undertook during the latter half of the 1980s. The site is in the southern part of the Izu Peninsula, at the top of a slightly elevated cape surrounded by the sea. By making an offset layout as if a set of square grids has been adapted to the topography, with the empty crevices between them as public spaces open to the sea, I proposed a hotel in which the sea may sensed with one's entire body.

1980年代後半に取り組んだホテルの計画である。敷地は伊豆半島南部、周囲を海に囲まれた小高い岬の上。そこに正方形グリッドの集合体を地形になじませるようにずらして配置し、その隙間の余白を海に開かれたパブリックスペースとして、全身で海を感じられるホテルを提案した。

1, 2 Image sketches.
1, 2 イメージスケッチ。

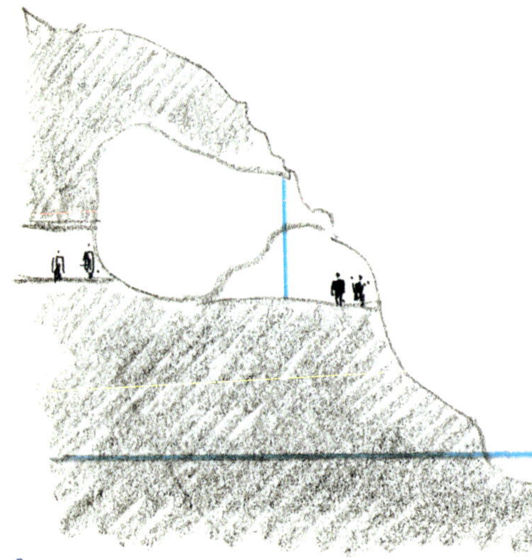

2

3

3 Perspective drawing.
4 Exploratory plan of the site layout. A collection of dwelling units clinging to the cliffs. Like a village on the Aegean, all the spaces are conceived in terms of sightlines toward the sea.

3 パースペクティブドローイング。
4 配置検討図。岸壁に張り付く住戸ユニットの集合体。エーゲ海の集落のように、すべてのスペースが海への視線を意識して考えられる。

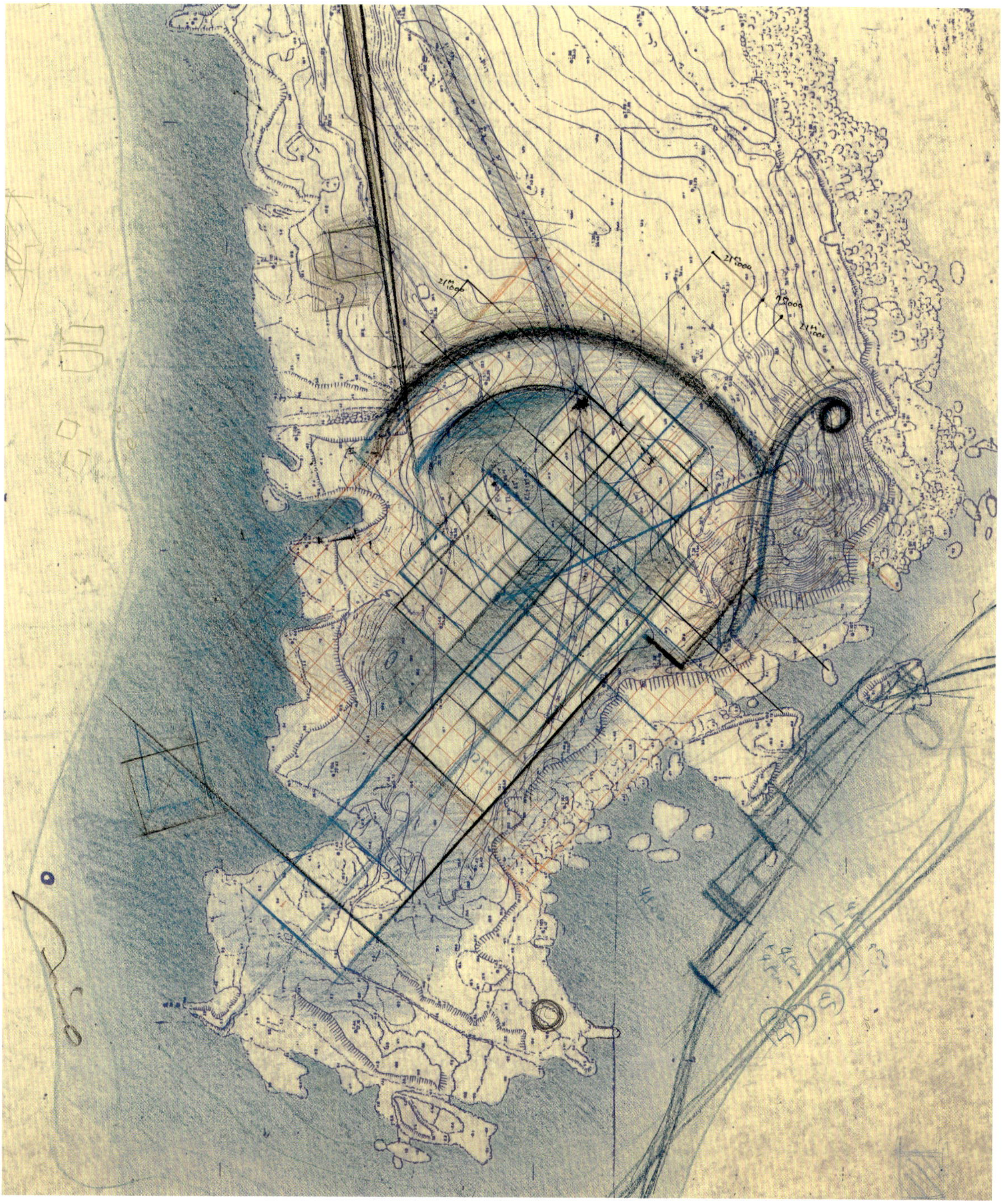

4

Children's Museum, Hyogo
兵庫県立こどもの館

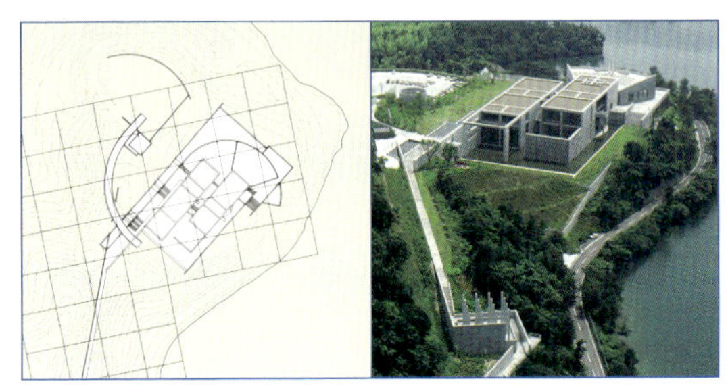

1. Himeji, Hyogo, Japan　兵庫県姫路市
2. 1987.3-1988.3
3. 1988.3-1989.7

This is a cultural and educational facility for children built facing a reservoir extending from the foot of verdant mountains on the outskirts of Himeji, Hyogo Prefecture. Here I thought of responding to the required program for the facility by using the entire site, merging the building into the natural environment. First the building is divided into three parts: the main hall, an intermediate exterior plaza with an array of concrete columns, and an atelier beyond. These were placed independently so as to fill the entire expanse of the 500m-long site. The architecture is a "garden" that subtly lures the children to stroll across the abundant nature of the site.

兵庫県姫路市郊外、緑深い山の裾野に広がる貯水池に面してつくられた、子供のための文化教育施設である。ここで考えたのは、建物を自然環境の中に溶け込ませ、場所全体をもって要求される施設のプログラムに応えること。まず建物を、メインの本館と、コンクリート柱の並ぶ野外の中間広場、その先の工房という、3つの部分に分けて考えた。それらを全長500mの敷地範囲いっぱいに離して配置する。子供たちを、知らずうちに自然豊かな敷地の散策に誘い出す〈庭園〉のイメージの建築である。

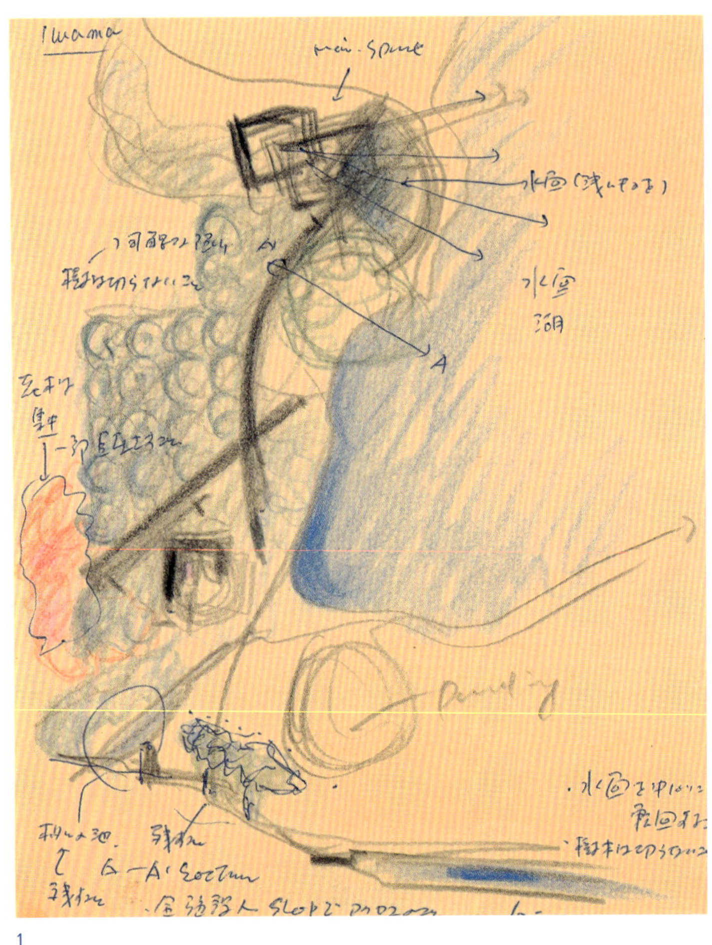

1

2

3

1 Site plan sketch. An image of dispersed functions and a broad waterfront.
2 Richly varied spatial sequence emerging from the integration with the topography.
3 Images of architecture integrated with the site through the medium of water.

1 配置検討スケッチ。機能を分散して、のびやかに広がる水辺のイメージ。
2 地形と一体化することで生まれる変化に富んだ空間のシークエンス。
3 水景を介して敷地と一体化する建築のイメージ。

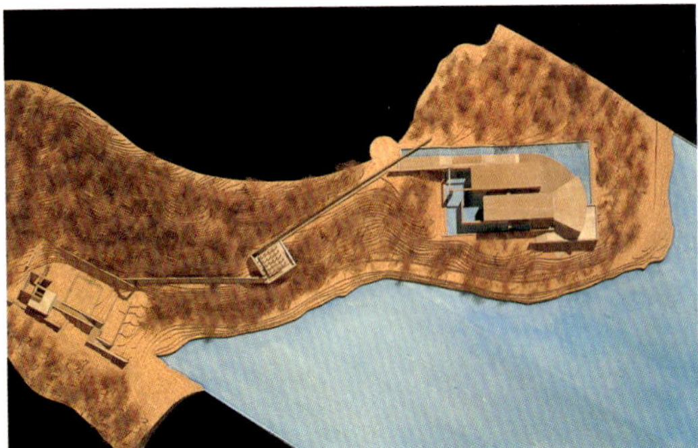

In the large volume of the main hall, "water" is used as a way to fit to the surroundings and moderate the sense of scale. The aim is architecture as an environmental sculpture that inhales the topography, greenery, and water.

大きなヴォリュームとなる本館部分では、そのスケール感を和らげ、周囲になじませる手立てとして、〈水〉を用いている。目指したのは地形と緑、水をたよりに場所に息づく、環境造形としての建築である。

1

1, 2 Sketches drawn while travelling. Various ideas inserted within a simple form.

1, 2 旅先で描かれたスケッチ。シンプルな造形の中に、さまざまなアイディアが組み込まれている。

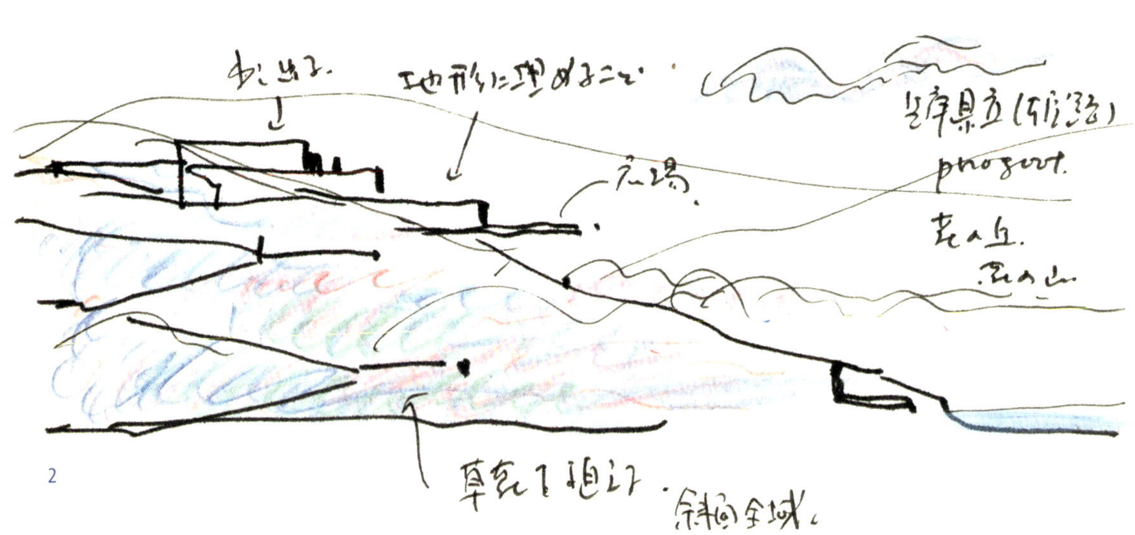

2

Benesse House / Naoshima
ベネッセハウス

1. Kagawa-gun, Kagawa, Japan　香川県香川郡
2. 1988.5-1990.10 (museum) / 1993.5-1994.9 (oval)
3. 1990.10-1992.3 (museum) / 1994.10-1995.6 (oval)

In the latter half of the 1980s, a cultural project was initiated for the regeneration of Naoshima, a small island floating in the Inland Sea, as an "island of nature filled with art." The first building was Benesse House Museum, a "lodging" art museum that includes accommodation facilities, constructed at the southern end of the island on a cape surrounded on three sides by the sea. Here I conceived an "invisible" architecture buried in the beautiful nature, and the image of a "borderless" art museum expanding into the seascape without distinctions between interior and exterior.

1980年代後半、瀬戸内海に浮かぶ小島、直島を〈自然あふれるアートの島〉として再生する文化プロジェクトがスタートした。その最初の建築である「ベネッセハウス ミュージアム」は、島の南端部、三方を海に囲まれた岬の上につくられた、宿泊施設を伴う〈滞在型〉美術館である。ここで考えたのは、美しい自然の中に埋もれて「見えない」建築、内外の区別なく海景の中に広がる「境界のない」美術館のイメージだ。

1

1 Regenerating bare mountain as a sacred place for nature and art—sketches of the project process laid out like an emakimono picture scroll.
2 This art museum is approached by boat from the sea. The scattered architectural elements are even more conspicuous in the rich natural landscape.

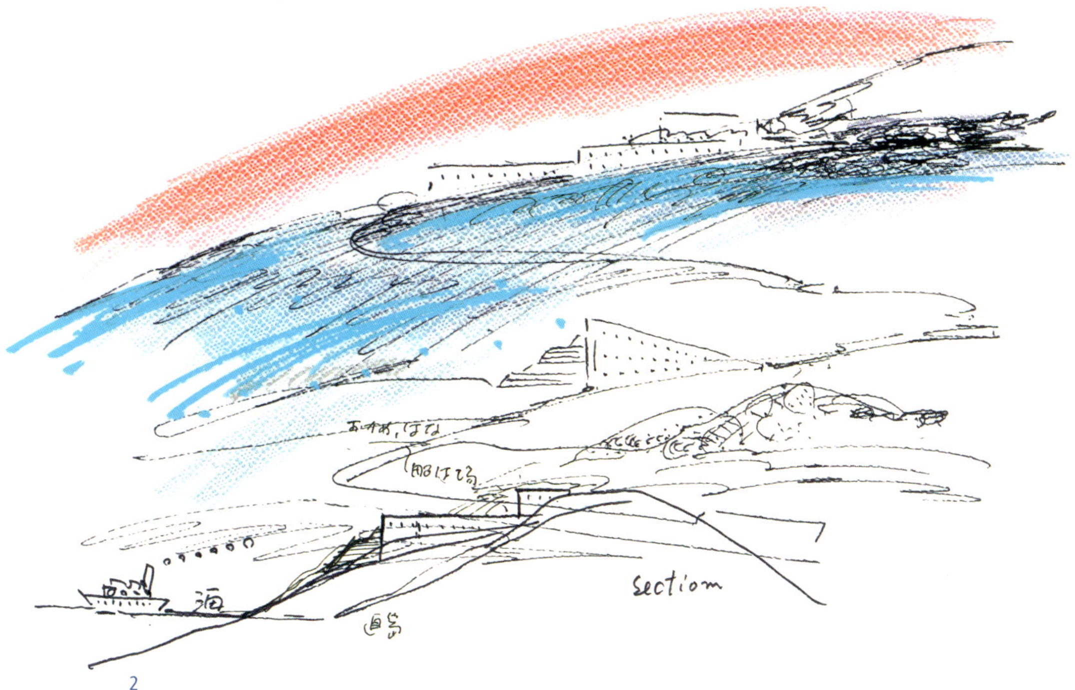

2

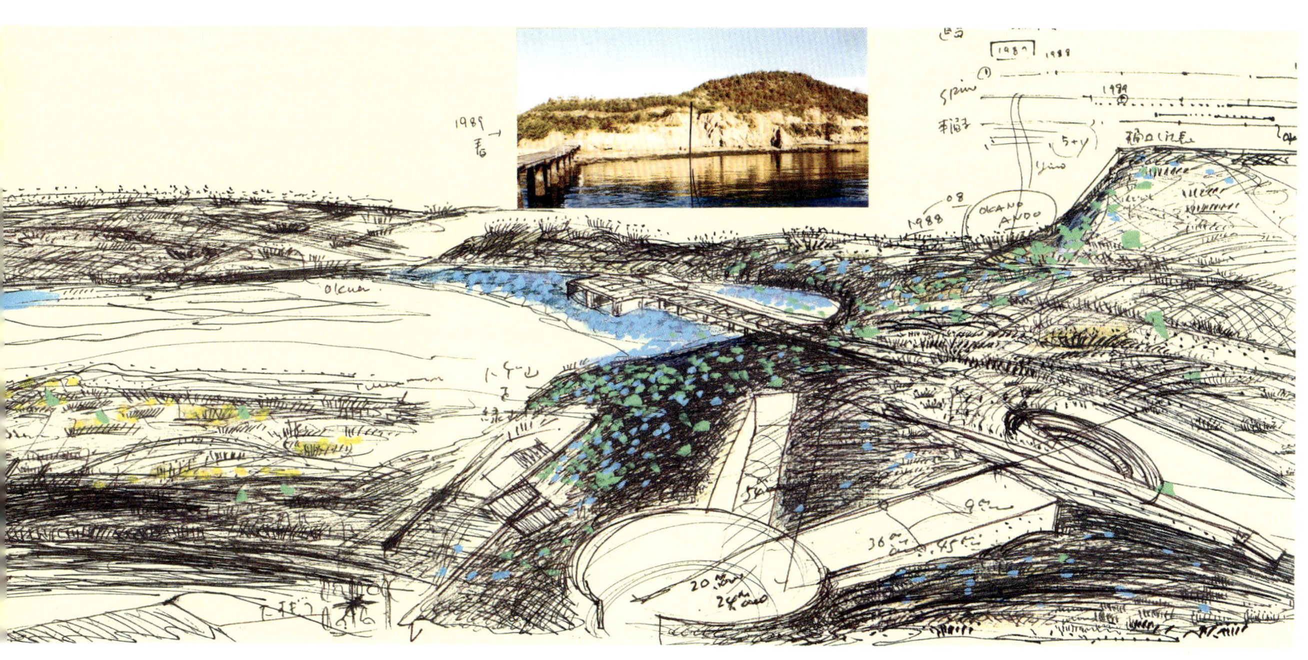

1 ハゲ山を自然とアートの聖地へと再生する——プロジェクトのプロセスを絵巻物のように綴ったスケッチ。
2 この美術館へは船に乗って海からアプローチする。散りばめられた建築のエレメントが、豊かな自然の風景をさらに際立たせる。

Three years after the completion of the museum I made a lodging wing called Oval, as an annex on the hill to the rear. A composition in which the guest rooms are arrayed around an elliptical water garden at the center, this architecture is intended as a microcosm of abstracted nature responding to the wide seascape of the Inland Sea.

ミュージアムの完成から3年後、その背後の丘の上にアネックスとして宿泊棟「オーバル」をつくった。楕円形の水庭を中心に宿泊室の並ぶ構成で、おおらかな瀬戸内の海景に呼応する、抽象化された自然の小宇宙を意図した建築だ。

1 Study sketch of the site layout. Oval is freely placed following the topography. It is connected to the museum by a cable car.
2 Image sketch. An elliptical space that vividly frames the sky.

1 配置検討スケッチ。地形に沿っておおらかに配される オーバル。ミュージアムとはケーブルカーで結ばれる。
2 イメージスケッチ。空を鮮やかに切り取る楕円の空間。

1

2

This was an unplanned addition, but on the other hand I think that the difference in timing is related to the natural development of the architecture. Over time, the greenery of the hill grows thicker and the geometry of the composition becomes further embedded.

予定外の増築であったが、逆にその時間のズレが自然な建築の展開につながったように思う。時とともに丘の緑は深まり、構成の幾何学は埋没していっている。

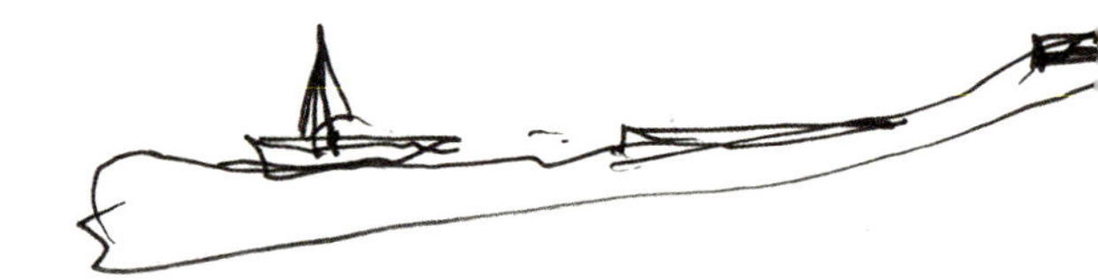

3

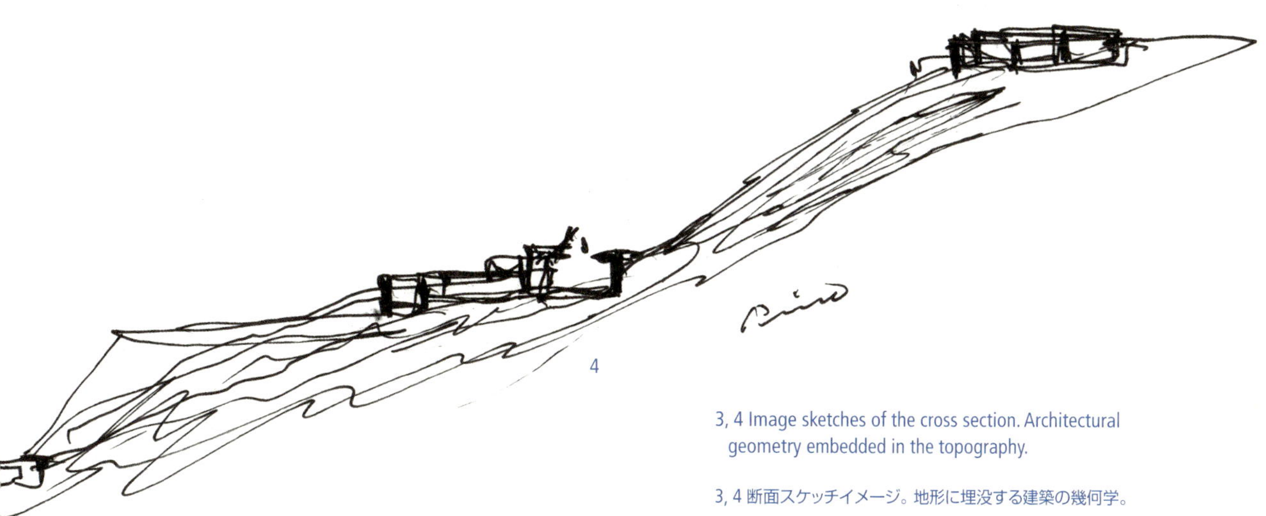

4

3, 4 Image sketches of the cross section. Architectural geometry embedded in the topography.

3, 4 断面スケッチイメージ。地形に埋没する建築の幾何学。

When I first visited Naoshima, I was surprised by the poor access to this isolated island and the destruction of its natural environment due to the effects of the steel smelting industry that is its major economic support, and I thought about the harshness of reality. However, on this island, with the strength of the client, who has made new relationships between place, art, and architecture, and the passion and tenacity of the art director, over time the project has enlarged in area and program, and staged additions have accumulated as if the buildings were propagating like living things. In this process of constant growth, a sense of life is the source of the energy of this place.

Sketches of the island while the museum was under construction. Through the great efforts involved in constantly making places, this small island in the Inland Sea—sculpted by isolation and time—has become a sacred place for presenting art to the world.

ミュージアム建設中の島のスケッチ。継続的な場所づくりの努力がひっそりと時間を刻んできた内海の小島を世界に発信するアートの聖地にした。

直島を初めて訪れたときは、離島というアクセスの悪さと、何より島を支えた金属精錬産業の影響で荒廃した自然環境に驚き、現実の厳しさを思った。だが、この島で、場所とアートと建築との新しい関係をつくるのだというクライアントと、アートディレクターの情熱と執念は逞しく、時を経るごとにプロジェクトはエリアとプログラムを拡大、建物も生物が増殖するように、段階的に増築が重ねられた。常に成長の過程にある、その生命感がこの場所のエネルギーの源である。

Museum of Literature, Himeji
姫路文学館

1. Himeji, Hyogo, Japan　兵庫県姫路市
2. 1988.7-1989.11 (phase Ⅰ) / 1993.9-1994.9 (phase Ⅱ)
3. 1989.7-1991.3 (phase Ⅰ) / 1994.10-1996.5 (phase Ⅱ)

The site is located in the center of Himeji City, 500m northwest of Himeji Castle at the foot of Mt. Otoko. This is a museum intended to introduce local authors related to the area, such as Tetsuro Watsuji, and their personal literary worlds. The theme here was to preserve the rich context of the place unaltered, bringing it into the building as "borrowed scenery." I thought of the site as a unified environment, actively preserving historical traces such as the old aristocratic residences remaining on the site, recomposing the whole as a garden, and embedding contemporary architecture mediated by a water garden. Beyond a mere archive, I wanted to make architecture that gives a strong sense of the uniqueness of this place.

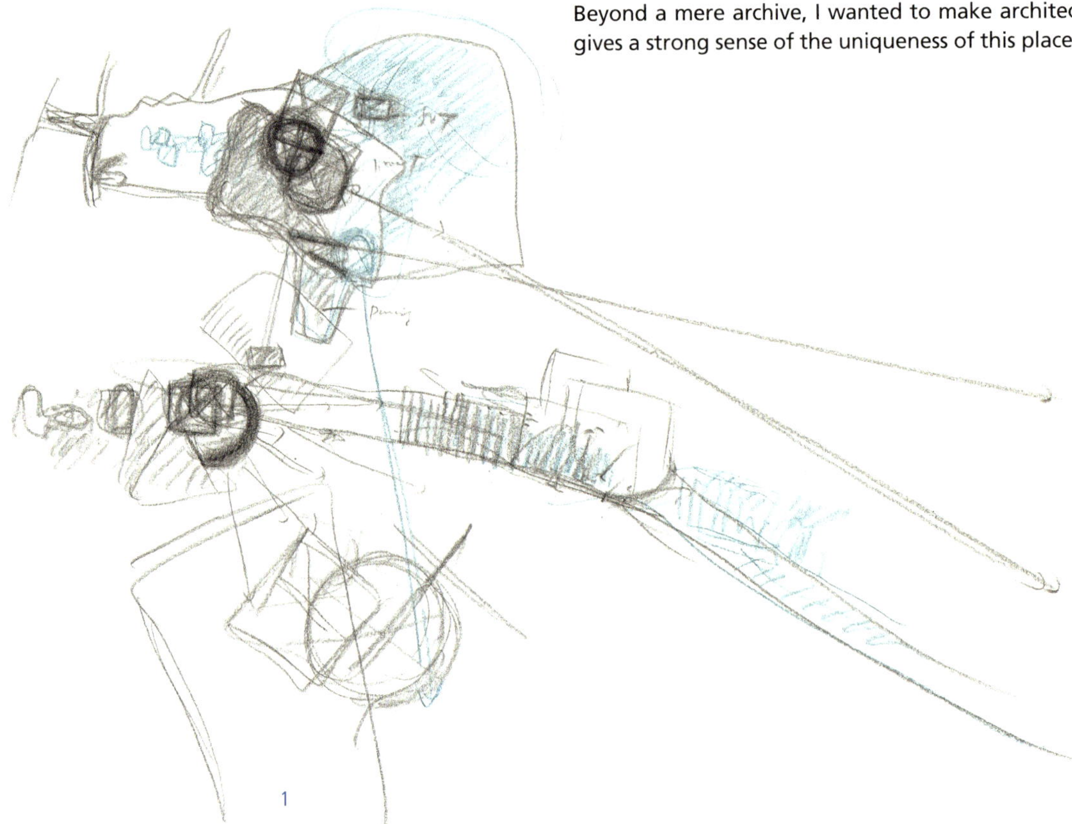

1

1, 2 Set in a location opposite Mt. Hime, where Himeji Castle stands, a very beautiful view of the castle can be obtained from the site. This view forms one axis of the architectural composition.

3 Detailed plan. The wooden house to the west, originally slated for removal, is preserved, and the house on the east side of the slope, in which Tetsuro Watsuji was born, is restored. The cascade of water is a buffer zone that gently connects the building with the site context.

2

敷地は姫路市の中心部、姫路城から500m西北の男山のふもとに位置する。和辻哲郎など地域ゆかりの文人たちとその文学世界を紹介する展示施設である。ここでは、場所のもつ豊かなコンテクストをそのまま、借景として建物に取り込むことを主題とした。そして考えたのが、敷地内に残る旧華族の屋敷など歴史の痕跡を積極的に残し、全体を庭園として再構成して、その中に水庭を介して現代建築を埋め込む環境一体型のサイト。単なる資料館を超えて、場所の個性を強く感じられるような建築をつくりたかった。

1, 2 姫路城の建つ姫山と対の位置にある、敷地からはお城の最も美しい眺めが得られる。その眺望を、建築構成のひとつの軸とする。

3 平面詳細図。当初撤去の予定であった西側の木造家屋を残し、東側の斜面には和辻哲郎の生家を再現する。それらの敷地のコンテクストと建築とを緩やかにつなぐ緩衝領域としての水のカスケード。

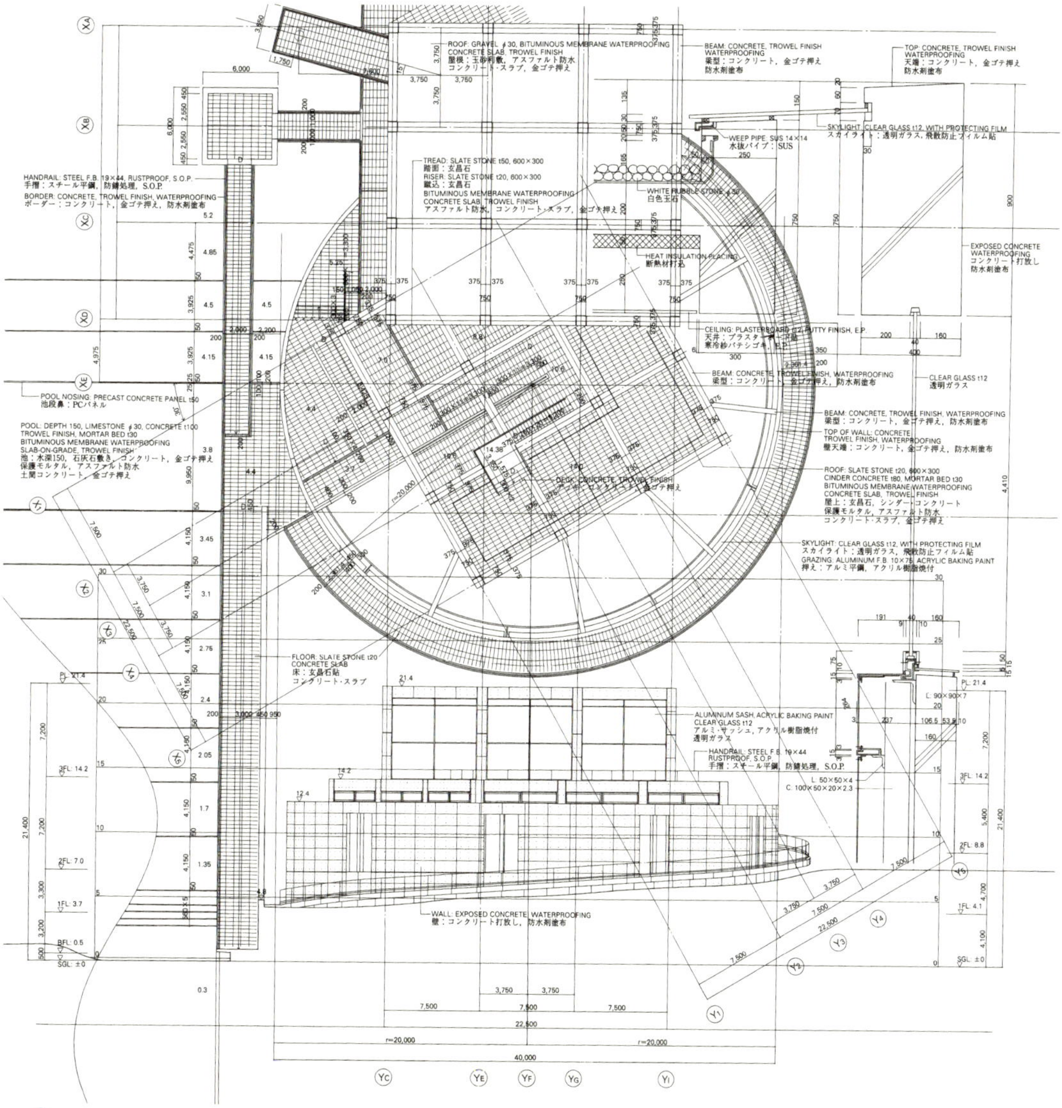

3

Five years after the completion of the Museum of Literature, I added a new south hall containing a library. The theme was to produce a "relationality" that brings about a new "ma" (intentionally empty space) in this place, while being integrated with the existing environment including the main hall. The theme was architecture with enhanced circulation routes integrated with the nature of the existing park, so a concrete box was combined with a glass box to make architecture with a buoyant expression.

文学館完成から5年後に、図書室をもつ新館（南館）を増築した。主題は、本館を含めた既存の環境の中に溶け込みつつ、場に新たな間をもたらす〈関係性〉をつくり出すことだった。既存の庭園の中に自然に溶け込み、その回遊性を増すような軽さをもった建築を主題に、コンクリートのボックスにガラスボックスを組み合わせた、軽快な表情の建築をつくった。

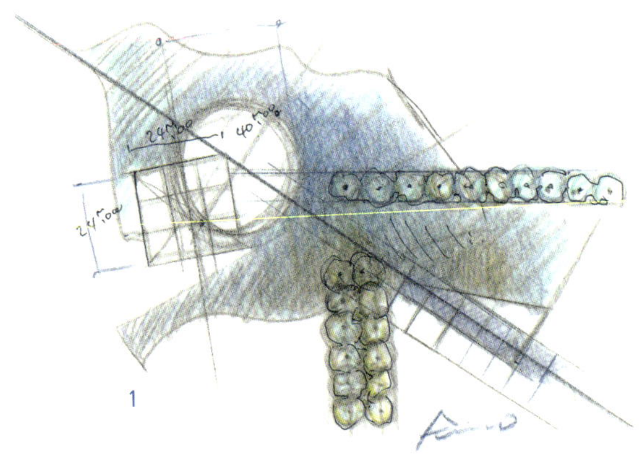

1

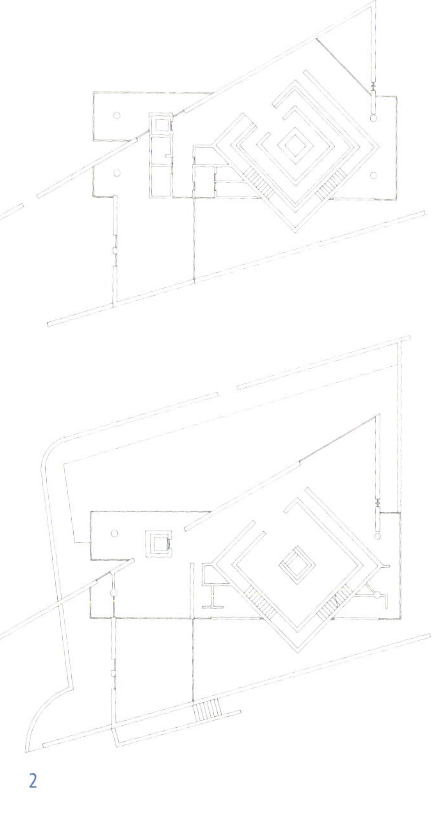

2

1 Image sketch.
2 Plans.
3 Exploratory drawing of the site layout. The main hall and the south hall, related in an axial composition, are gently connected by flowing water and lush greenery. Enhancing the circulatory character by means of an addition.

1 イメージスケッチ。
2 平面図。
3 配置検討図。構成の軸線をもって関係づけられる本館と南館は流れる水と生い茂る緑によって緩やかに結ばれる。増築により、回遊性が増した。

3

Suntory Museum+Plaza
サントリーミュージアム＋マーメイド広場

1. Osaka, Osaka, Japan　大阪府大阪市
2. 1989.8-1992.8
3. 1992.9-1994.8

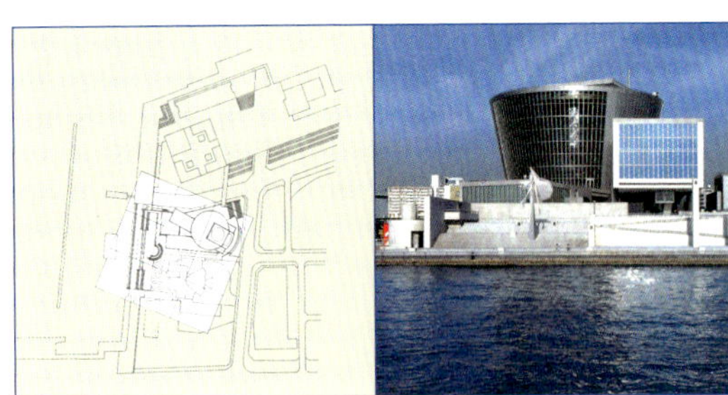

The site is located in a corner of Tempozan Harbor Village, a development that has been underway since the 1980s on Osaka's Nanko waterfront. This is an art museum with a total floor area of 2,700m^2. Here I conceived a building that exceeds the boundaries of the given site with a waterfront space extending to the sea. In other words, I tried to reorganize the entire public space, including the water edge belonging to the city and the sea belonging to the nation. The result is a water plaza, 100m wide and 40m deep, extending between the museum and the sea edge.

敷地は大阪南港、1980年代から大阪のウォーターフロントとして開発が進められてきた「天保山ハーバービレッジ」の一角に位置する。延床面積2,700m^{2}の美術館である。ここでは与えられた敷地の範囲を越えて建築を考え、そこから海に至るまでの水際空間、すなわち大阪市の所有する護岸、国の所有する海上をも含めた公共の空間全体の再編を試みた。その成果が美術館と海の水際線の間に広がる幅100m、奥行き40mの親水広場である。

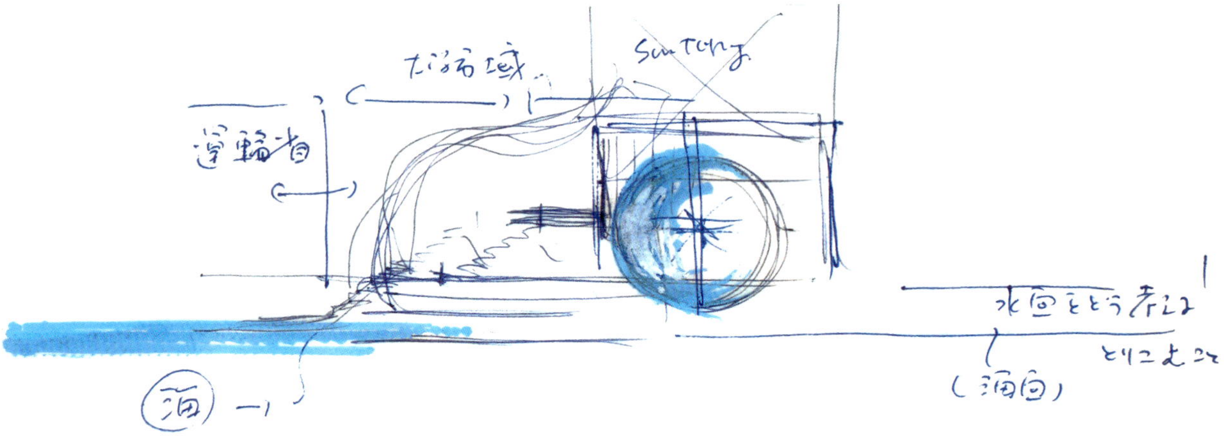

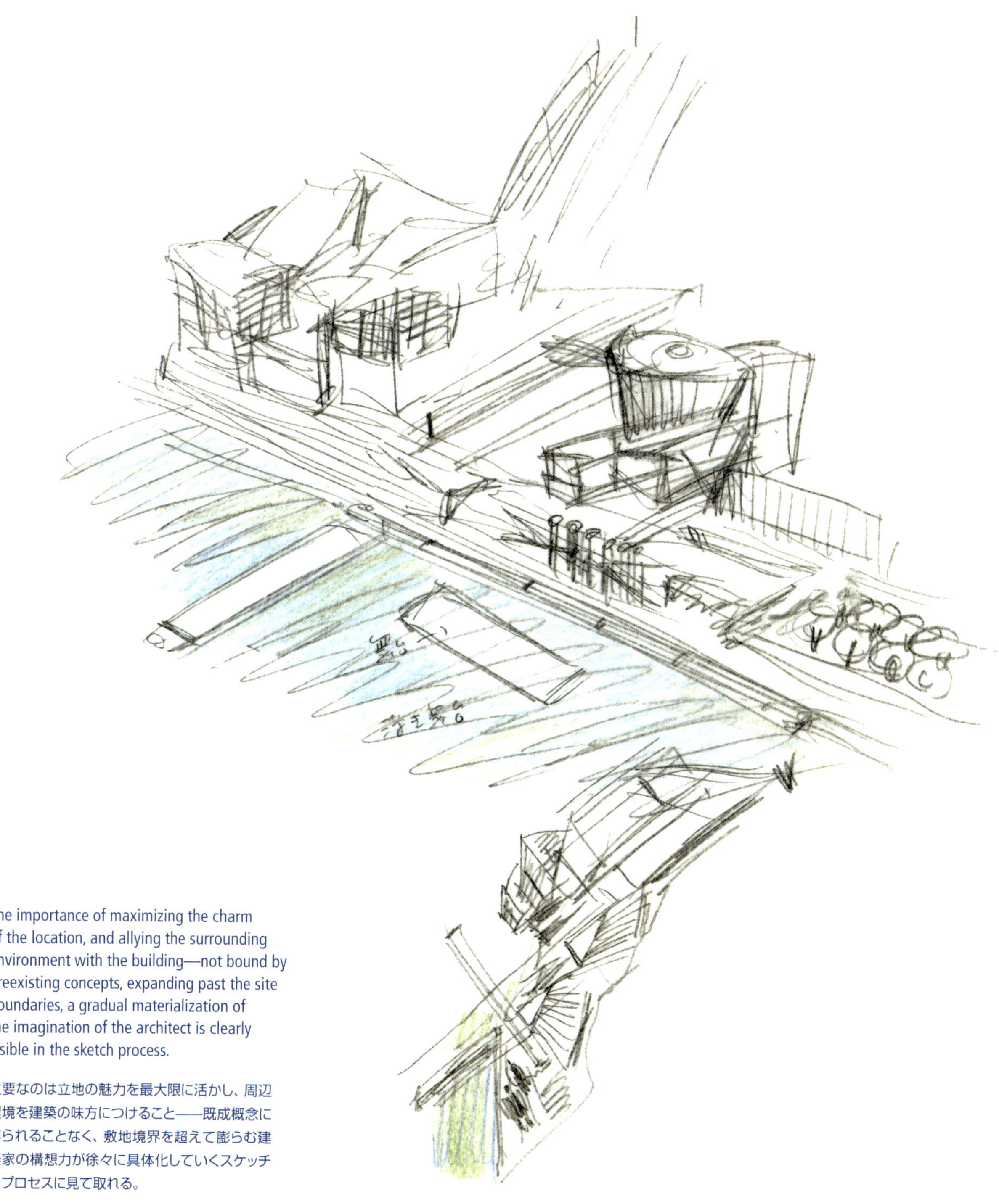

The importance of maximizing the charm of the location, and allying the surrounding environment with the building—not bound by preexisting concepts, expanding past the site boundaries, a gradual materialization of the imagination of the architect is clearly visible in the sketch process.

重要なのは立地の魅力を最大限に活かし、周辺環境を建築の味方につけること——既成概念に縛られることなく、敷地境界を超えて膨らむ建築家の構想力が徐々に具体化していくスケッチのプロセスに見て取れる。

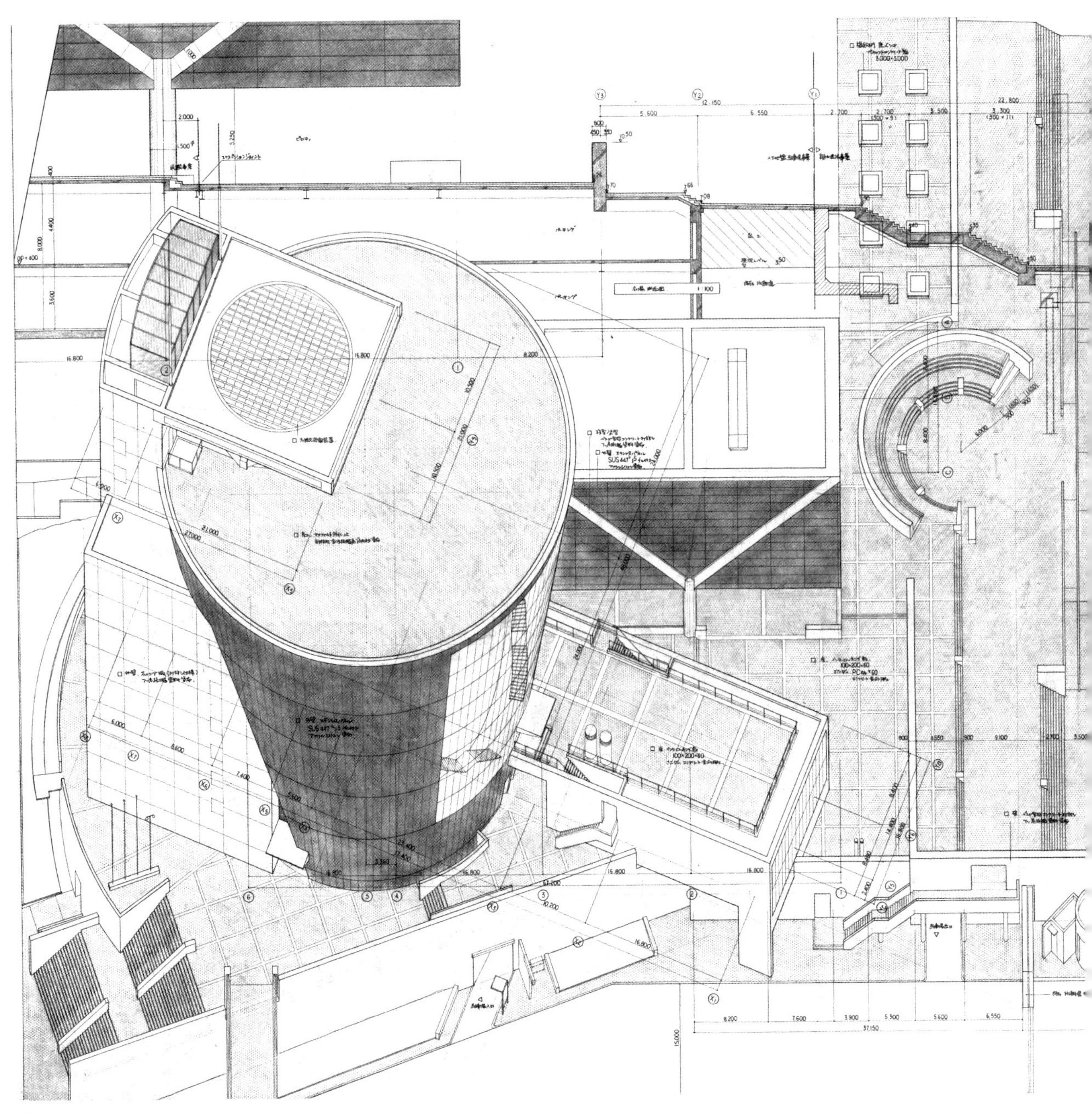

1

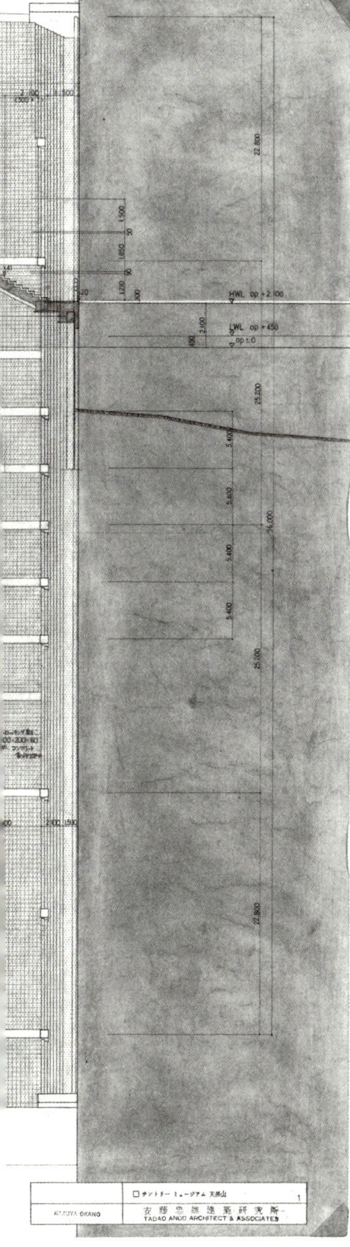

1 Axonometric. The main part of the museum is composed of two rectangular volumes projecting out to the sea at a different angles and different levels, on axis with an inverted conical cylinder containing a spherical 3D-theater. This architecture has a powerful expression, with a sense of scale and symbolism that holds its own within the maritime scenery.
2 Exploratory sketches of the plaza. It is gently connected to the sea by means of descending slopes and stairs. The five concrete columns standing tall at the water's edge give a rhythm to the scene.

1 アクソノメトリック。美術館本体は、球形の3Dシアターを内包する逆円錐型のシリンダーを軸に、2本の直方体が角度とレベルを違えて海に突き出す構成。湾岸部の風景の中で、海と対峙しても負けないスケール感と象徴性をもつ力強い建築表現。
2 広場の検討スケッチ。海に向かって降りていく階段とスロープで緩やかに海と接続する。水際に屹立する5本のコンクリート柱が風景にリズムをもたらす。

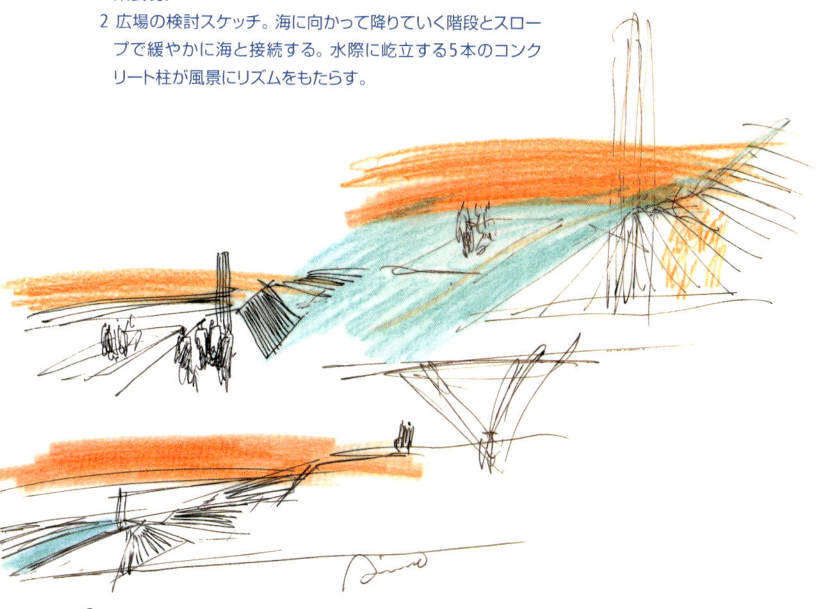

2

Water Temple
真言宗本福寺水御堂

1. Awaji, Hyogo, Japan　兵庫県淡路市
2. 1989.11-1990.12
3. 1990.12-1991.9

The site is located on top of a slightly elevated hill overlooking Osaka Bay in the northeast part of Awaji Island. This is a mido hall made as a freestanding addition to Honpuku-ji Temple, part of the Ninna-ji sect of Shingon Buddhism. Here, I wanted to enhance the significance of a temple as a "place for people to escape from everyday life and to take time for contemplation." The main theme of this architecture is the time and space of the dramatic shift from the profane to the sacred. A lotus pond awaits people at the end of a long approach route, and then a flight of steps sliced into the pond leads to the underwater hall space engulfed in vermilion light—the intention of the architecture is not a "simile" of tradition that relies on references to tangible shapes, but a "metaphor" by means of spaces.

1

2

敷地は淡路島北東部の大阪湾を一望する小高い丘の上に位置する。真言宗仁和寺派に属する本福寺の増築として、独立したかたちでつくった御堂である。ここではお寺がもつ意味を「人々が日常から抜け出し、考える時をもつための場所」という点に集約して考え、俗から聖への劇的な移行、その時間と空間による表現を建築の主題とした。長いアプローチの末に人々を待ち受ける蓮池、池を切り裂く階段が導く、朱色の光に包まれた水面下の御堂の空間——意図したのは具体的なかたちの参照にたよる伝統の〈直喩〉ではない、空間による〈隠喩〉の建築であった。

1 Making a circular flower basin on the gently sloping site—from the moment I received the commission, the image was a hall with an artificial flower basin as its roof.

2 Sketch of the scenery of the site in which the existing temple stands. A drawing of the flowers on the temple roof.

3 The early studies had a perfect circle as the plan shape of the pond. The idea was to give the hall a square plan with the same center, and cover this simple geometrical space with dense greenery.

1 緩やかな勾配の敷地に円形の水盤をつくる——依頼を受けた当初から、人工の水盤を屋根とする御堂のイメージがあった。

2 既存寺院が建つ敷地の風景スケッチ。寺の屋根に重ねて花の絵が描かれている。

3 当初検討していた池の平面形状は正円。御堂は中心を同じくした正方形平面とし、その純粋幾何学による空間を鬱蒼とした緑が覆うというアイディアだった。

3

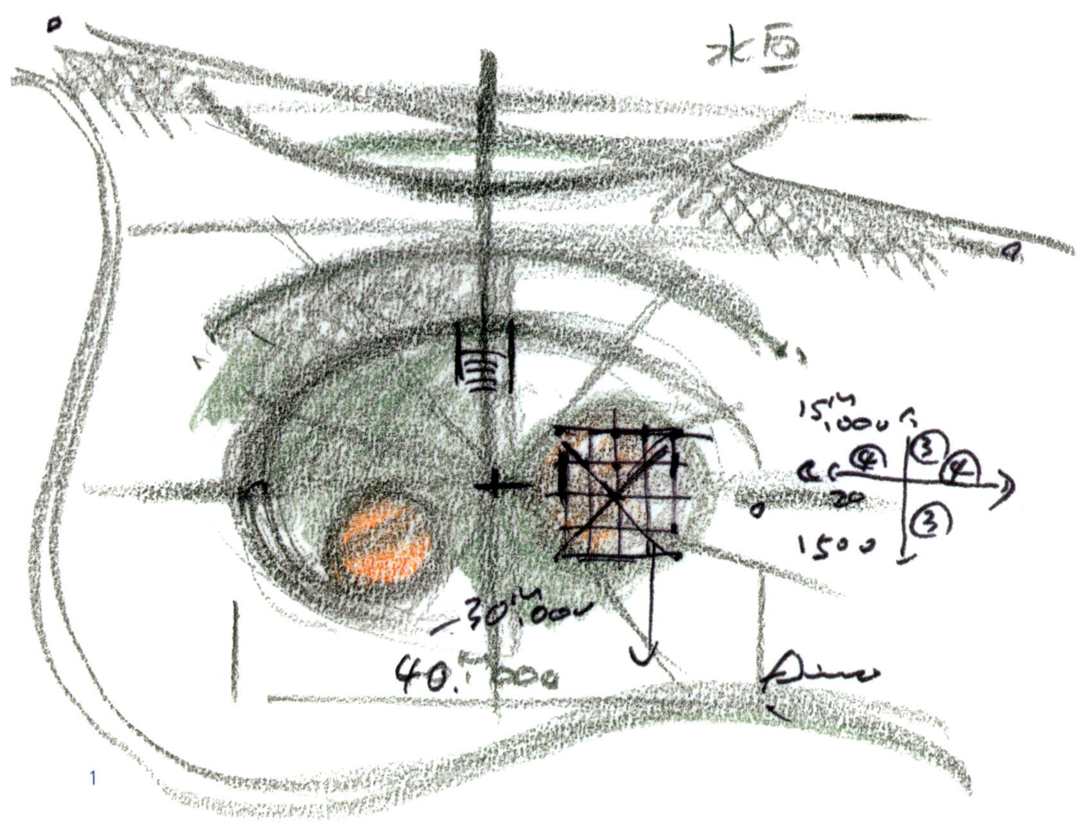

1

1 For Buddhist architecture, in which the roof gives an impression of authority, this is a bold proposal to bury the hall under a flower basin. A circular-plan main hall and a square-plan priest's quarters are arranged below an ellipse. The approach route to the underground level is an exterior staircase that divides the ellipse in two along its minor axis.

2, 3 Plan and section drafts. The main hall and the priest's quarters are both arranged as if buried in the sloping site. The square grid of the main hall faces west, with the idea that western light would shine in behind the sanctuary.

1 屋根を権威の象徴とする仏教建築にあって、御堂を水盤の下に埋め込むという大胆な提案。楕円の下には円形平面の本堂と正方形平面の庫裏が配される。地階へのアプローチは、楕円の短軸に沿って水盤を2分する外階段とした。

2, 3 平面、断面の検討図。本堂、庫裏ともに、傾斜地に埋め込むように配置されている。本堂の正方形グリッドは西向きとし、内陣の背後から西方の光が差し込むように考えられている。

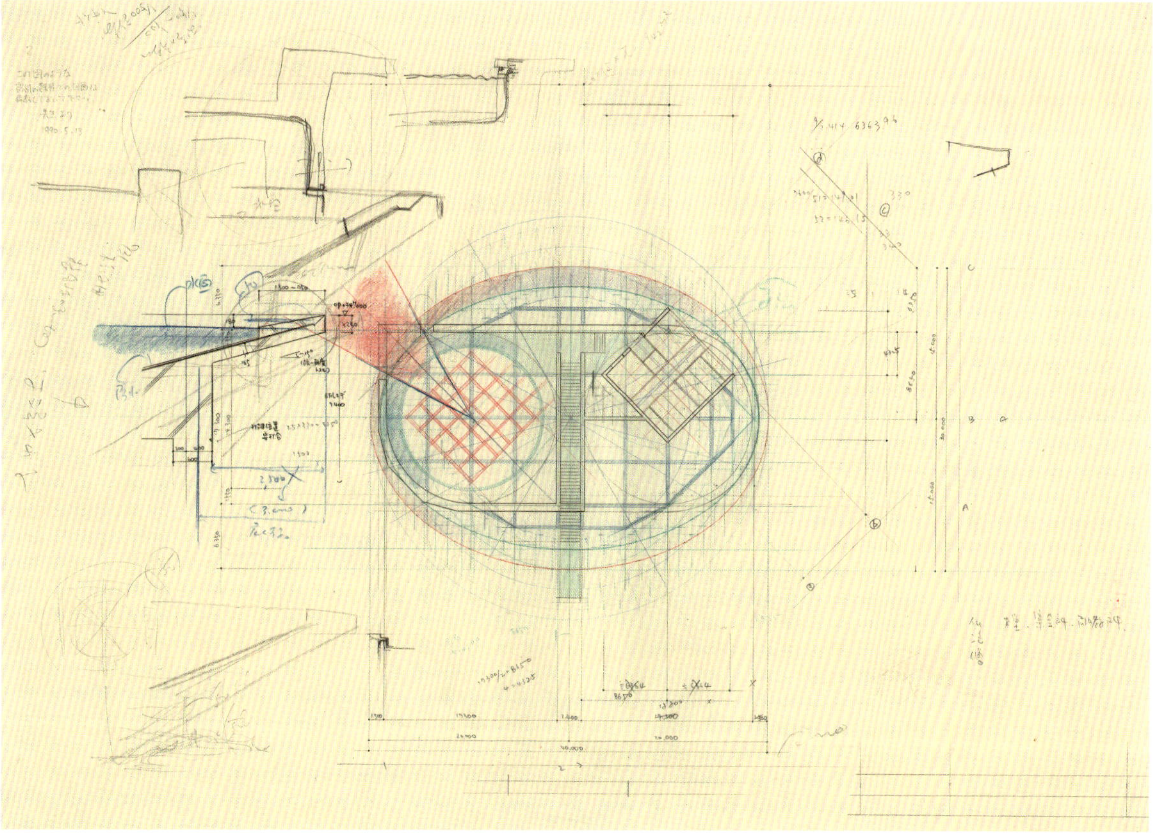

2

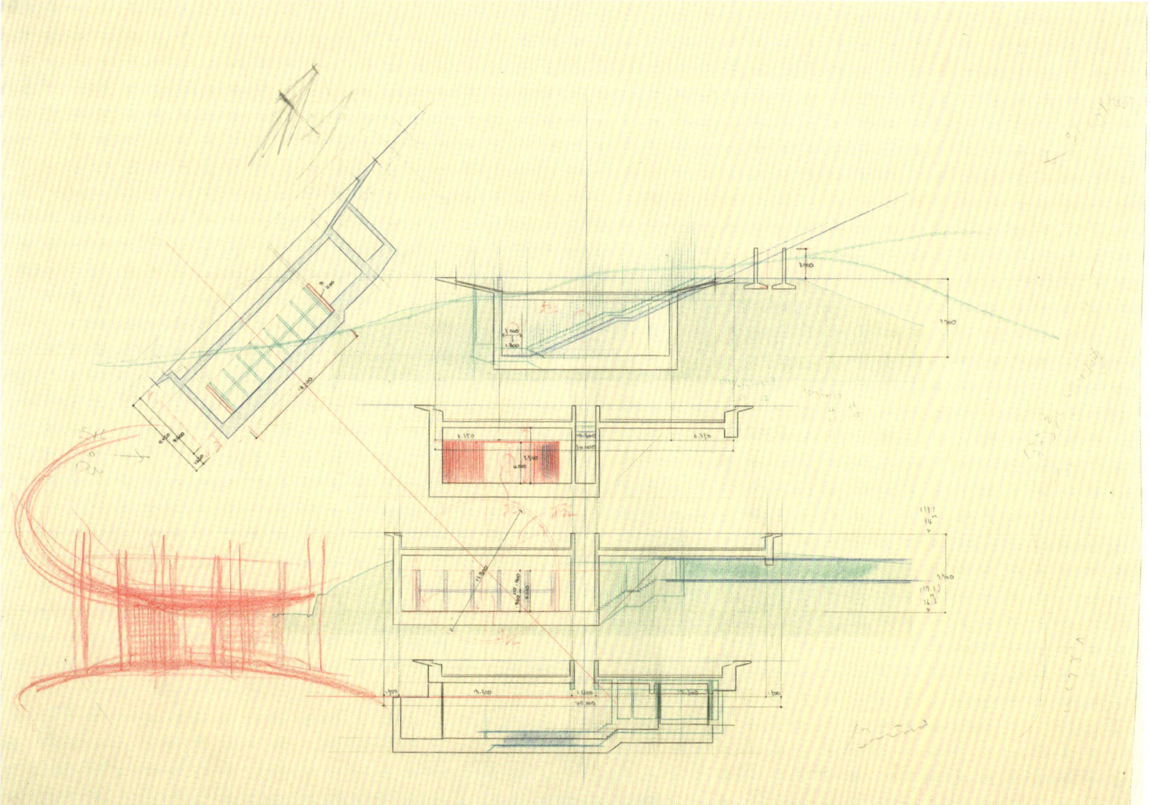

3

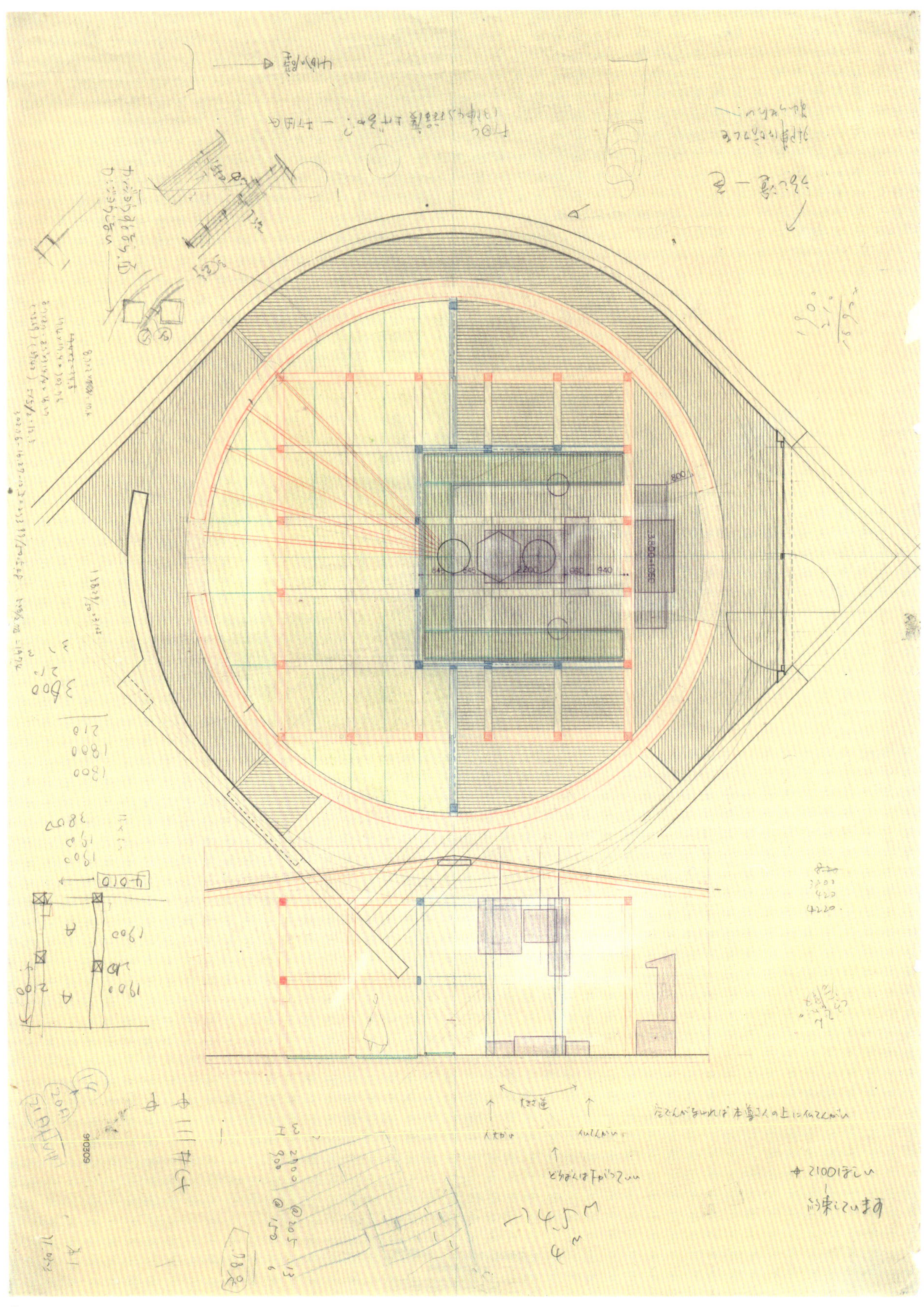

1

The main hall, with an elliptical flower basin as a roof, is a room with many closely spaced columns arrayed in a grid layout, all painted vermilion. The origin of the "vermilion" expression is the Jodo Hall of Jodo-ji temple in Ono City, Hyogo Prefecture. The powerful space produced by this structure is momentarily stained deep crimson by the light of the setting sun. I wanted to reproduce that magical scene with contemporary architectural techniques.

楕円形の水盤を屋根とする本堂内部は、グリッド状に柱が林立する多柱室として、そのすべてを朱色に塗ることにした。〈朱色〉の発想の原点は、兵庫県小野市に建つ浄土寺浄土堂だ。力強い構造むき出しの空間を、落日の光が一瞬真紅に染め上げる。あの幻想的光景を現代建築の手法で再現したいと考えていた。

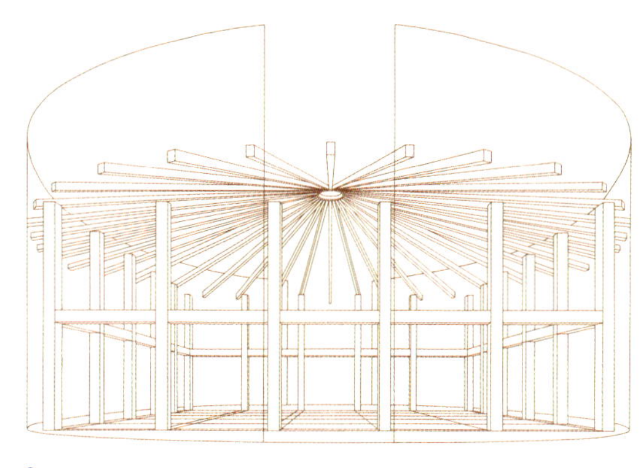

2

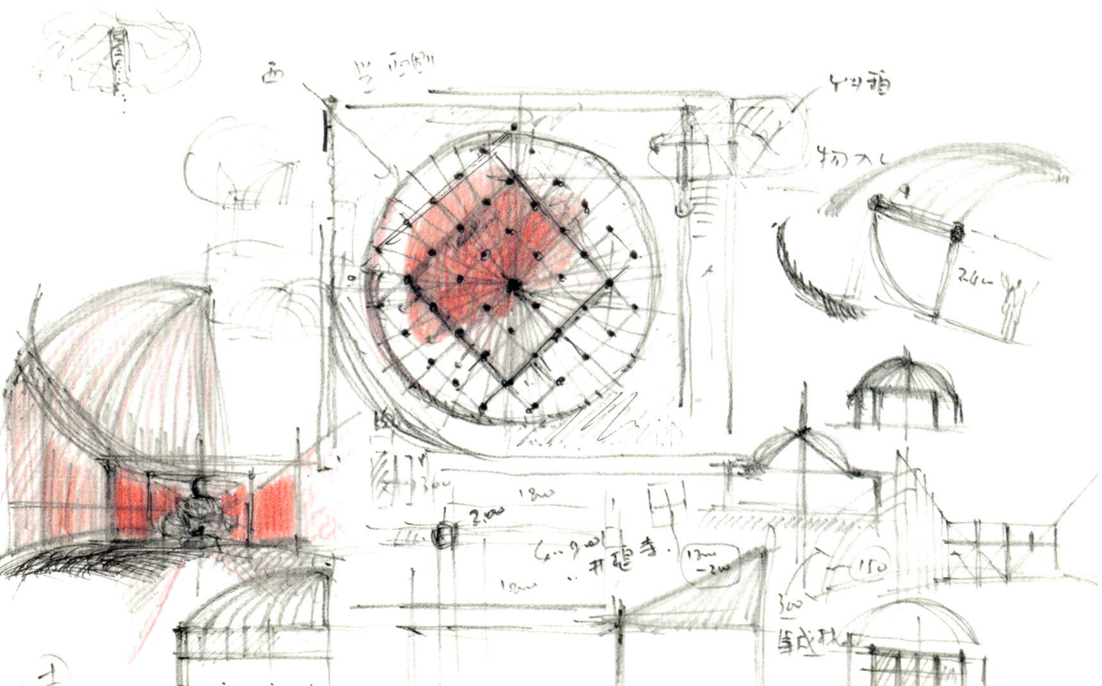

3

1 Detailed exploratory drawing of the main hall. The closely spaced grid of posts, and the lattice screens filling the gaps between the posts, partition the sanctuary and the outer space. Vermilion lattice windows facing due west are installed directly behind the sanctuary. Exterior light enters the room through this red filter, and the entire space is suffused with a soft vermilion.

2, 3 Initially, the intention was to install a suspended wooden ceiling in the upper part of the hall, but due to problems with the ceiling height it became an exposed concrete ceiling. As a result, the space further emphasizes the composition of nested boxes.

1 本堂の詳細検討図。グリッド状に林立する柱と、その柱間を埋める格子のスクリーンが内陣と外陣を区切っている。ちょうど内陣の背後の位置に、正確に西に向いた朱色の格子窓が設けられている。外光はこの赤いフィルターを通して室内に入り込み、空間全体を柔らかな朱色で包みこむ。

2, 3 当初、本堂上部は木造の化粧天井とする予定であったが、天井高さの問題で、コンクリートの直天井となった。その結果、入れ子状の構成がより強調された空間となった。

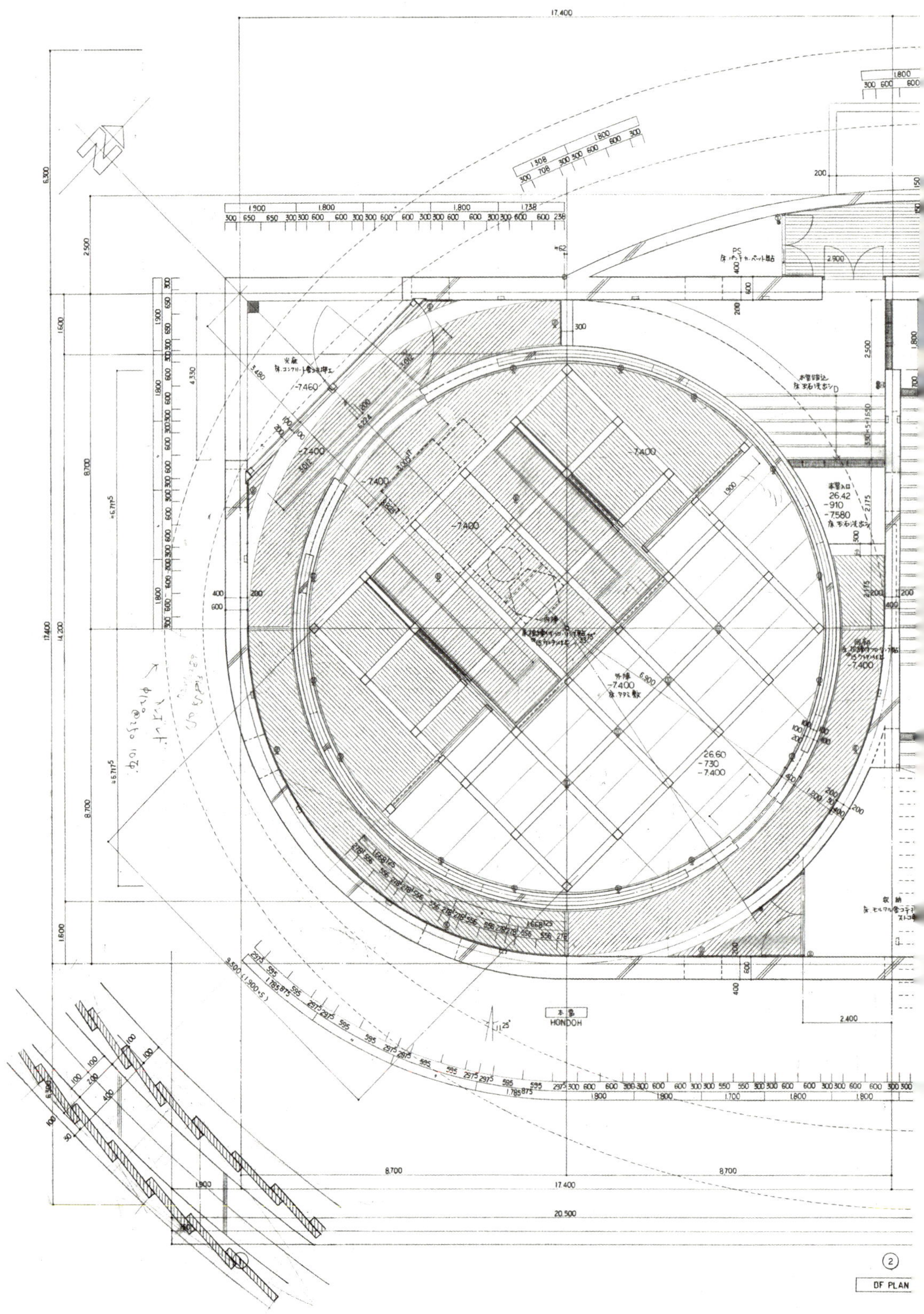

Detailed plan drawing of the underground level. Below the elliptical flower basin measuring 30m on its minor axis and 40m on its major axis, a circular main hall and a square priest's quarters are arranged at an angle according to their orientation.

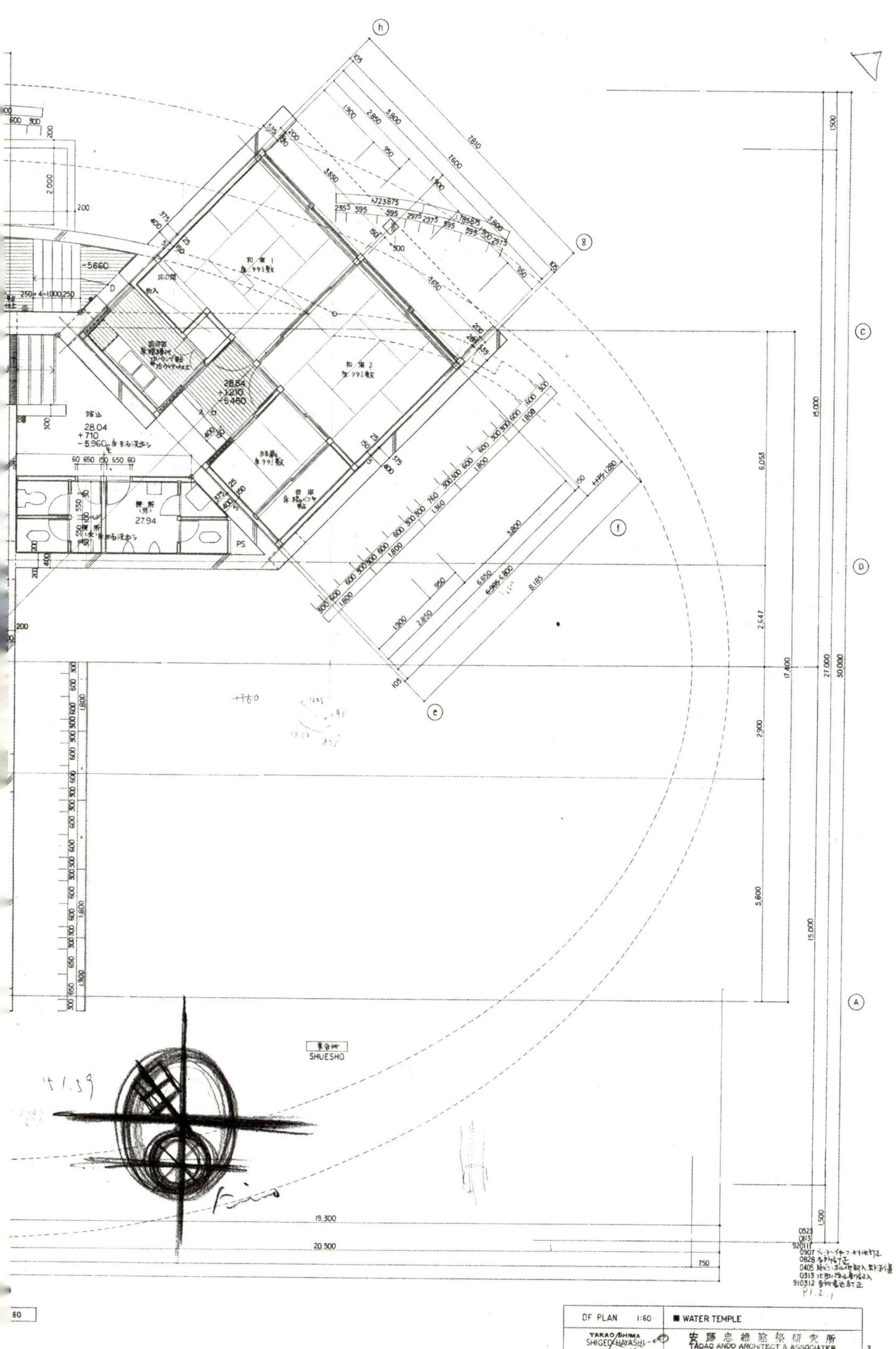

地下1階の平面詳細図。長径40m、短径30mの楕円形の水盤の下に、円形の本堂と正方形の庫裏が、方位に合わせて角度を振って配されている。

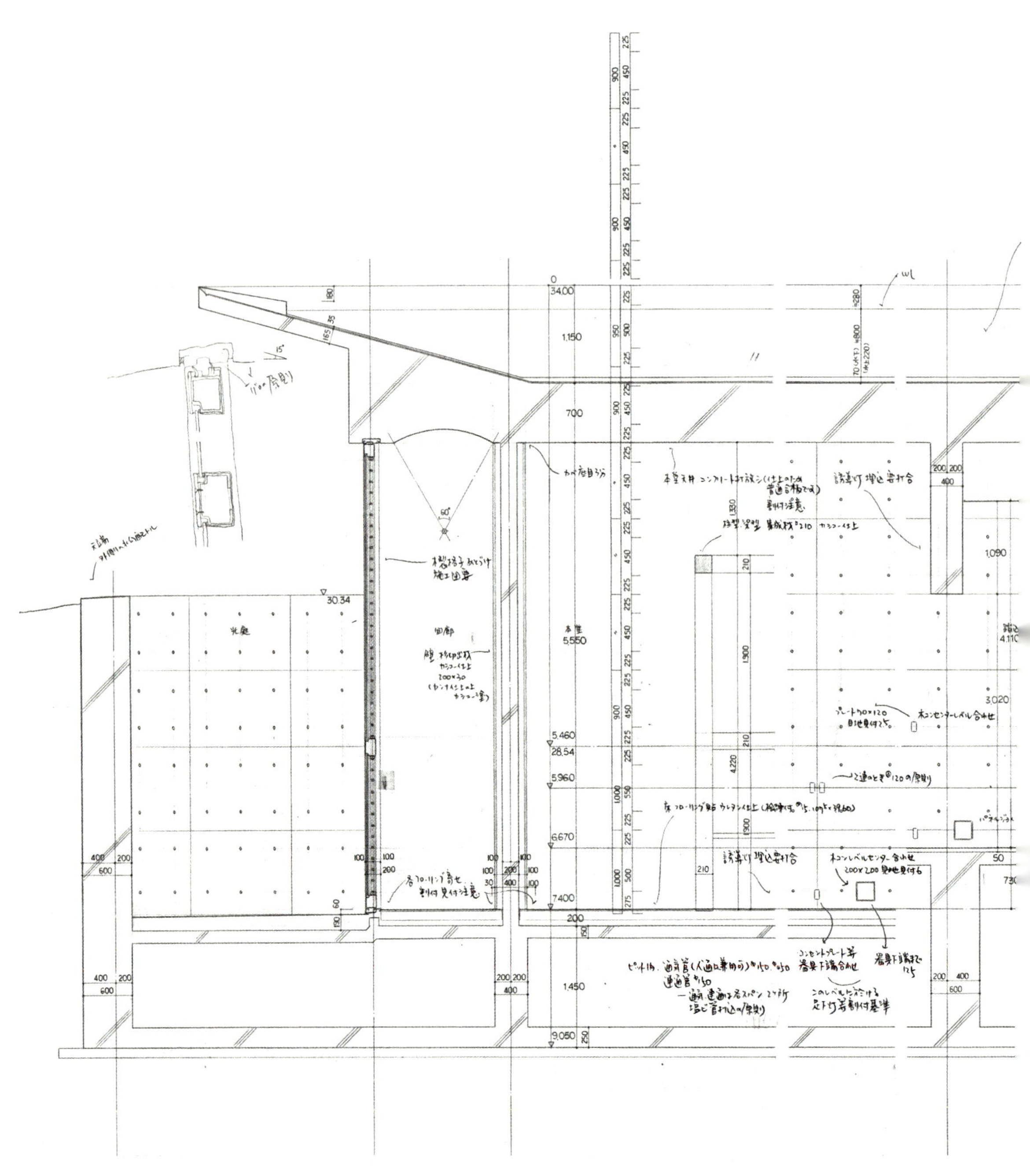

Detailed section and axonometric drawing of the priest's quarters.

断面詳細図と庫裏部分のアクソノメトリック。

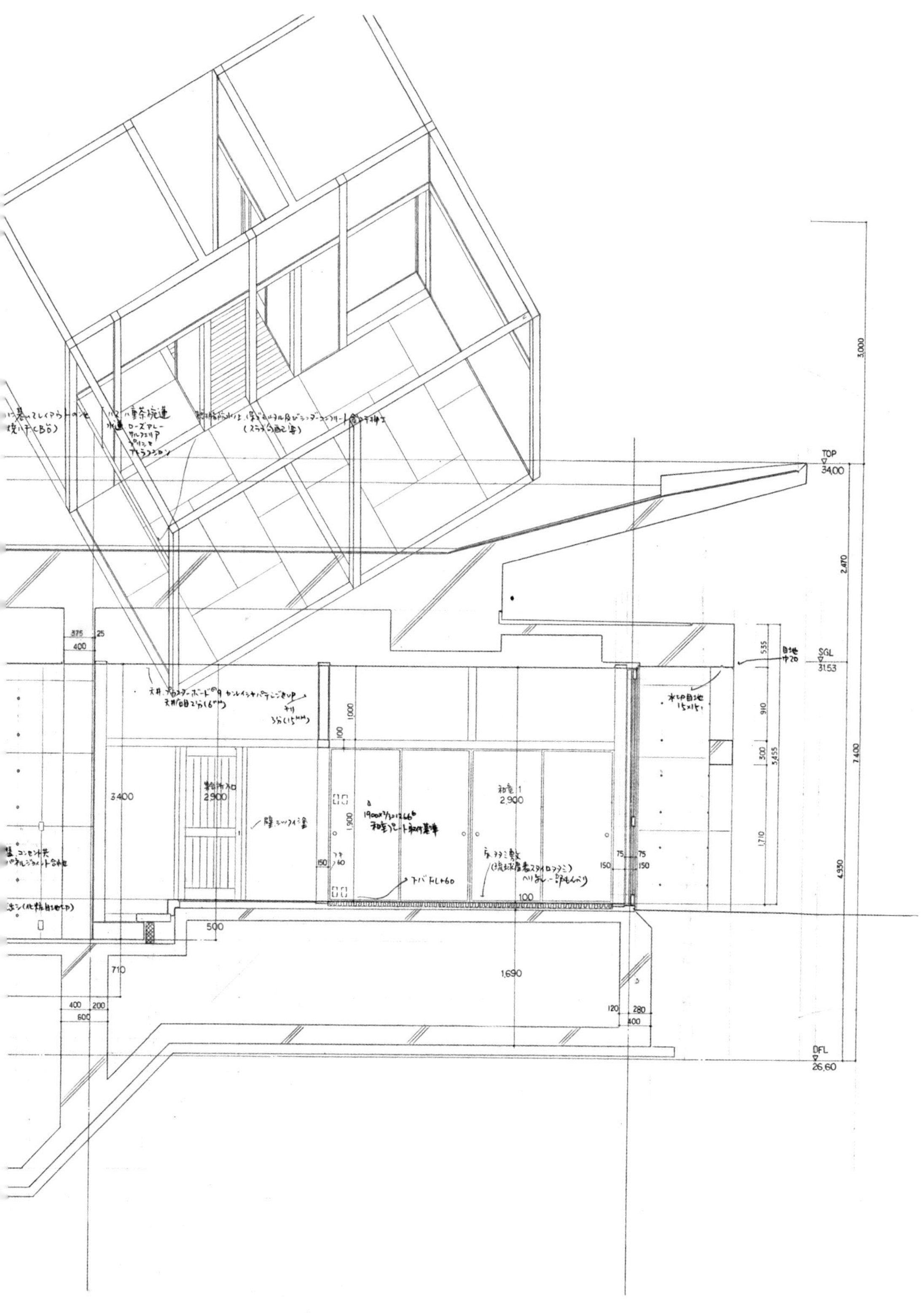

SECTION 1:30	■ WATER TEMPLE
TAKAO SHIMA	安藤忠雄建築研究所 TADAO ANDO ARCHITECT & ASSOCIATES

0604
920418
7

I once traveled through India during the rainy season, where I saw a scene of a temple standing in obscurity on the opposite side of a broad lotus pond, and I thought it resembled the image of one of the Buddhist paradises. The idea of a hall under a pond covered by the greenery of lotus flowers probably emerged from that memory.

かつて雨季のインドを旅したときに、広々とした蓮池の向こうに寺院がひっそりと建つ情景を見て、仏教徒のひとつの理想郷のイメージを見たように思った。緑の蓮に覆われた池の下のお堂というアイディアは、そんな過去の記憶から生まれたのかもしれない。

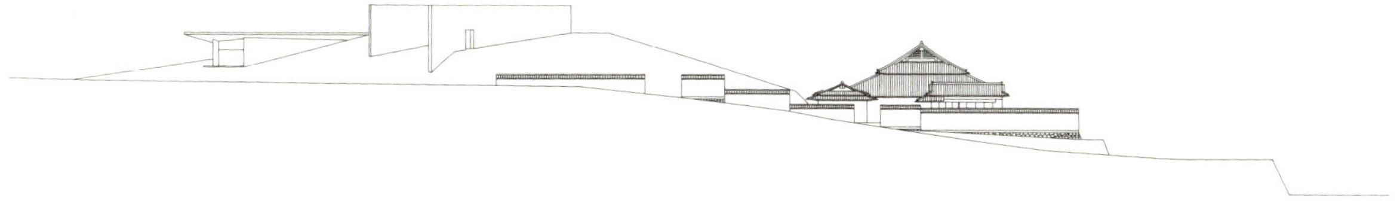

Forest of Tombs Museum, Kumamoto
熊本県立装飾古墳館

1. Yamaga, Kumamoto, Japan　熊本県山鹿市
2. 1989.12-1990.6
3. 1990.10-1992.3

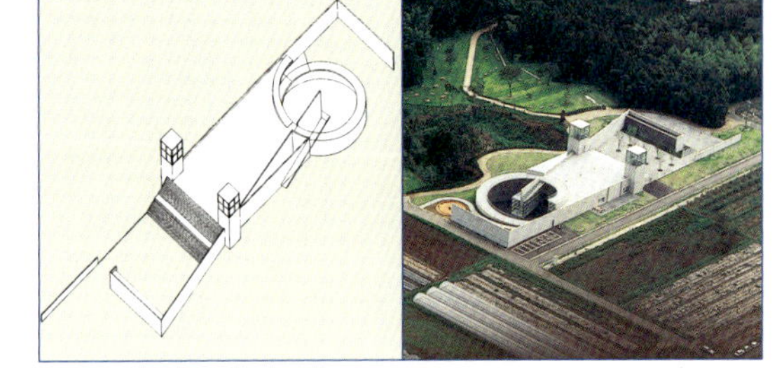

This is an ancient history museum built as a component of Kumamoto Artpolis, which was instigated as a new form of town planning. The site is a plain in northern Kumamoto Prefecture where the Iwabaru Tumulus cluster is located. Here I conceived the image of a building like a platform from where one can see the untouched scenery of tumulus mounds. The idea of an environmental museum as attempted here was later developed in the design of the Chikatsu-Asuka Museum.

新たな街づくりのかたちとして始まったくまもとアートポリスの一環としてつくられた古代博物館である。敷地は熊本県北部の岩原古墳群の分布する平地で、考えたのは、古墳のある風景をそのままに見せる基壇のような建物のイメージだ。ここで試みた環境博物館のアイディアが、後の近つ飛鳥博物館の計画に展開した。

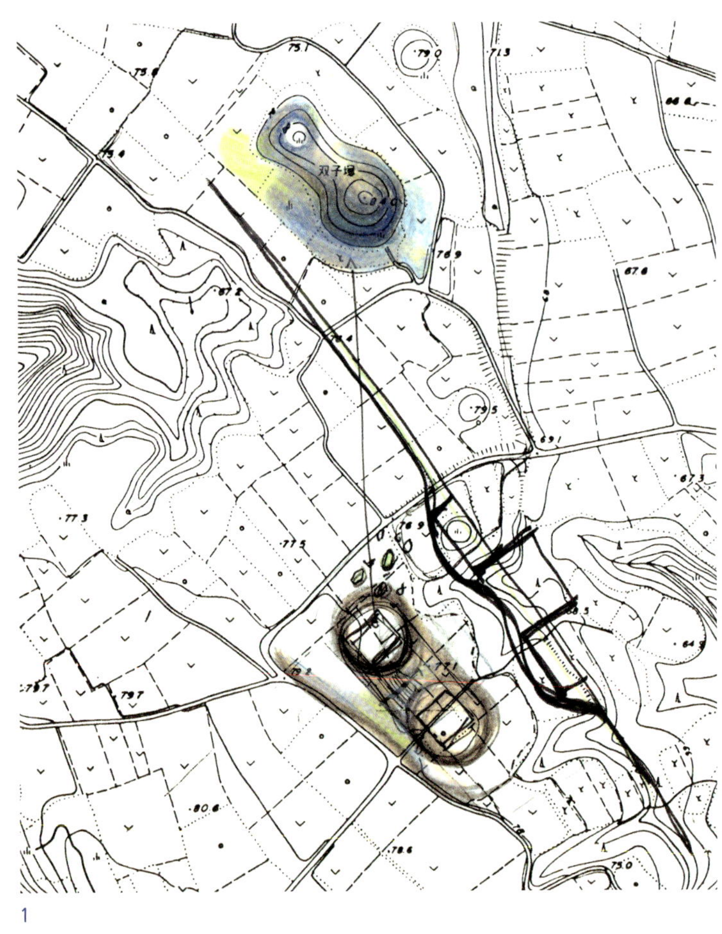

1

1, 2 Image sketches of the site layout. As well as its size and the beauty of its shape, the Futagozuka Tumulus is known as Japan's preeminent keyhole-shaped tumulus. An art museum is to be built on a site about 250m away.

3 The image of a building like an architecturalized flight of stairs arose from the desire for a platform that provides an unbroken view of the scenery. The volume is buried underground so the building does not intrude into the rural scenery, and is pierced by a circular void as a light garden.

1, 2 配置イメージスケッチ。双子塚古墳はそのかたちの大きさ美しさともに日本屈指の前方後円墳として知られる。そこから約250m離れた敷地につくられる博物館。

3 風景を一望にする基壇にとの思いから、建築化された階段のような建物のイメージが生まれる。田園風景の中で建物が突出しないよう、ヴォリュームは地下に沈め、その光庭として円形のヴォイドを穿つ。

2

3

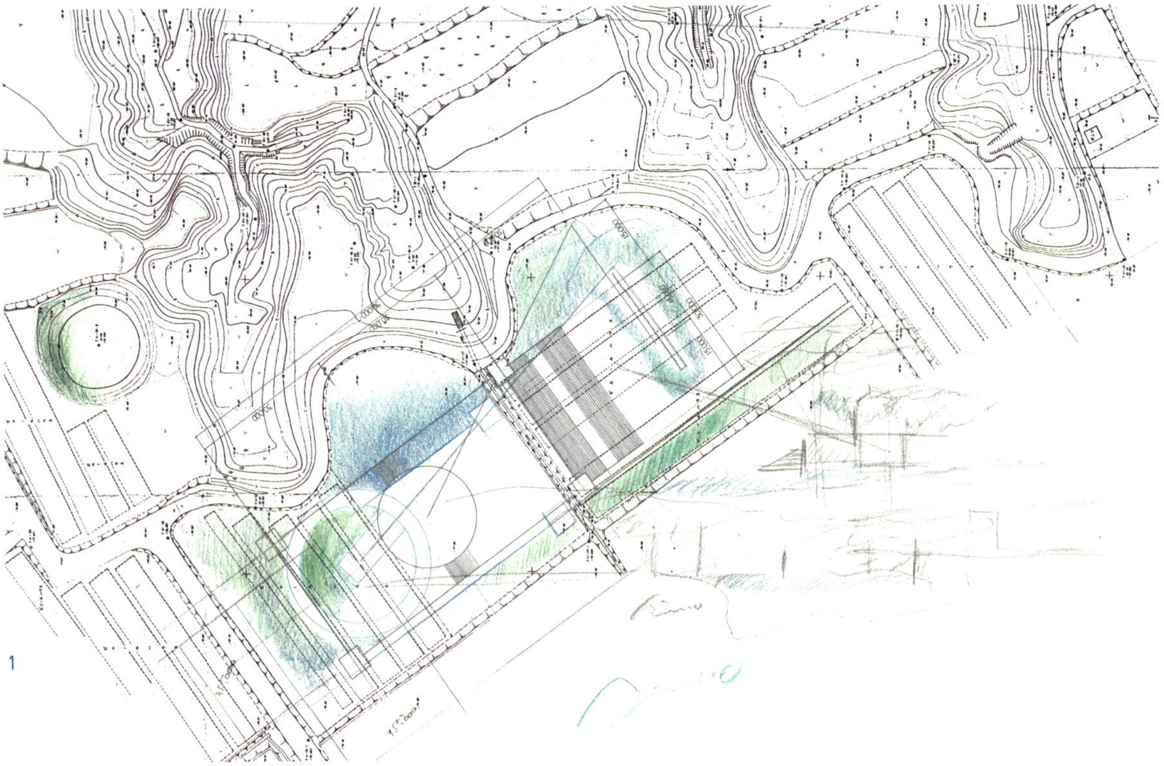

1

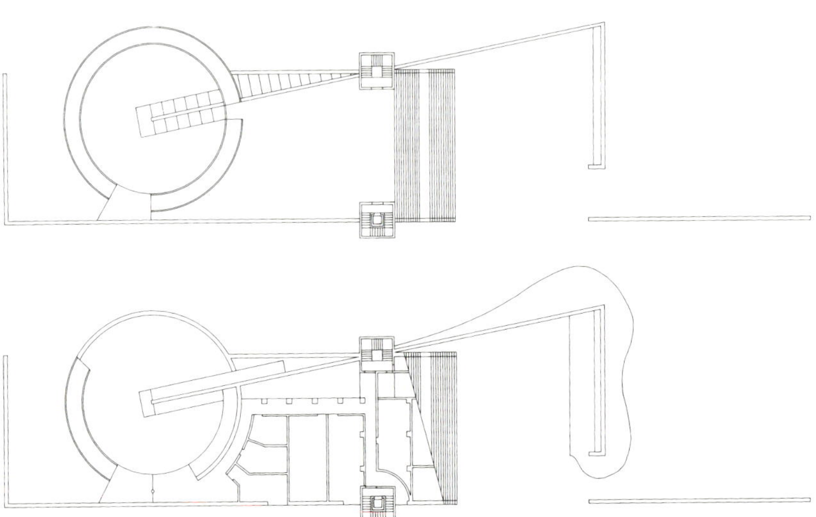

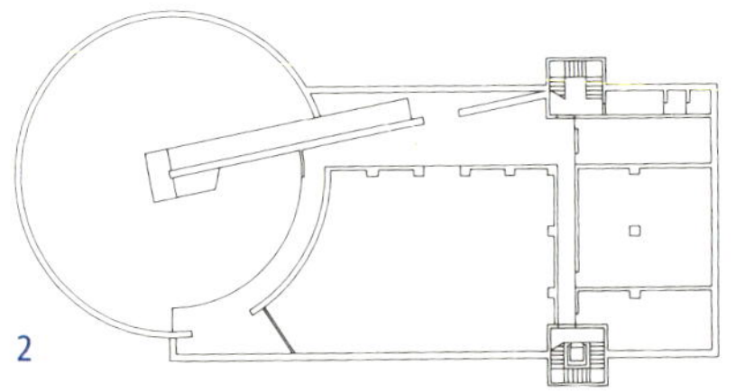

2

1 Building set in a point symmetry with the Futagozuka Tumulus. Architecture as geometry drawn on the earth, responding to the ancient grave markers.

2 From below: ground level plan, level 1 plan, top floor plan.

3 The excavation site is outside the 30m-diameter arc wall, and exhibits are placed inside. The spiral-shaped descending slope expresses the eternal flow of time connecting the past to the present.

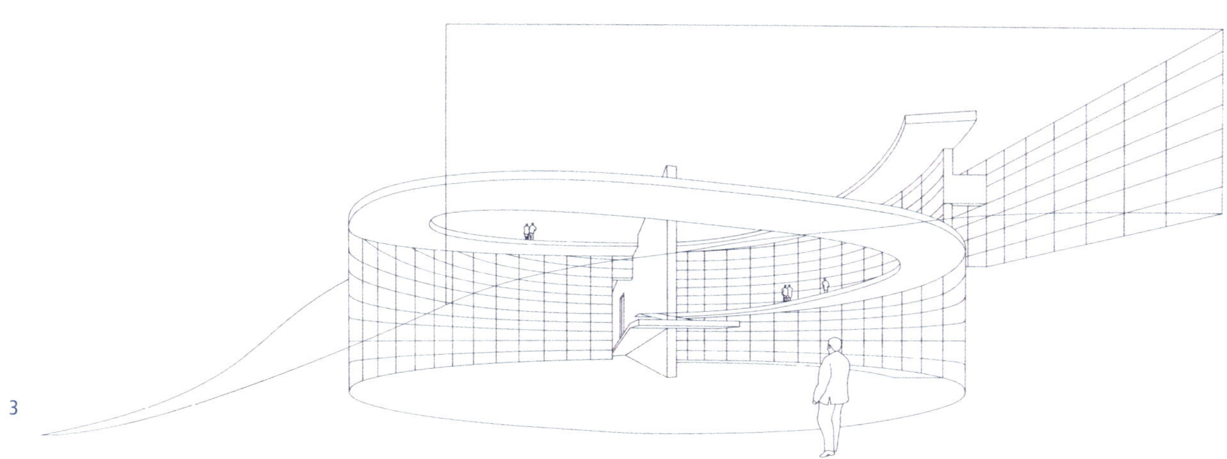

3

1 双子塚古墳と点対称をなすような建物配置。太古の墓標と呼応する、大地に描かれた幾何学としての建築。
2 下から地階、1階、屋上階平面図。
3 直径30m余りの円弧の壁の外側に発掘現場があり、その内側に展示物が置かれる。らせん状に下降するスロープが、過去から現代へとつながる悠久の時間の流れを表現する。

1990s

Chikatsu-Asuka Historical Museum, Osaka
Oyamazaki Villa Museum
Pulitzer Foundation for the Arts
Gallery Noda
Nariwa Museum
FABRICA (Benetton Communication Research Center)
House in Nipponbashi
Awaji-Yumebutai (Before 1995)
Sayamaike Historical Museum, Osaka
Langen Foundation / Hombroich
Seaside Housing Project
Omotesando Hills (Omotesando Regeneration Project)
Modern Art Museum of Fort Worth
Passerelle de Bercy-Tolbiac (International Design Competition)
Komyo-ji Temple

Chikatsu-Asuka Historical Museum, Osaka
大阪府立近つ飛鳥博物館

1. Minamikawachi-gun, Osaka, Japan　大阪府南河内郡
2. 1990.4-1991.11
3. 1991.12-1994.3

The site is located in a historical park established in a deep green valley in Osaka's Minamikawachi district, known as Japan's densest region of tumuli. This is a museum made for the purpose of research and display of tumulus culture. There are more than one hundred stone arrangements of tumuli remaining within the 300,000m^2 park, and the surrounding area is dotted with more than one hundred additional tombs in addition to four imperial tombs. Right in the middle of this superb historical environment, I thought of making architecture as a stage for the green valley, in which the entire roof of the building is a staircase plaza—the conception of an environmental experience museum as a first principle for confronting scenery sculpted by history.

1

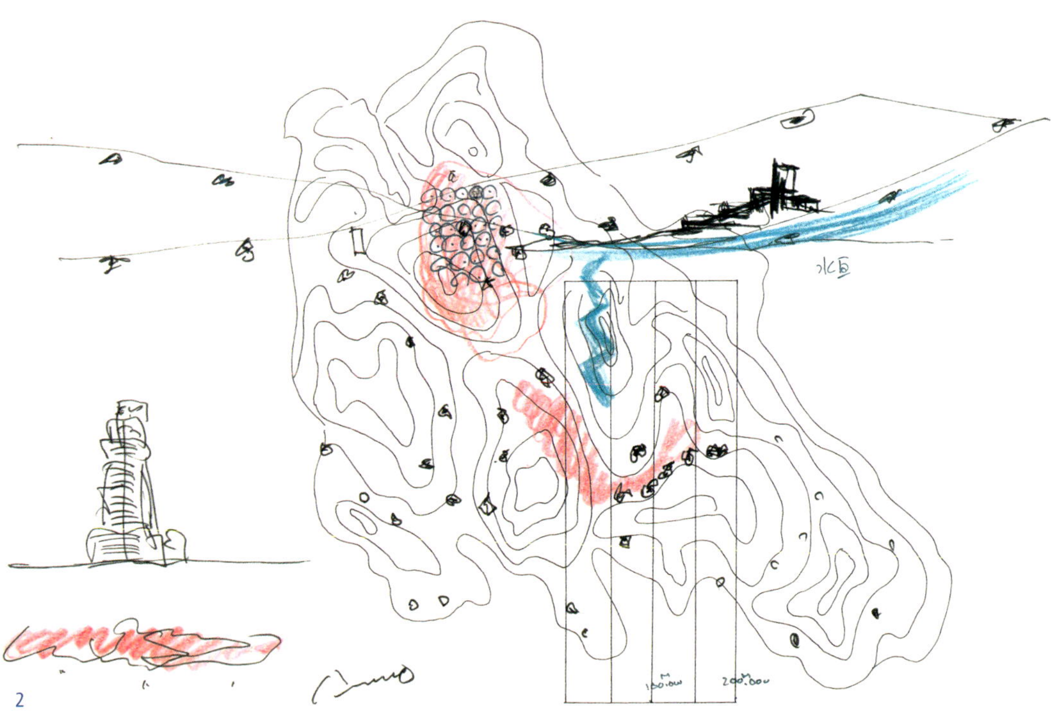

2

敷地は、日本有数の古墳密集地として知られる大阪府南河内郡の、緑深い谷間に設けられた史跡公園内に位置する。古墳文化の展示と研究を目的としてつくられた博物館である。30万m^2の広さをもつ公園内には、100基余りの古墳の石組みが残されており、周囲には、4基の天皇陵のほか、さらに100基以上の古墳が点在する。このすぐれた歴史的環境の只中で考えたのは建物の屋上をすべて階段広場とした緑の谷間のステージとしての建築、歴史の刻まれた風景との対峙を第一義とする、環境体験型博物館という構想である。

1 In terms of the scale of the plan, which is comparable with the Egyptian Pyramids, the tumulus of Emperor Nintoku is one of the world's largest structures. The magnificent conceptual power of the ancient Japanese people arouses the architect's imagination.
2 Image sketches drawn on top of a topographical map. The green hills, with a lake providing abundant water, are dotted with a huge number of historical landmarks. Contemporary architecture is conceived so as to maximize the potential of this place.
3, 4 Initial image sketches. A stage buried in a green ravine, architecture like a viewing plaza enabling an uninterrupted view of the surroundings, drawn as a silhouette.

3

4

1 仁徳天皇領古墳は、平面スケールにおいてはエジプトのピラミッドをもしのぐ世界最大級の構築物。古代日本人の壮大な構想力が建築家のイマジネーションをかきたてる。
2 地形図に重ねて描かれたイメージスケッチ。豊かな水をたたえた池をもつ緑の丘に無数の史跡が点在する。この場所のもつポテンシャルを最大限活かすような現代建築を考える。
3, 4 初期イメージスケッチ。緑の谷間に埋め込まれたステージ、周囲を一望にできる展望広場のような建築がシルエットとして描かれている。

1

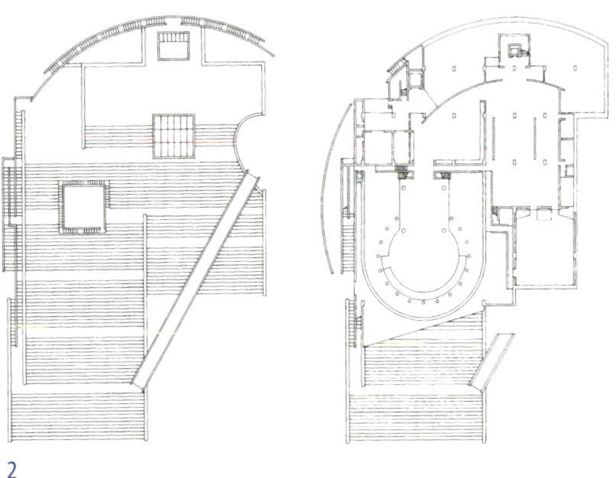

2

1 Early image sketch. Geometrical shapes dynamically layered on the topography produce a scene that is only possible in this place.
2 Plans.
3 Image sketches of the interior exhibition spaces. Plan diagrams imitating the tomb form combining circles and squares.
4 Image of a bold architecture covered with a large staircase, which may be called a contemporary tumulus.

1 初期イメージスケッチ。地形にダイナミックに幾何学を重ね合わせ、この場所にしかできない風景をつくる。
2 平面図。
3 内部の展示空間のイメージスケッチ。円と正方形を組み合わせた墳墓形状を模したような平面図式が描かれている。
4 大階段に覆われた、現代の古墳ともいうべき大胆な建築のイメージ。

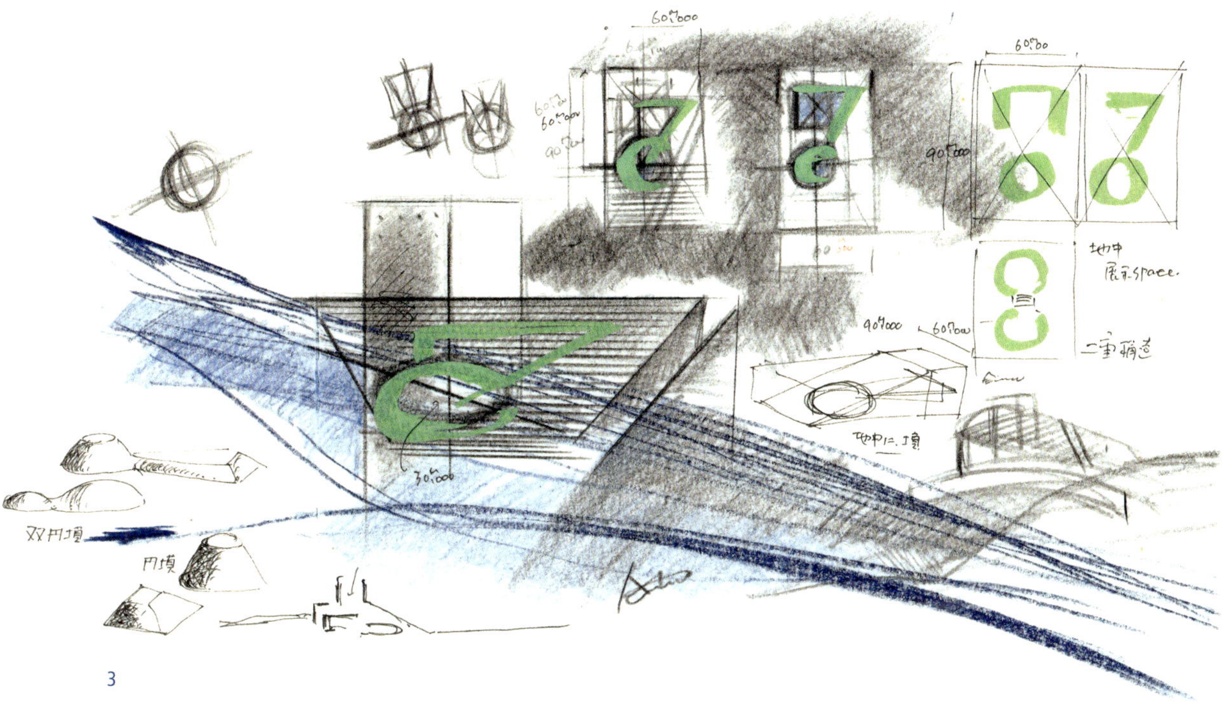

3

Ritz·Carlton

1228 OUEST, RUE SHERBROOKE ST. WEST
MONTREAL, QUEBEC, CANADA H3G 1H6
TEL.: (514) 842-4212 (800) 363-0366
FAX: (514) 842-3383 TELEX 05-24322

ANDO, TADAO MR
1188 SHERBROOKE WEST
MONTREAL, QUEBEC
H3A 3G2

ALCAN

HEURE DU DÉPART – 12:00 P.M. – CHECK OUT TIME

No CHAMBRE - ROOM No.	904
TAUX - RATE	130.00
DATE D'ARRIVEE - ARRIVAL DATE	3/20/90
DATE DEPART - DEPARTURE DATE	3/21/90

S'IL Y A UN CHANGEMENT AUX INFORMATIONS CI-DESSUS, VEUILLEZ EN AVISER LA RECEPTION IMMEDIATEMENT.
IF THERE IS ANY CHANGE IN THE ABOVE INFORMATION, PLEASE NOTIFY THE FRONT DESK IMMEDIATELY.

4

1

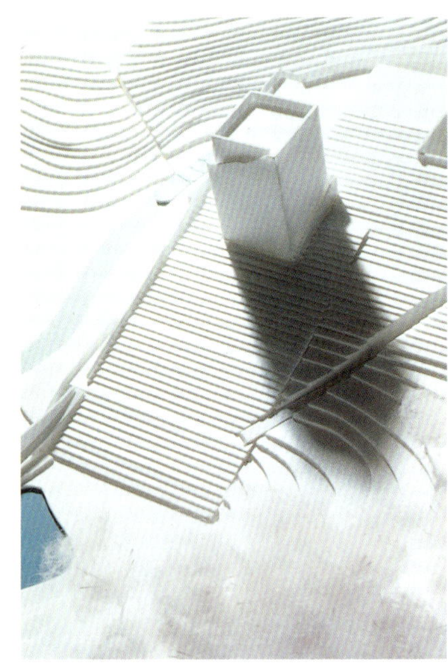

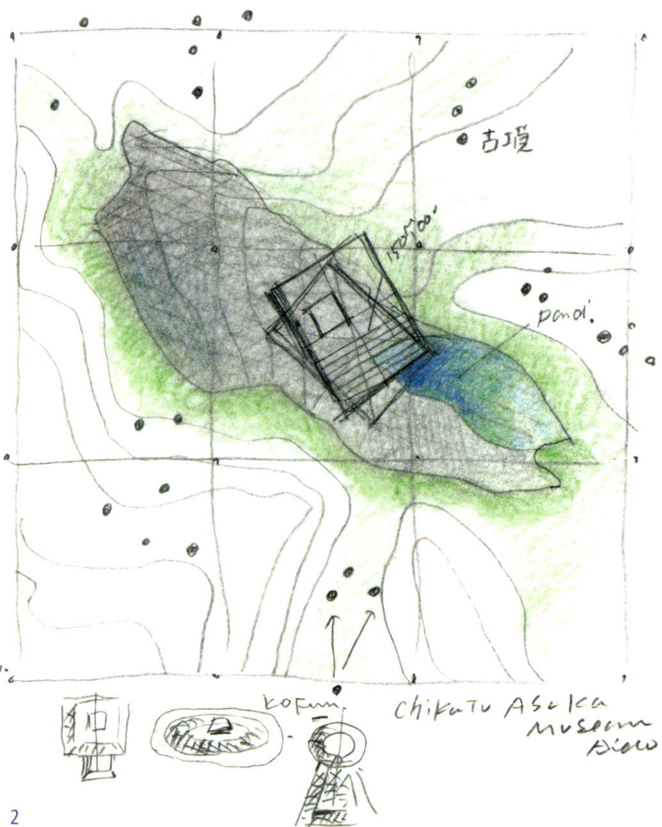

2

1 Image sketch of the rooftop stair plaza.
2, 4 Exploratory sketches of the site. The most appropriate relationships between the topography and the building volume are repeatedly drawn and studied.
3 Exploratory drawing of the cross section. The concrete tower is set as if piercing the stair plaza to make a deep, dark space in the interior. An image of the "underworld."

1 屋上階段広場のイメージスケッチ。
2, 4 サイトの検討スケッチ。地形と建物ヴォリュームの最もふさわしい関係を幾重にも図を重ね合わせ検討している。
3 断面検討図。階段広場に突き刺すように配されたコンクリートの塔が、内部に深い闇の空間をつくる。「黄泉の国」のイメージ。

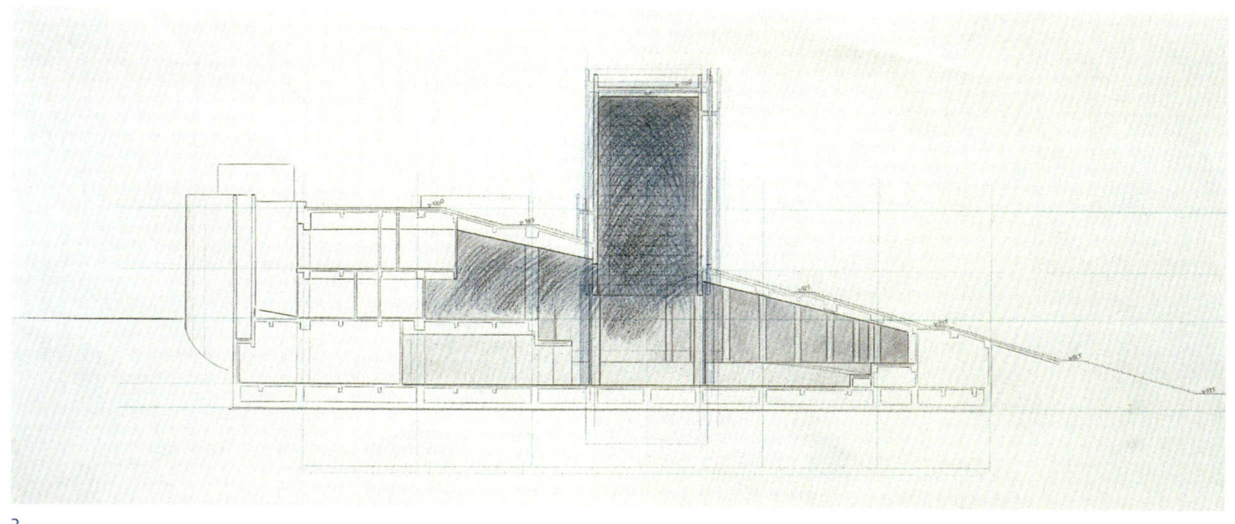

3

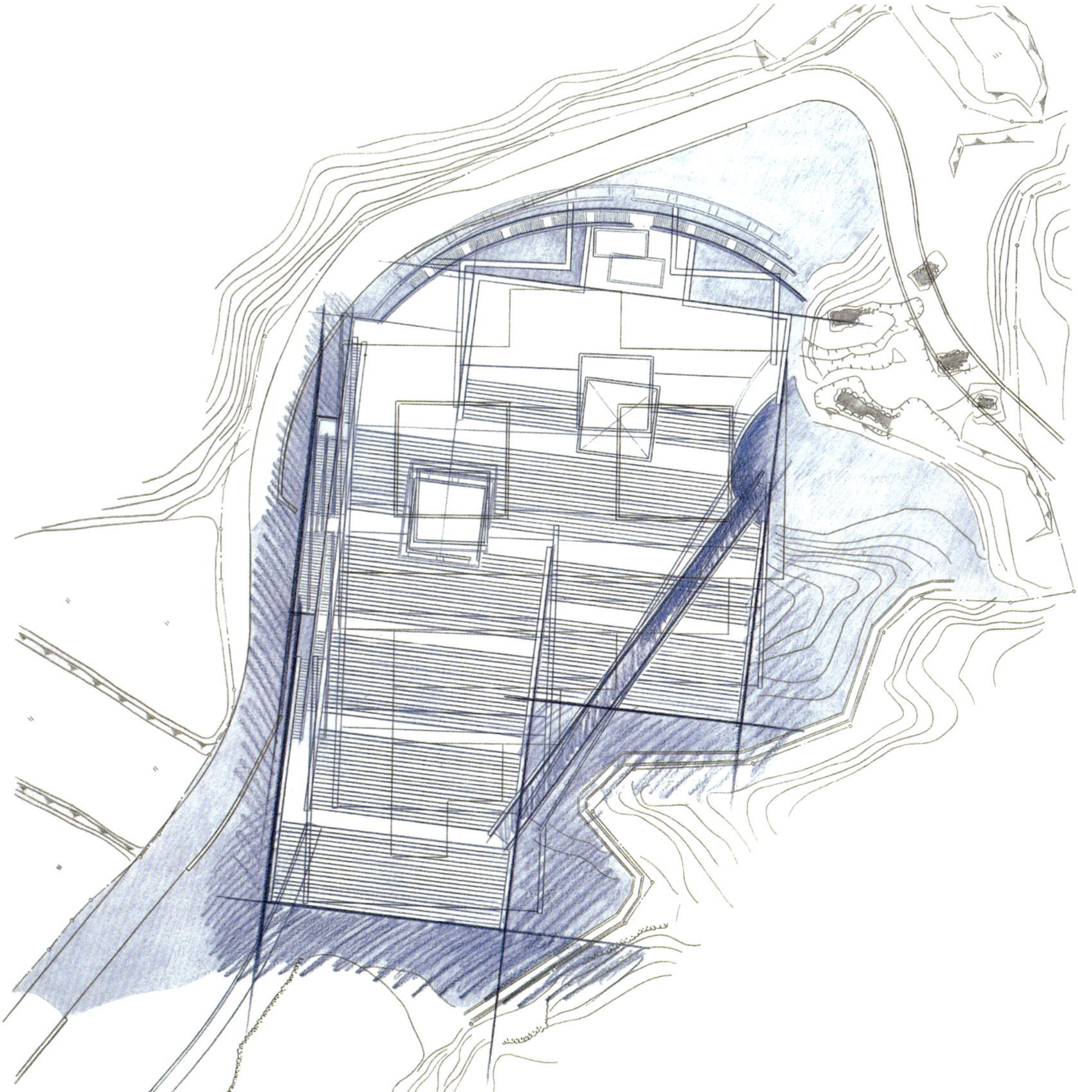

4

1

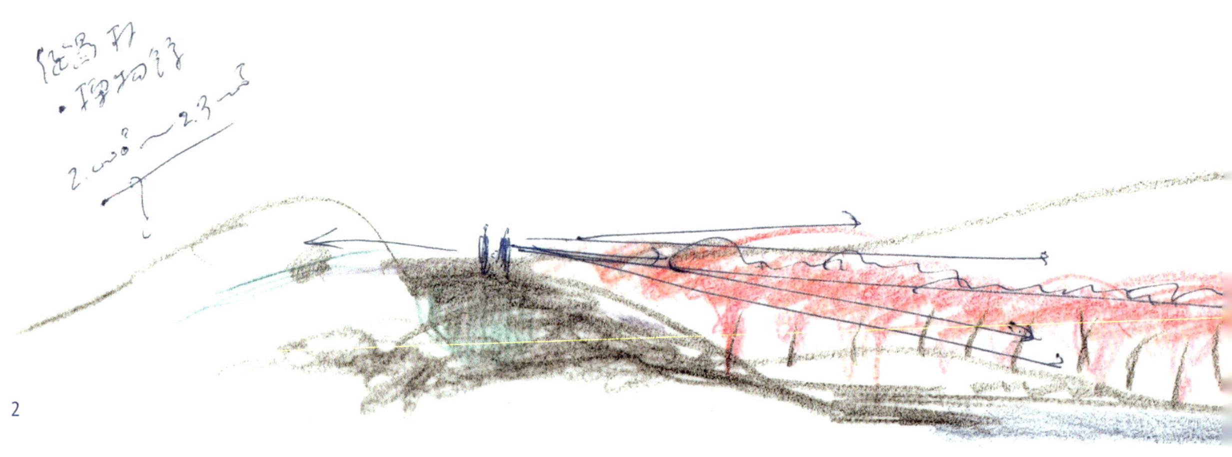

2

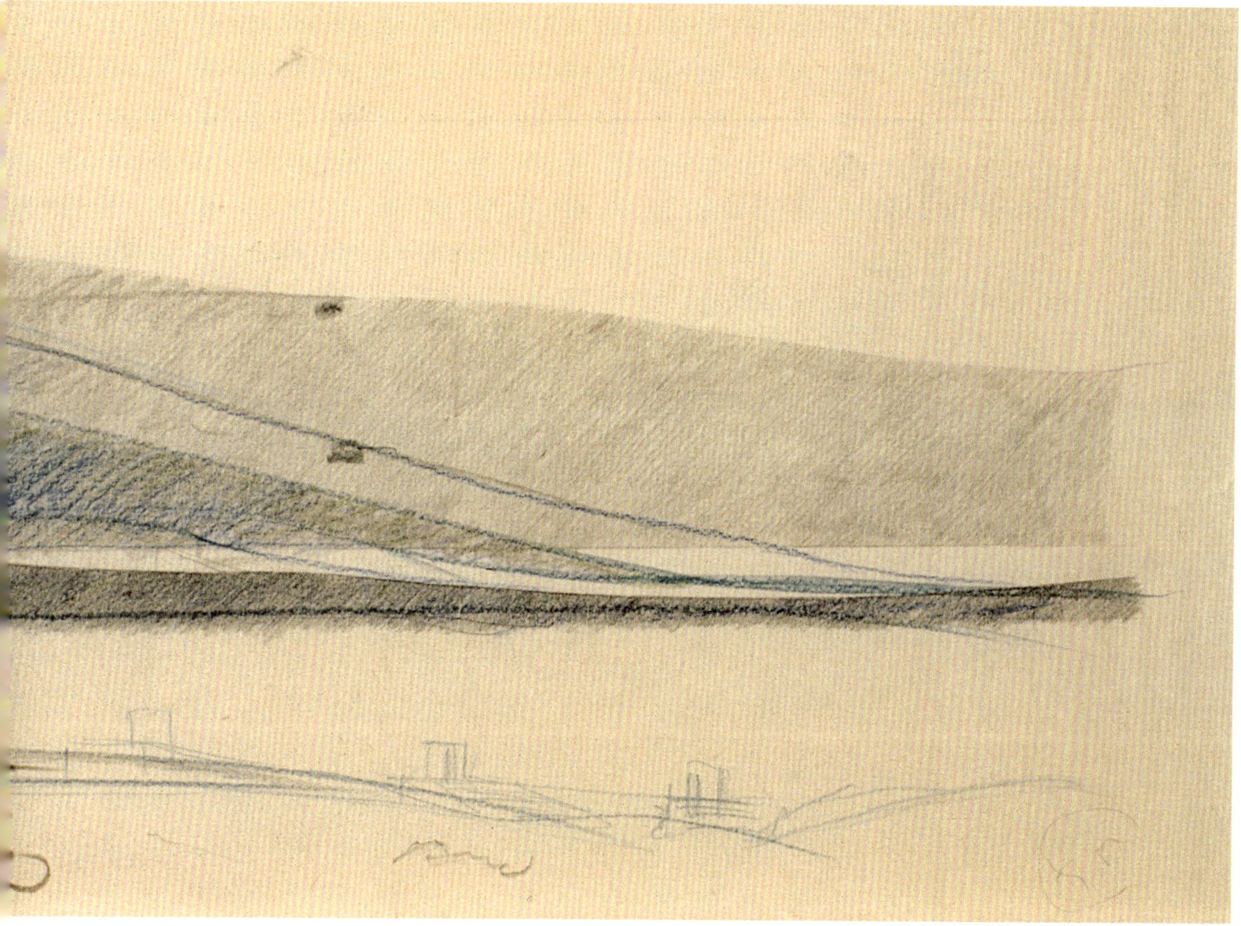

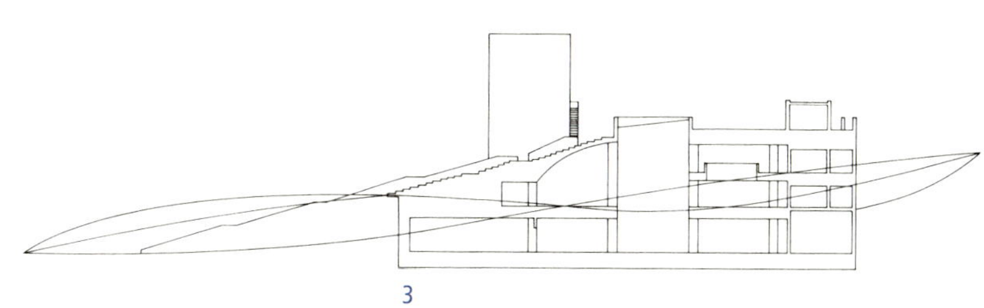

3

1 Elevation drawing.
2 Climbing a hill covered with plum trees and approaching along the lake. Image sketch of the approach to the building.
3 Section.

1 立面ドローイング。
2 梅林に包まれた丘を登り、池に沿ってアプローチする。建築の導入部のイメージスケッチ。
3 断面図。

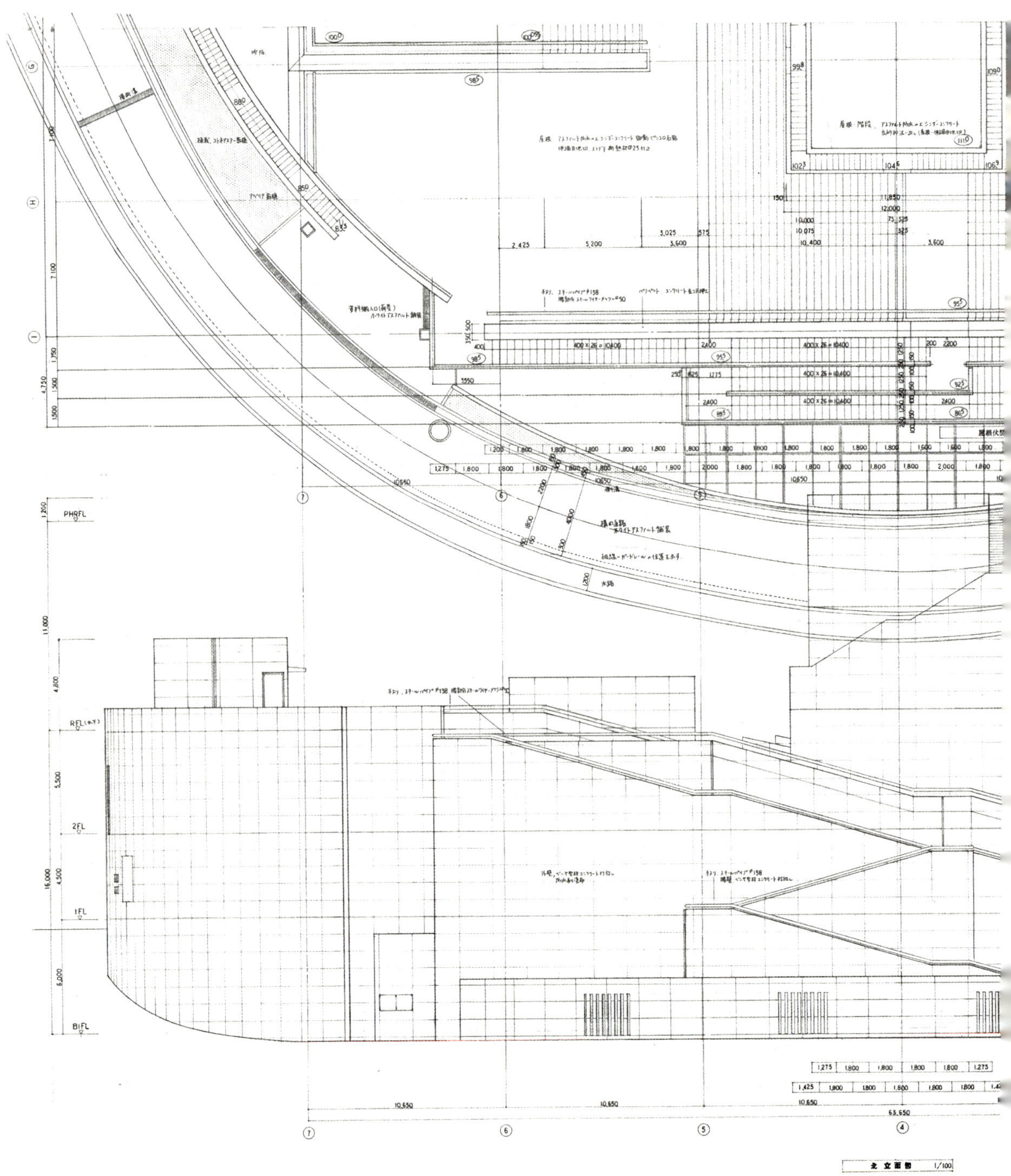

Detailed drawing of the rooftop stairs. The form of the stairs, covered by many hundreds of thousands of tiles, is also an expression of a façade oriented toward the sky.

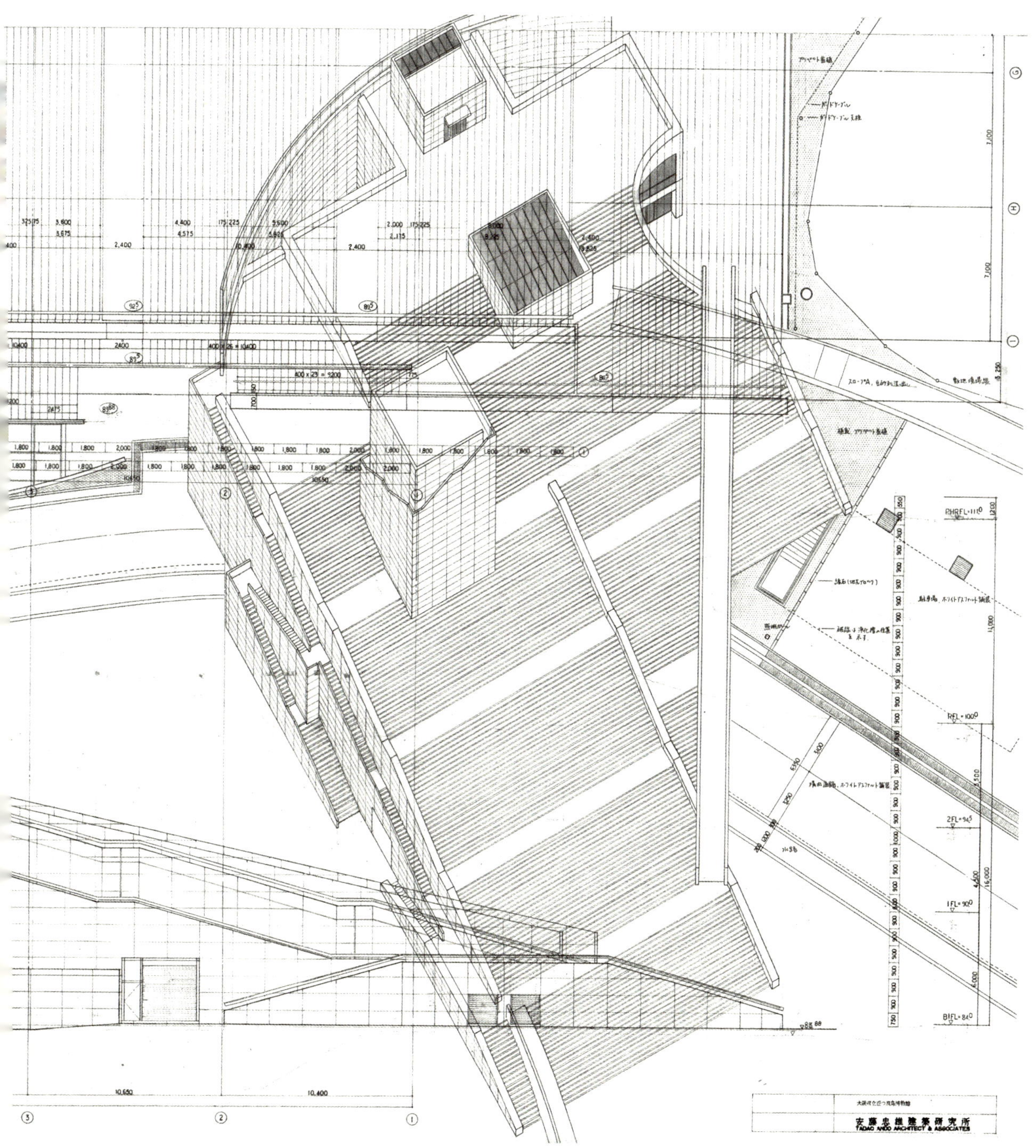

屋上階段の詳細図。何十万個の葺石で覆われた階段の造形は
空に向けたファサードの表現でもある。

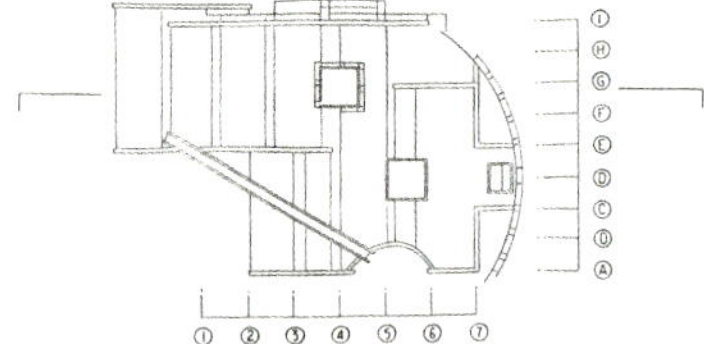

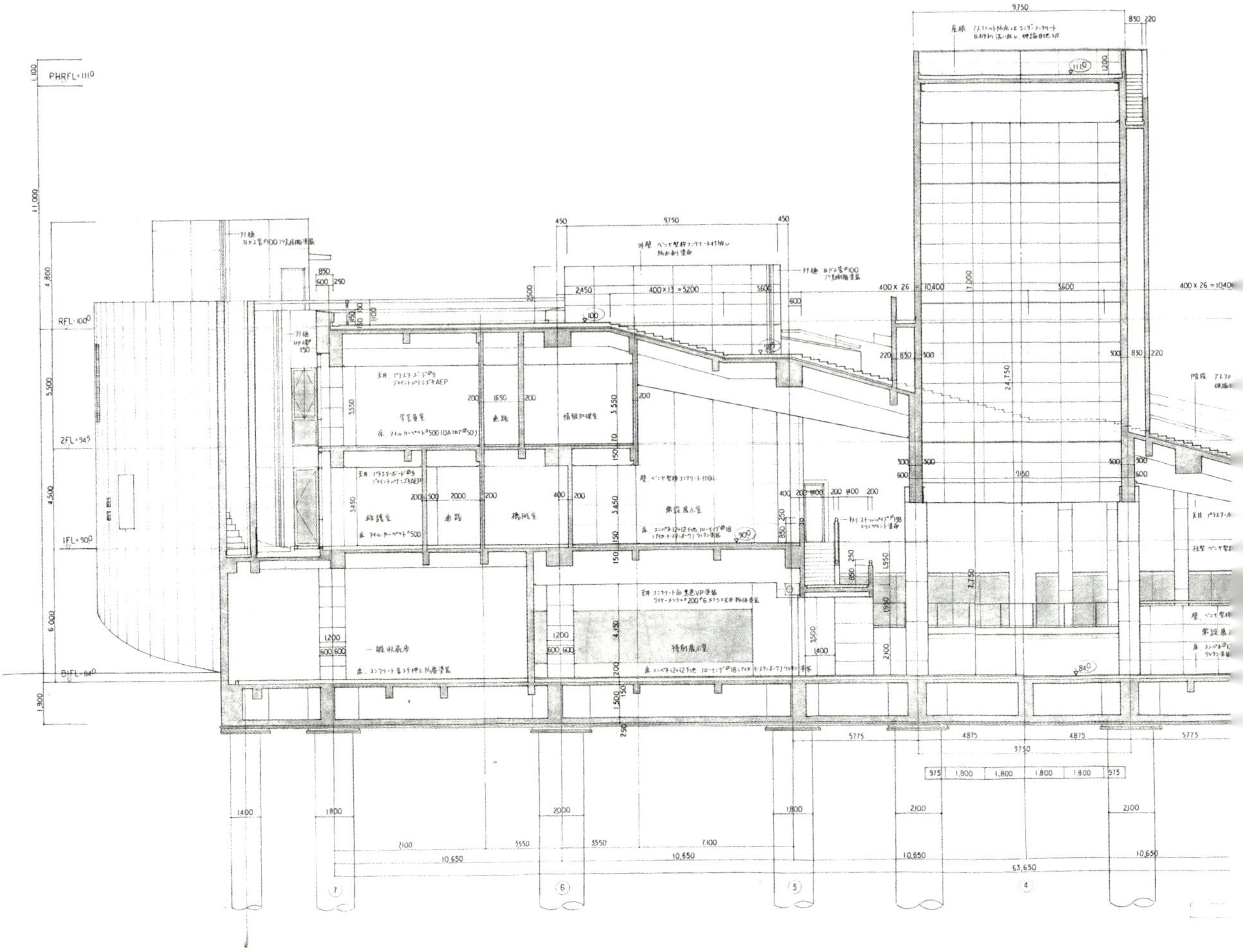

Section and axonometric drawing of the exhibition spaces. The tower rising from the rooftop stair plaza symbolizes the gloomy interior space.

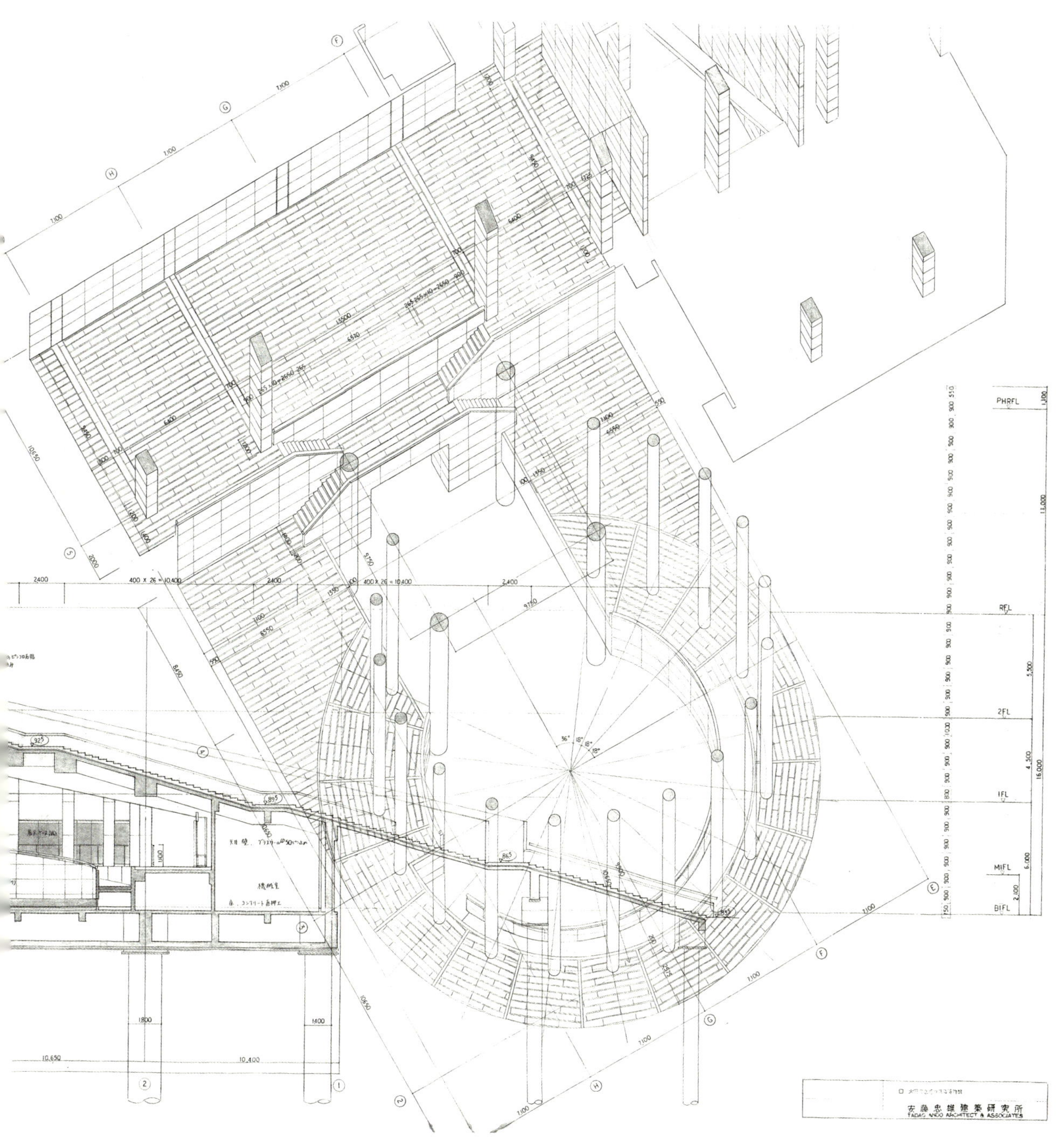

展示空間のアクソノメトリックおよび断面図。屋上階段広場に
屹立する塔が、内部の闇の空間を象徴する。

Oyamazaki Villa Museum
大山崎山荘美術館

1. Otokuni-gun, Kyoto, Japan　京都府乙訓郡
2. 1991.4-1994.7
3. 1994.8-1995.7

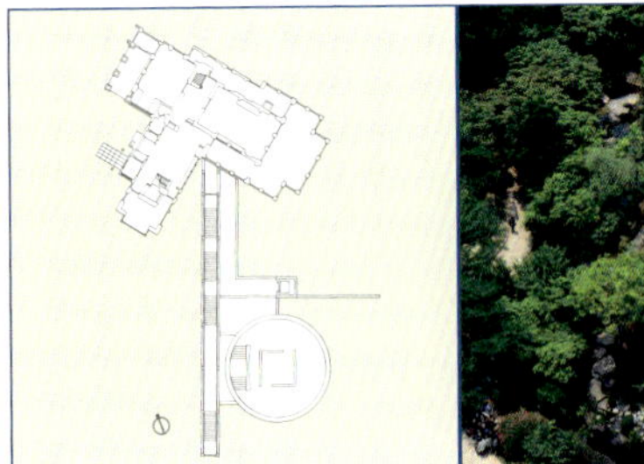

Halfway up Mt. Tenno in Oyamazaki, on the outskirts of Kyoto, the site is located in a place with an unbroken view of the confluence of the Kizu River, Katsura River, and Uji River into the Yodo River. This project involved the repair and restoration of an old mountain villa built in 1922, the Taisho period. The existing mountain villa, which imitates English Tudor style, has no historical value, but it is architecture wherein one can sense the desires of its maker in a way unlike contemporary architecture. Having conscientiously repaired and restored this charming building, I wondered if I could make new architecture in a shape that did not destroy the existing scenery, but provided mutually enhancing spaces.

1 I first considered a proposal for a ring-shaped gallery about 9m high and 5m wide, surrounding the old building. As if approaching the gallery by passing through the mountain villa, an egg-shaped special exhibition space is made at one end of the ring, like that considered for the Urban Egg (Nakanoshima Project 2).
2 Exploratory sketch of the site layout for the stage one proposal.

1 まず考えたのは、古い建物を取り巻くように幅5m、高さ9mほどのリング状のギャラリーをつくる案。ギャラリーへは、山荘の中を通ってアプローチするようにして、リングの一方の端には、中之島のアーバンエッグで考えた卵型の特別展示空間をつくる。
2 第1案配置検討図。

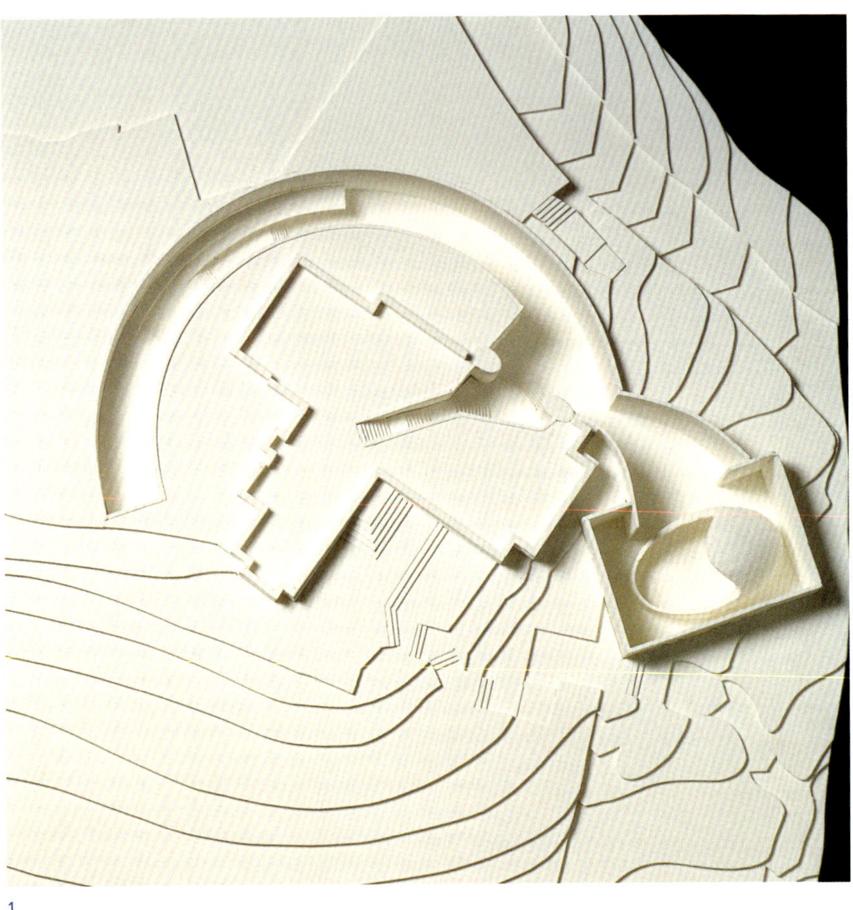

1

敷地は京都近郊大山崎の天王山の中腹、木津川、桂川、宇治川が合流して淀川となる様を一望に出来る場所に位置する。1922年、大正期に建てられた古い洋館の改修・増築を行った仕事である。イギリスのチューダー様式を模した既存の洋館は、史的価値があるものではなかったが、現代建築にはない、つくり手の思いが感じられる建築だった。この魅力的な建物を丁寧に修復、再生した上で、その空間と互いに刺激しあうような、新しい建築を既存の風景を壊さないかたちでつくろうと考えた。

2

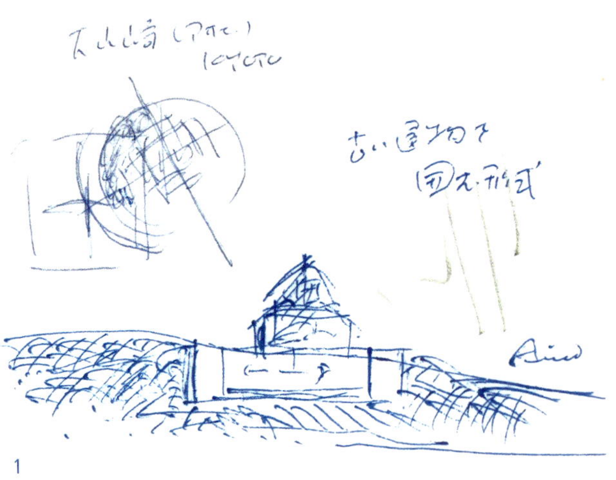

1

1 For the stage two proposal, I conceived a plan pattern that combines a perfect circle and square. Precisely because it is an underground space with an unseen shape, I was able to try and make a labyrinthine space by means of geometry.
2 Exploratory drawing of the site layout for the stage two proposal.

1 第2案として考えたのは、完結した円と正方形を組み合わせた平面パターン。かたちの見えない、地中の空間だからこそ可能な、幾何学による迷宮空間をつくろうとしていた。
2 第2案配置検討図。

2

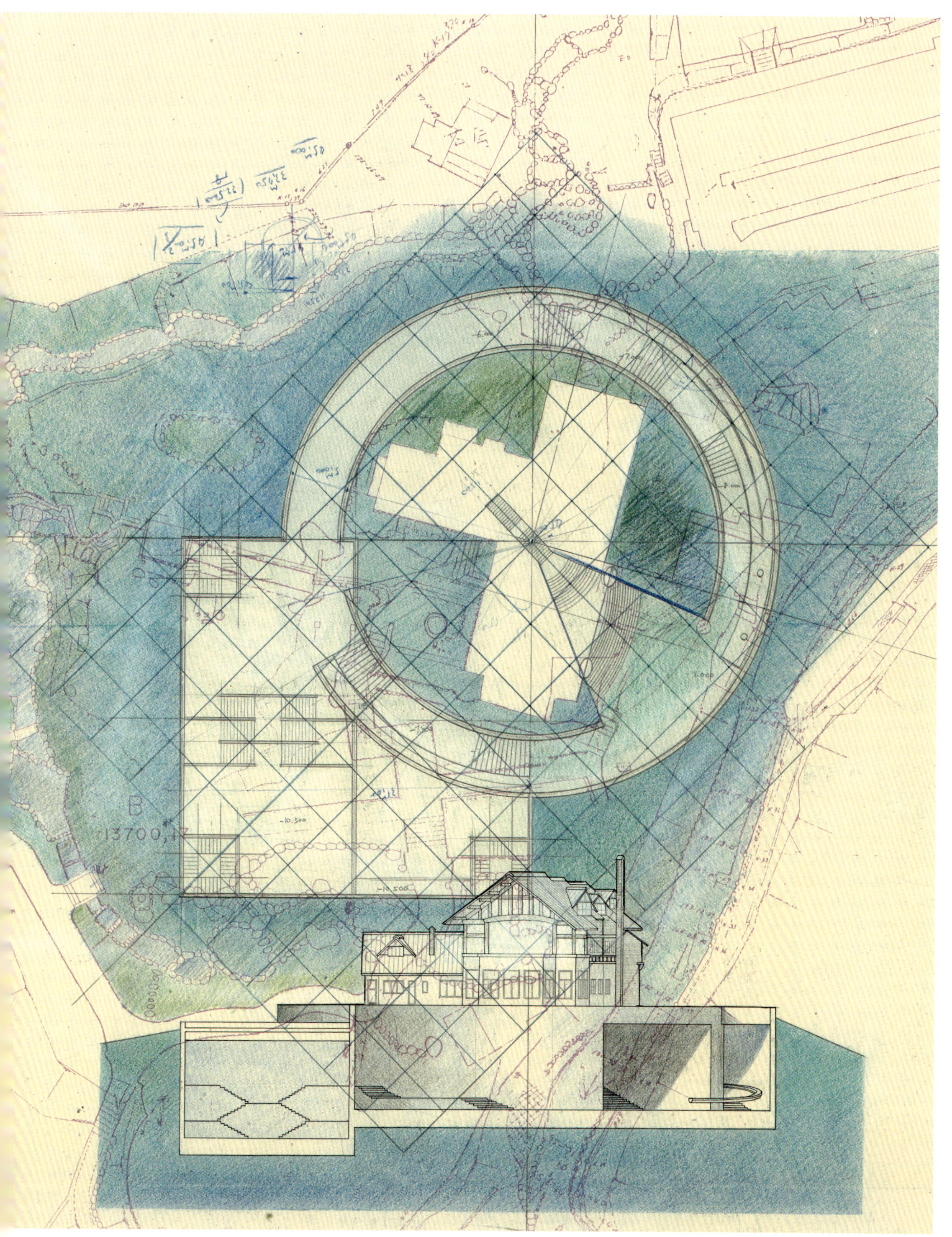

1

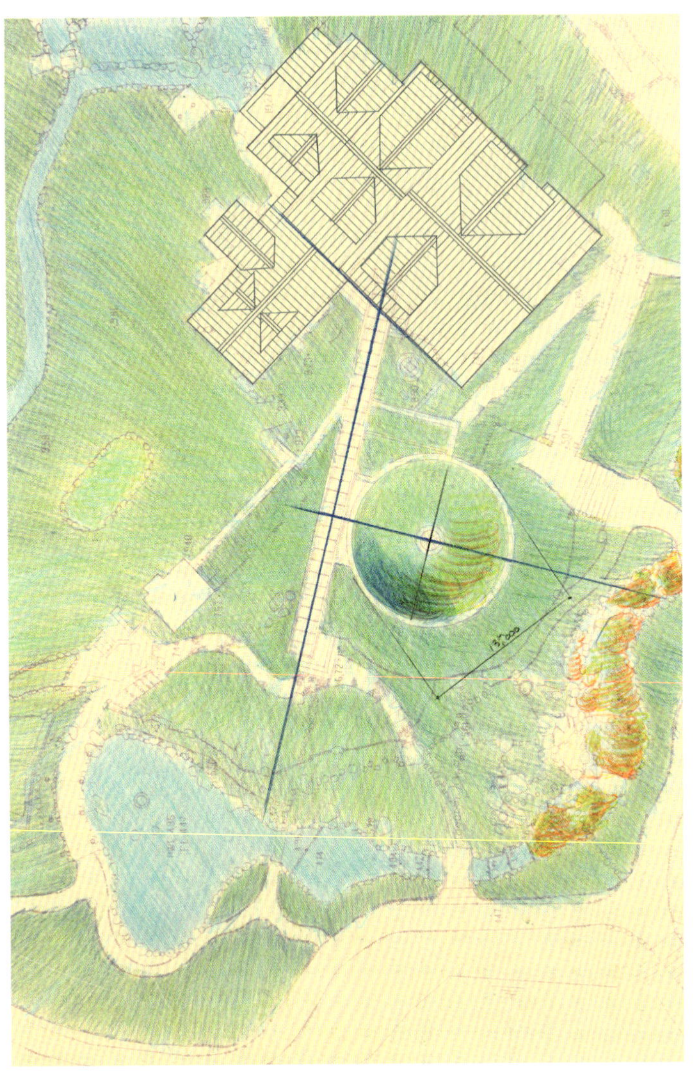

2

1 Because it did not fit well within the site boundaries, the ring-shaped gallery proposal was abandoned. The next stage was a cylindrical gallery in a shape detached from the mountain villa, but still set underground. I considered a proposal to traverse the space between new and old with a symbolic stair passage.

2 Exploratory drawing of the site layout for the stage three proposal (the realized proposal).

3 Concept drawing. In order to avoid spoiling the mood of the Japanese-style garden surrounding the mountain villa, the volume of the new addition is buried in the ground to reduce its height. In contrast with the dignified interior of the existing mountain villa, the stair room is a minimal space suffused with natural light from clerestories, and a 6.25m-diameter cylindrical exhibition room is set at the lower point.

1 敷地境界内にうまく納められないという理由で、リング状のギャラリー案は断念。今度は円筒形のギャラリーを山荘と切り離した形でやはり地中に配置。その新旧の間を象徴的な階段通路でつなぐ案を考える。

2 第3案（実現案）配置検討図。

3 コンセプトドローイング。山荘を取り囲む日本庭園の雰囲気を壊さぬよう、新築部のヴォリュームは地下に埋めて高さを抑える。階段室は既存山荘の重厚なインテリアとは対照的な、ハイサイドライトからの光に満たされたミニマルな空間とし、下りた先に直径6.25ｍのシリンダー型の展示室を配置する。

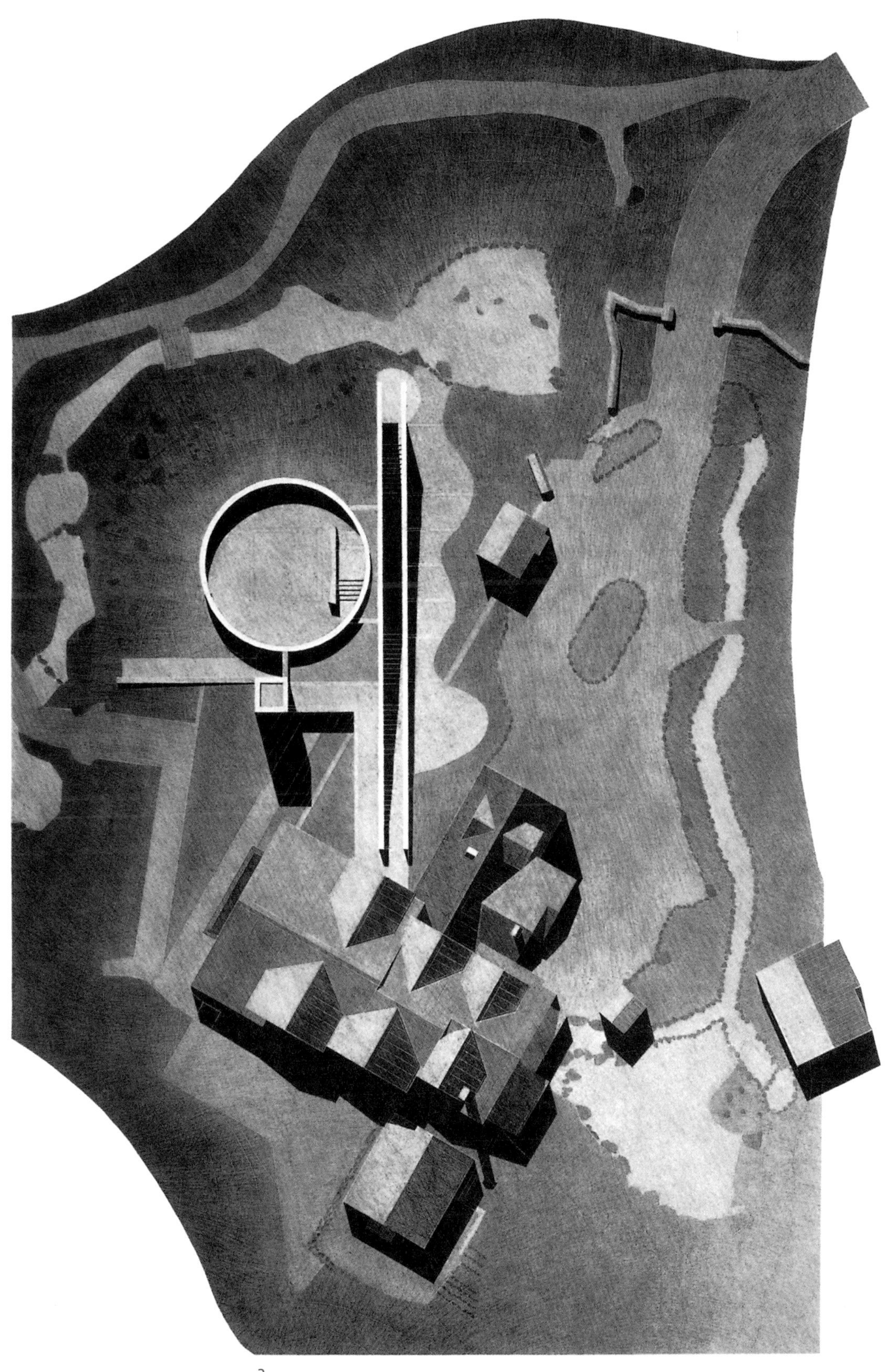

3

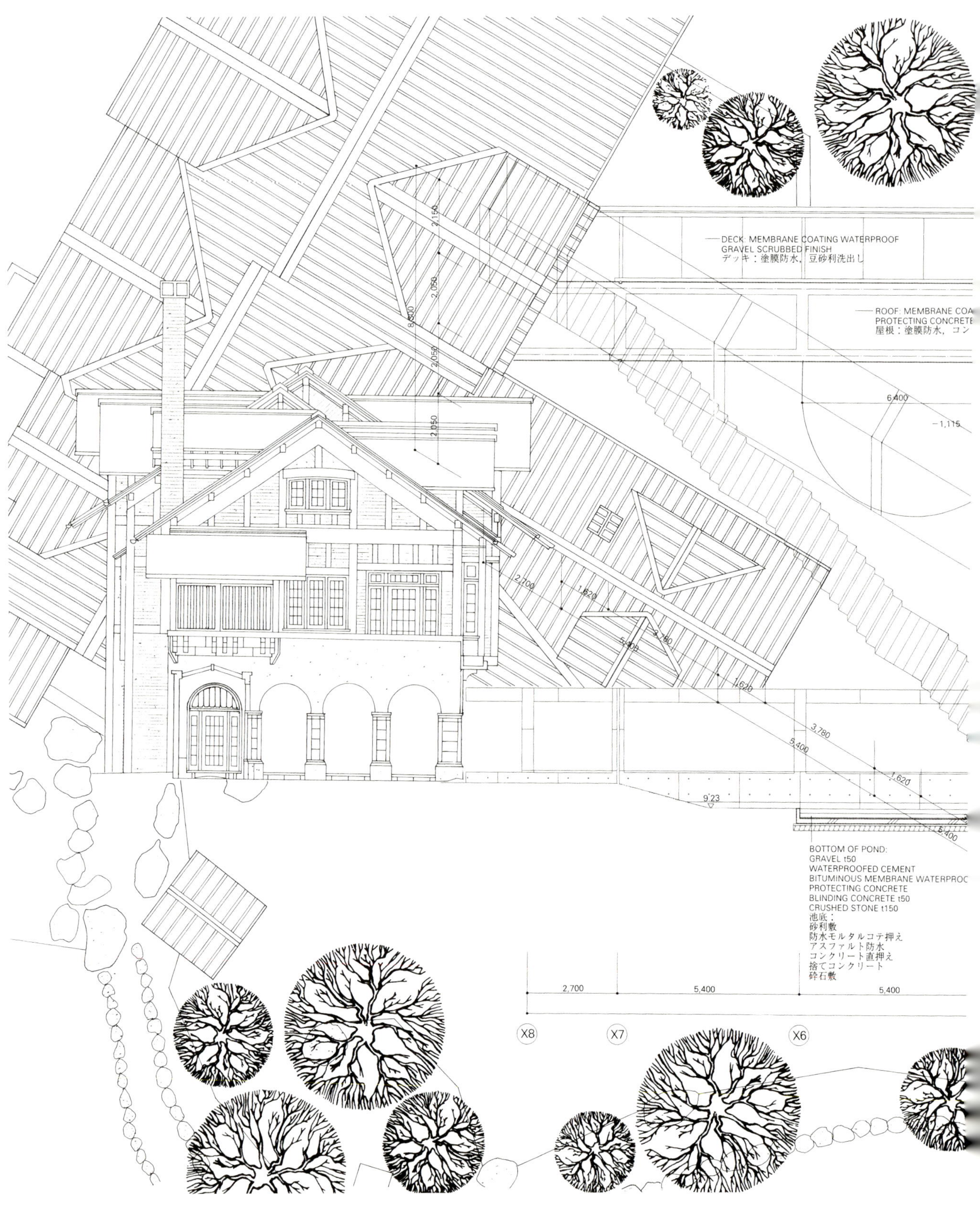

Axonometric

アクソノメトリック

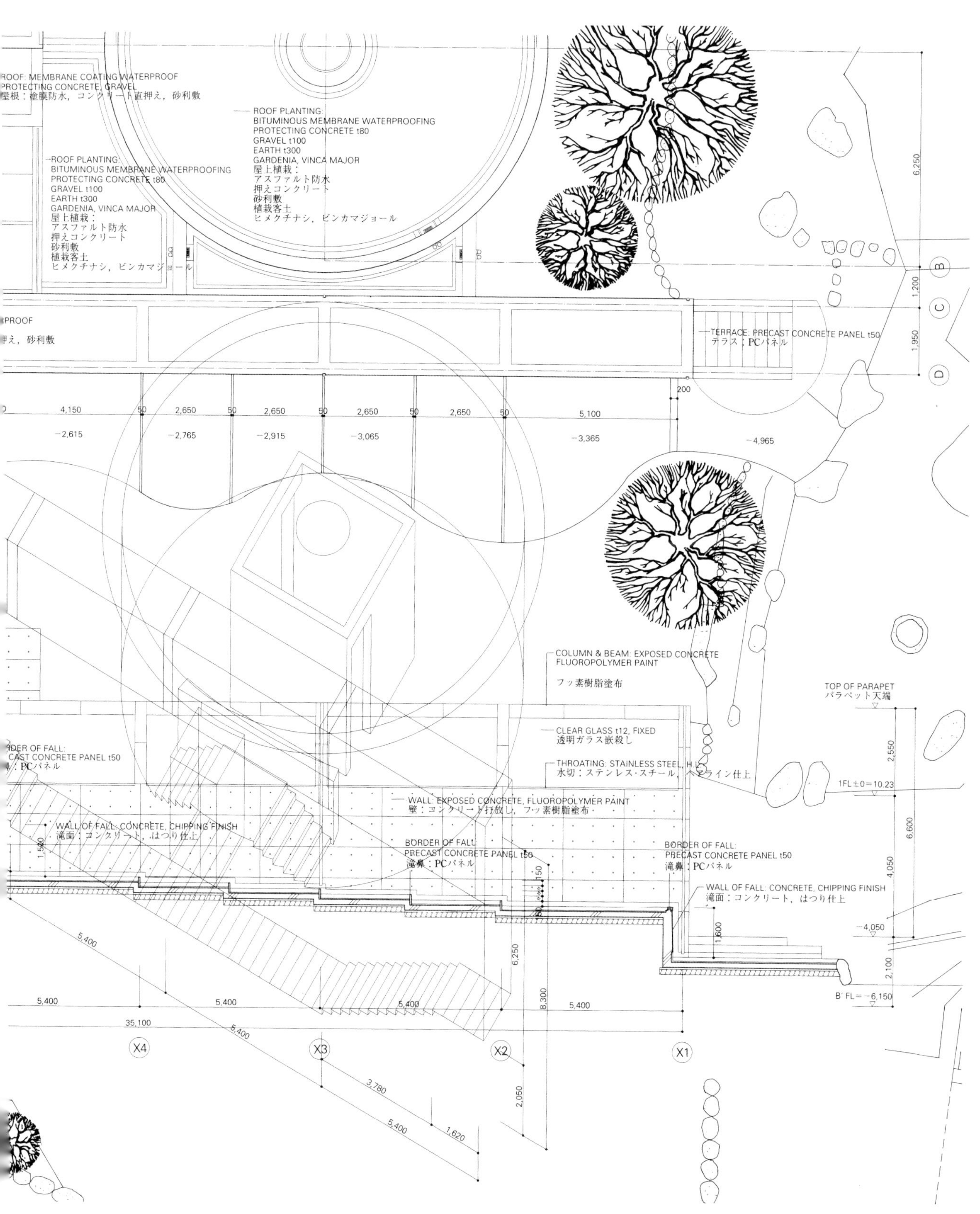

ROOF: MEMBRANE COATING WATERPROOF
PROTECTING CONCRETE, GRAVEL
屋根：塗膜防水，コンクリート直押え，砂利敷
ROOF PLANTING:
BITUMINOUS MEMBRANE WATERPROOFING
PROTECTING CONCRETE t80
GRAVEL t100
EARTH t300
GARDENIA, VINCA MAJOR
屋上植栽：
アスファルト防水
押えコンクリート
砂利敷
植栽客土
ヒメクチナシ，ビンカマジョール
ROOF PLANTING:
BITUMINOUS MEMBRANE WATERPROOFING
PROTECTING CONCRETE t80
GRAVEL t100
EARTH t300
GARDENIA, VINCA MAJOR
屋上植栽：
アスファルト防水
押えコンクリート
砂利敷
植栽客土
ヒメクチナシ，ビンカマジョール
TERRACE: PRECAST CONCRETE PANEL t50
テラス：PCパネル
COLUMN & BEAM: EXPOSED CONCRETE
FLUOROPOLYMER PAINT
フッ素樹脂塗布
TOP OF PARAPET
パラペット天端
CLEAR GLASS t12, FIXED
透明ガラス嵌殺し
THROATING: STAINLESS STEEL, HL
水切：ステンレス・スチール，ヘアライン仕上
1FL±0=10.23
WALL: EXPOSED CONCRETE, FLUOROPOLYMER PAINT
壁：コンクリート打放し，フッ素樹脂塗布
WALL OF FALL: CONCRETE, CHIPPING FINISH
滝面：コンクリート，はつり仕上
BORDER OF FALL:
PRECAST CONCRETE PANEL t50
滝鼻：PCパネル
BORDER OF FALL:
PRECAST CONCRETE PANEL t50
滝鼻：PCパネル
WALL OF FALL: CONCRETE, CHIPPING FINISH
滝面：コンクリート，はつり仕上
B' FL=−6,150
X4
X3
X2
X1

Detailed drawing of the exhibition space. The forms of the addition are thoroughly simplified, yet on the other hand, by ensuring that the approach route passes through the mountain villa, the contrasting old and new architectures are connected without difficulties, and an unprecedented new power is brought into this place.

展示詳細図。新築部の造形を徹底して簡素化し、一方でそのアプローチを必ず山荘を通るようにしたことで、対比的な新旧の建築が無理なく連続、かつてにはなかった新しい力が場に付加された。

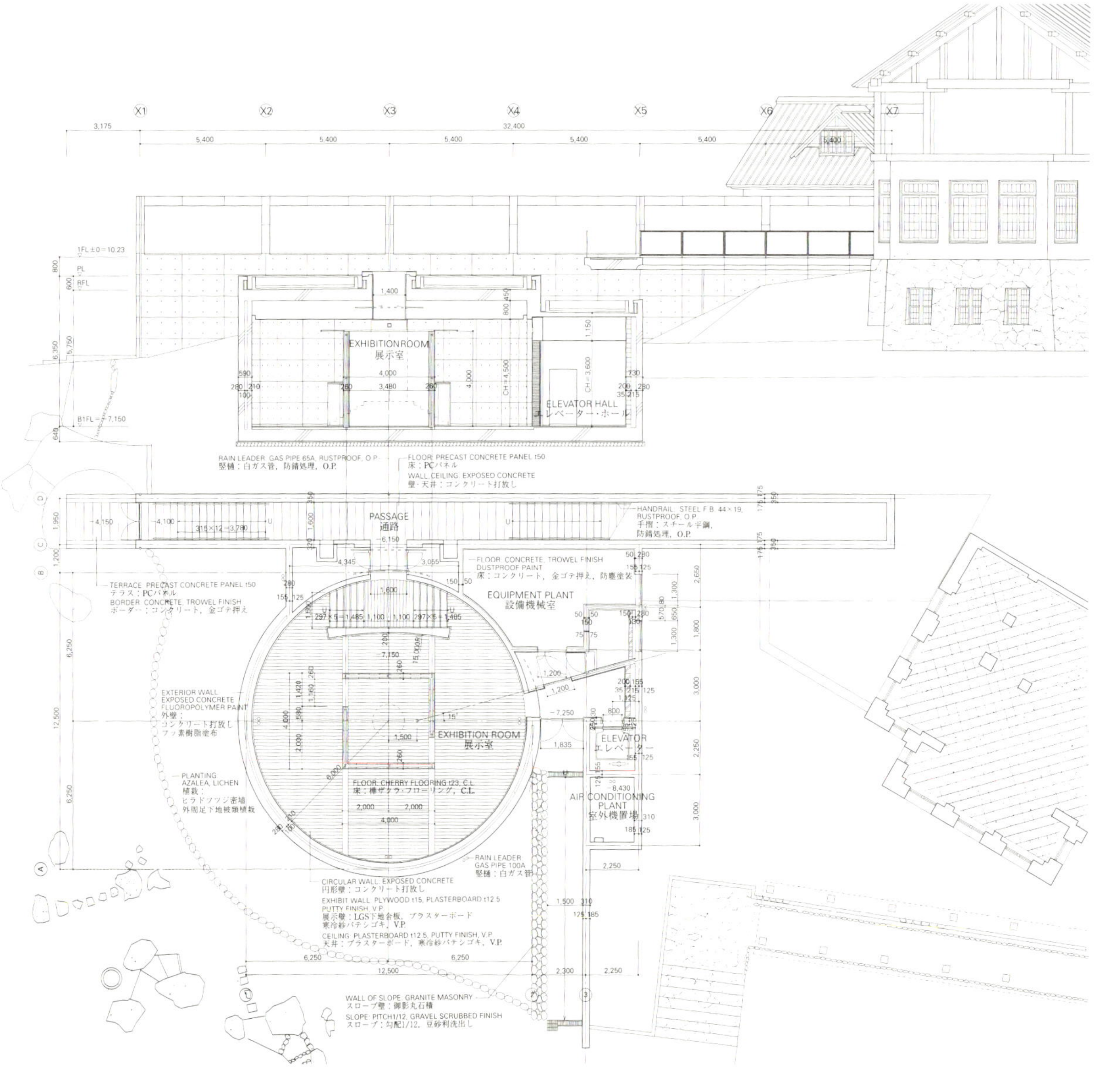

EXHIBITION ROOM
展示室
ELEVATOR HALL
エレベーター・ホール
RAIN LEADER: GAS PIPE 65A, RUSTPROOF, O.P.
竪樋：白ガス管，防錆処理，O.P.
FLOOR: PRECAST CONCRETE PANEL t50
床：PCパネル
WALL, CEILING: EXPOSED CONCRETE
壁・天井：コンクリート打放し
PASSAGE
通路
HANDRAIL: STEEL F.B. 44×19, RUSTPROOF, O.P.
手摺：スチール平鋼，防錆処理，O.P.
FLOOR: CONCRETE, TROWEL FINISH, DUSTPROOF PAINT
床：コンクリート，金ゴテ押え，防塵塗装
TERRACE: PRECAST CONCRETE PANEL t50
テラス：PCパネル
BORDER: CONCRETE, TROWEL FINISH
ボーダー：コンクリート，金ゴテ押え
EQUIPMENT PLANT
設備機械室
EXTERIOR WALL: EXPOSED CONCRETE, FLUOROPOLYMER PAINT
外壁：コンクリート打放し，フッ素樹脂塗布
EXHIBITION ROOM
展示室
ELEVATOR
エレベーター
PLANTING: AZALEA, LICHEN
植栽：ヒラドツツジ密植，外周足下地被類植栽
FLOOR: CHERRY FLOORING t23, C.L.
床：桜ザクラ・フローリング，C.L.
AIR CONDITIONING PLANT
室外機置場
RAIN LEADER: GAS PIPE 100A
竪樋：白ガス管
CIRCULAR WALL: EXPOSED CONCRETE
円形壁：コンクリート打放し
EXHIBIT WALL: PLYWOOD t15, PLASTERBOARD t12.5, PUTTY FINISH, V.P.
展示壁：LGS下地合板，プラスターボード，寒冷紗パテシゴキ，V.P.
CEILING: PLASTERBOARD t12.5, PUTTY FINISH, V.P.
天井：プラスターボード，寒冷紗パテシゴキ，V.P.
WALL OF SLOPE: GRANITE MASONRY
スロープ壁：御影丸石積
SLOPE: PITCH1/12, GRAVEL SCRUBBED FINISH
スロープ：勾配1/12，豆砂利洗出し

Pulitzer Foundation for the Arts
ピューリッツァー美術館

1. St. Louis, Missouri, U.S.A.　アメリカ合衆国 ミズーリ州 セントルイス
2. 1991.5-1994.12 (phase Ⅰ) / 1995.7-1997.10 (phase Ⅱ)
3. 1997.11-2001.7

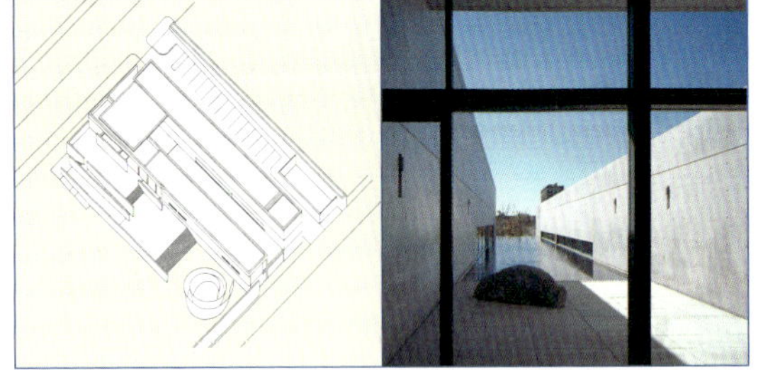

In the spring of 1991 I visited St. Louis at the invitation of Joseph Pulitzer Jr., now deceased but then head of the family that founded the Pulitzer Prize. Offering his own contemporary art collection in order to establish a cultural project for local urban renewal, Joseph's first plan was to make a gallery by refurbishing an old car factory located on a derelict site in the city center. In response to this, I proposed the idea of boldly setting the necessary new volume at some distance from the existing part, and turning the buffer space interposed between the new and old buildings into a water garden. In the middle of the brutal townscape I wanted to make a discreet pleasure garden for art, engulfed in water and greenery.

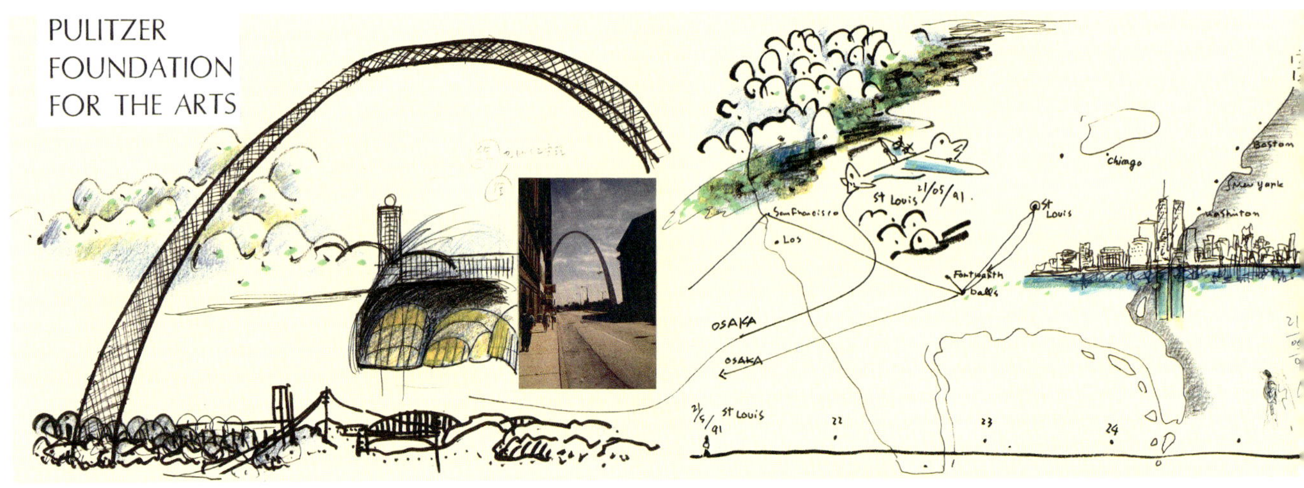

1

ピューリッツァー賞を創設したファミリーの当主、今は亡きジョセフ・ピューリッツァー・ジュニアの依頼でセントルイスを訪れたのは1991年の春だった。自らの現代美術のコレクションを提供し、地域再生のための文化プロジェクトを立ち上げる――ジョセフの当初の構想は、市中心部の荒廃した地域にある古い自動車工場を改修し、ギャラリーをつくろうというものだった。それに対し、私は、新たに必要なヴォリュームを、あえて既存部分と距離をおいて配置し、その新旧建物に挟まれる余白の部分を水庭とするアイディアを提案した。殺伐とした街並みの中に、水と緑に包まれたささやかなアートの楽園をつくりたいと考えていた。

2

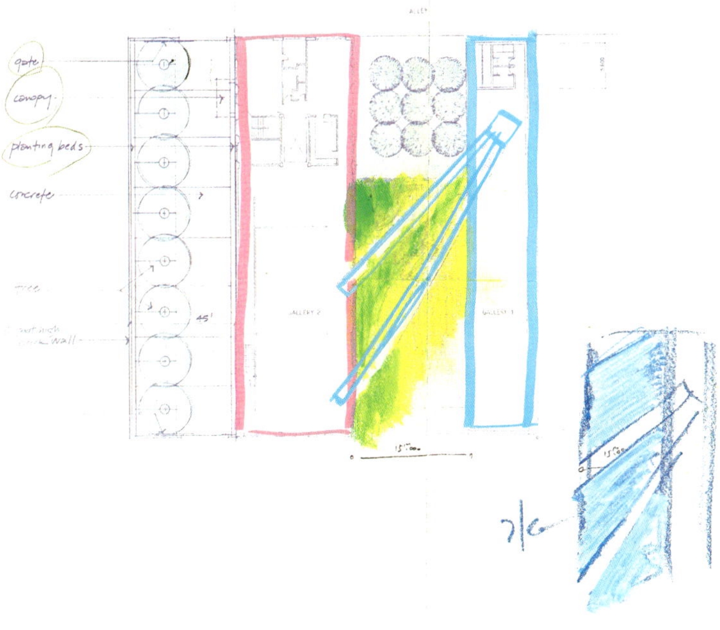

3

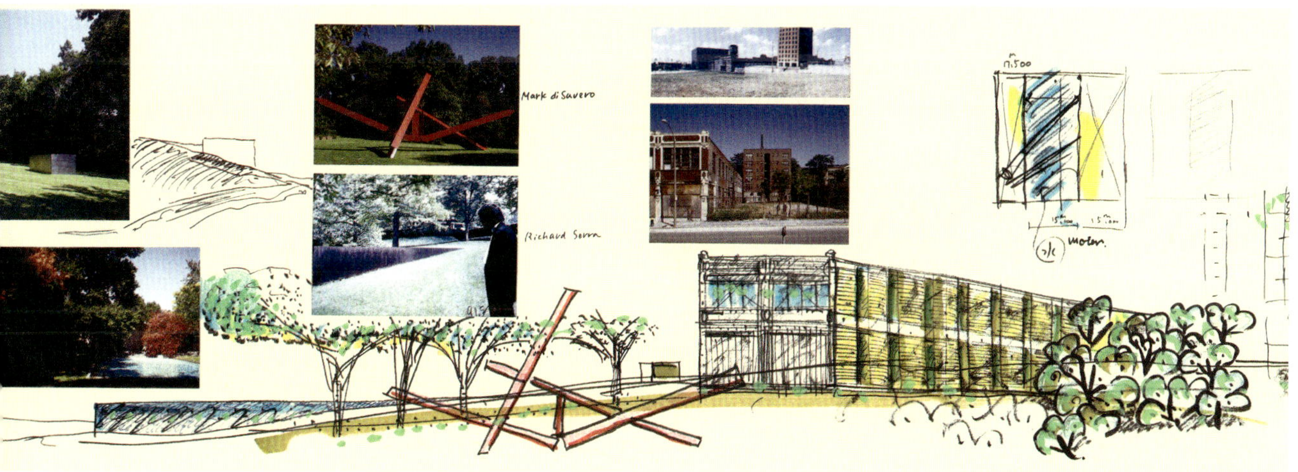

1 Part of a sketch done in the style of a traditional picture scroll (called "pata-pata"). It comprises a record of Ando's 1991 invitation to St. Louis to visit the site and the client's private residence.
2 An old car factory stood on the first construction site.
3, 4 Study sketches from the basic design stage. Delineating the idea of wedge-shaped walkways that three-dimensionally connect the old and new buildings through the medium of a water garden.

1 パタパタと呼ばれる絵巻物風のスケッチの一部。1991 年にセントルイスに招かれ、敷地とクライアントの自邸を訪れたときの記録が綴られている。
2 当初の建設地は古い自動車工場が建つ敷地だった。
3, 4 基本設計段階の検討図。水庭を介して、立体的に新旧建物をつなぐ楔形の歩廊のアイディアが描かれている。

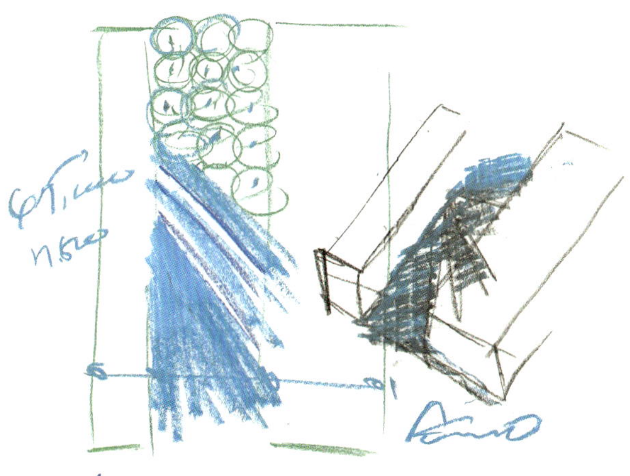
4

In 1994, the first design was suspended due to various circumstances. Before long, Joseph passed away, and it appeared that project had reached a standstill. However, his widow Emily Rauh Pulitzer took on her husband's cherished wish and fought to resume the project. The following year, the project was restarted as a new architectural project on a new site. The idea of placing a water garden as a buffer space in the center of the building was utilized unchanged. With the simplest possible form, it was composed as the ultimate box, completely stripped of all superfluous aspects. This architecture is an homage to Joseph Pulitzer Jr., who deeply loved the purity of modern art.

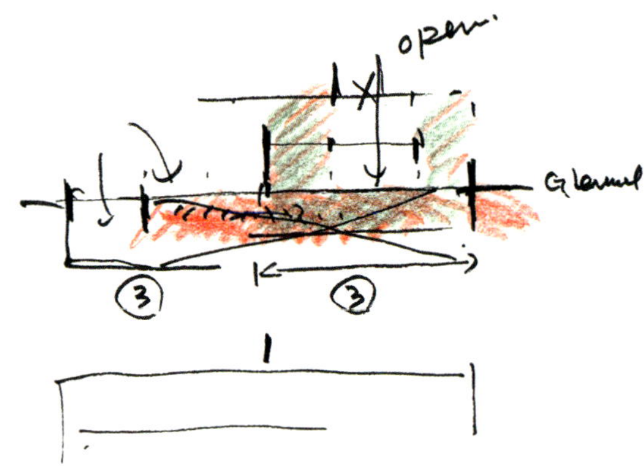

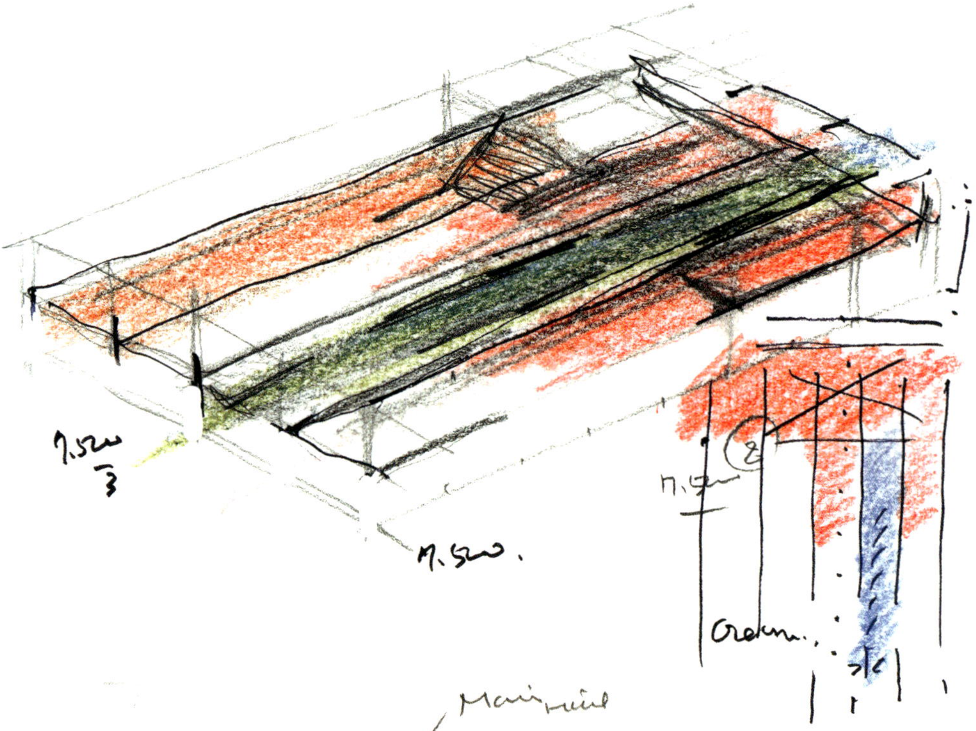

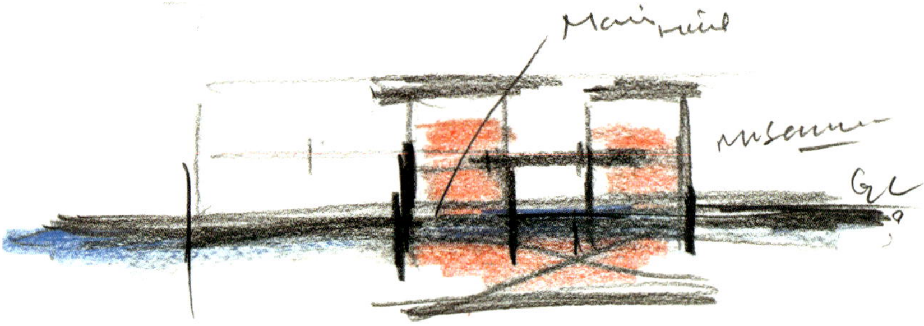

1994年、諸事情で第I期計画は中断した。ほどなくジョセフが亡くなり、プロジェクトは暗礁に乗り上げるかに見えたが、残されたエミリー・ラウ・ピューリッツァー夫人が夫の遺志を引き継ぎ、プロジェクトの続行のために奮闘。そして翌95年、プロジェクトは新たな敷地での新たな建築のプロジェクトとして再スタートを切った。建物中央を余白として水庭にあてるアイディアはそのままに生かした。それをできるだけ単純な形で、余分なものを一切剥ぎ取った究極の箱として構成する。モダンアートの純粋さをこよなく愛した、ジョセフ・ピューリッツァー・ジュニアへのオマージュとなる建築だ。

The intended architecture is embedded within a grid space based on an identical module in plan and section. How to insert the space of the water garden within a severe geometric composition, and how to draw the breath of nature into the building interior? Geometric ideas were iterated in order to fix the spatial diagram.

平面・断面ともに同じモジュールのグリッド空間の中に、目指す建築を切り取っていく。厳格な幾何学的構成の中に水庭のスペースをいかに組み込むか、その自然の息吹を建物内部にいかに引き込むか——空間の図式を固めるための数学的思考が繰り返される。

In this project, from the initial planning stage onward, it was necessary to have meetings with Ellsworth Kelly and Richard Serra, from whom Joseph had commissioned works. Kelly visited the site several times to examine the content and placement of his work. Every time I spoke to Serra, the size of the work that he was conceiving kept expanding, which finally forced changes in the design of the building apertures. Our opinions conflicted at times, but the potential of this art museum was certainly strengthened through the many uncompromising dialogues I had with them. As a collaboration between architecture and art right from the first stage of planning, this was an exceptional task, a pursuit of what I believe to be an ideal art museum.

このプロジェクトでは、ジョセフから作品制作を依頼されていたエルスワース・ケリー、リチャード・セラと、計画の初期段階から打ち合わせをする必要があった。ケリーは、何回も現場に訪れて作品の位置と内容を検討した。セラは、話を聞くたびに構想している作品の大きさが拡大し、挙句に開口部の設計変更を迫ってきたことさえあった。ときに意見は衝突したが、この妥協のない対話を彼らと繰り返していくうちに、美術館のポテンシャルは確実に強まっていった。計画の初期段階からの建築とアートのコラボレーションという、私の思う美術館の理想を追求し得た稀有な仕事だった。

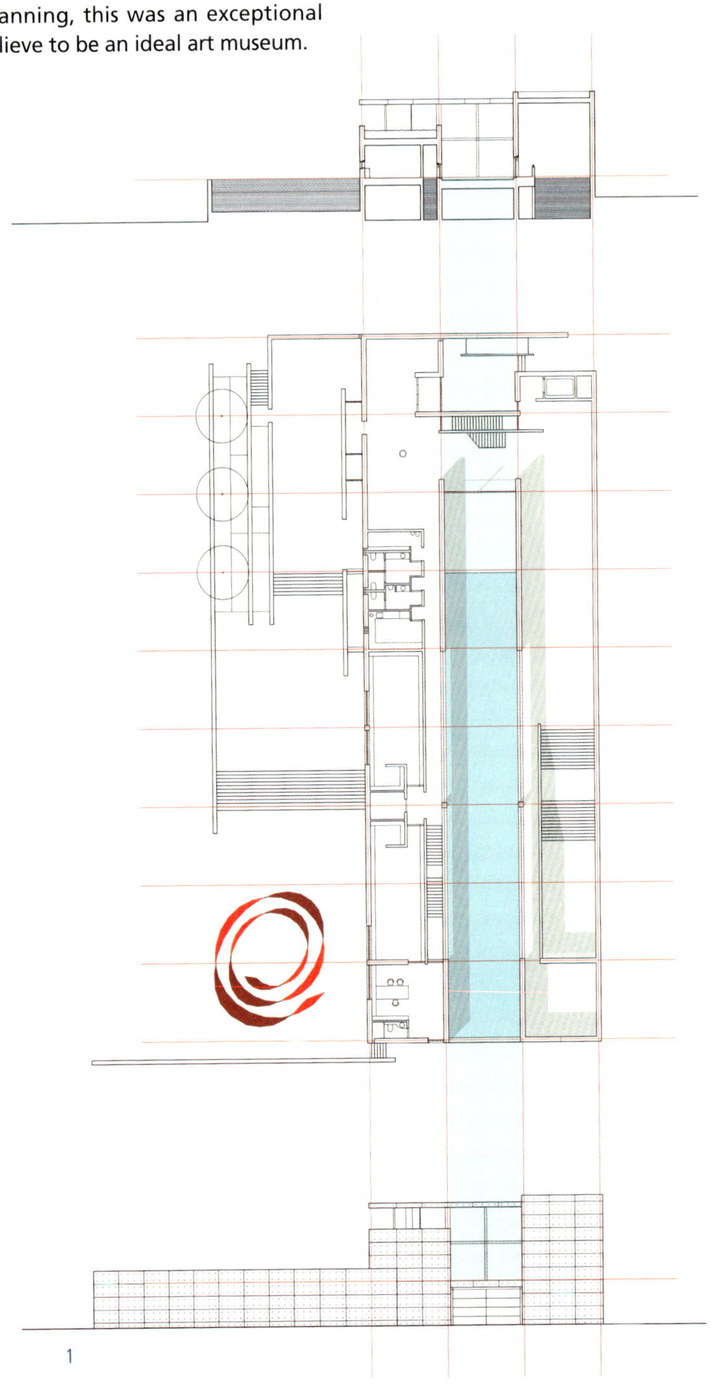

1

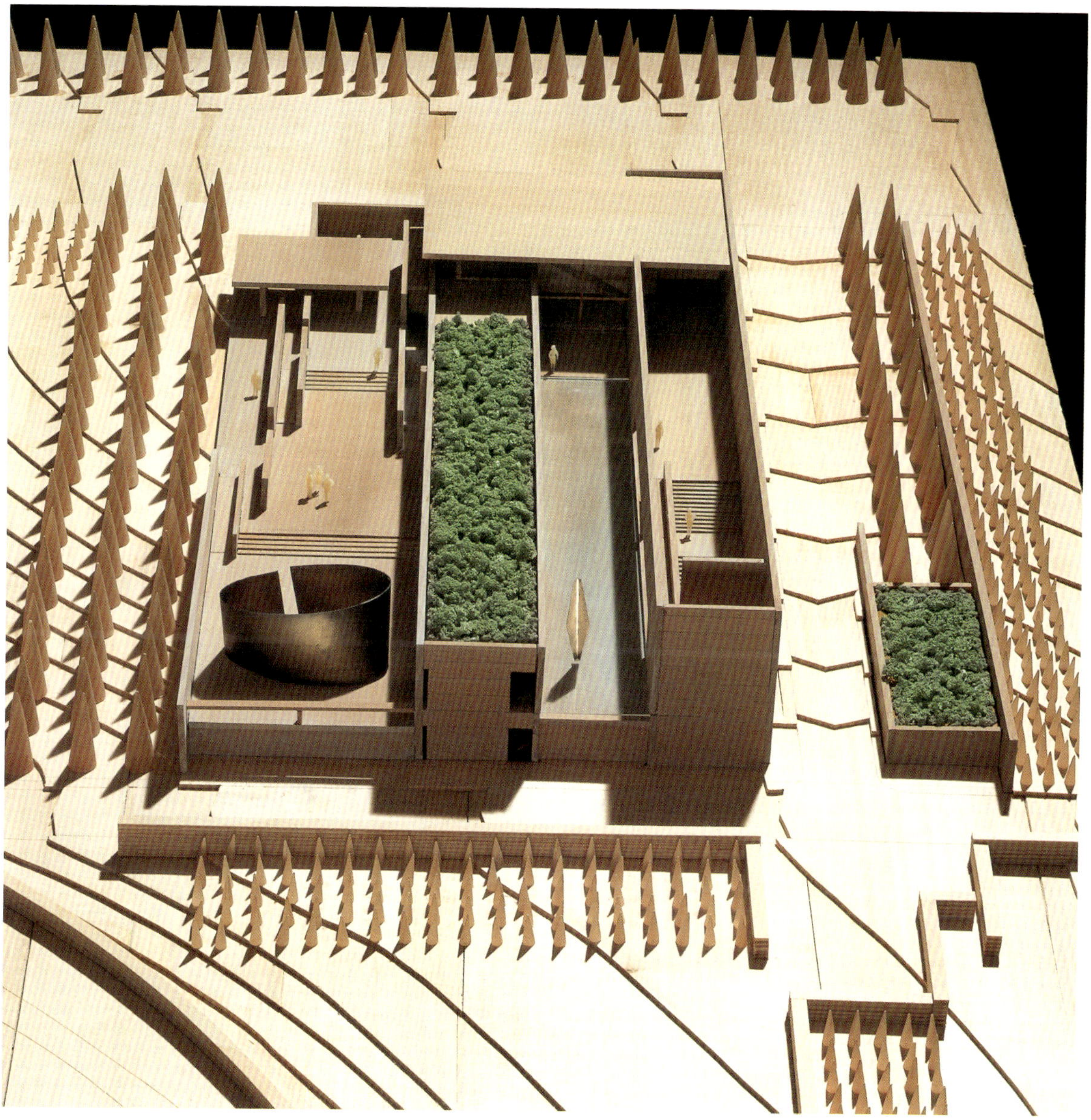

1 From above: section, plan, elevation. The water, as a buffer space piercing the building, produces a complex space in the center of a simple composition. Serra's Cor-ten steel work, which has a sense of scale equal to that of the building, is thought of as part of the architecture.

2 Longitudinal section of the gallery wing. Kelly's 8.54m-high "Blue Black" sculpture is placed on a wall that receives illumination from the skylight in the deepest part of the void space.

1 上から断面図、平面図、立面図。建物を貫く余白としての水が、単純な構成の中に、複雑な空間を生み出す。建物と同等のスケール感をもつセラのコールテン鋼の作品は建築の一部として考えられた。

2 ギャラリー棟の長手断面図。吹き抜け最奥部のトップライトの光を受け止める壁に、高さ 8.54 mのケリーの彫刻「ブルー・ブラック」が設置された。

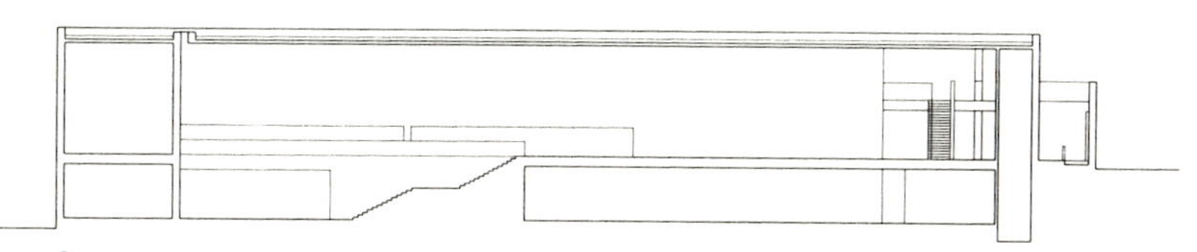

2

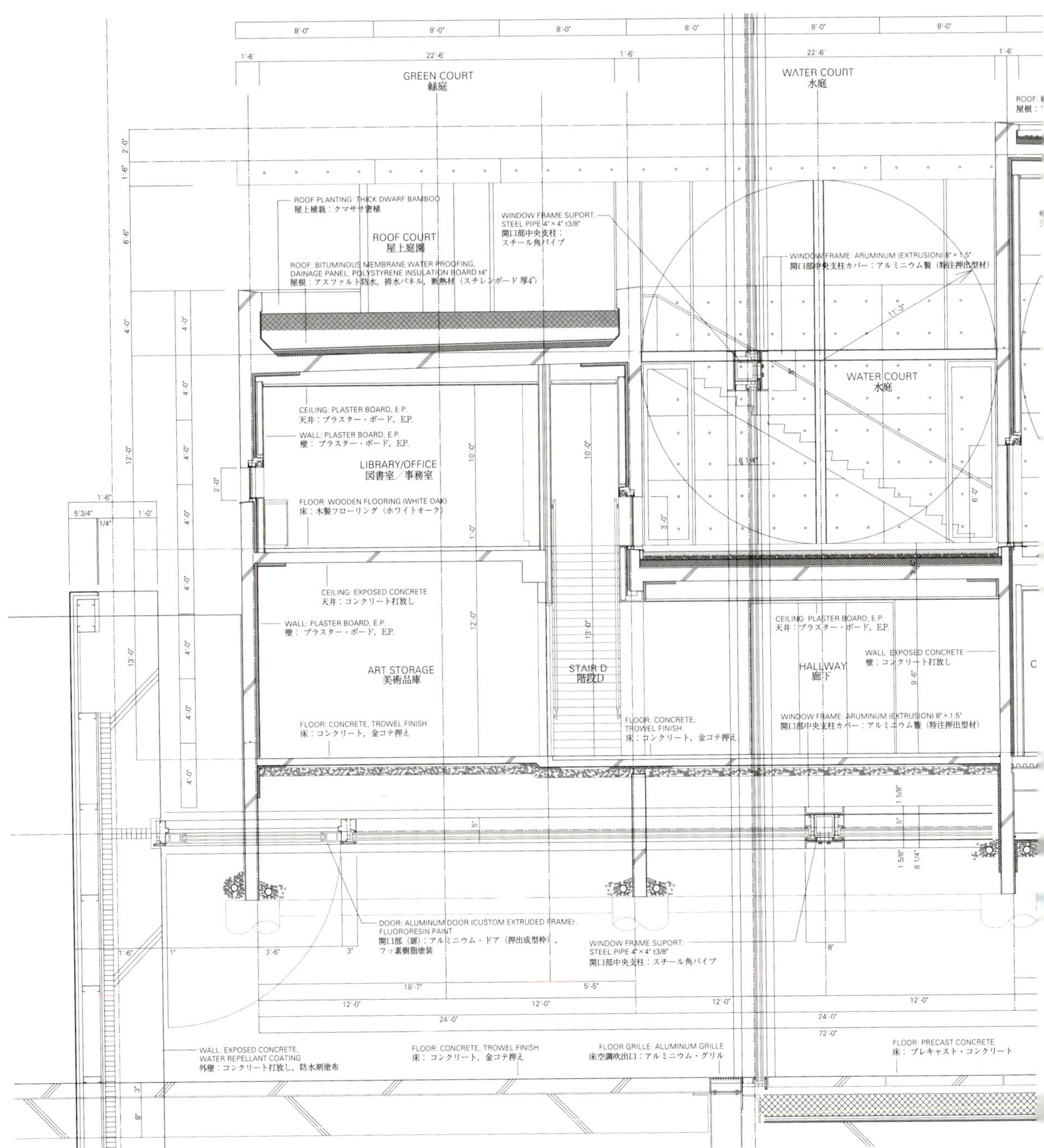

Sectional details. A pair of volumes with differing heights. Architecture aimed at a perfect geometric harmony.

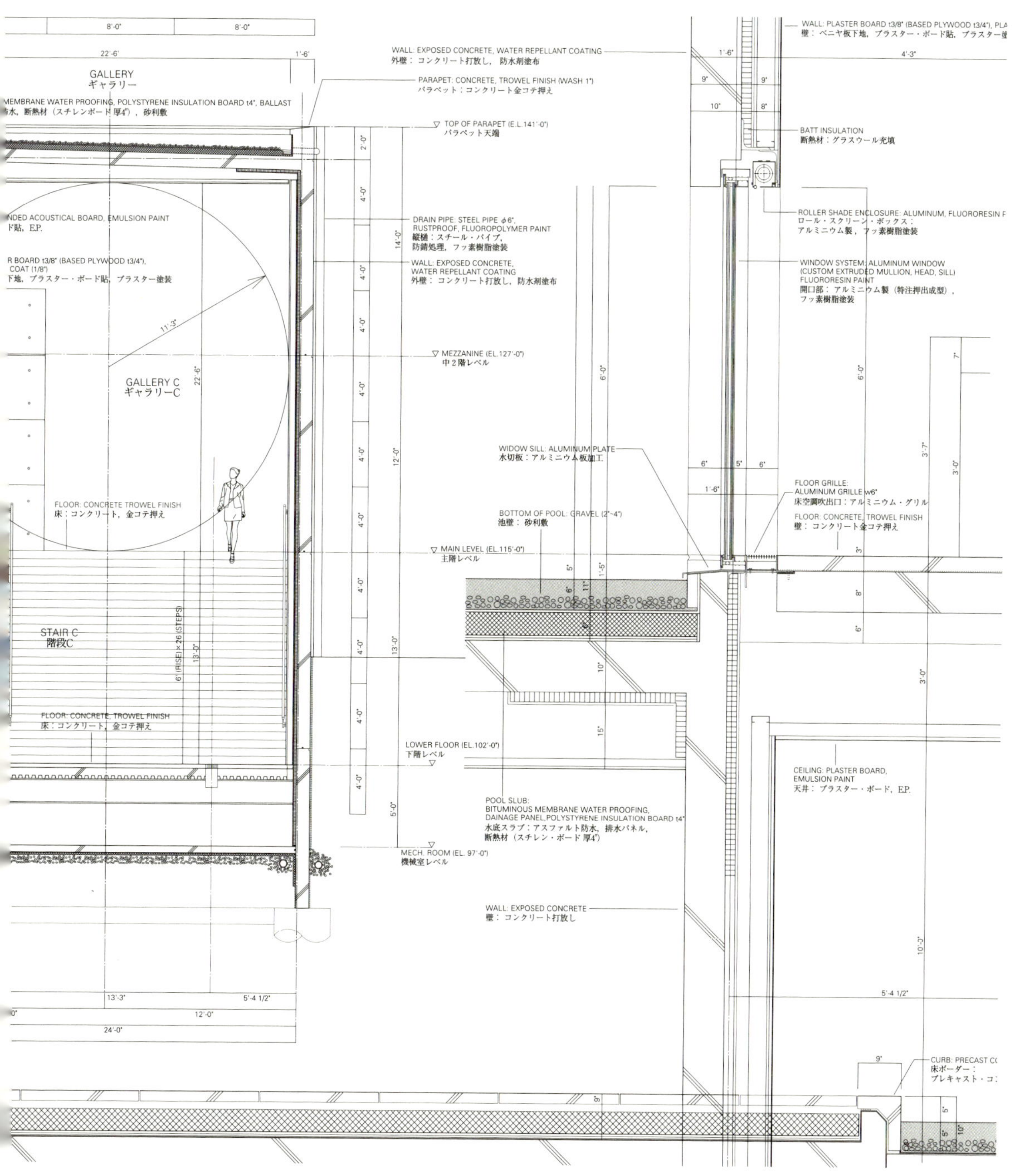

断面詳細図。高さの異なる一対のヴォリューム。
完全なる幾何学的調和を目指した建築。

Gallery Noda
ギャラリー野田

1. Kobe, Hyogo, Japan　兵庫県神戸市
2. 1991.12-1992.5
3. 1992.6-1993.1

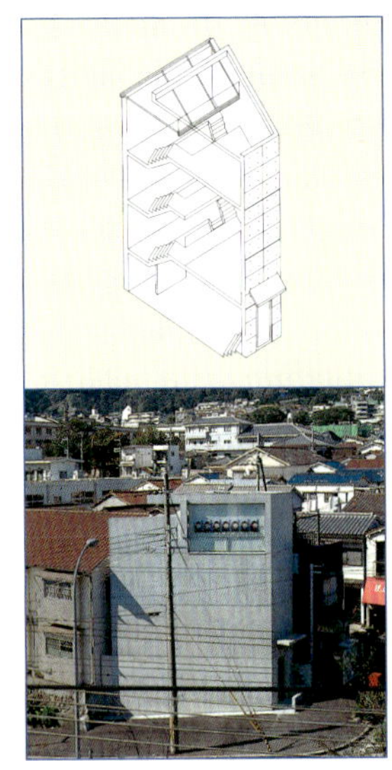

This is a tiny house built on a wedge-shaped site of less than 12 *tsubo* (40m^2) inserted between two roads set along a railway line. The client harbored the unreasonable hope to combine a gallery, an atelier, and a house, including a large bathtub in a living room with a high ceiling. Given the unbalanced conditions—cramped site, strict budget, the client's overinflated dreams—a unique house emerged as if a stairwell had been directly transformed into architecture.

線路沿いの2本の道路に挟まれた12坪足らずの楔形の敷地につくった極小の住宅である。クライアントはそこにギャラリーとアトリエと住居、天井の高い居間に大きなバスタブをつくろうと過大な思いを抱いていた。狭小な敷地と厳しい予算、膨らみすぎたクライアントの夢——アンバランスな条件の中で、吹き抜け階段をそのまま建築としたような、ユニークな家が生まれた。

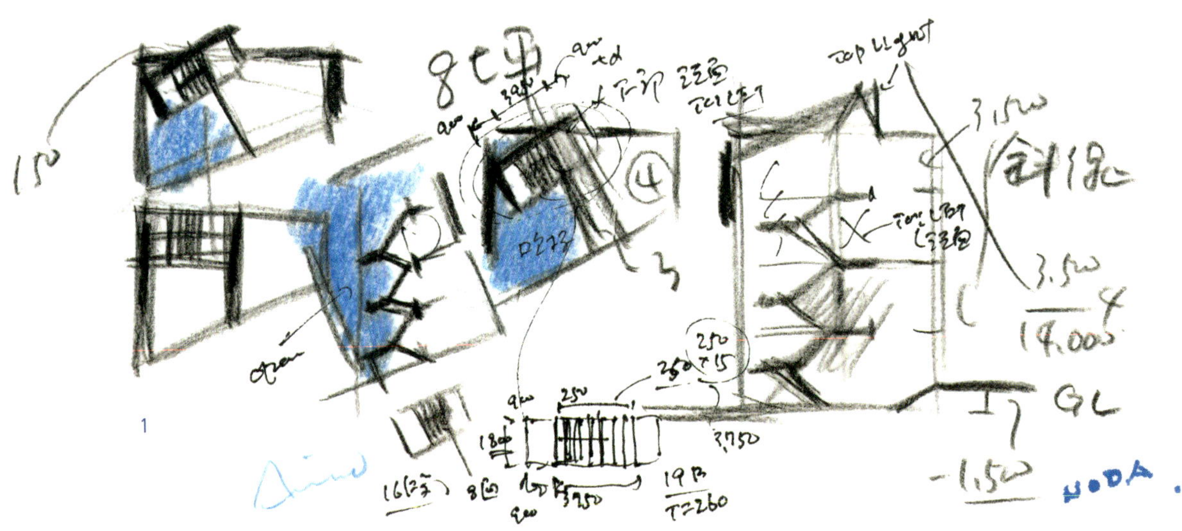

1

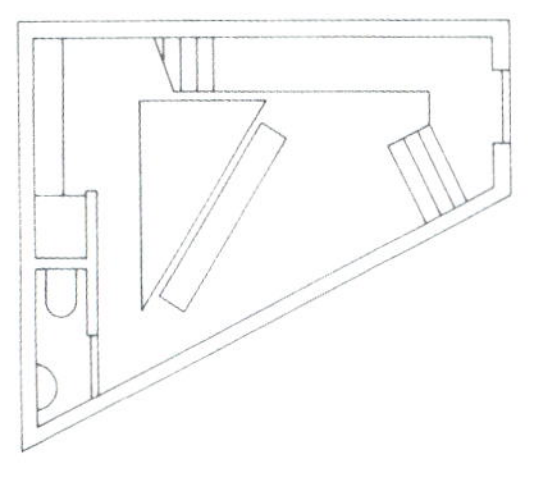
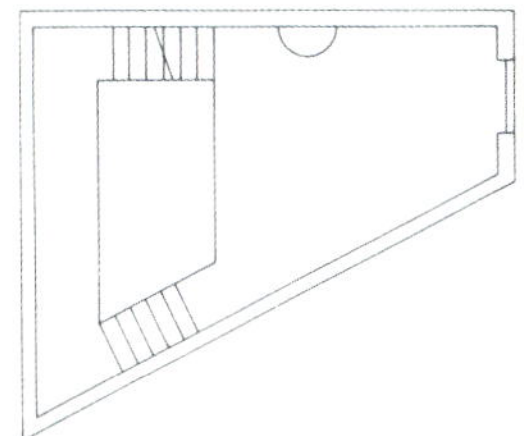
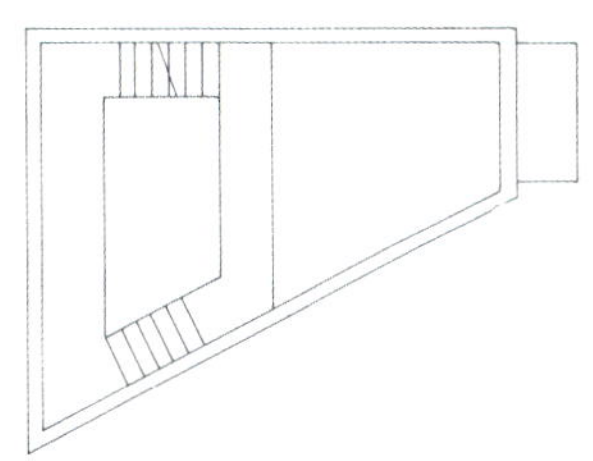
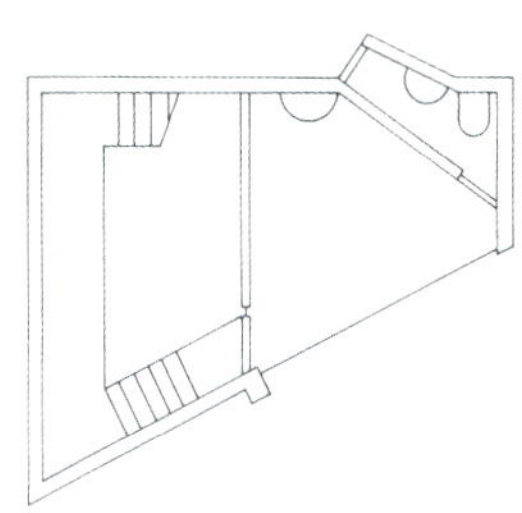

2

1 Image sketches. A composition with the stairwell itself extending in the vertical direction as the gallery, the landing on the second floor level as an atelier with a double-height ceiling, and the rooftop as a residence.
2 From left: first floor plan, second floor plan, void, rooftop plan.
3 Image sketch. Gallery in the shape of a flight of steps traversing the 10m-high void. Richly expressive natural light pours down from the skylight.

1 イメージスケッチ。吹き抜け階段そのものを垂直方向に伸びるギャラリーとして、2階レベルの踊り場を2層分の天井高さのアトリエに、最上階を住居とする構成。
2 左から1階、2階、吹き抜け、最上階平面。
3 イメージスケッチ。高さ10mの吹き抜けを巡る階段式のギャラリー。トップライトから表情豊かに自然光が降り注ぐ。

3

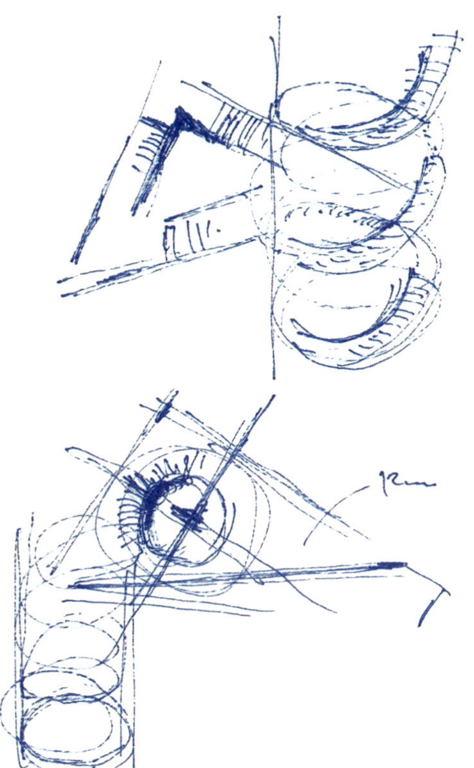

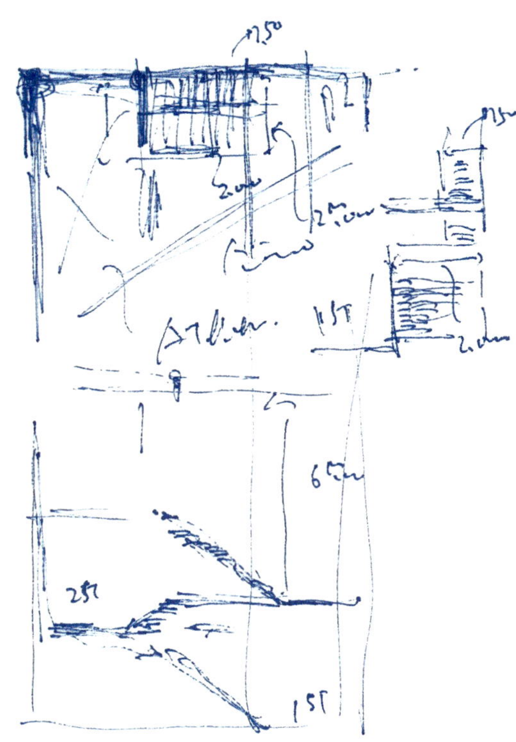

Exploratory sketches of the composition. While satisfying the minimum necessary functions within the strictly limited floor area, I wanted to make a rich space in which no hint of constriction may be felt—the theme was to connect the spaces vertically and combine the void and staircase in the layout, so a number of proposals were explored while searching for variations.

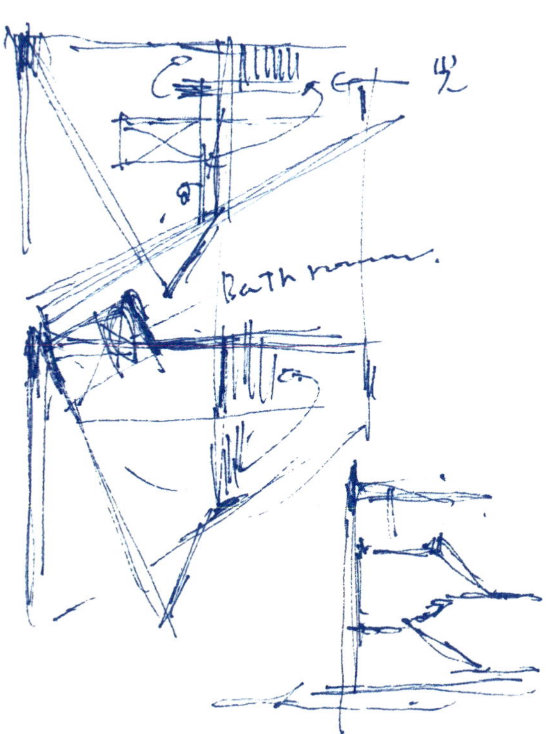

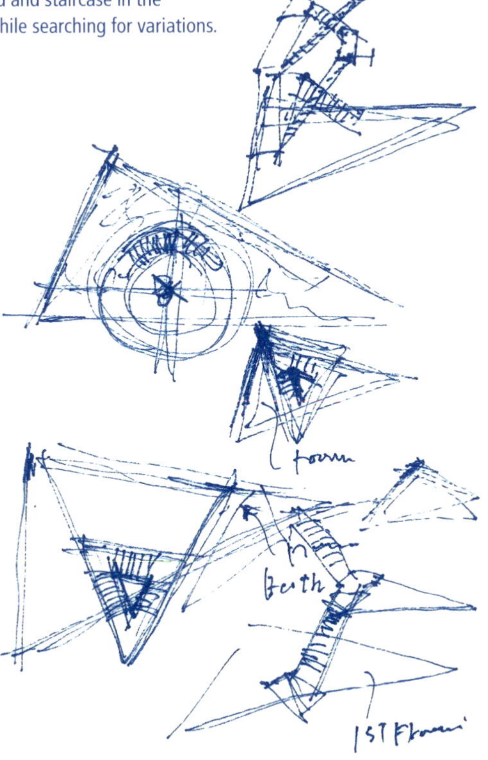

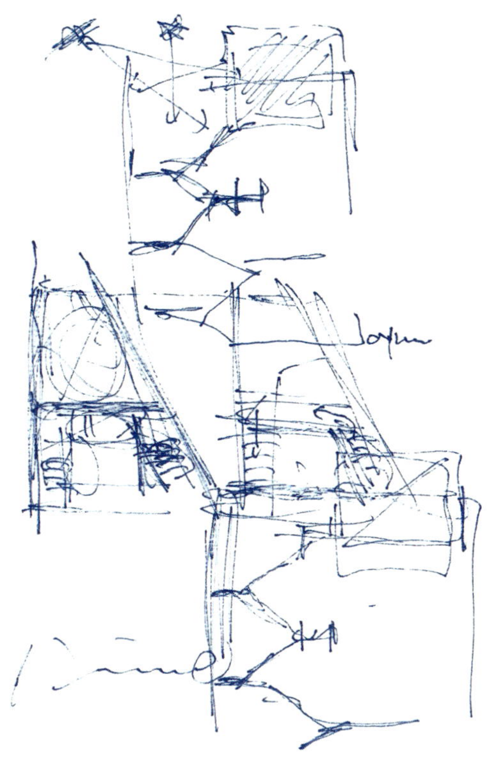

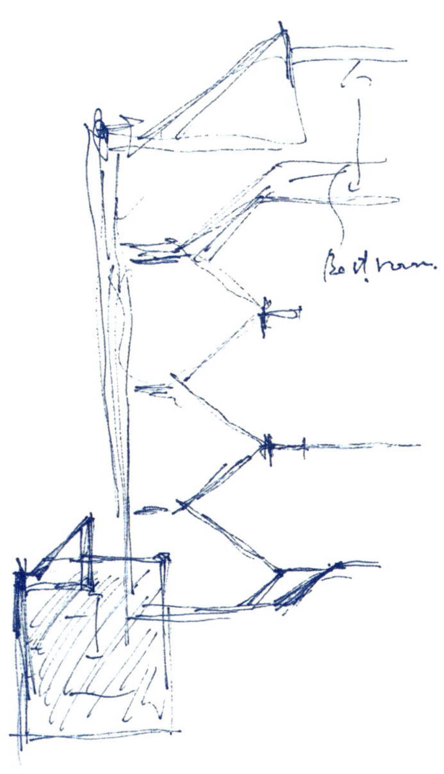

構成検討のスケッチ。厳しい面積の制約の中で、最低限必要な機能を満たしつつ、その狭さを微塵も感じさせない豊かな空間をつくりたい——主題は垂直方向の空間のつながり、階段と吹き抜けの配置に集約され、そのヴァリエーションを探るべく、いくつもの案が検討された。

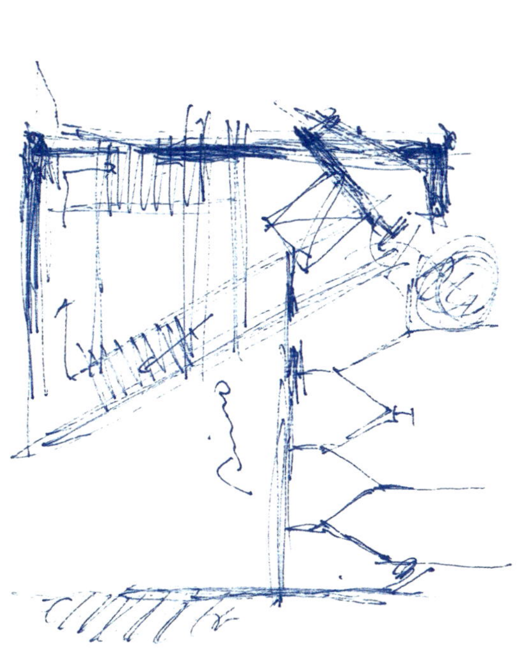

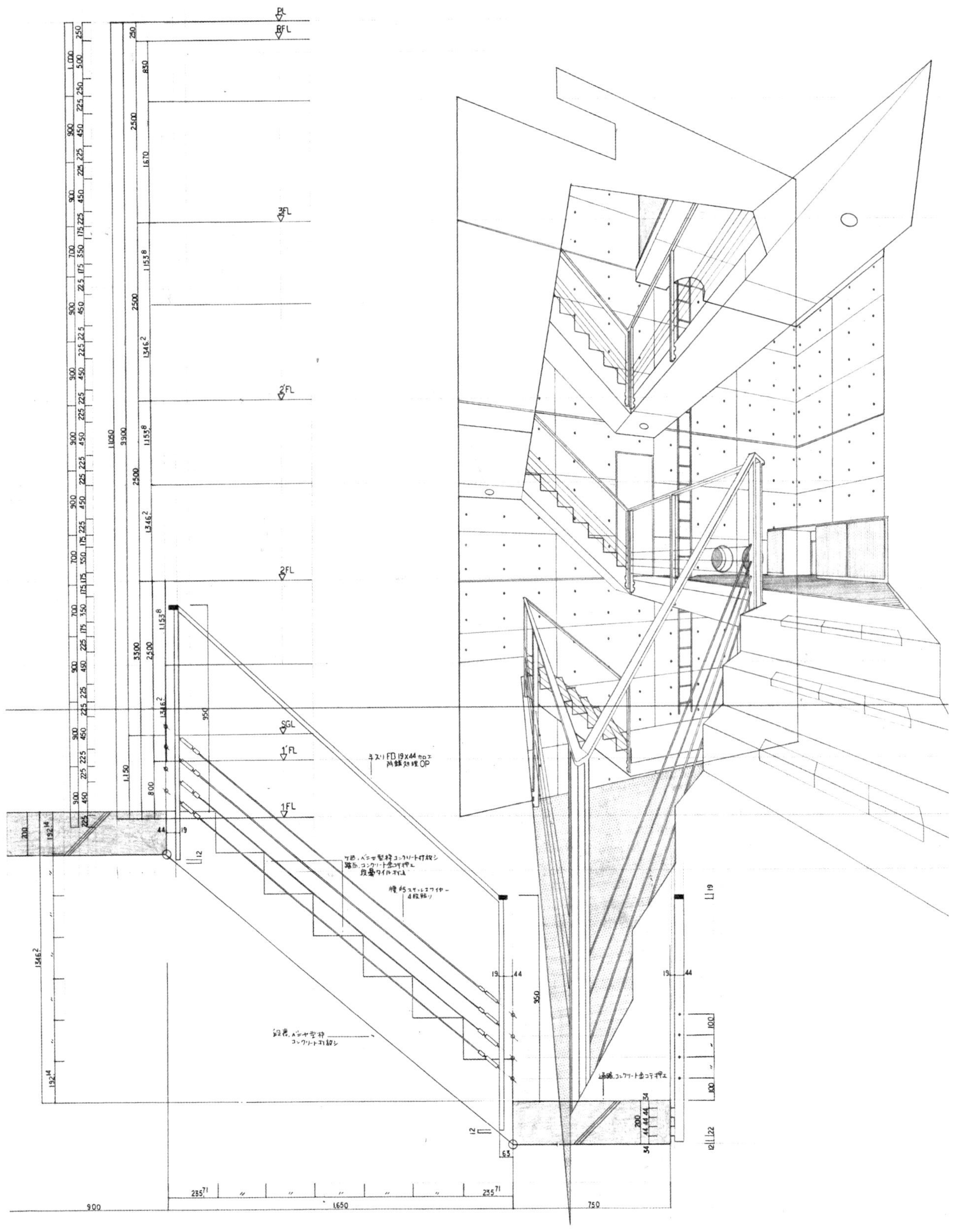

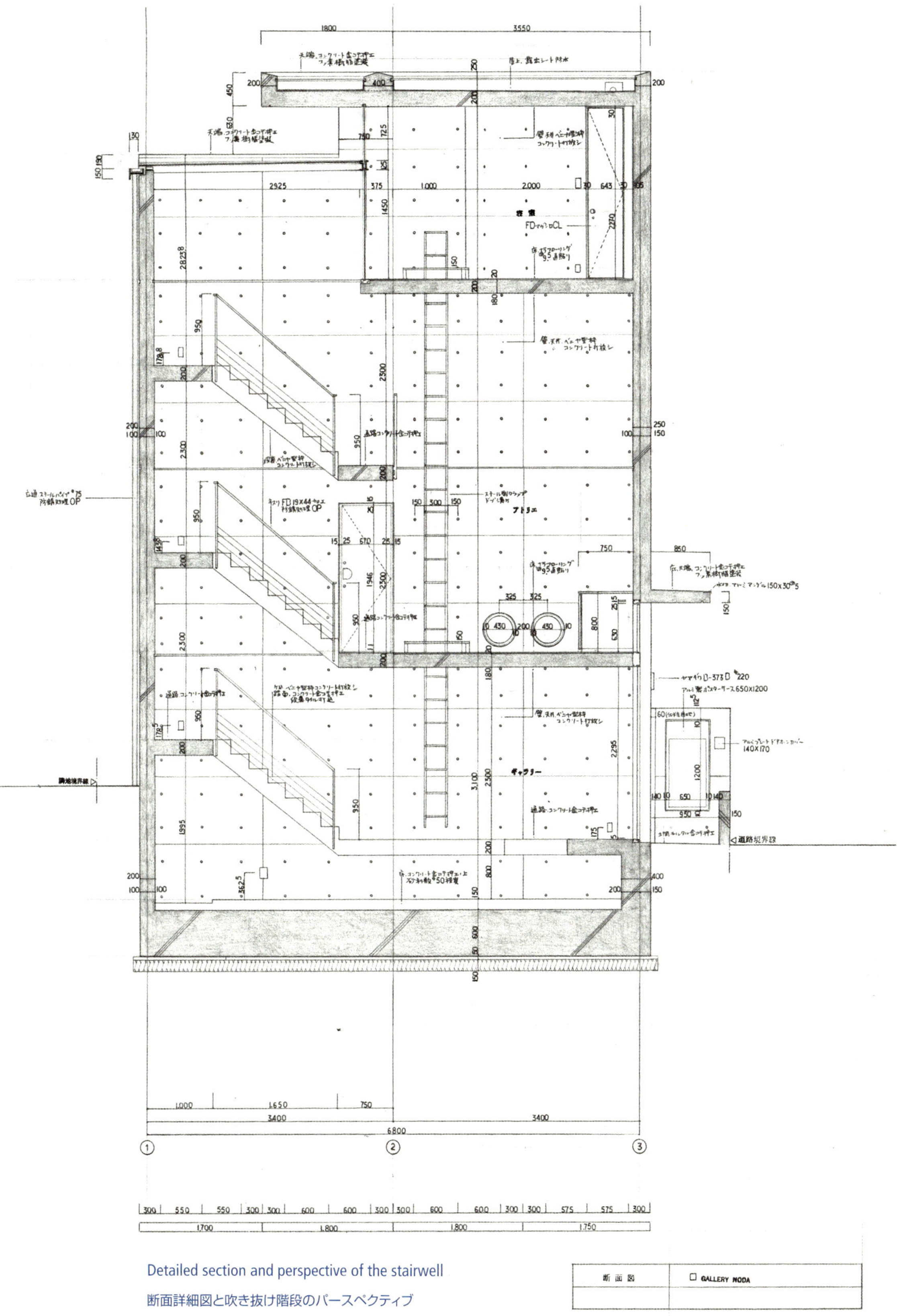

Detailed section and perspective of the stairwell

断面詳細図と吹き抜け階段のパースペクティブ

Nariwa Museum
成羽美術館

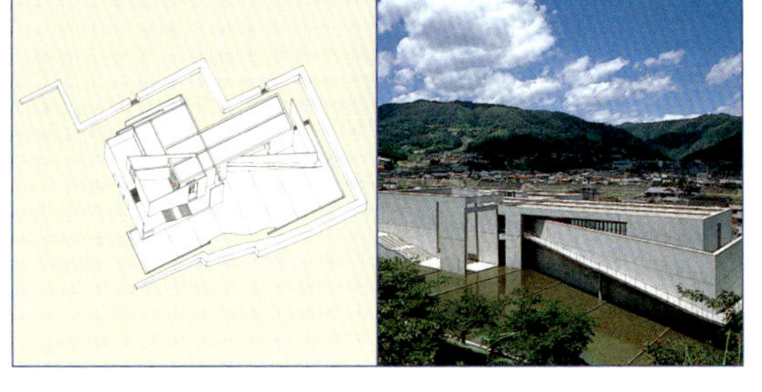

1. Takahashi, Okayama, Japan　岡山県高梁市
2. 1991.12-1993.3
3. 1993.4-1994.10

The site is in a provincial city located north of Kurashiki. This is a design for an art museum to exhibit a collection of Oriental art bequeathed by local artist Torajiro Kojima. On a site containing the ruins of an old mansion and a splendid stone wall, to the south there is a steep slope covered with lush greenery. Making maximum use of these site conditions, the theme was to create architecture that actualizes the individuality of the place.

敷地は倉敷の北に位置する地方都市。地元出身の画家児島虎次郎の残したオリエント美術のコレクションを展示する美術館の計画だ。旧屋敷跡であった敷地には立派な石垣があり、その南側には豊かな緑の急斜面が迫っていた。この立地条件を最大限に活かし、場所の個性を顕在化するような建築を主題としてつくった。

1

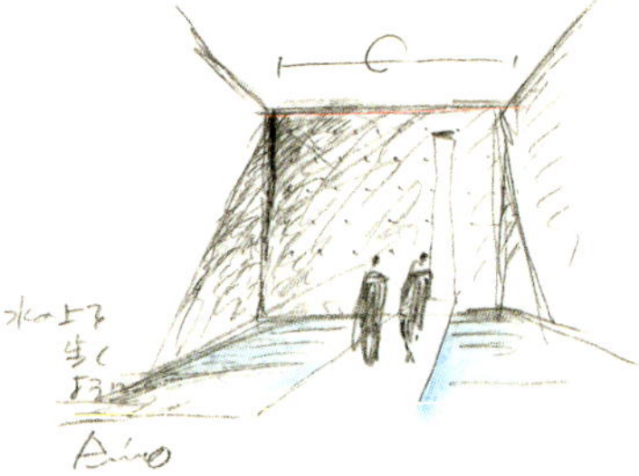

2

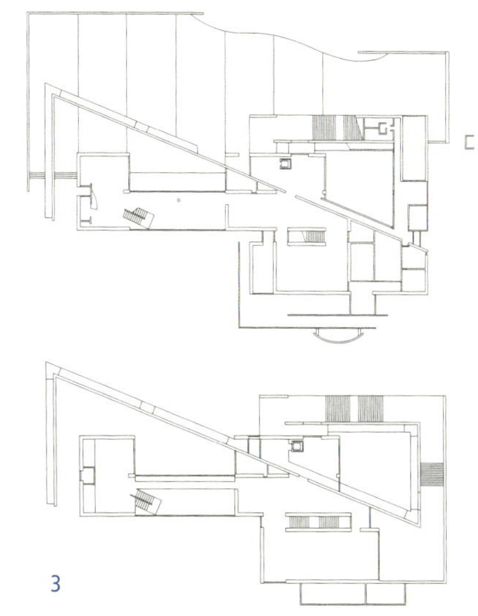

3

1 Exploratory compositional sketch of the stone wall in the topography, and local elements such as the scene of the tiled roofs of village houses visible from the site. Making a stark contrast with the geometrical composition of a square and an oblique line. Water is boldly drawn in so as to make a dramatic approach route and a quiet exhibition space.
2 Exploratory sketch of the approach route.
3 Plans.

1 石垣に地形、敷地から見える民家の瓦屋根の風景といった土着の要素と、構成検討スケッチ。強いコントラストをなす、1本の斜線と正方形による幾何学的構成。そこに大胆に水を引き込み、ドラマティックなアプローチと静謐な展示空間をつくる。
2 アプローチの検討スケッチ。
3 平面図。

FABRICA
(Benetton Communication Research Center)
FABRICA（ベネトンアートスクール）

1. Treviso, Italy　イタリア トレヴィソ
2. 1992.4-1994.12
3. 1992.10-2000.6

This is the design of an art school for young people studying craft and design. It was instigated by the fashion designer Benetton, whose main offices are located in Treviso, a small town in northeastern Italy. The site resembles the typical rural scenery of the Veneto area, so my concept was to begin with the repair and renovation of the Palladian villas remaining here. The repair and renovation of the existing parts gradually progressed while we had frequent conversations with the local artisans. I decided to bury most of the newly built parts under the ground. Rather than a futile clash between old and new buildings, I envisioned an architecture in which the old part is permitted to independently preserve its history unchanged, with new and old in sympathetic resonance.

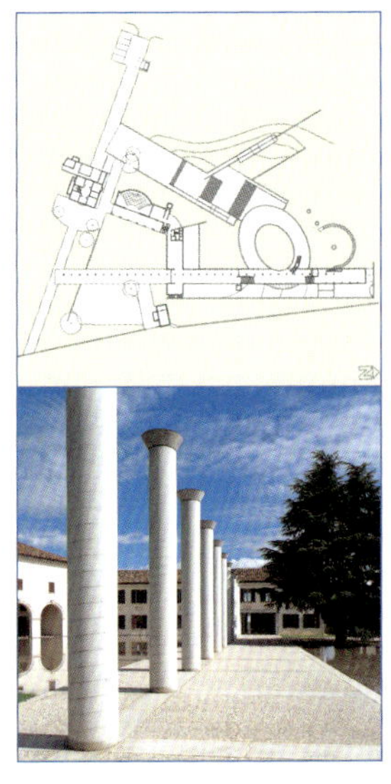

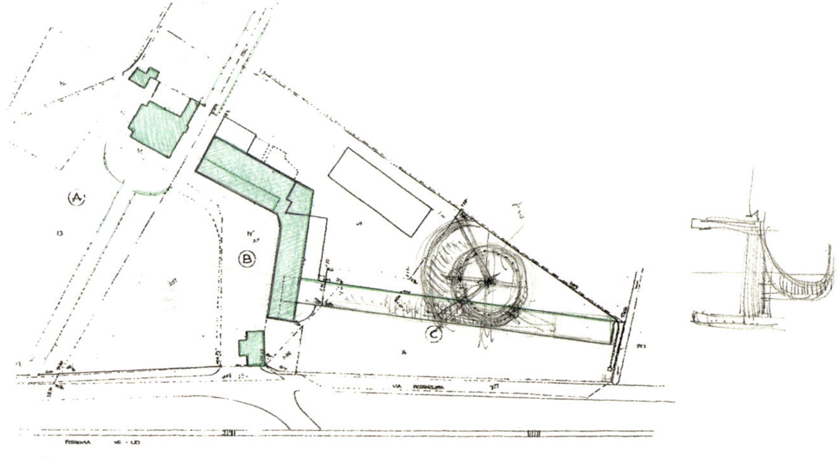

1

1, 2 First image sketches. Leaving the existing villa unchanged, adding underground architecture.
3 Exploratory drawing of the site layout. The geometries of the dry areas, and the gallery comprising a row of columns that pass through everything, make a beautiful contrast with the rural landscape.

1, 2 ファーストイメージスケッチ。既存ヴィラはそのままに、地下建築として増築する。
3 配置検討図。田園風景と美しい対比をみせるドライエリアの幾何学と全体を貫く列柱のギャラリー。

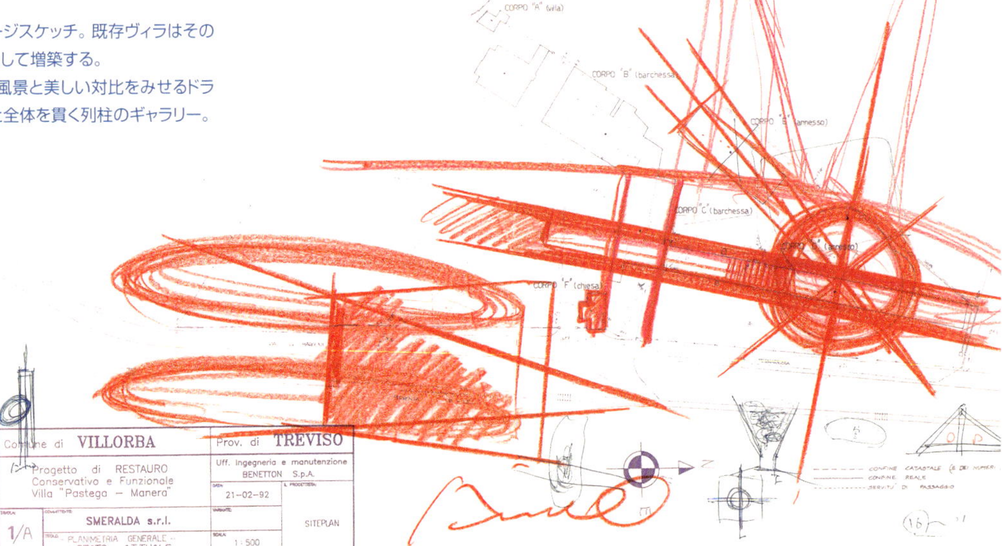

2

イタリア北東部の小さな街、トレヴィソに本社を置くファッションメーカー「ベネトン」の企画による、工芸やデザインを学ぶ若者のためのアートスクールの計画である。典型的なヴェネト地方の田園風景の様相を呈する敷地には、パッラーディオ風のヴィラ建築が残っており、それらの修復・再生を前提として構想した。既存部分の修復、再生に関しては現地の職人と対話を重ねながら時間をかけて進め、新たにつくる新築部分は、そのほとんどを地下に埋め込むよう考えた。新旧の建物を、いたずらに対立させるのではなく、古いものは古いなりにその歴史を自立的に保存、新旧が共振、共鳴しあうような建築を目論んだ。

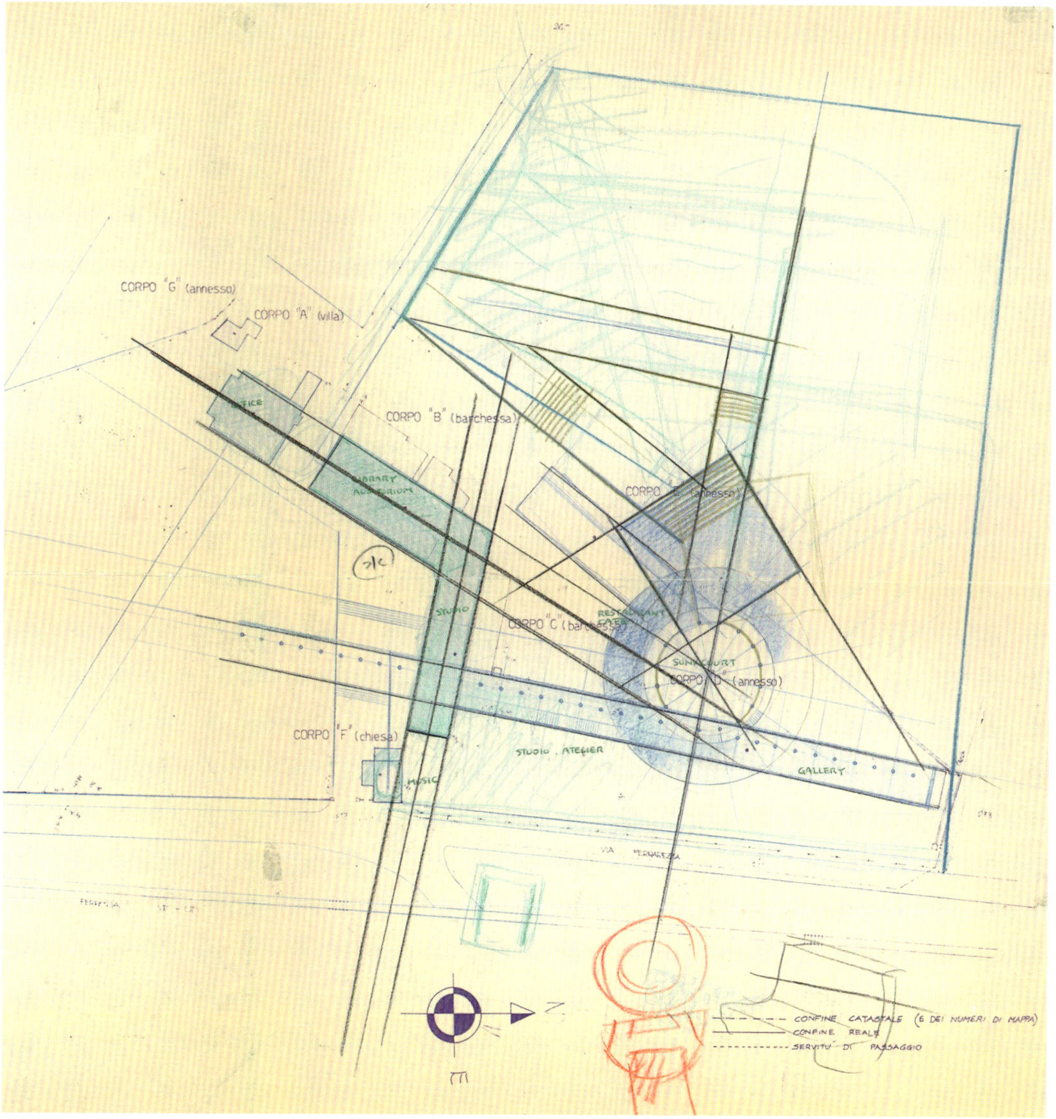

3

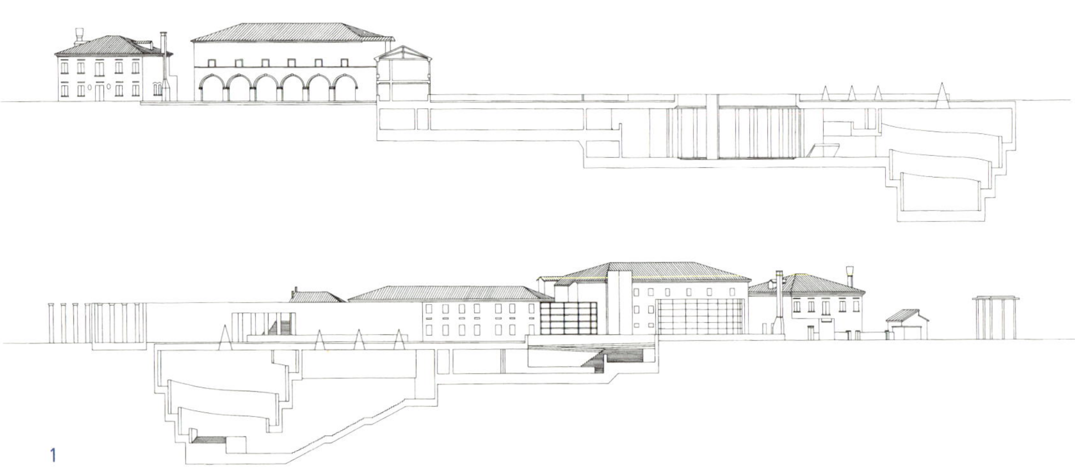

1

1 Sections.

2 Exploratory sketches of the composition of the new addition. Gallery following a row of columns passing through an existing building, the shape of the large stair luring people to the underground spaces, the circular sunken court that acts as a movement node—because it is underground architecture, awareness is concentrated on the design of the junctions with the outdoor spaces.

1 断面図。

2 新築部の構成の検討スケッチ。既存建物を貫く列柱に導かれるギャラリー、地下スペースへと人々をいざなう大階段の造形、交通の結節点となる円形のサンクンコート——地下建築ゆえに、外部空間との接合部のデザインに意識が集中される。

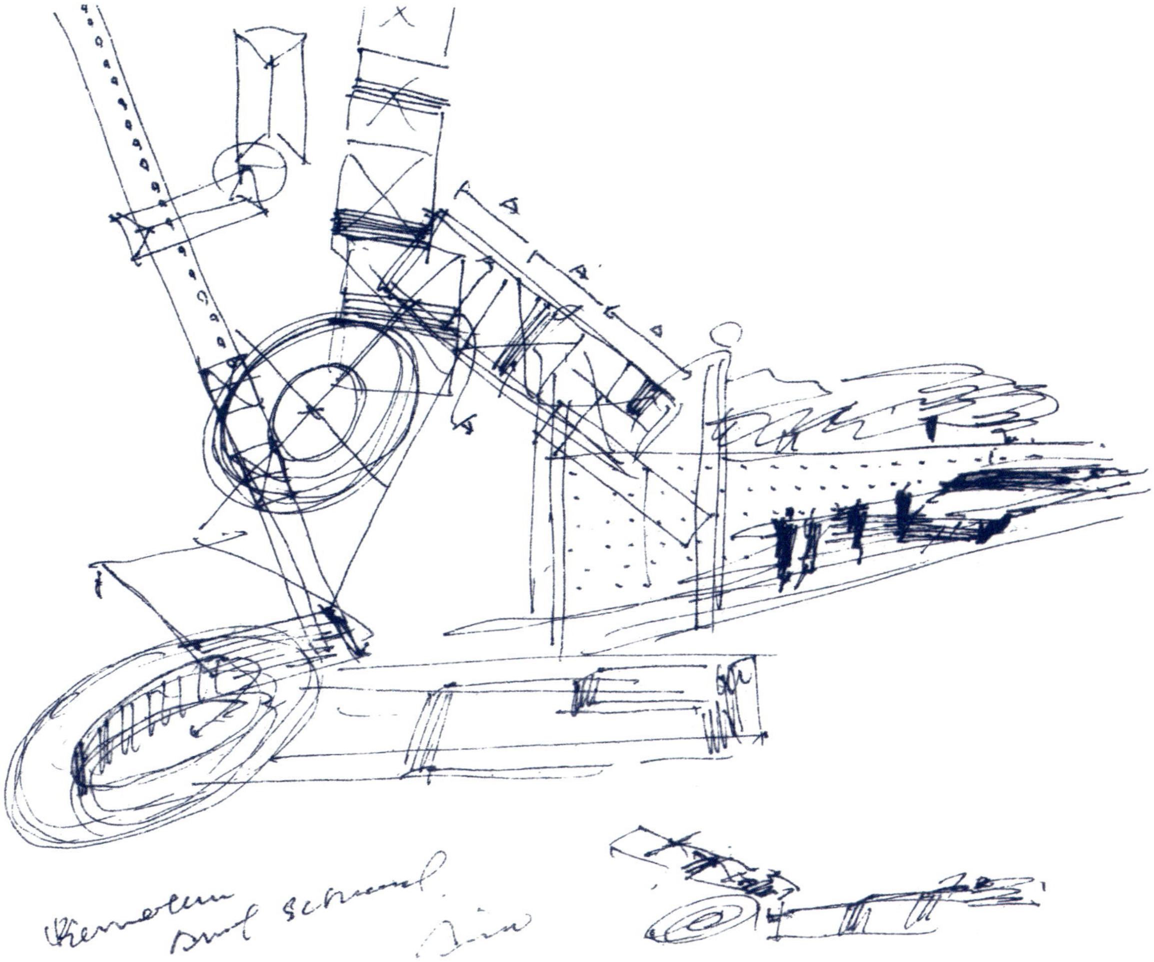

2

More than ten years after completion, the trees and shrubs grow thick on the ground, and FABRICA merges even further into the rural landscape. Now, in 2010, the next project underway is a proposal for student accommodation.

完成から10年余を経て、地上の樹木は生い茂り、FABRICAは一層田園風景の中に溶け込みつつある。2010年現在は、次なるプロジェクトとして学生たちの宿泊施設をつくる計画が進行中である。

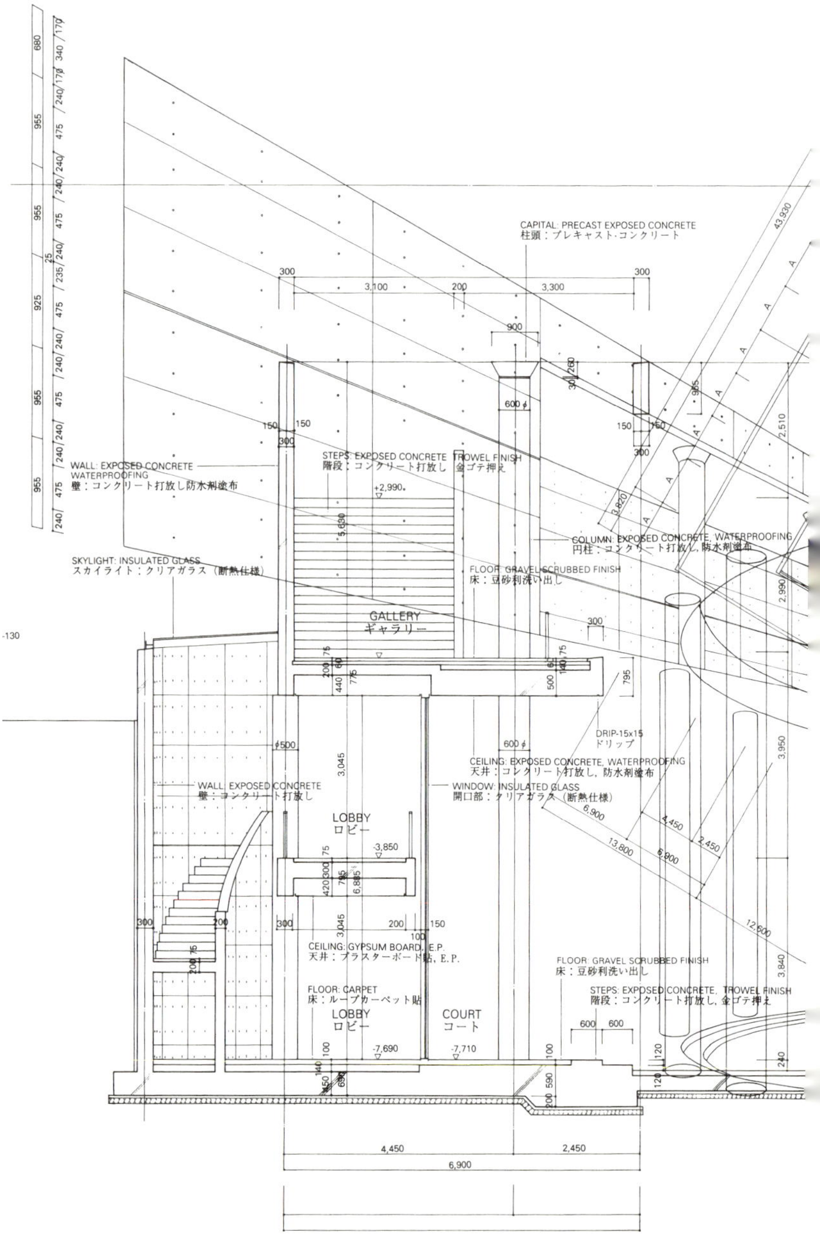

Drawing of the central court, which is the core of the composition of the new addition.

新築部分の構成の核となる中央コートのドローイング。

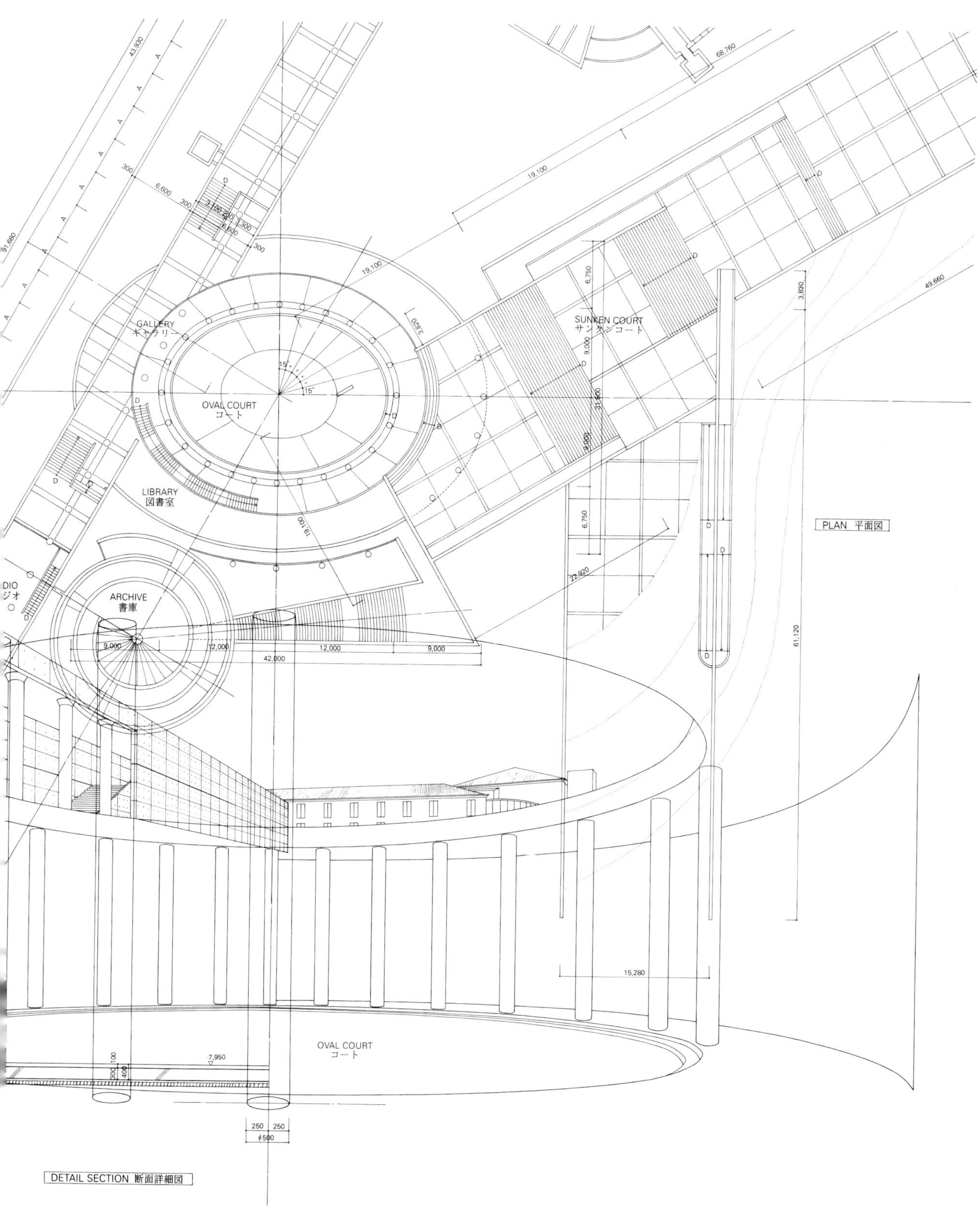
GALLERY
ギャラリー
OVAL COURT
コート
LIBRARY
図書室
ARCHIVE
書庫
SUNKEN COURT
サンクンコート
PLAN 平面図
OVAL COURT
コート
DETAIL SECTION 断面詳細図

House in Nipponbashi
日本橋の家

1. Osaka, Osaka, Japan　大阪府大阪市
2. 1993.3-1994.1
3. 1994.2-1994.9

Built on a narrow 2.9m-wide, 15m-deep site, this is a four-story-high joint residence in which the first floor is a shop. Within the simple sectional composition of four levels and four bays, I thought of inserting a void and a courtyard in two places then connecting all rooms to these. Energy was spent on studying the stairs that connect the vertically ascending living spaces.

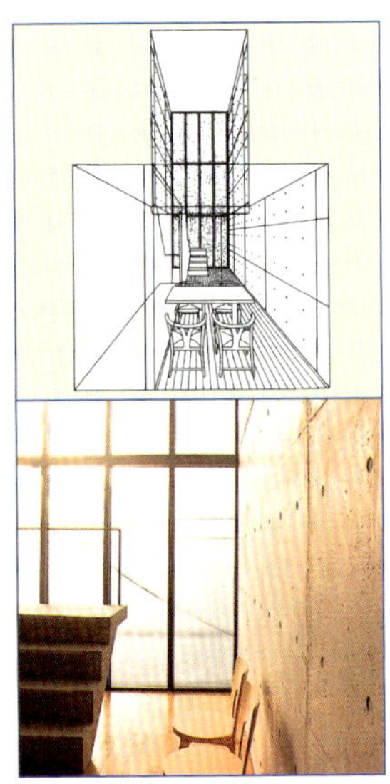

1 Initial image sketches. The forms of the folded and intersecting stairs, interlinked like a maze, give depth and expansiveness to the narrow interior space.

2, 3 Exploratory sketches of the detail dimensions. Precisely because the volume is limited, an exceptionally large void is made. This apparently absurd idea was realized through the architect's confident dimensional sensitivity.

1

間口2.9m、奥行き15mの狭小な敷地に建てた1階を店舗とする4階建ての併用住宅である。4層4スパンの単純な断面構成の中に、2か所の吹き抜けのヴォイド、中庭を組み込み、すべての部屋がこれらに接するように考えた。垂直に上昇する住空間をつなぐ階段のスタディにエネルギーが費やされた。

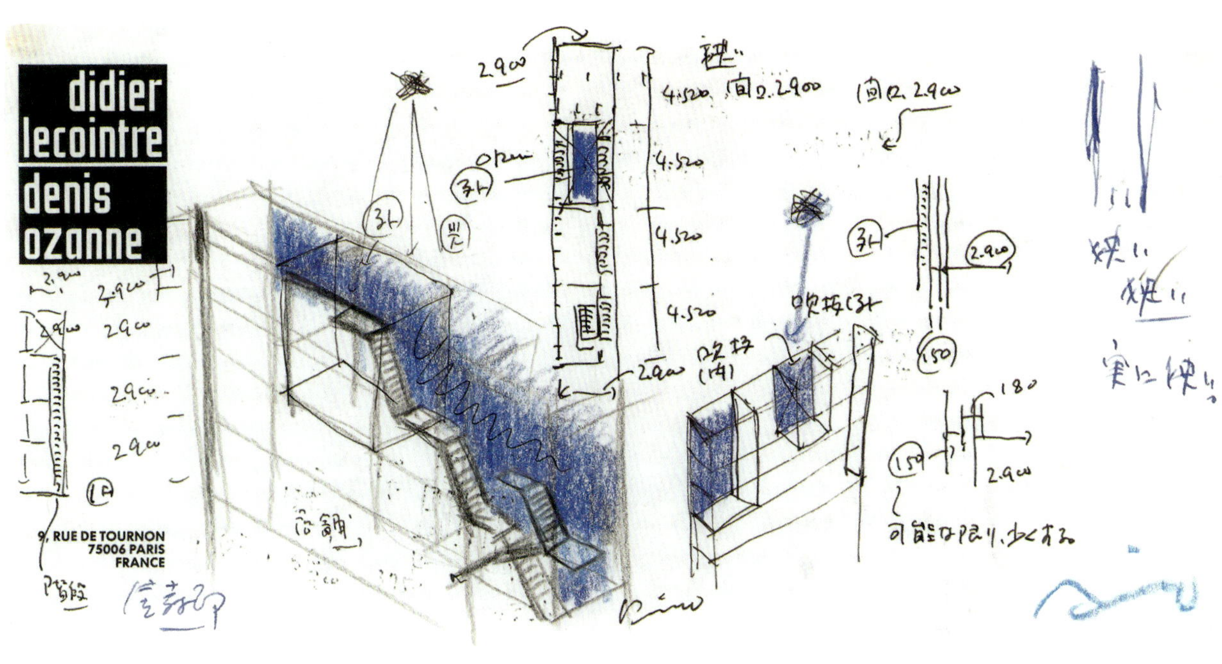

2

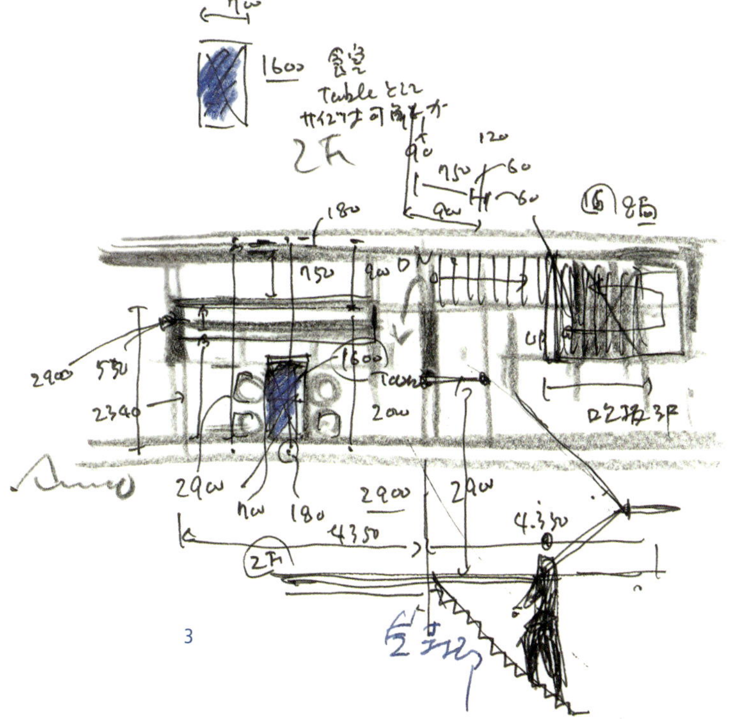

3

1 初期イメージスケッチ。折れ曲がり交差しながら迷路のようにつながっていく階段の造形が、狭い内部空間に奥行きとふくらみを与える。

2, 3 詳細寸法の検討スケッチ。限られた容積だからこそ、あえて大きな抜けの空間をつくる。一見無茶なアイディアを現実化するのは、建築家の確かな寸法感覚。

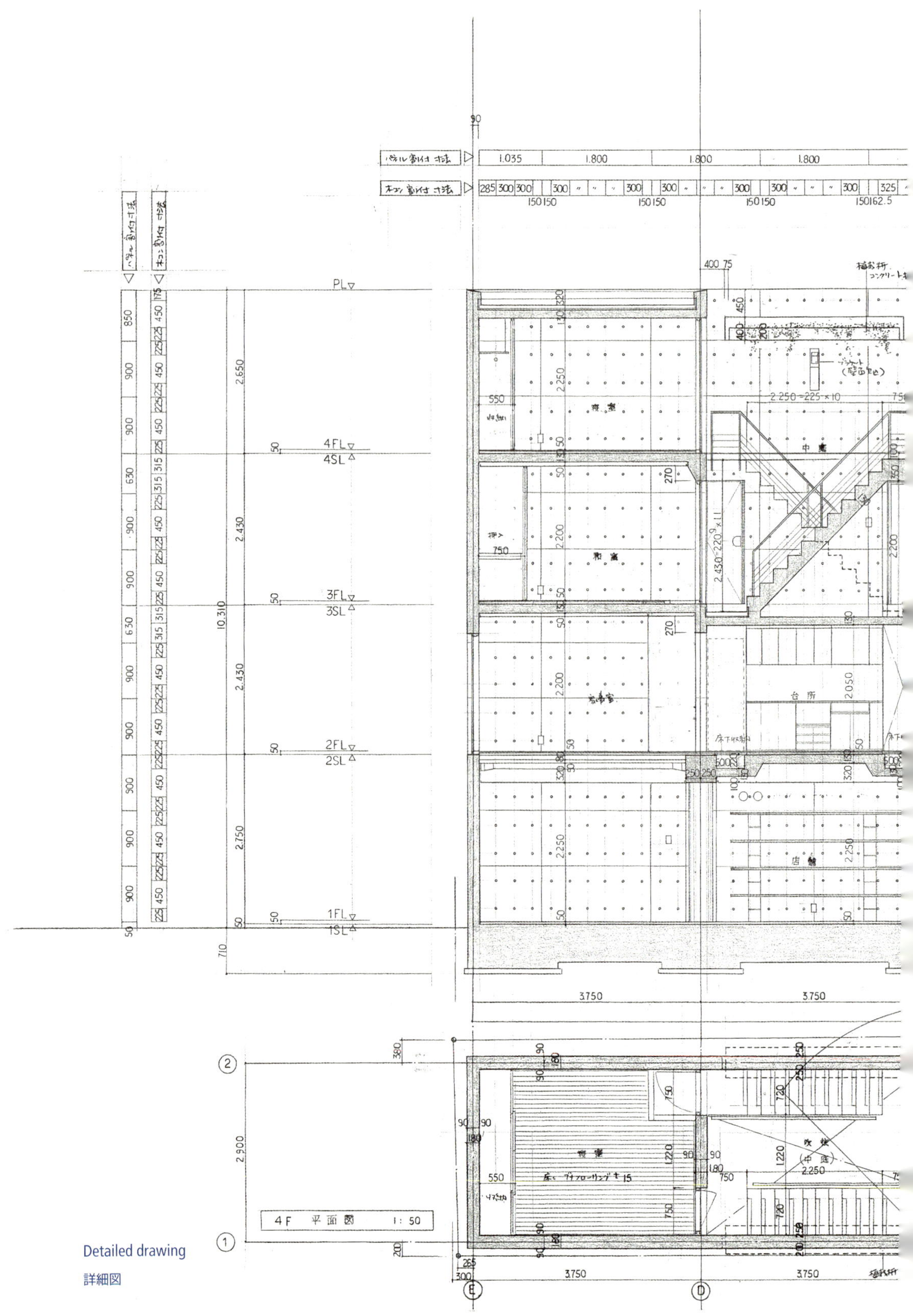

Detailed drawing

詳細図

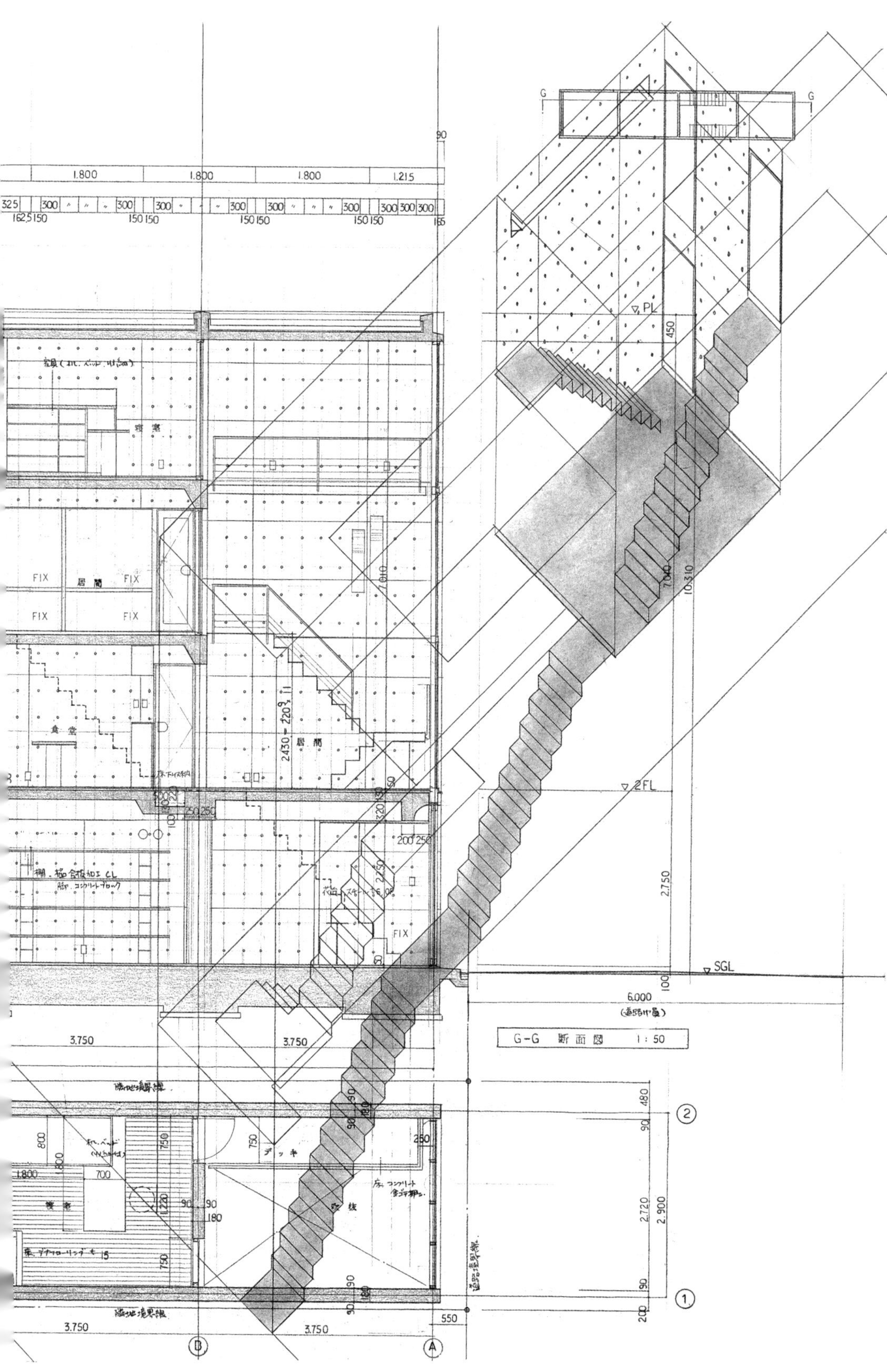
G-G 断面図 1:50
居間
食堂
寝室
FIX
デッキ
吹抜
▽PL
▽2FL
▽SGL
6,000
(道路巾員)
1.800
1.215
3.750
7.010
7.040
10.310
2.750
2.720
2.900

Awaji-Yumebutai (Before 1995)
淡路夢舞台（初期案）

1. Awaji, Hyogo, Japan　兵庫県淡路市
2. 1993.4-1994.12

This is a cultural complex designed as the central facility of the Awaji Island International Park City, which includes a prefectural park and a state park. On a former mining site that spans more than 1km and 28ha, I started the project with the theme of rejuvenating the greenery. Progress was temporarily interrupted by the 1995 earthquake and there were some design changes, but I persisted with the initial theme of environmental regeneration as in the first stage.

国営公園、県立公園を含む「淡路島国際公園都市」の中核施設として計画された、文化コンプレックスである。全長1km、広さ28haにおよぶかつての土砂採掘跡地に、緑の風景を取り戻すことを主題とし、プロジェクトはスタートした。1995年の地震で一時中断、計画変更を余儀なくされたが、環境再生というテーマは、当初のまま貫かれた。

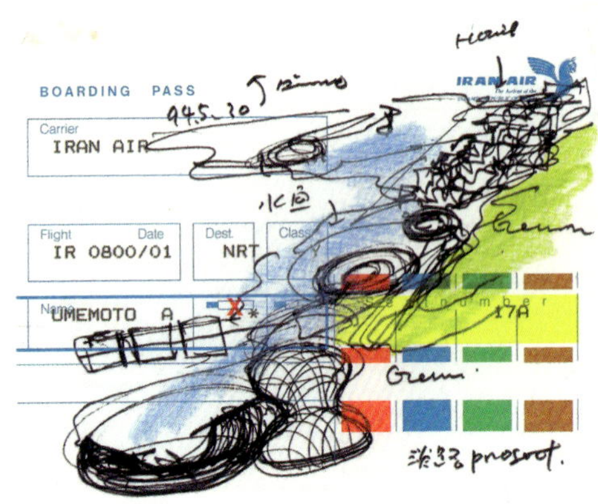

1

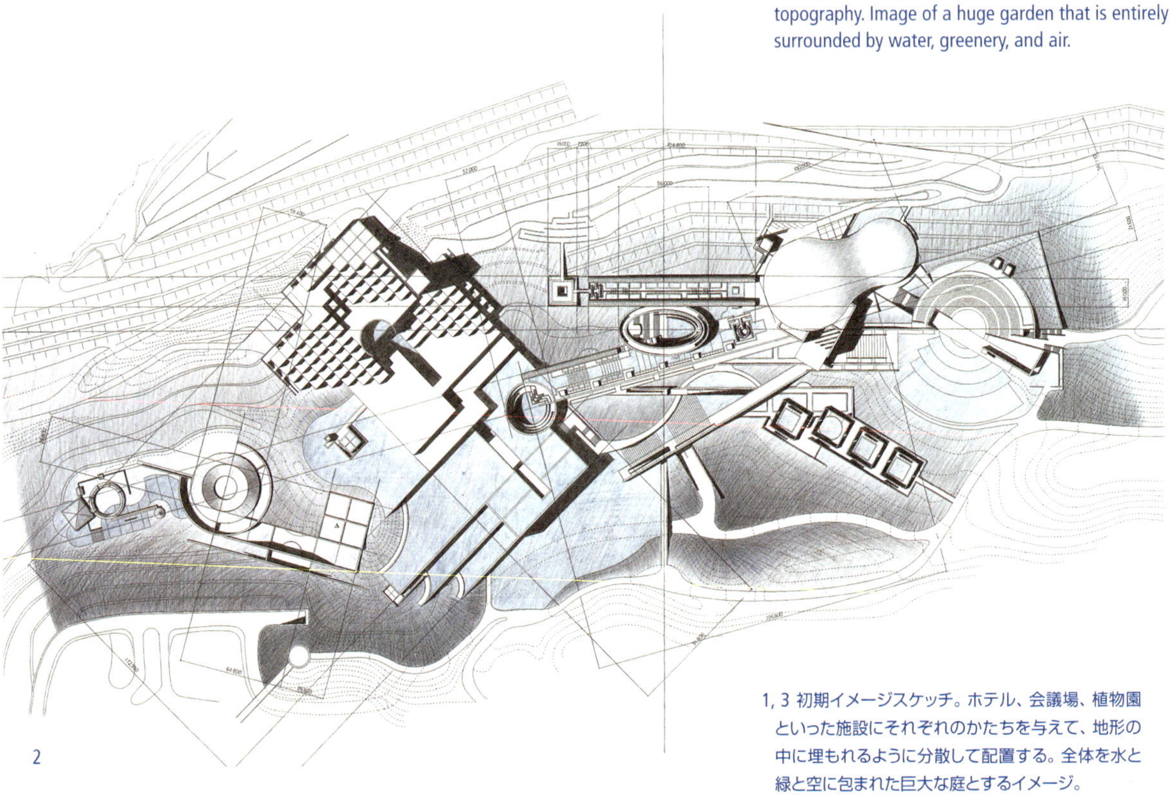

1, 3 Initial image sketches. Each of the facilities—hotel, conference hall, botanic garden—is given a shape, and they are dispersed as if buried into the topography. Image of a huge garden that is entirely surrounded by water, greenery, and air.

2

1, 3 初期イメージスケッチ。ホテル、会議場、植物園といった施設にそれぞれのかたちを与えて、地形の中に埋もれるように分散して配置する。全体を水と緑と空に包まれた巨大な庭とするイメージ。

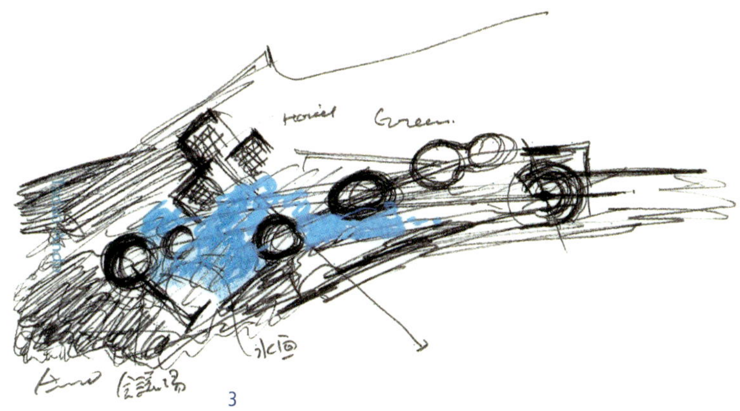

3

2 Site plan. While shifting the axial lines, the characteristic architectural spaces—changing in character according to the program—are buried in the slope running toward the sea. Water joins and unifies all into a single whole. Frequent references were made to large historical garden sites such as the Villa Adriana and the Alhambra.

2 配置図。海へと向かっていく斜面に、軸線をずらし重ねながら、プログラムに応じて異なる性格の建築空間を埋め込んでいく。それらをつなぎ合わせ、ひとつの全体に統合していく水。ヴィラ・アドリアーナやアルハンブラ宮殿といった歴史的な大庭園のサイトが繰り返し参照された。

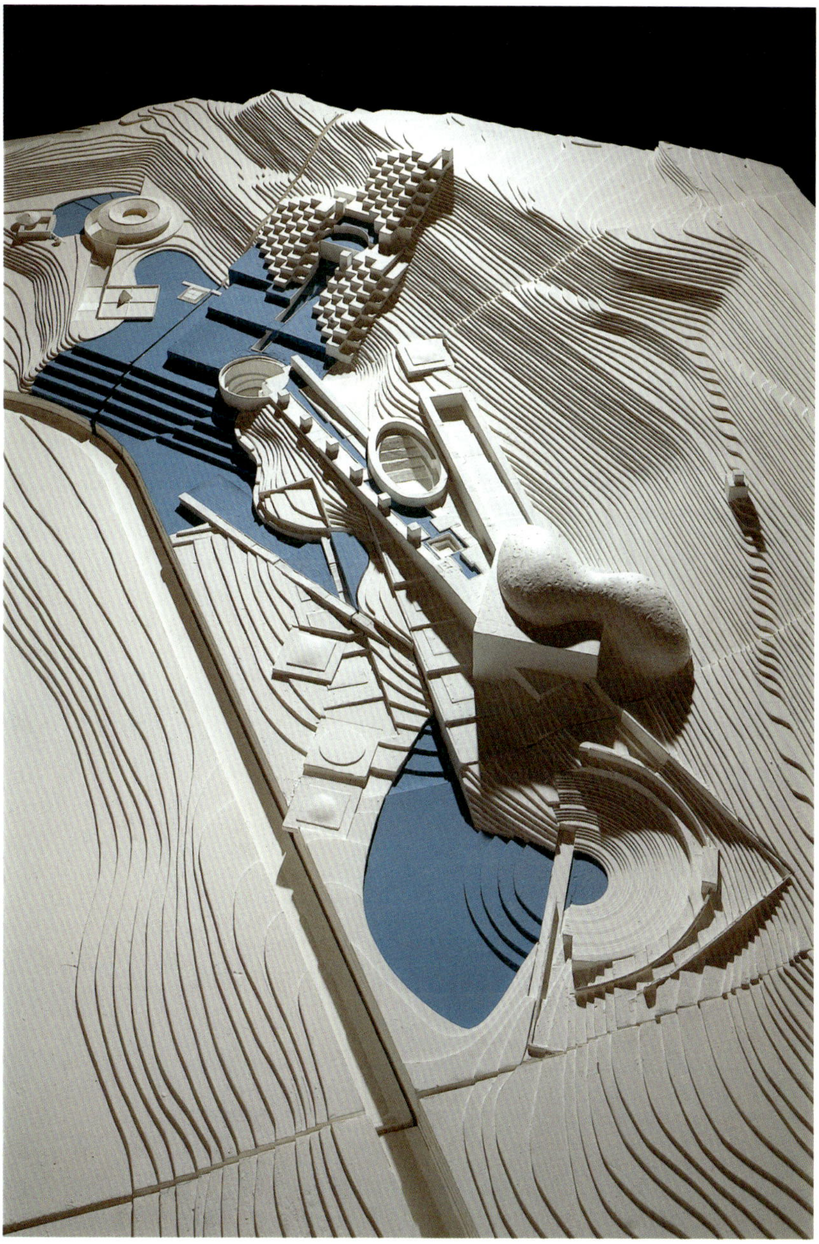

Sayamaike Historical Museum, Osaka
大阪府立狭山池博物館

1. Osakasayama, Osaka, Japan　大阪府大阪狭山市
2. 1994.6-1997.3
3. 1997.7-2001.3

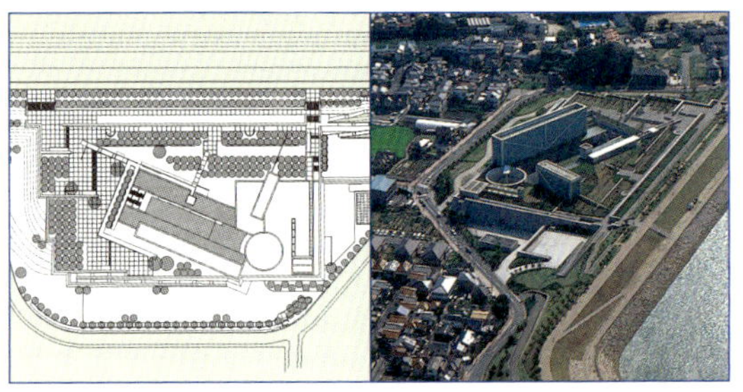

Built in the vicinity of Sayama Pond, Japan's oldest storage reservoir (constructed in the seventh century), about 10km west of the Chikatsu-Asuka Museum, this is a museum for conveying the history of Japan's flood control measures. The idea here is also based on the theme of an environmental museum, integrated with the locale of Sayama Pond. The main volume is embedded in the scenery as a base platform that gently continues the embankment, and only the exhibition wings and daylight towers appear above ground. As an extension of the embankment, this is a reticent architectural stance, but the intention is a dramatic space in which a turn in the approach route leads people to a magnificent historical world. What emerged here is a water garden space interposed between waterfalls on either side.

1, 2 Image sketches of a museum integrated with the Sayama Pond embankment. Since the completion of the museum in Sayama Pond, the planting of cherry trees along the embankment has been undertaken with the cooperation of local residents. The building will not be completed until the entire circumference of the embankment is lined with beautiful cherry trees.

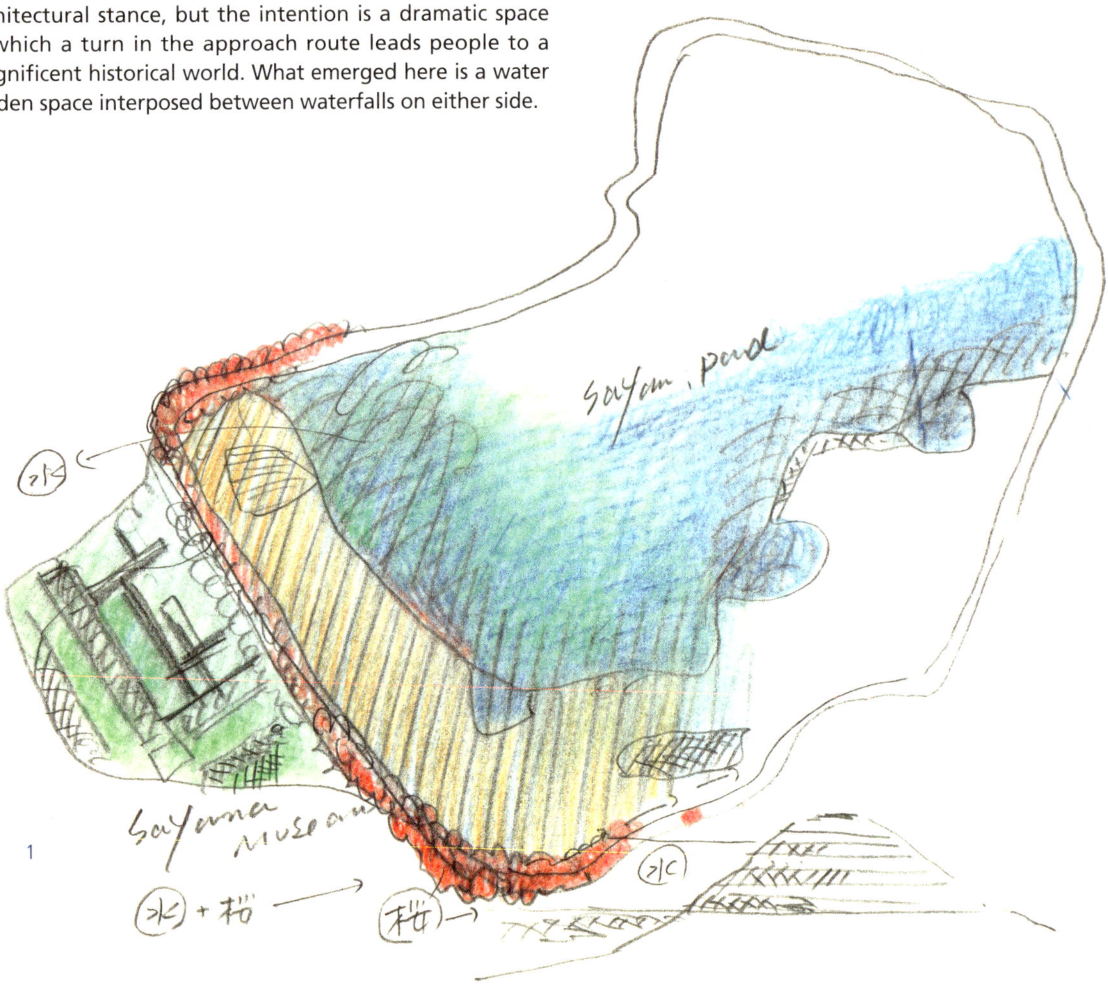

1

「近つ飛鳥博物館」から西に10kmほど離れた位置にある、7世紀に築造された日本最古のため池「狭山池」のほとりにつくられた、日本の治水事業の歴史を伝える博物館である。ここでも考えたのは、狭山池という場所と一体化してある環境博物館という主題だ。主要なヴォリュームは堤から緩やかに連続する基壇部として風景に埋没させ、地上には展示棟と採光塔だけが現れる。堤の延長としてある控え目な建築の構えだが、アプローチは一転して、人々を壮大な歴史の世界へと導くような劇的な空間にしたい。そこで生まれたのが両側を滝に挟まれた水庭の空間だった。

1, 2 狭山池の堤と一体化した博物館のイメージスケッチ。狭山池では博物館の竣工以来、地元住民の協力の下継続的に堤への桜の植樹が行われている。堤の全周を美しい桜並木が巡るまで建築は完結しない。

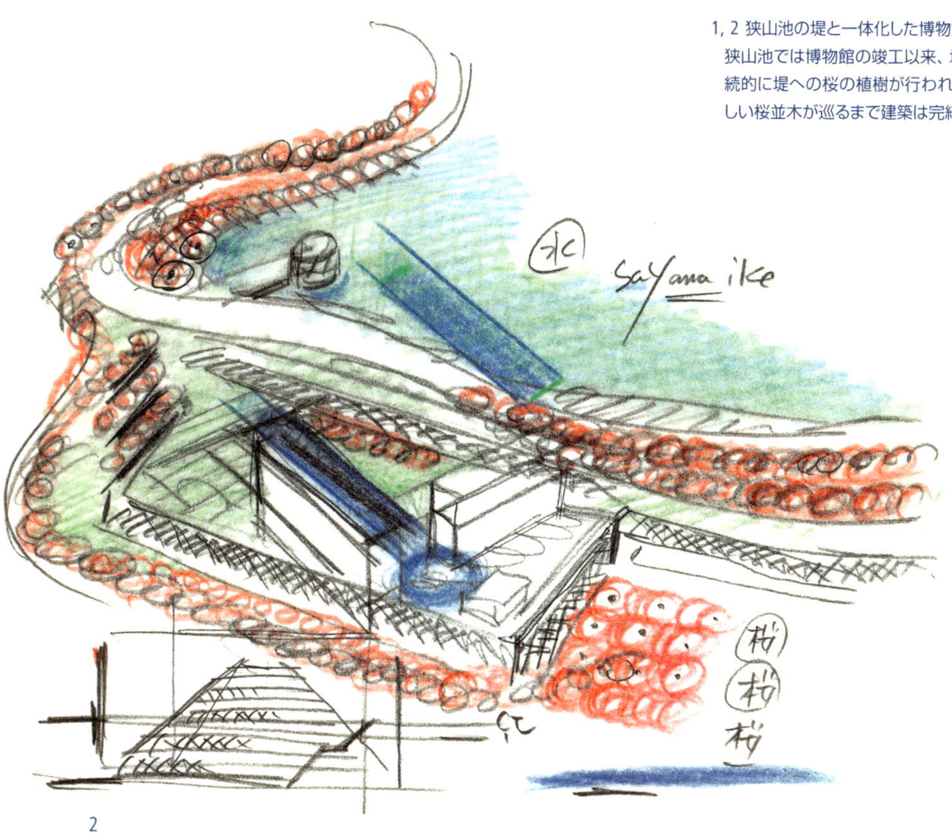

2

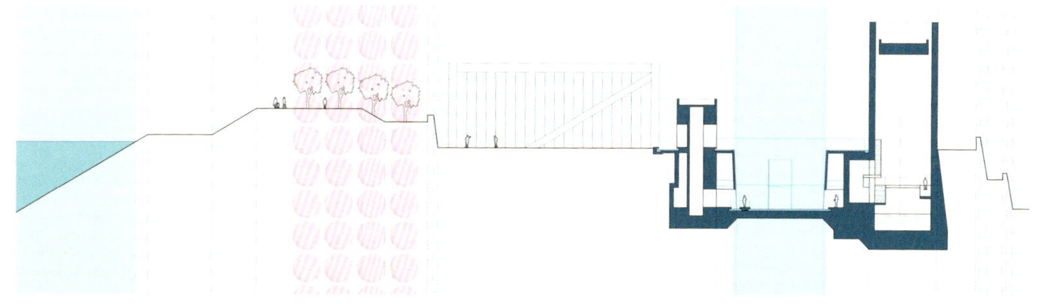

Langen Foundation / Hombroich
ホンブロイッヒ／ランゲン美術館

1. Neuss, Germany ドイツ ノイス
2. 1994.7-2002.3
3. 2002.8-2004.7

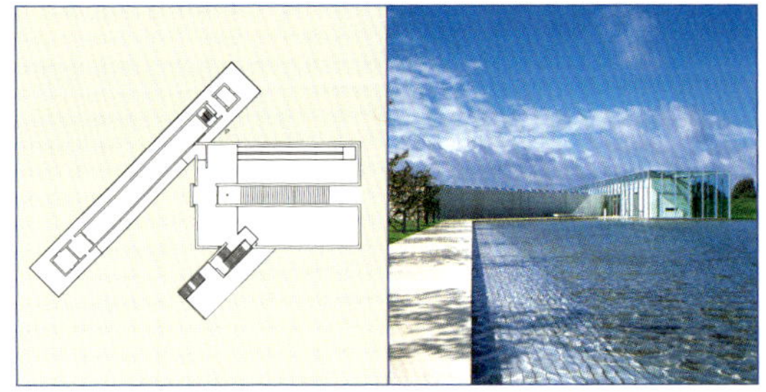

The site is close to Insel Hombroich, a famous art museum park in the outskirts of Dusseldorf. This is a plan for a gallery as part of a new art museum set in the remains of a NATO rocket launching base, for the person who also owns Insel. From about 1992, I had been nurturing the idea of a two-layered glass and concrete structure. The above-ground block of this art museum is where this idea has been implemented in its purest form.

敷地はデュッセルドルフ郊外、公園美術館として有名なインゼル・ホンブロイッヒ近くのNATOのロケット発射基地の跡に、インゼルと同じオーナーによって企画された新たな美術館の中のギャラリーである。1992年頃から、コンクリートとガラスの二重構造のアイディアを温めていた。それを最も純粋なかたちで実現できたのがこの美術館の地上棟だった。

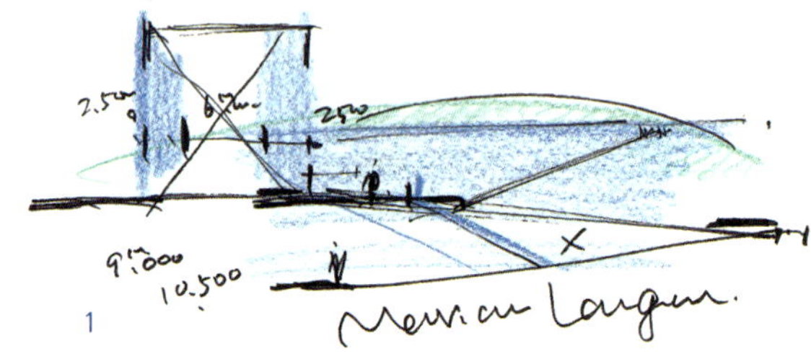

1

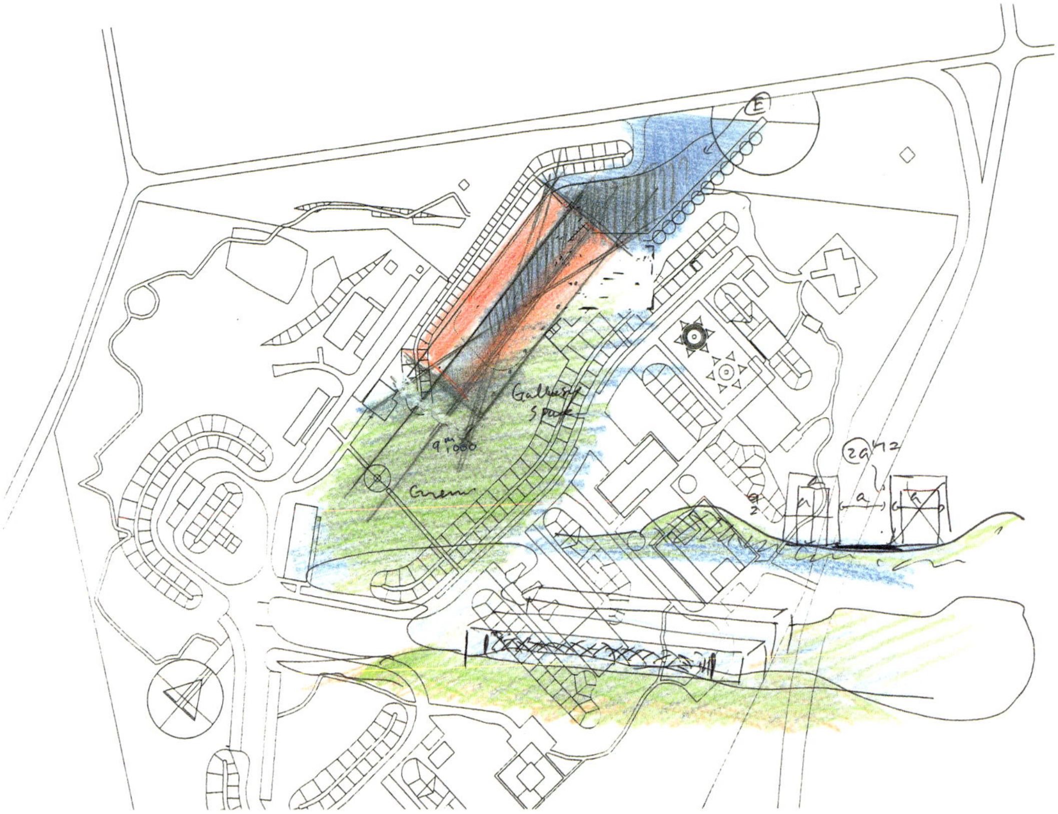

2

1, 2 Initial image sketches. The front of the site, interposed between green mounds, is made into a water garden, and a composition was first investigated in which two boxes with a double-layer structure of glass and concrete are arrayed. The idea of setting these complex boxes in parallel was simultaneously developed in a competition proposal for the Modern Art Museum of Forth Worth.

3 Detailed section of the above-ground block. Details for implementing the pure compositional image.

1, 2 初期イメージスケッチ。緑のマウンドに挟まれた敷地の前面を水庭とし、当初はコンクリートとガラスの二重構造のボックスを2本並べる構成を検討していた。この複数のボックスを平行配置するアイディアが、同時期のフォートワース現代美術館のコンペ案に発展する。

3 地上棟の断面詳細図。純粋な構成のイメージを実現するディテール。

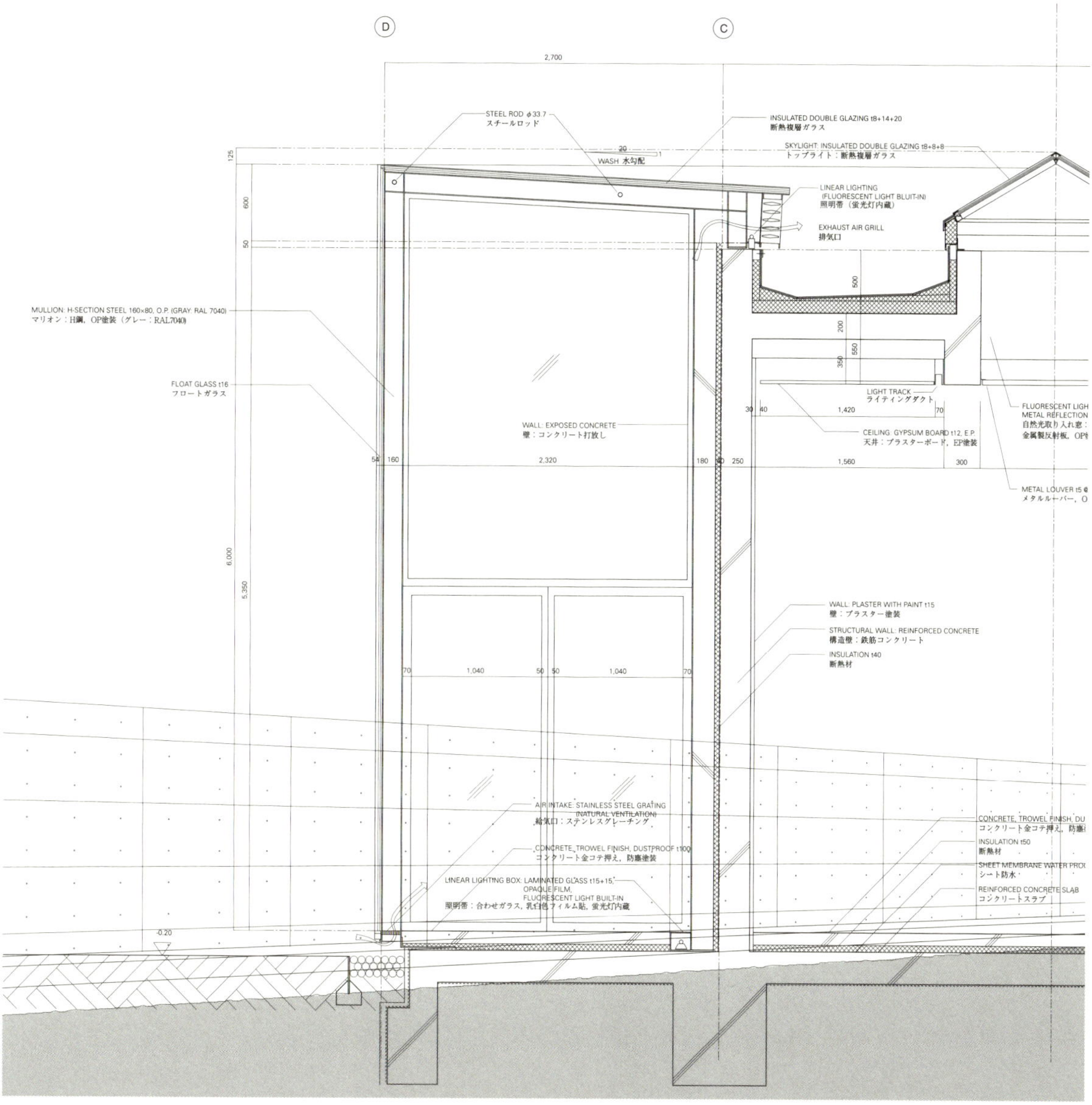

D
C
2,700
STEEL ROD φ33.7
スチールロッド
WASH 水勾配
INSULATED DOUBLE GLAZING t8+14+20
断熱複層ガラス
SKYLIGHT: INSULATED DOUBLE GLAZING t8+8+8
トップライト：断熱複層ガラス
LINEAR LIGHTING
(FLUORESCENT LIGHT BLUIT-IN)
照明帯（蛍光灯内蔵）
EXHAUST AIR GRILL
排気口
MULLION: H-SECTION STEEL 160×80, O.P. (GRAY: RAL 7040)
マリオン：H鋼，OP塗装（グレー：RAL7040）
FLOAT GLASS t16
フロートガラス
WALL: EXPOSED CONCRETE
壁：コンクリート打放し
LIGHT TRACK
ライティングダクト
CEILING: GYPSUM BOARD t12, E.P.
天井：プラスターボード，EP塗装
FLUORESCENT LIGH
METAL REFLECTION
自然光取り入れ窓：
金属製反射板，OP
METAL LOUVER t5 @
メタルルーバー，O
WALL: PLASTER WITH PAINT t15
壁：プラスター塗装
STRUCTURAL WALL: REINFORCED CONCRETE
構造壁：鉄筋コンクリート
INSULATION t40
断熱材
AIR INTAKE: STAINLESS STEEL GRATING
(NATURAL VENTILATION)
給気口：ステンレスグレーチング
CONCRETE, TROWEL FINISH, DUSTPROOF t100
コンクリート金コテ押え，防塵塗装
LINEAR LIGHTING BOX: LAMINATED GLASS t15+15,
OPAQUE FILM,
FLUORESCENT LIGHT BUILT-IN
照明帯：合わせガラス，乳白色フィルム貼，蛍光灯内蔵
CONCRETE, TROWEL FINISH, DU
コンクリート金コテ押え，防塵
INSULATION t50
断熱材
SHEET MEMBRANE WATER PRO
シート防水
REINFORCED CONCRETE SLAB
コンクリートスラブ
-0.20

3

Seaside Housing Project
海の集合住宅プロジェクト

1. Kobe, Hyogo, Japan　兵庫県神戸市
2. 1995.2-

This is an independent design proposal for a total of 7000 units of mass housing, made following the Hanshin Awaji Earthquake on January 17, 1995. The site is on the Kobe waterfront, in an area where many factories once stood. Since prior to the earthquake, regeneration proposals such as the New Eastern City Center had been underway, but precisely because this project is a symbol of revival there was no conventional economic precedent, so believing that urban development should be centered on housing, I grappled with this design despite not having been commissioned.

1995年1月17日の阪神淡路大震災の後、自主提案としてまとめた全7000戸の集合住宅計画案である。敷地は神戸市の臨海地区のかつて工場が林立していた地域。震災以前から「東部新都心」として再開発計画が進んでいたが、復興のシンボルとなるプロジェクトだからこそ、従来の経済性優先型ではない、住まいを中心とした都市づくりにすべきだと、頼まれもせずこの計画に取り組んだ。

1 The site is in a superb environment, interposed between the mountains and the sea in the area between Osaka and Kobe. Using the full potential of this site, I wanted to make a townscape "only possible in this place"—the project arose from the spirit of an architect who wanted to do something for a disaster area.

1 阪神間は山と海に挟まれた類まれな立地環境をもつ。その土地のもつ潜在力を活かした、「この場所にしかできない」街の風景をつくりたい——被災地のために自分ができることを何かしたいという建築家の心意気から始まったプロジェクト。

1

2

2 A seafront site with a total length of more than 1.5km. During the period of rapid economic growth this was an industrial zone packed with factories.

2 全長1.5kmにわたる海際の敷地。高度経済成長期には工場が林立する工業地帯だった。

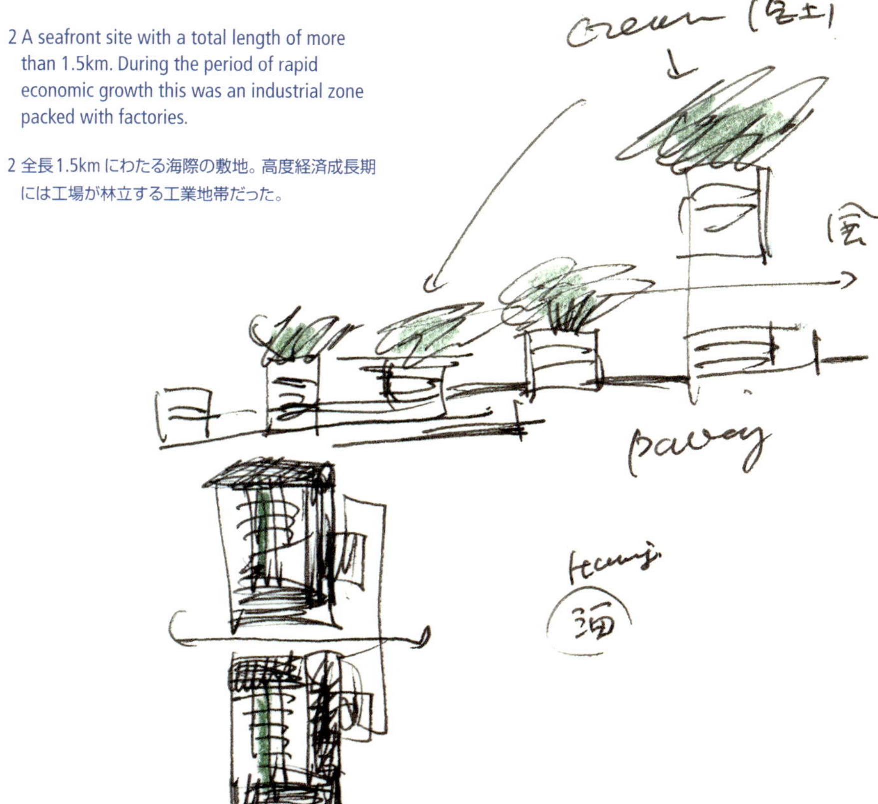

1 Exploratory sketches of the sectional design, characterized by high-rise, mid-rise, and low-rise blocks unified in a stepped composition. With elderly people in the highly grounded court houses of the low-rise part, families in the mid-rise part with rooftop gardens, and flats for singles in the high-rise part, there is a variety of housing appropriate for a mature city.

1 計画断面の検討スケッチ。特徴は高層·中層·低層を一体的に組み込んだ段状の構成。接地性の高い低層部のコートハウスは高齢者に、屋上庭園をもつ中層部は家族世帯に、高層部は単身者向けフラットと、成熟した都市にふさわしい、住戸ヴァリエーションをもつ。

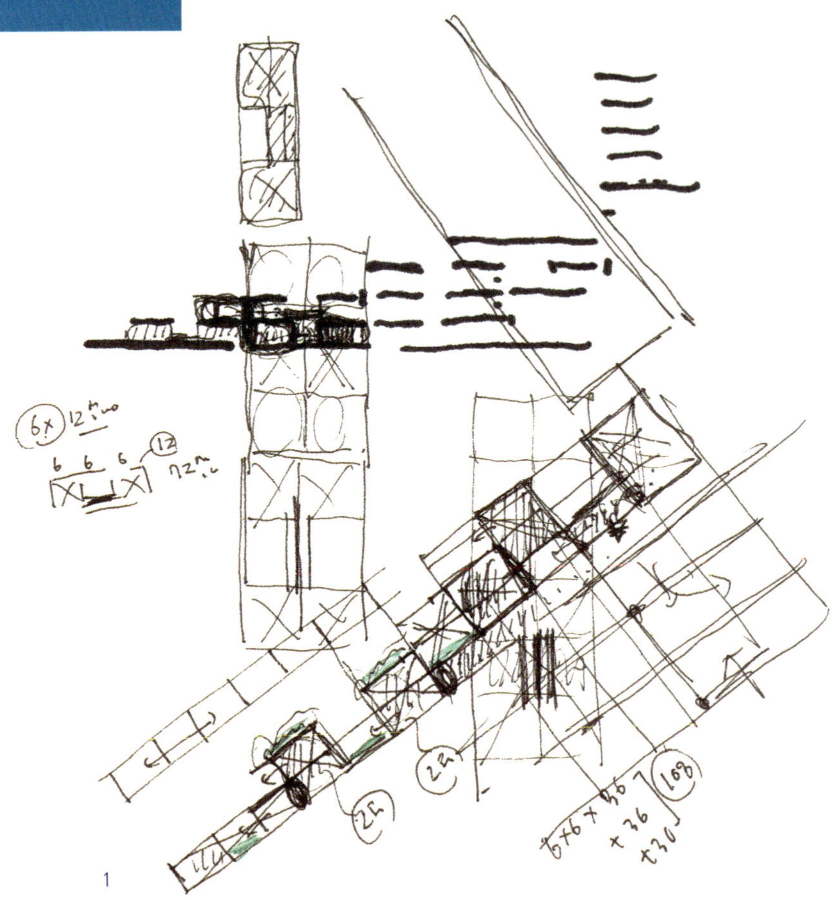

1

2 While making good use of the clarity of the grid, public spaces are created that connect with the sea at various levels. Terraces are established in each of the housing blocks from the living rooms of individual families, with seaside gardens for the entire housing development, and these gradations of public space nurture a sense of life in the new district.

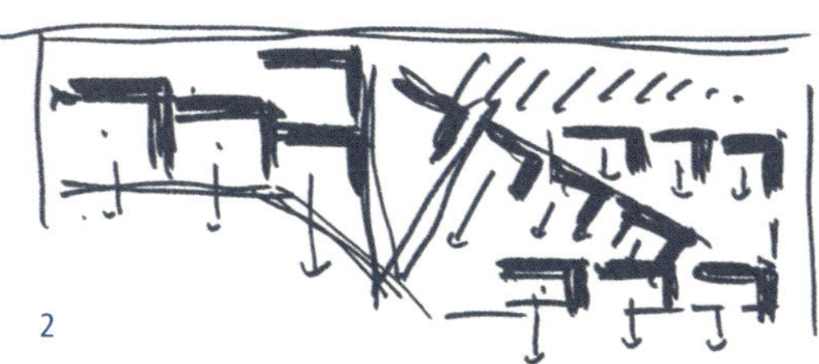

2

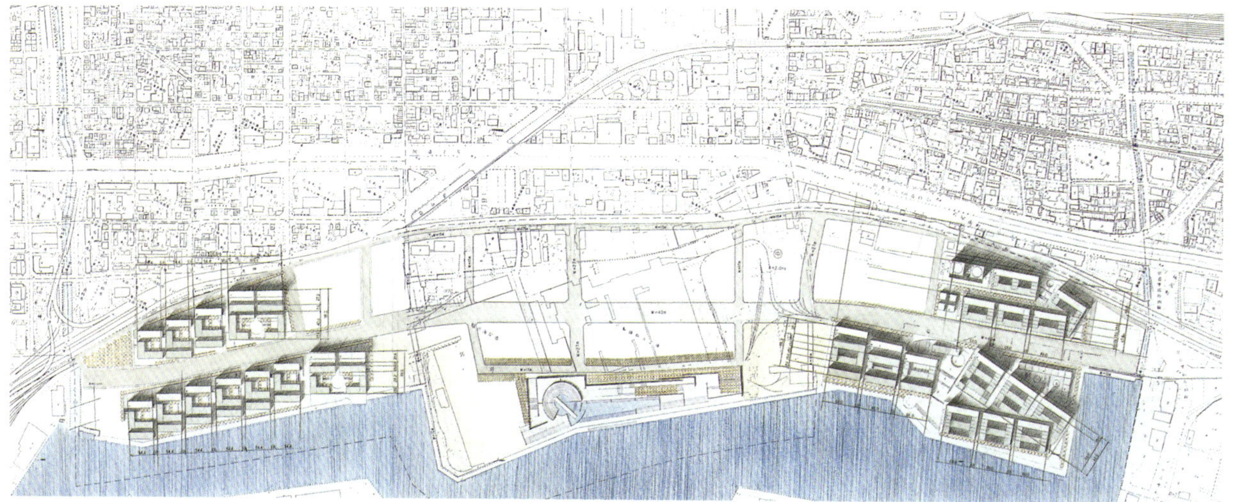

2 グリッドの明快性を活かしつつ、さまざまなレベルで海につながるパブリックスペースをつくり出す。1家族の居間から住棟ブロックごとに設けられたテラス、集合住宅全体の海際の庭と、このパブリックスペースのグラデーションが、新しい街の生命感を育んでいく。

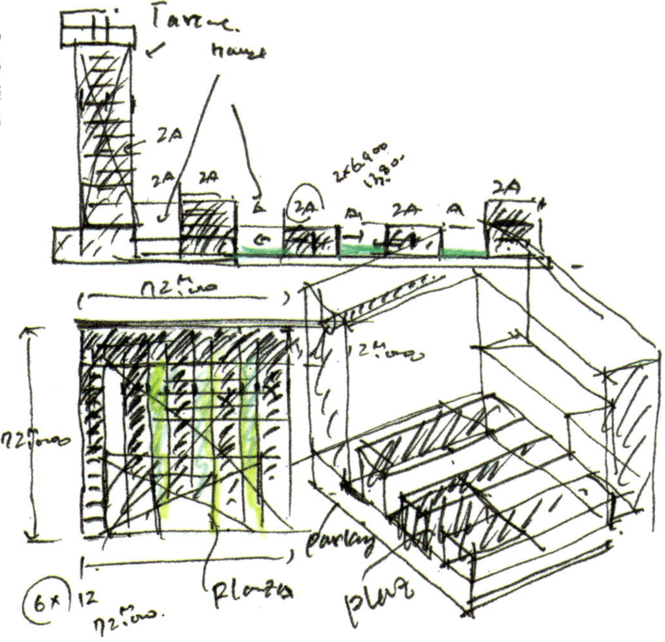

Part of the "Seaside Housing" conception was actually utilized in the New Eastern City Center plan, and the waterside plaza was realized as a garden for an art hall by combining it with the Hyogo Prefectural Museum of Art. What may an architect do for society? The earthquake caused a reconsideration of the architect's social responsibility.

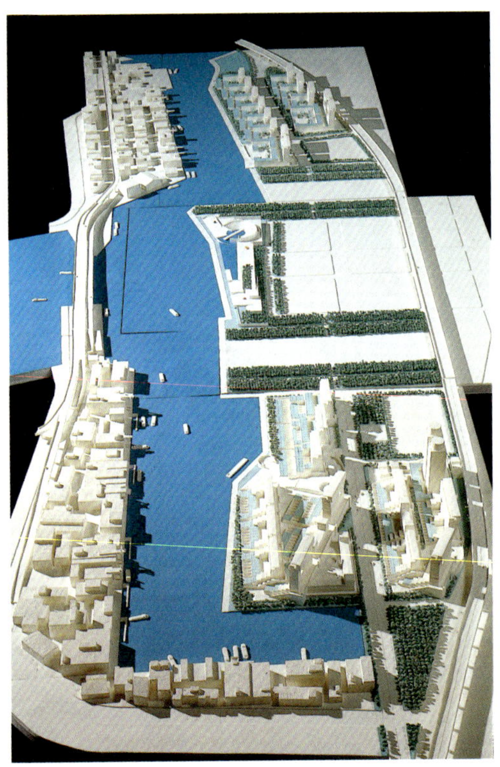

In a shape that interposes a central business district, this Seaside Housing is made oriented east-west. The seafront business district is a waterfront plaza with the function of disaster prevention, as a symbol for Kobe's revival.

「海の集合住宅」構想の一部は、現実の東部新都心計画に活かされることとなり、また水際の広場は兵庫県立美術館と併せ、芸術の館の庭として具現化することとなった。建築家は社会に対し一体何ができるのか——震災を通じて、建築家の社会的責任を改めて考えさせられた。

中央の業務地区を挟むかたちで、東西に「海の集合住宅」がつくられる。業務地区の海側は、地域全体、復興する神戸のシンボルとして防災機能もつ水際の広場とする。

Omotesando Hills
(Omotesando Regeneration Project)
表参道ヒルズ（同潤会青山アパート建替計画）

1. Shibuya-ku, Tokyo, Japan　東京都渋谷区
2. 1996.4-2003.3
3. 2003.8-2006.1

This is a residential and commercial complex built on the vestiges of the Dojunkai Aoyama apartments, which had been built as a reconstruction project following the Great Kanto Earthquake in the 1920s. Given that their repair and restoration was physically and economically impossible, I thought about ways to draw out the essence of this scene and translate it into new, contemporary architecture. By burying the majority of the required building volume into the ground, its height could be kept low, close to that of the zelkova trees lining Omotesando Street. Like the previous apartments, abundant public spaces are contained in the center. Throughout, I held on to these two precepts for the newly created architecture.

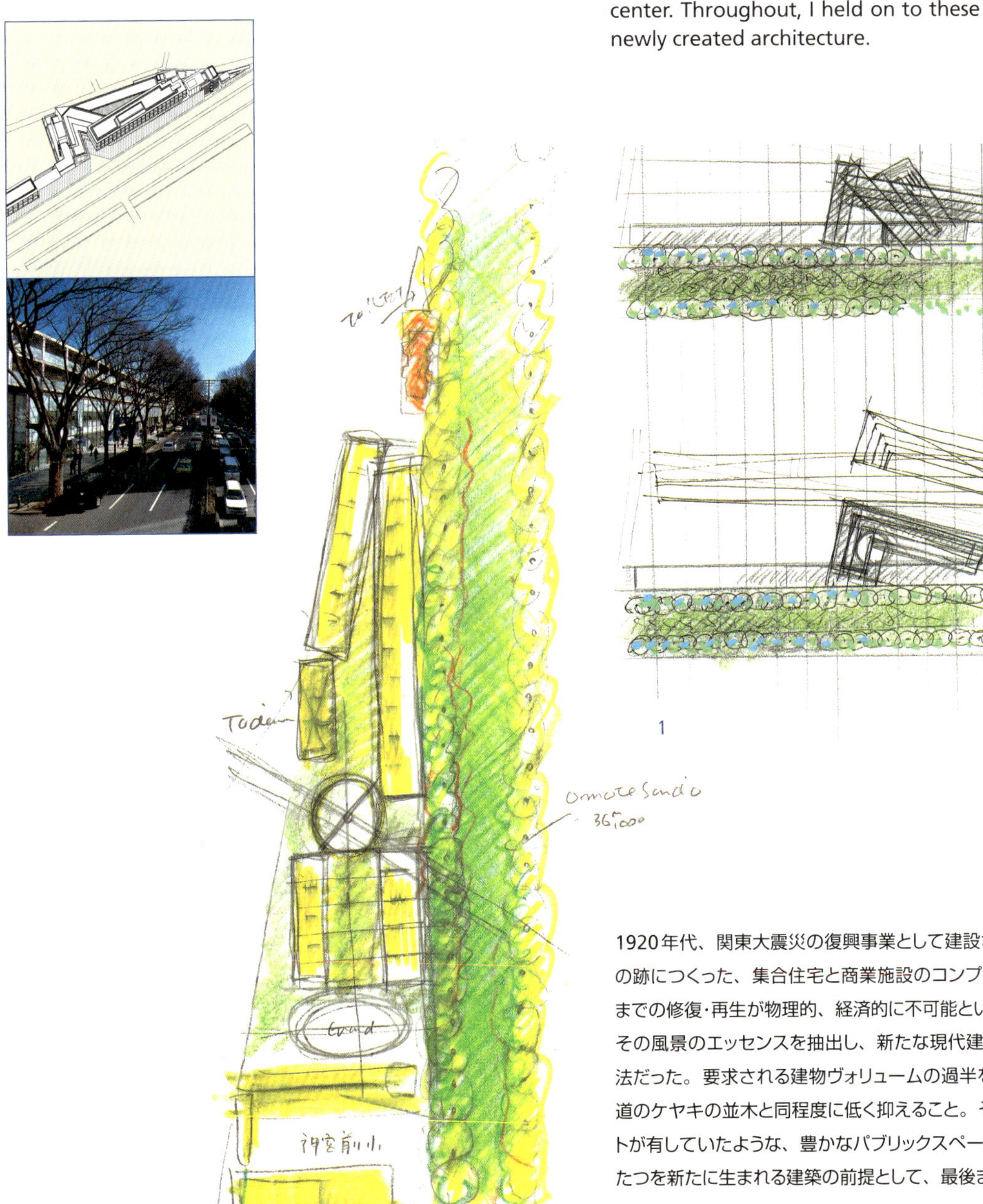

1

2

1920年代、関東大震災の復興事業として建設された同潤会青山アパートの跡につくった、集合住宅と商業施設のコンプレックスである。現状のままでの修復・再生が物理的、経済的に不可能という状況の中で考えたのは、その風景のエッセンスを抽出し、新たな現代建築として翻訳するという方法だった。要求される建物ヴォリュームの過半を地中に沈め、高さを表参道のケヤキの並木と同程度に低く抑えること。その中心にかつてのアパートが有していたような、豊かなパブリックスペースを内包すること。このふたつを新たに生まれる建築の前提として、最後まで守り抜いた。

1, 2 Exploratory sketches of the site layout composition. Investigation of a layout made by excising and enclosing voids.
3 Concept sketches drawn in order to show the design intentions.

1, 2 配置構成の検討スケッチ。ヴォイドを切り取る、囲み型配置の検討。
3 設計意図を示すために描かれたコンセプトスケッチ。

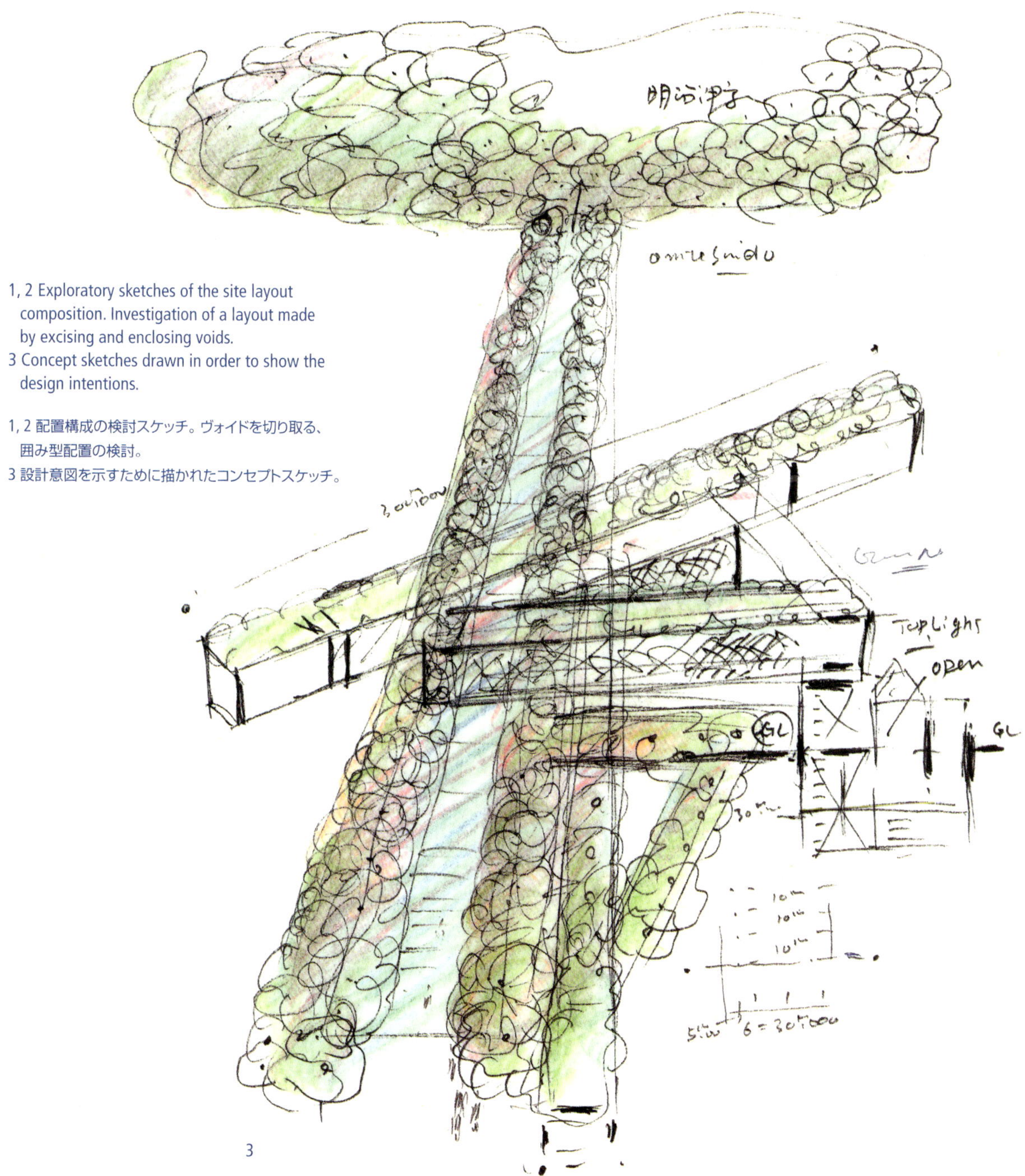

3

Modern Art Museum of Fort Worth
フォートワース現代美術館

1. Fort Worth, Texas, U.S.A.　アメリカ合衆国 テキサス州 フォートワース
2. 1996.8-1999.9
3. 1999.9-2002.9

This is in a place adjacent to the Kimbell Art Museum, a masterpiece by Louis Kahn located in a corner of a city park in the outskirts of Fort Worth, Texas. My proposal was chosen through an international competition on how to relate the now-classic Kimbell to a new art museum, and how to give character to this huge site. I had the idea of turning the site into a forest brimming with water and greenery, and making contemporary architecture that floats on a water garden with a rhythmical composition responding to the sense of order possessed by the Kimbell.

テキサス州フォートワース郊外の都市公園の一部、ルイス·カーンの傑作キンベル美術館に隣接する場所に位置する。現代の古典ともいうべきキンベルと新しい美術館とをどのように関係付けるか、その上で広大な敷地をどのように性格付けるかを争点に国際コンペが行われ、私の提案が選ばれた。私が考えたのは、敷地を水と緑にあふれた森とし、その水庭の上にキンベルのもつ秩序感に応えるリズミカルな構成の現代建築を浮かべるというアイディアだった。

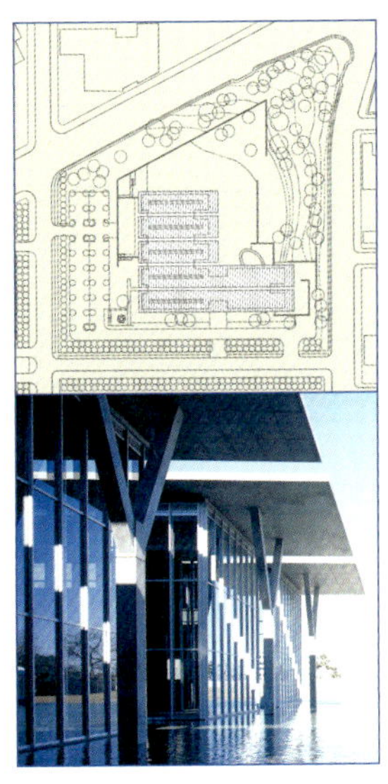

1

1, 2 Sketches of Kahn's Kimbell Art Museum drawn immediately after the decision to participate in the competition. A simple, clear composition, containing spaces with abundant light, clear order, and refined details. The abstracted essence of Kahn's building.

1, 2 コンペへの参加を決めた直後に描かれたカーンのキンベル美術館のスケッチ。単純明快な構成と豊かな光の空間、明快な秩序と洗練されたディテール——抽出されたカーンの建築のエッセンス。

2

3, 4 First image sketches. A broad water garden is placed on the east side of the site, a forest is oriented toward the busy intersection, and an environment surrounded by water and greenery is prepared. Architecture is inserted here in a composition of repeated linear shapes. A simple, clear concept responding to the difficult condition of proximity to the Kimbell Art Museum.

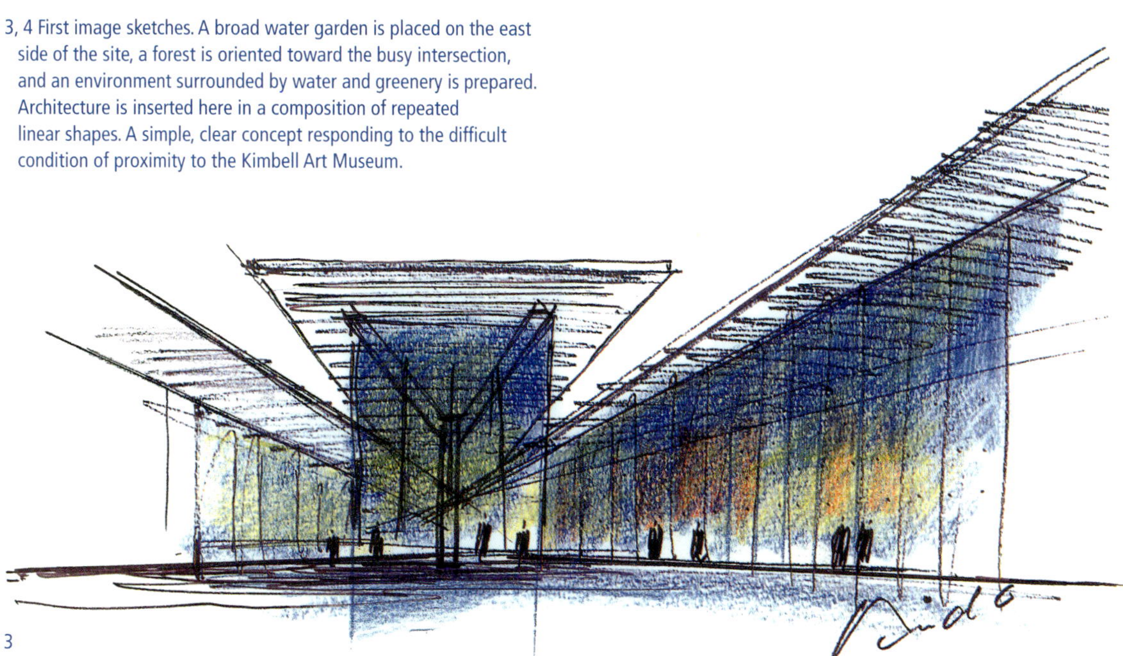

3

3, 4 ファーストイメージスケッチ。敷地東側に広い水庭を取り、交通量の多い交差点に対しては森を配して、水と緑で囲まれた環境を整える。そこにリニアな形態の繰り返しからなる構成の建築を挿入する。キンベル美術館のすぐそばという難しい与件に応える、単純、明快なコンセプト。

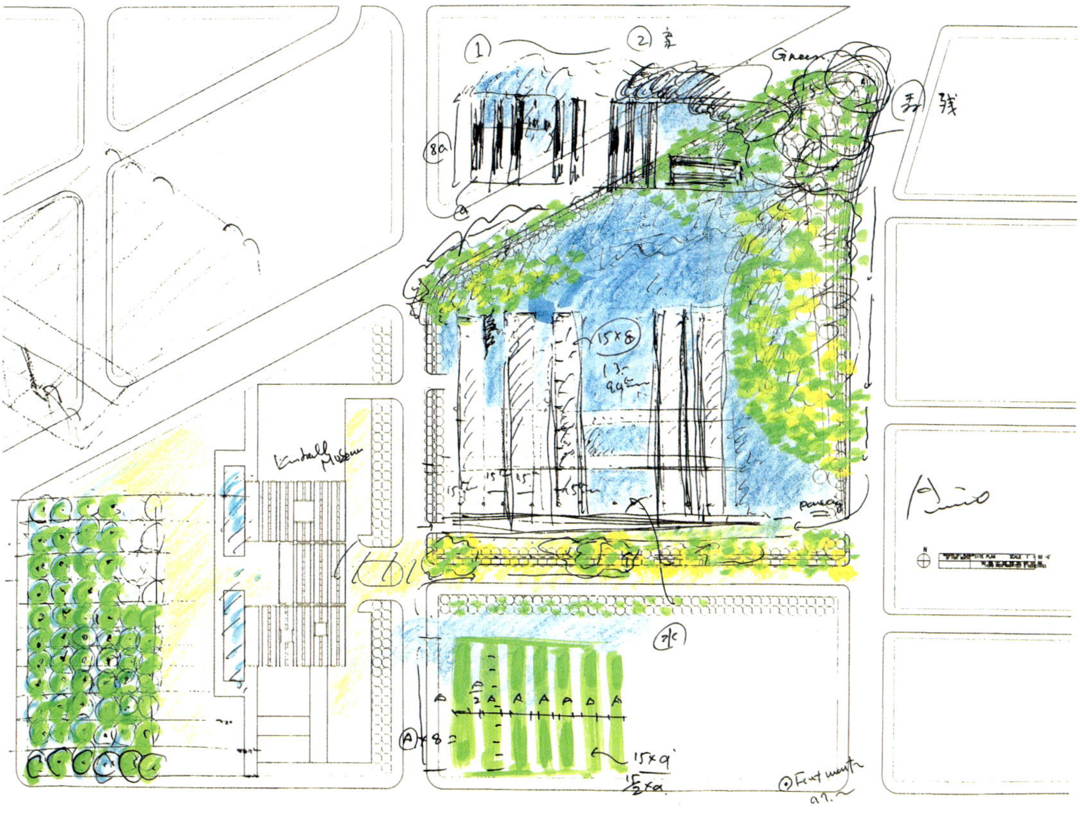

4

Using glass and concrete, the definitive materials of the twentieth century, I wanted to make architecture with an unprecedented new charm. The idea of a two-layered structure was one I had been nurturing since about 1992. In Fort Worth, by further developing this idea, I thought that the simplicity of the structure would, by contrast, give complex and varied interior spaces.

20世紀を代表するガラスとコンクリートという素材をもってなお、かつてない新しい魅力をもった建築をつくりたかった。二重構造のアイディアは、1992年頃から温めていたものだった。フォートワースでは、さらにそれを連続させることで、構成の単純さとは対照的な、複雑多様な内部空間をと考えていた。

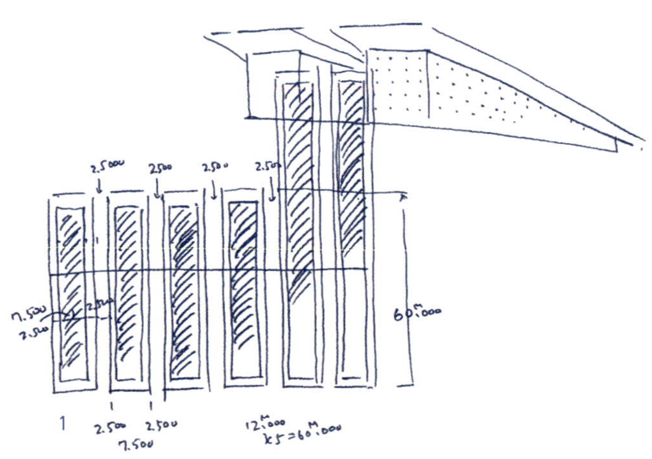

1, 3 A composition similar to that of the Kimbell, comprising a row of six connected boxes with a double-layer membrane structure. The existence of buffer spaces between the wings provides various possibilities in the plan composition.
2 Section diagram. The corridors inserted between concrete and glass are buffer zones, in various senses.
4 Plan (executed proposal*)
*At the execution stage, the six-wing composition became a five-wing composition.

1, 3 二重皮膜構造のボックスがキンベル同様に6列、連続する構成。棟間の余白の存在が、平面構成に多様な可能性をもたらす。
2 断面ダイアグラム。コンクリートとガラスに挟まれた回廊が、さまざまな意味でのバッファーゾーンとなる。
4 平面図（実施案※）
※実施段階で6棟構成は5棟構成になった。

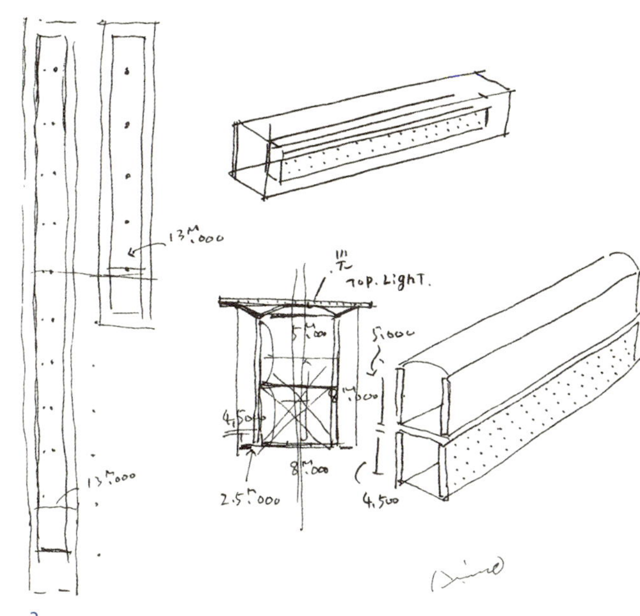

3

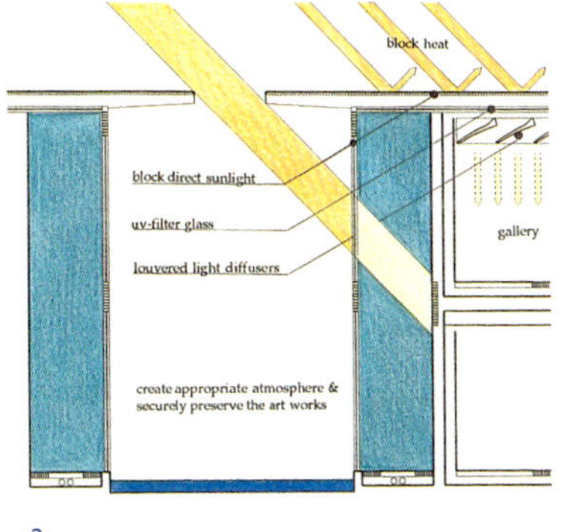

2

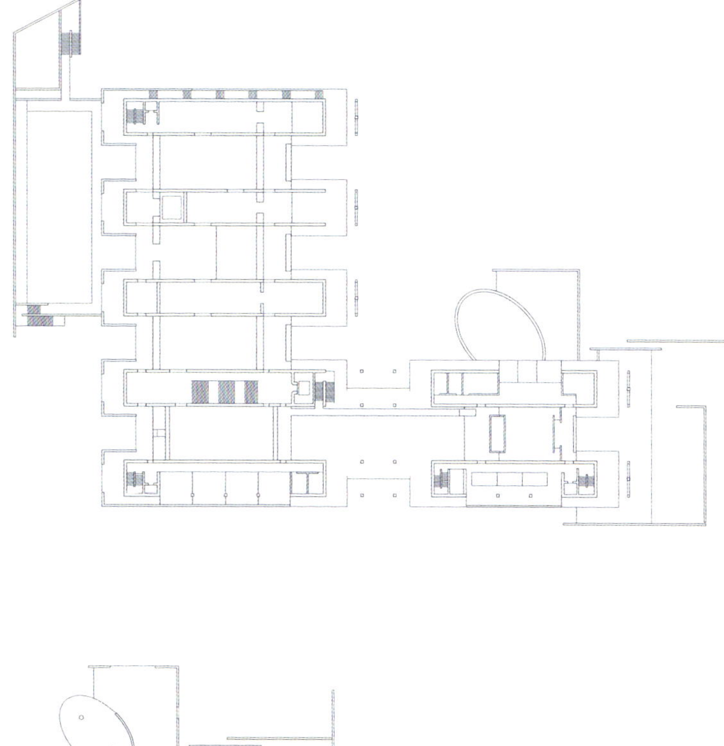

4

1

1 Section (executed proposal*).

2, 3 Study sketches of the shapes of the upper structure of the boxes, the roofs, and the skylights. In investigating an even simpler expression, the roofs were altered from louvers to concrete slabs. Various possibilities were investigated for inserting a system to obtain light.

1 断面図（実施案*）。

2, 3 ボックスの上部構造、屋根とトップライトの形状検討図。より簡潔な表現を検討する中で屋根はルーバーからコンクリートスラブになった。そこにいかなる採光のシステムを組み込みか、さまざまな可能性が検討された。

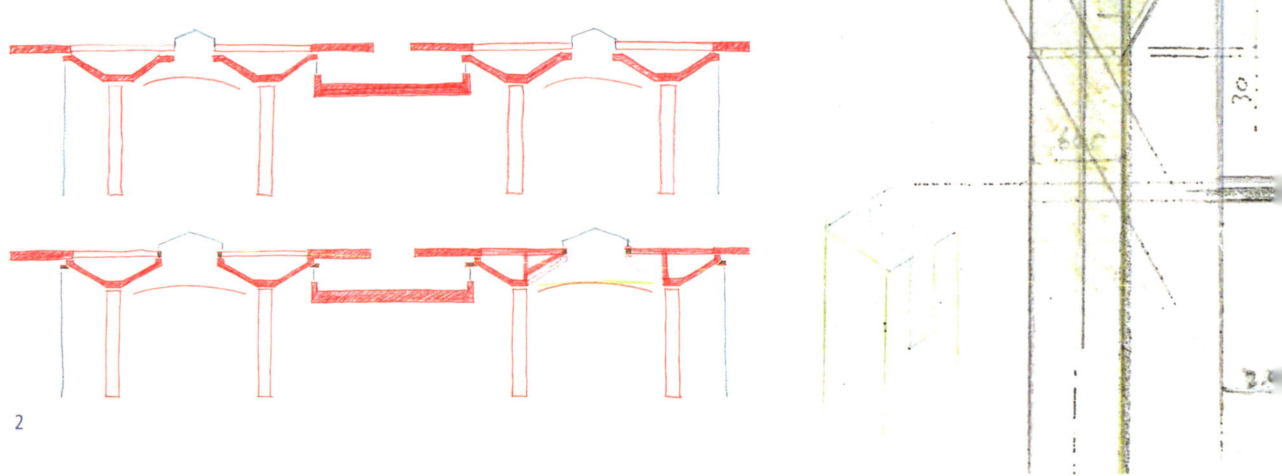

2

The characteristic spatiality of the interiors of the concrete boxes is completed by their illumination with skylights. I was thinking about how to respond with my architecture to the Kimbell's simple strength and delicate treatment of light. That is to say, this is architecture made in dialogue with the Kimbell.

コンクリートボックス内部の空間はトップライトの光により、それぞれに完結した独自の空間性をもつ。考えていたのはキンベルのシンプルな強さと繊細な光の扱いに、自身の建築の中でいかに応えるかということ。いわばキンベルとの対話の中でつくった建築だった。

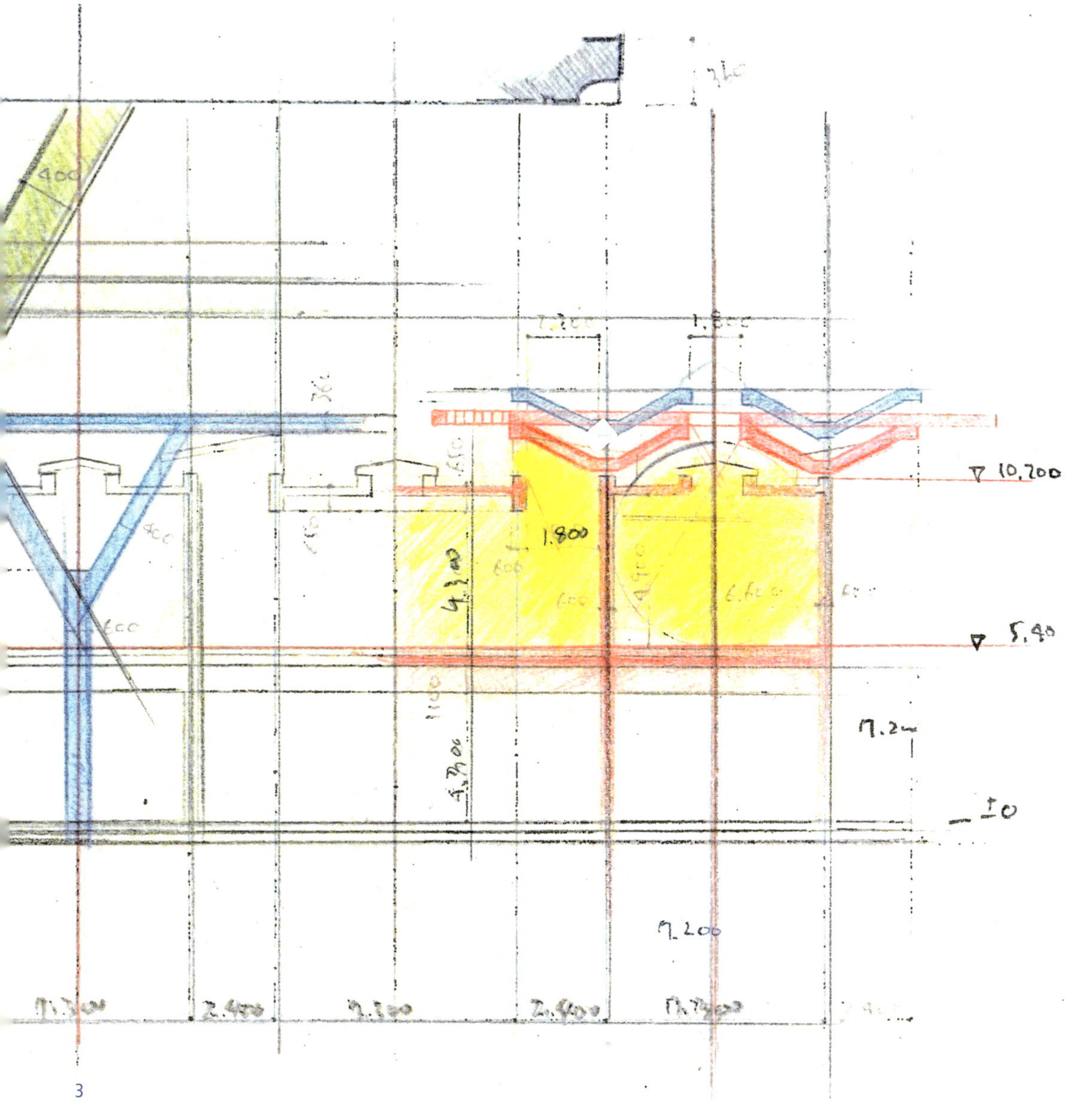

3

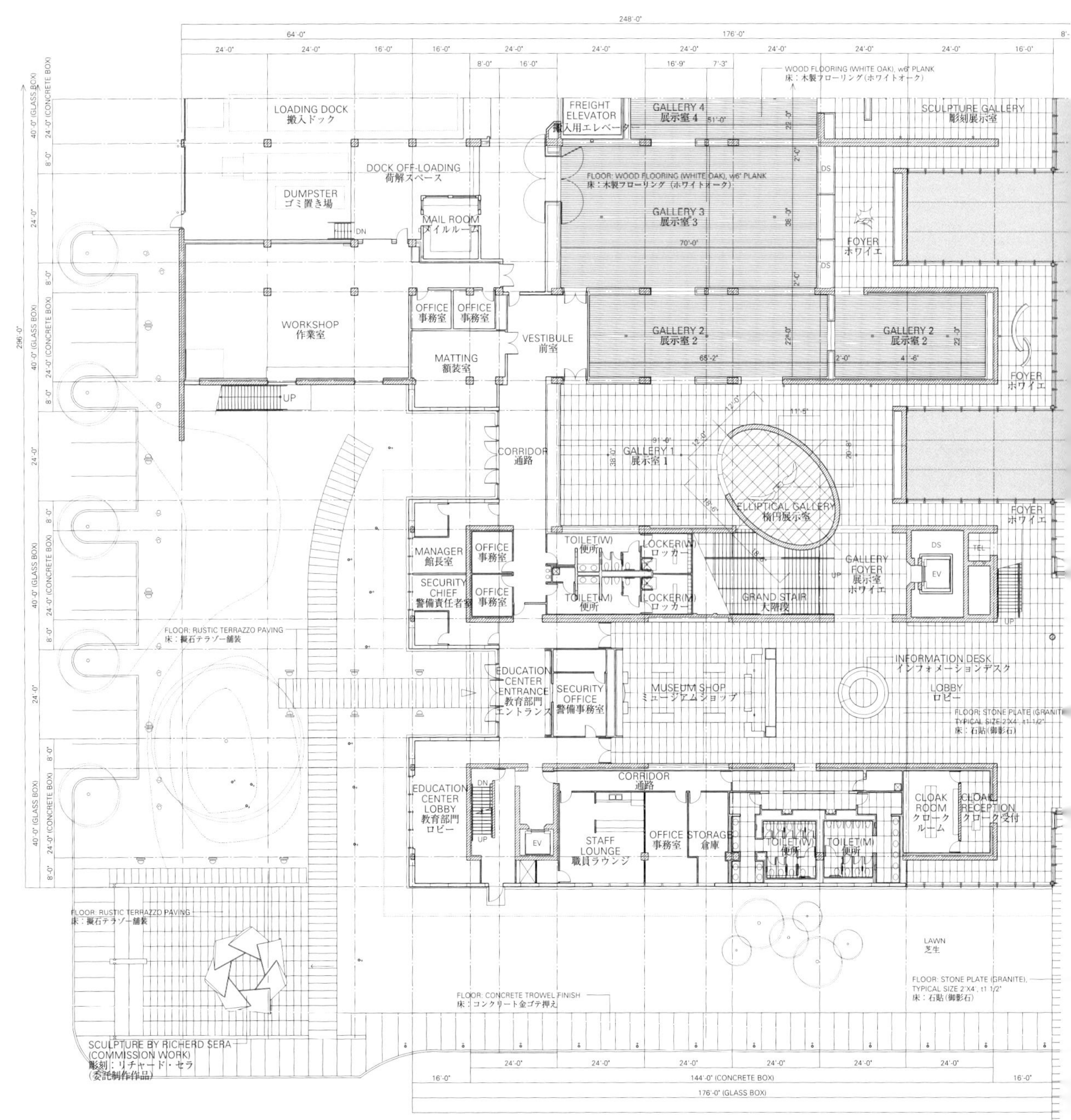

Detailed plan of the first floor

1階平面詳細図

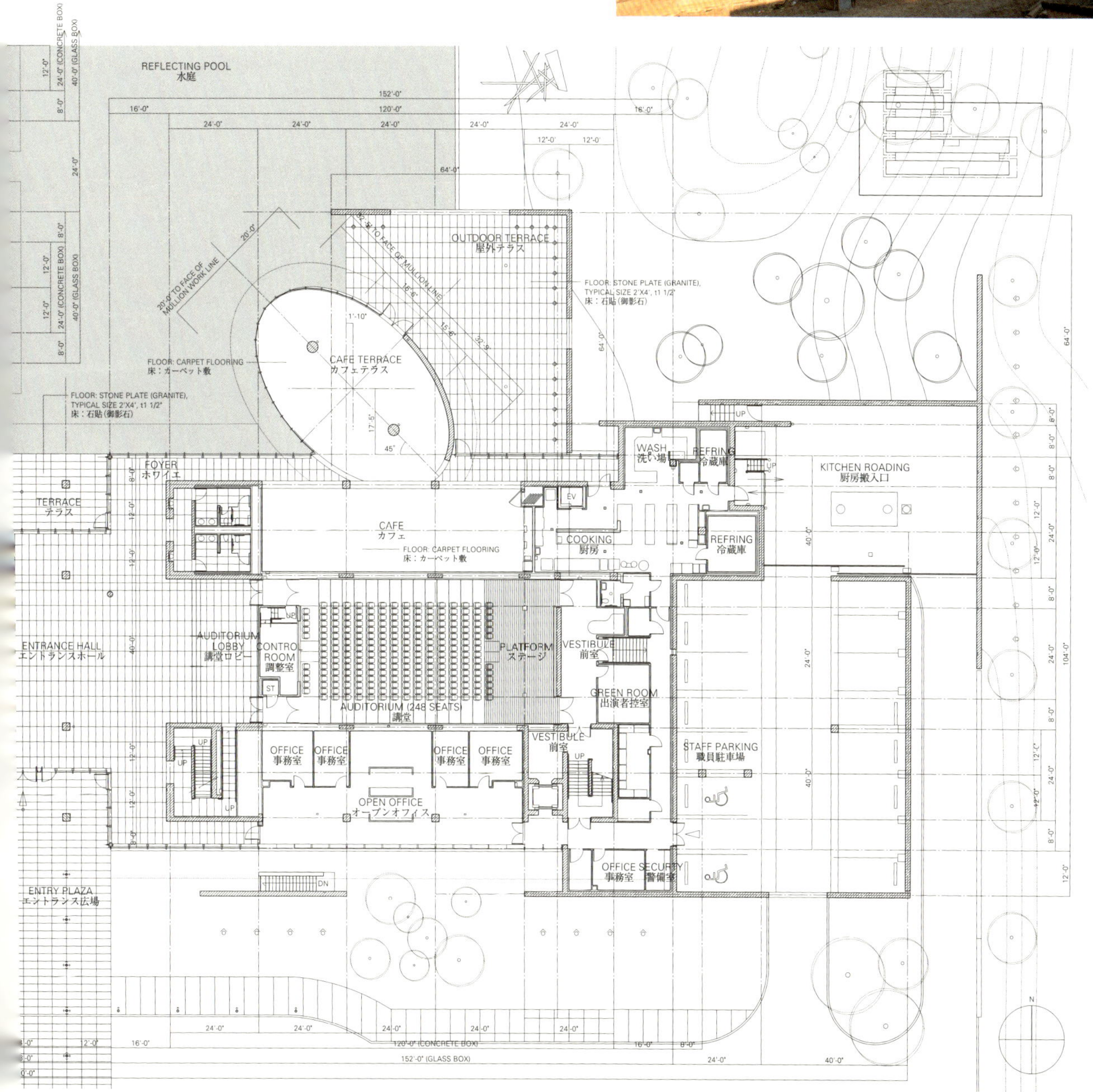

REFLECTING POOL
水庭

OUTDOOR TERRACE
屋外テラス

FLOOR: STONE PLATE (GRANITE), TYPICAL SIZE 2'X4', t1 1/2"
床：石貼（御影石）

20'-0" TO FACE OF MULLION WORK LINE

FLOOR: CARPET FLOORING
床：カーペット敷

CAFE TERRACE
カフェテラス

FLOOR: STONE PLATE (GRANITE), TYPICAL SIZE 2'X4', t1 1/2"
床：石貼（御影石）

FOYER
ホワイエ

TERRACE
テラス

CAFE
カフェ

FLOOR: CARPET FLOORING
床：カーペット敷

WASH
洗い場

REFRING
冷蔵庫

KITCHEN ROADING
厨房搬入口

COOKING
厨房

REFRING
冷蔵庫

EV

ENTRANCE HALL
エントランスホール

AUDITORIUM LOBBY
講堂ロビー

CONTROL ROOM
調整室

ST

AUDITORIUM (248 SEATS)
講堂

PLATFORM
ステージ

VESTIBULE
前室

GREEN ROOM
出演者控室

OFFICE
事務室

OFFICE
事務室

OFFICE
事務室

OFFICE
事務室

VESTIBULE
前室

STAFF PARKING
職員駐車場

OPEN OFFICE
オープンオフィス

OFFICE
事務室

SECURITY
警備室

ENTRY PLAZA
エントランス広場

UP

DN

N

120'-0" (CONCRETE BOX)

152'-0" (GLASS BOX)

Passerelle de Bercy-Tolbiac
(International Design Competition)
セーヌ川橋国際設計競技案

1. Paris, France　フランス パリ
2. 1998.8-1998.10

This is a proposal submitted to an international competition held in 1998 for a pedestrian bridge spanning the River Seine in Paris, France. The bridge is in a location that connects Dominique Perrault's Bibliothèque nationale de France, completed four years before this competition, to Parc Bercy on the opposite bank. I proposed the idea of a horizontal bridge, which extends straight along the axis of the library, joined to an arched bridge that crosses it diagonally.

1998年に開催された、フランスのパリ、セーヌ川に架かる歩道橋の国際コンペ提出案である。橋が架かる場所は、コンペの4年前に完成したドミニク・ペローのフランス国立図書館と、対岸のベルシー公園を結ぶ位置。そこで、私が提案したのは図書館の軸線に合わせてまっ直ぐ伸びる水平橋と、それと斜めに交差するアーチ橋を組み合わせた橋のアイディアである。

1

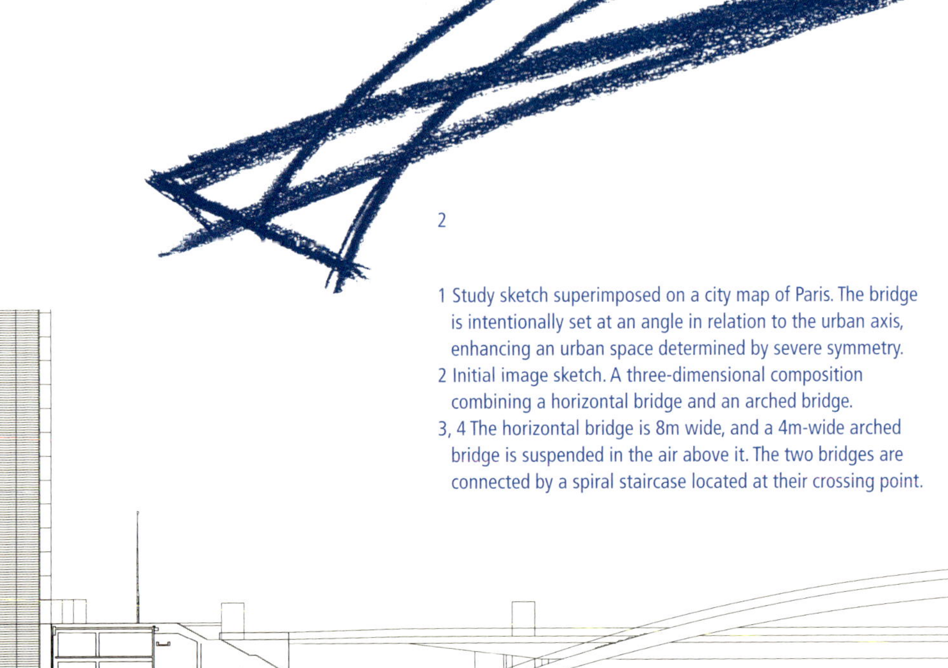

2

1 Study sketch superimposed on a city map of Paris. The bridge is intentionally set at an angle in relation to the urban axis, enhancing an urban space determined by severe symmetry.
2 Initial image sketch. A three-dimensional composition combining a horizontal bridge and an arched bridge.
3, 4 The horizontal bridge is 8m wide, and a 4m-wide arched bridge is suspended in the air above it. The two bridges are connected by a spiral staircase located at their crossing point.

3

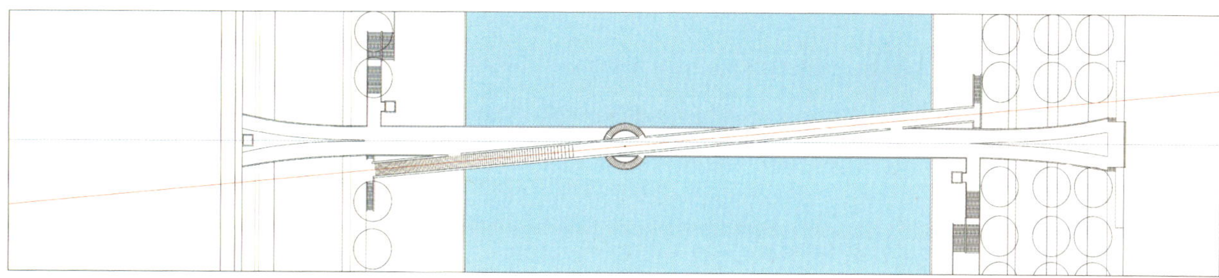

4

1 パリの都市地図に描き重ねられたスタディスケッチ。都市軸に対し意図的に角度を振った橋が、厳格なシンメトリーに支配された都市空間を刺激する。
2 初期イメージスケッチ。水平橋と太鼓橋とを組み合わせた立体的な構成。
3, 4 水平橋の幅員は8m、その上空に幅員4mのアーチ橋が架かる。2本の橋は、交差する位置の螺旋階段でつながっている。

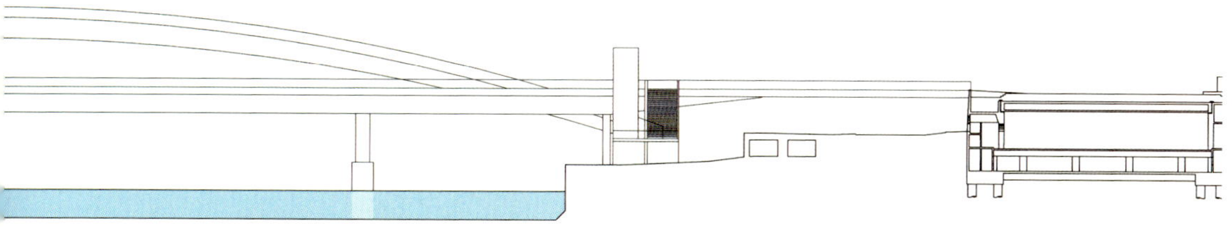

The shape of the sloping arched bridge takes the role of a structure supporting the horizontal bridge from above, and the role of a device for enjoying views of the ever-changing waterfront. This emerged from the idea that it would be interesting to provide an asymmetric place in a city of rigid symmetries.

斜めのアーチ橋は、水平橋を上部から吊る構造体としての役割と、変化に富んだ水辺の眺望を楽しむ装置としての役割を負う。「厳格なシンメトリーの都市に、ア・シンメトリーの場所をつくり出したら面白いのでは」という思いから生まれたかたちだった。

1

2

3

4

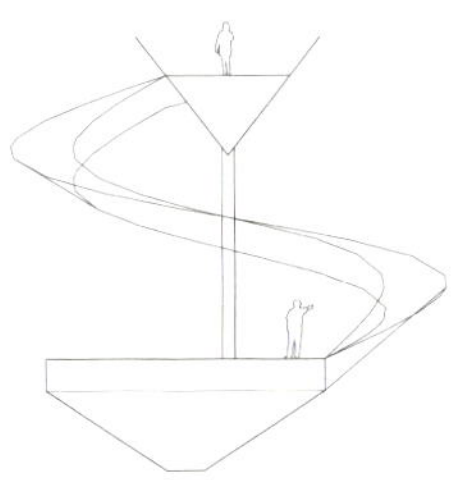

5

1-4 Richly varied sequence of urban spaces, achieved by the combination of two bridges. The views at different levels draw out new charms from Paris.
5 Sectional detail of the arched bridge, section of the horizontal bridge and the arched bridge.

1-4 ふたつの橋が組み合わされることで得られる、変化に富んだ都市空間のシークエンス。さまざまなレベルからの眺望が、新たなパリの魅力を引き出す。
5 アーチ橋の詳細断面図と、水平橋とアーチ橋の断面図。

Komyo-ji Temple
南岳山光明寺

1. Saijo, Ehime, Japan　愛媛県西条市
2. 1998.1-1999.3
3. 1999.4-2000.6

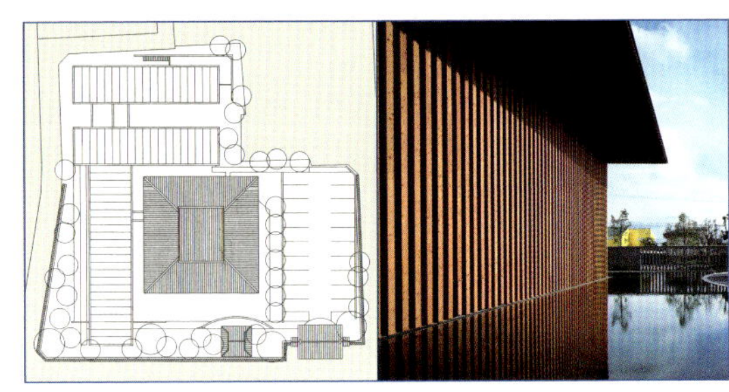

The site is located in a residential area at the center of Saijo City, Ehime Prefecture. This is the reconstruction of a Jodo Shinshu Buddhist temple that is more than 250 years old. As a "temple" in an area known for its abundant underground water, the concept is a wooden hall floating on a body of water engulfed in gentle light.
The theme is a contemporary timber structure that responds to Japanese tradition. Taking the *noki* (eave) and *kumimono* (bracket purlin) compositions characterizing Japanese architecture as a guide, I conceived a personal expression using wood.

敷地は愛媛県西条市中心部の住宅地に位置する。250年余り続く浄土真宗寺院の建て替えである。豊富な伏流水で知られる地域の〈お寺〉として、水面に浮かぶ柔らかな光に包まれた木のお堂を構想した。
主題は、日本の伝統に応える現代木造。日本建築特有の、深い軒の表現と組物的構成を手がかりに、自分なりの木の表現を考えた。

1

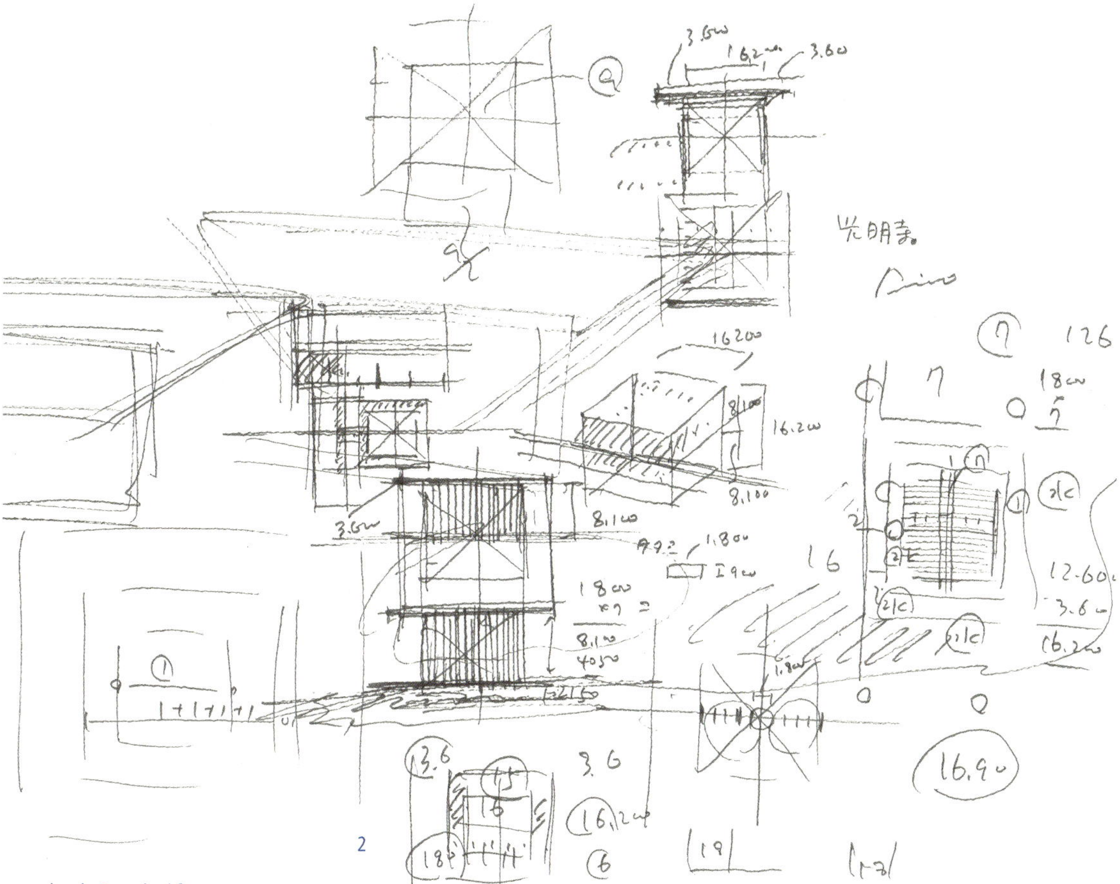

2

1 Initial image sketch. Detached from auxiliary facilities such as the visitor's hall, the reception hall, and the priests' quarters, the main hall is conceived as a symbolic place surrounded by water.

2, 3 Exploratory sketches of the composition. A cloister surrounds the square space on all four sides, above which a large roof is supported by four columns. The expression of the lattice is the core of the design. Because it is a timber structure building comprising an assemblage of wooden elements, dimensional coordination from part to whole is important.

1 初期イメージスケッチ。客殿、礼拝堂、庫裏などの付帯施設と切り離して、本堂を水に囲われ象徴的空間として考える。

2, 3 構成の検討スケッチ。方形の空間の四周を回廊が巡り、その上に4本の柱で支えられた大屋根が載る。デザインの核となるのは格子の表現。木部材の組み合わせとしてつくられる木造建築ゆえに、全体から部分へと一貫する寸法体系が重要となる。

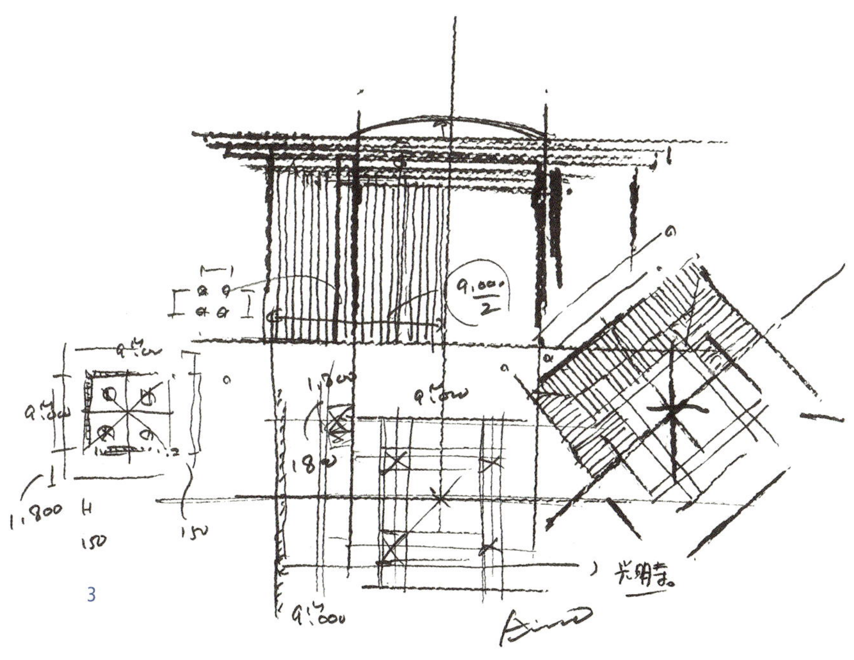

3

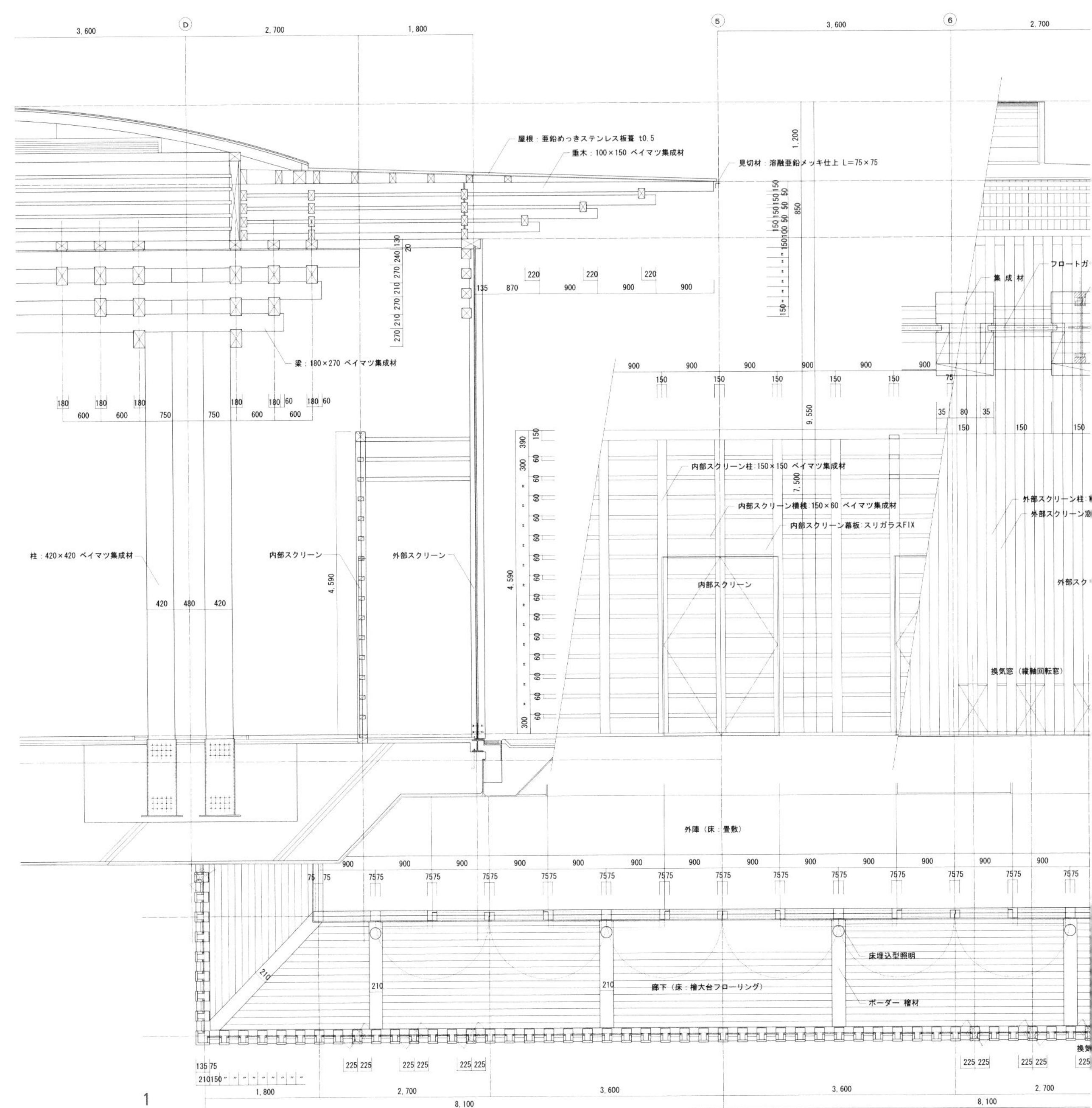
屋根：亜鉛めっきステンレス板葺 t0.5
垂木：100×150 ベイマツ集成材
見切材：溶融亜鉛メッキ仕上 L=75×75
梁：180×270 ベイマツ集成材
柱：420×420 ベイマツ集成材
内部スクリーン
外部スクリーン
内部スクリーン柱：150×150 ベイマツ集成材
内部スクリーン横桟：150×60 ベイマツ集成材
内部スクリーン幕板：スリガラスFIX
内部スクリーン
集成材
換気窓（縦軸回転窓）
外陣（床：畳敷）
床埋込型照明
廊下（床：檜大台フローリング）
ボーダー 檜材
1

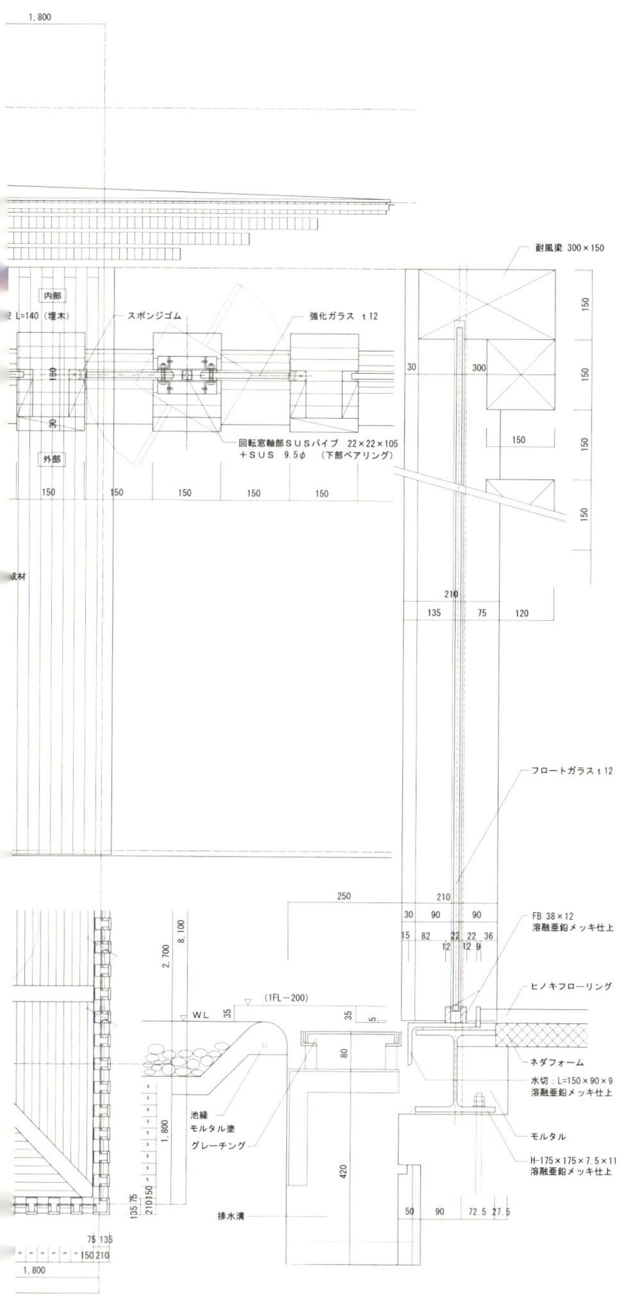

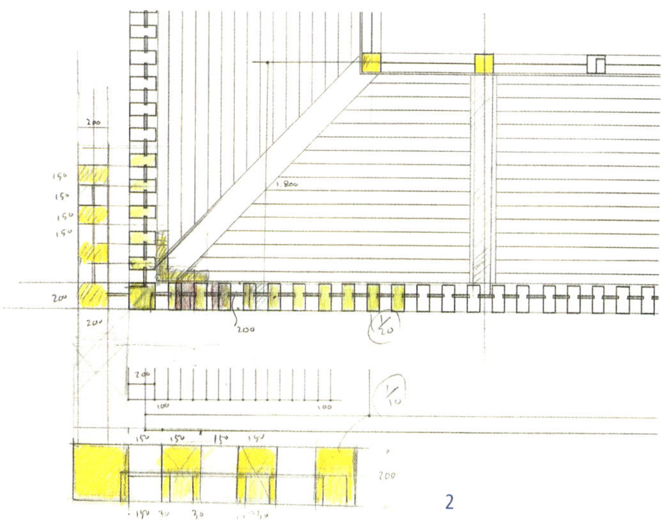

2

1 Detailed section. Below the assemblage that supports the contemporary *kumimono* made of laminated wood, by day the interior of the hall is suffused with gentle natural light coming in through the double-layer screens, whereas by night artificial light from the hall is dispersed and reflected in the pool, bringing about a magical atmosphere.

2 Detailed sketch of the exterior wall lattice. The vertical, closely spaced lattice of the exterior wall gently isolates the cloister surrounding all four sides of the hall from the pond surface. Glass is inserted in the gaps of the lattice, and one part may be opened and closed by axial rotation.

1 断面詳細図。集成材による現代的〈組物〉に支えられた架構の下、日中の堂内は、二重のスクリーンを経て入り込む柔らかな自然光で満たされ、逆に夜間は内部の光が散乱して池に反射し、幻想的な雰囲気を醸し出す。

2 格子の外壁ディテールスケッチ。ピッチの細かい縦格子の外壁が、本堂の四周を巡る回廊と池の水面とを緩やかに隔てる。格子の隙間にはガラスをはめ込み、その一部は軸回転で開閉可能にする。

2000s

Chichu Art Museum / Naoshima
François Pinault Foundation for Contemporary Art
Yokohama Local Meteorological Observatory
Interfaculty Initiative in Information Studies・Fukutake Hall, The University of Tokyo
Abu Dhabi Maritime Museum
Punta della Dogana Contemporary Art Centre
Shanghai Poly Theater

Chichu Art Museum / Naoshima
地中美術館

1. Kagawa-gun, Kagawa, Japan　香川県香川郡
2. 2000.8-2002.3
3. 2002.4-2004.6

This is another art museum built on a site in Naoshima, a small island in the Inland Sea. Named the Chichu Art Museum, this building contains a permanent exhibition of works by three artists: Impressionist Claude Monet, and the contemporary artists Walter de Maria and James Turrell. The site is located 600m west of the Benesse House Museum on a slightly elevated hill, carved into which are the remains of a stepped salt pan. Based on the potential of this place and the unique program of a permanent exhibition of spatial art, I proposed here an "underground architecture" that pursues to perfection the "architecture merged into the landscape" attempted at Benesse House Museum.

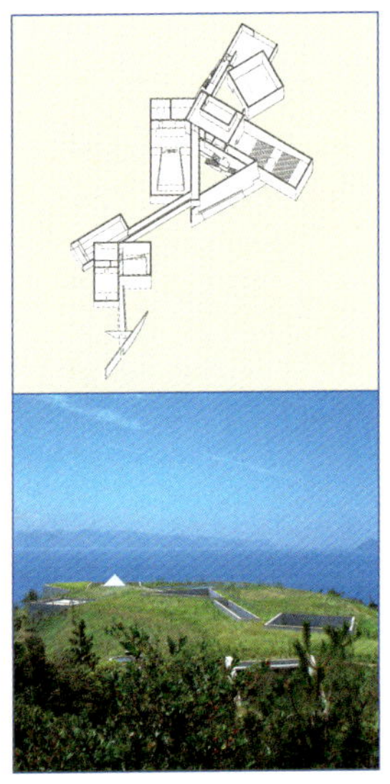

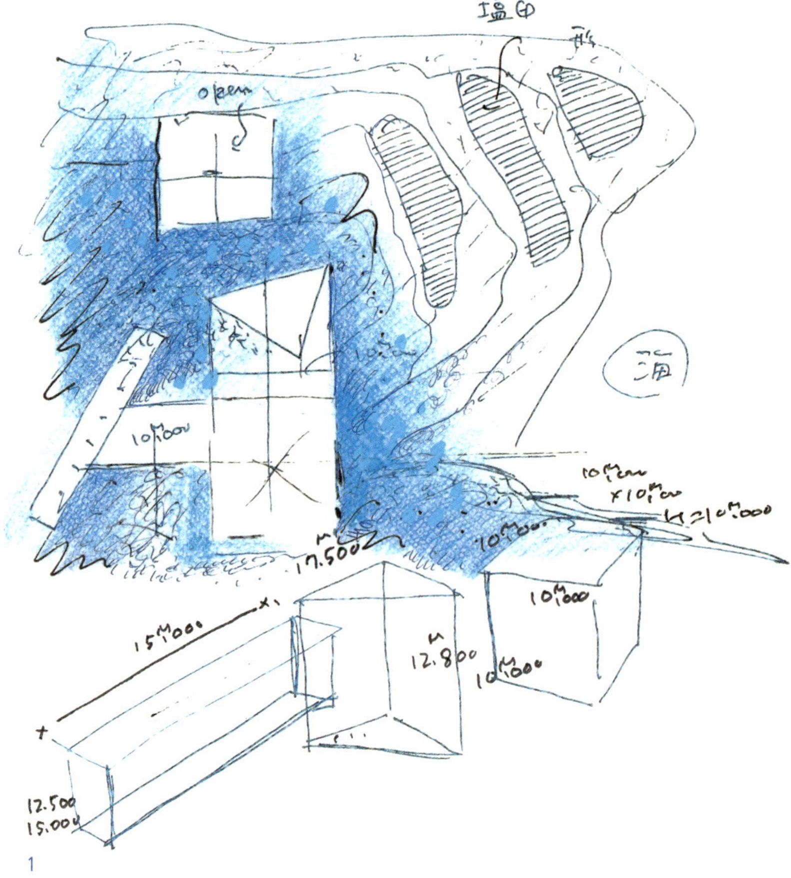

1

1 Initial image sketch. On the top of a hill, it comprises two voids—a square plan and an equilateral triangle plan—excavated along a north-south axis toward the sea.

2-4 Pure geometric spaces enabled by the fact that they are underground. How to combine them into a charming underground space full of variety? This three-dimensional image is dropped into the sketches and solidified.

1 初期イメージスケッチ。丘の上に、海へと向かう南北の軸線に沿って穿たれた、正方形と正三角形平面のふたつのヴォイドを軸として構成する。

2-4 地下だからこそ可能な純粋幾何学の空間。それらをいかに組み合わせて、変化に富んだ魅力的な地下空間とするか。3次元のイメージをスケッチに落として固めていく。

敷地は瀬戸内海の小島、直島につくられた、もうひとつの美術館である。「地中美術館」と名付けられた建物には、印象派のクロード・モネと現代美術のウォルター・デ・マリア、ジェームズ・タレルという3作家の作品が永久展示されている。敷地は「ベネッセハウス ミュージアム」の西方600m、段状塩田の遺構が刻まれた小高い丘の上に位置する。その場所のポテンシャルと〈空間アートの永久展示〉という特殊なプログラムを踏まえ、ここでは〈風景に溶け込む建築〉という「ベネッセハウス」での試みをさらに推し進めた完全なる〈地中建築〉を提案した。

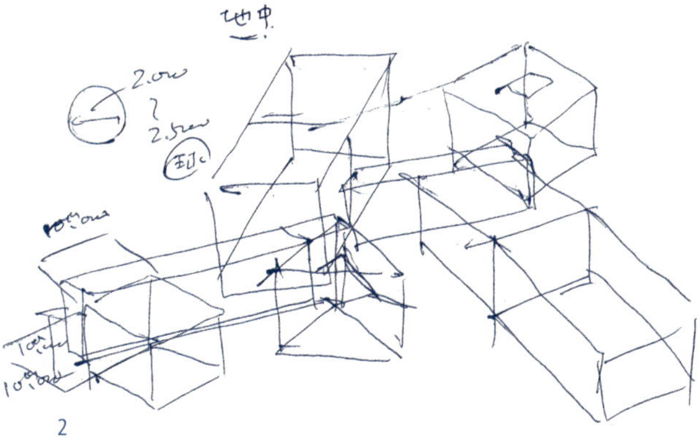

2

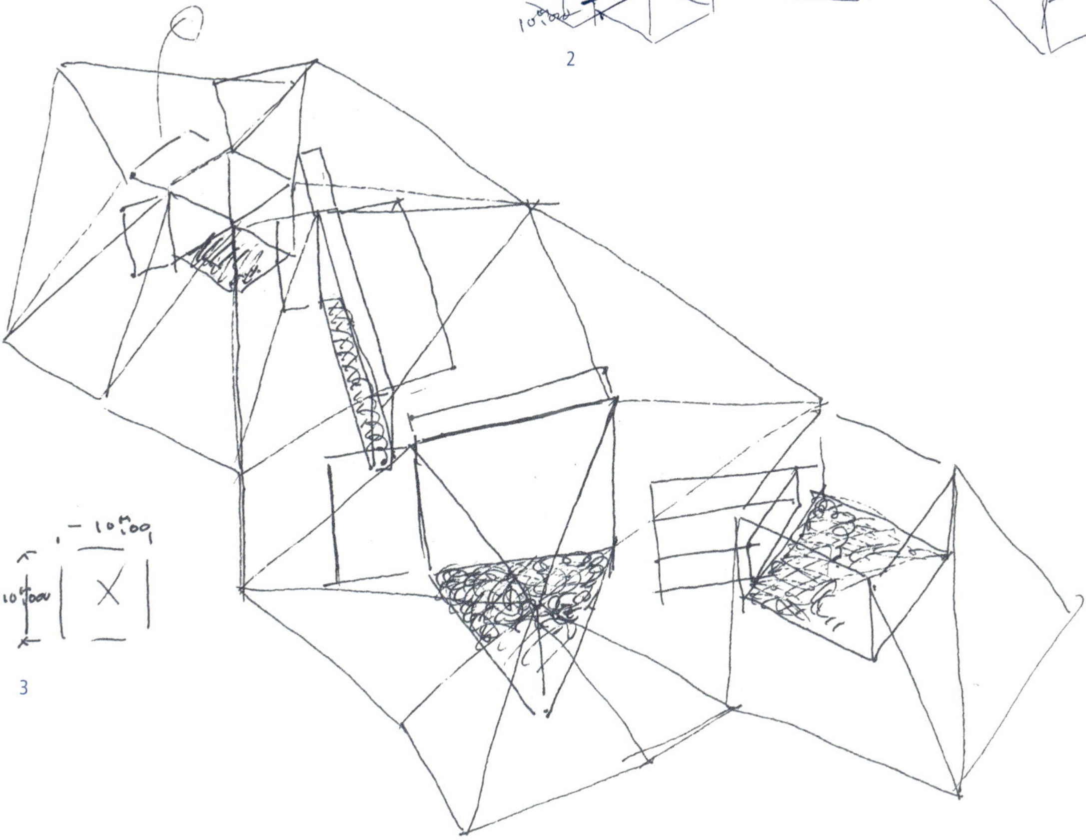

3

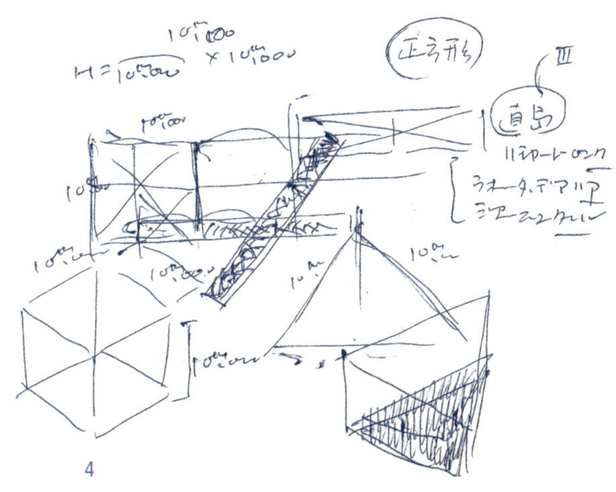

4

1 Exploratory sketch for the Walter de Maria room. Through uncompromising dialogues on the conflicting intentions of the artist, who develops images from an internal viewpoint, and the architect, who has overall control, an art space brimming with a sense of tension was made.
2 Detailed plan.

1 ウォルター・デ・マリア室の検討スケッチ。内部からの視点でイメージを膨らませていくアーティストと、全体をコントロールする建築家が互いの意思をぶつけあい、妥協なき対話を重ねていく中で、緊張感あふれるアートの空間がつくられていく。
2 平面詳細図。

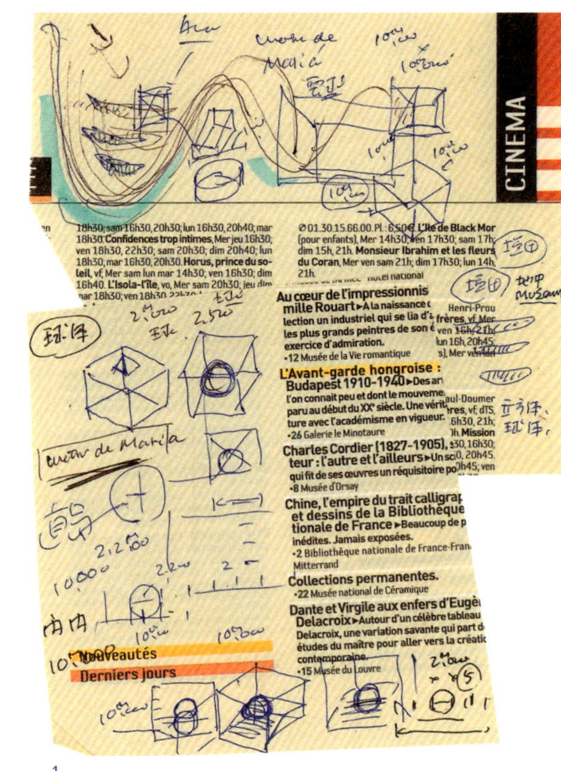

1

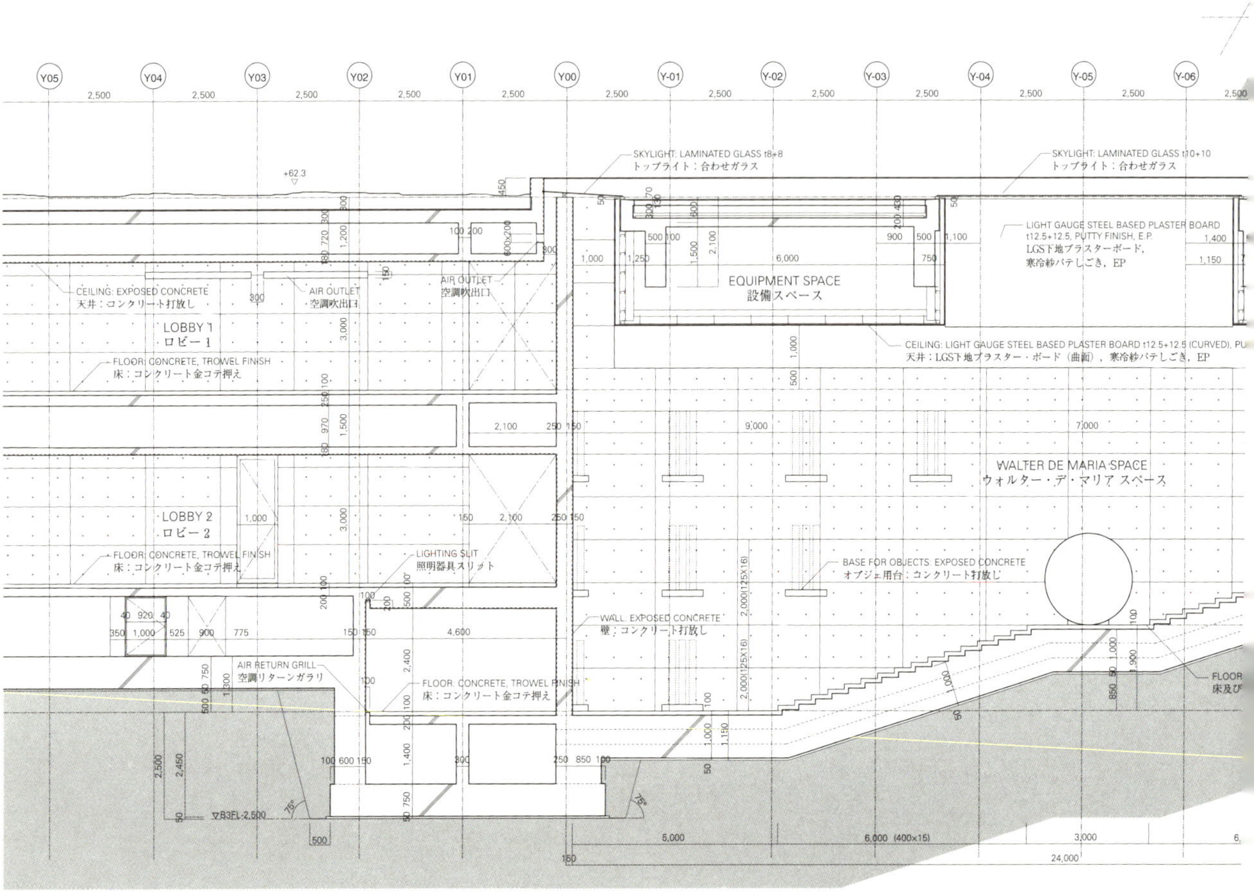

2

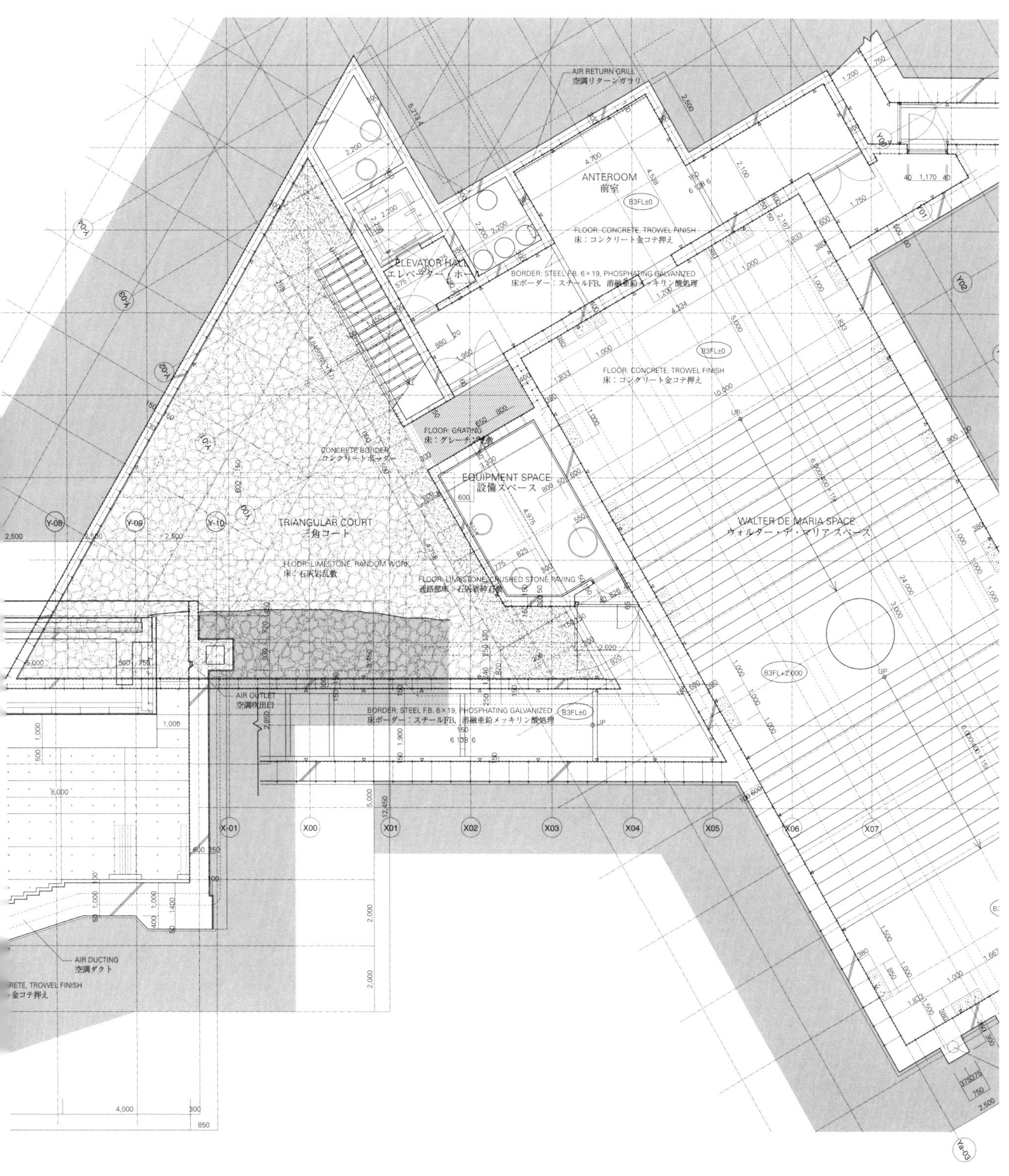

AIR RETURN GRILL
空調リターンガラリ
ANTEROOM
前室
FLOOR: CONCRETE, TROWEL FINISH
床：コンクリート金コテ押え
ELEVATOR HALL
エレベーターホール
BORDER: STEEL F.B. 6×19, PHOSPHATING GALVANIZED
床ボーダー：スチールFB，溶融亜鉛メッキリン酸処理
FLOOR: GRATING
CONCRETE BORDER
EQUIPMENT SPACE
設備スペース
TRIANGULAR COURT
三角コート
FLOOR: LIMESTONE, RANDOM WORK
床：石灰岩乱敷
FLOOR: LIMESTONE, CRUSHED STONE PAVING
WALTER DE MARIA SPACE
ウォルター・デ・マリアスペース
AIR OUTLET
空調吹出口
AIR DUCTING
空調ダクト

François Pinault Foundation for Contemporary Art
ピノー現代美術館

1. Ile Seguin, Paris, France　フランス パリ スガン島
2. 2001.1-2005.4

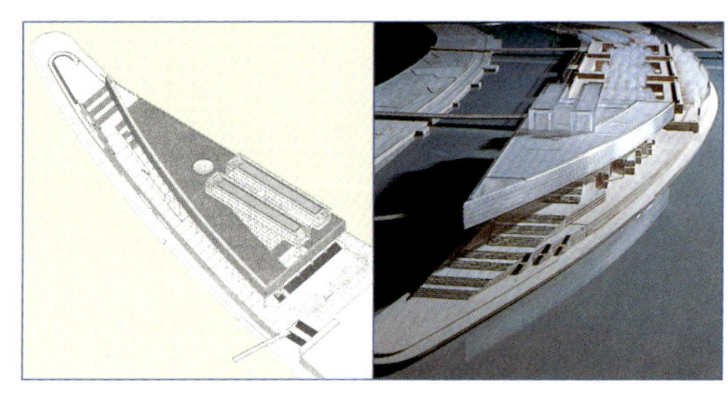

Through an international design competition held in October 2001, I was chosen as the designer for this art museum located on Ile Seguin in Paris, France. Making use of its unmatched position on an islet in the River Seine, I proposed architecture that inherits the memories of the place—the origin of Renault, and a revered site for the labor movement—with the periphery of the island architecturalized as a “plaza” and a glass volume floating above it. The construction documentation was completed and it was one step away from breaking ground, but the surrounding urban infrastructure improvements were stalled, and so the plan was cancelled. Together with the Pinault Foundation, we then began work on the design of Palazzo Grassi and Punta della Dogana in Venice.

2001年10月、国際コンペで私が設計者として選ばれた、フランスのパリ、スガン島を敷地とする美術館の計画。セーヌ川の中洲という類まれな立地を活かしつつ、ルノー発祥の地であり、労働運動のメッカであった場所の記憶を受け継ぐ建築として提案したのは、島の水際線なりに建築化された〈広場〉と、その上に浮遊するガラスのヴォリュームによる建築だった。実施設計まで完了し、着工まであと一歩というところまで進んだが、周辺の都市インフラ整備が進まず、計画は中止となった。そして新たにピノー財団と組んで始まったのが、ヴェネツィアの「パラッツォ・グラッシ」とそれに続く「プンタ・デラ・ドガーナ」の再生計画だった。

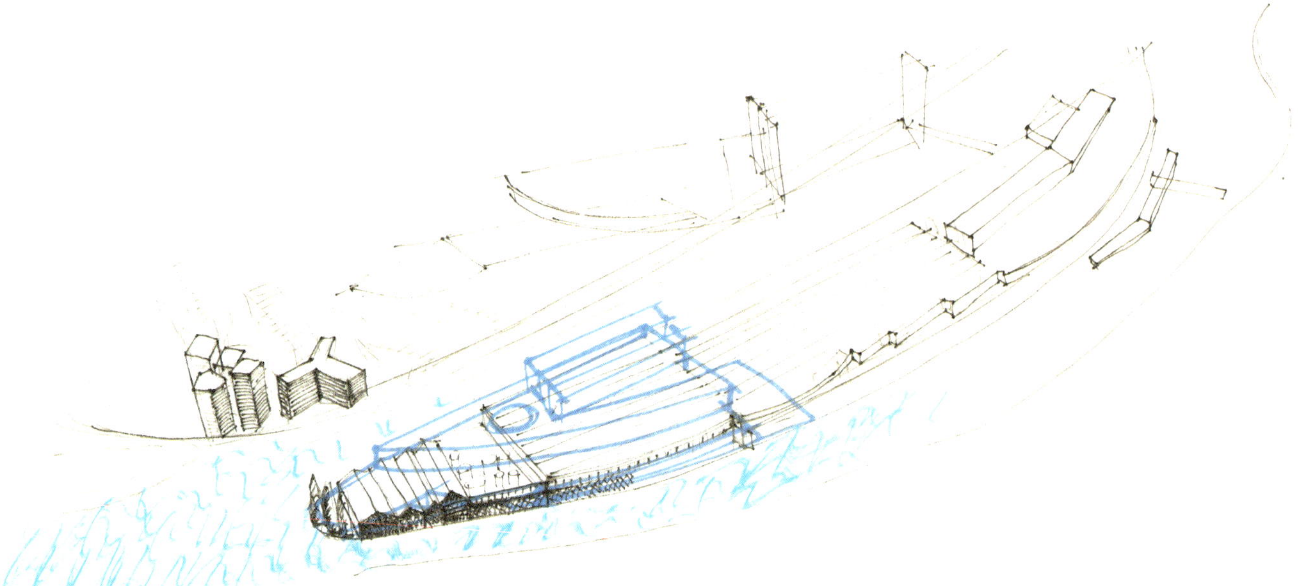

1

1 Early image sketch.
2 The Renault factory rising along the contours of the island. Sketch of the site scenery.
3 A composition of a floating glass volume and a base platform integrated with the island, connected by rectangular volumes.

1 初期イメージスケッチ。
2 ルノーの工場が島の輪郭に沿って起ち上がる。敷地の風景スケッチ。
3 浮遊するガラスのヴォリュームと、島と一体化する基壇部、それをつなぐ矩形のヴォリュームによる構成。

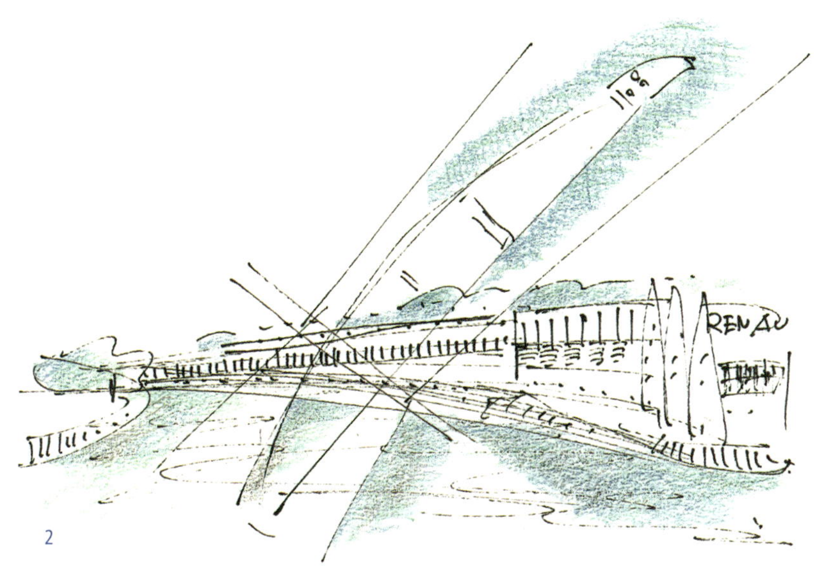

2

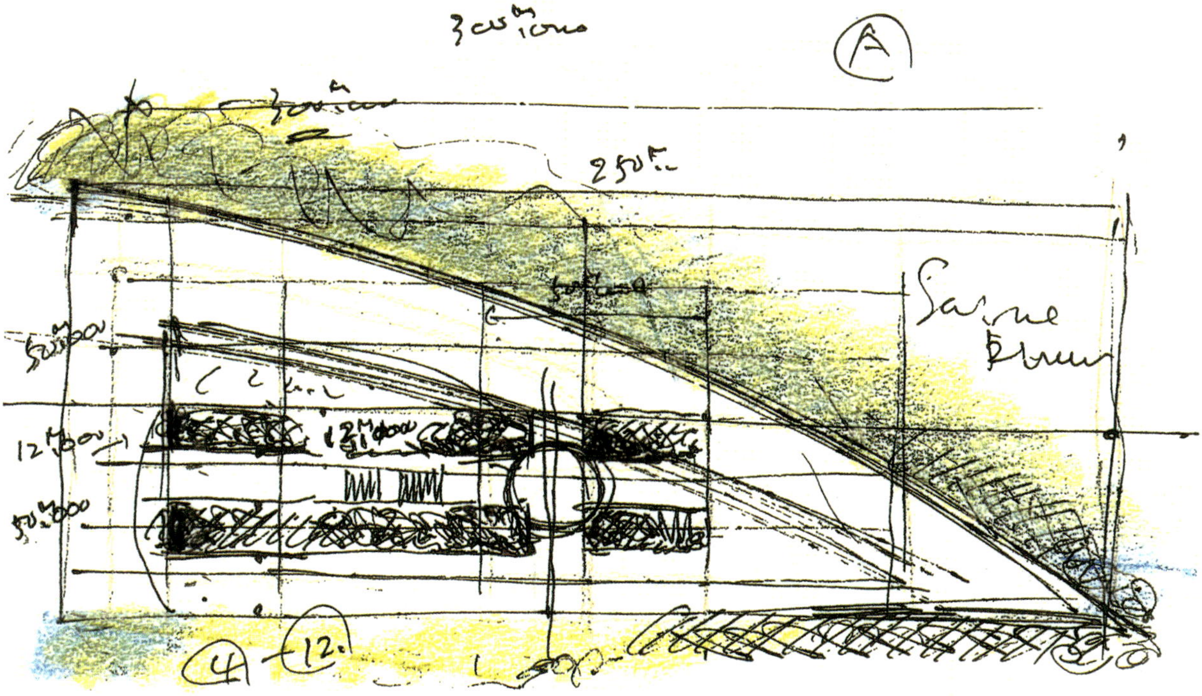

3

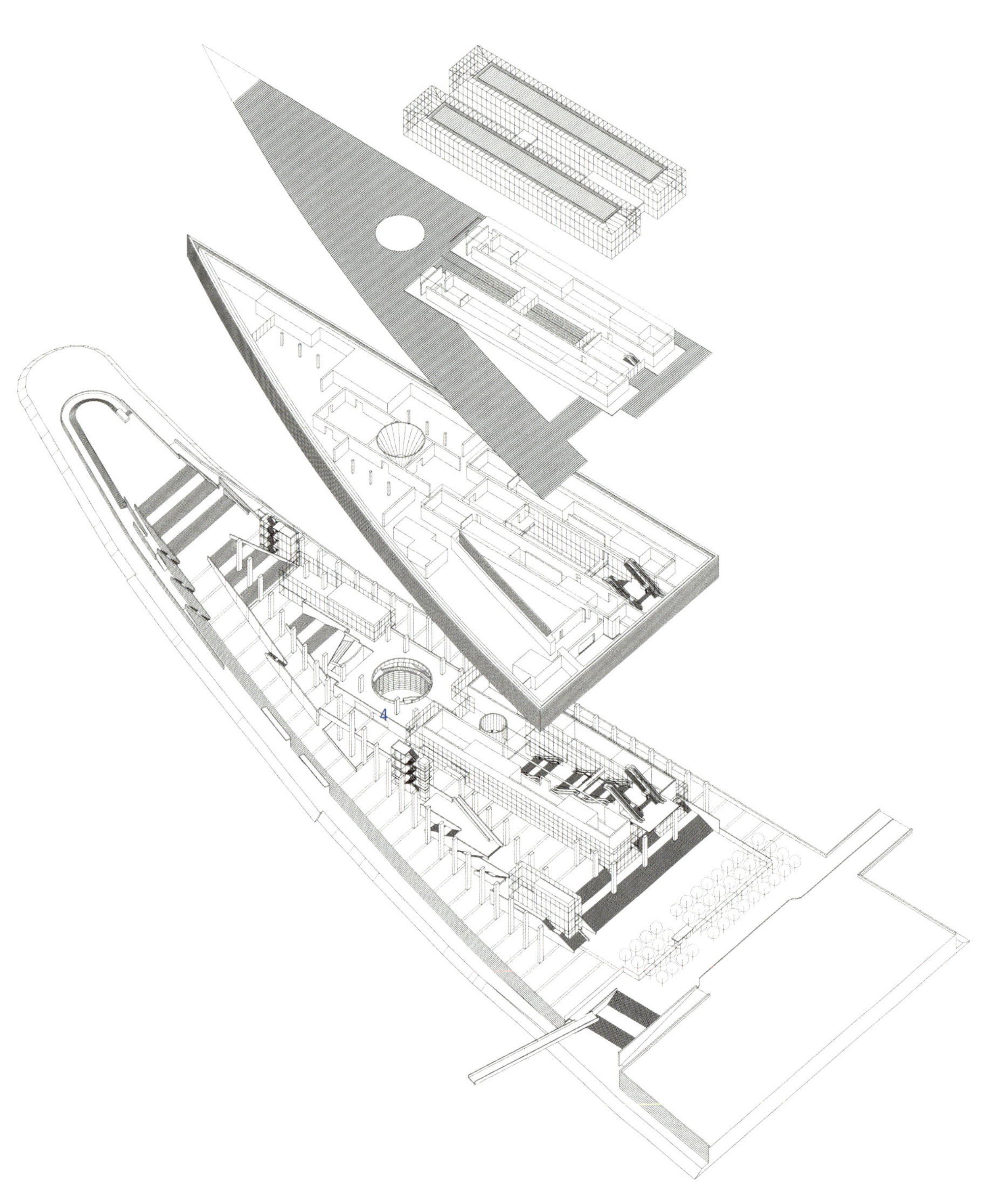

Compositional diagram using axonometrics.
アイソノメトリックによる構成図式。

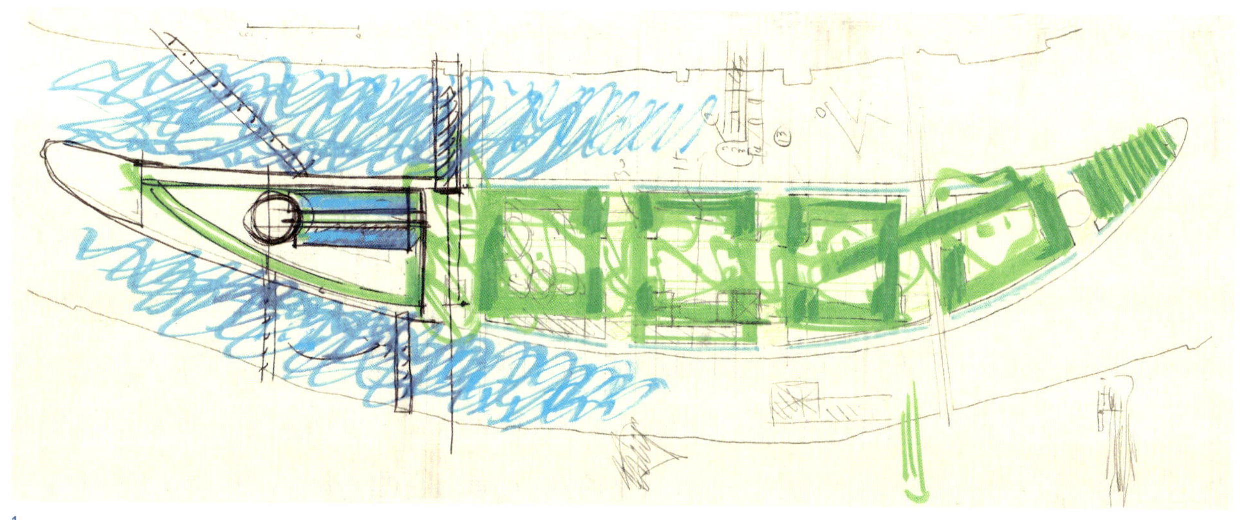

1

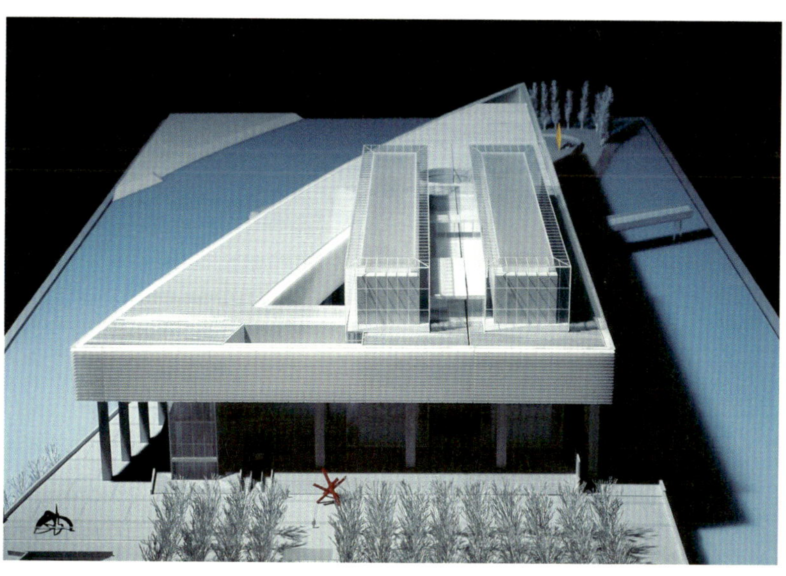

1, 2 Image sketches drawn during the design of the art museum. Not only an island with an art museum, a new, uncommissioned proposal has been drawn to the rear. This design proposal for a masterplan of the entire island was taken to the stage of construction documentation and a model was built. Due to various circumstances it ended up unfinished, but the dream of regenerating of a former industrial fortress as a cultural fortress, not attained in Paris, has been realized in Venice in a different place and different form.

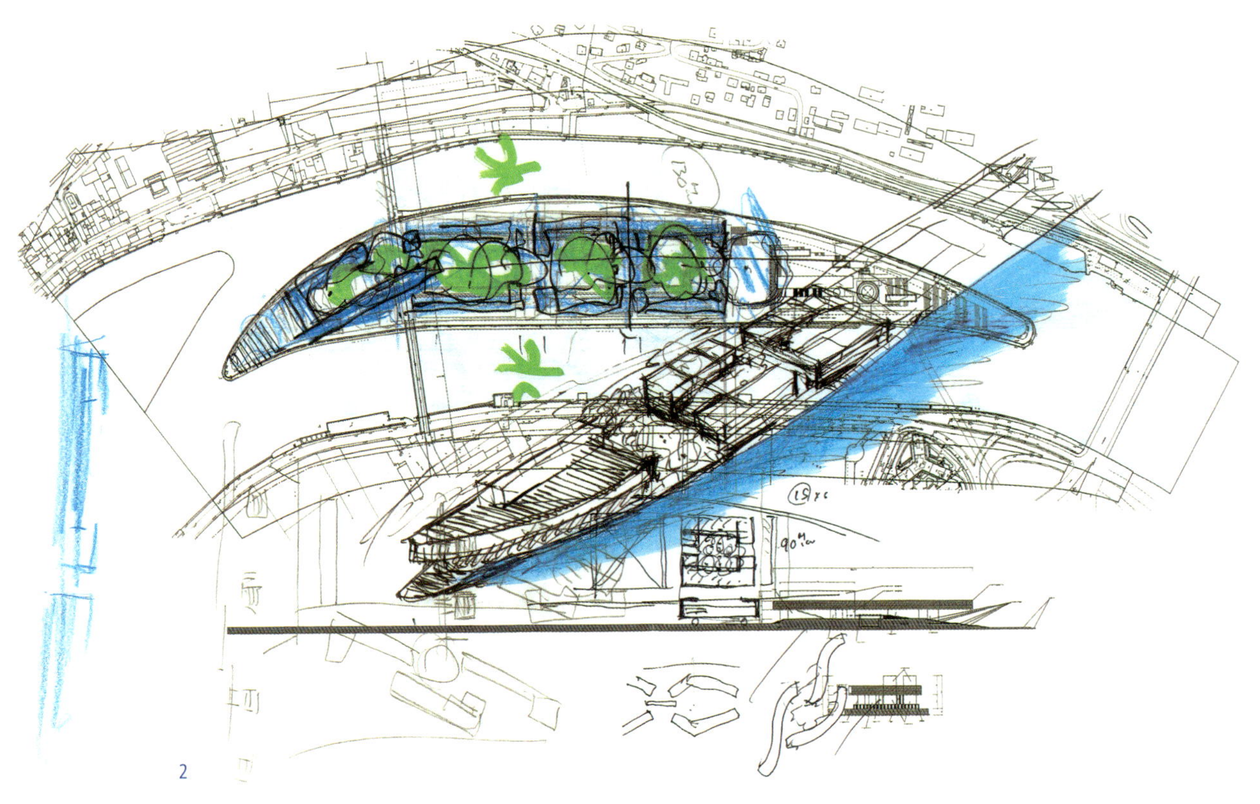

2

1, 2 美術館設計時に描かれたイメージスケッチ。美術館のある島のへさきだけでなく、依頼を受けていないその背後の部分まで、新たな提案が描かれている。実施設計時点で島全体のマスタープランの提案計画が完成、模型化されていた。諸事情で未完に終わったが、かつての産業の砦を文化の砦に再生する——パリでかなわなかった夢は、場所を変え、かたちを変えてヴェネツィアで実現することになった。

Yokohama Local Meteorological Observatory
横浜地方気象台

1. Yokohama, Kanagawa, Japan　神奈川県横浜市
2. 2004.9-2006.3
3. 2006.1-2009.3

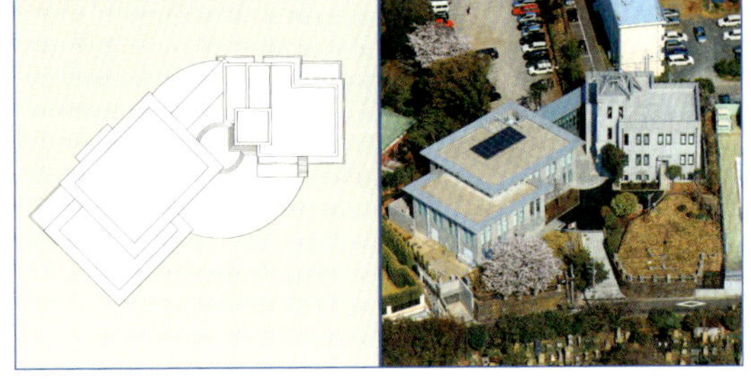

This is an addition to the Yokohama Local Meteorological Observatory, built on high ground looking down on Yokohama Bay. Completed in 1927, the Yokohama Local Meteorological Observatory is an early Modernist building designed by Shigezo Shigeno, a prefectural engineer then in his twenties, as "the latest style, primarily simple and practical." Possessing a nostalgic warmth, this building is saturated with the desires of its maker and is loved by the local residents. Having renovated the existing facility, a new wing was constructed.

The main theme was how to handle the "ma" (intentionally empty space) between old and new. Here I conceived a form set at a certain distance, acting as a counterpoint to the existing facility. The old part and new part are each treated as independent objects, and the space between them is a buffer zone in which new and old collide. This is a simple diagrammatic design, but the realized "ma" space manifests a force that exceeds the expectations of the designer.

横浜港を見下ろす高台に建つ、横浜地方気象台の増築である。昭和2年に完成した横浜地方気象台は、当時20代前半の県技師、繁野繁造が〈簡素実用を主とした最新式〉として設計した初期モダニズムの建築だ。古きよき時代の温もり――つくり手の思いの沁み込んだその建築は、地元住民にも〈ハマの気象台〉として愛されている。この既存施設の改修を行った上での新たな棟の建築だった。

主題は新旧の〈間〉の取り方。そこで考えたのが既存施設と一定の距離をおいて向き合い、対をなすかたちの増設である。古い部分と新しい部分をそれぞれ自立したものとして扱い、その隙間を新旧の衝突する緩衝スペースとする。単純な図式の計画だが、実際に建ち上がった〈間〉の空間は、設計者の予想を超えた力をもって現れた。

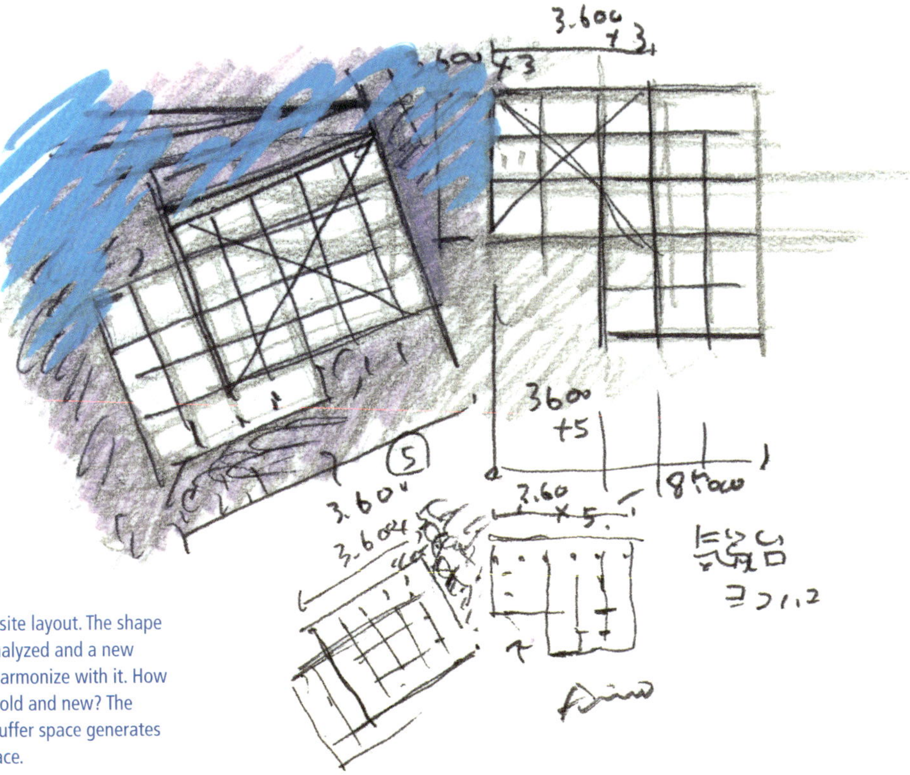

1

1, 4 Exploratory sketch of the site layout. The shape of the existing building is analyzed and a new wing is composed so as to harmonize with it. How to make the "ma" between old and new? The existence of a moderating buffer space generates a sense of tension in this place.
2, 3 Exterior image sketches.

2
3

4

1, 4 配置検討のスケッチ。既存建物の形を分析し、それと呼応するような新たな棟の構成を考える。新旧の〈間〉をいかに取るか。適度な余白の存在が、場に緊張感を生み出す。
2, 3 外観イメージスケッチ。

Interfaculty Initiative in Information Studies Fukutake Hall, The University of Tokyo
東京大学情報学環・福武ホール

1. Bunkyo-ku, Tokyo, Japan　東京都文京区
2. 2005.9-2006.9
3. 2006.12-2008.3

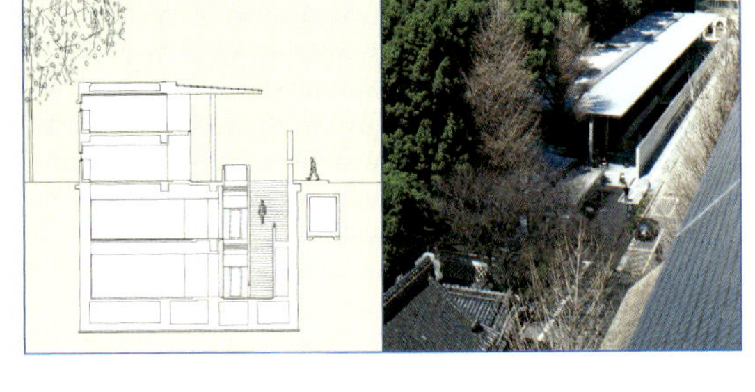

Located within the Hongo Campus of the University of Tokyo, this is an educational facility built in commemoration of the 130th anniversary of the establishment of the university. The site is within a green belt and adjacent to the Akamon (Red Gate), the oldest structure on the campus. The long and narrow site, 100m wide and 15m deep, was filled with splendid camphor trees more than 100 years old. Taking the continuation of the scene of existing camphor trees as the theme, I initially had the idea of a completely underground building in which the volume is placed under the campus road and a sunken court is established on the Hongo Street side. During planning, it was established that there were public utility conduits under the road and so this proposal was abandoned, but I persevered with the basic idea.

東京大学本郷キャンパス内に、大学創立130周年を記念してつくられた校舎施設である。敷地は、キャンパス内最古の建造物である「赤門」に隣接する、緑地帯の一角。間口100m、奥行き15mの細長い敷地には、樹齢100年を超える見事なクスノキが繁っていた。このクスノキの風景の継承を主題として、当初考えていたのは、構内道路下にヴォリュームを置き、本郷通り側にドライエリアを設ける完全な地下建築のアイディア。計画途中で、道路下に共同溝があることが判明し断念したが、基本となる考え方はそのまま貫いた。

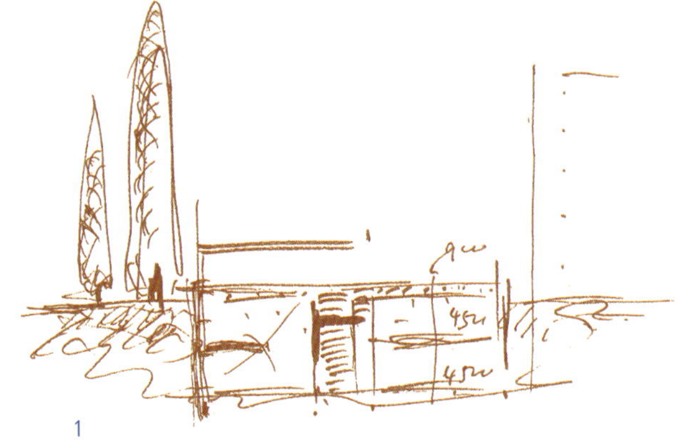
1

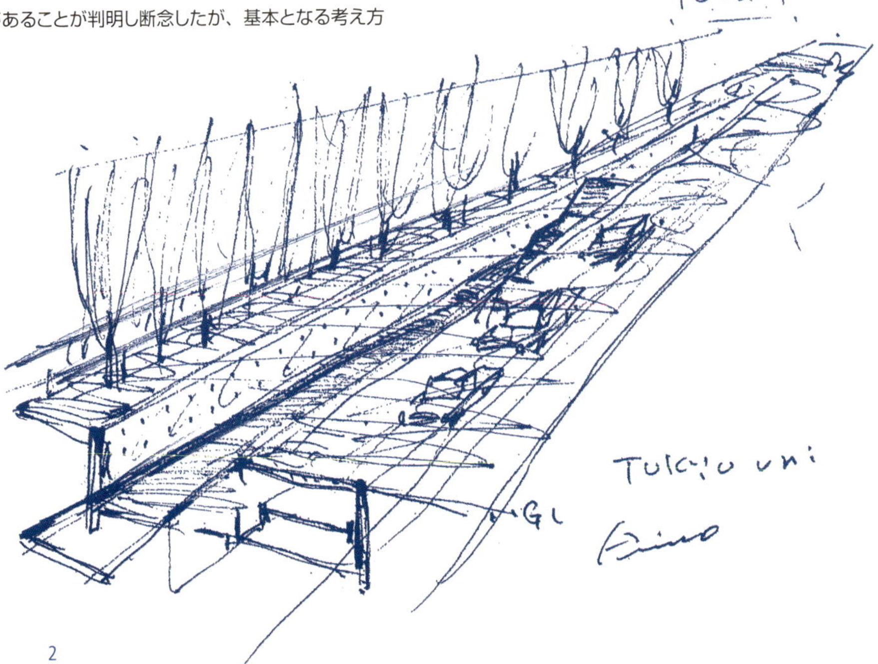

2

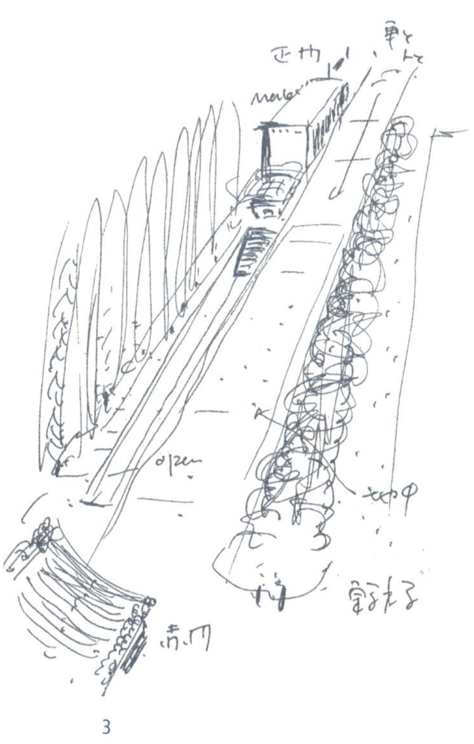

3

1, 2 Arranging the rooms below the campus road, and making an open court on the Hongo Street side. A design proposal that differs from the realized building.

3 Image sketch of an aerial view of the site from the direction of the Akamon gate. A proposal for underground architecture, arising from the desire to avoid obstructing the scene of dense camphor trees.

4 Looking at the camphor trees across the dry area from the rooms under the road.

1, 2 構内道路の下に部屋を配して、本郷通り側をオープンコートとする。実現案とは異なるもうひとつの設計案。

3 赤門方向から、敷地の鳥瞰を描いたイメージスケッチ。クスノキの生い茂る風景を遮らないという配慮から生まれた地下建築案。

4 道路下の部屋からドライエリア越しにクスノキを見る。

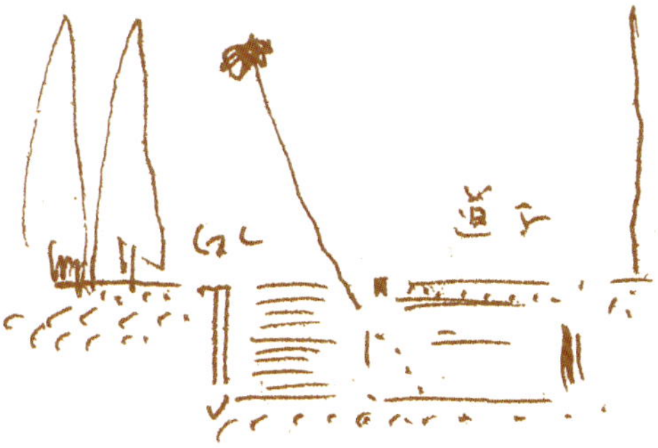

4

Abu Dhabi Maritime Museum
アブダビ海洋博物館

1. Abu Dhabi, UAE　アラブ首長国連邦 アブダビ
2. 2006.6-

This building will be made as a component in a large-scale development for a site on Saadiyat Island off the coast of Abu Dhabi, the capital of the United Arab Emirates. The program is a maritime museum that will introduce the local culture of Abu Dhabi. Given the character of the project, a type of symbolism rooted in its locale is expected from the newly created building. Accordingly, I conceived an architecture that takes the form of a shell-shaped void carved out of a rectangular volume. Furthermore, this void is inverted in the vertical direction to make a huge exhibition water tank. The source of the image is a vault of "wind."

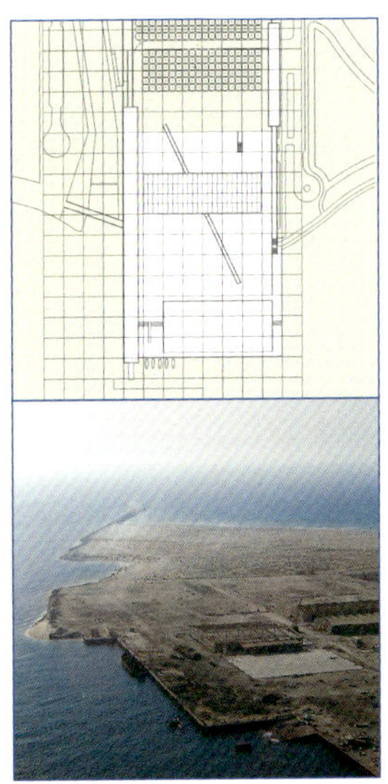

1

2

敷地はアラブ首長国連邦の首都アブダビ、その沖合の島サアディヤット島の大掛かりな開発計画の一環としてつくられる建物である。プログラムは地元アブダビの文化を紹介する海洋博物館というもの。プロジェクトの性格上、新たに生まれる建築には、場所に根差したある種のシンボリズムが期待された。そこで考えたのが、矩形平面のヴォリュームから、シェル状のヴォイドをくり抜いたかたちの建築だ。さらに、そのヴォイドを鉛直方向に反転して、巨大な展示水槽をつくる。イメージの源泉は、吹き抜ける〈風〉である。

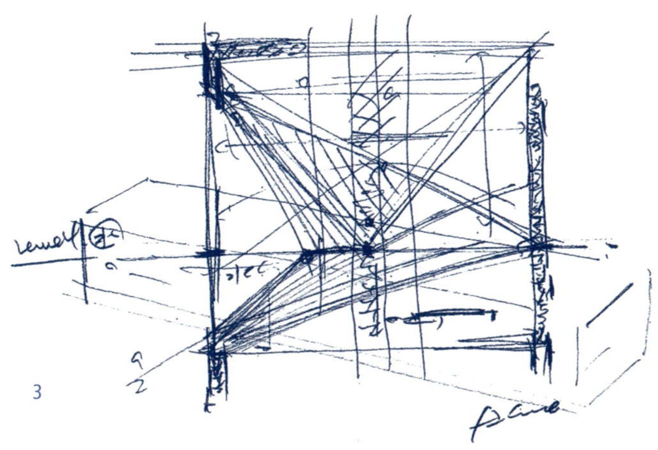

3

1 Image sketch.
2, 3 Architecture that gives shape to the invisible wind.
4 Section diagrams.

1 イメージスケッチ。
2, 3 目に見えない風をかたちにする建築。
4 セクションダイアグラム。

4

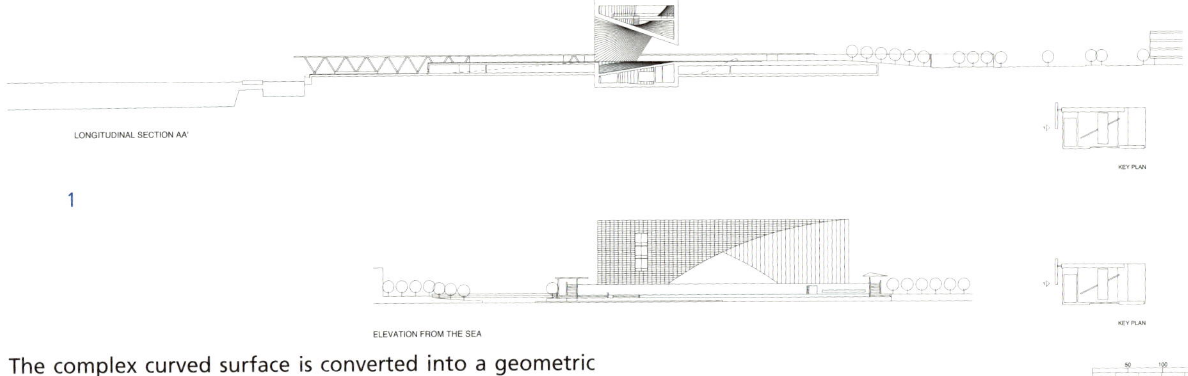

1

The complex curved surface is converted into a geometric system. The void is defined by the curved surface of a hyperbolic paraboloid shell.
The interior of the building is a dynamic space that has an exterior image just like a ship's hull. In this huge void space, floors float at various levels and ramps traverse between them, producing a three-dimensional spatial composition.

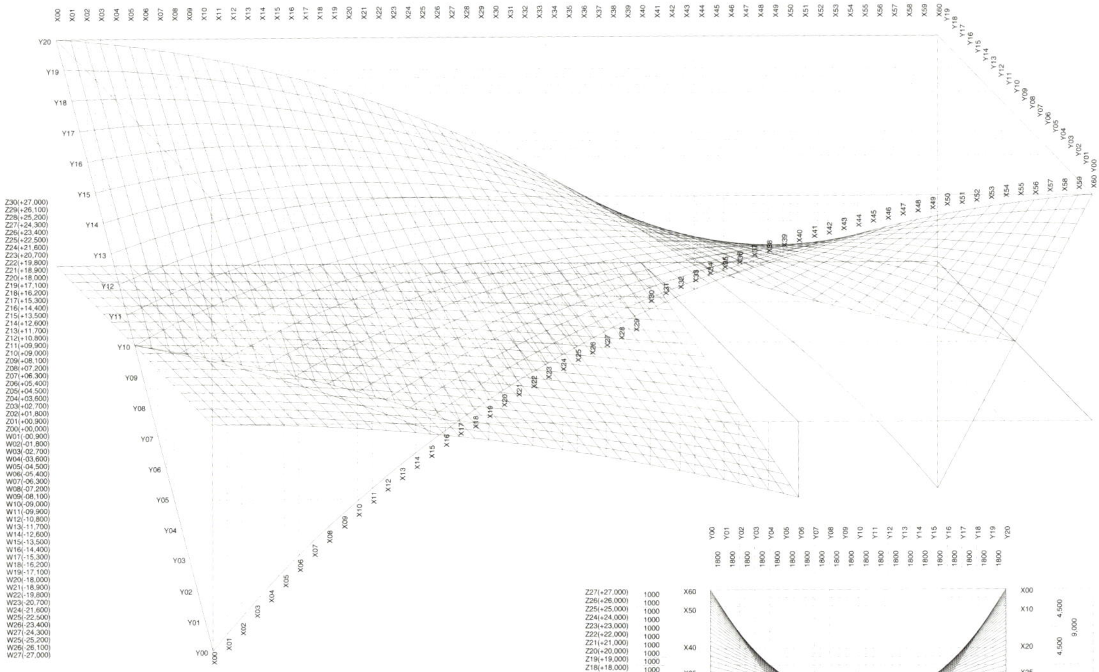

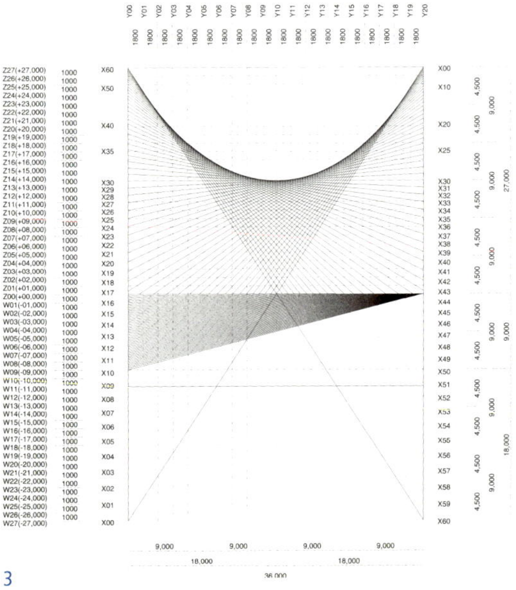

1 Section and elevation.
2 Plans.
3, 4 Geometrical study of the composition.
A strong space generated by excavating a rectilinear volume to create a void defined by a hyperbolic paraboloid shell curved surface.

1 断面図と立面図。
2 平面図。
3, 4, 構成の幾何学的検討図。直方体ヴォリュームからHP シェル曲面で規定されるヴォイドをくり抜くことで生まれる力強い空間。

Geometrical analysis

A bold space in geometrical form by hollowing out the void defined by a HP shell curve surface from a rectangular solid – our image of the shape of a wind = the shape of the ship sail filled by a wind – is reflected in the building design.

3

2 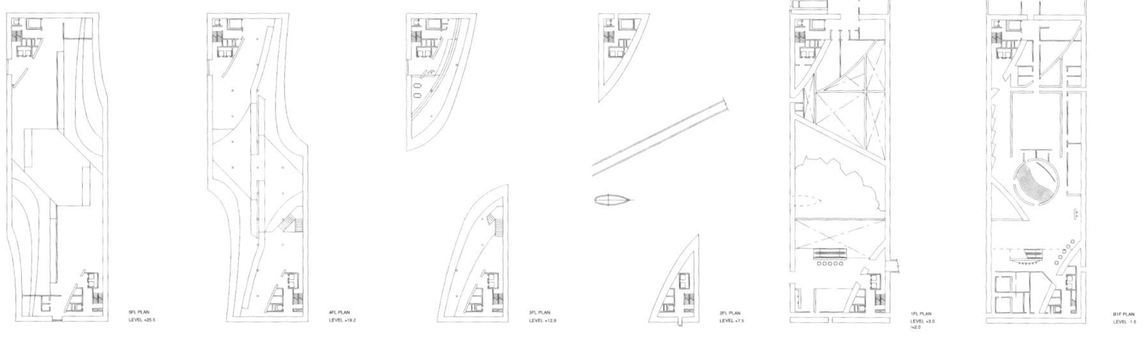

複雑な曲面形状を幾何学的システムに変換する。ヴォイドを規定するのはHPシェル曲面。

建物内部は、外観のイメージそのままの船の底のような動的な空間となっている。その巨大な吹き抜け空間の中にはさまざまなレベルのフロアが浮かべられ、その間をスロープが巡り、立体的な空間構成をつくり出す。

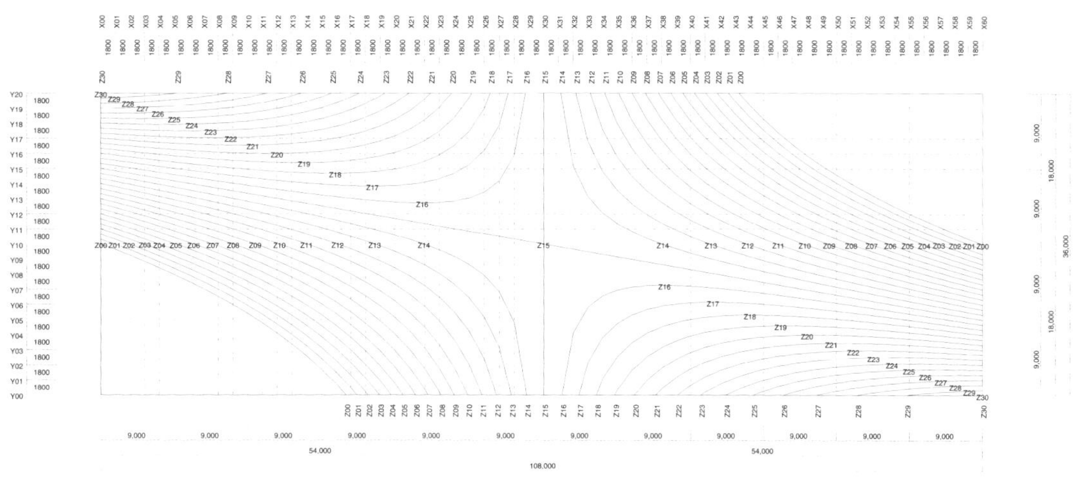

4 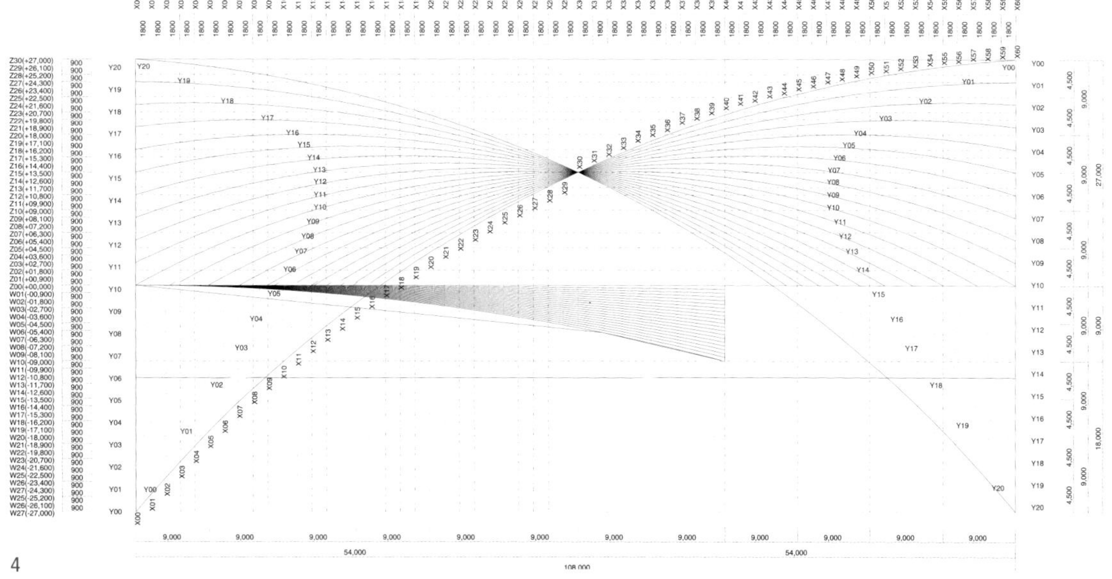

Punta della Dogana Contemporary Art Centre
プンタ・デラ・ドガーナ

1. Venice, Italy　イタリア ヴェニス
2. 2006.1-2007.9
3. 2007.10-2009.5

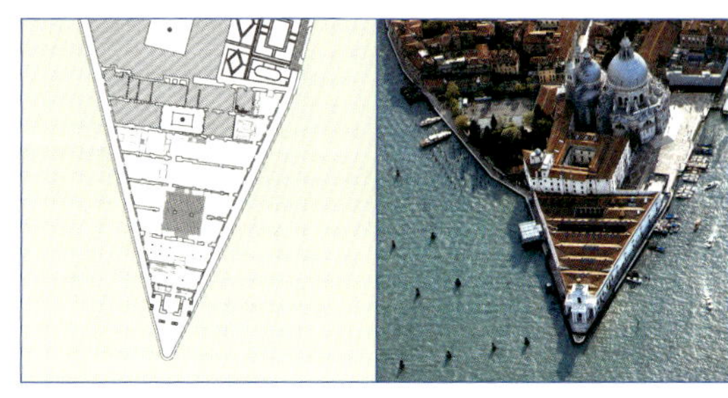

Following on from the Palazzo Grassi, this is a renovation project for a historical structure built on the Grand Canal in Venice, Italy. The site is Punta della Dogana, the tip of Dorsoduro, on the bank opposite Piazza San Marco. This is a plan to remodel the Dogana di Mare (Customhouse in the Sea), which has been standing here since the fifteenth century, into a contemporary art museum. With regard to this great historical structure, I thought to return everything to its original state, thus linking a time and making a place, then further linking that time to the future by inserting a new space in the center.

「パラッツォ・グラッシ」に続き、イタリア、ヴェニスで関わった大運河に建つ歴史的建造物の改造プロジェクト。敷地はサン・マルコ広場の対岸にある、ドルソドーロ島の先端、「プンタ・デラ・ドガーナ」。そこに15世紀から建つ「海の税関（Dogana di Mare）」を現代美術館に改造するという計画だ。この偉大な歴史的建造物に向かうにあたり考えたのは、すべてを建設当初のかたちに戻し、時間をつなぐ場所をつくること、さらにその時間を未来へとつなぐ新しい空間を中心に挿入することだった。

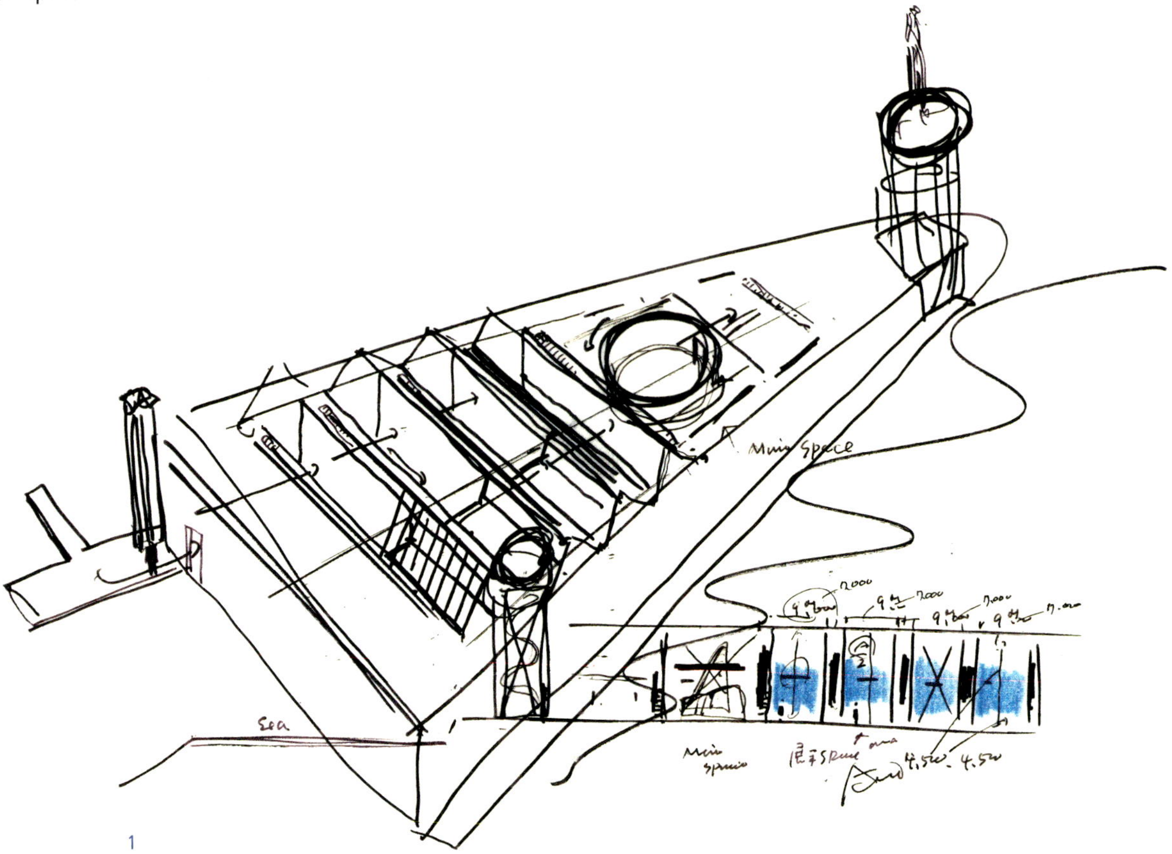

1

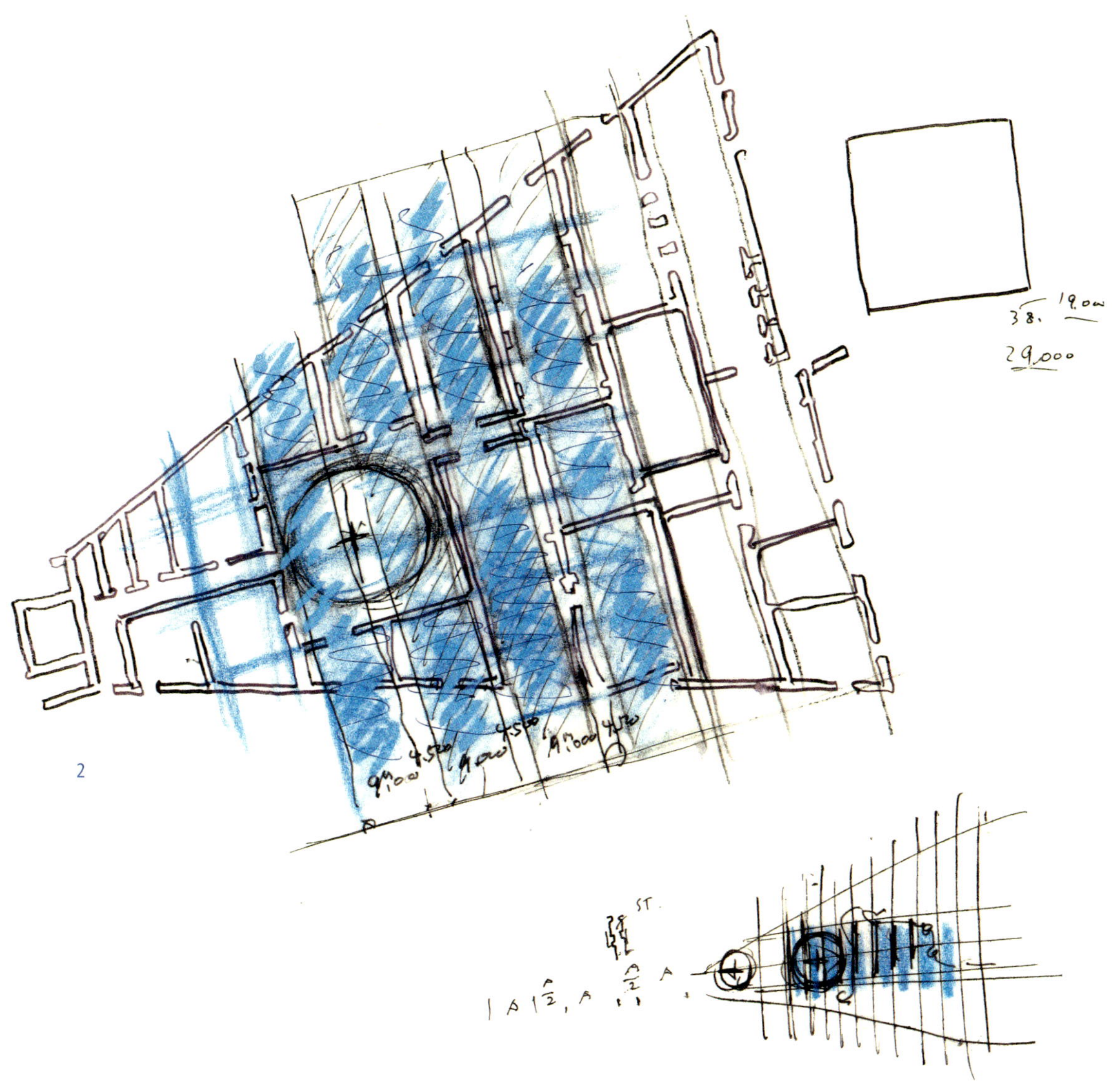

2

1, 2 First image sketches. The spatial essence of the old building is interpreted and abstracted.

1, 2 ファーストイメージスケッチ。古い建物のもつ空間のエッセンスを読み解き、抽出する。

1, 2 Following the shape of the promontory, the Punta della Dogana has a clear architectural composition comprising a triangular plan divided into narrow strips by north-south walls. Respecting the original shape of the building, all the partition walls added during its frequent renovations are removed, and the building is returned to the shape of its initial construction. Special significance is given to the space at the center of the building (where two bays had been turned into one room during a later renovation) as a space for dialogue between new and old.

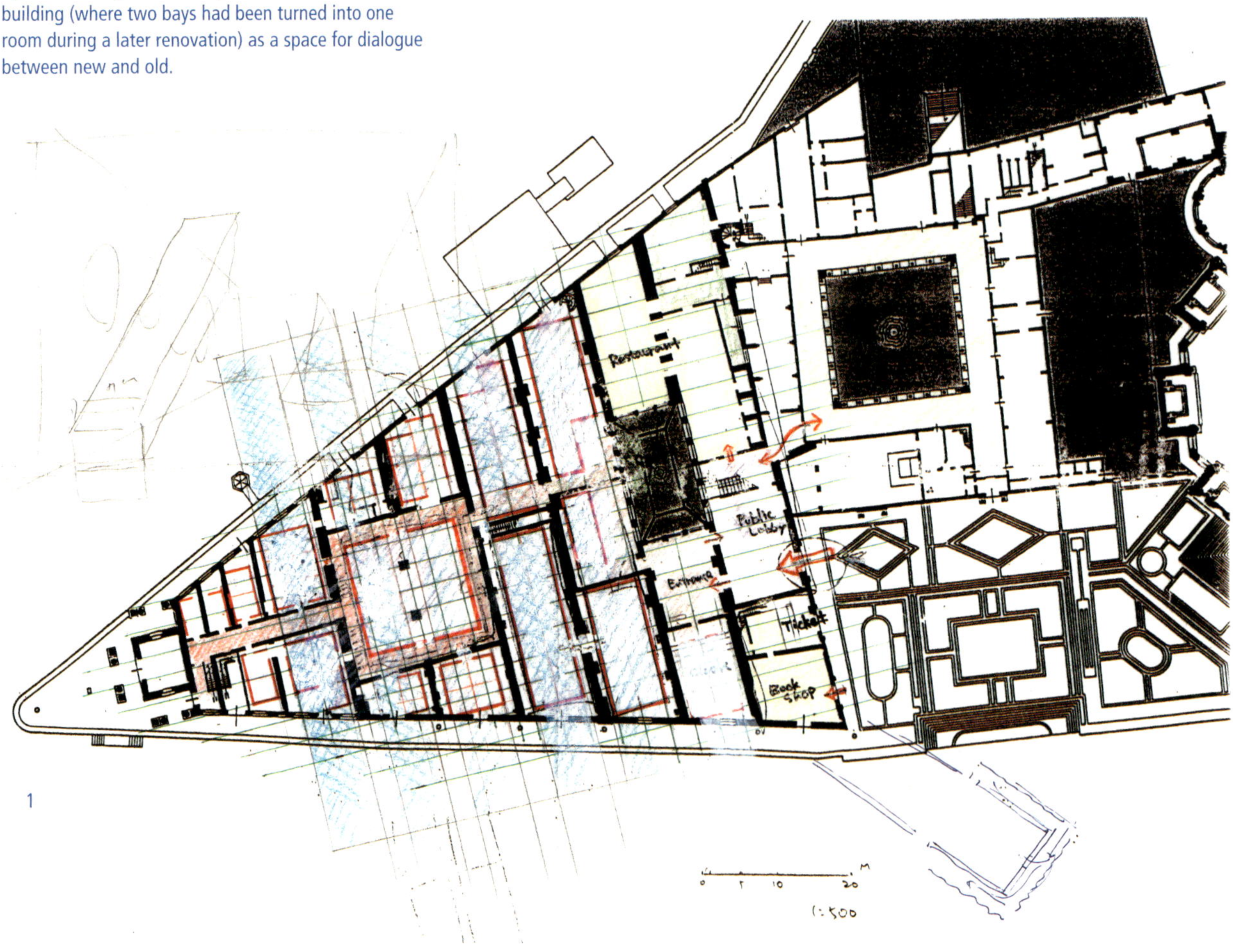

1

1, 2「プンタ・デラ・ドガーナ」は、岬の形状に沿った三角形平面を南北方向の壁が短冊状に区切る、明快な構成による建築である。その建物本来の形を尊重し、度重なる改造の中で加えられた仕切り壁などをすべて撤去して、建物を建設当初の形に戻す。その中で建物中央の、後の改造による2列分を1室としたスペースを、新旧の対話の場として特別な意味を与える。

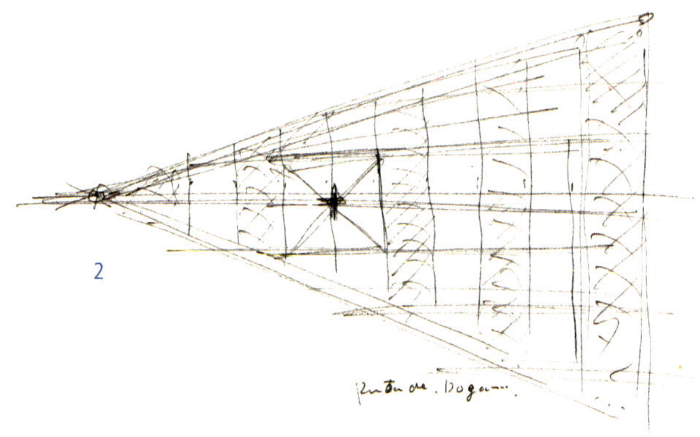

2

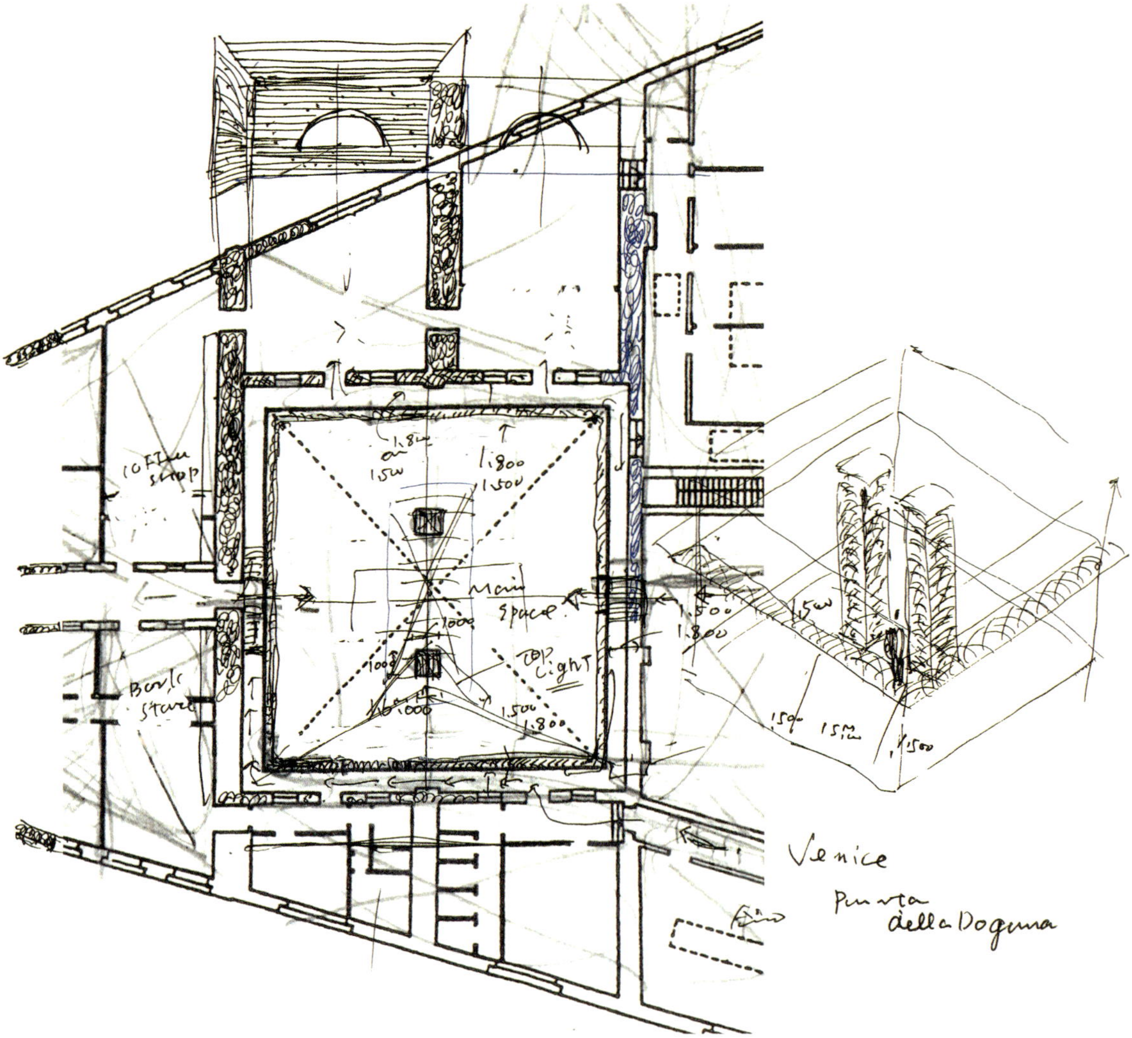

Exploratory sketch of the central court. This part is the exception, left in an unchanged form, and a concrete box is inserted to create a new space. The dialogue between new and old generated here is a dynamic force that connects the traces of time in the building to the present day and on to the future.

セントラルコートの検討スケッチ。この部分だけは、例外的にそのままのかたちに留め、さらにそのうちにコンクリートボックスを挿入して新たな空間をつくり出す。そこに生ずる新旧の対話が、建築に刻まれてきた時間を、現代、未来へと結びつける原動力となる。

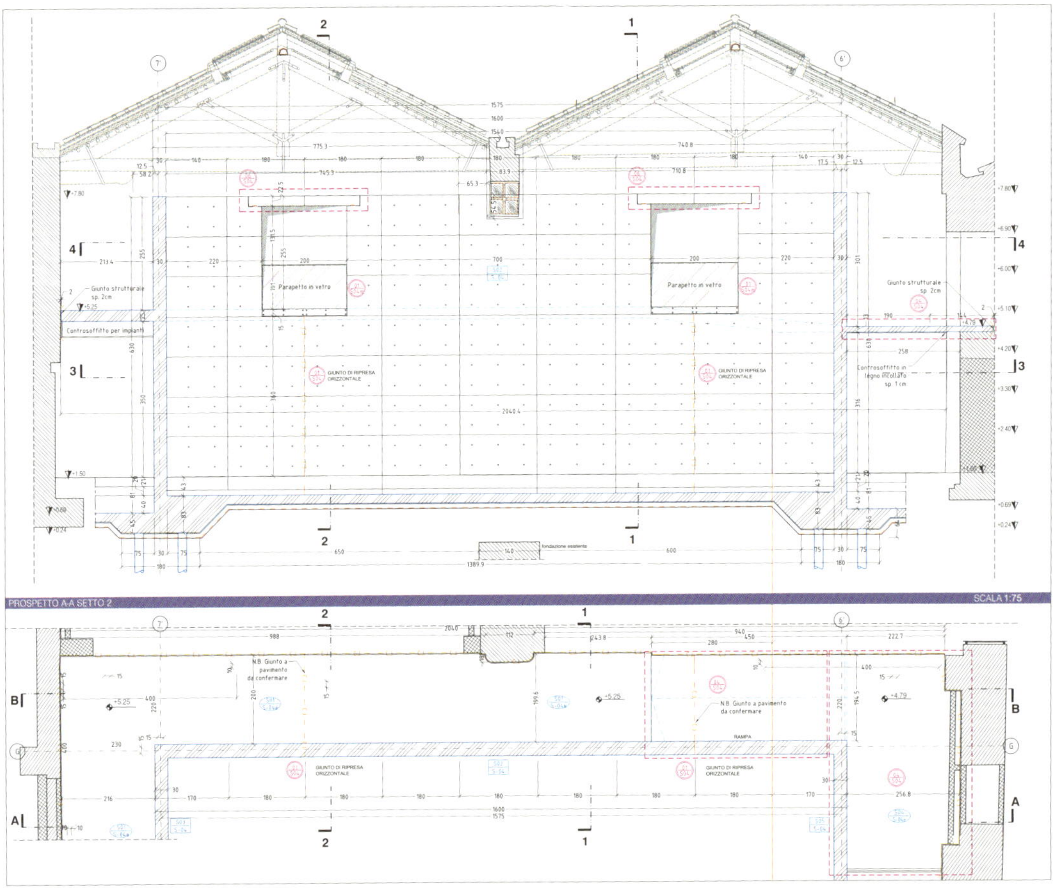

PROSPETTO A-A SETTO 2

SCALA 1:75

Detailed drawing of the central court.　セントラルコート詳細図

The light shining through the dynamic ceiling trusses makes the smooth wall surfaces of the concrete box seem to float within the yellowish brown of the bricks.

ダイナミックな天井小屋組みからこぼれる光が、れんがの茶褐色の
中に挿入されたコンクリートの滑らかな壁面を浮かび上がらせる。

1

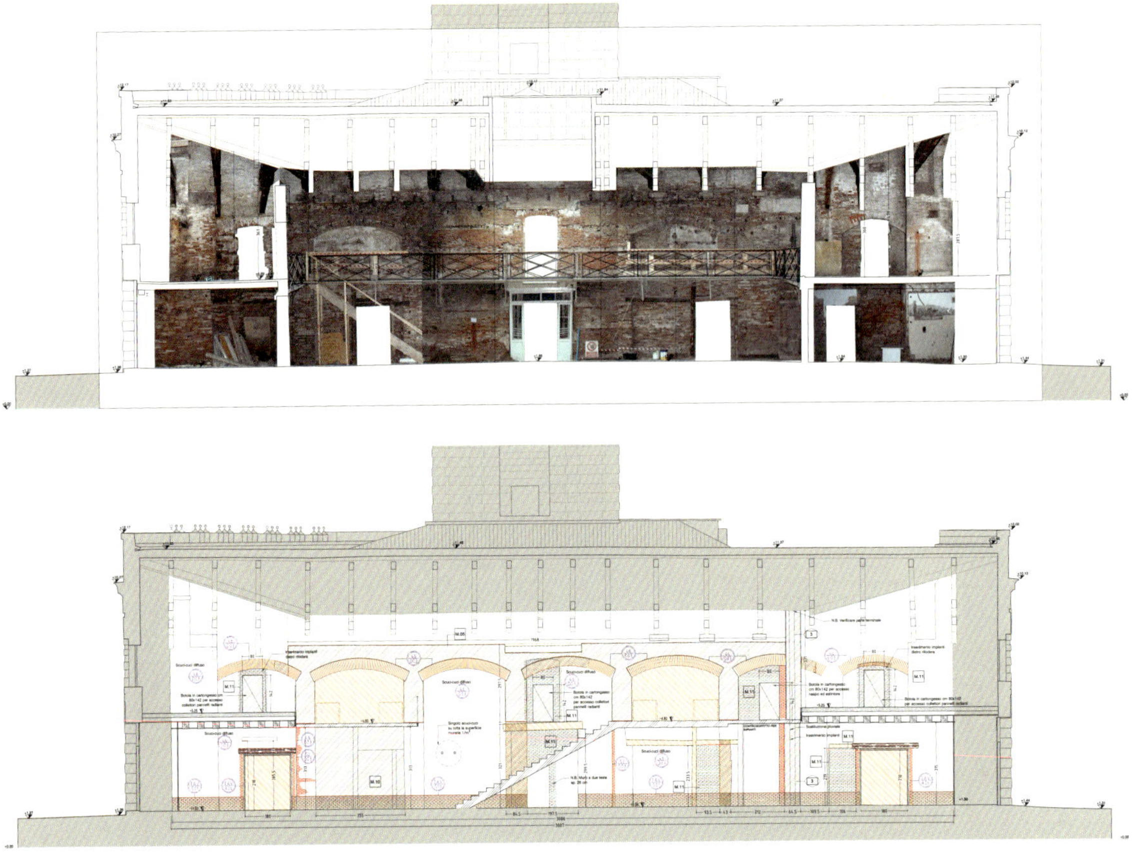

2

1 The construction was carried out by a team of artisans that has supported Ando's work in Italy from FABRICA onward. From collecting materials at old lumberyards through to legal negotiations, their experience and passion has been a strong driving force for the project.
2 Renovation drawings.

1 施工にあたったのは、「FABRICA」から、安藤のイタリアでの仕事を支えてきた技術者チーム。古材バンクでの材料の収集から、法的な折衝ごとまで、彼らの経験と情熱が、プロジェクト推進の大きな力となった。
2 改修計画図。

I initially planned to make a pair of concrete columns flanking the building entrance. Yet during the design process we ascertained that urban infrastructure, such as telephone lines, passes directly below, and so finally I abandoned the construction of the columns. Renovation projects for old buildings generally do not proceed as planned. However, I make my architecture in the belief that it is precisely the collisions and frictions arising between new and old that provide the motive power for creating the future of the city.

当初建物エントランスの脇には、一対のコンクリート柱をつくろうと計画していた。が、計画途中でその真下に通信線などの都市インフラが通っていることが判明、結局柱の建設は断念することとなった。古い建物の再生プロジェクトは、大抵が予定調和的には進まない。だが、そこに生じる新旧の衝突と摩擦こそが、都市の未来をつくる原動力だと信じて私は自身の建築をつくっている。

PROSPETTO SUL CANAL GRANDE - PROSPETTO NORD

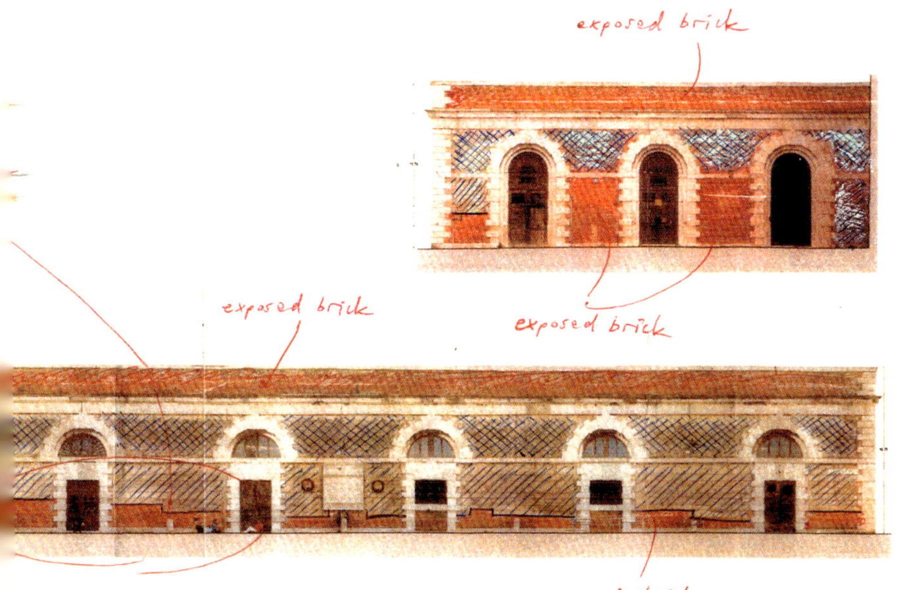

On the exterior, the existing façade is restored and repaired, but all the bricks parts that had been exposed for a long time were left visible rather than being covered with plaster.

外観は、現状ファサードの復元・修復に徹したが、年月を経て露出したれんが部分はすべて漆喰で覆うのではなく、そのまま見せるようにした。

Shanghai Poly Theater
上海保利大劇場

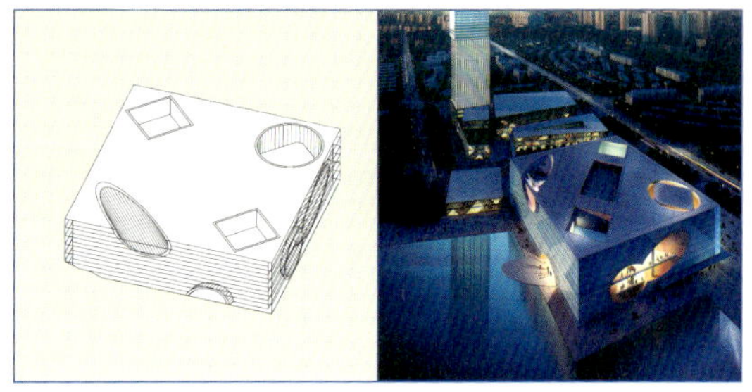

1. Shanghai, China　中華人民共和国 上海
2. 2009.3-2010.3
3. 2010.5-

1

The site is in Jiading, on the outskirts of Shanghai, an area currently undergoing rapid urban development. This is a proposal for a cultural complex centered on an opera house, made as a cultural center for a new town of $100km^2$.
The building faces an artificial lake in a lush green park. The exterior is a simple, 30m-high rectangular volume, with a square plan of 100m per side. Inserted into this are 18m-diameter cylindrical void spaces set at various angles. Taking these freely developed three-dimensional spaces as the framework for the building composition, a 1600-seat main hall is placed at the center.
Shanghai is called a magical city of the Orient, and I wanted to make architecture that responds to the energy of this city not through its exterior skin but through the violence of the interior space, in which solids and voids collide.

敷地は現在急激な都市開発が進む上海郊外の嘉定区に位置する。$100km^2$のニュータウンの文化的中心としてつくられる、オペラハウスを中心とした文化コンプレックスの計画である。
建物は緑豊かな公園の中の人工湖に面して建つ。外形は1辺100mの正方形平面で高さ30mの単純な矩形のヴォリューム。そこに直径18mの円筒状のヴォイド空間を上下左右様々な角度から挿入し、その自在に展開する3次元的空間を建物構成の骨格として、中央に1600席のメインホールを配置する。
かつて東洋の魔都と呼ばれた上海、その都市のエネルギーに対し、表層のかたちでなく、ソリッドとヴォイドの交錯する内部の空間の激しさで応えたいと考えた建築である。

1 Initial image sketch.
2 Compositional diagram. Cylindrical void spaces inserted into a simple 100m x 100m x 30m rectangular volume. Spaces of varied character are created through the collision of cube and tubes. Expression of urban symbolism through interior spaces.
3 Exploratory cross section. The main theater floats at the center of a composition in which tube-shaped public spaces expand three-dimensionally.

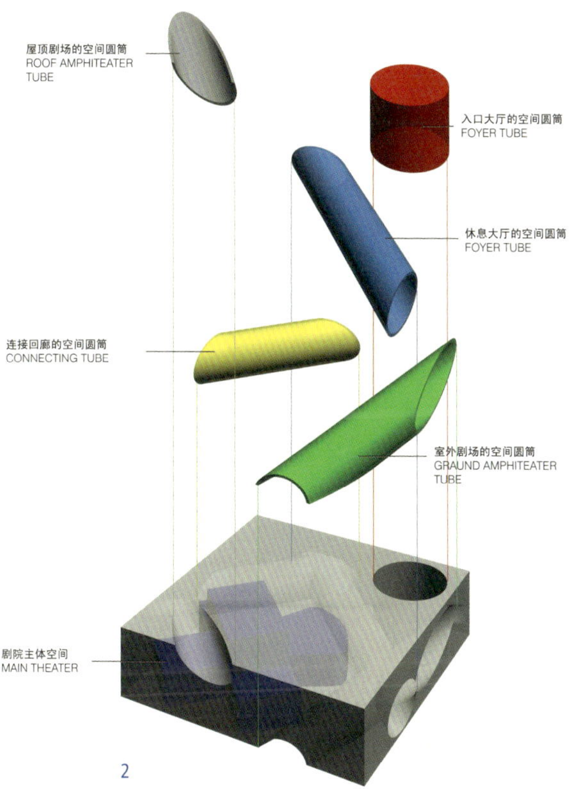

2

1 初期イメージスケッチ
2 構成のダイアグラム。100m×100m×30m の単純な矩形のヴォリュームに円筒状のヴォイド空間を挿入。キューブとチューブの交錯によって、さまざまな性格の場所をつくり出す。内部の空間による、都市のシンボリズムの表現。
3 断面検討図。チューブ状のパブリックスペースが3次元的に展開する構成の中央に、メインのシアターが浮かぶ。

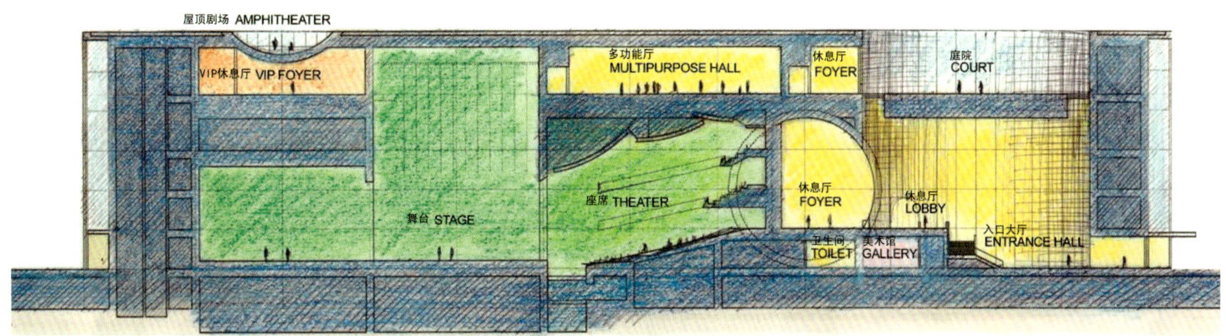

3

1 Image perspective of the exterior. Reflected in the water, the façade appears as a cross section of the dynamic composition.

2 Study model of the spatial diagram for the interior of the rectangular volume. Architecture that conceals an inner violence.

1

1 外観イメージパース。ダイナミックな構成の切断面として現れるファサードが水面に映し出される。
2 矩形ヴォリューム内部の空間ダイアグラムのスタディ模型。内なる激しさを秘めた建築。

2

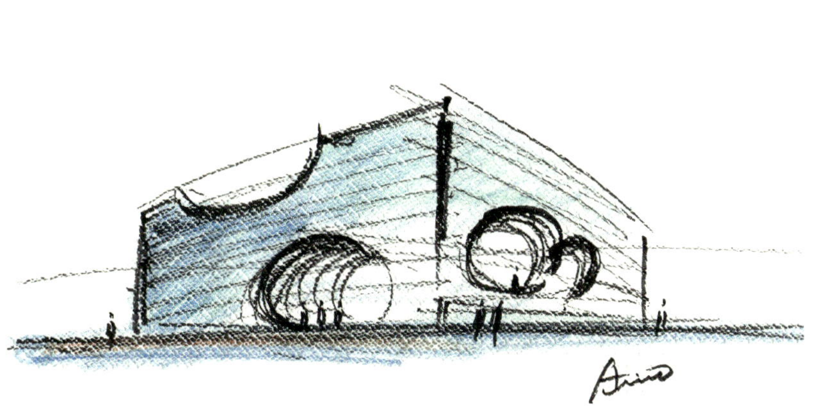

MVRDV
FARMAX
100 CUBES
CANTZ
TADAO ANDO

CONCORDE

Profile 略歴
Tadao Ando 安藤忠雄

Profile

1941 ● Born in Osaka, Japan
1962-69 ● Self-educated in architecture
1969 ● Established Tadao Ando Architect & Associates

Awards

1979 ● Annual Prize, Architectural Institute of Japan "Row House in Sumiyoshi"
1985 ● The 5th Alvar Aalto Medal, The Finnish Association of Architects, Finland
1989 ● Gold Medal of Architecture, Académie d'Architecture (French Academy of Architecture), France
1993 ● Japan Art Academy Prize, Japan
1995 ● The Pritzker Architecture Prize, U.S.A.
1996 ● The 8th Premium Imperiale
2002 ● Gold Medal of the American Institute of Architects, U.S.A.
● Honorary Degree, Università Degli Studi di Roma, Italy
● Honorary Degree, Tongji University, Shanghai, China
● The Kyoto Prizes, Japan
2003 ● Person of Cultural Merit, Japan
2005 ● Gold Medal of Union Internationale des Architectes
● Chevalier de l'Ordre National de la Légron d'Honneur, France

Affiliations

2002 ● Honorary Academician, The Royal Academy of Arts in London

Academic Activities

1987 ● Visiting Professor, Yale University
1988 ● Visiting Professor, Columbia University
1990 ● Visiting Professor, Harvard University
1997- ● Professor, The University of Tokyo
2003- ● Emeritus Professor, The University of Tokyo
2005 ● Special University Professor Emeritus, The University of Tokyo
● Regent Professor, University of California, Berkeley
2006- ● General Director, Tokyo 2016 Olympic Games Bid Committee

Representative Works

1983 ● Rokko Housing I, Kobe, Hyogo
1989 ● Church of the Light, Ibaraki, Osaka
1992 ● Benesse House Museum, Naoshima, Kagawa
1993 ● Rokko Housing II, Kobe, Hyogo
1994 ● Chikatsu-Asuka Historical Museum, Kanan, Osaka
1995 ● Benesse House Oval, Naoshima, Kagawa
1999 ● Rokko Housing III, Kobe, Hyogo
2000 ● Awaji-Yumebutai (Awaji Island Project), Awaji, Hyogo
● Komyo-ji Temple, Saijo, Ehime
● FABRICA (Benetton Communications Research Center), Treviso, Italy
2001 ● Pulitzer Foundation for the Arts, St. Louis, U.S.A.
● ARMANI / TEATRO, Milan, Italy
● Sayamaike Historical Museum, Osaka-Sayama, Osaka
2002 ● Hyogo Prefectural Museum of Art, Kobe, Hyogo
● The International Library of Children's Literature, Taito-ku, Tokyo
● Modern Art Museum of Fort Worth, Fort Worth, U.S.A.
2003 ● 4×4 House, Kobe, Hyogo
2004 ● Chichu Art Museum / Naoshima, Naoshima, Kagawa
● Langen Foundation / Hombroich, Neuss, Germany
2006 ● Omotesando Hills (Omotesando Regeneration Project), Shibuya-ku, Tokyo
● Palazzo Grassi, Venice, Italy
2007 ● 21_21 DESIGN SIGHT, Minato-ku, Tokyo
2008 ● Fukutake Hall, the University of Tokyo, Bunkyo-ku, Tokyo
● Tokyu Toyoko-Line Shibuya Station, Shibuya-ku, Tokyo
2009 ● Punta della Dogana Contemporary Art Centre, Venice, Italy

略歴	1941	●大阪に生まれる
	1962-69	●独学で建築を学ぶ
	1969	●安藤忠雄建築研究所を設立
受賞	1979	●「住吉の長屋」で昭和54年度日本建築学会賞
	1985	●フィンランド建築家協会から、国際的な建築賞 アルヴァ・アアルト賞（第5回）
	1989	●1989年度フランス建築アカデミー大賞（ゴールドメダル）
	1993	●日本芸術院賞
	1995	●1995年度プリツカー賞
	1996	●高松宮殿下記念世界文化賞
	2002	●2002年度アメリカ建築家協会（AIA）ゴールドメダル
		●ローマ大学名誉博士号
		●同済大学（上海）名誉教授
		●京都賞
	2003	●文化功労者
	2005	●国際建築家連合（UIA）ゴールドメダル
		●レジオン・ドヌール勲章（シュバリエ）叙勲
名誉会員	2002	●イギリス ロイヤルアカデミー オブ アーツ名誉会員

教職	1987	●イェール大学客員教授
	1988	●コロンビア大学客員教授
	1990	●ハーバード大学客員教授
	1997-	●東京大学教授
	2003-	●東京大学名誉教授
	2005	●東京大学特別栄誉教授
		●カリフォルニア大学バークレー校客員教授
	2006-	●2016年東京オリンピック招致活動の総監督を務める
主な作品	1983	●六甲の集合住宅Ⅰ（兵庫 神戸）
	1989	●光の教会（大阪 茨木）
	1992	●ベネッセハウス ミュージアム（香川 直島）
	1993	●六甲の集合住宅Ⅱ（兵庫 神戸）
	1994	●大阪府立近つ飛鳥博物館（大阪 河南）
	1995	●ベネッセハウス オーバル（香川 直島）
	1999	●六甲の集合住宅Ⅲ（兵庫 神戸）
	2000	●淡路夢舞台（兵庫 淡路）
		●南岳山光明寺（愛媛 西条）
		●FABRICA（ベネトンアートスクール）（イタリア トレヴィソ）
	2001	●ピューリッツァー美術館（アメリカ セントルイス）
		●アルマーニ・テアトロ（イタリア ミラノ）
		●大阪府立狭山池博物館（大阪 大阪狭山）
	2002	●兵庫県立美術館（兵庫 神戸）
		●国際子ども図書館（東京 台東区）
		●フォートワース現代美術館（アメリカ フォートワース）
	2003	●4×4の住宅（兵庫 神戸）
	2004	●地中美術館（香川 直島）
		●ホンブロイッヒ／ランゲン美術館（ドイツ ノイス）
	2006	●表参道ヒルズ（同潤会青山アパート建替計画）（東京 渋谷区）
		●パラッツォ・グラッシ（イタリア ヴェニス）
	2007	●21_21 DESIGN SIGHT（東京 港区）
	2008	●東京大学情報学環・福武ホール（東京 文京区）
		●東急東横線渋谷駅（東京 渋谷区）
	2009	●プンタ・デラ・ドガーナ（イタリア ヴェニス）

Credits クレジット

Photography 写真

Mitsumasa Fujitsuka 藤塚光政
006-007, 016-017, 091 right, 260 left-middle, 314-315

Hiroyuki Hirai 平井広行
172-173 top

Kaori Ichikawa 市川かおり
cover, 221

Andrea Jemolo
298 right-top, 301, 303,
306 top (except first right) & second top (except second right)

Mitsuo Matsuoka 松岡満男
044 left-middle, 100 left-bottom, 168 right-top, 182 right-top,
200 right-top, 212 center-top, 220 left-top, 222 right-top,
236 right-top 237 center-top, 250 right-top, 262 left-middle,
274 right-top & right-middle, 292 right-top, 293 right-top

Shigeo Ogawa 小川重雄
291 left-middle & right-top, 302 bottom, 304 bottom, 307,
308-309 top

Tomio Ohashi 大橋富夫
141 middle & bottom, 146 right-top & left-bottom,
162 right-middle, 166 left-top & left-middle, 167,
171 middle (4 photos), 175 top, 181 top, 212 bottom,
214 left-bottom, 216 right-top, 240 top, 241 top, 249 bottom
254 top, 256 left-top, 258 bottom, 271 top, 273

Francesco Radino
238 left-middle

Tohmas Riehle / arter
253 top

Shinkenchiku-sha 新建築社
055, 056 right-middle, 063 top, 076 left-top, 079, 095 bottom,
100 right-top, 138 left-bottom, 139, 148 left-middle,
153 left-top, 176 top, 196 left-middle, 237 bottom, 242 left-top,
252 right-top, 277 right-bottom,

Yoshio Shiratori 白鳥美雄
029, 116 right-top, 138 left-top

Yoshio Takase 高瀬良夫
227 top

David Woo
269 top

Courtesy of Casa BRUTUS/Magazine House Co,. LTD.
写真提供：マガジンハウス カーサ ブルータス
006-007, 016-017, 091 right, 314-315

Other photographs courtesy of Tadao Ando Architect & Associates
上記以外の写真：安藤忠雄建築研究所

Drawings 図版

Tadao Ando Architect & Associates 安藤忠雄建築研究所

English Translations 英訳

Hiroshi Watanabe 渡辺 洋
008-011

Thomas Daniell & Ellen Van Goethem
トーマス・ダニエル & エレン・ヴァン・フーテム
Project descriptions and captions

The source of following drawings:
"TADAO ANDO DETAILS" volume 3 and 4 by
A.D.A. EDITA Tokyo
以下の図版初出：『TADAO ANDO DETAILS』3巻および4巻
（A.D.A. EDITA Tokyo 刊）
228-229, 253 bottom, 268-269 bottom, 286-287 bottom

Tadao Ando Architect & Associates
安藤忠雄建築研究所

Tadao Ando	安藤忠雄
Masataka Yano	矢野正隆
Fumihiko Iwama	岩間文彦
Kazuya Okano	岡野一也
Takaaki Mizutani	水谷孝明
Hironobu Wakayama	若山泰伸
Hidehiro Yano	矢野英裕
Kanya Sogo	十河完也
Yoshinori Hayashi	林 慶憲
Shimao Mori	森詩麻夫
Tatsuhito Ono	小野龍人
Takeharu Suzuki	鈴木丈晴
Tomonori Miura	三浦朋訓
Kosuke Sakai	酒井康介
Kazutoshi Miyamura	宮村和寿
Seiichiro Takeuchi	竹内誠一郎
Kensuke Suto	須藤謙介
Hajime Moriyama	森山 一
Gonzalo Velez Jaramillo	ヴェレス・ハラミジョ・ゴンザロ
Peter Boda	ボダ・ピーター
Yosuke Kanemaki	印牧洋介
Chisato Kodaira	古平知沙都
Akiko Hayashida	林田安紀子
Ayano Higuchi	樋口彩乃
Tamao Shichiri	七里玉緒
Yumiko Kato	加藤由美子

安藤忠雄の建築 0

Tadao Ando 0
Process and Idea

2010年3月31日　初版 第1刷発行

著者……………安藤忠雄

発行者…………遠藤信行

デザイン…………太田徹也

プリンティング
ディレクション……高柳　昇

印刷・製本………株式会社東京印書館

発行所…………TOTO出版
（TOTO株式会社）
〒107-0062 東京都港区南青山1-24-3
TOTO乃木坂ビル2階
[営業] tel:03(3402)7138
fax:03(3402)7187
[編集] tel:03(3497)1010
URL:http://www.toto.co.jp/bookshop/

ISBN978-4-88706-309-9